W9-DJM-299

Accessories After The Fact

The Warren Commission, The Authorities and The Report

Accessories After The Fact

The Warren Commission, The Authorities, and The Report

by Sylvia Meagher

Preface by Senator Richard S. Schweiker
Introduction by Peter Dale Scott

Vintage Books
A Division of Random House

New York

FIRST VINTAGE BOOKS EDITION, March 1976

Copyright © 1967 by Sylvia Meagher
Preface and Introduction Copyright © 1976 by
Random House, Inc.

Library of Congress Cataloging in Publication Data

Meagher, Sylvia.
  Accessories after the fact.

  Includes bibliographical references.
  1. United States. Warren Commission. Report
of the President's Commission on the Assassination of President John F. Kennedy. 2. Kennedy,
John Fitzgerald, Pres. U.S., 1917–1963—Assassination. I. Title.
[E842.9.M39 1976]   364.1′524′0973   75–39081
ISBN 0–394–71630–2

Manufactured in the United States of America

CAT. 9/79

*This book is dedicated to
the innocent victims of a society which
often inflicts indignity, imprisonment, and even death
on the obscure and helpless.*

Contents

Preface

As a Senator investigating certain aspects of the Warren Commission inquiry, I have found Sylvia Meagher's *Accessories After the Fact* to be an indispensable research tool.

Yet to appreciate fully the significance of Mrs. Meagher's work, it is necessary to go back to the fall of 1964, when the Warren Commission Report was released.

Most Americans initially accepted the Commission's findings that Lee Harvey Oswald, acting alone, assassinated President Kennedy. Some had doubts but dismissed them because of the reputation of the men and agencies who served the Commission, the major media's immediate endorsement of the Report, and the hyperbolic and wildly speculative assertions of some Warren Commission skeptics.

Fortunately, Sylvia Meagher had the courage to cast a critical eye—and, more importantly, an objective eye—on the Warren Report.

It wasn't until Watergate and my services on the Senate Intelligence Committee that I began to question much of what I had accepted about the Report. And when I had questions, there always seemed to be answers in *Accessories After the Fact*.

The significance of this book cannot be overstated. It is by far the most meticulous and compelling indictment of the Warren Commission Report. Through her painstaking attention to detail, Sylvia Meagher has exposed the gross inconsistencies between the Commission's Final Report and the twenty-six volumes of evidence it reviewed. One only need read her passage on the appearance of the "magic bullet" at Parkland Hospital, or the Oswald police lineup, to appreciate the degree to which the Report has been devastated.

In addition to *Accessories After the Fact*, Mrs. Meagher has made a second major contribution to research in this field by compiling a complete index to the Warren Report and exhibits. For reasons yet unknown, the

Warren Commission chose not to index its twenty-six volumes. Thus until she compiled her comprehensive index, critical analysis of the Warren Report was, in Mrs. Meagher's words, "tantamount to a search for information in the *Encyclopaedia Britannica* if the contents were untitled, unalphabetized, and in random sequence." It was virtually impossible for a serious student of the assassination to wade through the more than 20,000 pages of documentation. This accomplishment, together with *Accessories After the Fact* and its own index, clearly establish Sylvia Meagher's major contribution to understanding this tragic incident in our nation's history.

As this is written, I am investigating the effectiveness and truthfulness of United States intelligence agencies in investigating the assassination for the Warren Commission. Where our inquiry will lead only time will tell. Whether a full-scale reopening of the entire assassination investigation will result is still uncertain. But one thing is clear: Sylvia Meagher's *Accessories After the Fact* was instrumental in finally causing a committee of Congress—with full subpoena power, access to classified documents, and a working knowledge of the nuances of the FBI and CIA—to take a second official look at what happened in Dallas November 22, 1963.

SENATOR RICHARD S. SCHWEIKER (R-PA)
Washington, D.C.   October 5, 1975

Introduction

In 1965 Sylvia Meagher produced her *Subject Index to the Warren Report and Hearings and Exhibits,* which may someday be remembered as the only index to have altered the history of U.S. politics. If she had written nothing else, she would have been remembered for the way this index drew order out of chaos, defined a subject matter for serious scholarship and invited anyone who cared to drive a wedge between the findings of the Warren Report and its own twenty-six volumes of published Hearings.

Two years later, with *Accessories After the Fact,* Ms. Meagher showed how effectively this analysis of published documentation challenged not just the conclusions of the Warren Commission, but the methods of distortion, suppression and apparent intimidation, which were used to arrive at untenable conclusions. She was not the first to labor in these Augean stables, and she herself freely acknowledged the invaluable help and support she had received from other early researchers.

But, like Linnaeus in the age of the great botanical voyagers, Sylvia Meagher, in her second book as much as in her first, brought a new degree of order and method to the vast tracts of previously unmanageable detail. The nearly encyclopedic scope of this task produced a book that, like any encyclopedia, is coherent in particular sections rather than its entirety. Its coherence and importance lie in its method: its demonstration that, in the great welter of irrational rumor and falsehood, rigorous analysis is both fruitful and urgently needed.

The first press response to her book confirmed her charge that important elements of the media had taken over the defense of the indefensible Report. Of the six reviews quoted in *Book Review Digest,* only one can be called favorable. *The New York Times* dismissed the book as a "bore" without "any important disclosures"; it predictably did not mention her disclosures about *The New York Times* (cf. infra. p. 458). John Sparrow, Warden of

All Souls College, Oxford, writing in the *Times Literary Supplement* of London, dismissed Ms. Meagher as a "demonologist" with a "gift for innuendo" and deplorable vituperation, "ready to sling at the authorities any stone and any mud that presents itself." These were revealing charges from a don who readily admitted that he had "not had time to study" the book.

Despite such reviews, and with no promotional campaign to correct them, the book managed quietly to sell out within three years. Since that time it has proliferated in bootlegged Xeroxed copies, while searchers for the original have driven the second-hand price to fifty dollars or more. In all these years the reputation of the Warren Report has continued to sink, and that of Sylvia Meagher's critique to grow.

This is not to claim that Sylvia Meagher is infallible. The second edition of this book has had to correct a few slips and misunderstandings, a few apparent anomalies for which explanations could later be supplied. The miracle is, how few. Her main charges still stand. John Sparrow, Warden of All Souls, like the rest of his breed, has not yet backed up his invective with a single specific refutation. He is not likely to.

The worst that can be said of Sylvia Meagher's book today is that it did not have access to facts learned since 1967. Most of these have come from the thousands of unpublished Warren Commission documents and memoranda in the National Archives. Some of these are still withheld; some are slowly being released. The rest are slowly being read and compared by researchers, many of whom (like myself) would still name Sylvia Meagher's book as their chief inspiration and guide.

Some day new information may supplant Ms. Meagher's book; to date it has for the most part strengthened it. Here I can give one example from a story that didn't break until early September, 1975. On pp. 215–16 of this book Ms. Meagher assembled evidence to support the hypothesis that, despite sworn testimony to the contrary, Lee Harvey Oswald had met with Dallas FBI Agent James Hosty, had for some reason been irritated with Hosty, and "had stopped at the downtown office of the FBI . . . and left a note." This was not only a direct challenge to the claim of the Report (and the FBI) that Oswald had never contacted Hosty or the Dallas FBI, it was pertinent to her larger claim that the FBI was covering up the truth about its relations to Oswald (p. 210), that it initially withheld from the Commission the presence of Hosty's name in Oswald's notebook (p. 211), and that the Warren Commission *never* (as it claimed, *WR 327*) made an "independent review" of FBI files to determine whether or not Oswald was an FBI informant (p. 350). Sylvia Meagher concluded that:

> The real relationship between Oswald and the FBI remains to be uncovered, and the tactics used to conceal it merely increase suspicion of the nature of that relationship (p. 219).

On the initial issue of fact, Sylvia Meagher has now been proven right, the Warren Commission wrong, and the FBI deceitful. On August 30, 1975, FBI Director Clarence J. Kelley confirmed that Oswald *had* left a threatening note for Hosty at the FBI office; according to *Time,* the FBI, on orders from

Washington Headquarters, had later destroyed the note and perhaps altered FBI records to conceal it. Thus her concluding suspicion is even more justified than it was before. Meanwhile, readers of Clarence Kelley's admission were able to appreciate its significance only if they knew the related facts in Sylvia Meagher's eighth chapter.

In another equally important example, unpublished documents have corroborated Sylvia Meagher's charge that the Warren Commission covered up misbehavior and lies of the Dallas police. On pp. 304–9, Sylvia Meagher assembled facts to challenge Dallas Police Chief Curry's sworn testimony that Oswald "was arraigned for the assassination of the President" and that Curry himself "was present at the time" (*4H 156*). This was audacious skepticism in the face of considerable testimony in support of Curry, including that of Detective Captain Will Fritz (*4H 221*). Sylvia Meagher was one of the first to entertain seriously Oswald's own surprising claim that he had not been charged with the murder of President Kennedy, or even heard anything from the Dallas police about such a charge (*WR 201, cf. infra*, p. 306).

Astonishingly, the unpublished Warren Commission Documents support Ms. Meagher against the alleged "eye-witnesses." According to an early FBI report, based on information from Fritz's office, Oswald was arraigned only on the charge of murdering Officer Tippit:

> No arraignment on the murder charges in connection with the death of President Kennedy was held inasmuch as such arraignment was not necessary in view of the previous charges filed against Oswald and for which he was arraigned.
>
> (Commission Document 5, p. 400)

To review such examples is to see even more clearly the social pathology of the Warren Commission syndrome in this country, to see the importance of Sylvia Meagher's healing challenge, and the difficulty of that challenge's being heard. To believe Sylvia Meagher is to entertain the possibility that FBI agents could lie, that Dallas police could lie, and that a blue-ribbon Commission of leading public figures could transmit these lies in the form of an elaborately footnoted report. For many Americans, to adjust to such possibilities is to tread on the borders of paranoia. It is to accept that someone, something, has gone insane.

Sylvia Meagher's book promises even worse discomforts for the reluctant reader. It is not just that Oswald had unexplained relationships to the FBI, or Jack Ruby to the Dallas police. There is also the unexplained behavior of the State Department, where Sylvia Meagher rightly detected a "radical deviation from orthodox practice where Oswald was involved" (p. 336). There is the serenity of the CIA, along with the FBI and State, in the face of Oswald's alleged threats to disclose classified data to the Soviet Union. Ms. Meagher, like most researchers, saw this serenity "as an indication that they knew there was nothing to get excited about" (p. 342). She showed how the Warren Report, despite contrary evidence, simply altered the chronology of Oswald's travel to the Soviet Union, to reconcile it with the CIA's account of the available commercial air flights (p. 331). "There is reason," she added, "to wonder if he went on a commercial flight at all."

In confronting these anomalies and irregularities in high levels of government, the unaccustomed reader may mistakenly think that the only alternative to the Warren Report is a vast conspiracy of thought control and the rewriting of history at every level of U.S. society. Here I think the more recent experience of Watergate will help us to dispel such paranoia and to understand the mechanics of the Warren Commission syndrome in a more rational perspective. If Oswald had ever, at any point in his career, been involved with any government agency or in any national security matter, it is clear (we now know) that numbers of relatively innocent public servants would participate in a cover-up where they were told that national security was involved. What was possible in 1972 would have been even more possible in 1964, when the CIA's and FBI's numerous illegal activities had not yet been exposed and documented.

Sylvia Meagher herself concluded her book, in a bold chapter entitled "The Proof of the Plot," with a hypothesis that would, if correct, have provoked just such a bureaucratic cover-up in the name of national security. Oswald and Ruby, she suggests, may have been involved in anti-Castro activities of the CIA. She points out how anti-Castro Cubans, and also Americans involved in their conspiratorial activities, were related to the Oswald case in a way that no non-conspiratorial hypothesis could explain. The strong support of the CIA for these Cubans, the quick disaffection of President Kennedy for the CIA's

> incredible bungling . . . suggested an early end to what has been called 'the invisible government,' and a threat to their Cuban proteges (p. 385).

Sylvia Meagher noted that Oswald exhibited a sustained interest in Cuba and had contact with Cuban intriguers. The same was true of Jack Ruby. A retired U.S. Army colonel had reportedly seemed to be "playing the role of an intelligence officer in his contacts with the Cubans" in Dallas, and "trying to arouse the feelings of the Cuban refugees in Dallas against the Kennedy administration." She asks whether it is far-fetched to postulate the formation of a plot amongst members of such circles (p. 386).

Such speculations seem much less outlandish today, after the Watergate break-in, and after the arrest of some of the CIA's other top Cubans on serious narcotics charges. Since Sylvia Meagher wrote, we have also learned that the CIA was collaborating closely on anti-Castro matters with figures from the underworld of organized crime in Chicago, and we know more about Jack Ruby's extensive links to that same underworld. Once again, unpublished Warren Commission documents corroborate Ms. Meagher's disturbing hypothesis, and it is surely significant that some of the key documents in this sensitive area are still withheld.

The implications of Sylvia Meagher's hypothesis are so serious and far-reaching that it will indeed be difficult for any Congressional committee to explore the matter further. The wound is too painful to be re-opened gratuitously: the public must understand and insist on the need for the truth. But that is precisely why it is so urgent that this book be widely read, and that the demand grow that its questions and criticisms be answered. What is at stake, I believe, is nothing less than the political and spiritual well-being of the republic, the choice whether reason or unreason will prevail.

PETER DALE SCOTT
October, 1975

President's Commission on the Assassination of President Kennedy

CHIEF JUSTICE EARL WARREN, *Chairman*

SENATOR RICHARD B. RUSSELL
SENATOR JOHN SHERMAN COOPER
REPRESENTATIVE HALE BOGGS
REPRESENTATIVE GERALD R. FORD
MR. ALLEN W. DULLES
MR. JOHN J. McCLOY

J. LEE RANKIN, *General Counsel*

Assistant Counsel

FRANCIS W. H. ADAMS
JOSEPH A. BALL
DAVID W. BELIN
WIL███ █. COLEMAN, JR.
M██████ ██ EISENBERG
B█ ██████ █IN
L███ ███ERT, JR.

ALBERT E. JENNER, JR.
WESLEY J. LIEBELER
NORMAN REDLICH
W. DAVID SLAWSON
ARLEN SPECTER
SAMUEL A. STERN
HOWARD P. WILLENS*

S███ ██ ██bers

PHILLIP BARSON
EDWARD A. CONROY
JOHN HART ELY
ALFRED GOLDBERG
MURRAY J. LAULICHT
ARTHUR MARMOR

RICHARD M. MOSK
JOHN J. O'BRIEN
STUART POLLAK
ALFREDDA SCOBEY
CHARLES N. SHAFFER, JR.
LLOYD L. WEINREB

---

* *Mr. Willens also acted as liaison between the Commission and the Department of Justice.*

Key to Symbols

Citations not otherwise designated refer to the Report of the President's Commission on the Assassination of President John F. Kennedy *(The Warren Report) (U.S. Government Printing Office, 1964), symbol "WR" followed by page numbers; or to the* Hearings Before the President's Commission on the Assassination of President Kennedy, *i.e., "Hearings and Exhibits" (U.S. Government Printing Office, 1964), for which the symbols utilized in the footnotes to the Warren Report are used. References to testimony indicate the volume number of the Hearings, followed by the page number (e.g., 2H 301 designates Volume II of the Hearings, page 301); and references to the Exhibits indicate the name and/or numbers of the Exhibit (e.g., Kantor Exhibit No. 3; or CE 150). Page numbers which follow Exhibit designations may refer either to the pages of the Exhibit itself, or to the pages of the volume on which it appears.*

Foreword

During the eight o'clock news that morning the face of Dallas Police Chief Jesse E. Curry filled the television screen with assurances that every possible precaution had been taken to ensure the safety of President John Fitzgerald Kennedy. At two o'clock New York time I sat in my office with white-faced colleagues, listening to news bulletins over a transistor radio. President Kennedy had been shot while riding in a motorcade in Dallas.

We all remembered the indignities suffered by UN Ambassador Adlai Stevenson in Dallas less than a month before when a spitting, savage mob of right-wing extremists had subjected him to the hatred and fury they felt for the United Nations, which he represented and symbolized. The screaming insults, the blows, and the spittle were intended for all who believed in the United Nations. They were intended for those who hoped and worked for an end to the cold war and a beginning of genuine peace, for equality and mutual respect among men, for the rule of law and an end to brute violence—aims which had inspired President Kennedy's historic speech at American University in June '63.

At 2:p.m. the voice on the radio said with solemn anguish, "The President is dead." Someone in the room screamed with shock and grief. Someone cursed the John Birch Society and its kind. "Don't worry," I said derisively, "you'll see, it was a Communist who did it."

An hour later, back at the television screen on which Curry earlier had reassured the audience, I heard that Lee Harvey Oswald—a man with a Russian wife and a history of pro-Castro activities—had been taken into custody.

This is the personal background for my instantaneous skepticism about the official version of what happened in Dallas on November 22, 1963. In the three years that have followed, intensive study of the evidence against the alleged lone assassin has convinced me, as intuition alone could not, that the truth about Dallas remains unknown and that Lee Harvey Oswald may well have been innocent.

President John Fitzgerald Kennedy arrived at Love Field in Dallas, Texas, on Friday, Novmber 22, 1963 at 11:40 a.m. In his party were his wife Jacqueline Kennedy, Vice President Lyndon B. Johnson and Mrs. Johnson, Governor of Texas John B. Connally, Jr., and Mrs. Connally, and several prominent members of the Senate and the House. One purpose of the Presidential visit to Texas was to seek a reconciliation between warring factions within the state's Democratic Party. Despite apprehension about the President's safety in this city of right-wing activities, the President proceeded in his open car in a motorcade from the airfield toward the Trade Mart Building, where he was to be guest of honor at a luncheon organized by Dallas civic and business leaders.

At 12:30 p.m. the Presidential car proceeded from Houston Street to Elm Street, approaching a triple underpass. Shots rang out. The President and Governor Connally, who was seated directly in front of him, were hit.

The car raced to Parkland Hospital, where the President was taken to an emergency room and futile attempts were made to save his life. He was declared dead at 1 p.m. Governor Connally was seriously wounded, underwent surgery, and in due course recovered from his bullet wounds.

After President Kennedy was pronounced dead, Vice President Johnson left Parkland Hospital under heavy security protection, proceeding to Love Field. He boarded the Presidential airplane and at 2:38 p.m. took the oath of office and became the thirty-sixth President of the United States.

As Johnson was sworn into office, Lee Harvey Oswald was undergoing interrogation at the Dallas police headquarters on suspicion of shooting to death a patrolman, J. D. Tippit, who was murdered shortly after 1 p.m. on a street in Oak Cliff, a section of Dallas some distance from the scene of the assassination. Oswald was employed at the Texas School Book Depository on Elm Street, where witnesses had reported a man shooting at the motorcade from the sixth-floor southeast corner window. Within little more than a minute after the President and the Governor were shot, Oswald had been encountered on the second floor of the Book Depository by a motorcycle officer and the Book Depository superintendent; they found in Oswald's demeanor and appearance no cause for suspicion and proceeded immediately to the roof of the build..ing. encounter

Some time later, apparently 30 or 40 minutes after the ..ge of hom..e that intendent reported to the Dallas police captain in cha..spicion of th..ssassi- Oswald was missing. The captain placed Oswald under su..n learned tha..Oswald nation but before sending out an alarm for the missing ma.. was under arrest for the Tippit killing.

Oswald remained in police custody from Friday afternoon until Sunday morning. The Dallas police and district attorney quickly identified him as a defector who had lived in the Soviet Union, returned to the United States with a Russian wife, and become active in pro-Castro activities. While they acknowledged that Oswald steadfastly claimed that he was innocent of both the assassination and the murder of the policeman, the Dallas authorities repeatedly told the press and the public that his guilt was certain, giving a running account of evidence—real and imaginary—which they regarded as conclusive.

The police announced that Oswald would be transferred to the county jail on Sunday morning. Anonymous telephone calls the night before the transfer threatened that Oswald would be seized and killed, yet the plans for a public transfer proceeded.

Handcuffed to a detective and flanked by officers, Oswald was escorted to the police basement to begin the removal to the county jail. Suddenly, a man in the crowd of reporters and plainclothesmen fired a revolver point-blank, felling the prisoner. Oswald was removed to Parkland Hospital, where he died about two hours later. His killer, Jack Ruby, proprietor of a strip-joint, was to die of cancer in the same hospital some three years later.

The police charges that Oswald, a Marxist, had committed the assassination caused public misgivings, for it was a most strange denouement to the widespread assumption immediately after the President's death that he had been killed by the same right-wing fanatics who had abused Adlai Stevenson. The public's anxieties were compounded by the murder of Oswald in the police basement by Ruby, a known police buff. Dallas officials were denounced on every side for their mishandling of events at every stage; not even the authoritative weight of the Federal Bureau of Investigation sufficed in this instance to make the police version of the assassination credible to the American public or to observers abroad.

No one outside of Dallas was prepared to agree that, as police spokesmen said upon Oswald's death, "the case was closed." One week after the assassination, on November 29, 1963, President Johnson appointed a Commission, chaired by the Chief Justice of the U.S. Supreme Court, to "satisfy itself that the truth is known as far as it can be discovered and to report its findings and conclusions to him [the President], to the American people, and to the world."

The Report of the President's Commission—the Warren Report—was published at the end of September 1964. In essence, its conclusions were the same as those of the Dallas authorities: Lee Harvey Oswald, acting alone and unaided, had assassinated the President and murdered a police officer. Two months later, at the end of November 1964, 26 volumes of Hearings and Exhibits were published, assertedly presenting the testimony and evidence upon which the Warren Report was predicated.

This book examines the correlation, or lack of correlation, between the Report on the one hand and the Hearings and Exhibits on the other. The first pronounces Oswald guilty; the second, instead of corroborating the verdict reached by the Warren Commission, creates a reasonable doubt of Oswald's guilt and even a powerful presumption of his complete innocence of all the crimes of which he was accused.

On the day of the assassination the national climate of arrogance and passivity in the face of relentless violence—beatings, burnings, bombings, and shootings—yielded in some quarters to a sudden hour of humility and self-criticism. The painful moment passed quickly, for the official thesis of the lone, random assassin destroyed the impulse for national self-scrutiny and repentance. Thus, the climate of cruelty and barbaric hatred was restored after what was scarcely an interruption, and it was possible for Cuban émigrés—virtually with impunity and without regard for the hundreds of people who might be killed or injured—to fire a bazooka at the United Nations Headquarters building to express displeasure at the presence there of Che Guevara. Thus it was possible for American Nazi thugs to assault peaceful citizens assembled at a public meeting in Dallas at Christmas 1965. Thus it is possible for Americans to look upon the napalmed children of Vietnam and listen to their terror and agony nightly over the television tubes, and to go about their daily business as usual.

Few people who have followed the events closely—and who are not indentured to the Establishment—conceive of the Kennedy assassination as anything but a political crime. That was the immediate and universal belief on November 22 before the opinion-makers got to work endorsing the official explanation of the complex mystery as Gospel and entreating all good citizens to do the same.

What is noteworthy about the advocates of the Report is that they defend their position largely by rhetoric, asking how anyone can possibly question the probity of Chief Justice Warren or Senator Russell (much as one may disagree with his views on race) or even Allen Dulles. They do not argue on evidence, because frequently they are uninformed, and in preaching their faith in the Warren Commission there is scarcely a platitude they are not willing to use. As a general rule, partisans of the Report have not read it, much less the 26 volumes of Hearings and Exhibits. In discussion and debate, they expose their unfamiliarity with the facts and expound all kinds of irresponsible errors and assumptions. The critics of the Report, on the other hand, have by and large performed arduous labor and taken great pains to master and document the available information with the scrupulousness which was to be expected but is not found in the Warren Report. Only a few of the critics who question or reject the Report have been guilty of careless or incomplete research; and while that is not to be condoned, it is nevertheless the Commission and not the lone critic which had the responsibility of establishing and reporting the truth, with virtually unlimited manpower and funds at its disposal.

It is not the critic's responsibility to explain why the Chief Justice signed such a Report or why Robert Kennedy accepts it or to answer other similar questions posed by the orthodox defenders. As critic Tom Katen has pointed out, instead of evaluating the evidence in terms of Robert Kennedy's acquiescence, his acquiescence should be evaluated in the light of the evidence. Nor is it the critic's responsibility to name the person or persons who committed the assassination if Oswald did not—another characteristic *non sequitur*. It is, on the other hand, clearly the responsibility of the authors and advocates of the Report to explain and justify its explicit documented defects. If they cannot or will not, then let the Government which has given us such a profoundly defective document—at a cost to the people of well over a million dollars—scrap the Report and commission one that will sustain its assertions and conclusions and survive the test of close scrutiny.

One of the most reprehensible actions of the Warren Commission is that it disbanded the moment it handed over its Report, leaving no individual or corporate entity to answer legitimate questions arising from demonstrable misstatements of fact in the Report. On September 27, 1964 the Commission, in effect, attempted to close the case no less firmly than the Dallas police tried to close it on November 25, 1963. Letters to Commission members or counsel posing factual questions on the basis of material cited in the official volumes have gone either completely unanswered, or unanswered in substance. The policy of silence is an affront to concerned citizens and invites the irresistible inference that the authors are unable to defend or justify the points at issue.[1]

The haste with which the Warren Commission closed its case is arresting, because when all is said and done it is the very same case that the Dallas police tried to close before Oswald's corpse grew cold. Chief Jesse E. Curry and Captain J. Will Fritz of the Dallas Police and Dallas District Attorney Henry Wade said that Oswald was guilty. The Commission says so. Curry, Fritz, and Wade said that he acted alone and had no accomplices. The Commission says so. Curry, Fritz, and Wade said that he shot Tippit. The Commission says so. The Commission adds the charge that he tried to kill Major General Edwin A. Walker—but that is no tribute to its investigatory skill as opposed to that of the Dallas police. It is merely a story told by Marina Oswald and accepted by the Commission too readily by far, in disregard for the inconsistency between her story and the objective facts recorded contemporaneously or determined later, and in disregard for the doubts which arose about Marina Oswald's credibility when unyielding facts forced the Commission to reject her matching story of an attempt by her husband to assassinate Richard M. Nixon.

The Commission's blatant bias for and against witnesses and its double standard of judging credibility are in themselves beyond belief. Marina Oswald's testimony is treated as impeccable, despite the ludicrous Nixon story and her poor showing under the sole cross-examination (by Senator Russell) to which she was subjected. Helen Markham is another star witness. If Mrs. Markham did not misstate the truth one can only say—as Counsel Joseph Ball said on a public platform—that she is an "utter screwball." It is not necessary to belabor the Commission's desperation in declaring her wild testimony as having "probative value." Having deemed "reliable" the testimony of Marina Oswald and Helen Markham, how does the Commission deal with witnesses who on the face of it have neither fabricated nor become embroiled in blatant self-contradiction nor raved confusedly? The Commission decided that Seth Kantor was "mistaken." Buell Wesley Frazier and his sister—mistaken. W. W. Litchfield—mistaken or "lying." Wanda Helmick—mistaken or "lying." It dealt in the same way with

---

1 In mid-1965 I addressed letters to former members of the Warren Commission (Gerald R. Ford, John Sherman Cooper, Earl Warren) and to members of the staff (lawyers J. Lee Rankin, Albert E. Jenner, Jr., Wesley J. Liebeler, and Melvin E. Eisenberg; and historian Alfred Goldberg), requesting clarification on various points of evidence. In four cases (Cooper, Goldberg, Liebeler, and Rankin) no reply was received. In one case, a former assistant counsel agreed to discuss the questions put to him by telephone, on a confidential basis and not for attribution. He was not able to resolve the relevant problems—indeed, he was not even aware of the existence of one piece of evidence (the actual full-page ad of Klein's Sporting Goods in the February 1963 *American Rifleman*, from which it is evident that the rifle ordered by "Hidell" was a different model from the rifle found in the Depository), which I sent to him at his request.

In the remaining cases, I received replies of a purely formal nature, referring me to others for the requested information, only to have the redirected queries go without reply. One such reply promised that the writer would send a substantive response to the questions raised in my letter during the week of July 19, 1965; the promised response has yet to arrive.

Gertrude Hunter, Edith Whitworth, Roger Craig, Arnold Rowland, Victoria Adams, William Whaley, Albert Guy Bogard, Dial Ryder, C. A. Hamblen, Wilma Tice, and still others.

All those "mistaken" or "lying" witnesses have one thing in common: they gave evidence which in whole or in part was inconsistent with or antithetical to the official thesis of the lone psychotic assassin and the lone psychotic killer of the lone psychotic assassin. That was the thesis of the Dallas police and district attorney on November 25, 1963, and, with minor and inconsequential variations, the thesis of the Warren Commission a year later.

It has been said jokingly that the Dallas police are not so bad—look how quickly they caught Jack Ruby. Not so bad? They are brilliant. In some 48 hours they solved three murders of unparalleled complexity and mystery with the same conclusions as those reached a year later by the Chief Justice and his six eminent colleagues, the stable of bright young lawyers, the legions of investigators, and the regiment of criminology experts. The Dallas police achieved in a matter of some three days what the Commission achieved after an investigation said to be unprecedented in scope, depth, duration, and, we daresay, expense. Not many police departments can match the Dallas force.

In addition to the crimes and brutalities often committed by police and other officers of the law—not only in the South but in other regions—it is frequently alleged that police officers are found increasingly among the members of right-wing extremist organizations, several of which are known to collect arsenals and plan acts of violence and destruction.

The Dallas police permitted the most important prisoner in the history of Texas to be gunned down in their basement while handcuffed to a detective and flanked by officers. A few months later the Dallas police lost another prisoner, a woman who said she had worked for Ruby once, by suicide in one of their jail cells. Yet the same police solved the mystery of the assassination and the murder of Tippit with enough speed, authority, and skill to make one's mind reel. (Unfortunately they did not do nearly so well in the shooting of Warren Reynolds, a witness at the Tippit scene, a case which has remained unsolved since January 1964.) It seems unfair that editorial writers first assailed the Dallas force with contempt, and then wrote dazzling tributes to the Warren ·Commission without retracting their unkind words about the hapless Dallas police. If one accepts and endorses the Warren Report, one must also commend the Dallas police for their swift, sure work, and vindicate them in their finding that Oswald was the lone assassin and that the case was closed.

The difficulty is that the editorial writers and partisans of the Report rushed into a chorus of superlatives before they could read the 888-page Report with requisite care, and long before the supporting documents and testimony were made available for study and comparison. When the Hearings and Exhibits were issued two months after the Report, there was another concert of praise, equally extravagant and premature. None of the favorable appraisals was conditional on study of the Hearings and Exhibits to see if they corroborated the assertions in the Report (except perhaps for a critique by Professor Herbert Packer) and few have been followed by a restatement, reiterating or modifying the initial appraisal on the basis of such study.

There is much mention of the 26 volumes of the Hearings and Exhibits but little familiarity with their contents, organization, or character. The first 15 volumes consist of transcripts of the testimony of witnesses. Volumes I through V present the testimony of witnesses heard by the Warren Commission itself—not by the full Commission, as a rule, but with two or three members present—in the chronological sequence of their appearances. Volumes VI through XV present the testimony taken in depositions—that is, testimony under oath taken by a Commission lawyer, usually in Dallas, in the presence of a court reporter—arranged not chronologically but in rough approximation of the area of evidence on which a witness testified.

Volumes XVI through XXVI consist of Exhibits. The first three volumes in this group consist of exhibits identified by number (*CE 1, CE 2*, etc.) which were read into the record during the examination of the witnesses who testified before the Commission and whose testimony is found in Volumes I through V, as mentioned already. The next three volumes (Volumes XIX through XXI) consist of exhibits read into the record during the testimony of witnesses who provided the depositions contained in Volumes VI through XV; these exhibits, unlike the first group, are identified by the name of the witness and then by number (*Armstrong Exhibit No. 1, Paine Exhibit No. 2*, etc.). Finally, the last five volumes (XXII through XXVI) revert to numbered exhibits (*CE 2003, CE 2905*, etc.) selected by an unspecified criterion and not linked with specific testimony or entered on the record during the Hearings. (Thousands of cubic feet of Commission documents, consisting of reports and papers not converted into exhibits or published, are in the custody of the National Archives in Washington, D.C. Still other documents and materials are "classified" and not available for examination even at the Archives.)

Scrutiny of the Hearings and Exhibits, it must be acknowledged, is a monumental undertaking, involving the mastering of 26 thick volumes consisting of some 20,000 pages and more than ten million words. Few people have the time or fortitude for such a task. There are imposing obstacles even to the study of one or two distinct elements of the evidence in their entirety, to determine whether there is fidelity between the raw data and the account given in the Report. Such clearly delimited study would not require exorbitant time or effort if the Commission had included a subject index to make possible the tracing of the relevant testimony and documents to any single item of evidence.[2] The sheer mass of unclassified, unexplored data is enough to discourage an attempt to take inventory. It would be tantamount to a search for information in the *Encyclopedia Britannica* if the contents were untitled, unalphabetized, and in random sequence. It is hard to be unsympathetic to the student who shuddered and declined to read the Hearings and Exhibits word by

2 Sylvia Meagher, *Subject Index to the Warren Report and Hearings and Exhibits* (New York: Scarecrow Press, 1966).

word; however, it is equally hard to be sympathetic to the apologist for the Report who read the Report superficially, without skepticism or notice of its internal contradictions, publicly endorsing the findings and influencing opinion in favor of the Report while not bothering to read the Hearings and Exhibits.

It has been said that the American people are the only jury that Lee Harvey Oswald will ever have. It is our responsibility, then, to examine with utmost care and objectivity the evidence for and against him, and to reach an independent verdict. That responsibility cannot be delegated to others, however exalted their reputations and their honors. The first step must be the patient reading of the Hearings and Exhibits, imposing as the task is. If that reading demonstrates that the Report is an inaccurate, incomplete, or partisan synthesis of the raw material on which it supposedly relies, the authors—the Warren Commission—must account for the discrepancies in a manner that satisfies all doubt about their competence and their motives. If they cannot, or will not, provide such satisfaction, the people are entitled to a new investigation and a new report, by a competent and disinterested body submitting to the adversary procedure and permitting Oswald the maximum defense which can be given an accused man posthumously—an act of justice thus far denied him.

A new investigation utilizing the adversary procedure may theoretically also find that Oswald was the lone assassin. If such a finding is supported by unambiguous evidence which cannot be successfully challenged by the defense and if it is based on procedural decorum and equity, it will be acceptable. If there is a different finding, implicating co-assassins or absolving Oswald entirely, that too must meet the strictest tests of evidence and procedure.

A new investigation is imperative, because study of the Hearings and Exhibits has destroyed the grounds for confidence in the Warren Report. Study has shown the Report to contain (1) statements of fact which are inaccurate and untrue, in the light of the official Exhibits and objective verification; (2) statements for which the citations fail to provide authentication; (3) misrepresentation of testimony; (4) omission of references to testimony inimical to findings in the Report; (5) suppression of findings favorable to Oswald; (6) incomplete investigation of suspicious circumstances which remain unexplained; (7) misleading statements resulting from inadequate attention to the contents of Exhibits; (8) failure to obtain testimony from crucial witnesses; and (9) assertions which are diametrically opposite to the logical inferences to be drawn from the relevant testimony or evidence.

In this constellation, as in the case of the "mistaken" witnesses, there is one constant: the effect of each inaccuracy, omission, or misrepresentation is to fortify the fragmentary and dubious evidence for the lone-assassin thesis and to minimize or suppress the contrary evidence. To that constant must be linked the Commission's unashamed refusal to permit Oswald a defense, as formally requested by his mother, in contravention of the most elementary concept of fairness and judicial procedure. The excuse that Marina Oswald, chief witness for the prosecution, did not desire a defender to represent the man whose guilt she proclaimed and reiterated hardly merits discussion. If that position had any moral or legal merit, it was vitiated completely when the Commission appointed the President of the American Bar Association, Walter Craig, "to participate in the investigation and to advise the Commission whether in his opinion the proceedings conformed to the basic principles of American justice."[3] This compromise was worse than meaningless. The Commission should not have required a reminder from the head of the ABA to recall that an accused person has a fundamental right to self-defense and the benefit of reasonable doubt—even posthumously—and in any case no such reminder issued from Mr. Craig or his appointed observers. Craig and his representatives participated in the examination of witnesses from February 27 to March 12, 1964 (after Marina, Marguerite, and Robert Oswald had completed their 468 pages of testimony), the most memorable of their infrequent interventions being a question hostile to Oswald's interests. Thereafter, by agreement with the Commission's chief counsel, the ABA representatives "made suggestions" to counsel instead of participating directly in the proceedings. Therefore, it became impossible to isolate any contribution on their part, much less to infer that there was any safeguard of the interests of the accused or the propriety of the proceedings. Moreover, the ABA observers took no part whatever in the examination of 395 witnesses who did not appear before the Commission but were deposed by counsel. The whole sorry arrangement was a mockery that further compromised the Commission's claim to impartiality.

Although the Commission excluded the use of the adversary procedure, it did not hesitate to take advantage of its prerogatives—for example, engaging in the preparation of witnesses. The records show repeated instances of "dry runs" in which counsel questioned the witness in advance of his formal testimony. Such prior rehearsal is essential in a trial where the witness's story will be challenged in cross-examination, but in a fact-finding investigation resort to dry runs in advance of testimony can only feed suspicion that there was no search for truth but only for testimony which would buttress a preconceived and fixed conclusion.

A reading of the full testimony also leads to the irresistible conclusion that the witnesses fall into two general categories—the "friendly" and the "unfriendly"—which again is alien to the impartial fact-finding process. In the case of some "unfriendly" witnesses the Commission went beyond a show of antipathy and set out to discredit character. As Paul L. Freese wrote in the *New York University Law Review*, "The technique of character impeachment used by the Commission has disturbing implications."[4] While Freese ascribes the Commission's publication of defamatory comments on certain witnesses to its "zeal to publish the full truth,"[5] it is susceptible to other interpretations. It is striking that the Commission regarded as unimpeachable a number of witnesses whose testimony is inherently disordered and strongly suggestive of falsification or mental incompetence, or both. When Jack Ruby, a convicted murderer, gave testimony in conflict with the testimony of Seth Kantor, a responsible and re-

3 WR xiv.
4 Paul L. Freese, *New York University Law Review*, Vol. XL, No. 3, May 1965, pp. 424-465.
5 *Ibid.*, p. 449.

spected member of the White House press corps, the Commission chose to believe Ruby and decided that Kantor was mistaken. As already mentioned, it
relied on Marina Oswald and Helen Markham, both of whom became flagrantly
ensnarled in self-contradiction if not outright falsification. By contrast, the
Commission set out to impeach the character of a number of witnesses who
were disinterested and whose testimony was corroborated by others, apparently
for the sole reason that their testimony came into conflict with a theory which
was not subject to change regardless of the evidence.

Moreover, it is arresting that off-the-record discussion took place well over
two hundred times during the examination of witnesses, on occasion at crucial
points in the testimony and as frequently as seven or eight times per witness.
Some of those off-the-record passages undoubtedly were innocuous; in many
instances, this discussion was placed on the record immediately afterward.
However, one witness who was deposed by counsel subsequently appeared
before the Commission at his own request to report that during an off-the-
record interruption, counsel had accused him of perjury and had threatened
him with the loss of his job. If the witness had not placed those facts on the
record himself, they would have remained completely concealed from public
knowledge. We are therefore entitled to regard the constant resort to off-the-
record discussion as an unsatisfactory if not a suspicious practice.

Of the 489 witnesses who gave testimony, less than one-fourth appeared
before the Commission itself. Even in those cases, the seven members of the full
Commission were never present as a body or throughout an entire session. The
Chairman was in attendance at least part of the time for all 94 witnesses who
came before the Commission, but his colleagues heard only the following estimated numbers of witnesses:

Representative Ford	70	Mr. McCloy	35
Mr. Dulles	60	Representative Boggs	20
Senator Cooper	50	Senator Russell	6

Some of the difficulties encountered by the members in finding time to
spare from other duties for the Commission's needs were almost comical, as
may be seen in the following colloquy.

Chairman: Senator Cooper, at this time I am obliged to leave for our all-day
conference on Friday at the Supreme Court, and I may be back later in the
day, but if I don't, you continue, of course.

Cooper: I will this morning. If I can't be here this afternoon whom do you
want to preside?

Chairman: Congressman Ford, would you be here this afternoon at all?

Ford: Unfortunately, Mr. McCloy and I have to go to a conference out
of town.

Chairman: You are both going out of town, aren't you?

Cooper: I can go and come back if it is necessary.

Chairman: I will try to be here myself. Will Mr. Dulles be here?

McCloy: He is out of town.   (3H 55)

But if attendance was irregular, at least some members of the Commission heard some of the testimony of some of the 94 witnesses who came before the panel. None of the members heard any of the witnesses (well over 350) who testified by deposition; they included such important witnesses as Forrest V. Sorrels, Billy Lovelady, Seymour Weitzman, Earlene Roberts, Sheriff Bill Decker, Abraham Zapruder, Harry Holmes, Domingo Benavides, Nelson Delgado, George De Mohrenschildt, George Bouhe, Jean Lollis Hill, James Tague, Albert Guy Bogard, Dial Ryder, Sylvia Odio, Carlos Bringuier, Gertrude Hunter, Edith Whitworth, George Senator, Harry Olsen, Karen Carlin, and Curtis (Larry) Crafard. A number of witnesses who should have been examined with particular care are represented in the Hearings only by an affidavit. Most appalling of all are the numbers of persons whose names are found nowhere in the list of the Commission's witnesses, from whom no testimony in any form was taken despite indications that they possessed important or crucial information. The failure to examine or, in some instances, to locate such witnesses—including those who gave an account of the Tippit shooting wholly different from the official one—is one of the most serious defects in the Commission's work, and suggests, at the very least, a high degree of negligence.

The Commission's housekeeping is another area in which its performance was inept and undeserving of public confidence. Because of the Commission's inability to maintain control over its internal records, disclosures flowed steadily to the press, including the complete transcript of the examination of Jack Ruby. The Chairman and other spokesmen made a series of ill-advised public statements; the former made an unwarranted attack on the character of a witness and never retracted it, even when the witness exonerated himself from suspicion and requested a retraction. The Chairman also made the shocking statement, still unexplained, that the whole truth might never be known in our lifetime. At least one Commission member capitalized commercially on his experience by publishing an article[6] and later a book[7] purporting to provide a "portrait of the assassin." Apparently the same Commission member is unwilling or unable to explain ambiguities in the Report, including those revealed in his own book, to the taxpayer.

The Commission's failures manifest a contempt for the citizens whom this body pretended to serve—a contempt not for their rights alone but for their intelligence. It must be said, without apology to the authors and advocates of the Warren Report, that it resembles a tale told for fools, full of sophistry and deceit, signifying capitulation to compromise and the degradation of justice by its most eminent guardians.

In June 1966 publication of Edward Jay Epstein's book, *Inquest*,[8] sparked a long overdue national debate on the Warren Report. *Inquest* was followed almost immediately by the private editions *Whitewash* by Harold Weisberg

---

6 Representative Gerald R. Ford, "Piecing Together the Evidence," *Life,* October 2, 1964, pp. 42-50B.

7 Representative Gerald R. Ford, *Portrait of the Assassin* (New York: Simon and Schuster and Ballantine Books, 1965).

8 *Inquest* (New York: Viking Press, 1966).

(issued later by Dell as a paperback)[9] and *Forgive My Grief* by Penn Jones, Jr.;[10] and by *Rush to Judgment* by Mark Lane,[11] *The Oswald Affair* by Léo Sauvage,[12] and *The Second Oswald* by Richard Popkin.[13] *The Oswald Affair* had appeared in the original French edition (Éditions Minuit, Paris) early in 1965, the first full-length book to assess the official findings on the basis of both the Warren Report and the 26 volumes of Hearings and Exhibits. Unfortunately, it did not become available to American readers until a year and a half after publication in France.

The writers of these books began to be heard on radio and television; news stories and editorials began to appear in respected newspapers, reflecting serious concern about the validity of the Warren Report and suggesting—or demanding, in some cases—that the Commission answer the charges against its Report or that a new investigation be carried out. As this is written, a long list of prominent names are on record as favoring one or another form of new inquiry. Representative Theodore R. Kupferman (R., N.Y.) has presented a joint resolution in the Congress calling for a reappraisal of the Warren Report and, if need be, a new investigation. Former Assistant Counsel Wesley J. Liebeler, embarrassed by his acknowledged contributions to *Inquest*—the book without which no public controversy might now be raging—has launched an attempt to rehabilitate himself. He has organized a new investigation with the stated purpose of reinstating the discredited findings of the Warren Commission, perhaps by re-interpreting the evidence or finding new information. Liebeler is conducting this new investigation with the assistance of 20 law students at the University of California. (*New York Times,* Oct. 23, 1966, p. 66; News broadcast, WINS (N.Y.C.) radio, Oct. 22, 1966.) That a spokesman for the Commission cannot defend the Report as it stands but is seeking a means by which to restore its respectability is in itself a total default to the opposition. Liebeler seems unaware of that.

The critical books and articles that began to appear in June 1966 (and those published earlier that had been ignored before the new wave of skepticism) served as catalytic agents for several major events. One was the sudden announcement early in November 1966 that the notorious autopsy photographs and X rays had been deposited in the National Archives by the Kennedy family, at the request of the Justice Department (admittedly made as a result of the mounting criticism and questions about the Warren Report). But the terms of the transfer of this evidence to the Archives were such that the photographs and X rays will not be made available to any individual or organization except a new governmental investigatory body, if one is appointed to further investigate the assassination.[14]

---

9   *Whitewash* (Hyattsville, Maryland: Weisberg, 1966); and *Whitewash: The Report on the Warren Report* (New York: Dell Publishing Co., Inc., 1966).

10   *Forgive My Grief* (The Midlothian (Tex.) Mirror, 1966).

11   *Rush to Judgment* (New York: Holt, Rinehart, & Winston, 1966).

12   *The Oswald Affair* (New York: World Publishing Co., 1966).

13   *The Second Oswald* (New York: Avon Books/The New York Review of Books, 1966).

14   *The Reporter,* December 15, 1966, p. 46.

On the third anniversary of President Kennedy's death, *Life,*[15] *Ramparts,*[16] and other influential publications called editorially for further investigation and openly questioned the evidence and the findings of the Warren Commission. The silent principals suddenly spoke up; Governor Connally, Senator Russell, Commander Boswell, and J. Edgar Hoover, among others, tripped over each other in their haste to issue public statements, which, deliberately or inadvertently—and in some instances, unintentionally contravening the purpose of the statement—created new doubt and mystery. The gambit of "producing" the missing autopsy photographs and X rays, if it was a gambit, in no way stilled the controversy.

We now have a climate in which the news media and public opinion acknowledge what was formerly unthinkable: that the Warren Commission may have erred, or worse. This healthier climate perhaps signifies recovery of the skepticism, independence of mind, and sense of justice to which Americans as a people lay claim as national attributes. Too often, and especially in the Oswald case, the public has been apathetic, ready to accept government "truth," callously indifferent to injustice.

If closed minds continue to open, to receive and evaluate objectively the facts which are on the record, we may yet proceed to pursue the truth to its ultimate reaches—regardless of attendant dangers and doubts—so that history will know with certainty what happened in Dallas, and why.

To that end, investigation into the assassination and the related murders should be reopened, entrusted to an uncompromisingly independent, competent, and impartial body—a body committed to the use of adversary procedure, the rules of evidence, and total respect for justice, in both the letter and the spirit. In other words, a body different from the Warren Commission.

Whether or not that comes to pass in the immediate future, the country owes profound gratitude to the critics and researchers whose work, published or unpublished, has helped to destroy the myth of the Warren Report. Because of their courage, intelligence, and integrity, "it is the majestic Warren Commission itself that is in the dock today, rather than the lonely Oswald," as Anthony Howard wrote in the *London Observer* on August 7, 1966.[17] The Commission must receive justice—that justice which was denied to Oswald in death as in life—but nothing less than justice.

Sylvia Meagher
December 1966

---

15 *Life,* November 25, 1966, pp. 38-48.
16 *Ramparts,* November 1966, p. 3.
17 "The Clamour Rises for Kennedy X Rays," *The London Observer,* August 7, 1966, p. 10.

PART I
THE ASSASSINATION

Chapter 1
The Motorcade and the Shots

The Speed of the Presidential Car

After the assassination, reports that the President's car had stopped after the first shot was fired were interpreted in some quarters as evidence that the driver believed that the shot came from somewhere in front of the car. The Warren Report dismissed the allegation:

> The Presidential car did not stop or almost come to a complete halt after the firing of the first shot or any other shots. The driver, Special Agent William R. Greer, has testified that he accelerated the car after what was probably the second shot. Motion pictures of the scene show that the car slowed down momentarily after the shot that struck the President in the head and then speeded up rapidly. *(WR 641)*

This passage is found under "Rumors and Speculations," an appendix to the Warren Report which the Commission used as a graveyard for the claims of various early critics of the lone-assassin theory. One such critic, Mark Lane, testified on March 4, 1964 that he believed that the car had come to a halt when the shooting began, on the basis of statements by

> ... various witnesses, including Mr. Chaney, a motorcycle policeman, Miss Woodward, who was one of the closest witnesses to the President at the time that he was shot, and others. I think that is . . . conceded by almost everyone, that the automobile came to—almost came to a complete halt after the first shot. . . . *(2H 45)*

According to Lane, reporter Mary Woodward had corroborated, in a telephone conversation, the statement in her story in the *Dallas Morning News* of November 23, 1963 that "instead of speeding up . . . the car came to a halt." *(2H 43)*

3

Lane's allegation about Chaney is corroborated in the testimony of another motorcycle officer, M. L. Baker. Baker testified on March 24, 1964 that his fellow officer, James Chaney, had told him:

> He was on the right rear of the car or to the side, and then at the time the chief of police, he didn't know anything about this, and he moved up and told him, and then that was during the time that the Secret Service men were trying to get in the car, and at the time, after the shooting, from the time the first shot rang out, the car stopped completely, pulled to the left and stopped. . . . Mr. Truly was standing out there, he said it stopped. Several officers said it stopped completely.   *(3H 266)*

When he testified on March 24, 1964, Roy Truly corroborated Baker's statement.

> *Truly:* I saw the President's car swerve to the left and stop somewheres down in this area. . . .
> *Belin:* When you saw the President's car seem to stop, how long did it appear to stop?
> *Truly:* It would be hard to say over a second or two or something like that. I didn't see—I just saw it stop. I don't know. I didn't see it start up. . . . The crowd in front of me kind of congealed . . . and I lost sight of it. *(3H 221)*

Various other witnesses said that the car had come to a complete stop or almost a standstill when the noise of the shot was heard—Senator Ralph Yarborough *(7H 440)*, for example, and Mrs. Earle Cabell *(7H 487)*, among others. Policeman Earle V. Brown, who was stationed on the triple overpass farther down Elm Street, testified on April 7, 1964 that:

> *Brown:* Actually, the first I noticed the car was when it stopped. . . . After it made the turn and when the shots were fired, it stopped.
> *Ball:* Did it come to a complete stop?
> *Brown:* That, I couldn't swear to.
> *Ball:* It appeared to be slowed down some?
> *Brown:* Yes; slowed down.   *(6H 233)*

In sum, at least seven eyewitnesses to the assassination indicated that the President's car had come to a complete stop, or what was tantamount to a stop. Two of those witnesses (James Chaney and Mary Woodward) were not asked to testify before the Commission on this or on other observations of some importance reported to the Commission as hearsay (see, for example, *2H 43-45* and *CE 2084*). Apparently the witnesses were mistaken in remembering that the car had stopped; motion pictures, according to the Commission, contradicted them. Yet it seems clear from the way in which counsel led witnesses that the Commission had considerable resistance to inferences which might be drawn from evidence that the car had stopped at the first shot. "Stopped" was transformed into "seemed to stop" and then into "slowed down." Such leading of witnesses, which would have been challenged in a courtroom, was facilitated by the Commission's closed hearings, to which there was only one exception, by request of the witness concerned. *(2H 33)*

The films of the assassination have not been released for public showing, although it is possible to see the most important one, the Zapruder film—taken by amateur photographer Abraham Zapruder—at the National Archives. That film does not seem to support the witnesses who said that the car stopped dead. This being so, it is baffling that counsel conducted the questioning somewhat improperly and why the Report presents this evidence with some lack of impartiality (in a passage failing to indicate that some seven witnesses mistakenly believed that the car had stopped at the first shot). Yet in dismissing an allegation related to the source of the first shot, the same passage seemingly yields ground on the source of the third. The statement that "the car slowed down momentarily after the shot that struck the President in the head" is consistent with other evidence, to be discussed later, that the fatal shot came not from the Texas School Book Depository, as the Report maintains, but from a point in front of the car and to its right.

The Mark on the Curb and the Cut on the Face

In order to attempt to solve the mystery of the assassination, it is vital to establish the number and direction of the shots. Utilizing certain physical evidence and eyewitness testimony, the Warren Commission concluded that only three shots were fired and that they came from the sixth floor of the Texas School Book Depository, at the corner of Elm and Houston Streets. Was that conclusion based upon the conscientious and disinterested examination of all the evidence, the impartial consideration of all the testimony, and the rational, objective assessment of the information? Here is the chronology of two pieces of evidence vital to the determination of the number and direction of the shots.

November 22, 1963   Shortly after the shooting it was known that a bystander, James Tague, had been struck on the face by an apparent bullet fragment, and that a fresh bullet mark was found on the curb near the place where Tague had been standing. The Tague incident was reported to a deputy sheriff and his superior *(7H 546-547)*, to Dallas Police Officer Haygood *(WR 116)* and the Dallas police at City Hall *(7H 556)*. Although Tague went to City Hall and reported his experience, the police report on the assassination *(CE 2003)* does not include any affidavit from or any reference to Tague.

November 23, 1963   Two Dallas newsmen, Tom Dillard and James Underwood, took films or photographs of the mark on the curb. *(Shaneyfelt Exhibit No. 26)*

November 25, 1963   Dillard was interviewed by FBI Agent Kreutzer. Presumably he reported the bullet mark on the curb. However, the FBI report on the interview is omitted from the Exhibits although it was in the possession of the Warren Commission. *(6H 166)*

April 1, 1964   Dillard and Underwood were examined by Commission Counsel Ball, who failed to elicit by his questions information from either of the witnesses about the mark on the curb. Ball referred explicitly to the FBI interview of Dillard *(6H 166);* if that report included information about the mark on the curb, it must be inferred that Ball deliberately excluded this from the scope of his examination.

April 9, 1964   Officer Haygood gave testimony before Commission Counsel Belin in which he reported that a bystander was hit on the face during the shooting. *(6H 298)*

May 1964   Disclosures to the press indicated that the Warren Commission had concluded that the first bullet that struck the President had also hit the Governor and caused all of his wounds.

End of May 1964   Tague took films at the scene of the assassination, observed without his knowledge by unknown investigators who informed the Warren Commission of the incident. He later said, "I didn't think anyone knew about that." *(7H 555)*

June 11, 1964   Two FBI agents interviewed James Underwood about the mark on the curb. *(Shaneyfelt Exhibit 26)* The report on the interview is not included in the Commission's Exhibits. It is not known what led the FBI to interview Underwood at this time; it should be noted that Dillard was not interviewed now, perhaps because he had already told the FBI about the mark on the curb when he was interviewed on November 25, 1963.

Unspecified date before July 7, 1964   Martha Jo Stroud, Assistant U. S. Attorney for Dallas, sent a communication to the Warren Commission transmitting a photograph of the mark on the curb which had been taken by Dillard. *(Shaneyfelt Exhibit 26)*

July 7, 1964   The Commission formally requested the FBI to investigate the mark on the curb. *(Shaneyfelt Exhibit 26)*

July 15, 1964   FBI agents interviewed Dillard and Underwood and, accompanied by them, tried to locate the mark on the curb but reported that they were unable to find it. This information was sent to the Commission in a letter dated July 17, 1964. *(Shaneyfelt Exhibit 26)*

July 23, 1964   Tague and Deputy Sheriff Walthers gave testimony before Commission Counsel Liebeler, both reporting the cut and the mark on the curb. *(7H 544-558)* There is no indication in the record that Tague had been interviewed before this date by any investigative agency, although he had reported his experience to the Dallas police on the day of the assassination and apparently was under official surveillance at the end of May when he took films at the scene.

August 5, 1964   FBI Expert Shaneyfelt located the mark on the curb and removed a piece of curbing for examination at the FBI Laboratory. *(15H 697-701)*

August 12, 1964   In a report to the Commission, the FBI stated: "In response to your inquiry, assuming that a bullet shot from the sixth-floor window of the . . . Depository struck the curb . . . evidence present is insufficient to establish whether it was caused by a fragment of a bullet striking the occupants of the Presidential limousine . . . or whether it is a fragment of a shot that may have missed. . . ." *(Shaneyfelt Exhibit 27)*

September 3, 1964   The FBI informed the Commission that the distance from the President's car to the mark on the curb at the time of the head shot (Frame 313) was about 260 feet. *(Shaneyfelt Exhibit 36)*

September 27, 1964   The Warren Report revealed that a bystander had been hit on the cheek by an object during the shooting and that an apparent bullet mark had been found on a curb nearby. The Report stated:

> . . . the mark on the south curb of Main Street cannot be identified conclusively with any of the three shots fired. Under the circumstances it might have come from the bullet which hit the President's head, or it might have been the product of the fragmentation of the missed shot upon hitting some other object in the area.   *(WR 117)*

Appraisal of the Facts

It is indisputable that in a methodical, impartial investigation Tague would have been interviewed and the mark on the curb would have been examined at an early stage—certainly before conclusions were formulated about the number and the source of the shots. The evidence was known immediately to the Dallas police and sheriff's officers and almost certainly to the FBI as well, from the interview with Dillard if not from local police officers. Yet the first overt indication of FBI interest in the curb came only on June 11, 1964, and the records do not specify what provoked action at that time. It may have been the communication from Martha Jo Stroud; that too has been withheld from the Exhibits and the date is not known. Whatever that date, it is perfectly clear from the documents that it was her communication that led the Commission on July 7, 1964 to request an FBI investigation of the curb, and it is entirely legitimate to wonder if the public would have learned anything whatever about this or the Tague matter in the absence of such an external stimulus. The omission from the Exhibits of the FBI reports on interviews with Underwood and Dillard and the letter from Mrs. Stroud betrays a lack of candor on the Commission's part and perhaps an attempt to conceal its persistent inattention, and the FBI's, to vital evidence—evidence which irresistibly creates uncertainty about the actual number of shots.

If the Commission now concedes that the mark on the curb was made by a bullet, or a bullet fragment, it does so on the same undeviating assumption that the shots came exclusively from the Book Depository. To assume a priori that the mark was produced by a missile from that source, as both the Commission and the FBI did without even considering any other possibility, betrays the commitment to a hypothesis with which this evidence has little compatibility. Straining to force the evidence into harmony with preconceived conclusions, the Commission suggests two rather frail possibilities.

It suggests that a fragment from the bullet that hit the President's head might have produced the mark on the curb, ignoring the fact that two large fragments (equivalent respectively to one-fourth and one-eighth of the mass of the whole bullet) had dropped into the car without even penetrating the windshield or the relatively soft surfaces on which they were found. *(WR 76-77, 557; 5H 66-74)* If those fragments suffered such a dramatic loss of velocity upon impact and fragmentation, how could a different piece of the bullet retain sufficient momentum to travel "about 260 feet" farther, and to cut Tague's face and/or mark the curb?

Alternatively, the Commission suggests, the mark was made by a bullet that missed and fragmented upon hitting "some other object in the area." There is no evidence to support this conjecture. It is all but untenable, because the preponderance of testimony indicates that the shot that struck the President's head was the last shot fired.

For a proper understanding of the dilatory way in which the Commission and its servant agencies pursued the investigation of the Tague injury and the mark on the curb, one should appreciate the energy and tenacity with which other inquiries were conducted. A case in point is the report that Oswald had visited the Irving Sports Shop to have a scope mounted on a rifle. That story received a degree of corroboration from two women who gave a detailed description of a man, accompanied by his wife and two little girls, who had come into a furniture shop to inquire about the new location of the gunsmith who had formerly occupied the premises. The two women identified Marina Oswald as the woman. Marina Oswald denied that she had been in the furniture store with Oswald and her babies. Invariably taking Marina Oswald's testimony as gospel even when her story was inherently implausible or in conflict with credible and disinterested testimony, the Commission took considerable pains to disprove the story told by the two women in the furniture shop. This is seen in the following excerpt from an FBI report:

> By letter dated June 30, 1964, the President's Commission requested that a check be made of the public record of births for the area which encompasses both Dallas and Irving, Texas, to ascertain the names and addresses of female babies born on October 20, 1963. It was requested that parents of these babies be interviewed to determine whether any of these families have an older female child approximately two and one-half years old and whether any of these families were in Mrs. Whitworth's furniture store in early November, 1963, and under what circumstances.   *(CE 1338)*

Although the FBI applied itself diligently to this assignment, no suitable family was found. But the matter is mentioned here solely to demonstrate the lengths to which the Commission went in some instances, in contrast to its inaction in others.

In the case of the mark on the curb and Tague's injury, the Commission's investigation and conclusions are inadequate and unsatisfactory. We are left with evidence of a bullet or bullet fragment that almost certainly did not come from any of the three bullets which the Commission—reasoning that only three shells were found and downgrading objective evidence of more than that number of bullets fired—concludes were involved.[1]

---

1 On pages 37-38 of his book *Whitewash II* (privately published at Hyattstown, Maryland, 1966) Harold Weisberg discloses evidence of a second apparent bullet mark on the sidewalk on the north side of Elm Street. This mark, considered by two witnesses to be a bullet mark, was called to the attention of the FBI two days after the Warren Report, without any mention of such a mark, was issued.

On Elm Street between Houston and the triple underpass the FBI located a "wide-dug-out scar," about four inches long and half an inch wide, and reported to the Warren Commission (presumably defunct) that "this scar lies in such a direction that if it had been made by a bullet, it could not have come from the direction of the window" of the Book Depository.

Where Did the Shots Come From?

I do not agree with the contention in the Warren Report *(WR 61-117, 639-642)* that all the shots fired at the Presidential car came from the sixth-floor window of the Book Depository. I do agree that an assassin, or a decoy, was at that window. I also agree that the known facts appear to eliminate shots fired from the overpass.

The Commission has not, however, given adequate consideration to the possibility of assassins at locations other than the window or the overpass; this possibility has certainly not been ruled out. There is a considerable body of evidence suggesting that shots were fired from the grassy knoll on Elm Street between the Book Depository and the overpass. In his article "Fifty-One Witnesses: The Grassy Knoll,"[2] Harold Feldman has provided an impressive analysis of eyewitness testimony and has demonstrated that fifty-one of the witnesses represented in the Hearings and Exhibits thought that the shots had come from the grassy knoll.

In discussing the source of the shots, I shall consider a number of specific elements in the testimony and evidence:

(1) The inconsistent and baffling reaction of bystanders and police officers, if all the shots indeed came from the sixth-floor window of the Book Depository.

(2) The strong suggestion that shots were fired from the grassy knoll and that a man or men were seen to flee the scene.

(3) The incompleteness and selectivity of the eyewitness testimony and photographic evidence on which the conclusions in the Warren Report are based.

(4) Suspicious circumstances, ignored by the Warren Commission, which point to the method of escape of assassins who may have fired at the President from the grassy knoll.

Inconsistent and Baffling Reactions

This is a case in which appearances constantly and repeatedly belie the "facts" asserted by the Warren Commission. The Commission insists that all the shots came from the sixth-floor window of the Book Depository, yet the testimony and photographs show that after the shooting there was a mass surge of police and spectators to the grassy knoll and the railroad yards, and that for some five or ten minutes no attention was paid to the Book Depository. The building had not been effectively sealed as late as 12:50 p.m. (if it was ever sealed at all),

---

2 *The Minority of One,* March 1965, pp. 16-25.

although according to the Warren Report a number of eyewitnesses told the police immediately that they had seen a rifle, or a man with a rifle, in the sixth-floor window. No one rushed to that window; no one even rushed to the sixth floor.

It was not until 1:12 p.m. that signs of a sniper's nest were noticed for the first time, by a sheriff's deputy—not because a witness had alerted him but because he was in the course of a floor-by-floor search of the whole building.

The belated and accidental discovery of the sniper's nest presented a self-evident and signal problem: Why did the police ignore eyewitness reports of a rifle in the sixth-floor window? Why didn't they send a search party immediately to the sixth floor to trap or intercept the sniper? That elementary question was not posed by the Warren Commission to the police witnesses who received the eyewitness reports or who organized the floor-by-floor search of the building. The Warren Report ignores the very existence of this pivotal and potentially disruptive question.

Among those who reported a man with a weapon in the sixth-floor window, Howard L. Brennan is one of the Commission's star witnesses. It is Brennan whom the Commission regards as "most probably" the source of the description of the suspect that was called in by Inspector J. Herbert Sawyer and broadcast over the police radio at 12:45 p.m. But Brennan testified that he gave the description to Secret Service Agent Forrest V. Sorrels (3H 145-146), who arrived on the scene well after the description was broadcast. And Inspector Sawyer did not remember speaking to Brennan or to anyone resembling Brennan or wearing (as Brennan was) a hard-top hat. (6H 322-323) Moreover, Sawyer in his testimony (6H 322) verified an entry in the radio log (CE 1974, p. 171) which indicated that only a minute or two after calling in the 12:45 description, Sawyer had told the dispatcher that "it's unknown whether he is still in the building or *not known if he was there in the first place.*" (Italics added) Had Brennan or anyone else who gave the description of the suspect to Sawyer specified that the man was at the sixth-floor window, Sawyer would hardly have said that it was not known if the assassin was in the Book Depository "in the first place." Although the Report omits it in paraphrasing the description called in by Sawyer (WR 144), Sawyer specified that the suspect was armed with a 30-30 rifle or some type of Winchester. (CE 1974, p. 170)

The burden of this evidence is that an unknown witness gave Sawyer a description of a suspect armed with a 30-30 rifle that looked like a Winchester and that the witness did not place the suspect in the Book Depository building, much less in a particular window. It is surprising, therefore, that the Commission proclaims that the description was "based primarily on Brennan's observations" (WR 5) and that Brennan's description "most probably led to the radio alert at 12:45 p.m." (WR 144, 649)

A faithful rendition of the evidence should have led the Commission to say, rather, that Brennan almost certainly was not the source of the description and that the witness who really provided the description has remained unidentified.

The surge of people to the grassy knoll and the railroad yards, and the lack of activity at the Book Depository in the aftermath of the shots, is recurrent in the testimony of many witnesses. An FBI report of an interview with T. E. Moore states:

> Mr. Moore noticed some of the bystanders on the north side of Elm Street below the concrete pavilion rushing away from the street, across the grass towards the concrete pavilion in the direction of some railroad tracks behind the concrete pavilion. Mr. Moore stated that at the sound of the first shot he looked up towards the Texas School Book Depository because the shot sounded like it had come from a high area; however, he did not observe anything noteworthy at the . . . Depository. He stated that approximately ten minutes later, the . . . Depository was surrounded by police officers. *(CE 2102)*

James Tague testified that it was "five or six or seven minutes in there before anybody done anything about anything. . . . If Oswald was in that building, he had all the time in the world to calmly walk out of there." *(7H 558)*

Motorcycle officer Bobby Hargis testified:

> I looked over to the Texas School Book Depository Building, and no one that was standing at the base of the building was—seemed to be looking up at the building or anything, like they knew where the shots were coming from. . . . Some people looking out of the windows up there, didn't seem like they knew what was going on. . . . About the only activity I could see was on the bridge, on the railroad bridge . . . and I thought maybe some of them had seen who did the shooting and the rifle.   *(6H 295)*

James Altgens of the Associated Press, who took the famous "doorway" photographs *(CEs 203, 1407-1408),* told the Commission:

> I saw a couple of Negroes looking out of a window which I later learned was the floor below where the gun—the sniper's nest was supposed to have been, but it didn't register on me at the time that they were looking from an area that the bullet might have come from.   *(7H 518-519)*

Altgens' observations should be regarded in the light of the central importance given by the Warren Report to the accounts of those witnesses who were looking out of the window. According to the Report *(WR 70-71)* Harold Norman heard a bolt of a rifle operate and shells dropping to the floor and said at once that the shots were coming from over his head. Bonnie Ray Williams is said to have had "debris" fall onto his head, which he brushed away before it was seen by anyone other than his two companions. The Report tells us that James Jarman confirmed what Norman had said about the source of the shots and that debris had fallen on Williams' head; it does not mention that Jarman testified that he himself thought that the shots had come from below the fifth-floor window from which he was watching the motorcade. *(3H 209)* Nor does the Report emphasize or even mention that the three men did not act at the time as if they believed that the shots had been fired from over their heads. They neither went up to the sixth floor nor immediately notified the police that the shots had come from there. The Report states that "after pausing for a few minutes, the three men ran downstairs" and reported their experience. *(WR 71)* According to the testimony, it was about fifteen minutes before the three men reached the street and told their story. *(3H 183)* They had first rushed to the west windows on the fifth floor, because, as Harold Norman explained:

> . . . it seems as though everyone else was running towards the railroad tracks, and we ran over there. Curious to see why everybody was running that way for. . . . We saw the policemen, and I guess they were detectives, they were searching the empty cars. . . .   *(3H 192-193)*

Bonnie Ray Williams told a similar story.

> We saw the policemen and people running, scared, running—there are some tracks on the west side of the building, railroad tracks. They were running towards that way. And we thought maybe—well, to ourself, we know the shots practically came from over our head. But since everybody was running, you know, to the west side of the building, towards the railroad tracks, we assumed maybe somebody was down there.   *(3H 175)*

After looking at the scene to the west of the building, the three men next went to the fourth floor. *(3H 182, 207)* Jarman, who thought the shots had come from below the fifth floor, and Williams both testified that they had gone to the floor below—surely peculiar behavior for men who had reason to think the shots had come from the floor above—but Counsel Ball showed no interest, and this is not mentioned in the Report.

Then the men continued down the stairs and reached the street, where they saw Brennan talking to a police officer "and they then reported their own experience," according to the Report. If that is what happened, it is very strange indeed that the police did not immediately send a search party to the sixth floor, as already pointed out; and equally strange that the three men were not taken immediately to the sheriff's office or to police headquarters, as were many other witnesses whose stories were far less important, to make a formal statement. Of the three, only Williams gave an affidavit that afternoon, in which he said that he had heard shots which sounded as if they came from just above him. *(CE 2003, p. 65)* Jarman gave an affidavit on November 23, 1963 in which he did not even mention that he had watched the motorcade from the fifth floor, much less what Norman had said or the debris on Williams' head. *(CE 2003, p. 34)* Norman, the only one of the three who had heard the rifle bolt and the falling shells, was never taken to police headquarters at all and gave no affidavit.

Norman was questioned, for the first time apparently, on November 26 by FBI Agent Kreutzer. The report on that interview has been withheld from the Exhibits, although Norman was questioned about the interview during his testimony before the Warren Commission and disputed some of the statements attributed to him by the FBI. *(3H 196)* He was next interviewed on December 4 by Secret Service Agent Carter *(CE 493),* but in his Commission testimony he denied that he had said, as the Secret Service reported, that he knew "the shots came from directly above us." *(3H 194)*

In spite of Norman's disclaimer (and Jarman's), the Warren Report asserts that "three employees of the Book Depository, observing the parade from the fifth floor, heard the shots fired from the floor immediately above them." *(WR 61)* It cites the observations of Howard Brennan—whose story is marked by internal contradictions and absurdities, and who admitted that he had lied to the police *(WR 144-146)*—in support of the presence of a man in the sixth-floor window. The Commission asserts that it does not rely on Brennan's "identification" in reaching the conclusion that the man in the window was Oswald but is satisfied that he saw someone who at the least resembled Oswald and whom Brennan believed to be Oswald. *(WR 146)* According to Wesley J. Liebeler, former assistant counsel to the Commission, the conclusion that it was Oswald at the window is supported by

> . . . the least direct evidence of all, because there isn't any eyewitness . . . to rely on. . . . The fact that Oswald's fingerprints were on the cartons has no probative value whatsoever on the issue of whether he was in the window or not, because he worked at the Depository, he could have put his prints there at any time.[3]

On the same occasion Liebeler's colleague Burt Griffin listed as evidence of Oswald's presence at the window the "fact" that he had shot Tippit![4]

Nor did the Commission rely on fifteen-year-old Amos Euins, who told a reporter immediately after the shooting that he had seen a colored man firing from the window *(6H 170)* but who testified ultimately that he did not know whether the man he saw in the window was colored or white. *(WR 147)*

Other witnesses saw a rifle-like object or a rifle protruding from the window but not a man. *(WR 64-65)* All these witnesses gave testimony before the Commission or by deposition. One of them, James Richard Worrell, Jr., told the Commission when he testified on March 10, 1964 that he had seen six inches of a rifle protruding from the window and that he had heard a total of four shots. Taking alarm, he had run around the corner on Houston Street and upon stopping to catch his breath had seen a man rush out of the Book Depository and run out of sight; he did not see the man's face. *(WR 253)* The Report mentions Worrell only once; the Commission does not evaluate his testimony or confront the possibility that his story, if true, may implicate a man other than Oswald. (Worrell was killed on November 5, 1966 in a motorcycle crash in Dallas—the third important witness to die in a motor vehicle accident in less than a year.[5])

Amos Euins provides some corroboration for the allegation that a man ran out of the Book Depository after the shooting. He testified that the policeman to whom he had reported his own observations, whose name he did not remember ("he was kind of an old policeman"), had interviewed another man and that the man had said "he seen a man run out the back" and that the running man "had some kind of bald spot on his head." *(2H 205-206)* Nothing in the published record indicates that the Commission made any attempt to identify or question the unknown witness who had reported that "a man run out the back," probably giving that information to Inspector Sawyer or Sergeant Harkness, the officers who seem to have been in contact with Euins at the relevant time. The unidentified witness could not have been Worrell, because the latter said nothing about

---

3 Public discussion on September 30, 1966, and WBAI-New York, Radio Broadcast, December 30, 1966.
4 *Ibid.*
5 See Chapter 16.

his observations until the next day. Clearly, then, two witnesses unknown to each other reported independently that a man *who was not Oswald* had run out of the Book Depository and fled.

Another eyewitness who gave testimony antithetical to the lone-assassin thesis, Arnold Rowland, became the victim of cruel disparagement and unjust character defamation at the hands of the Commission. *(WR 250-252)*[6] Rowland testified that some 15 minutes before the shooting he saw in the south*west* corner window of the sixth floor of the Book Depository a man holding a rifle—a rifle which Rowland described with considerable accuracy before the discovery of the Mannlicher-Carcano, which he thought might be a .30-06 caliber deer rifle. *(2H 170)* Rowland told his wife about the man, whom he took to be a Secret Service agent, before the assassination; immediately after the shooting, he told the police that he had seen a man with a rifle in the southwest corner window and a second man—an elderly Negro—in the south*east* corner window.

The Commission rejected Rowland's story because of alleged doubt about his observation of a second man. The Commission suggests that Rowland never mentioned the second man until he testified, on March 10, 1964. Rowland, on the other hand, asserted that he had told the FBI about the second man when he was interviewed the day after the assassination and that he had been told, in effect, to forget it. *(2H 183)* Rowland's was not an isolated report of FBI indifference to vital information offered by witnesses; moreover, a deputy sheriff corroborated that right after the shooting Rowland had reported seeing two men. *(WR 251)* Rowland's wife also confirmed essential parts of his testimony. The Commission nevertheless repudiated his story and—while crediting such unreliable witnesses as Marina Oswald, Howard Brennan, and Helen Markham, and while ignoring prima-facie misrepresentation in the testimony of police witnesses (to be discussed later)—impeached his character.

The Commission succeeded in proving that Rowland, like most eighteen-year-old males, sometimes exaggerated his endowments and accomplishments—he inflated his grades at school and, with more naïveté than cunning, boasted that his vision was better than 20-20, and the like. On such irrelevant and immaterial grounds, Rowland's testimony, corroborated as it was, was dismissed as untrustworthy. No attention was paid to the striking fact that Rowland's description of the second man, the one in the south*east* corner window, seems to correspond with the initial description allegedly given by Euins of the man he had seen in the same window. Since the Commission itself acknowledges that Rowland's testimony posed the spectre of "an accomplice," its rejection of his story on contrived grounds speaks for itself.

Another witness who saw two men at a Book Depository window escaped the danger of defamation; her story was ignored. Mrs. Carolyn Walther told the FBI soon after the assassination that she had seen two men in a window of an upper floor, one of whom was holding a rifle pointed toward the street below. He wore a white shirt and had blond or light hair; his companion wore a brown

---

6 Exhaustive accounts of the Rowland affair were published in the article by Paul L. Freese in the *New York University Law Review,* in *Inquest* by Edward Jay Epstein, and in *Whitewash II* by Harold Weisberg.

suit coat. *(CE 2086)* Mrs. Walther was never asked to give testimony on her observations.

There were still other witnesses who might have given valuable information. Stanley Kaufman, a lawyer and friend of Jack Ruby's, testified that one of his clients at the county jail on Houston Street and his fellow inmates had congregated at the jail windows to watch the motorcade. The Book Depository was in their line of sight. The client, Willie Mitchell, told Kaufman that "he didn't see anyone in that window." *(15H 525-526)* When he gave his deposition, Kaufman tactfully suggested that "it might be helpful to the Commission to know that there were people in jail who saw the actual killing."

Mitchell, who saw no one in the sixth-floor window, was not questioned by the Commission or, apparently, by anyone on the Commission's behalf. The record indicates no attempt to obtain the names of other inmates. Perhaps the Commission felt that their testimony would be superfluous and there was sufficient evidence already to establish Oswald's presence in the window. (Remember, one of the Commission's lawyers, Wesley J. Liebeler, admitted that there was "the least direct evidence of all" to support the finding in the Warren Report that Oswald was present in the window at the time of the shooting.[7]) But the original problem which arose from the testimony of those who had seen and reported shooting from that window—the failure of the police to act on the information—was never confronted by the Commission and remains unresolved and disquieting.

The Warren Commission must have been aware that the response of the Dallas police to the stories ostensibly told by witnesses shortly after the shooting was inconsistent with those stories; however, the Commission failed to acknowledge the inconsistencies or obtain satisfactory explanations. Why were the police so slow to seal off the Book Depository and to search the sixth floor? One possible explanation which has been suggested by Thomas Buchanan[8] and others is that the police were implicated in the assassination and had their own reasons for allowing the assassin time to escape. Another explanation, which seems consistent with the known facts, is that the police were convinced that shots had come from the grassy knoll area and were genuinely skeptical of any reports by witnesses of an assassin in the window of the Book Depository.

The Grassy Knoll and the Fleeing Man

Certainly there were numerous reasons for believing that shots had come from the grassy knoll. The knoll rises to a height of about 25 feet; on it there are trees and bushes, a fence, concrete monuments, and colonnades, all offering a place of concealment and a clear line of fire to the Presidential limousine. As the testimony shows, many witnesses believed that the shots came from the grassy knoll area: some saw a puff of smoke in the trees there and some saw a fleeing man.

---

7 *Loc. cit.*

8 Thomas Buchanan, *Who Killed Kennedy?* (London, Secker and Warburg, 1964), pp. 110-126.

Forrest Sorrels, the head of the Dallas office of the Secret Service, was riding in the lead car. He testified that he heard shots and "turned around to look up on this terrace part there, because the sound sounded like it came from the back and up in that direction." *(7H 345)*

James Tague, who was standing on the south side of Main Street near the triple underpass and was cut on the face, apparently from a ricocheting bullet, testified:

> *Tague:* My first impression was that up by the, whatever you call the monument, or whatever it was . . . that somebody was throwing firecrackers up there, that the police were running up there to see what was going on. . . .
> *Liebeler:* You thought [the shots] had come from . . . behind the concrete monument here . . . ?
> *Tague:* Yes.   *(7H 557)*

William E. Newman, Jr., who was watching the motorcade from a position on Elm Street "near the west end of the concrete standard," said in his affidavit of November 22, 1963:

> We were standing at the edge of the curb looking at the car as it was coming toward us and all of a sudden there was a noise, apparently gunshot. . . . I was looking directly at him [the President] when he was hit in the side of the head. . . . Then we fell down on the grass as it seemed that we were in direct path of fire . . . everybody in that area had run up on top of that little mound. I thought the shot had come from the garden directly behind me. . . . I do not recall looking toward the Texas School Book Depository. I looked back in the vicinity of the garden.   *(CE 2003, p. 45)*

Abraham Zapruder, who was standing on a concrete slab on the grassy knoll taking motion pictures of the motorcade, with his secretary standing beside him, testified:

> I remember the police were running behind me . . . right behind me. Of course, they didn't realize yet, I guess, where the shot came from—that it came from that height. . . . Some of them were motorcycle cops . . . and they were running right behind me, of course, in the line of the shooting. I guess they thought it came from right behind me. . . . I also thought it came from back of me.   *(7H 571)*

Billy Lovelady, the man seen in the doorway of the Book Depository in the Altgens photograph, thought that the shots had come from "right there around that concrete little deal on that knoll . . . between the underpass and the building right on that knoll." *(6H 338)* This is the only reference we have found to a building on the grassy knoll. We have not been provided with information about its physical structure and its occupancy, or the feasibility of its use as a firing site or a hiding place after the shooting.

Lovelady's boss, Roy Truly, testified:

> I thought the shots came from the vicinity of the railroad or the WPA project, behind the WPA project west of the building. . . . There were many officers running down west of the building. It appears many people thought the shots came from there because of the echo or what.   *(3H 227, 241)*

O. V. Campbell, Vice President of the Book Depository, told Mrs. Robert Reid that the shots "came from the grassy area down this way . . . in the direction . . . the parade was going, in the bottom of that direction." *(3H 274)*

Mrs. Charles Hester told the FBI that she and her husband had been standing on the south side of Elm Street near the underpass when they heard gunshots. According to the FBI report, her husband then grabbed her and shoved her to the ground. Both Mrs. Hester and her husband believed that they had actually been in the direct line of fire. *(CE 2088)*

John Arthur Chism said in an FBI interview that he had been standing on the curb "in front of the concrete memorial on Elm Street which is just east of the triple underpass" and that he was "of the opinion that the shots came from behind him." *(CE 2091)*

In an affidavit dated November 22, 1963, Emmet Hudson said that he had been on the steps leading up the grassy slope, with another spectator. Hudson said, "The shots that I heard definitely came from behind and above me." *(Decker Exhibit No. 5323,* Vol. XIX, p. 481)

The other spectator may have been Malcolm Summers. Summers said in an affidavit dated November 23, 1963 that he had been standing on the terrace of the small park on Elm Street when he heard a shot, and then a second shot. He hit the ground . . .

Then all of the people started running up the terrace. . . . Everybody was just running around towards the railroad tracks and I knew that they had somebody trapped up there. . . . I stayed there 15 or 20 minutes and then went over on Houston Street to where I had my truck parked.

I had just pulled away from the curb and was headed toward the Houston Street viaduct when an automobile that had three men in it pulled away from the curb in a burst of speed, passing me on the right side, which was very dangerous at that point, then got in front of me, and it seemed then as an afterthought, slowed in a big hurry in front of me as though realizing that they would be conspicuous in speeding. . . . They were in a 1961 or 1962 Chevrolet sedan, maroon in color. I don't believe I could identify these men, but I do believe I could identify the automobile if I saw it again.
(*Decker Exhibit No. 5323,* Vol. XIX, p. 500)

Jack W. Faulkner of the Sheriff's Office reported on November 22, 1963 that he had been standing on Main and Houston when he heard three shots and the crowd began to move *en masse* toward Elm Street.

When I reached Elm Street there was much confusion. I asked a woman if they had hit the President, and she told me that he was dead, that he had been shot through the head. I asked her where the shots came from, and she pointed toward the concrete arcade on the east side of Elm Street, just west of Houston Street.   (*Decker Exhibit No. 5323,* Vol. XIX, p. 511)

L. C. Smith of the Sheriff's Office also reported on November 22 that he had "heard a woman unknown to me say the President was shot in the head and the shots came from the fence on the north side of Elm." *(Decker Exhibit 5323,* Vol. XIX, p. 516)

Mary Woodward, a reporter on the staff of the *Dallas Morning News,* was an eyewitness to the assassination. She described her experience in a story which appeared under her by-line in the November 23, 1963 issue of the *Dallas Morning News*.[9] She was not interviewed by any official agency until December 7, 1963, when she told the FBI that she and three companions had been watching the motorcade from the north side of Elm Street, near the second light post, when she heard shots.

> She stated that her first reaction was that the shots had been fired from above her head and possibly behind her. Her next reaction was that the shots might have come from the overpass which was to her right. . . . She never looked at any time towards the Texas School Book Depository building. . . .   *(CE 2084)*

In her story in the *Dallas Morning News*, Miss Woodward had written also that:[10] "About ten feet away a man and his wife had thrown a small child to the ground and were covering his body with theirs; apparently the bullets had whizzed directly over their heads."

In widely published photographs (e.g. *Newsweek*, December 2, 1963, p. 21 and elsewhere) this man and woman can be seen on the grass, near the steps leading to the top of the grassy knoll.

Lee H. Bowers,[11] railroad tower-man, testified that at the time of the shooting "there seemed to be some commotion" and that immediately afterward a motorcycle officer mounted nearly all the way to the top of the grassy knoll. Asked by counsel what he meant by "a commotion," Bowers replied, "I just am unable to describe rather than it was something out of the ordinary, which attracted my eye for some reason, which I could not identify." *(6H 288)* Malcolm Couch, a television reporter who was riding in the motorcade, testified: "And people were pointing back around those shrubs around that west corner and—uh—you would think that there was a chase going on in that direction." *(6H 160)* James Underwood testified:

> . . . most of the people in the area were running up the grassy slope toward the railroad yards just behind the Texas School Book Depository Building. Actually, I assumed, which is the only thing I could do, I assumed perhaps who[ever] had fired the shots had run in that direction. . . .   *(6H 170)*

Frank Reilly testified, too, that the shots seemed to "come out of the trees . . . on the north side of Elm Street, at the corner up there . . . where all those trees are . . . at that park where all the shrubs is up there . . . up the slope." *(6H 230)*

---

9   *Dallas Morning News*, November 23, 1963, p. 3.

10   *Ibid.*

11   Mr. Bowers, one of the most important witnesses to the assassination because of his vantage point of the whole area from the top of the railroad tower, testified also to the presence of two cars behind the fence on the grassy knoll during the half-hour before the assassination. A third car entered the area only a few minutes before the shooting. Two of the cars had out-of-town license plates and displayed Goldwater stickers. Bowers testified also that he had seen two men standing near the fence on the grassy knoll just before the shots were heard.

Bowers was killed on August 9, 1966 at the age of 41 when his car struck a bridge abutment two miles west of Midlothian, Texas.

Some witnesses reported that they had seen a puff of smoke in that same location.[12] S. M. Holland testified:

> I counted four shots and about the same time all this was happening, and in
> this group of trees . . . there was a shot, a report, I don't know whether it
> was a shot. I can't say that. And a puff of smoke came out about six or eight
> feet above the ground right out from under those trees. . . . There were
> definitely four reports. . . . I have no doubt about it. I have no doubt about
> seeing that puff of smoke come out from under those trees either. . . . I
> definitely saw the puff of smoke and heard the report from under those
> trees. . . . The puff of smoke I saw definitely came from behind the arcade
> to the trees.   *(6H 243-245)*

Asked by Counsel Ball if he had seen smoke from his vantage point on the overpass, Royce G. Skelton replied: "No sir; I just stated to your secretary that I
heard people say they did, but I didn't." *(6H 238)* Austin Miller, a railroad
worker who was also standing on the overpass, said in his affidavit of November
22, 1963:

> One shot apparently hit the street past the car. I saw something which I
> thought was smoke or steam coming from a group of trees north of Elm off
> the railroad tracks. I did not see anyone on the tracks or in the trees. A large
> group of people concreated [sic] and a motorcycle officer dropped his
> motor and took off on foot to the car.   *(CE 2003, p. 41)*

Deputy Sheriff A. D. McCurley in his report of November 22, 1963 said
that when he heard the shots,

> I rushed towards the park and saw people running towards the railroad
> yards beyond Elm Street and I ran over and jumped a fence and a railroad
> worker stated to me that he believed the smoke from the bullets came from
> the vicinity of a stockade fence which surrounds the park area.
>   *(Decker Exhibit No. 5323,* Vol. XIX, p. 514)

Deputy Sheriff J. L. Oxford and Chief Criminal Deputy Allan Sweatt also
reported that they had been told by bystanders that the shots had come from the
fence; a witness told Oxford that he had seen smoke "up in the corner of the
fence." *(Decker Exhibit No. 5323,* Vol. XIX, pp. 530-531)
Other spectators said that they had seen someone running away from the
scene. J. C. Price said in an affidavit of November 23, 1963 that he had been

---

12 An FBI report *(CE 3133)* states that the alleged assassination rifle was fired both in
direct sunlight and in full shade, at the Commission's request, to determine whether any
flame was visible. No flame was seen, but "a small amount of white smoke was visible."
   S. M. Holland told the Associated Press in November 1966 that "four or five of us saw
it, the smoke . . . one of my employees even saw the muzzle flash. The way the Warren
Commission published my testimony, it was kind of watered down some." (*The New York
Times,* November 23, 1966, p. 25.)
   Despite the FBI report and the testimony of Holland and other witnesses who saw a puff
of smoke under the trees on the grassy knoll, Warren Commission Senior Counsel Joseph A.
Ball stated publicly on November 17, 1966 at San Diego, California, "Since when did rifles
give off a puff of smoke? They don't do it." (*Dallas Morning News,* November 27, 1966.)
Apparently Ball is not familiar with the exhibits which bear directly on his area of responsi-
bility in the investigation: to develop evidence which identified the assassin.

watching the motorcade from the roof of the Terminal Annex Building (a short distance from the Book Depository) and continued:

> There was a volley of shots, I think five, and then much later, maybe as much as five minutes later another one. I saw one man run towards the passenger cars on the railroad siding after the volley of shots. This man had a white dress shirt, no tie, and khaki colored trousers. His hair appeared to be long and dark and his agility running could be about 25 years of age. He had something in his hand. I couldn't be sure but it may have been a headpiece. (*CE 2003*, p. 52)

Secret Service Agent Paul Landis, Jr., who was riding in the motorcade on the right rear running board of the car behind the Presidential limousine, said in a report dated November 30, 1963:

> I was not certain from which direction the second shot came, but my reaction at this time was that the shot came from somewhere towards the front, right-hand side of the road. . . . I scanned the area to the right of and below the overpass where the terrain sloped toward the road on which we were traveling.
>
> The only person I recall seeing clearly was a Negro male in light green slacks and a beige colored shirt running from my left to my right, up the slope, across a grassy section, along a sidewalk, towards some steps and what appeared to be a low stone wall. He was bent over while running and I started to point towards him, but I didn't notice anything in his hands and by this time we were going under the overpass at a very high rate of speed. . . . (*CE 1024*, Vol. XVIII, p. 755)

Arnold Rowland told the Commission that "some lady said someone [had] jumped off one of the colonnades and started running." *(2H 181)*

Jean Lollis Hill testified that she had seen and attempted to pursue a man running or trying to get away from the top of the slope west of the Book Depository and gave the following account of a conversation with Mark Lane:

> *Mrs. Hill:* I told him that my story had already been given, that they had an affidavit down there, and he said, "Were you ever at any time . . . told not to say something or this, that, and the other," and I said, "The only thing that I was told not to say was not to mention the man running," and he said, "And why?"
>
> And I said, "Well, it was an FBI or Secret Service that told me not to, but they came in to me just right after I was taken—I was there in the pressroom—and told me in fact—I told him it was Featherstone [a reporter on the *Dallas Times-Herald*] that told me. He [Featherstone] said, "You know you were wrong about seeing a man running." He said, "You didn't. . . ." I told Mr. Lane that Mr. Featherstone had told me that, and I said, "But I did," and he said, "No; don't say that any more on the air." . . . And I made it clear to Mark Lane, because I mentioned his name several times. . . .
>
> *Specter:* You mean Featherstone?
>
> *Mrs. Hill:* Yes; that the shots had come from a window up in the Depository and for me not to say that any more, that I was wrong about it, and I said, "Very well," and so I just didn't say any more that I ran across the street to see the man. . . . (*6H 221-222*)

Incompleteness and Selectivity

It is not clear from Mrs. Hill's testimony whether it was only Featherstone or an FBI or Secret Service agent as well who told her to stop saying that she had seen a man running away and who insisted that the shots had come from a window in the Book Depository. Nor is it clear how soon after the shooting this pressure was applied to Mrs. Hill. It would have been desirable to interrogate Featherstone on this point, but he was not questioned. Normally, one would think, any reporter would have hastened to print the sensational news that Mrs. Hill offered; yet this reporter wanted only to shut her up. This material investigation by the Commission.

Price and Landis, who also saw someone running away, were not even called to testify before the Commission. Other spectators who believed that the shots had come from the grassy knoll and were never asked to give testimony included Mary Woodward and her three companions, Mrs. Charles Hester, John Arthur Chism, Malcolm Summers, O. V. Campbell, William E. Newman, and Abraham Zapruder's secretary, the latter not even being represented by an affidavit or an FBI interview. Of the 23 witnesses mentioned here, only 11 gave testimony before the Commission; in the case of one witness, Austin Miller, counsel did not elicit information which appeared in his affidavit: that is, that he had seen smoke or steam coming from a group of trees near the railroad tracks.

Another witness was never interviewed by the FBI or the Secret Service, much less questioned by the Commission, although she possessed important information. In an affidavit of November 22 (*Decker Exhibit 5323,* Vol. XIX, p. 483) Julia Mercer said that on the morning of the assassination while she was driving toward the overpass, she had seen a man carrying a rifle case walk across the grass and up the grassy hill which forms part of the overpass. She gave a detailed and precise description of the incident. In an apparent reference to Julia Mercer, Forrest Sorrels testified:

> . . . this lady said she thought she saw somebody that looked like they had a guncase. But then I didn't pursue that any further—because then I had gotten the information that the rifle had been found in the building and shells and so forth. *(7H 352)*

It would have been logical at that point to ask Sorrels how he could be sure, within an hour after the assassination and presumably before the arrest of the lone Oswald, that the discovery of the rifle in the Book Depository was sufficient to eliminate other assassins in other locations. No such question was asked by counsel for the Commission.

The presentation of photographic evidence by the Commission is also incomplete and selective. Few crimes other than the murder of Oswald by Ruby have been so fully recorded on film as the assassination of President Kennedy. One would have expected the Commission to requisition every known still or motion picture and to examine this photographic evidence with the utmost care, in order to establish as firmly as possible the location of the assassin or assassins and other clues recorded in photographs or enlargements. Surprisingly, the Commission has mentioned in the Report and shown in the Exhibits only some of the photographic record, omitting films and photographs of obvious importance.[13]

Even the Zapruder frames, perhaps the most complete record available of the fatal stretch of the motorcade, are not presented in their entirety (CE 885); segments at the beginning and the end have been omitted, perhaps to conserve space and also possibly for reasons of delicacy (Mrs. Kennedy is shown crawling onto the back of the car). Moreover, Frames 208 through 211 have been omitted without explanation even though expert testimony suggested that the President may have been struck by the first bullet between Frames 210 and 225.[14] Ironically, these four strategic frames were "accidentally torn," according to a spokesman for Life magazine, in the excitement of examining the film immediately after it was purchased. However, the missing segments are included in the copies of the film made in Dallas before the original was damaged.[15] The irony is augmented with the transposition and misnumbering of two later frames, which Ray Marcus discovered early in 1965. The President was struck in the head in Zapruder Frame 313, and the subsequent frames assume vital importance because they indicate the physical reaction to impact of the head shot, which in turn throws light on the direction from which the bullet came. Yet the Commission's presentation of black-and-white reproductions transposes and mislabels Frames 314 and 315; J. Edgar Hoover has acknowledged this as a "printing error."[16]

Only a few frames from motion pictures taken by Orville Nix and Mary Muchmore were included in the Exhibits and neither Mr. Nix nor Mrs. Muchmore was asked to testify before the Commission. Furthermore, there is no affidavit or FBI report found in the Exhibits to indicate what these eyewitnesses saw or what they thought about the number and direction of the shots.

Photographs which may have revealed the state of the sixth-floor window at the time of the shooting or which took in the grassy knoll area have not been offered in support of the conclusion that all the shots came from the window. Consider, for example, the affidavit of Hugh William Betzner, Jr., who was

---

13   I am grateful to Richard E. Sprague for making available a list compiled by him of photographs and films which seem to have been overlooked entirely by the Warren Commission and its investigative agencies. The list includes: a movie taken by bystander John Martin, which shows the grassy knoll seconds after the last shot; a photograph taken by Art Rickerby of Life magazine from a camera car in the motorcade, which also shows the grassy knoll after the last shot; a movie film which shows the Dealey Plaza and Book Depository area, beginning before the first shot and ending several minutes after the last, taken by David Weigman of NBC while riding in the motorcade in a camera car; and photographs taken by Wilma Bond, Ron Reiland, Darnell, Alyea, Craven, Atkins, Stoughton, Burrows, Brandt, Dorman, Cancellare, Foley, Beck, Weaver, and Powell.

Not only was this invaluable body of photographic evidence untapped and ignored: the eyewitnesses who held the cameras were not asked to testify or (with one exception) questioned by federal agents or the local authorities. The observations of these 19 or more persons might have produced new information of inestimable importance.

14   WR 98.

15   A spokesman for Life magazine in a conversation with the author in December 1966.

16   In a letter dated December 14, 1965.

standing on the south side of Elm Street (across the road from the Book Depository) taking photographs of the President when he heard shots:

Police and a lot of spectators started running up the hill on the opposite side of the street from me to a fence of wood. I assumed that that was where the shot was fired from. . . . Police officers and the men in plain clothes were digging around in the dirt as if they were looking for a bullet. . . . I went on across the street and up the embankment to where the fence is located . . . as the rumor had spread that that was where the shot had come from.

    I started figuring where I was when I had taken the third picture and it seemed to me that the fence row would have been in the picture. . . . Deputy Sheriff Boone took my camera and asked me to wait. . . . An hour or two [later] he brought my camera back and told me that as soon as they were through with the film and they were dry that they would give me the film. A little later he came in and gave me the negatives and told me they were interested in a couple of pictures and implied that the negatives was all I was going to get back.   (*Decker Exhibit No. 5323,* Vol. XIX, pp. 467-468)

That is the first and the last that is heard of Mr. Betzner or his photographs. Despite the fact that a police officer indicated "interest" in the photographs which included the fence from which some people thought the shots had come, the Warren Commission did not examine or inquire about the photographs (so far as is known) or make them available.

There is also a report from Allan Sweatt, Chief Criminal Deputy in the Sheriff's Office, that after the shooting a woman who had taken some photographs was brought in to him. According to Sweatt, "One picture was taken just shortly before the shooting of the President which showed the Sexton Building [i.e., and perhaps the Book Depository] in the background. This picture was turned over to Secret Service Agent Patterson. . . ." (*Decker Exhibit No. 5323,* Vol. XIX, p. 533) The Commission has provided us with neither the photograph nor any indication of what if anything it showed at the sixth-floor window where the lone assassin was presumably waiting for his victim to appear.

The Report does mention that a film which included the Book Depository sixth-floor window was taken by Robert J. Hughes only minutes before the shooting *(WR 644);* the Commission "found" that Hughes's film did not show two silhouettes at the window, as had been speculated, but a shadow from cartons near the window. Nothing would have been simpler than to document that "finding" by means of the frame from the film taken by Hughes "just before the assassination," but the Commission does not exhibit it. One may ask if it is not strange that the film failed to show the assassin, who was seen just before the shooting standing at the window with his gaze fixed on the overpass, by at least one witness. *(WR 146)*

Still another film of the assassination was taken by Ralph Simpson, a Canadian then vacationing in Dallas. Simpson told Sergeant Patrick Dean of the Dallas Police that he had stationed himself on the southwest side of Dealey Plaza to see the motorcade and had taken films with a movie camera with a wide-angle lens that he believed had included the Book Depository and the motorcade at the time the shots were fired. Simpson offered to airmail the films from Victoria, British Columbia, according to Sergeant Dean in his Commission testimony of June 8, 1964 *(5H 256)* as well as in an earlier deposition. *(12H 443-446)* Again, this is the first and last that is heard of the film: the Commission has told us nothing beyond what is contained in Dean's testimony. Was the film received? Was it viewed? What did it show?

Finally, a clue to the apparent suppression of possibly another significant film or photograph is found in the testimony of Mrs. Eva Grant, when she is questioned about Tom Howard, one of the lawyers defending Jack Ruby in his trial for the murder of Oswald:

Mrs. Grant: We had found a mistrust in him . . . where information has come to us that Tom Howard is trying to sell a picture of the late President Kennedy being shot and half his skull is in the air, to *Life* magazine . . . and Earl [Ruby] told me to get ahold of the Secret Service, they came out to see me . . . and we went in the alley because I don't know if my place is bugged or not, and the Secret Service stepped in to either squash the sale of this particular picture or got ahold of it—the films and everything. . . .
(14H 479)

Hubert: Did you ever find out whether it was true that Mr. Howard was doing this?

Mrs. Grant: Well, since then I heard it was true, but doubly true there's some girl that works for one of your departments who heard and who told another person that there is evidence there is a picture of that kind in existence.

Hubert: You have never seen the picture?

Mrs. Grant: No, I haven't . . . but Earl told me to get ahold of the men here and I did and I called the office and [Secret Service Agent] Elmer Moore came out and I told him.
(14H 480)

Tom Howard was not questioned about the film or photograph, and now he cannot be questioned. He died of an apparent heart failure in May 1965, one of a growing list of persons directly or indirectly involved in the Oswald case who have died within the three years following the assassination. The Secret Service was not questioned. *Life* magazine was not questioned. The trail ends, as it begins, in Mrs. Grant's testimony.

Another film that leads to frustration is the documentary *Four Days in November*. Including newsreel footage of the motorcade, it was shown commercially every year for a time in New York City on the anniversary of the assassination. On viewing the picture for the first time in 1965, I was impressed by the quality, volume, and variety of the sound track: it seemed exactly as if one were hearing the event in person, standing right there or riding in the motorcade. And when the Presidential car turned on to Elm Street in the newsreel, I expected, with rising excitement, to hear the actual "crack!" of the first shot.

Instead, both the film and the sound stopped abruptly, and a still photograph showing the President after he was shot in the head was projected onto the screen in awful, heart-stopping solemnity.

No doubt this is excellent dramatic technique. But if the original unedited sound track recorded the swell of crowd noise and the sirens and the motor-cycles' guttural reports, why couldn't it resolve the problem of how many shots were fired, and of the interval between the shots?

The Warren Report, like the sound track at the crucial moment, is silent.

Sinister Circumstances Ignored

The Commission's incomplete and unsatisfying exposition of the film and photo-graphic evidence is compounded by a stone-deafness to certain testimony which shrieks of the strange and sinister. By way of prologue, let us recall this state-ment in the Warren Report:

> [The Secret Service agents assigned to the motorcade] remained at their posts during the race to the hospital. None stayed at the scene of the shoot-ing, and none entered the Texas School Book Depository at or immediately after the shooting. . . . Forrest V. Sorrels, special agent in charge of the Dallas office, was the first Secret Service agent to return to the scene of the assassination, approximately 20 or 25 minutes after the shots were fired.
> *(WR 52)*

Although I am seldom able to concur without qualification in the Com-mission's factual assertions, it is possible in this instance to agree, on the basis of an independent check of all available information: there was no Secret Service agent at the scene of the assassination until Sorrels returned to Elm Street and entered the Book Depository at 12:50 or 12:55 p.m. The whereabouts of all the Secret Service agents in the White House detail are indicated in their individual reports. *(CE 1024)* They stayed with the Presidential party through-out, returning to Washington with the new President and his entourage on Friday afternoon. The agents who had been stationed at the Trade Mart or at Love Field either went to Parkland Hospital or remained at their posts at the airfield until departure. Not one agent from the Washington contingent went to the Book Depository area, claimed that he went there, or could possibly have been there.

The evidence indicates that none of the Secret Service agents from the Dallas field office were at the scene of the shooting either. Headed by Forrest V. Sorrels, the office is staffed by six agents, including Mike Howard, who is actually stationed at Fort Worth. *(13H 57; CE 2554)* Of the remaining five, two were assigned to the Trade Mart (J. J. Howlett and Robert Steuart) and two (William Patterson and Roger Warner) to Love Field. *(CE 1024, CE 2554)* There is no information on the whereabouts of the sixth agent, Elmer Moore, who was not assigned to the task of Presidential protection during the Dallas visit; the fact that he is the only agent who did not provide a report on his activities that day suggests that he was off duty or away from Dallas. There is no indication that he was at the scene of the shooting.

In the light of these facts, how are we to interpret the testimony given by Deputy Constable Seymour Weitzman, Sergeant D. V. Harkness, and Patrol-man J. M. Smith?

Weitzman testified that someone said the shots had come from the wall between the railroad overpass and the monument area where Elm Street becomes a dead end; immediately he had scaled the wall and gone into the railroad yards, where "other officers, Secret Service as well, also were present." *(7H 107)*

Sergeant Harkness testified that he had reached the rear of the Book Depository before 12:36 p.m., to make sure that the building was sealed off. When he arrived, "there were some Secret Service agents there. I didn't get them identified. They told me they were Secret Service agents." *(6H 312)* Note that they *told* Harkness that they were Secret Service agents.

J. M. Smith was stationed at Elm and Houston Streets, to control the crowds and vehicular traffic. He did not observe anything unusual when he glanced at the Book Depository from time to time. After the shots, a woman came up to him "just in hysterics" and told him that "they were shooting the President from the bushes." Smith proceeded at once to the area "behind the concrete structure" in the grassy space back from Elm Street toward the railroad tracks, where he checked the bushes and the cars in the parking lot. He testified:

> *Smith:* Of course, I wasn't alone. There was some deputy sheriff with me, and I believe one Secret Service man when I got there. I got to make this statement, too. I felt awfully silly, but after the shot and this woman, I pulled my pistol from my holster, and I thought, this is silly, I don't know who I am looking for, and I put it back. Just as I did, he showed me that he was a Secret Service agent.
>
> *Liebeler:* Did you accost this man?
>
> *Smith:* Well, he saw me coming with my pistol and right away he showed me who he was.
>
> *Liebeler:* Do you remember who it was?
>
> *Smith:* No, sir, I don't . . .   *(7H 535)*

I suggest that he was one of the assassins, armed with false credentials. The men who identified themselves as Secret Service agents, to Harkness and to Smith, by the Commission's own account could not have been genuine agents. The incidents occurred well before Sorrels returned to the scene; in any event, he was by himself and must be ruled out. Who, then, were the men who claimed to be but could not have been Secret Service agents? Was there any conceivable *innocent* reason for such impersonation?

Few mysteries in the case are as important as this one, and it is appalling that the Commission ignored or failed to recognize the grounds here for serious suspicion of a well-planned conspiracy at work. It seems inconceivable that none of the many investigators and lawyers saw the significance of the reports made by these witnesses or realized that assassins positioned on the grassy knoll— behind the fence or the trees—might have been armed with forged Secret Service credentials and lost themselves in the crowd that surged into the area.

That may well be what happened in fact; whether or not such a theory is valid, it was a dereliction of duty for the Commission to ignore the testimony given by Harkness and Smith as well as, in effect, the substantial body of testimony from other witnesses who believed that the shots came from the grassy knoll.

Appraisal

In the aggregate the unanswered questions, the distorted interpretation of testimony, the failure to call important witnesses and to investigate important circumstances reported, and the fragmentary nature of the photographic evidence which was taken into account call into question the Warren Commission's conclusions about the source of the shots that struck the President and the Governor. By no standard can its investigation be considered conclusive, complete, or objective. Perhaps it is not too late to do what the Commission left undone —by conducting a painstaking examination of all the photographic evidence that has been withheld from the public, including the photographs taken during the autopsy (discussed elsewhere in this study), and by undertaking the other essential inquiries thus far neglected.

The Zapruder Film

Without daring to state it as a conclusive finding, the Warren Report makes a prodigious effort to persuade us that a single shot struck the President in the neck and proceeded on to strike the Governor, causing all of his wounds. The authors state that there is "very persuasive evidence from the experts to indicate that the same bullet which pierced the President's throat also caused Governor Connally's wounds." They acknowledge that there is a difference of opinion about that hypothesis (including the firm dissent of the Governor himself), but they claim that "it is not necessary to any essential findings of the Commission to determine just which shot hit Governor Connally." (*WR 19*)

Surely that is one of the most misleading statements in the whole Report. The Commission insists that all the shots came from the Book Depository. If the Governor was wounded by a pristine bullet and not by either of the two missiles which struck the President, it is self-evident under the Commission's reconstruction of the crime that the assassin made three hits in three tries, in a span of five and one-half seconds. Not one of the sharpshooters who tested their skill with the Mannlicher-Carcano rifle (the alleged murder weapon) achieved such accuracy, even though the experiments utilized stationary rather than moving targets. It is therefore impossible to make a serious claim that the Commission's essential findings do not hinge upon a determination of the shot that struck the Governor—if, indeed, only one bullet inflicted all of his wounds.

One might expect the Zapruder film to establish the moment at which the Governor was hit in relation to the shot that struck the President in the neck. Unfortunately, neither the film nor the color slides made for the Commission by the *Life* magazine photo laboratory (now available for examination at the National Archives) enable the viewer to pinpoint this moment. Nevertheless, careful study of the color slides has other rewards.

A significant fact recorded on the slides is that several persons are seen to move abruptly, as if reacting to a stimulus such as the sound of a shot, before the earliest point at which the Commission believes the President could have been hit by the first bullet. Mrs. Kennedy makes a sudden sharp turn toward the President, bending her head as if to look at him, in Frame 204. Howard Brennan is seen sitting on a wall and looking over his left shoulder at the Presidential car until Frame 207, when he turns his head suddenly to look at the right. The Secret Service agent riding on the front right running board of the follow-up car, directly behind the Presidential limousine, also looks sharply to his right in Frame 207.

If the interpretation of those movements is valid, it implies strongly that the first shot was fired before Frame 204, during the sequence in which the President was concealed from the Book Depository window by tree foliage (Frames 166 to 210) and when a sniper positioned in that window could not have seen or aimed at him. That was the decisive factor to a Commission predisposed to "find" that all the shots came from that window. Thus the Commission says:

> . . . the evidence indicated that the President was not hit until at least Frame 210 and that he was probably hit by Frame 225. The possibility of variations in reaction time in addition to *the obstruction of Zapruder's view by the sign precluded a more specific determination* than that the President was probably shot through the neck between Frames 210 and 225. . . . (Italics added)   *(WR 105)*

The Commission has stated, in effect, that Zapruder did not see the President at the moment that he was first shot because of the intervention of the traffic sign. This is a contradiction of Zapruder's testimony: *"I heard the first shot and I saw the President lean over and grab himself like this* [holding his left chest area]." *(7H 571)* (Italics added) As Harold Weisberg has pointed out in his book *Whitewash*, Zapruder's testimony in itself strongly suggests that the President was hit before he disappeared behind the sign at Frame 210 and while he was still invisible to a rifleman in the sixth-floor window. The lawyer who took Zapruder's testimony failed to appreciate or explore this important observation, and the Warren Report, ignoring the Zapruder testimony, inaccurately asserts that he did not see what he so inconveniently saw.

At Frame 225 the President is reacting to the bullet in the back but the Governor shows absolutely no evidence of being shot. Students of the Zapruder film and color slides differ with each other in identifying the frame or approximate frame at which the Governor was shot. The earliest point suggested is Frame 228; the Governor himself designates Frames 231-234; others believe that he was not struck until considerably later—some on the basis of his unperturbed appearance, and others reasoning that his right hand appears to grip a metal bar at the side of the car as late as Frame 233 and that his hand must still have been uninjured at that point by the bullet that ultimately smashed the right wristbone.

It is frustrating and ironic that the Zapruder film does not enable the viewer to pinpoint the exact moment of impact of the bullet in the President's back or of the bullet (or bullets) that struck the Governor.[17] But the film does establish a definite delay between the wounding of the two men—a delay too short for the Carcano rifle to be fired twice by one man, and too long to leave the single-missile hypothesis with credibility.[18] That time lapse therefore compromises the single-bullet theory and destroys the Commission's pretense that a determination of just which shot hit Governor Connally was "not necessary to any essential findings" (as even Lord Devlin, supremely uncritical partisan of the Warren Report, belatedly conceded in the London *Observer* of September 25, 1966).[19]

The problem posed by the time lapse between the wounding of the two men is discussed in the following passage from the testimony:

Dulles: But you would then have the problem you would think if Connally had been hit at the same time, [he] would have reacted in the same way, and not reacted *much later* as these pictures show. [Italics added]

Shaneyfelt: That is right.

Dulles: Because the wounds would have been inflicted.

McCloy: That is what puzzles me.

Dulles: That is what puzzles me.   *(5H 155)*

The Commission tried to dispose of the puzzlement by suggesting that the Governor had experienced a delayed reaction to his wounds. *(WR 112-113)* In presenting this proposition, the Commission does not cite supporting medical testimony. However, the records show that the Commission in fact did solicit medical opinion on the possibility of a delayed reaction by the Governor to a bullet that smashed his rib, collapsed his lung, and fractured his wrist.

Specter: Could that missile have traversed Governor Connally's chest without having him know it immediately or instantaneously?

---

17   The article "A Matter of Reasonable Doubt" in *Life* magazine of November 25, 1966 (p. 48) reviewed the Zapruder color frames and reported an interview with Governor Connally in which he reiterated his absolute certainty that he was hit by a separate bullet, in Frame 234. (Ray Marcus of Los Angeles has concluded from his expert analysis of the Zapruder frames that Connally was hit in Frame 238.)

18   Senator Richard B. Russell joined Governor Connally in rejecting the single-bullet theory, in the wake of the *Life* article, as did Malcolm Kilduff *(The New York Times,* November 22, 1966, p. 1).

19   Apologists for the Warren Report such as Professor Alexander M. Bickel of Yale and former Assistant Counsel Wesley J. Liebeler have tried to validate the Commission's untenable pronouncement by suggesting that Oswald could have fired the first shot and struck Kennedy earlier, at Frame 185 of the Zapruder film, when there was a break in the foliage of an obstructing oak tree for one-eighteenth of a second. That improvisation can be discarded immediately, for an earlier shot would have meant a steeper downward trajectory, leaving the so-called exit wound in the anterior neck unaccounted for and thus reintroducing at least one more assassin.

Liebeler developed the theme of a first shot that hit the President "while the limousine was partly obscured from the window by the tree" during a public discussion at the Theater for Ideas in New York City on September 30, 1966. After pronouncing hmself at some length on the plausibility of that theory, he was asked where that bullet would have wound up. Liebeler replied:

"Where did that bullet end up? Well, that was the bullet—that was the bullet that came into the President's back, and then—and then, came out his throat. [Pause] Well, that raises a problem, doesn't it? [Laughter] Wait a minute, just a minute [Mixed voices of audience and panel]. . . . And that is why, Mr. Popkin, I think it *did* go through the President first and hit the Governor. . . ." (WBAI radio, New York City, broadcast December 30, 1966)

Dr. Humes: I believe so. I have heard reports, and have been told by my professional associates, of any number of instances where people received penetrating wounds in various portions of the body and have only the sensation of a slight discomfort or slight slap or some other minor difficulty from such a missile wound. *I am sure that he would be aware that something happened to him,* but that he was shot, I am not certain. [Italics added]

Ford: Would that have been the potential reaction of the President when first hit, as shown in [CE] 385?

Dr. Humes: It could very easily be one of some type of an injury—I mean the awareness that he had been struck by a missile, I don't know, but people have been drilled through with a missile and didn't know it. *(2H 376)*

Specter: Dr. Dziemian, Governor Connally testified that he experienced the sensation of a striking blow on his back which he described as being similar to a hard punch received from a doubled-up fist. Do you have an opinion as to whether that sensation would necessarily occur immediately upon impact of a wound such as that received by Governor Connally, or could there be a delayed reaction in sensing that feeling?

Dr. Dziemian: I don't have too much of an opinion on that. All I can say is that some people are struck by bullets and do not even know they are hit. This happens in wartime. But I don't know about that.

Specter: So that it is possible in some situations there is some delay in reaction?

Dr. Dziemian: I couldn't say.

Specter: Is it a highly individual matter as to the reaction of an individual on that subject?

Dr. Dziemian: I don't know.

Dulles: But take a wrist wound like the wound of Governor Connally. He couldn't get that without knowing it, could he?

Dziemian: I think he said that he didn't know he had a wrist wound until much later.

(Discussion off the record)

Specter: I have no further questions of Dr. Dziemian. *(5H 93-94)*

McCloy: Let me ask you this, Doctor, in your experience with gunshot wounds, is it possible for a man to be hit some time before he realizes it?

Dr. Shaw: Yes. There can be a delay in the sensory reaction.

McCloy: Yes; so that a man can think as of a given instant he was not hit, and when actually he could have been hit.

Dr. Shaw: There can be an extending sensation and then just a gradual building up of a feeling of severe injury.

McCloy: But there could be a delay in any appreciable reaction between the time of the impact of the bullet and the occurrence?

Dr. Shaw: Yes; but in the case of a wound which strikes a bony substance such as a rib, usually the reaction is quite prompt. *(4H 115-116)*

The Commission was wise to omit reference to the doctors' testimony, even in a footnote. It would be hard to argue that they supported the farfetched conjecture of a delayed reaction, despite the pressure of leading questions. It is true, as Dr. Arthur J. Dziemian said, that the Governor was not aware of his wrist wound until much later; yet it seems obvious from the Governor's own account that severe pain from the chest wound blocked out awareness of lesser pain. Perhaps that point was clarified during the off-the-record discussion.

The net effect of the medical testimony is hardly favorable to the proposition of a delayed reaction, and it would be idle to pretend that this further vitiation of the single-missile thesis is immaterial to the Commission's "essential findings."

The Commission is far more persuasive when it discusses the relative positions of the President and the Governor as evidence for the single-missile theory, but its arguments are by no means conclusive so long as the time of the Governor's shot and his posture at that time remain uncertain. Moreover, there is a cut-off point after which the Governor could not have received his injuries from a shot that came from the Book Depository window, whether or not that shot first struck the President. The Warren Report states that "at some point between Frames 235 and 240 is the last occasion when Governor Connally could have received his injuries, since in the frames following 240 he remained too far to his right." *(WR 106)* A footnote to that statement cites the testimony of FBI Expert Robert Frazier. *(5H 170)* However, Frazier's actual testimony *(5H 170-171)* is misrepresented in the Report, since he places the cut-off point at Frame 225. He states repeatedly that the Governor could have been struck between Frames 207 and 225 and sustained his actual wounds; and he specifically excludes Frames 235 and 240.[20]

Both Frazier and the Commission predicate the cut-off point on a shot that came from the Book Depository window, refusing to confront the possibility that he might have been shot from another location—a possibility that must be examined in the light of the Governor's lack of reaction before or at the cut-off time. Instead of examining all the possibilities in an impartial and scientific spirit, the Commission resorted to pure conjecture and, as laymen, posed the highly implausible and obviously dubious "delayed reaction" sub-hypothesis. The argument that the bullet that passed through the President's neck must have struck the Governor because it did not strike the car or any other occupants or objects (and it had to go *somewhere*) seems compelling at first glance. Against that argument one may cite the repeated published reports after the assassination that a bullet had lodged in the President's body and testimony indicating that a bullet had hit the pavement near the Presidential car during the shooting.[21]

Liebeler: So, you were standing directly in front of the Depository and on the same side of Elm Street that the Depository is located?

---

20   Frazier testified that "there is only one position beyond Frame 225 at which the Governor could have been struck," *(5H 170)* but he did not specify that position, nor was he asked by examining counsel to do so.

21   The *Washington Post* reported on December 18, 1963—and *The New York Times* on January 26, 1964—that the bullet that hit the President in the right shoulder several inches below the collar-line had lodged in the body. The *Washington Post* said on May 29, 1966 (page A3, column 4) that "on December 18, 1963, the *Washington Post* and other newspapers reported on the basis of rumors from Dallas that the first bullet to strike the President 'was found deep in his shoulder.' *This report was confirmed prior to publication by the FBI.*" (Italics added)

Mrs. Baker: Yes.

Liebeler: Tell me what you saw.

Mrs. Baker: Well, after he passed us, then we heard a noise and I thought it was firecrackers, because I saw a shot or something hit the pavement.

Liebeler: And you heard that immediately after the first noise; is that right?

Mrs. Baker: Yes . . . I saw the bullet hit on down this way, I guess, right at the sign, angling out.   *(7H 508-509)*

Thanks to the initiative of another witness, Royce Skelton, we know that he too saw a bullet hit the pavement. He volunteered, when counsel had already thanked and dismissed him, that he had seen a bullet hit the pavement at the left front of the Presidential car. *(6H 238)* In addition to the observations of Skelton and Mrs. Baker, there is the fact (discussed earlier) that a bystander was cut on the cheek and a curbstone was hit by a bullet or bullet fragment. Taken as a whole, this evidence scarcely permits the Commission to postulate that the first bullet that struck the President must have hit the Governor because it did not hit anything else.

Other anomalies cannot be ignored in an evaluation of the single-missile thesis—the trajectory of the shots, for example. Arlen Specter, the assistant counsel who was primarily responsible for the medical and ballistics evidence, repeatedly posed to witnesses a hypothetical set of circumstances in which the shots that struck Kennedy and Connally followed a 45° angle of descent. *(See 3H 362; 3H 373; 5H 92; and 6H 110)* Dr. J. J. Humes testified that the trajectory of the wounds sustained by both men was about 45°. *(2H 370)* In his autopsy report, however, Dr. Humes said that the shots came from a point "behind and somewhat above the level of the deceased" *(WR 543)*, which does not seem to agree with a sixth-story window or a 45° trajectory.

The 45° trajectory postulated repeatedly by Specter and others was abandoned abruptly when Dr. Robert Shaw told the Commission that its diagram of the Governor's wounds gave an incorrect position for the exit wound in the chest. He corrected the diagram by raising the exit wound *(4H 105, 112)*, thus reducing the trajectory to 25°, the figure quoted in the Report. *(WR 93)*

The Report, however, does not base the trajectory of the bullets that hit the President on medical or physical findings; it utilizes other data. *(WR 106-107)* The trajectory from the Book Depository window to the car in Frames 210-225 (the interval during which the President was shot in the back, according to the Commission) ranged from 21°34′ to 20°11′, somewhat less than that of the bullets that hit the Governor. In absolute terms, that might suggest that the Governor was hit before Frame 210, when the car was closer to the Book Depository (but concealed from the sixth-floor window by thick tree foliage); on the other hand, if the 45° trajectory for the President's non-fatal wounds put forward by Dr. Humes and by Specter was maintained after the trajectory for Connally was corrected, it might have compelled the conclusion that the Governor was shot considerably later than the President.

How did the Commission establish the trajectory? According to the testimony *(5H 153, 162)* and the Report *(WR 106)*, it was established by taking an average of the angle from the window to the car between Frames 210 and

225, which (after adjustment to allow for the 3° slope of the street) came to 17°43'30"; and by "piercing" stand-ins for Kennedy and Connally with a rod held at that angle of descent. *(CE 903)* Thus, it is hardly surprising that the rod went through the stand-ins at points "approximating" the sites of the wounds actually sustained by the victims. The disparity of almost 8° in the trajectory of Connally's wounds is written off to either a slight deflection of the bullet or a slight shift in the Governor's posture. *(WR 107)*

Thus, by virtue of those ingenious calculations, approximations, and speculations, a trajectory of 45° is reduced to one of about 17°, without regard for the physical law stating that the line between two fixed points (the Book Depository window and the car positioned at the Stemmons Freeway sign) is a constant. The Warren Commission has formulated a new law: The shots came from the Book Depository window and no other point in the universe; everything else is mutable.

To regard such capriciously fluctuating "evidence" as authoritative or authentic would be folly, all the more so when the testimony of the groundskeeper at Dealey Plaza, Emmett Hudson, reveals that one of the two fixed points—the Stemmons sign—had been shifted from its place after the assassination and removed completely by early in 1965. *(7H 562-563)* Nevertheless, Liebeler, the counsel who examined Hudson, failed to ask a single question about the removal of the sign or to take the slightest interest in this provocative information. Consequently, we do not know if the sign was moved before or after the FBI re-enactment tests of May 24, 1964 or, for that matter, before or after the Secret Service re-enactments of December 5, 1963.

The repositioning and ultimate disappearance of the Stemmons sign is a mystery with ominous undertones. Having no interest in evidence which did not incriminate Oswald, the Warren Commission took not the slightest interest in the Stemmons sign and, needless to say, made no investigation into when and why it was moved.

Before leaving the subject of the Zapruder film (to which I shall return later), it is apropos to quote from a report written by Thomas Stamm after seeing a screening of the film at the National Archives in September 1965. Stamm wrote, in an unpublished manuscript:

Of greatest importance in the film is the sequence of the fatal shot and its aftermath. This sequence shows President Kennedy thrust violently back against the rear seat, from which he bounces forward and spins off to his left into Mrs. Kennedy's arms. Almost immediately he begins to fall away from Mrs. Kennedy as she rises in obvious shock, revulsion, and horror and climbs onto the back of the limousine from which she is thrust back into the car by Secret Service Agent Hill.

The sudden explosive violence with which President Kennedy is slammed back against the rear seat is unmistakable. It is within the realm of speculative possibility that the violent backward thrust of the President was caused by the sudden acceleration of the limousine, as Secret Service Agents Kellerman and Greer, in the front seats, made their effort to escape the murder site and obtain medical help at Parkland Hospital. Against that thesis is the fact that Mrs. Kennedy is obviously not thrust back but maintains her position while the President gyrates back, forward, and into her arms.

Against that thesis, also, is the testimony of Governor and Mrs. Connally, as noted in the Report: "Mrs. Connally heard a second shot fired and pulled her husband down into her lap. . . . The Governor was lying with his head on his wife's lap when he heard a shot hit the President. At that point, both Governor and Mrs. Connally observed brain tissue splatter over the interior of the car. According to Governor and Mrs. Connally, it was after this shot that Kellerman issued his emergency instruction and the car accelerated." *(WR 50)* No other testimony relating to this point is adduced in the Report, and the Commission apparently accepted the testimony of the Governor and his wife as accurate and factual.

The violent backward thrust of President Kennedy occurs, to the eye, at the instant of impact of the fatal shot. The two events appear to be simultaneous and to have the obvious relationship of cause and effect. The service of truth requires no other explanation.

That President Kennedy could have been thrust back violently against the rear seat in consequence of a bullet fired from above and behind him seems a manifest impossibility. This sequence in the Zapruder film, occupying a mere fraction of a second, invalidates the official autopsy finding and demolishes the Commission's thesis and findings of a lone gunman firing from the southeast corner sixth-floor window of the Depository. It makes of the Report a monstrous fabrication erected to obscure the truth which must now be disinterred despite the official verdict.

Subsequently other researchers have viewed the Zapruder film (thanks to the courtesy of Mr. Edward Kern of *Life* magazine, I was able to view some 25 screenings of the film and excellent color transparencies of the individual frames). Without exception or hesitation, each of the viewers has corroborated the dramatic thrust of the President's body back and to the left in reaction to the bullet that hit his head in Frame 313. Vincent J. Salandria and Gaeton Fonzi conclusively demonstrated the backward recoil by tracing the position of the body in successive frames, using two projectors and projecting one slide upon the other. The resultant diagram[22] constitutes conclusive and irrefutable proof that the bullet that sent the President violently backward and to his left was fired in front of and to the right of the car and not from the Book Depository. Some six months after that diagram was published no spokesman for the Warren Commission has challenged the data or the accompanying conclusion that the fatal shot came from somewhere on the grassy knoll.

The Zapruder film was screened many times for viewing by "Commission representatives and representatives of the FBI and Secret Service" in the Commission's building. *(5H 138)* The film was viewed also by doctors who had operated on Governor Connally, and by the Governor. To the critic who has seen the Zapruder film and gasped at this graphic proof of a conspiracy to kill the President—for there must have been a gunman in front of the car as well as behind it—one thing arouses even more alarm and anguish than the sight of his exploding head: the silence of the Warren Commission (and its lawyers,

---

22   *The Greater Philadelphia Magazine,* August 1966, p. 44.

investigators, and witnesses) in regard to this visible evidence clearly implicating at least two riflemen in the crime.

That silence, as much as any other single abuse of logic or misrepresentation of evidence in the Warren Report, convicts the Commission of dishonesty and calculated deception. The Commission did not acknowledge the slam of the body against the back of the seat; it did not solicit opinion from experts as to whether that body recoil conceivably could be reconciled with a shot from behind the car; and it did not inform the public—the vast majority of whom will never view the Zapruder film at the National Archives—that the camera had recorded events central to the establishment of the truth and utterly inconsistent with the lone-assassin thesis.[23]

---

23   In January 1967 *Ramparts* published the results of a study conducted for the magazine by Dr. R. A. J. Riddle, assistant professor of physics at UCLA. After studying the relevant segment of the Zapruder film, Dr. Riddle pointed out that the law of conservation of momentum governs the movement of an object hit by a projectile and gives the object a motion in the same direction as the motion of the projectile. After applying that principle to Frames 310-323, Dr. Riddle reached a conclusion that "contradicts the findings of the Warren Commission"—that is, that the shot came from the front and right of the car.

Chapter 2
The Book Depository

Prior Knowledge of the Motorcade Route

Late in the afternoon of Thursday, November 21, 1963, Lee Oswald was driven by his fellow worker Buell Wesley Frazier from Dallas to Irving, Texas, where his wife and two daughters lived in the home of their friends Ruth and Michael Paine. This visit on the night before the assassination was unexpected and is, at first glance, an embarrassment to those who question his guilt. The Warren Commission believes that Oswald went to Irving in order to retrieve his rifle and take it to Dallas the next morning. This, of course, presupposes Oswald's knowledge of the Presidential visit and of the motorcade route. While the Commission was conducting its hearings, advocates of the theory that Oswald was a fall guy and had been framed claimed that he could not have known the route of the Presidential motorcade and therefore could not have planned the crime in advance.

The Warren Report, when it appeared, seemed to dispose of the argument, pointing out that the motorcade route was published in both Dallas newspapers on November 19, 1963, and was therefore available for at least 72 hours before Oswald reported for work on November 22. *(WR 642)*[1]

---

1 The Warren Report states that "on the morning of the President's arrival, the [*Dallas*] *Morning News* noted that the motorcade would travel through downtown Dallas onto the Stemmons Freeway, and reported that "the motorcade will move slowly so that crowds can get a good view of President Kennedy and his wife." *(WR 40)* The footnote to the statement refers to a cropped photocopy of the front page of the *Dallas Morning News* of November 22, 1963 *(CE 1365)*, showing only the headline and one column of print, with five columns blanked out. Examination of the uncropped first page reveals that the Commission deleted a map of the Presidential motorcade route on which the motorcade travels down Main Street, *without* turning on to Elm Street, through the triple underpass and then to the Trade Mart.

In addition to excising the map that indicated no detour from Main Street along Houston to Elm, the Commission asserts that "the Elm Street approach to the Stemmons Freeway is necessary in order to avoid the traffic hazards which would otherwise exist if right turns were permitted from both Main and Elm into the freeway." *(WR 39)* But Traffic Patrolman Joe Marshall Smith testified that he knew of nothing that would have prevented the motorcade from going directly down Main Street under the triple underpass and on to the Stemmons Freeway. *(7H 538-539)*

The Commission is on solid ground in demonstrating that Oswald *could* have known the motorcade route as early as Tuesday, November 19, and that he might have been aware a day or more in advance that the President's car would pass the Book Depository. But nothing in the testimony indicates that Oswald *did* know the motorcade route.

Most of the Book Depository employees who were questioned on their own prior knowledge of the route indicated that they did not learn until Friday morning that the motorcade would pass the building *(3H 178, Williams; 3H 209, Jarman);* among them, apparently, it had not been a topic of general conversation. For that matter, FBI Agent Hosty, who had participated in the advance preparations for the President's protection during the Dallas visit, did not know until Thursday evening that there was to be a motorcade and "never realized that the motorcade would pass the Texas School Book Depository Building." *(WR 441)*

Obviously the Commission has inferred (but not established) that Oswald was aware of the exact route early enough for premeditation, as manifested by his return to Irving. It does appear that Oswald's visit on Thursday evening without notice or invitation was unusual. But it is not clear that it was unprecedented. An FBI report dealing with quite another matter—Oswald's income and expenditures—strongly suggests that Oswald had cashed a check in a grocery store in Irving on Thursday evening, October 31, 1963 *(CE 1165,* p. 6); the Warren Commission decided arbitrarily that the transaction took place on Friday, November 1. *(WR 331)* Neither Oswald's wife nor Mrs. Ruth Paine, both of whom were questioned closely about the dates and times of Oswald's visits to Irving during October and November, suggested that he had ever come there —with or without prior notice—on a Thursday. It is possible, though implausible, that Oswald came to Irving on Thursday, October 31, 1963, solely to cash a check and then returned to Dallas without contacting his wife or visiting the Paine residence. More likely, Marina and Mrs. Paine forgot that visit or, for reasons of their own, preferred not to mention it. Either way, it is clear that Oswald's visit to Irving on Thursday night, November 21, may not have been unprecedented.

The possibility of a previous Thursday visit introduces an element of doubt about the degree to which the November 21 visit in fact incriminates Oswald, and about the validity of the inference that his primary purpose was to obtain the rifle. Furthermore, there is very serious doubt about Oswald's prior knowledge of the motorcade route. James Jarman, Jr., a fellow employee of Oswald at the Book Depository, testified on March 24, 1964 that he had talked to Oswald between 8 and 9 a.m. on Friday about an order and that "later in the morning" he had encountered Oswald on the first floor. Jarman told the Commission:

> ... he was standing up in the window and I went to the window also, and he asked me what were the people gathering around on the corner for, and I told him that the President was supposed to pass that morning, and he asked me did I know which way he was coming, and I told him, yes; he probably come down Main and turn on Houston and then back again on Elm. Then he said, "Oh, I see," and that was all.   *(3H 200-201)*

Jarman said that he himself had first learned of the motorcade route at about 9 a.m. on Friday, when he overheard a conversation between two people who worked in the building. *(3H 209)* Asked whether it was he or Oswald who had initiated the conversation about the motorcade passing the Book Depository, Jarman replied, "He asked me." *(3H 209-210)*

Jarman's testimony is acknowledged in the report *(WR 183)* but not in the context of Oswald's access to advance information about the exact motorcade route. It is mentioned without comment or evaluation in a section dealing with Oswald's statements under detention.

But Oswald himself did not mention his conversation with Jarman after his arrest, according to the relevant testimony and documents. He did not cite that conversation as support of his protestations of innocence, although he did offer other facts or allegations. This is a crucial point in evaluating Oswald's questions to Jarman.

Why did Oswald ask questions which suggested that until spectators began to gather there, he did not know the Presidential motorcade would pass the building? There are two possibilities. One is that he really did not know that the motorcade was to pass the Book Depository. The consequences which flow from that assumption are irrefutable: that he did not plan or execute the assassination.

The other possibility is that Oswald did know that the motorcade would pass the building and that his questions to Jarman were a "plant" to divert suspicion in the event that such suspicion of him arose after he carried out his monstrous crime. But if that was true, why then did he not use the "plant" for the very purpose that had led him to set it up—to indicate his innocence—when he was actually arrested and accused of the assassination? Moreover, there is no other sign of methodical advance planning to escape suspicion or create the impression of innocence. On the contrary, Oswald left an abundant trail of incriminating evidence, on his person as well as among his possessions in both Dallas and Irving. An assassin subtle and calculating enough to plant the suggestion that he did not even know the motorcade route until just before the shooting would not be so careless or self-defeating as to carry incriminating documents in his wallet or leave photographs of himself holding the murder rifle where the police could scarcely fail to find them.

One may defend or attack either of the two assumptions; certainly there are ample arguments to be made in each case. But the Warren Commission has kept silent, neither taking a position nor defending it. It has merely mentioned Jarman's testimony as though it were of no import. We have no clue to the Commission's reasoning, but unquestionably the Commission discounts the possibility that Oswald really did not know the motorcade route and that his questions to Jarman resulted from honest curiosity. It seems reasonable to infer that in deciding that Oswald's questions were planted, the Commission was not seriously troubled by any inconsistency in relation to its conclusions about Oswald's behavior before or after the assassination.

Others will not be satisfied so easily and will continue to ask why, if the questions were a plant, Oswald himself never confronted the police with the fabrication designed for that very purpose. Without an answer to that puzzle, one may well feel haunted by the thought that the questions, and the questioner, were wholly innocent.

The Chicken Lunch

Students of the events of November 22 will remember that the remains of a chicken lunch were found on the sixth floor of the Book Depository, together with a soda pop bottle and an empty cigarette package. It was thought that a sniper had been hiding out, waiting for his victim. A news broadcast on Dallas radio-TV station KRLD on the night of the assassination reported:

> A Dallas police inspector named J. H. Sawyer said the police found the remains of fried chicken and paper on the 5th floor indicating he said that apparently the person had been there for quite a while waiting for this moment in history.   *(CE 2174)*

The theory went through several transformations in the next days. One version was that the chicken bones were several days old and had no connection with the assassination. It was next said that one of the workers had eaten the chicken during a coffee break that morning. The empty cigarette package was dropped from mention.

The final version of the story is found on page 68 of the Warren Report: Bonnie Ray Williams had gone up to the sixth floor to eat his lunch and had left behind his paper lunch sack, chicken bones, and an empty pop bottle. The Report does not specify just where Williams left this debris, and small wonder. Judging from the highly contradictory testimony of the police officers who searched the sixth floor, the chicken must have been shot out of a cannon.

Deputy Sheriff Luke Mooney, who discovered a pile of cartons stacked in the form of a protective barrier at the southeast window, testified that he saw one partially eaten piece of chicken on top of those boxes and a small paper bag about a foot away, on the same carton as the chicken. *(3H 288-298)* Sergeant Gerald Hill saw a chicken leg bone and a paper sandwich bag on top of the cartons. *(7H 46)* But Officer L. D. Montgomery saw "one piece of chicken on a box and there was a piece on the floor—just kind of scattered around right there"; but he didn't remember if the paper bag was on top of the cartons or on the floor. The soda pop bottle was "a little more to the west of that window." *(7H 97-98)*

Officer E. L. Boyd, on the other hand, saw chicken bones on top of some boxes about 30 or 40 feet west of the southeast corner window where the cartons stood. *(7H 121)* Officer Marvin Johnson recalled remnants of fried chicken and a soda bottle "by some other window . . . toward the west," perhaps at the second pair of windows from the southeast corner. *(7H 105)* R. L. Studebaker, who photographed the evidence found on the sixth floor, saw chicken bones, a brown paper bag, and a soda bottle in the third aisle from the east wall, near a two-wheel truck, but the chicken bones were inside the paper bag. He did not see chicken bones on the pile of cartons or on the floor (where Mooney, Hill, and Montgomery had seen them). *(7H 146)* Bill Shelley, foreman at the Book Depository, also remembered that the chicken bones were at the third window from the southeast corner, "laying on a sack . . . with a coke bottle sitting in the window," and while remembering the chicken bones on top of the paper bag instead of inside it, he, like Studebaker, remembered seeing no lunch remains elsewhere on the sixth floor. *(6H 330-331)*

E. D. Brewer, however, remembered seeing the paper lunch bag and some chicken bones or partially eaten chicken together with a pop bottle at the southeast corner window, near the rifle shells. *(6H 307)*

Lieutenant J. C. Day is in the third-aisle faction. He remembered seeing the lunch bag and the pop bottle at the third set of windows, with the two-wheel truck. The bag of chicken bones and the empty bottle were brought to the police laboratory and may still be there, except for "the chicken bones, I finally threw them away that laid around there." When he heard that one of the workers had eaten his lunch on the sixth floor, Day explained, he realized that the chicken bones had no connection with Oswald. He had checked the bottle for Oswald's fingerprints, with negative results, and then put aside the chicken and the paper bag. *(4H 266)*

Day was not asked if there were fingerprints other than Oswald's on the bottle and, if so, whether those prints had been identified. An attempt should have been made to determine whether Bonnie Ray Williams had left fingerprints on that bottle, for while he was linked to the lunch remains some time after the assassination, Williams, in his affidavit of November 23 *(CE 2003),* did not make any mention of the chicken lunch.

Four of the nine witnesses, then, remembered seeing the chicken remains at the southeast corner window on top of the barrier of cartons. One of the four remembered chicken on the floor there, as well. One witness saw the chicken remains at the second pair of windows from the east wall; and four witnesses saw them with the soda bottle at the third pair of windows. But none of them saw chicken remains except at the place he specified; and no one admitted having moved the chicken or the lunch bag. Neither the chicken nor the paper bag is visible in any of the photographs taken on the sixth floor, but there are photographs showing the empty bottle standing on the floor near the two-wheel truck in the third aisle.

All the witnesses remember seeing the chicken leg or bones unwrapped, except Studebaker—who insisted that the bones were inside the paper bag, "wrapped up and put right back in" together with "a little piece of Fritos in the sack, too."

Finally, we have an opinion from Captain Will Fritz: "I will tell you where that story comes from. At the other window above there, where people in days past, you know, had eaten their lunches, they left chicken bones and pieces of bread, all kinds of things up and down there. That isn't where he [Oswald] was at all. He was in a different window, so I don't think those things have anything to do with it." *(4H 239)* Well, everything is clear at last.

But it is not quite so simple as the Captain suggests. It is a matter for concern that the stalwart men of the Dallas police department have such faulty visual perception, or faulty recall—if in fact the conflicts in their stories really result from impaired faculties.

The predisposition of the Dallas police is apparent from their concentration on evidence identifiable with Oswald. Lieutenant Day saw no need to check the empty bottle for fingerprints other than Oswald's. We will never know if fingerprints were on the bottle, or whose they were.

The confused and contradictory testimony on the chicken remains permits little trust in a case that rests largely on evidence gathered by investigators of such dubious competence. The Warren Commission has nevertheless seen to it that this chicken will not come home to roost in the quarters of the Dallas police: there is no sign that the Commission was perturbed by the mad variety of the testimony.

The Shield of Cartons

According to the Warren Report, police officers arrived at the Book Depository shortly after the assassination and began a search for the assassin and the evidence; around 1 p.m. Deputy Sheriff Luke Mooney noticed the pile of cartons in front of the window in the southeast corner of the sixth floor; searching the area, at approximately 1:12 p.m. he found three empty cartridge cases on the floor near the window. *(WR 79)*

The Commission's exhibits include a photograph *(CE 723)* captioned "shield of cartons around sixth-floor southeast corner window." *(WR 80)* The photograph shows eight stacks of cartons, three or four to a stack, arranged in a crude semi-circle so as to conceal the window area from view, from the floor up, to the height of the bottom frame of the upper half of the window. The Commission suggests that the purpose of the arrangement was "shielding Oswald from the view of anyone on the sixth floor who did not attempt to go behind them" and that Oswald needed no assistance in stacking the cartons. *(WR 248)* Other photographs *(CE 1310-1312)* indicate that a man of Oswald's height, if standing, would be visible behind the shield of cartons from the top of his head to about the middle of his chest.

Perplexing questions arise about this shield of cartons and, indeed, about the selection of the southeast corner window by a sniper—questions which, it would seem, did not occupy the Commission.

A first question which arises from the account in the Report of the discovery of the sniper's nest *(WR 79)* is why it should have taken Luke Mooney 12 minutes, once having discovered the shield of cartons, to notice the three cartridge cases. It turns out, as will be seen, that the Report is inaccurate and that there was no 12-minute delay.

A more baffling question which is not illusory is why almost half an hour elapsed between the report by three employees who had watched the motorcade from the fifth-floor windows that shells had been ejected overhead, and the moment that Mooney stumbled into the sniper's nest. The police had also heard witnesses who reported immediately after the shots that they had seen a rifle or an object like a rifle, or a man, or a man with a rifle, in the sixth-floor window. By any rule of criminal investigation, the police should have rushed immediately to the southeast corner of the sixth floor. Instead, as Mooney testified, the sniper's nest was discovered by chance during a floor-by-floor search.

Mooney testified that after the shots were heard, he and other officers ran and jumped over a fence into the railroad yards, because . . .

> From the echo of the shots, we thought they came from that direction. . . . We were there only a few seconds until we had orders to cover the Texas Depository Building. . . . I noticed there was a big elevator there. So I jumped on it. . . . And how come I get off the sixth floor, I don't know yet. But, anyway, I stopped on six, and I didn't even know what floor I was on. . . . I was alone at the time. . . . I assume there had been other officers up there. But I didn't see them. And I began crisscrossing it, round and round, through boxes, looking at open windows—some of them were open over on the south side . . . .
>
> Then I decided—I saw there was another floor. . . . So I went on up to the seventh floor. . . . We looked around up there for a short time. And then I says I am going back down on six. . . . So I went back down. . . . I went straight across to the southeast corner of the building, and I saw all these high boxes. Of course they were stacked all the way around over there. And I *squeezed between two*. And the minute I squeezed between these two stacks of boxes, I had to turn myself sideways to get in there—that is when I saw the expended shells and the boxes that were stacked up looked to be a rest for the weapon. [Italics added]   *(3H 283-284)*

Mooney's description indicates that very soon after the shooting, orders were given to cover the Book Depository, but not any particular floor of the building and certainly no particular window. Mooney went first to the sixth floor, without even realizing that it was the sixth, and although he crisscrossed through boxes and looked at open windows on the south side, he did not then see the shield of cartons or anything else to arouse suspicion. No one else was present on the sixth floor. It was only after Mooney went to the seventh floor for a while and then returned to the sixth floor that he discovered the shield of cartons and the shells. His testimony shows that he found the shells at once and not, as the Report suggests, 12 minutes after he noticed the shield of cartons.

How is it that Mooney did not notice the shield on his first inspection when, he testified, he took particular notice of the open windows on the south side? Is it possible that the stacks of cartons were not arranged in the form of a shield on his first search and that the structure was hastily assembled while he was on the floor above for about ten minutes? Or was the shield of cartons set up by an assassin or assassins before the shooting? If the latter, we should consider why an assassin, if he were an "inside" man, would have selected the southeast corner window on the sixth floor as the place from which to fire with a minimum of risk of being observed or trapped.

The fifth, sixth, and seventh floors of the Book Depository are storage floors where employees came to obtain books as they were needed to fill orders but where no personnel are normally at work throughout the day. During the week of the assassination, however, a floor-laying crew was working full-time on the sixth floor. That floor was therefore the least "safe" of the three unoccupied floors for any assassin fearful of unexpected intrusion. An inside man had to expect that one of the workers might return unpredictably to retrieve cigarettes (as Charles Givens said he did) or that some of the floor-laying crew might elect to watch the motorcade from the sixth floor (as Bonnie Ray Williams testified, before lunch "everybody was talking like they was going to watch from the sixth floor"). Far less risk would attach to the seventh floor—not only was it deserted, but, according to the diagram, there is an enclosure at the southeast corner that would ensure privacy at the southeast corner window. *(CE 507)*

But if the assassin nevertheless selected the sixth-floor window and went to that position as soon as the crew went to lunch, he was interrupted almost at once by the return of Bonnie Ray Williams with his chicken lunch. The assassin had no way of knowing how long Williams might linger, or whether he might not even decide to remain there to observe the motorcade. Then, if not before, the assassin should have turned his thoughts to the seventh floor. If it was too late to leave without calling attention to himself, he then had to wait motionless and silent for almost 20 harrowing minutes.

Williams finally departed, at about 12:20 p.m. The motorcade was due to pass the Book Depository at 12:25 p.m. The assassin could not have counted on the five-minute delay which in fact occurred. He had only a few short minutes after Williams' departure, then, in which to reassemble the rifle and set up cartons on the window ledge to serve as a gun-rest.

Did he have enough time also to assemble a shield of cartons? Did he even need such a shield?

According to the Report, "cartons had been stacked on the floor, a few feet behind the windows, thus shielding Oswald from the view of anyone on the sixth floor who did not attempt to go behind them." *(WR 248)* Again the Commission seems to have ignored the dictates of common sense; in this case, the salient fact is that there was a natural, built-in shield on the sixth floor. There are six rows of columns across the floor, from north to south, with five columns in each row. There are seven sets of double windows on the south facade. If the southeast corner window where the shield of cartons was found is numbered *1* and the southwest corner window is *7,* the elevators on the north wall would face window *5;* the staircase would face window *7.* No one arriving on the sixth floor, either by elevator or by stairs, would see the southeast corner window— his view would be obstructed by the 30 columns and the random stacks of book cartons (some as high as a man) scattered along the floor. Existing obstructions would also appear to shield the area from the view of any of the men in the floor-laying crew who returned to the southwest corner of the floor. *(CE 723)* The fact that the normal state of the Book Depository floors obstructs the view is borne out in the testimony of motorcycle officer M. S. Baker:

> *Cooper:* ... As you walked up the stairs could you see into each floor space as you passed from floor to floor?

Baker: Partly. Now, this building has got pillars in it, you know, and then it has got books, cases of books stacked all in it. And the best that I could, you know, I would look through and see if I could see anybody. *(3H 267)*

An intruder on the sixth floor, therefore, would have to walk along the north wall to the northeast corner before he could obtain an unobstructed view of the southeast corner window; while he was walking, an assassin would have ample time to assume the pose of an innocent spectator.

An assassin was far more vulnerable to observation by spectators on the street than by intruders inside; in fact, some witnesses claimed that they had seen a man at the window.

The Commission has blandly disregarded the illogical and contradictory nature of the alleged assassin's actions: it infers that he assembled a shield of cartons against witnesses inside the Book Depository—which served little purpose other than to call attention to the window afterwards—and yet ignored taking precaution against being observed by witnesses outside the building.

If all those considerations are put aside, it is still necessary to explain the fact that during the ten minutes in which the alleged assassin presumably made the necessary preparations for his deed, he was observed by a spectator on the street standing idly at the window, "like he was looking down toward the . . . triple underpass . . . just was there transfixed." *(WR 146)*

The Commission has not suggested when, according to its reasoning, the alleged assassin assembled a shield consisting of some 24 cartons, each of which weighed about 50 pounds *(WR 249)*, most of which had to be lifted physically and placed atop one, two, or three other cartons. This would require substantial exertion and considerable time. Could Oswald *or any other solitary assassin* accomplish this and still have time to assemble a rifle, arrange a gun-rest, sit still long enough to leave a palmprint on the carton on which he sat, and finally gaze motionless and transfixed at the underpass—all in the 10 or 15 minutes at his disposal after the departure of Bonnie Ray Williams?

One must wonder if the Commission believed in its own inferences and conclusions about the shield of cartons, especially when the Report maintains silence about the presence—or absence—of fingerprints on the individual cartons in the shield. It seems inconceivable that Oswald could have lifted and positioned those 24 cartons or more without leaving his prints. Yet neither the Report nor the Hearings and Exhibits suggest that any inquiry was made about the number and identification of prints on those cartons—an incomprehensible omission to which Léo Sauvage first called attention in a magazine article.[2]

Progressing to the moment when the last shot was fired and the assassin began his escape, rifle in hand, how did he penetrate his self-constructed barrier of cartons? As they assertedly stood when they were discovered, the space between stacks was too narrow for human passage. Mooney testified that he had to squeeze through. The assassin, similarly, would have had to squeeze out—unless, of course, he first removed and then replaced some of the cartons. Either way, he would be slowed down somewhat in leaving the window. To accept the

---

2   "The Oswald Affair," *Commentary*, March 1964, pp. 55-65.

findings in the Report, one must believe that he penetrated the shield, carefully concealed a rifle elsewhere on the floor, ran down the stairs to the second floor and into the lunchroom in time to stand there calmly (whether he held a bottle of coke or not is discussed elsewhere), *all in less than 80 seconds.*

This reconstruction presents so many implausibilities, such hairbreadth timing, that almost any alternative comes as a relief to one's sense of logic. It taxes credulity that an assassin should have taken momumental pains to barricade himself from observation from within, which was remote if not impossible, while flaunting himself with extreme nonchalance before spectators on the street, well before the shooting, when there was no need to show himself staring and immobile.

The Warren Report does not confront those problems or attempt to answer the oustanding and relevant questions: Where was Oswald while Williams ate his chicken? When did he arrange the shield of cartons? Were fingerprints or palmprints on those cartons, and were they Oswald's? Why did he re-seal the shield when he emerged from behind the cartons? And why did Luke Mooney overlook the shield of cartons on his first inspection of the sixth floor? Without credible answers to those questions, the pronouncements in the Report about the shield of cartons are unacceptable.

The Short, Bulky Package

In order to sustain the conclusion that Oswald was the lone assassin, the Warren Commission had to establish Oswald's presence at the place it designated as the source of all the shots. In subsequent chapters I shall discuss the Commission's failure to establish Oswald's presence on the sixth floor of the Book Depository despite the claim in the Report that he was at that location shortly before the shooting.

But even if there were persuasive evidence that Oswald was on the sixth floor, the Commission had to confront an equally important problem: to prove, beyond a reasonable doubt, that the "assassination weapon" was present too, that it had been introduced into the building by Oswald, and that he had fired it.

Like the question of his foreknowledge of the motorcade route, Oswald's introducing the rifle into the building—and therefore his trip to Irving the night before to obtain the rifle, and his alleged construction of the paper bag in which to carry it—is crucial to the question of premeditation and the finding of guilt.

The Commission realized the importance of this aspect of the case. Two of its main findings are (a) that the Mannlicher-Carcano 6.5 mm. rifle was owned by and in the possession of Oswald, and (b) that Oswald carried that rifle into the Book Depository on the morning of November 22. *(WR 19)*

What is remarkable is that if the statements in the Report in defense of those findings are compared with the actual testimony and evidence, every link in the Commission's chain of reasoning proves to be feeble. Let us retrace the

Commission's steps and see if the evidence leads us to the same conclusions, or if at the end of the journey we are burdened with a heavy weight of reasonable doubt.

> The Commission considered the circumstances surrounding Oswald's return to Irving, Texas, on Thursday, November 21, 1963 and concluded that Oswald told the curtain rod story to Frazier to explain both the return to Irving and the obvious bulk of the package which he intended to bring to work the next day. *(WR 129, 137)*

There is no reason to doubt Wesley Frazier's story that Oswald asked him for a ride to Irving on Thursday night, saying that he wanted to pick up some curtain rods. According to the reports on Oswald's interrogation by the police, he denied having told Frazier anything about curtain rods. *(WR 604)* There is no transcript of the interrogation, but if Oswald actually contradicted Frazier, he was almost certainly untruthful. If Captain Fritz, the interrogator, thought Oswald was lying when he denied the curtain rod story, it is a pity that he did not proceed to ask him why he did return to Irving on Thursday; no one seems to have asked that question at any time during Oswald's detention.

In any event, a lie about the purpose of a visit or the contents of a package is a far cry from proof of criminal purpose, and there is some question about whether in fact the Thursday visit was as unusual or unprecedented as the Report suggests. An FBI report on Oswald's income and expenditures contains an interview with the cashier of the A & P Store in Irving, Mrs. Georgia Tarrants, who said that Oswald had appeared at the cashier's cage and cashed a $33.00 unemployment check on Thursday night, October 31, 1963. *(CE 1165)* Troy Erwin, the manager of the store, told the FBI that the check in question had definitely been cashed there sometime after 3 p.m. on Thursday, October 31, 1963, and before the "close of business" on Friday, November 1, 1963. The Commission states merely that Oswald cashed the $33.00 check on Friday, November 1 *(WR 331),* and although Mrs. Tarrants had said that the transaction took place on Thursday night, she was not requestioned and no further attempt was made to pinpoint the date.

Both Marina Oswald and Ruth Paine testified that they believed that Oswald had come to Irving on the night before the assassination to make up with his wife over a quarrel they had had. As will be discussed later, there is reason to question Marina Oswald's account of the quarrel; but, assuming for the sake of argument that Oswald went to Irving to reconcile with his wife, his subsequent actions are susceptible to an interpretation that is not necessarily incriminating. Like most husbands, Oswald would have been disinclined to reveal the marital contretemps to Frazier, a casual bachelor acquaintance. It is even conceivable that Oswald, having told an innocent fiction about curtain rods, carried an improvised package to work in order to support the story. Moreover, there *were* curtain rods stored in the Paine garage. Counsel Jenner and Secret Service Agent Joe Howlett accompanied Mrs. Paine to the garage and found two curtain rods on a shelf. *(9H 425)* The rods were measured and found to be 27½ inches long—a figure which should be borne in mind, for reasons to be discussed a bit later.

Mrs. Paine maintained that only those two curtain rods had been stored in the garage and that consequently Oswald did not take curtain rods from the premises on the fatal morning. Her husband, however, was not certain of the number of curtain rods which had been stored in the garage, before *or* after the assassination. *(9H 424, 9H 461)*

All the same, the Commission's čonclusion that the curtain rod story was an invention to cover Oswald's unscheduled visit to Irving for a different purpose would be reasonable and plausible—*if* the collateral evidence were established beyond reasonable doubt.

> The Commission considered the disappearance of the rifle from its normal place of storage and concluded (1) that Oswald took paper and tape from the wrapping bench of the Depository and fashioned a bag large enough to carry the disassembled rifle, and (2) that he removed the rifle from the blanket in the Paines' garage on Thursday evening. *(WR 129, 137)* The period between 8 and 9 p.m. provided ample opportunity for Oswald to prepare the rifle for his departure the next morning.   *(WR 130)*

The Commission has not indicated its reasoning as to when and where Oswald fashioned the paper bag from materials taken from the Book Depository. Presumably he did so only after the motorcade route became known on Tuesday, November 19, 1963, and before departing for Irving after work on Thursday. (Amateur psychiatrists who suggest that Oswald became insane on Thursday night when his wife spurned him overlook the clear element of premeditation if, as the Commission believes, the paper bag was fabricated by Oswald.) But there is no evidence to back the Commission's assumption that Oswald took wrapping paper and sealing tape from the wrapping bench. On the contrary, Troy West, the wrapping clerk, testified that to his knowledge Oswald had never borrowed or used those materials and that he bad never seen Oswald near the roll of wrapping paper or the tape dispenser. Moreover, Harold Weisberg in his book *Whitewash* has pointed to a significant fact which escaped mention in the Warren Report: when tape is pulled from the Book Depository tape dispenser it is automatically moistened by a mechanism like a water wheel.[3]

> *Belin:* If I wanted to pull the tape, pull off a piece without getting water on it, would I just lift it up without going over the wet roller and get the tape without getting it wet?
> *West:* You would have to take it out. You would have to take it out of the machine. See, it's put on there and then run through a little clamp that holds it down, and you pull it, well, then the water, it gets water on it. *(6H 361)*

Although counsel should have delved into this matter in greater detail so as to make it clear just what procedures were necessary in order to remove a length of tape without wetting it, Troy West's testimony makes it evident at least that normally the tape emerges from the dispenser in wet condition. Anyone wishing to remove tape without wetting it would have to inactivate the apparatus in such a way as to produce dry tape showing the "series of small markings in the form of half-inch lines" by which the Warren Commission established that

---

3 *Whitewash* (Dell Publishing Co., New York, 1966), p. 61.

the tape actually used to seal the improvised paper bag had originated in the Book Depository tape-dispensing machine. *(WR 579-580)* West does not suggest any way to obtain dry tape except by removing the roll of tape from the machine. That would produce tape lacking the markings found on the paper bag tape. The Commission failed to ascertain whether or not there is a way to obtain a length of dry tape *without* removing the roll of tape from the machine. While conceding that there may be such a method—for example, removing the wet roller—the burden of proof is the Commission's. On the basis of the facts the Commission has made available, it would appear that the tape used in the fabrication of the paper bag was removed in wet condition or that the tape-dispenser was adjusted in such a way as to make the removal of the tape a conspicuous operation. Yet no one saw Oswald at the tape-dispenser or with a length of wet tape in his possession.

Despite the lack of supporting evidence and in the face of serious constraints such as lack of the needed privacy and time, the Commission implicitly asks us to assume that Oswald filched the necessary materials and secretly fabricated a paper bag at the Book Depository or in his rented room in Dallas after working hours (there was no opportunity to fashion the bag without being detected during his overnight visit to Irving).

The Commission adds blandly that he made the bag to hold the *disassembled* rifle. Why not the assembled rifle, while he was at it? That would have eliminated avoidable complications—the disassembling of the weapon, if it was not already disassembled, and certainly the reassembling of the weapon at the Book Depository, where there was little privacy to be had. Perhaps Oswald did not remember the actual length of the assembled rifle (40.2 inches) or perhaps he was under the impression that he had received the rifle he actually had ordered, which was only 36 inches long in assembled state.[4]

According to the Commission's findings, Oswald must have carried the paper bag concealed on his person when he accompanied Frazier to Irving on Thursday. Frazier saw no paper bag or any sign that Oswald had concealed on his person the six-foot length of wrapping paper necessary to construct a bag consisting of two sheets, each about three feet long, sealed at the edges. Neither Marina Oswald *(1H 120)* nor Ruth Paine *(3H 49, 77)* noticed anything which provided the smallest corroboration for the Commission's assumption. According to an FBI interview of December 3, 1963:

> Marina stated that when Oswald visited the Paine house on Thursday evening, November 21, 1963, he did not bring anything with him when he arrived at the house. . . . She further advised that she does not know of any-

---

4   The Commission asserts that the rifle was ordered on a coupon cut from a full-page advertisement by Klein's Sporting Goods Co. in the February 1963 issue of the *American Rifleman* magazine *(WR 119),* but the actual advertisement (which is not included in the Commission's Exhibits) offers a 36-inch Carcano rifle weighing 5½ lbs. with catalogue number C20-T750. The same catalogue number without the "T" identifies the 40.2-inch Carcano shown in Klein's full-page ad in the November 1963 *Field & Stream (Holmes Exhibit No. 2).* Thus, the rifle *ordered* by "Hidell" does *not* correspond with the longer, heavier rifle found in the Book Depository. The Commission never mentions this descrepancy, which apparently was overlooked or disregarded. It is possible that Klein's made an error in filling the order. But can we merely *assume* that?

thing that Oswald took with him from the Paine house to work the next morning, November 22. . . . She examined this sack and said she had never seen anything like it and that she had not seen such a sack or such paper in the possession of Oswald on November 21, 1963, or at any time prior thereto.   (*CE 1401*, p. 272)

To accept the Commission's inferences, then, we must credit Oswald with great adroitness in concealing the paper bag not only from Wesley Frazier and Ruth Paine but also from his wife, in the privacy of their bedroom at the Paine home.

Regrettably, the Commission made no attempt to determine when Oswald made the paper bag, or where. There is no foundation for the conclusion that he made the bag and took it to Irving other than its convenience to the Commission's fixed theory.

The "disappearance of the rifle" and the finding that Oswald removed it from the blanket in the Paine garage between 8 and 9 p.m. on Thursday are also marked by uncertainty.[5] Before dealing with the "disappearance" of the rifle, we should examine the question of its appearance in the Paine garage by reviewing the steps between the shipping of the rifle by Klein's Sporting Goods store in Chicago and the dramatic moment in the garage when the blanket was found to be empty.

Klein's Sporting Goods, a large mail-order weapons house, mailed the rifle to "A. Hidell" at Dallas Post Office Box 2915. That box had been rented by Oswald. The Commission asserts that the relevant post office record form had been destroyed and that it is not known whether or not Oswald, in renting the box, had authorized "A. Hidell" to receive mail there. (*WR 121*) This statement flatly contradicts an FBI report of June 3, 1964 that states:

Our investigation has revealed that Oswald did not indicate on his application that others, including an "A. Hidell," would receive mail through the box in question, which was Post Office Box 2915 in Dallas. This box was obtained by Oswald on October 9, 1962, and relinquished by him on May 14, 1963.   (*CE 2585*, Question 12)

The Commission has an answer for this problem, too, even though it has suggested that Hidell might have been authorized to receive mail at the box when its own exhibit indicates that he was not. The Commission says that it does not matter one way or the other, because Oswald would have had no difficulty in obtaining the package from Klein's. He had only to present the notice which would have been placed in his box and he would have received the package without even having to identify himself.

Apparently no inquiry was made at the post office to determine whether any employee recalled handling the package from Klein's or handing it over to a person presenting a notice, nor was any attempt made to trace the notice or any other documentary evidence relating to the delivery of the package.

---

5 Commission Counsel Liebeler himself considered that there was no actual evidence that the rifle was in the Paine home on the eve of the assassination (*Inquest*, p. 138).

The Report presents only assumptions as to the ease with which Oswald might have obtained the package addressed to Hidell, on the basis of testimony from a post office inspector at a sub-station. It offers no interviews with or testimony from the employees at the main post office where Box 2915 was acually maintained and where stricter procedures may have been in force. The Commission certainly should have looked for concrete proof rather than accept a theoretical likelihood as sufficient—especially when the assurance that Oswald would have had no difficulty in obtaining a parcel addressed to Hidell rested on the testimony of a single witness, Post Office Inspector Harry Holmes, who is also an FBI informer. *(CE 1152)*

There is no proof that the rifle addressed to Hidell was handed over to Lee Harvey Oswald by the postal authorities, and Marina Oswald's testimony is the only basis cited in the Report for the conclusion that Oswald came into possession of a rifle shortly before the attack on General Walker. (The notorious photograph of Oswald, holding a rifle, that appeared "retouched" on the cover of *Life* is discussed in a later chapter.) Marina Oswald is also the sole authority for the conclusion that the rifle was taken from Dallas to New Orleans, and from New Orleans to Irving, where it remained on the floor of the garage wrapped in a blanket. She testified that soon after returning from New Orleans, she had gone to the garage to search for parts to the baby's crib and that she had lifted a corner of the blanket and seen part of the stock of a rifle. *(WR 128)*

Against that testimony, we must weigh the fact that all the information carefully obtained by the Commission about the Oswalds' luggage indicates that their suitcases and other baggage were too small to hold the Carcano rifle. There was a large, soft-sided canvas zipper suitcase, 15 inches high and 25-30 inches wide *(2H 463);* a rectangular suitcase 21½ inches by 14 inches *(2H 264);* a small blue zipper canvas bag which appears *(CE 126)* less than 24 inches long *(1H 50, 115; 6H 436; and 11H 462);* a small cloth bag, about 14 inches long *(8H 134);* an inexpensive canvas bag, about 26 inches long *(6H 415);* some ordinary suitcases about 28 inches long; and two Marine Corps duffel bags.

> *Jenner:* Now, Mrs. Paine, the staff is interested in Lee Harvey Oswald's luggage. . . . Would you please, to the best of your recollection, tell us what pieces of luggage he had . . . what they looked like, their shape and form?
>
> *Mrs. Paine:* Yes. He had two large Marine duffel bags with his name on them, and probably his Marine serial number. It was marked with a good deal of white paint. It stood quite high.
>
> *Jenner:* Were they up-ended when you say high? You mean standing on end, they were high?
>
> *Mrs. Paine:* Standing on their end they would come well above this table.
>
> *Jenner:* I see. About 40 inches?
>
> *Mrs. Paine:* Something like that; I would guess so.
>
> *Jenner:* Excuse me, I am interested in just that. Would you go over to the drawing board and move your hand, judge from the floor, and stop right there? . . . That is just about 45 inches. . . . Was there any appearance as to either duffel bag, which, to you, would indicate some long, slim, hard—
>
> *Mrs. Paine:* I assume them both to be full of clothes, very rounded.

Jenner: I don't wish to be persistent, but was there anything that you saw about the duffel bags that led you at that time to even think for an instant that there was anything long, slim and hard like a pole?

Mrs. Paine: No.

Jenner: Or a gun, a rifle?

Mrs. Paine: No.

Jenner: No? Nothing?

Mrs. Paine: Nothing.   *(2H 462-463)*

Jenner: Now would you please tell us what there was in the way of luggage placed in the station wagon?

Mrs. Paine: There again the two large duffels which were heavier than I could move, he put those in.

Jenner: Describe their appearance, please.

Mrs. Paine: Again stuffed full, a rumply outside.

Jenner: Rumply? No appearance of any hard object pushing outwards?

Mrs. Paine: No.

Jenner: Against the sides or ends of the duffel bags?

Mrs. Paine: No.

Jenner: You saw nothing with respect to those duffel bags which might have led you to believe—

Mrs. Paine: A board in it, no.

Jenner: A tent pole, a long object, hard?

Mrs. Paine: No.

Jenner: Nothing at all?

Mrs. Paine: No.   *(3H 19)*

Jenner's crescendo of frustration is an index to the importance that was attached to showing that the rifle could have been carried in Oswald's luggage. Counsel was persistent, but thwarted. Some weeks later Jenner put the same kinds of questions to Lillian Murret, Oswald's aunt in New Orleans, and got the same kinds of answers from her as from Ruth Paine. *(8H 135, 140)* The tone and substance of the dialogue indicate such an anxiety to determine how the rifle was transported from city to city that it is surprising that in its Report the Commission made no comment about the futility of its inquiry.

The attempt to establish the packing or unloading of a parcel that could have held the rifle was equally futile.

Jenner: Was there a separate package of any character wrapped in a blanket?

Mrs. Paine: No. There was a basket such as you use for hanging your clothes. It carried exactly that, clothes and diapers, and they weren't as neat as being in suitcases and duffels would imply. There was leftovers stuffed in the corner, clothes and things, but rather open.

Jenner: So you saw no long, rectangular package of any kind or character loaded in or placed in your station wagon?

Mrs. Paine: No, it doesn't mean it wasn't there, but I saw nothing of that nature.

Jenner: You saw nothing?

Mrs. Paine: I saw nothing. . . .

Jenner: Now in the process of removing everything other than the two duffel bags on the occasion on the 24th of September, 1963 when you reached Irving, Texas, did you find or see any long, rectangular package?

Mrs. Paine: I recall no such package.

Jenner: Did you see any kind of a package wrapped in the blanket?

Mrs. Paine: Not to my recollection. . . . I don't recall seeing the blanket either . . . not until later. . . .

Ford: Did you see the blanket in New Orleans?

Mrs. Paine: On the bed or something. I am asking myself. I don't recall it specifically. . . . My best recollection is that I saw it [for the first time] on the floor of my garage sometime in late October. . . .   *(3H 20-21)*

In response to further questions Mrs. Paine repeated that she did not see the blanket in the Oswald apartment in New Orleans in the spring or in the fall and that she did not see it in her station wagon. She also reiterated that she did not see the blanket in her garage until October sometime, no earlier than October 7, she was sure. *(3H 42)*

Michael Paine was no more helpful than his wife had been. He testified:

. . . I do remember that my wife asked me to unpack some of their heavy things from their car. I only recall unpacking duffel bags but any other package, that was the heaviest thing there and they were easy also. . . . I unpacked whatever was remaining in the station wagon into the garage. So sometime later, I do remember moving about this package which, let's say, was a rifle, anyway it was a package wrapped in a blanket.   *(2H 414)*

I have read since that Marina looked in the end of this package and saw the butt end of a rifle. Now I didn't remember that it was something easy to look into like that. I thought it was well wrapped up.   *(9H 440)*

Still seeking to corroborate that the blanket in the garage had held a rifle, the Commission tried an experiment with Ruth Paine.

Jenner: For the record, I am placing the rifle in the folded blanket as Mrs. Paine folded it. This is being done without the rifle being dismantled. May the record show, Mr. Chairman, that the rifle fits well in the package from end to end, and it does not—

Mrs. Paine: Can you make it flatter?

Jenner: No; because the rifle is now in there.

Mrs. Paine: I just mean that—

Jenner: Was that about the appearance of the blanket-wrapped package that you saw on your garage floor?

Mrs. Paine: Yes; although I recall it as quite flat.

Jenner: Flatter than it now appears to be?

Mrs. Paine: Yes. But it is not a clear recollection.

Jenner: You have a firm recollection that the package you saw was of [this] length?

Mrs. Paine: Yes, definitely.

Jenner: That is 45 inches, approximately.   *(3H 23)*

Now, Mr. Chairman, may I reinsert the rifle in the package, on the opposite side from what it was before, and have the witness look at it. . . . Mr.

Chairman, I have now placed the opposite side of the rifle to the floor, and may the record show that the package is much flatter. . . . Does the package look more familiar to you, Mrs. Paine?

Mrs. Paine: I recall it as being more like this, not as lumpy as the other had been. *(3H 25)*

With Michael Paine, there was also an experiment. He was given the blanket and the Carcano rifle and asked to construct a package that resembled or duplicated the one in the garage.

Paine: It seemed to me this end up here was not as bulky as the whole. . . .

Liebeler: . . . You are having difficulty making it as small as when you re-member it in the garage?

Paine: Yes . . . I should say this end was a little bit too big here and it is not quite big enough here. . . . I thought of the package pretty much as all of the same thickness. . . .

Liebeler: Are we saying now that its thickness is not as you remember the package in your garage or the same width?

Paine: Well, most likely this end down here is perhaps, the butt end of the rifle. . . . As I have it wrapped is a little bit too full. . . .

Liebeler: And as far as the middle is concerned, you say that is what, not as thick or not as wide?

Paine: Yes; somehow it should be a little wider, or a little fuller.

Liebeler: It was a package which wasn't quite so tapering?

Paine: Quite so tapered. . . . *(9H 442-443)*

Liebeler: Would you measure the length of that package and tell us what it is?

Paine: That is 41 inches.

Liebeler: Now, after going through the process that we have gone through here, of trying to wrap this rifle in this blanket, do you think that the pack-age that you saw in your garage could have been a package containing a rifle similar to the one we have here?

Paine: Yes; I think so. This has the right weight and solidness. *(9H 443)*

Although both Ruth and Michael Paine ultimately agreed that the recon-structed package containing the Carcano rifle was similar to the blanket-wrapped package in the garage, FBI hair-and-fiber expert Paul Stombaugh introduced a new problem when he testified that in examining the blanket, he had found:

Stombaugh: . . . a hump approximately ten inches long, located approxi-mately midway. . . . It would have had to have been a hard object, approxi-mately ten inches in length, which protruded upward, causing the yarn in the blanket to stretch in this area, and it would have had to have been tightly placed in the blanket to cause these yarns to stretch.

Eisenberg: Now, when you say the object was ten inches long, do you mean that the object itself was ten inches long or that there was an object ten inches—an object protruding at a point ten inches from the place you have marked *A*?

Stombaugh: No, sir; the object itself would have had to have been approxi-mately ten inches long to have caused this hump.

> *Eisenberg:* It couldn't have been any longer than ten inches?
> *Stombaugh:* Not at this point; no, sir.   *(4H 58)*

Eisenberg clearly had in mind the telescopic sight on the rifle—but that was at least 11 inches long. *(CE 139)* The Commission disposed of the problem with the bland statement that the bulge "could have been caused by the telescopic sight of the rifle, which was approximately 11 inches long." *(WR 129)*

Since when is a finite, material object in the possession of the authors *approximately* this or that many inches long? The Commission had no reason not to give the precise measurements of the scope—no reason other than to divert attention from still another weakness in its chain of so-called evidence.

How strong are the Commission's grounds for the conclusion that Oswald visited the garage on Thursday evening between 8 and 9 p.m.? That finding rests solely on Ruth Paine's testimony that she found a light burning in the garage at 9 p.m. and her assumption that Oswald must have been there and neglected to turn off the light switch when he left. Neither she nor Marina Oswald could provide any positive evidence that Oswald had entered the garage at all at any time during the overnight visit.

> *Jenner:* You say your home is small and you can hear even the front door opening. Does the raising of the garage door cause some clatter?
> *Mrs. Paine:* Yes; it does.
> *Jenner:* And had the garage door been raised, even though you were giving attention to your children, would you have heard it?
> *Mrs. Paine:* If it was raised slow and carefully, no; I would not have heard it.
> *Jenner:* But if it were raised normally?
> *Mrs. Paine:* Yes.
> *Jenner:* You would have heard it. And it is your recollection that at no time that evening were you conscious of that garage door having been raised.
> *Mrs. Paine:* That is correct.   *(3H 64)*

> *Jenner:* You did not see Lee Oswald in the garage at any time that evening?
> *Mrs. Paine:* Did not see him in the garage; no.   *(3H 67)*

Marina Oswald, for her part, acknowledged that she had had no reason to think that Oswald had been in the garage until Ruth Paine told her that she had found a light burning there. *(1H 66-67)*

> The Commission considered Oswald's arrival at the Depository Building on November 22, carrying a long and bulky brown paper package, and concluded that Oswald carried the rifle into the building, concealed in the bag.
> *(WR 129, 137)*

> The Commission weighed the visual recollection of Frazier and Mrs. Randle against the evidence that the bag Oswald carried contained the assassination weapon and concluded that Frazier and Randle are mistaken as to the length of the bag.   *(WR 134)*

Here we encounter the central weakness of the Commission's thesis: The only two witnesses who saw Oswald with the "long and bulky" package said that it was too short to hold the Carcano rifle, even in disassembled form, and their testimony was consistent, disinterested, and persuasive. Had Oswald come to trial, his defense might have relied heavily on the statements of Wesley Frazier and his sister, Linnie Mae Randle, whom the Commission has arbitrarily dismissed as "mistaken." The transcript of their testimony on March 11, 1964 provides a good basis for assessing their credibility:

Ball: What did the package look like?

Frazier: Well, I will be frank with you, I would just, it is right as you get out of the grocery store, just more or less out of a package, you have seen some of these brown paper sacks you can obtain from any, most of the stores, some varieties, but it was a package just roughly about two feet long.

Ball: It was, what part of the back seat was it in?

Frazier: It was in his side over on his side in the far back.

Ball: How much of that back seat, how much space did it take up?

Frazier: I would say roughly around two feet of the seat . . . around two feet, give and take a few inches.

Ball: How wide was the package?

Frazier: . . . say, around five inches, something like that. Five, six inches or there. . . .   *(2H 226)*

Ball: Did it look to you as if there was something heavy in the package?

Frazier: Well, I will be frank with you. I didn't pay much attention to the package because like I say before and after he told me that it was curtain rods and I didn't pay any attention to it, and he never had lied to me before so I never did have any reason to doubt his word.[6]   *(2H 228)*

Ball: Now we have over here this exhibit for identification which is 364 which is a paper sack made out of tape, sort of a homemade affair. Will you take a look at this. . . . Does it appear to be about the same length?

Frazier: No, sir.

Ball: . . . Was one end of the sack turned over, folded over? Do you remember that?

Frazier: Well, you know, like I was saying, when I glanced at it, but I say from what I saw I didn't see very much of it, I say the bag wasn't open or anything like it where you can see the contents. If you was going to say putting—to more or less a person putting in carefully he would throw it in carefully, you put it more toward the back. If he had anything folded up in it I didn't see that.

Ball: When you saw him get out of the car, when you first saw him when he was out of the car before he started to walk, you noticed he had the package under the arm?

---

6   When Frazier was asked if Oswald's package appeared to contain "some kind of weight," he replied that it did, that he had worked in a department store and had uncrated curtain rods when they had come from the factory, bundled up "pretty compact," so that when Oswald had told him that his package held curtain rods Frazier "didn't think any more about the package whatsoever." *(2H 228-229)* Frazier, had he been more articulate, might have said what he appeared to mean—that on the basis of his own experience in a department store, he had found the appearance of Oswald's package entirely consistent with the appearance of a wrapped bundle of curtain rods.

   It is the Commission's peculiar misfortune that several witnesses whom it chose to regard as "mistaken" were particularly qualified by training or experience to make the particular judgments in question. Frazier had handled shipments of curtain rods; and Seymour Weitzman, whom the Commission holds responsible for the erroneous identification of the rifle as a Mauser, ironically enough had acquired familiarity with rifles because he was "in the sporting goods business awhile." *(7H 108)*

Frazier: Yes, sir.

Ball: One end of it was under the armpit and the other he had to hold it in his right hand. Did the package extend beyond the right hand?

Frazier: No, sir. Like I say if you put it under your armpits and put it down normal to the side.

Ball: But the right hand on, was it on the end or the side of the package?

Frazier: No; he had it cupped in his hand.   *(2H 239)*

Ball: You will notice that this bag which is the colored bag, FBI Exhibit No. 10, is folded over. Was it folded over when you saw it the first time, folded over to the end?

Frazier: I will say I am not sure about that. . . .

Ball: . . . When you were shown this bag, do you recall whether or not you told the officers who showed you the bag—did you tell them whether you thought it was or was not about the same length as the bag you saw on the back seat?

Frazier: I told them that as far as the length there, I told them that it was entirely too long.   *(2H 240)*

Ball: It has been suggested that you take this bag, which is the colored bag . . . and put it under your arm just as a sample, or just to show about how he carried the bag. . . . Put it under your armpit. . . . Are you sure that his hand was at the end of the package or at the side of the package?

Frazier: Like I said, I remember I didn't look at the package very much, paying much attention, but when I did look at it he did have his hands on the package like that.

Ball: But you said a moment ago you weren't sure whether the package was longer or shorter.

Frazier: . . . What I was talking about, I said I didn't know where it extended. It could have or couldn't have, out this way, widthwise not lengthwise.

Ball: In other words, you say it could have been wider than your original estimate?

Frazier: Right.

Ball: But you don't think it was longer than his hands?

Frazier: Right.   *(2H 241)*

Warren: Could he have had the top of it behind his shoulder, or are you sure it was cupped under his shoulder there?

Frazier: Yes; because the way it looked, you know, like I say, he had it cupped in his hand. . . . And I don't see how you could have it anywhere other than under your armpit because if you had it cupped in your hand it would stick over it.

Ball: Could he have carried it this way?

Frazier: No, sir. Never in front here. Like that. Now, that is what I was talking to you about. No, I say he couldn't because if he had you would have seen the package sticking up like that. From what I seen walking behind, he had it under his arm and you couldn't tell that he had a package, from his back.   *(2H 243)*

Frazier was given a dismantled gun in a paper bag and asked to hold it in the same position as he had seen Oswald hold his package. As the Report indicates, the package extended almost to the level of Frazier's ear when the bottom was cupped in his hand; when he placed the top of the package under his arm-pit, the bottom extended eight to ten inches below his hand. At this point, Counsel Ball gave up. But before we leave Wesley Frazier we should take note that he is just over six feet tall, while Oswald was five feet nine inches. His inability to fit the package containing the dismantled rifle between his armpit and his palm would be even more marked in Oswald's case, if the difference in height applied proportionately to the length of the arm.

Mrs. Randle testified next, giving the following description:

Mrs. Randle: He was carrying a package in a sort of a heavy brown bag,[7] heavier than a grocery bag it looked to me. It was about, if I might measure, about this long, I suppose, and he carried it in his right hand, had the top sort of folded down and had a grip like this, and the bottom, he carried it this way, you know, and it almost touched the ground as he carried it.

Ball: . . . And where was his hand gripping, the middle of the package?

Mrs. Randle: No, sir; the top with just a little bit sticking up. . . . *(2H 248)*

Ball: We have got a package here. . . . You have seen this before, I guess, haven't you, I think the FBI showed it to you. . . . Now, was the length of it any similar, anywhere near similar?

Mrs. Randle: Well, it wasn't that long, I mean it was folded down at the top as I told you. It definitely wasn't that long. . . .

Ball: This looks too long?

Mrs. Randle: Yes, sir. . . .

Ball: . . . You figure about two feet long, is that right?

Mrs. Randle: A little bit more.

Ball: . . . There is another package here. You remember this was shown you. It is a discolored bag. . . . What about length?

Mrs. Randle: . . . There again you have the problem of all this down here. It was folded down, of course. . . .

Ball: Fold it to about the size that you think it might be.

Mrs. Randle: This is the bottom here, right? This is the bottom, this part down here.

Ball: I believe so, but I am not sure. But let's say it is.

Mrs. Randle: . . . Do you want me to hold it?

Ball: Yes. . . . Is that about right? That is 28 and ½ inches.

Mrs. Randle: I measured 27 last time.

Ball: You measured 27 once before?

Mrs. Randle: Yes, sir.   *(2H 249-250)*

Raymond F. Krystinik testified on March 24, 1964, and contributed a singular piece of information about his friend Michael Paine in the following excerpt from his testimony:

Krystinik: I don't feel that he had anything to do with it. I think if he had been of a more suspicious nature, he could possibly have avoided the President being shot. He told me after the President was killed and after it had

---

7 The Warren Report *(WR 131)* states that Oswald was carrying a heavy brown bag, according to Mrs. Randle's testimony, giving the impression that the package rather than the paper was "heavy."

come out that the rifle had possibly been stored at his home, that he had moved in his garage some sort of heavy object about this long wrapped up in a blanket, and he had the impression when he moved it this was some sort of camping equipment, and that it was considerably heavier than camping equipment he had been dealing with, and it never occurred to him it might be a gun or rifle that had been broken down.

Liebeler: Would you indicate approximately how long the package was?

Krystinik: He said something about like that [indicating].

Liebeler: How long would you say that was?

Krystinik: Looking at it, I would say 26 or 28 inches. Maybe 30 inches.

Liebeler: [Measuring] The witness indicates a length of approximately 27 inches.

Krystinik: Michael might have had his hands up two or three inches different from that.

Liebeler: To the best of your recollection, Michael indicated the length of about 27 inches?

Krystinik: Yes.   *(9H 475-476)*

Dimensions of approximately 27 inches crop up persistently. As already mentioned, the curtain rods stored in the Paine garage measured 27½ inches. If the paper bag actually held a 35-inch object, it is an extraordinary coincidence that all the estimated and actual measurements in the relevant testimony invariably gravitate around the number *27*.

Another puzzle is the fate of the package after Oswald entered the back door of the Book Depository. The Warren Report states that Jack Dougherty saw Oswald enter the building, "but he does not remember that Oswald had anything in his hands as he entered the door." *(WR 133)* This is a subtle and disingenuous transformation of what Dougherty really said:

Dougherty: I'll put it this way; I didn't see anything in his hands at the time.

Ball: In other words, your memory is definite on that, is it?

Dougherty: Yes, sir.

Ball: In other words, you would say positively he had nothing in his hands?

Dougherty: I would say that—yes, sir.   *(6H 377)*

Dougherty was quite explicit. Had the Commission reflected faithfully what he actually said, we might have found the usual rejoinder that the witness was probably mistaken. In this instance, however, the Report merely replaces Dougherty's positive statement with a negative, of quite a different value. Anyone who searches the Report for an analogous editorial liberty that works to Oswald's advantage is doomed to frustration.

Whatever it contained, the paper bag disappears from view once Oswald moves out of Frazier's sight. No attempt has been made to determine where Oswald concealed the package all morning or how he managed to take it to the sixth floor unseen. The Commission believes that he did so, for stated reasons which we now examine.

The Commission considered the presence of a long, handmade brown paper bag near the point from which the shots were fired, and the palmprint, fiber, and paper analyses linking Oswald and the assassination weapon to this bag,

and concluded that Oswald left the bag alongside the window from which
the shots were fired.   *(WR 129, 137)*

The presence of the bag in the southeast corner is cogent evidence that it
was used as the container for the rifle.   *(WR 135)*

Oswald's palmprint on the bottom of the paper bag indicated, of course,
that he had handled the bag. . . . The palmprint was found on the closed
end of the bag. It was from Oswald's right hand in which he carried the long
package as he walked from Frazier's car to the building.   *(WR 135)*

Stombaugh was unable to render an opinion that the fibers which he found
in the bag had probably come from the blanket. . . . In light of the other
evidence linking Oswald, the blanket, and the rifle to the paper bag found
on the sixth floor, the Commission considered Stombaugh's testimony of
probative value in deciding whether Oswald carried the rifle into the building in the paper bag.   *(WR 137)*

Still another set of ambiguities marks the discovery of the long paper bag
on the sixth floor of the Book Depository. The Report states that it was found
alongside the southeast window but does not specify when or by whom it was
found. Surprisingly, the testimony reveals that Deputy Sheriff Luke Mooney,
who discovered the shield of cartons and the rifle shells that focused suspicion
on the southeast corner window, did not see the homemade paper bag which
was lying right near the shells. *(3H 288)* Deputy Sheriff Roger Craig remembered the small paper lunchbag but not the long paper bag. *(6H 268)* Sergeant
Gerald Hill remembered the lunchbag but said, "that was the only sack I saw.
. . . If it [the long paper bag] was found up there on the sixth floor, if it was
there, I didn't see it." *(7H 65)* J. B. Hicks of the police crime laboratory testified that he had not seen a long paper sack among the items taken from the
Book Depository. *(7H 289)*

Other police officers testified that they saw the paper bag, but they did not
make it clear who saw the bag first or why it was not photographed before the
scene was disturbed. Detective Richard Sims said:

> . . . we saw some wrappings—a brown wrapping there . . . by the hulls. . . .
> It was right near the stack of boxes there. I know there was some loose
> paper there. . . . When the wrapper was found Captain Fritz stationed
> Johnson and Montgomery to observe the scene there where the hulls were
> found. . . . I was going back and forth, from the wrapper to the hulls.
> *(7H 162)*

This was a clever trick of Sims's, since the wrapper and the shells were separated
by a distance of perhaps two feet.

Montgomery and Johnson, said by Sims to have been guarding the window
scene so that it wasn't disturbed, gave somewhat differing accounts. Montgomery testified that he had arrived on the sixth floor after the shells were
found but before the rifle was discovered. Asked what he had seen in the southeast corner, he replied that he had seen boxes and a sack and pieces of chicken.

Ball: Where was the paper sack?

Montgomery: Let's see—the paper sack—I don't recall for sure if it was
on the floor or on the box, but I know it was just there—one of the pictures
might show exactly where it was.

Ball: I don't have a picture of the paper sack.

Montgomery: You don't? Well, it was there—I can't recall for sure if it was on one of the boxes or on the floor there. . . the southeast corner of the building there where the shooting was.

Ball: Did you turn the sack over to anybody or did you pick it up?

Montgomery: Yes—let's see—Lieutenant Day and Detective Studebaker came up and took pictures and everything, and then we took a Dr. Pepper bottle and that sack that we found that looked like the rifle was wrapped in. . . .

Ball: . . . Did you pick the sack up?

Montgomery: . . . Yes . . . wait just a minute—no; I didn't pick it up. I believe Mr. Studebaker did. We left it laying right there so they could check it for prints.   *(7H 97-98)*

After describing the discovery of the rifle, the shells, the chicken bones, the lunch sack, and the pop bottle, Johnson was asked if there had been anything else.

Johnson: Yes, sir. We found this brown paper sack or case. It was made out of heavy wrapping paper . . . right in the corner . . . southeast corner.

Belin: Do you know who found it?

Johnson: I know that the first I saw of it, L. D. Montgomery, my partner, picked it up off the floor, and it was folded up, and he unfolded it.

Belin: When it was folded up, was it folded once or refolded?

Johnson: It was folded and then refolded. It was a fairly small package . . . it was east of the pipes in the corner. To the best of my memory, that is where my partner picked it up. I was standing there when he picked it up. . . . The Crime Lab was already finished where I was, and I had already walked off to where he was. . . . Just from memory, I would say that that sack would be a little longer than those book cartons. . . . Like I said, my partner picked it up and we unfolded it and it appeared to be about the same shape as a rifle case would be. In other words, we made the remark that that is what he probably brought it in. That is why, the reason we saved it.   *(7H 103-104)*

E. D. Brewer said that he had seen a "relatively long paper sack there" and that it was "assumed at the time that it was the sack that the rifle was wrapped up in when it was brought into the building. . . ."

Belin: Well, you mean you assumed that before you found the rifle?

Brewer: Yes, sir; I suppose. That was discussed.   *(6H 307)*

Although the police officers speculated with uncommon deductive brilliance—before the rifle had been found—that the paper bag had been used to bring it into the building, no one took the trouble to photograph it where it lay. Johnson reiterated that his partner Montgomery had picked up and unfolded the bag, and although Montgomery said that he did not lift it from the floor, he seemed uncertain. If Montgomery did pick up the bag—which might explain why it was not photographed at the scene—he should have left his fingerprints on it.

But Lieutenant Day testified that he had examined the outside of the paper bag and found no prints at all. The bag had gone to the FBI laboratory that same night. When it was returned two days later, there was a legible print on it, apparently raised by the application of silver nitrate. *(4H 266-268)*

Day's assistant, R. L. Studebaker, gave a different account. When he was asked if at any time he had seen a paper sack around the southeast window, he replied:

Studebaker: Yes, in the southeast corner of the building—folded. . . . It was a paper—I don't know what it was. . . . I drew a diagram in there for the FBI, somebody from the FBI called me down—I can't think of his name—and he wanted an approximate location of where the paper was found. . . .

Ball: Was it folded over?

Studebaker: It was doubled—it was a piece of paper about this long and it was doubled over.

Ball: How long was it, approximately?

Studebaker: I don't know—I picked it up and dusted it and they took it down there and sent it to Washington and that's the last I have seen of it, and I don't know.

Ball: Did you take a picture of it before you picked it up?

Studebaker: No . . . no; it doesn't show in any of the pictures. . . .

Ball: You say you dusted it? . . . Did you lift any prints?

Studebaker: There wasn't but just smudges on it—is all it was. There was one little ole piece of a print and I'm sure I put a piece of tape on it to preserve it . . . just a partial print.

Ball: The print of a finger or palm or what?

Studebaker: You couldn't tell, it was so small. . . .

Ball: When you say you taped it, what did you do, cover it with some paper?

Studebaker: We have—it's like a Magic Mending Tape, only we use it just strictly for fingerprinting. . . . I put a piece of one-inch tape over it—I'm sure I did.   *(7H 143-144)*

But strangely enough there was no tape and no "little ole piece of a print" on the bag when it arrived in Washington and was examined by FBI fingerprint expert Sebastian Latona. He testified that when he received the bag, there was "nothing visible in the way of any latent prints"; or, needless to say, of the tape placed on the bag by Studebaker. *(4H 3-8)* The Commission made no attempt to reconcile those contradictions, if it even noticed them.

In sum, the testimony about the discovery of the paper bag is vague and contradictory. Luke Mooney, who stumbled on the "sniper's nest" first and might have been expected to see the long paper bag in his inventory of the scene, did not see it. The bag was not photographed. There is a strong suggestion that Montgomery picked it up prematurely; however, while that might explain the lack of a photograph, it raises the new problem of the absence of Montgomery's fingerprints—and the presence of Oswald's palmprint.

The Commission, as we have seen, interprets the palmprint as evidence that Oswald handled the bag but does not acknowledge that it also serves to corroborate Frazier's story that Oswald carried his package between his armpit and his right palm, which would have been impossible if the package had contained the rifle.

As for the fibers, the experts were unable to say—even "probably"—that they had come from the blanket. That the material of the bag matched the supplies in the Book Depository is interesting but not very significant, since any employee might have made it for wholly innocent reasons.

The Commission has offered no firm physical evidence of a link between the paper bag and the rifle. The Report does not mention the negative examination made by FBI expert James Cadigan. Cadigan said explicitly that he had been unable to find any marks, scratches, abrasions, or other indications that would tie the bag to the rifle. Those negative findings assume greater significance in the light of an FBI report *(CE 2974)* which states that the rifle found on the sixth floor of the Book Depository was in a well-oiled condition. It is difficult to understand why a well-oiled rifle carried in separate parts would not have left distinct traces of oil on the paper bag, easily detected in laboratory tests if not with the naked eye. The expert testimony includes no mention of oil traces, a fact which in itself is cogent evidence against the Commission's conclusions.

Equally significant, there were no oil stains or traces on the blanket in which a well-oiled rifle ostensibly had been stored—not for hours but for months. This serves further to weaken, if not to destroy, the Commission's arbitrary finding that the Carcano rifle had been wrapped in that blanket until the night before the assassination.

Appraisal of the Known Facts

Many other questions must be asked about the assassination weapon (see Chapter 4 entitled "The Rifle"); the preceding pages have dealt only with matters pertaining to Oswald's ownership of the rifle and with the manner of its arrival at the Book Depository. The defects of the Commission's assumptions, reasoning, and conclusions can be summarized as follows:

(1) The rifle was shipped by Klein's Sporting Goods Store of Chicago to "A. Hidell"; the Commission did not try to establish that it was delivered to Lee Harvey Oswald.

(2) Despite the Commission's reliance on the testimony of Marina Oswald, compelling evidence virtually excludes the use of the Carcano rifle in the attempt on the life of General Walker. This will be discussed in detail in a later chapter.

(3) Repeated attempts by the Commission to prove that the rifle was carried in Oswald's luggage on the trips to and from New Orleans failed completely.

(4) It is not certain when, how, or if the rifle appeared in the Paine garage.

(5) There is no firm evidence that Oswald entered the garage on Thursday night or at any other time before his departure for Dallas on Friday.

(6) The Commission's claim that Oswald returned to Irving on Thursday in order to pick up the rifle is questionable. His visit is susceptible to other interpretations; and evidence shows that a Thursday visit to the Paine home was not unprecedented.

(7) Evidence is entirely lacking that Oswald made the paper bag at the Book Depository between November 19 and 21, or at any other time.

(8) The bag that Oswald carried on the morning of November 22 was entirely too short to hold the disassembled rifle.

(9) There were no oil stains on the blanket or the paper bag, or any other objective signs that the bag had been used to carry the Carcano rifle.

(10) The blanket evidence is at least doubtful, and there is serious ground to question that the blanket ever served to hold the Carcano rifle with its 11-inch telescopic sight.

(11) The testimony on the discovery of the paper bag at the Book Depository is highly confused and contradictory.

(12) We do not know what Oswald actually said about the paper bag during the interrogations; his *reported* explanation, insofar as it comes into conflict with Wesley Frazier's testimony, is not credible. But, as discussed in another section of this study, those present at the interrogations gave incomplete and contradictory accounts of the questioning, and a number of Oswald's assertions which were assumed to be false later proved to be truthful.

In short, the entire history of Oswald's supposed connection with the alleged assassination rifle is defective at every point. If Oswald had lived to stand trial, any competent defense attorney would have demanded that the prosecution prove each of the contentions made in the Warren Report with that immunity from official challenge which the authors enjoyed by virtue of arrogating unto themselves the functions of the prosecution, the judge, and the jury. In an adversary proceeding, the prosecution would have been hard put to sustain the validity of any of the arguments posed in the Warren Report, and defense counsel would have delighted in demolishing the so-called evidence, point by point.

And herein lies the terrible and bitter irony of the case of Oswald's cold-blooded execution by the hand of Jack Ruby, before Oswald had even acquired legal counsel. It is easy to understand why many people are convinced that herein also lies the cause.

In addition to points 7 through 12 above, new questions about the paper bag arise from singular information in an FBI report which came to light in the National Archives in May 1967. (*CD 205*, p. 148) The document indicates that an undeliverable package addressed to "Lee Oswald" was discovered, on December 4, 1963, in the dead-letter section of the Irving post office, where it had rested for an unknown length of time. The package contained "a brown paper bag made of fairly heavy brown paper which bag was open at both ends" and measured about 18 inches. It was addressed to Oswald at a non-existent address in Dallas, with no postage on the outer wrapper. No post office personnel knew anything about the parcel or remembered handling it.

The FBI report does not indicate whether the parcel was addressed by hand or by typewriter. There is no sign that any effort was made by the FBI or the Warren Commission to identify the sender, or to compare the paper bag or the outer wrapper with materials in the Book Depository or the Paine residence.

How did this paper bag find its way into the Irving post office? Since it had no postage or sender's name, it was probably dropped into a mailbox, presumably with the postage to be collected from the addressee upon delivery. Was this done before or after the assassination? It seems certain that if it had come into the hands of the postal authorities after November 22, 1963 it would have been reported immediately to the investigative agencies, for even the lowliest mail clerk could not have failed to recognize the name "Lee Oswald" on that day or subsequently.

Assuming, as it seems reasonable to do, that the parcel was dispatched before the assassination, it must still be determined *who* sent it. Did Oswald send the paper bag to himself? Surely not, since he had no demonstrable opportunity to make either the other paper bag or this one, and since he undoubtedly knew his own correct address. (If the address on the parcel was handwritten, the FBI report does not suggest that it was Oswald's writing.) In all probability, then, the paper bag was mailed to Oswald by an unknown person who did not wish to indicate his identity and whose reasons seem indisputably questionable. No one not implicated in the assassination could have known before the event that a homemade paper bag would become a piece of key evidence against a suspect who was said to have acted alone. The sender was implicated, either as Oswald's co-conspirator or as a member of a plot *not only* to assassinate the President but also to frame an innocent man, in advance, for the crime.

These inferences seem logical, even inevitable, although there may be some other combination of circumstances that might account for the mysterious parcel found in the dead-letter section of the post office. The same inferences must have suggested themselves to the members of the Commission and/or its staff who processed the FBI report. The implications did not lead to further investigation but the report was merely put aside without further ado or mention in the Report or the Exhibits.

A startling clue to the possibility of a conspiracy to incriminate Oswald in the assassination by those who planned and executed it has been thrust under the rug by the Warren Commission.

The Sixth Floor at Noon

According to the Warren Report

The Report links Oswald with "the point from which the shots were fired" by a number of means, including the assertion that he was present on the sixth floor about 35 minutes before the assassination. That assertion rests on the testimony of Charles Givens, "the last known employee to see Oswald inside the building prior to the assassination," and on the discovery of Oswald's clipboard on the sixth floor on December 2, 1963. According to the Report:

1. At about 11:45 a.m. the floor-laying crew used both elevators to come down from the sixth floor. The employees raced the elevators to the first floor. Givens saw Oswald standing at the gate on the fifth floor as the elevator went by.

2. Givens testified that after reaching the first floor, "I discovered I left my cigarettes in my jacket pocket upstairs, and I took the elevator back upstairs to get my jacket with my cigarettes in it." He saw Oswald, a clipboard in hand, walking from the southeast corner of the sixth floor toward the elevator.

3. Givens said to Oswald, "Boy, are you going downstairs?**** It's near lunch time." Oswald said, "No, sir. When you get downstairs, close the gate to the elevator." Oswald was referring to the west elevator which operates by pushbutton and only with the gate closed. Givens said, "Okay," and rode down in the east elevator. When he reached the first floor, the west elevator—the one with the gate—was not there.

4. Givens thought this was about 11:55 a.m. None of the Depository employees is known to have seen Oswald again until after the shooting.

5. The significance of Givens' observation that Oswald was carrying his clipboard became apparent on December 2, 1963, when an employee, Frankie Kaiser, found a clipboard hidden by book cartons in the northwest corner of the sixth floor at the west wall a few feet from where the rifle had been found. This clipboard had been made by Kaiser and had his name on it. Kaiser identified it as the clipboard which Oswald had appropriated from him when Oswald came to work at the Depository.   *(WR 143)*

According to the Hearings and Exhibits

Study of the testimony and documentary evidence demonstrates that the assertions in each of the five paragraphs are characterized by omission of relevant facts, failure by the Warren Commission to note logical and logistical defects, misrepresentation, or uncritical gullibility. Let us analyze the paragraphs one by one.

Paragraph (1) suffers from the omission of relevant facts. Two witnesses other than Givens saw Oswald standing at the elevator gate on the fifth floor. One of them was Bonnie Ray Williams, who testified on March 24, 1964:

On the way down I heard Oswald. . . . On the way down Oswald hollered "Guys, how about an elevator?" I don't know whether those are his exact words. But he said something about the elevator. . . . I think he asked Charles Givens—I think he said, "Close the gate on the elevator, or send one of the elevators back up."   *(3H 168)*

Billy Lovelady gave a similar version of the encounter with Oswald, from which it is apparent that Oswald was waiting impatiently to board an elevator as the employees were racing each other to the first floor and that he asked them to send one of the elevators back up for him. This took place at about 11:45

a.m. It should have been made clear in the Report that Oswald was not merely standing at the gate but was waiting to get on an elevator and descend.

Paragraph (2) suffers from logistical defects. Givens had left his cigarettes in his jacket near the southwest corner of the sixth floor, where he and the other members of the floor-laying crew had been at work. He testified that he returned to get his cigarettes, using the east elevator which he left waiting for his return trip down. As he was "fixing to get on" again, he saw Oswald walking straight down the aisle along the east wall. But the east elevator is some 50 feet from the east wall and some 80 feet diagonally from the point at which Givens said that he saw Oswald, according to the floor plan. *(CE 483)* More graphically, the elevators oppose the fifth of seven sets of windows, counting from the southeast window from which it is claimed that the shots were fired. The intervening space is cluttered with columns (there are 36 columns on the floor in rows of six) and stacks of cartons, some even as high as a man, as can be seen in a photograph of the southeast window taken from the northeast corner. *(CE 725)* It appears that it would have been physically impossible for Givens to see Oswald, as he testified he did *(6H 353),* unless without any reason for doing so he walked far to the east of the elevator.

Paragraph (3) is illogical. According to Williams and Lovelady, Oswald had tried at 11:45 a.m. to board the elevator and had addressed a request to Givens to send the elevator back up. Why, then, should he decline to accompany Givens down at 11:55, and ask him again to send the elevator up as if he had not already asked the same thing ten minutes before? The first request is corroborated by a number of witnesses, but we have only Givens' unsupported account of the second request.

There are additional reasons for suspecting that Givens' story of the encounter with Oswald at 11:55 a.m. is a complete invention, originating in complicity between this witness and Dallas police officers. Curious and disturbing questions arise from the testimony of Lieutenant Jack Revill. Revill told the Warren Commission that he and Lieutenant Dyson, accompanied by three detectives, were conducting a systematic search of the Book Depository and that as he was about to leave, shortly after two o'clock, he encountered and recognized Charles Givens, who was known to the police on narcotics charges. Revill said:

> I asked him if he had been on the sixth floor and . . . he said, yes, that he had observed Mr. Lee, over by this window. . . . So I turned this Givens individual over to one of our Negro detectives and told him to take him to Captain Fritz for interrogation. . . .   *(5H 35-36)*

When Revill gave this testimony in May 1965, Givens had already provided a different version of the incident in which there was no mention of Revill or of seeing "Mr. Lee" on the sixth floor. Givens testified on April 8, 1964:

> Officer Dawson [*sic*] saw me and he called me and asked me was my name Charles Givens, and I said "Yes." And he said, "We want you to go downtown and make a statement." And he puts me in the car and takes me down to the city hall and I made a statement to Will Fritz down there. *(6H 355)*

Givens' statement, in an affidavit dated November 22, 1963, does not contain a word about his alleged return to the sixth floor at 11:55 a.m. or about "Lee" or Oswald. The affidavit says:

> I worked up on the sixth floor until about 11:30 a.m. Then I went downstairs and into the bathroom. At twelve o'clock I took my lunch period. I went to the parking lot at Record and Elm. . . .   (*CE 2003*, p. 27)

When Givens reached City Hall and gave his statement, Oswald was already under interrogation by Captain Fritz. It is immensely implausible if not inconceivable that no mention should have been made of Givens' encounter with Oswald at 11:55 a.m. if that encounter had actually taken place and had already been discussed with Revill.

It is apropos to remember that Givens, like Oswald, was missing from the Book Depository after the assassination. According to the verbatim transcript of the police radio log (*CE 1974*, p. 83), Inspector J. Herbert Sawyer called the dispatcher a few seconds after 1:46 p.m. and said:

> We have a man that we would like to have you pass this on to CID [Criminal Investigation Division] to see if we can pick this man up. CHARLES DOUGLAS GIVENS, G-I-V-E-N-S. He is a colored male . . . a porter that worked on this floor up here. He has a police record and he left.

This entry was not included in an earlier edited transcript of the police radio log, for reasons which are not clear. Inspector Sawyer testified about the alert for Givens on April 8, 1964.

> *Sawyer:* I put out another description on the colored boy that worked in that department.
> *Belin:* What do you mean, the colored boy that worked in that depository?
> *Sawyer:* He is the one that had a previous record in the narcotics, and he was supposed to have been a witness to the man being on that floor. He was supposed to have been a witness to Oswald being there.
> *Belin:* Would Charles Givens have been that boy?
> *Sawyer:* Yes, I think that is the name, and I put out a description on him.
> *Belin:* How do you know he was supposed to be a witness on that?
> *Sawyer:* Somebody told me that. Somebody came to me with the information. And again, that particular party, whoever it was, I don't know. I remember that a deputy sheriff came up to me who had been over taking these affidavits, that I sent them over there, and he came over from the sheriff's office with a picture and a description of this colored boy and he said that he was supposed to have worked at the Texas Book Depository, and he was the one employee who was missing, or that he was missing from the building. He wasn't accounted for, and that he was suppose to have some information about the man that did the shooting. . . . I think we caught the man in the crowd later and sent him . . . directly down to Captain Fritz's office. . . .   (*6H 321-322*)

Sawyer's testimony is in conflict with Givens'. It is also in conflict with Revill's. No corroboration for his story is found in the reports of personnel in the Sheriff's Office on their activities after the shooting. Most significant is that Sawyer's story suffers from an anachronism, since Givens had no knowledge that the shots were thought to have come from the Book Depository until he returned to the building, well after the alert by Sawyer at 1:46 p.m.! No wonder Sawyer could not identify the "particular party" who told him that Givens had information about the man who did the shooting, when Givens himself did not yet realize that he was the custodian of such information—assuming for the sake of argument that the 11:55 a.m. encounter had in fact occurred. But if by some miracle of intuition he nevertheless volunteered information to anyone about the 11:55 incident, he would have been detained right then and there and there would have been no later alert for him on the police radio.

Because of all of the defects which attach to paragraphs (1), (2), and (3), I reject as false the story that Givens returned to the sixth floor at 11:55 a.m. and that he met and spoke to Oswald at that time. The circumstances suggest that Givens, a Dallas Negro with a police record and vulnerable to intimidation, was persuaded to fabricate this story and that at least two Dallas police officials attempted to authenticate the invention by testifying that Givens acknowledged verbally the meeting with Oswald on November 22, shortly after the assassination, even though the meeting is not reflected in Givens' affidavit of the same date but subsequent to the alleged verbal report.

Returning to paragraph (4) of the Warren Commission's assertions about the 11:55 encounter, I must challenge the statement that none of the Book Depository employees was known to have seen Oswald again until after the shooting. Eddie Piper testified in his affidavit of November 22, 1963 and in his appearance before counsel of the Warren Commission on April 8, 1964 that he saw and spoke to Oswald "just at twelve o'clock, down on the first floor." *(6H 383)* William Shelley testified on April 7, 1964 that he saw Oswald when he (Shelley) "came down to eat lunch about ten to twelve." *(6H 328)* And Givens himself was asked during his testimony if he had ever told anyone that he had seen Oswald in the domino room (on the first floor) at about ten minutes of noon—which he of course denied. *(6H 354)*

One person who should have seen Oswald after 11:55 a.m., if Givens' story was true, is Bonnie Ray Williams. Williams returned to the sixth floor at twelve o'clock to eat the famous chicken lunch; but he saw neither Oswald nor Givens there. *(3H 169-170)*

Finally, how does paragraph (5) on the discovery of the clipboard fare when subjected to critical examination? Not very well. The clipboard was discovered among cartons on the sixth floor near where the rifle had been found, on or about December 2, 1963, something like ten days after the assassination. Frankie Kaiser, who found the clipboard, testified on April 8, 1964:

> *Ball:* How did you happen to find the clipboard?
> *Kaiser:* I was over there looking for the Catholic edition—teacher's edition.
> *Ball:* Where did you see the clipboard?
> *Kaiser:* It was just laying there in the plain open—and just the plain open boxes—you see, we've got a pretty good space back there and I just noticed it laying over there.
> *Ball:* Laying on the floor?
> *Kaiser:* Yes, it was laying on the floor.   *(6H 343)*

It is hard to understand how even the Dallas police and their counterparts from the Sheriff's Office, much less subsequently the FBI and Secret Service agents, could have managed to overlook a clipboard "laying there in the plain open." There had been an intensive search of the sixth floor after the rifle shells were found. According to Deputy Sheriff Luke Mooney, "the floor was covered with officers. . . . We were searching . . . we was just looking everywhere." *(3H 289)*

Nevertheless, the clipboard did not enter the picture until about ten days had elapsed, and in its anxiety to place Oswald on the sixth floor, the Warren Commission saw only that it was "significant" in that respect, without any apparent uneasiness about the invisibility of the clipboard for a prolonged period—after which it was found because it was so conspicuous!

Appraisal of the Known Facts

The testimony and exhibits fail to sustain the assertions and conclusions related to the five paragraphs in the Report and in several fundamental respects contradict the official version of events. The testimony contains flagrant conflicts among the witnesses, of a nature which compels strong suspicion of misrepresentation and collusion. Oswald's presence on the sixth floor has *not* been established, and evidence indicates that he was actually on the first floor during the crucial period of time. Ignoring both the glaring and the subtle contradictions, the Warren Commission again has loaded the dice against the accused.

Chapter 3
The Escape

The Departure from the Book Depository

According to the Warren Report

As the action is reconstructed *(WR 149-156, 648)*, Oswald shot the President from the southeast corner window of the sixth floor at 12:30 p.m., and then within the next minute and a half crossed the floor to the northeast corner, hiding the rifle on his way, and took the stairs down. He reached the second floor and entered the vestibule leading to the lunchroom before Roy Truly and police officer Marrion L. Baker, ascending from the first floor, had reached the second-floor landing. Tests established that Baker's minimum time to reach the second-floor landing after the shots was 1 minute 18 seconds; in the event, he probably took longer. Further tests established that Oswald could have reached the second floor vestibule in 1 minute 14 seconds.

Victoria Adams, an employee who testified that she went down the same stairs from the fourth floor to the first within one minute of the shooting, did not meet Oswald, or Truly and Baker. She claimed that when she arrived on the first floor she noticed Billy Lovelady and William Shelley, other Book Depository employees. However, according to the Report, Lovelady and Shelley had gone to the railroad yards after the shooting and did not re-enter the Book Depository until some minutes had passed. Miss Adams is therefore mistaken in her belief that she descended the stairs within one minute of the shots and must have come down later than Oswald and after Truly and Baker had climbed above the fourth floor.

Meanwhile, the Report asserts, after the encounter with the police officer, Oswald obtained a soft drink from a machine and walked through the second

70

floor, where he was seen by Mrs. Robert Reid when she returned to her desk, probably at 12:32 p.m. Oswald walked east and south to the stairway, descended to the first floor, and departed from the main entrance at about 12:33 p.m., before the building was effectively sealed off by the police.

According to the Hearings and Exhibits

Roy Truly testified on March 24, 1964 about the circumstances under which he and Baker encountered Oswald:

Truly: [Immediately after the shooting] I saw a young motorcycle policeman run up to the building, up the steps to the entrance of our building. He ran right by me. And he was pushing people out of the way. . . . I ran up and . . . caught up with him inside the lobby of the building, or possibly the front steps. . . . I ran in front of him. . . . I went up on a run up the stairway. . . . This officer was right behind me and coming up the stairway. By the time I reached the second floor, the officer was a little further behind me than he was on the first floor . . . a few feet. It is hard for me to tell. I ran right on around to my left, started to continue on up the stairway to the third floor, and on up.

Belin: Now, when you say you ran on to your left, did you look straight ahead to see whether there was anyone in that area, or were you intent on just going upstairs?

Truly: If there had been anybody in that area, I would have seen him on the outside. . . .   *(3H 221-223)*

I suppose I was up two or three steps before I realized the officer wasn't following me. . . . I came back to the second-floor landing. . . . I heard some voices, or a voice, coming from the area of the lunchroom, or the inside vestibule. . . . I ran over and looked in this door. . . . I think I opened the door. I feel like I did. I don't remember. . . .

I opened the door. . . . I saw the officer almost directly in the doorway of the lunchroom facing Lee Harvey Oswald. . . . He was just inside the lunchroom door . . . two or three feet possibly. . . . When I reached there, the officer had his gun pointing at Oswald. The officer turned this way and said, "This man work here?" And I said, "Yes." . . . Then we left Lee Harvey Oswald immediately and continued to run up the stairways. . . .

Belin: All right . . . how far was the officer's gun from Lee Harvey Oswald when he asked the question?

Truly: . . . it seemed to me like it was almost touching him. . . .

Belin: Did you hear Lee Harvey Oswald say anything? . . . Did you see any expression on his face? . . .

Truly: He didn't seem to be excited or overly afraid or anything. He might have been a bit startled, like I might have been if somebody confronted me. But I cannot recall any change in expression of any kind on his face.
(3H 224-225)

The next day, March 25, 1964, Officer Baker described the same incident:

Baker: As I came out to the second floor there, Mr. Truly was ahead of me, and as I come out I was kind of scanning, you know, the rooms, and I caught a glimpse of this man walking away from this—I happened to see him through this window in this door. I don't know how come I saw him, but I had a glimpse of him coming down there.

Dulles: Where was he coming from, do you know?

Baker: No, sir. All I seen of him was a glimpse of him go away from me. . . . He was walking away from me about 20 feet away from me in the lunchroom. . . . I hollered at him at that time and said, "Come here." He turned and walked right straight back to me. . . .

Boggs: Were you suspicious of this man?

Baker: No, sir; I wasn't.   *(3H 250-251)*

Boggs: When you saw him, was he out of breath, did he appear to have been running or what?

Baker: It didn't appear that to me. He appeared normal, you know.

Boggs: Was he calm and collected?

Baker: Yes, sir. He never did say a word or nothing. In fact, he didn't change his expression one bit.   *(3H 252)*

Baker may have had more light to shed on his encounter with Oswald and the other events of the day. His testimony was taken off the record no less than five times.

The impassive Oswald was seen next by Mrs. Robert Reid, a clerical supervisor whose office was on the second floor of the Book Depository. She had been watching the motorcade from the street. She testified on March 25, 1964 that when she heard the shots:

Mrs. Reid: . . . the thought that went through my mind, my goodness I must get out of this line of shots, they may fire some more. . . . I ran into the building. I do not recall seeing anyone in the lobby. I ran up to our office . . . up the stairs . . . the front stairs. . . . I went into the office. . . . I kept walking and I looked up and Oswald was coming in the back door of the office. I met him by the time I passed my desk several feet. . . . I had no thoughts of anything of him having any connection with it at all because he was very calm. He had gotten a coke and was holding it in his hands and I guess the reason it impressed me seeing him in there I thought it was a little strange that one of the warehouse boys would be up in the office at that time, not that he had done anything wrong.   *(3H 274)*

Belin: . . . Was there anything else you noticed about him? . . . Anything about the expression on his face?

Mrs. Reid: No; just calm.   *(3H 278)*

Dulles: Was he moving fast?

Mrs. Reid: No; because *he was moving at a very slow pace*. I never did see him moving fast at any time. [Italics added]   *(3H 279)*

We revert now to Victoria Adams, bearing in mind that if her story is accurate it decisively invalidates the Warren Commission's hypothesis about Oswald's movements between 12:30 and 12:33 p.m. Miss Adams testified that she had watched the motorcade from an open window on the fourth floor (the third set of double windows from the southeast corner), in company with other employees in the Scott, Foresman Co. publishing office where she worked. After the last shot, she and Sandra Styles immediately ran down the back stairs to the first floor, where she saw Lovelady and Shelley standing near the elevator.

Belin: How long do you think it was between the time the shots were fired and the time you left the window to start toward the stairway?

Miss Adams: Between 15 and 30 seconds, estimated, approximately.

Belin: How long do you think it took you to get from the window to the bottom of the stairs on the first floor?

Miss Adams: I would say no longer than a minute at the most. *(6H 392)*

It is true that the testimony given by Lovelady and Shelley on the same day as Victoria Adams, April 7, 1964, suggests that she is mistaken in her estimate of the time. Both men said that after the shooting they had gone together to the railroad tracks and observed the searching of cars for about a minute and a half before returning to the Book Depository by the rear door. Neither man remembered clearly whether or not he saw Victoria Adams on arrival. *(6H 329-330, 339-340)*

However, this testimony is not consistent with affidavits executed by the same two men on the day of the assassination for the Dallas police. Lovelady's affidavit *(CE 2003,* p. 36) states that he heard shots and *"after it was over we went back into the building* and I took some police officers up to search the building." Nothing about railroad tracks. [Italics added]

Shelley's affidavit *(CE 2003,* p. 59) stated:

"I heard what sounded like three shots. . . . I ran across the street to the corner of the park and ran into a girl crying and she said the President had been shot. . . . *I went back to the building* and went inside and called my wife and told her what happened. I was on the first floor and I stayed at the elevator. . . ." [Italics added]

Nothing about railroad tracks.

In their original stories, then, both Lovelady and Shelley accounted for their movements after the shooting in a manner that is completely consistent with Victoria Adams' testimony.

Appraisal of the Known Facts

The Warren Commission spared neither pains nor runners in straining to make Oswald's alleged actions fit within the strictly limited time available. Tests were conducted in which Baker ran his distance twice, a stand-in for Oswald ran twice, and Mrs. Reid (gallant woman!) did her sprint no less than three times. Among those runners and alleged runners, only Victoria Adams was exempted from re-enacting her dash from the fourth floor to the first so that her estimate of one minute could be tested by stop watch. Why was she left aside when the tests were run? Why was her companion, Sandra Styles—who was in a position to confirm or contradict her testimony—not called before the Commission and questioned?

Witnesses Lovelady and Shelley salvaged the Commission's hypothesis from the brink of disaster by giving testimony that seemed to discredit Victoria Adams' story. But the Commission had in its hands their affidavits of November 22, which supported her testimony. The affidavits were sworn while events were still fresh. Is it conceivable that both men should have forgotten to mention the railroad yards at that time, and that both should have remembered in April—so providentially?

If we are to believe what is credible instead of what is essential to the patchwork official theory, we must believe Victoria Adams' testimony and the affidavits of Lovelady and Shelley. The testimony of the latter two suggests the possibility of collusion and misrepresentation.

Let us re-examine the stair episode described in the Report. Oswald has reached the second floor, only to be hailed by a policeman with a gun in hand. He walks "right straight back" to the officer, looking "calm and collected," "normal," and merely "a bit startled" by the weapon pointed at him. But now the assassin has the great good luck to have his supervisor vouch for him and to see the two men resume their rush upstairs. He is safe and free to escape from the building.

At that moment Oswald had merely to return to the back stairs, walk down one flight to the first floor, and walk out the back door. The longer he delayed, the greater the danger that the building would be sealed off by the police and he would not be permitted to leave. He was alone and had no audience to impress with a pretense of relaxed innocence. The imperative was to slip downstairs and get as far away as possible.

Instead of using his advantage, Oswald apparently decided to use the most distant and dangerous exit—the main door on Elm Street where police and spectators were plentiful. But he was in no hurry to get there. He first obtained a Coca-Cola from the dispensing machine, then ambled across the second floor "at a very slow pace." No one saw him again until he boarded a bus that was headed back to the scene of the crime. For a murderer to return to the scene of the crime is, of course, in the best classical tradition, but isn't a little time supposed to elapse before such a compulsion prevails?

The Commission has speculated about Oswald's movements between the second floor, where he was seen by Mrs. Reid, and the bus, where he was seen by other witnesses. But no attempt was made to determine where Oswald left the Coca-Cola bottle, or whether it was still full when abandoned.[1] No inquiry was made among the police officers guarding the front door of the Book Deposi-

---

[1] The timing of Oswald's purchase of a coke from the dispensing machine on the second floor is very important in evaluating the assertion that he had sufficient time to descend from the sixth floor and encounter Truly and Officer Baker, and in assessing Oswald's "escape." The original story out of Dallas was that Oswald had a bottle of coke in his hand when he was stopped by Baker. Léo Sauvage wrote in *Commentary (ibid., p. 56)* that the "police officer and the manager of the building had described Oswald as holding a Coca-Cola bottle in his hand," and that that was one of the details announced by Chief of Police Jesse Curry on Saturday, November 23. The Warren Report, however, insists that Oswald had nothing in his hands when Baker and Truly saw him. *(WR 151)* That is what both Baker and Truly said when they testified before the Commission, whatever they may have said on earlier occasions.

Baker, for some reason, was asked to provide a further statement attesting to his encounter with Oswald, only a few days before the Warren Report was released. In that brief handwritten statement of September 23, 1964, Baker states that he entered the Book Depository to determine if the shots might have come from that building and that on the second floor he *"saw a man standing in the lunchroom drinking a coke."* However, a line is drawn through the phrase "drinking a coke," so as to delete it, the deletion being initialed by Baker. *(CE 3076)* The very fact that Baker said spontaneously that Oswald was drinking a coke, regardless of the later deletion, has self-evident significance of great persuasiveness.

tory after the shooting to determine whether Oswald had been allowed to walk out of the building (although one of the policemen testified that he was in position within two to three minutes and permitted no one to leave without authorization). *(7H 543)* No examination was made of all films and photographs taken at the scene to see whether Oswald's departure was recorded by a camera. No attempt was made to check Oswald's story, after his arrest, that a Secret Service agent had stopped him in front of the Book Depository to ask where the nearest telephone was located.[2]

It is curious, in fact, that Captain Fritz and the other interrogators never even asked Oswald which exit he had used or whether a policeman had been stationed at the door, and if so, whether he had tried to prevent him from leaving or had checked his credentials. The authorities who questioned Oswald should have been eager to learn how he had managed to leave a building which had been sealed by the police, perhaps within three minutes after the shooting, and whether his safe departure had been facilitated by an accomplice or merely by carelessness. The reports on the interrogation of Oswald *(WR Appendix XI)* reflect no attempt to obtain such information from him. Indeed, the reports do not indicate that Oswald was ever asked whether he had accomplices and who they were.

Despite the remarkable defects of the investigation at all stages, we still have clear knowledge of Oswald's whereabouts immediately after the shooting and after his encounter with Baker and Truly. The three witnesses who saw him in the Book Depository testified to his normal demeanor and unhurried pace. Clearly, Oswald's known actions and reactions seem wholly consistent with innocence, but would seem preposterous if he were guilty.

The Bus Ride

Before the Warren Report

District Attorney Henry Wade held a press conference on Sunday night after Oswald was murdered, of which it has been said that he was not guilty of a single accuracy. Wade asserted that Oswald had boarded a bus[3] after leaving the Book

---

2 Pierce Allman, WFAA-TV (Dallas) newsman, was within a few feet of the President just as he was shot, according to a B.B.C. radio broadcast. Allman telephoned the news to his station from a Book Depository telephone. He was not questioned by the Warren Commission but Allman told the Secret Service *(CD 354 National Archives)* that he was directed to a phone in the Book Depository and that Oswald mistook him for a Secret Service agent. Allman says that the incident occurred just as Oswald described it, and that it must have been Oswald who directed him to the telephone. The incident is noteworthy not only because it corroborates Oswald's story, which the Commission did not trouble to investigate, but because it suggests that Oswald lingered at the building—an action hardly compatible with the Commission's reconstruction of his movements or with "escape."

3 At a press conference Friday night in police headquarters the news that Oswald had taken a bus after leaving the Book Depository provoked an incredulous reporter to ask if this was the first time that the Dallas Public Transport system was used as a "getaway car." *(CE 2170)*

Depository and had laughed aloud as he told a woman passenger that the President had been shot. In Wade's own words:

> The next we hear of him is on a bus, where he got on a bus at Lamar Street; told the bus-driver the President had been shot. The President [he] told a lady who—all this was verified by statements—told a lady on the bus that the President had been shot. He said, how'd he know. He said that a man back there had told him. He went back to talk to him. The defendant said, "Yes, he's been shot," and laughed very loud.   *(CE 2168)*

According to the Warren Report

The Report explains that the bus-driver, Cecil J. McWatters, testified that it was actually another passenger, teen-ager Milton Jones, who had exchanged words with a woman passenger during the bus ride. The Commission considered that "McWatters' recollection alone was too vague to be a basis for placing Oswald on the bus," and quotes Mary Bledsoe, a former landlady of Oswald's, to establish his presence. As Mrs. Bledsoe told it, Oswald had boarded the bus looking "like a maniac," his shirt undone, his "sleeve was out here," he was dirty, he "looked so bad in his face, and his face was so distorted."

Mrs. Bledsoe did not mention any altercation between a man and a woman passenger, but the Report states that "in a later interview, Jones confirmed that he had exchanged words with a woman passenger on the bus during the ride south on Marsalis." *(WR 159-160)*

According to the Hearings and Exhibits

The "later interview" with Milton Jones is very interesting indeed. An FBI report dated April 3, 1964 states:

> On March 30, 1964, ROY MILTON JONES . . . advised he is an eleventh-grade student attending half-day sessions at the N. R. Crozier Technical High School . . . and is employed part time as a clerk at Buddies Supermarket. . . . JONES stated that he used the name "MILTON JONES" rather than his full name and is better known by this name at school and at work.
>
> He said that on November 22, 1963 he attended the usual morning session of classes at high school and got out of school at about 11:45 a.m. He said he walked to Elm Street near the Capri Theatre, where he waited for the Marsalis bus, which arrived at approximately 12:10 or 12:15 p.m. He said that, upon boarding the bus, he sat in the first seat facing forward on the curb side of the bus and was alone. He recognized the driver by sight as one who frequently drove the bus at this time of day, but stated he did not know him by name. JONES advised that the bus proceeded in the direction of Houston Street and, approximately four blocks before Houston Street, was completely stopped by traffic which was backed up in this area.
>
> He recalled that at this time *a policeman notified the driver the President had been shot and he told the driver no one was to leave the bus until police officers had talked to each passenger*. JONES estimated that there were about fifteen people on the bus at this time and *two police officers boarded the bus and checked each passenger to see if any were carrying firearms*. [Italics added]

JONES advised that before the bus was stopped, the driver made his last passenger pickup approximately six blocks before Houston Street, that one was a blond-haired woman and the other was a dark-haired man. He said the man sat in the seat directly behind him. . . . JONES advised that when the bus was stopped by traffic, and prior to the appearance of the police officers . . . the man who was sitting behind him left the bus by the front door while it was held up in the middle of the block. JONES stated that he did not observe this man closely since he sat behind him in the bus, but, on the following Monday when he caught the same bus going home from school with the same driver, the driver told him he thought this man might have been LEE HARVEY OSWALD.

According to the FBI report, Jones described the man as a white male, about thirty to thirty-five years, 5 feet 11 inches, 150 pounds, dark brown hair receding at temples, no glasses or hat, dressed in a light blue jacket and gray khaki trousers. The report continues:

JONES estimated the bus was held up by the police officers for about one hour and, after they were permitted to resume, they crossed the Marsalis Bridge, where a woman . . . boarded the bus . . . and the driver asked her whether she had heard that the President had been shot. She replied that she had not heard anything in this regard, and stated she did not believe it was true.

The driver then pointed to JONES and said, "Ask him, he saw it." JONES said the driver was smiling at this time and the woman turned to him and he told her, "I don't know anything about it. I just heard some others say that the President had been shot." He said that because of the expression on the woman's face both he and the driver were smiling at this time, and she then said, "You are both smiling, so I don't believe it."

JONES advised he could not recall any conversation between the bus-driver and himself or any other person on the bus about the President being shot in the temple. He said he did not hear any person make this remark on the bus. . . . He said that, in conversation with this same bus-driver on the following Monday, the driver told him the Dallas Police Department had him up until one o'clock on Saturday or Sunday morning questioning him about the passenger on his bus who looked like LEE HARVEY OSWALD.   *(CE 2641)*

The bus-driver, McWatters, had given a different version of the incident later described by Jones. When McWatters testified before the Commission on March 12, 1964 he said that about seven blocks before the Book Depository a man had knocked on the door and mounted the bus, dressed in "what I would call work clothes, just some type of little old jacket on, and I didn't pay any particular attention to the man. . . ." *(2H 264)* Asked where he was when he first heard that the President had been shot, McWatters said:

Well, I was sitting in the bus, there was some gentleman in front of me in a car, and he came back and walked up to the bus and I opened the door and he said, "I have heard over my radio in my car that the President has been—" I believe he used the word—"has been shot."   *(2H 265)*

The bus-driver testified that this incident had occurred while the bus was stalled in traffic. While the driver of the passenger car was talking to him, the

man later identified as Oswald had left the bus. The bus then proceeded toward
Houston street, turning at the corner of Elm and Houston, where . . .

> . . . the traffic was still tied up, but the police, they opened up a lane there,
> they had so many buses and everything that was tied up, they opened up,
> moved traffic around that they run quite a few of these buses through there.
> . . . They weren't letting any cars through at that time but they just ran a
> bunch of those buses through . . . right on down here to Houston. . . .
>
> *(2H 265-266)*

McWatters related the progress of the bus to Oak Cliff and the incident with
the woman passenger.

> Well, there was a teen-age boy, I would say seventeen or eighteen years of
> age, who was sitting to my right on the first cross seat and me and him had,
> we had conversationed a little while we was tied up in the traffic, you know,
> of the fact of we wondered where all, what all the excitement was due to
> the fact of the sirens and others, and . . . I made the remark, I wonder
> where the President was shot, and I believe he made the remark that it was
> probably in the head if he was in a convertible or something to that effect.
> . . . It was a conversation about the President, in other words, to where he
> was shot. . . .
>
> Now, as we got on out to Marsalis . . . there was a lady who was . . .
> getting on, and I asked her had she heard the news of the President being
> shot . . . and she said, "No, what are you—you are just kidding me."
>
> I said, "No, I really am not kidding you." I said, "It is the truth from
> all the reliable sources that we have come in contact with," and this teen-age
> boy sitting on the side, I said, "Well, now, if you think I am kidding you
> . . . ask this gentleman sitting over here," and he kind of, I don't know
> whether it was a grinning or smile or whatever expression it was, and she
> said, "I know you are kidding now, because he laughed or grinned or made
> some remarks to that effect." And I just told her no it wasn't no kidding
> matter, but that was part of the conversation that was said at that time.
>
> *(2H 266-267)*

Senator Cooper later questioned McWatters about the passenger subsequently identified as Oswald and about other people on the bus.[4]

> *Cooper:* Was the passenger that got on near Murphy Street the same pas-
> senger that you later have testified about who told you that the President
> had been shot in the temple?
> *McWatters:* Well, they told me later that it was, but at the time they didn't
> tell me.
> *Cooper:* Who didn't tell you?
> *McWatters:* The police didn't.   *(2H 277)*
>
> *Cooper:* Then the one who told you the President had been shot in the
> temple was not the one you later identified in the police line-up?
> *McWatters:* No, sir.   *(2H 278)*

---

4 McWatters failed to make a positive identification of Oswald as the passenger on his bus.
The Dallas police report on the assassination (*CE 2003*, p. 293) nevertheless lists McWat-
ters as having made a positive identification on viewing the line-up. Similarly, Howard
Brennan failed to make a positive identification when he viewed the line-up; the same
Dallas police report omits Brennan entirely from the list of witnesses who viewed the suspect.

McWatters explained that he had not actually identified any man in the police line-up, contrary to the impression conveyed by his affidavit of the same day, but had indicated that the "No. 2 man" looked most like the passenger, because:

> *McWatters:* . . . he was the shortest man in the line-up, in other words, when they brought these men out there, in other words, he was about the shortest, and the lightest weight one, I guess, was the reason I say that he looked like the man, because the rest of them were larger men. . . .
>
> *Ball:* Were you under the impression that this man that you saw in the line-up and whom you pointed out to the police, was the teen-age boy who had been grinning?
>
> *McWatters:* I was, yes, sir; I was under the impression that was the fellow. . . . In other words, when I told them, I said, the only way is the man, that he is smaller, in other words, he kind of had a thin like face and he weighs less than any one of them. The only one I could identify at all would be the smaller man on account he was the only one who could come near fitting the description. . . . I really thought he was the man who was on the bus . . . that stayed on the bus.   *(2H 281)*

The longer McWatters testified, the more he became embroiled in self-contradiction and faulty logic. He was unable to explain how it was that all of his statements and his affidavit on the day of the assassination could have related to Milton Jones, as he now claimed, when Jones had not taken a bus transfer and when it was the transfer given to Oswald and found on his person that had led the police to McWatters. He was unable to explain why he had not told the police about the second man on the bus, who had knocked on the bus door to be admitted. *(2H 289)* He acknowledged that the statement in his affidavit of November 22 that he had picked up a man at Elm and Houston was "wrong," saying that he had not read the document with sufficient care before signing it.

Since McWatters insisted that he had completely confused Oswald with the teen-ager Jones on the day of the assassination, Senator Cooper logically enough asked McWatters if the two looked alike. *(2H 291)* McWatters replied in vague, if not evasive, terms that Jones and Oswald were the same height and the same build. Apparently the Commission made no independent check on the alleged resemblance, although McWatters' demeanor justified the most serious doubt about his veracity—even when the FBI report on the interview with Milton Jones *(CE 2641)* indicated that he was only five feet two inches tall, or some seven inches shorter than Oswald as well as seven years younger.

On top of his utterly confused testimony about Jones and Oswald, McWatters had no recollection at all of the third important passenger on that bus ride, Mary Bledsoe *(2H 288)*, the witness quoted with obvious and excessive satisfaction by the Commission as establishing Oswald's presence on the bus. Mrs. Bledsoe, Oswald's former landlady, testified on April 2, 1964 that Oswald had boarded the bus looking like a maniac, wearing a brown shirt with "all the buttons torn off" and a hole in the sleeve at the right elbow. She said:

> *Mrs. Bledsoe:* Motorman said, "Well, the President has been shot," and I say—so, and the woman over—we all got to talking about four of us sitting

around talking, and Oswald was sitting back there, and one of them said, "Hope they don't shoot us," and I said, "I don't believe that—it is—I don't believe it. Somebody just said that." And it was too crowded, you see, and Oswald got off.

Ball: Did he say anything to the motorman when he got off?

Mrs. Bledsoe: They say he did, but I don't remember him saying anything. *(6H 409-410)*

Ball: Was there traffic? Was the traffic heavy?

Mrs. Bledsoe: Oh, it was awful in the city, and then they had roped off that around where the President was killed, shot, and we were the first car that came around there, and then all of us were talking about the man, and we were looking up to see where he was shot and looking—and then they had one man and taking him, already got him in jail, and we got—Well, I am glad they found him.

Ball: You were looking up at where?

Mrs. Bledsoe: At where the boy was shot . . . [School Book Depository— S. M.] . . . because we were right four blocks from there, you see. *(6H 411)*

Mrs. Bledsoe went on to relate that she had notified the police on Friday evening that she had seen Oswald on the bus. The next night (Saturday) she had gone to the police headquarters where she had identified Oswald, not in a line-up but from photographs of him holding a gun. At some later time, Secret Service agents had come to her home, bringing a brown shirt which she had recognized, from the hole in the sleeve and the color, as the one Oswald had worn on the bus. *(6H 412-413)*

The record with respect to that shirt is somewhat unclear. When arrested, Oswald was wearing a shirt *(CE 150)* that corresponds generally with the shirt described and identified by Mrs. Bledsoe as the one he was wearing on the bus. But it is difficult to accept the identification as conclusive, because of Mrs. Bledsoe's obviously confused testimony; one cannot judge whether the shirt he wore when arrested (displayed to her on an unspecified date by the Secret Service) was one which she had previously seen. *(6H 412-413)*

So far as is known, Oswald's shirt was intact until the scuffle in the Texas Theater which culminated in his arrest. If so, the fact that Mrs. Bledsoe saw the shirt already torn, an hour before the scuffle, would be an anachronism. (None of the witnesses who saw Oswald before the bus ride—Wesley Frazier, Officer Baker, and Roy Truly—suggested that his shirt was ripped or torn.)

Moreover, Oswald told Captain Fritz that during his brief visit to his room he had changed his trousers *and his shirt*, "because they were dirty," and that he had placed them "in the lower drawer of his dresser." *(WR 604-605, 622)* The police officers who searched the room did not indicate on the police property list that discarded trousers and shirt were found there. The police did not volunteer information on that point and the Commission did not attempt to elicit such information. Nevertheless, the Commission asserts on the strength of Mrs. Bledsoe's testimony and the bus transfer found on Oswald that "although Oswald . . . claimed to have changed his shirt, the evidence indicates that he continued wearing the same shirt he was wearing all morning and which he was still wearing when arrested." *(WR 124-125)*

If I agree with this conclusion, it is less in the way of agreement with the Commission's reasoning than for the fact that in a photograph taken while the shots were being fired, a man is seen in the doorway of the Book Depository who strongly resembles Oswald and who is wearing a shirt that strongly resembles the one Oswald wore when he was arrested; this shirt bears no resemblance at all to the red-and-white-striped short-sleeved shirt worn by Billy Lovelady, yet the Commission identifies him as the man in the doorway (without publishing his picture) in debunking the "rumor" that this man was Oswald, the lone assassin —then supposedly at the sixth-floor window. (An elaborate scientific analysis was carried out by FBI Expert Lyndal Shaneyfelt, at the Commission's request, to establish that the shirt worn by Oswald in photographs taken in the police building was the same as the shirt he is seen wearing in photographs taken at the Texas Theater. It was far more urgent to make such a scientific analysis of the shirt worn by the man in the doorway, but this was not requested or done.)

In a more conscientious and impartial investigation, an attempt would have been made to check out Oswald's claim that he had changed his shirt. Even if there were no evidence to support his statement, it would still have been necessary to evaluate Mrs. Bledsoe's apparently premature observation of holes and torn buttons. It was still necessary to ask why, if she saw Oswald on the bus, her description ("looking like a maniac," etc.) stands in flagrant contradiction to the descriptions given by others on the bus. And it was still necessary to ask why, if Mrs. Bledsoe was really on the bus, neither the driver nor the only other passenger who was questioned had any recollection of her.

There is reason to wonder whether either Mrs. Bledsoe *or* Oswald was on the bus, together or separately. Indeed, if we tend to believe that Oswald was on the bus, it is more because of Milton Jones's report about the police boarding party than because of the incomplete and inconsistent evidence presented by the Commission.

Appraisal of the Known Facts

There were three witnesses from the bus on which Oswald apparently was a brief passenger. The bus-driver is the only one of the three who testified before the Commission, and his testimony gives a poor impression of his judgment and candor. The landlady provided a deposition in which she exhibited some degree of confusion and frank malice toward Oswald. Her statement that he entered "looking like a maniac" and with his face "so distorted" is completely at variance with all other descriptions and scarcely justifies the confidence which the Commission placed so readily in her testimony. The teen-ager was not asked to give testimony. The Commission seems to have paid inadequate attention to his statements to the FBI.

Two of the three witnesses—the bus-driver and the teen-ager—said that Oswald was wearing a jacket. The teen-ager described it as light blue. The taxi-driver who picked Oswald up after the bus ride also said that Oswald was wearing a jacket, which he described as faded blue. *(2H 255)* Only the landlady described Oswald as wearing no jacket—but it will come as no surprise that the Commission chose to accept her testimony and apparently considered that the three men were "mistaken." Two of the men said that Oswald was wearing a blue jacket. Oswald owned a blue jacket. But the Commission found that he left it behind at the Book Depository (WR 155), where it was discovered "subsequently." "Subsequently" was "late in November" (WR 163); and it is not inconceivable that the jacket was placed there, to be discovered once the police reconstruction of Oswald's movements was composed. The possibility that the blue jacket had been placed in the Book Depository in order that its discovery there might lend credence to the story of Oswald's "escape" seems never to have occurred to the Commission.

The witnesses disagreed also about how the bus-driver had learned that the President had been shot. The statement to the press by Dallas District Attorney Henry M. Wade that Oswald himself had announced the news and had "laughed very loud" was an irresponsible invention. The teen-ager, Milton Jones, said that a policeman had given the news to the driver. The driver himself said, with some corroboration from the landlady (CE 1985), that a motorist had told him the news.

But there is a more serious conflict. The driver testified that traffic was at a standstill, but that the police had allowed buses to proceed while holding up passenger cars. Milton Jones, however, gave the surprising report that two policemen had boarded the bus and searched the passengers, just after Oswald had left. If that is true, it suggests the following implications:

(1) McWatters, whose testimony betrays the fact that he permitted the police to influence him improperly (2H 277), may have withheld from the Commission the important information that the police had searched his bus.

(2) Police officials were unaware of or suppressed information about the search of the bus by policemen.

(3) Instructions for such a search, if transmitted on the police radio, have been omitted from the official transcripts of the radio log.

(4) The search of a bus on which Oswald had been a passenger, just after he had debarked—and in the absence of city-wide roadblocks or interference with movement of all other vehicles—raises the possibility that the police were pursuing Oswald before his absence from the Book Depository was even noticed. If such a pursuit in fact took place, one would wish to know the identity of the policemen and their reasons for their interest in Oswald—especially considering the fact (discussed in Chapter 13) that two policemen in a patrol car appeared in front of Oswald's rooming house and sounded their horn while he was in his room.

The implications of the information obtained from Milton Jones must have been apparent to the Commission when it received the FBI report of April 3, 1964 on the interview with him. Witnesses continued to give testimony for some five months, but the Commission did not call Milton Jones or make any attempt to test his story. They did not even dismiss his statements as "mistaken," as they did with so many other witnesses who reported circumstances embarrassing to the official findings; they just ignored the whole thing.

The Commission also ignored significant parts of Mrs. Bledsoe's testimony —for example, that she had identified Oswald from photographs in the police station at a time when Oswald was in custody and appearing in line-ups. Mc-Watters, who did view a line-up, suggested that there was a marked difference in size between Oswald and the other men—which speaks for the "fairness" of the line-ups that "satisfied" the Commission. *(WR 169)* More important is the landlady's disclosure that the bus passengers were aware, very soon after the shooting, that the shots had come from a specific window in the Book Depository and that a suspect had been arrested and jailed. The Commission showed an extraordinary lack of curiosity about that suspect and has given us no information whatsoever about him.

A fact-finding body that is repeatedly deaf to such alarm bells as these invites questions about its competence. Such questions are compounded by the manipulation of data that is discussed next.

The Cab Ride

According to the Warren Report, Oswald walked from the point where he had left the bus to the Greyhound Bus Terminal. There he took a taxicab driven by William Whaley, saying that he wished to go to 500 North Beckley. As the cab was about to start, Oswald seemed about to yield his place to an elderly woman who wanted a taxi too, but apparently she refused his offer. The cab proceeded to North Beckley, where Oswald got out in the 700 block, paying a meter charge of 95 cents. The Report *(WR 163)* states that the elapsed time of the reconstructed run from the Greyhound Bus Station to Neely and Beckley Streets was 5 minutes 30 seconds, in a retracing of the route performed during an interview with Whaley in Dallas. The Commission suggests that if the cab ride lasted approximately 6 minutes, Oswald could have walked the distance to his rooming house in time to arrive there by 1 p.m.

Comments on the treatment of the taxi ride by the Warren Commission can be brief. It is immediately obvious that Oswald's actions were inconsistent with those of an escaping assassin in two respects: he took a taxi to a local address instead of taking advantage of the possibilities in the Greyhound Bus Station for leaving Dallas or the State of Texas altogether; and he was ready to surrender the taxi to a lady who wanted it, as if he had no cause for anxiety or urgency.[5] These surprising actions are not discussed in the Report in the context of Oswald's alleged guilt, although the mere fact of his departure from the Book Depository is considered incriminating.

---

5   It is increasingly difficult to reconcile Oswald's demeanor with what the Commission calls "escape." Whaley testified to the "slow way" Oswald had walked up to the taxi, saying: "He didn't talk. He wasn't in any hurry. He wasn't nervous or anything." *(2H 261)*

The estimate of six minutes for the taxi trip merits a few remarks. Whaley[6] first testified before the Commission on March 12, 1964. At that time he estimated the distance between the points where he had picked up and discharged Oswald as two and a half miles. Asked for an estimate of the time it took to cover that distance, Whaley said:

> *Whaley:* I run it again with the policeman because the policeman was worried, he run the same trip and he couldn't come out the same time I did. . . . I got the two minutes on him he never could make up. So I had to go back with him to make that trip to show him I was right.
> *Ball:* How much time, in that experiment, when you hit the lights right, how long did it take you?
> *Whaley:* Nine minutes.   *(2H 259)*

The estimate of nine minutes for the taxi ride apparently created difficulties, since Oswald's movements from the Book Depository to the Tippit scene, as reconstructed by the Warren Commission, had him on a tight schedule without a minute to spare. Whaley was re-interviewed in Dallas on April 8, 1964, after again retracing the route on which he had transported Oswald, this time in a Secret Service car. It was this re-enactment that served as the basis for the Commission's estimate of six minutes *(6H 434)*, with a slightly altered point of termination of the ride (the 700 instead of the 500 block of North Beckley Street), three blocks (instead of five) from the rooming house, to which Whaley now agreed. He readily acknowledged that his original recollection—that Oswald had left the cab in the 500 block—was wrong.

In allowing six minutes for the taxi ride,[7] the Commission has made no allowance for traffic conditions immediately after the assassination. Yet in the case of testimony that Jack Ruby was seen at Parkland Hospital an hour after the assassination, the Commission solemnly concluded that the witnesses were mistaken, basing this decision in part on the assumption that Ruby could not have made the drive in the available time, 10 to 15 minutes, because of traffic conditions. Since the normal time for the drive was 9 to 10 minutes, the Commission apparently considered that Ruby would have experienced a slowdown of 50 per cent.

It is difficult to reconcile the Commission's reasoning in the case of Ruby with its calculations in the case of Oswald. His trip was actually speeded up by 33⅓ per cent in relation to the driver's first attempts to retrace the route, which took nine minutes. In the later experiment, the Commission failed to check the six-minute ride against the taxi meter to see if it registered 95 cents at the end of the ride, the amount that Oswald paid.

These discrepancies are not raised to support a claim that Oswald took

---

6   William Whaley was an important, naïve, and likeable witness. He provided significant testimony not only on the cab ride but on the nature of the police line-ups and the methods of official investigators, probably without even realizing the full importance of what he contributed, in well-intended desire to give his full co-operation to the investigation. He died on December 18, 1965, in a head-on collision, as discussed in a later chapter.

7   The first chapter, presenting the Summary and Conclusions, refers to "five or six minutes" *(WR 6)*, while on a later page *(WR 163)* the estimate is "about six minutes."

more time, or Ruby took less, than the estimates given in the Warren Report; they are raised to call attention to the use of a double standard which enabled the Commission to reach whatever conclusions were desirable or necessary to its fundamental thesis, and to underline the difficulty of fixing the real facts with precision and confidence. If it is assumed that normal driving times prevailed despite the traffic conditions and that Ruby could have gone to Parkland Hospital, the possibility of conspiracy is raised. If, on the other hand, it is allowed that there was a marked slowdown in traffic, the possibility arises that Oswald reached his rooming house too late to walk to the Tippit scene in time to shoot Tippit.

The Commission, of course, avoids these dismaying alternatives by a stratagem which has no merit except transparency.

Establishing a Link Between the Tippit Suspect and the Assassination

According to the Warren Report

The circumstances under which Captain Fritz of the Dallas Police discovered that the suspect wanted in connection with the assassination had already been arrested for the murder of Tippit are described in the following excerpts:

> As Fritz and Day were completing their examination of this rifle on the sixth floor [of the Texas School Book Depository], Roy Truly, the building superintendent, approached with information which he felt should be brought to the attention of the police. Earlier, while the police were questioning the employees, Truly had observed that Lee Harvey Oswald, one of the 15 men who worked in the warehouse, was missing. After Truly provided Oswald's name, address, and general description, Fritz left for police headquarters. He arrived at headquarters shortly after 2 p.m.   *(WR 9)*

> When he entered the homicide and robbery bureau office, he saw two detectives standing there with Sergeant Gerald L. Hill, who had driven from the theater with Oswald. Hill testified that Fritz told the detective to get a search warrant, go to an address on Fifth Street in Irving, and pick up a man named Lee Oswald. When Hill asked why Oswald was wanted, Fritz replied, "Well, he was employed down at the Book Depository and he had not been present for a roll call of the employees." Hill said, "Captain, we will save you a trip . . . there he sits."   *(WR 180)*

According to the Hearings and Exhibits

Roy Truly testified on March 24, 1964 on his realization that Oswald was missing from the Book Depository and the steps he took to bring his absence to the attention of the police.

> *Truly:* When I got back to the first floor, at first I didn't see anything except officers running around, reporters in the place. There was a regular mad-

house. . . . I noticed some of my boys over in the west corner of the shipping department, and there were several officers over there taking their names and addresses, and so forth. . . . I noticed that Lee Oswald was not among these boys. So I picked up the telephone and called Mr. Aiken down at the other warehouse who keeps our application blanks. . . . So Mr. Campbell [vice-president of the Book Depository] is standing there, and I said, "I have a boy over here missing. I don't know whether to report it or not." Because I had another one or two out then. I didn't know whether they were all there or not. . . . So I picked the phone up then and called Mr. Aiken, at the warehouse, and got the boy's name and general description and telephone number and address at Irving. . . . I knew nothing of this Dallas address. I didn't know he was living away from his family. . . .

Belin: Did you ask for the names and addresses of any other employees who might have been missing?

Truly: No, sir. . . . That is the only one that I could be certain right then was missing.   *(3H 229-230)*

Truly testified a second time on May 14, 1964, on another matter, but his notification of the police that Oswald was missing was also discussed.

Truly: When I noticed this boy was missing, I told Chief Lumpkin that, "We have a man here that's missing." I said, "It may not mean anything, but he isn't here." I first called down to the other warehouse and had Mr. Aiken pull the application of the boy so I could get—quickly get his address in Irving and his general description, so I could be more accurate than I would be. . . .   *(7H 382)*

Ball: You didn't talk to any police officer before you called the warehouse and got the address?

Truly: Not that I remember.

Ball: You did that on your own without instructions?

Truly: That's right.   *(7H 383)*

Captain Will Fritz in testimony before the Warren Commission on April 22, 1964 took up the tale:

. . . Mr. Truly came and told me that one of his employees had left the building, and I asked his name and he gave me his name, Lee Harvey Oswald, and I asked his address and he gave me the Irving address. . . . After he told me about this man almost, I left immediately after he told me that. . . . I felt it important to hold that man. . . .

I told them [Police Officers Sims and Boyd] to drive me to City Hall and see if the man had a criminal record. . . . My intentions were to go to the house at Irving. When I got to the city hall . . . I asked when I got to my office who shot the officer, and they told me his name was Oswald, and I said, "His full name?" And they told me and I said, "That is the suspect we are looking for in the President's killing."   *(4H 206)*

A different version of this incident, however, had been given by Dallas Police Officer C. W. Brown, when he testified on April 3, 1964. He described the situation at police headquarters just after Oswald had been brought in from the Texas Theater under arrest:

Brown: . . . the phones were ringing. I answered the phone. It was Captain Fritz. He was still at the scene on the sixth floor of the School Book Depository, and I told him that the officers had just brought in a suspect that had shot the police officer, and told him about Mr. Shelley [employee at the Depository] telling me that this boy that was identified as Lee Harvey Oswald, was also an employee there. He said, "I will be right up in a few minutes."

Belin: Where was Captain Fritz at this time?

Brown: He was still at the scene of the shooting . . . he called from there. I told him it looked like we might have the boy that was responsible for that. He said, "Okay, I will be up in a few minutes."

Belin: What did you mean by "that," for the assassination?

Brown: For the President's assassination. That was my personal opinion at that time.   *(7H 248)*

Brown's account is confirmed by Sheriff J. E. Decker in a report on the assassination and in his testimony of April 16, 1964:

After my first arrival at the Texas School Book Depository Building from Parkland Hospital, Captain Fritz of the DPD, Homicide Division arrived and he went on up into the Texas School Book Depository Building, leaving a pair of his officers downstairs where they opened up their automobile and brought out rifles to assist them in securing the building. Shortly thereafter Captain Fritz came to my office where he contacted his department by telephone and advised me that the suspect, Lee Harvey Oswald, had been apprehended in the Texas Theater in Oak Cliff. Also he advised me that Oswald had been employed in the Texas School Book Depository.
(Decker Exhibit No. 5323)

In his testimony, two weeks after Brown's, Sheriff Decker referred to the incident somewhat more curtly: "Then, I talked to Fritz after he arrived . . . then we went across the street and he phoned and that's when I learned Oswald had been formerly employed there at that building." *(12H 46)*

The same counsel (David Belin) who had questioned Brown on April 3, 1964 heard from Sergeant Gerald Hill on April 8, 1964 the testimony on which the Warren Report relies in relating these events.

. . . Captain Fritz walked in. He walked up to [Detectives] Rose and Stovall and made the statement to them, "Go get a search warrant and go out to some address on Fifth Street," and I don't recall the actual street number, in Irving, and "pick up a man named Lee Oswald." And I asked the Captain why he wanted him, and he said, "Well, he was employed down at the Book Depository and he had not been present for a roll call of the employees." And we said, "Captain, we will save you a trip," or words to that effect, "because there he sits."   *(7H 59)*

The police officers who were present at the arrest of Oswald at the Texas Theater testified that they were pursuing the suspect in the Tippit murder and were unaware at the time that the man arrested was involved in the assassination. However, Johnny Calvin Brewer, the shoe salesman who was present at the arrest, testified on April 2, 1964:

. . . there were a couple of officers fighting him and taking the gun away from him . . . and he was fighting, still fighting, and I heard some of the police holler, I don't know who it was, "Kill the President, will you." And I saw fists flying and they were hitting him.   *(7H 6)*

[The Warren Report dismisses as "unlikely" the report that a police officer made that remark. *(WR 179)*]

The cashier at the theater, Julia Postal, testified on April 2, 1964 that during the arrest a police officer came into the box office to use the telephone and that he remarked, "I think we have got our man on both accounts." *(7H 12)*

Appraisal of the Known Facts

Roy Truly encountered Oswald less than two minutes after the shots were fired under circumstances so clearly eliminating Oswald from suspicion that Truly did not hesitate to vouch for him, in effect, to Officer M. L. Baker. Hence, Truly seems to have over-reacted to Oswald's absence shortly afterward (according to his testimony, Truly remembered that he had noticed and reported Oswald's absence about half an hour earlier than the time stated in the Warren Report, about 1:20 p.m.). Truly seems almost embarrassed when he testifies to his own industry and initiative in obtaining Oswald's address even before reporting his absence to the police, as if he himself recognizes the contradiction between his encounter with Oswald and his response to Oswald's absence soon afterward.

Captain Fritz, in turn, over-reacted to Truly's report. Though not clairvoyant, Fritz "felt it important to hold that man" and "left immediately" with the intention of going "to the house at Irving." Extraordinary: The President had been shot, everyone was in shock and consternation, the anxiety for Kennedy's safety in Dallas had been brutally shown to be well-founded, and in the Book Depository an abandoned chicken lunch at a sniper's nest pointed to the feared conspiracy against the Head of State. In this setting, Fritz put aside everything to go outside the city limits searching for a missing working man—not the only one missing, for Charles Givens was absent too, and perhaps others as well—a man already encountered and let go by a police officer.

Was such urgent action warranted by the circumstances? Captain Fritz needed only to put out an alert on the police radio to have Oswald picked up by officers having lesser responsibilities at that moment than the Chief of Homicide—an alert such as the one sent out for Charles Givens (a man with a Dallas police record) when Givens had not appeared by 1:30 p.m. Fritz could also have telephoned the Irving Police Department and asked them to check at the Paine address to see if Oswald was there, instead of leaving the scene of the assassination to go there personally, when the Paine home was not even within Dallas police jurisdiction.

Instead of taking such reasonable steps, Fritz left the Book Depository without even giving Oswald's name and description to the police radio dispatcher so that police throughout the city would be alerted if they saw him. Moreover, Fritz stopped to see Sheriff Decker and, according to his own version of events, next went to the police building, before even setting out to look for

Dulles: There are no reports; you found no reports in your files?

Fritz: No, sir. . . . We had no reports on him at all.   *(4H 248)*

But the Dallas office of the FBI, and FBI Agent James P. Hosty, Jr., in particular, did know about Oswald. Lieutenant Jack Revill of the Dallas Police criminal intelligence section, the section that handles subversive activities, claimed that it was only after Oswald had been arrested that Hosty told him for the first time that Oswald was an FBI case. Revill testified that the conversation took place when he and Hosty encountered each other in the police basement at about 3 p.m. on Friday and proceeded together to the elevators.

And Mr. Hosty ran over to me and he says, "Jack"—now as I recall these words—"a Communist killed President Kennedy . . . Lee Oswald killed President Kennedy." I said, "Who is Lee Oswald?" He said, "He is in our Communist file. We knew he was here in Dallas. . . ."   *(5H 34)*

I asked him why he had not told us this, and the best [of] my recollection is that he said he couldn't. Now, what he meant by that I don't know. Because in the past our relations had been such that this type of information, it surprised me that they had not, if they had such information he had not brought it or hadn't made it available to us.   *(5H 37)*

Revill's testimony suggests that the FBI normally would have notified the Dallas police about Oswald's presence in the city and his activities; Revill could not understand why Hosty did not or could not inform the police about Oswald before the day of the assassination. (Perhaps it did not occur to Revill that, as will be discussed in Chapter 20, Oswald might have been an FBI functionary or informant—in which case there was no need for the FBI to report to the Dallas police, and no prospect that Hosty would make any admissions about Oswald's real status once he was under arrest.)

Revill testified that he informed his superiors about Hosty's statements to him about Oswald in a memorandum which he dictated at about 3:30 p.m. on the same day. His story received corroboration from Detective V. J. Brian, who heard part of the conversation between Revill and Hosty, and from the stenographer who typed Revill's memorandum. *(WR 441-442)*

When Revill was writing his memorandum at about 3:30 on Friday afternoon, Oswald was under interrogation by Captain Fritz. Upon his arrest at the Texas Theater at 2 p.m., Oswald had refused to give his address. He had no identification on his person which indicated that he was living in a furnished room on North Beckley Street. The Book Depository records on Oswald listed his address as the Paine residence in Irving. Neither Marina Oswald nor Ruth Paine knew the Beckley Street address. Nevertheless, Captain Fritz testified that when he returned to the police building and began to question Oswald, ". . . or maybe just before I started to talk to him, some officer told me outside of my office that he had a room on Beckley, I don't know who that officer was. . . ." *(4H 207)*

The Warren Commission, understandably, was curious about the identity of that officer, since his knowledge of Oswald's address under those circumstances was inconsistent with the claim by the Dallas police that they had no knowledge of Oswald until his arrest on November 22, 1963. The Commission's interest is apparent from the record. *(4H 207-210)* In response to further questions on the matter, Fritz said, "I thought he lived in Irving and he told me he didn't live in Irving. He lived on Beckley as the officer had told me outside." *(4H 210)* Nevertheless, the officer was never identified, and the means by which he acquired information about Oswald's Beckley Street address remain a mystery.

When we revert to Revill's memorandum, the mystery deepens, for at the top of the memorandum *(CE 709)* we find the following words:

Subject: Lee Harvey Oswald
605 Elsbeth Street

Oswald had lived on Elsbeth Street at the end of 1962 and in early 1963—but since the Dallas police had no previous record of him, and no information about his old addresses at the time that Revill's report was written, the Commission found this part of the memorandum arresting.

> *Dulles:* This is an address he once lived at. . . . I want to find out what he [Revill] knows about it.
>
> *Revill:* Is this a—is this an incorrect address on Mr. Oswald where he was living at the time?
>
> *Rankin:* If you check it up I think you will find—it is an incorrect address at the time. I think you will also find that 602 Elsbeth Street is where he lived at one time. . . .   *(5H 41)*
>
> *Dulles:* . . . Where did you get this address that you put on of 605 Elsbeth Street, do you recall?
>
> *Revill:* Yes, sir; from Detective E. B. Carroll or Detective Taylor. . . .
>
> *Dulles:* You have never ascertained where they got it?
>
> *Revill:* No, sir. . . . I never even thought about it until you brought up the point. . . .
>
> *Dulles:* Can you find out where they got this address?
>
> *Revill:* Yes, sir; I can.
>
> *Dulles:* I think that would be useful. I would like to know that. I would like to know where they got this address also.   *(5H 42)*

Although Revill promised to obtain the information, and Dulles was very anxious to have it, the answers are not to be found in the 26 volumes of the Hearings and Exhibits. Did Revill fail to send the information? Or did the Commission decide to withhold his report? Dulles was astute enough to recognize the implications of the Elsbeth Street address on Revill's memorandum: it suggested strongly that the Dallas police, despite their denials, did have prior knowledge of Oswald.

All the more frustrating, then, is the fact that no one, including Dulles, seems to have paid any attention to an equally bizarre and incomprehensible entry on another document—a list of the names and addresses of Book Depository employees compiled on Revill's instructions within a few hours of the assassination. *(5H 34; CE 2003, p. 127)*

The list appears in a memorandum dated November 22, 1963, addressed to Captain W. P. Gannaway, through Lieutenant Jack Revill, and signed by

Detectives W. R. Westphal and P. M. Parks. *(CE 2003,* p. 127) At the top of the page is a handwritten notation from Gannaway to Fritz: "All contacted except as noted." The list contains about 55 names, of which 12 are marked in the margin "not home." All the others, according to Gannaway's notation, had been contacted.

The very first entry on the list, without any notation in the margin, is: Harvey Lee Oswald . . . . . 605 Elsbeth.

Where did Westphal and Parks get that address? It was not known at the Book Depository, where they compiled the list, nor did they have access to Oswald or his possessions. Neither Westphal nor Parks, nor any other of the police officers who were involved, was ever questioned about the source of the Elsbeth Street address, or even about the implication that Oswald had been contacted at his home and was cleared.

The quality of the detective work performed by the Dallas police, and scarcely improved upon by the Warren Commission, is more suitable to a Marx Brothers comedy than to the awful tragedy of Kennedy's assassination. The Commission, having overlooked one anachronism completely and failed to explain another—leaving unresolved the strange indications that the police were familiar with Oswald before the assassination—asserts and reiterates, in its Report, that the Dallas police did not know that Oswald was in the city before the assassination. *(WR 660-661)* That evasive phraseology falls short of saying that the police had no knowledge of Oswald's existence until his arrest on November 22.

Indeed, Oswald seems to have been encountered by the Dallas police sometime between April 6 and 24, 1963, while distributing pro-Castro literature on the streets of Dallas *(WR 406-407),* as the Commission acknowledges somewhat too tentatively. If we compare Oswald's description of the incident in a letter to the Fair Play for Cuba Committee *(V. T. Lee Exhibit No. 1)* with the Dallas police report to the Warren Commission of May 19, 1964 on "an unidentified white male passing out pro-Castro literature at Main and Ervay Streets" in the late spring of 1963 *(CE 1407),* it becomes quite clear that the "unidentified white male" was Oswald.

But the police report was written a year after the actual event; contemporaneous records of the incident, if they exist, have been withheld. Can we be certain that the pro-Castro picket remained "unidentified," despite the two police memoranda of November 22, 1963 which indicate—without any apparent legitimate source—details of Oswald's life which suggest that he was known to the police long before the assassination?

While these anachronisms remain unresolved, as the Warren Commission has left them, it is premature to dismiss the notion that Oswald may have been framed for a crime committed by others.

Chapter 4
The Rifle

The rifle is physical evidence of central importance. In this section, it will be shown that the Warren Commission has given an incomplete, misleading, and at times false account of this evidence. The Commission failed to pin down the circumstances under which the rifle was first said to be a Mauser and presented a misleading and incomplete explanation of the "mistake." The Commission glossed over the poor and decrepit condition of the weapon and the defects in several of its parts, even going so far as to convert one defect into an "advantage." Its assertion that the serial number on the rifle was the only such in existence is open to serious doubt. It relied on rifle tests which were not valid because they lacked any semblance of comparability to the feat ascribed to Oswald; even so, the results of those tests do not support the inference that Oswald had the capability which the Commission has attributed to him on the basis of a perverse "interpretation" of the scores achieved.

The Commission failed to investigate an expert's report that the rifle scope was installed as if for a left-handed man. Oswald was not left-handed. It failed to mention in the Report negative results of a canvass conducted to trace the rifle ammunition to Oswald and presented no evidence of his purchase or possession of such ammunition. It made claims about the recency of the ammunition which are completely false. It made unsupported and questionable assertions about the ammunition clip.

I have already raised questions about the alleged appearance in and disappearance of this rifle from the Paine garage. By adding to those considerations and anomalies to be discussed in the pages which follow, one arrives at a point at which all the Commission's assertions about the murder rifle must be rejected because of the specious nature of many of its pronouncements.

The Vanished Mauser

On the afternoon of November 22, 1963 Dallas television station KBOX broad-cast the following news item:

> A rifle [has been] found in a staircase on the fifth floor of the building on which the assassin is believed to have shot the President of the United States. Sheriff's deputies identify the weapon as a 7.65 Mauser, a German-made Army rifle with a telescopic sight. It had one shell in the chamber. Three spent shells were found nearby.   *(CE 3048)*

Shortly after midnight, Dallas District Attorney Henry Wade replied to a reporter who asked the make of the rifle: "It's a Mauser, I believe." *(CE 2169)*

On Saturday, November 23, 1963, Deputy Constable Seymour Weitzman signed an affidavit for the Dallas police in which he said that he and Deputy Sheriff Boone had discovered the rifle during a search of the sixth floor of the Book Depository, and that, "This rifle was a 7.65 Mauser bolt action equipped with a 4/18 scope, a thick leather brownish-black sling on it." *(CE 2003*, p. 63)

A copy of this affidavit came into the hands of Mark Lane; during the months which followed, he and other critics of the police theory of the assassina-tion cited this affidavit, on the public platform and in print, as a serious and suspicious defect in the case against Oswald. There was a clear inference that there may have been substitution and fabrication of evidence.

When the Warren Report was issued, it was learned that Weitzman, who saw the rifle only at a glance and did not handle it, thought the weapon looked like a 7.65 Mauser bolt-action rifle *(WR 81);* that Wade, on one occasion, re-peated the error that the murder rifle had been a Mauser *(WR 235)*—although the Report did not explain how the district attorney made contact with Weitz-man, presumably the source of his error, or why he accepted as authoritative information obtained from a deputy constable at a time when he was in consul-tation with the chief of police and the captain in charge of homicide; and the following passages are found in the appendix on "speculations and rumors":

> *Speculation:* The rifle found on the sixth floor of the Texas School Book Depository was identified as a 7.65 Mauser by the man who found it, Deputy Constable Seymour Weitzman.[1]
>
> *Commission finding:* Weitzman, the original source of the speculation that the rifle was a Mauser, and Deputy Sheriff Eugene Boone found the weapon. Weitzman did not handle the rifle and did not examine it at close range. He had little more than a glimpse of it and thought it was a Mauser, a German bolt-action rifle similar in appearance to the Mannlicher-Carcano. Police laboratory technicians subsequently arrived and correctly identified the weapon as a 6.5 Italian rifle.   *(WR 645-646)*

---

[1] This so-called "speculation" is, of course, a mere statement of known fact, accepted as fact by the Commission itself. The real speculation—that there was a substitution of rifles to incriminate Oswald—was not confronted explicitly by the Report.

Now that we are acquainted with the official findings, let us make an independent check of the facts which led the Warren Commission to its conclusions. The question of the identification of the rifle as a Mauser arose first when Mark Lane testified before the Commission, on March 4, 1964.

Now, in reference to the rifle, there is on file—I assume that you have it or copies of it—in the Dallas district attorney's office or the police office in Dallas, an affidavit sworn to by Officer Weitzman, in which he indicates that he discovered the rifle on the sixth floor of the Book Depository Building at, I believe, 1:22 p.m., on November 22, 1963.

Now, in this affidavit, Officer Weitzman swore that the murder weapon —that the rifle which he found on the sixth floor was a 7.65 Mauser, which he then went on to describe in some detail, with reference to the color of the strap, etc. Now, the prosecuting attorney, of course, took exactly the same position, and for hours insisted that the rifle discovered on the sixth floor was a German Mauser, adding the nationality. A German Mauser is nothing at all like an Italian carbine. I think almost any rifle expert will indicate that that is so. I have been informed that almost every Mauser . . . every German Mauser has stamped on it the caliber, as does almost every Italian carbine.   *(2H 46)*

Having heard Lane's comments on March 4, the Commission proceeded on March 24 to question, not Weitzman, but Deputy Sheriff Eugene Boone, co-finder of the rifle. Boone testified on his activities at the time of the shooting and the subsequent search of the Book Depository, describing the discovery of the rifle. He received the thanks of the Chairman and was about to depart when Counsel Joseph Ball, perhaps to his later chagrin, intervened.

Ball: There is one question. Did you hear anybody refer to this rifle as a Mauser that day?
Boone: Yes, I did. And at first, not knowing what it was, I thought it was a 7.65 Mauser.
Ball: Who referred to it as a Mauser that day?
Boone: I believe Captain Fritz. He had knelt down there to look at it, and before he removed it, not knowing what it was, he said that is what it looks like. This is when Lieutenant Day, I believe his name is, the ID man was getting ready to photograph it. We were just discussing it back and forth. And he said it looks like a 7.65 Mauser.
Ball: Thank you.
The Chairman: Thank you very much, Sheriff. You have been very helpful.   *(3H 295)*

We can only agree: very helpful. Not only in his informative testimony, but also in his written reports to his superior, Sheriff Decker, which the Commission and its counsel obviously had not read in advance and perhaps not even subsequently. In a report dated November 22, 1963, Boone said, ". . . I saw the rifle, that appeared to be a 7.65 mm. Mauser with a telescopic site [*sic*]. . . ." (*Decker Exhibit 5323*, p. 508) Boone reported the same thing in a second written report of the same date. But nowhere in the Report is there a hint of the startling fact that not only Weitzman but Boone as well believed the rifle a 7.65 Mauser; nor a murmur of Boone's testimony that Captain Fritz himself had thought the rifle a 7.65 Mauser.

The next witness heard by the Commission on this question was not Weitzman but Chief Curry. He testified on April 22, 1964 that he did not know who made the original identification of the rifle, and that he did not know whether or not it was true that the original identification was a 7.65 Mauser.

> *Ford:* Do you know when it was finally determined that it was not a 7.65 Mauser?
> *Curry:* No, sir; I don't know that.
> *McCloy:* As far as I know there was no police report that it was a 7.65 rifle.
> *(Discussion off the record.)*
> *Rankin:* Chief Curry, do you know of any police records of your police department that showed that this weapon that was purportedly involved in the assassination was a Mauser rifle?
> *Curry:* No, sir; not to my knowledge.   *(4H 181)*

Both the questions and the answers are surprising when one recalls that Commissioner McCloy and his confreres had already learned of the Weitzman affidavit, and that this affidavit is among the documents in the Dallas police report on the assassination *(CE 2003)*, which Curry presumably read. Curry, who had had some five months in which to inform himself on this matter, responded that he "did not know" no less than five times in the brief testimony on the identification of the rifle.

Captain Fritz and Lieutenant Day also testified on April 22, 1964. Captain Fritz pointed out that the rifle had been called "most everything" and denied that he himself had thought it was a Mauser.

> *Fritz:* No, sir; I knew—you can read on the rifle what it was and you could also see on the cartridge what caliber it was.
> *Ball:* Well, did you ever make any—did you ever say that it was a 7.65 Mauser?
> *Fritz:* No, sir; I did not. If I did, the Mauser part, I won't be too positive about Mauser because I am not too sure about Mauser rifles myself. But I certainly am sure that I never did give anyone any different caliber than the one that shows on the cartridges.   *(4H 205-206)*

Captain Fritz, advancing from answers that seemed evasive to a kind of acknowledgment that he might have called the rifle a Mauser, vindicates Deputy Sheriff Boone—but traps himself with a categorical statement under oath that he never gave any caliber except the one that shows on the cartridges. He was quoted in *The New York Times* of November 23, 1963 as saying that the rifle was of an "unusual undetermined caliber."[2] If the Commission was aware of this newspaper story, it ignored it. Acting as something of a scapegoat in this case (in the following chapter on autopsy and medical findings see the section on anterior

---

2 Gladwin Hill wrote in *The New York Times* of November 23, 1963 (p. 4, col. 2) that police ballistics experts were still studying the rifle, apparently with no conclusive findings, and that "Captain Fritz said it was of obscure foreign origin, possibly Italian, of about 1940 vintage, and of an unusual, undetermined caliber."

neck wound), the press was probably "inaccurate" again. A pity, though, that Fritz did not complain that he was misquoted.

Lieutenant Day, the least uncomfortable of the witnesses, was asked if he had ever described the rifle as anything other than a 6.5 caliber carbine. He replied, "I didn't describe the rifle to anyone other than police officers." *(4H 263)*

We come now not to Weitzman but the testimony of District Attorney Henry Wade. *(5H 250)* In the transcript (which is undistinguished by any clarity or precision) Wade conceded that he had said that the rifle was a Mauser, and that he had been inaccurate, because he got his information secondhand. Counsel Rankin did not ask the logical question: From whom? We will have to surmise whether it was Weitzman, Boone, or a higher official.

After Wade's testimony on June 8, 1964, Mark Lane made a second appearance before the Commission, on July 2. On this occasion he was permitted to examine the rifle, as he had requested earlier.

> Although I am personally not a rifle expert, I was able to determine that it was an Italian carbine because printed indelibly upon it are the words "Made Italy" and "caliber 6.5." I suggest it is very difficult for a police officer to pick up a weapon which has printed upon it clearly in English "Made Italy, Cal. 6.5" and then the next day draft an affidavit stating that it was in fact a German Mauser, 7.65 millimeters. *(5H 560-561)*

But Weitzman never picked up the weapon, as we learned from the Report. It will be obvious by now that the Commission itself never examined this key witness. Weitzman gave a deposition on April 1, 1964, at which time he was questioned by Counsel Ball.

> *Ball:* In the statement you made to the Dallas Police Department that afternoon, you referred to the rifle as a 7.65 Mauser bolt action?
> *Weitzman:* In a glance, that's what it looked like.
> *Ball:* That's what it looked like—did you say that or someone else say that?
> *Weitzman:* No; I said that. I thought it was one.
> *Ball:* Are you fairly familiar with rifles?
> *Weitzman:* Fairly familiar because I was in the sporting goods business awhile. *(7H 108)*

Ball then asked the witness questions about his service in the U.S. Armed Forces, learning that he had been a flier and had ended up in a prison camp in Japan. Ball then reverted to the rifle.

> *Ball:* Now, in your statement to the Federal Bureau of Investigation, you gave a description of the rifle, how it looked.
> *Weitzman:* I said it was a Mauser-type action, didn't I?
> *Ball:* Mauser bolt action.
> *Weitzman:* And at the time I looked at it, I believe I said it was a 2.5 scope on it and I believe I said it was a Weaver but it wasn't; it turned out to be anything but a Weaver, but that was at a glance.
> *Ball:* You also said it was a gun-metal color?
> *Weitzman:* Yes.
> *Ball:* Gray or blue?

Weitzman: Blue metal.

Ball: And the rear portion of the bolt was visibly worn, is that worn?

Weitzman: That's right.

Ball: And the wooden portion of the rifle was what color?

Weitzman: It was a brown, or I would say not a mahogany brown but dark oak brown.

Ball: Rough wood, was it?

Weitzman: Yes, sir; rough wood.

Ball: And it was equipped with a scope?

Weitzman: Yes, sir.

Ball: Was it of Japanese manufacture?

Weitzman: I believe it was a 2.5 Weaver at the time I looked at it. I didn't look that close at it; it just looked like a 2.5 but it turned out to be a Japanese scope I believe. *(7H 109)*

Appraisal of the Known Facts

Although the Warren Report assigns the sole responsibility for the confusion about the identity of the rifle found in the Book Depository to Seymour Weitzman, it is clear from the testimony and the documents that Deputy Sheriff Eugene Boone and probably Captain Fritz of the Dallas Police also described the rifle as a Mauser, Boone in two written reports. The Report is therefore misleading, if not deceptive, on this point.

Henry Wade admitted that he publicly identified the rifle as a Mauser, on the basis of secondhand information from someone. The Commission failed to ask who that person was, a key question so obvious that one cannot escape the impression that it desired to avoid the answer and the possible complications it might have introduced. Wade was not asked whether he had had any contact with Weitzman; nor was Weitzman asked if he had told Wade, or anyone else, that the rifle was a Mauser. In the absence of that information, the attempt in the Report to attribute to Weitzman the full responsibility for the misidentification of the rifle by Wade or others is wholly unwarranted.

The Commission itself heard testimony from Curry, Fritz, Boone, Day, and Wade on the "Mauser." The only witness blamed for the erroneous identification in the Report is the only witness who did not appear before the Commission; he was deposed by Counsel Ball. In that deposition, Ball and Weitzman discuss an FBI interview with Weitzman, on an unknown date, apparently on the basis of an FBI report on that interview. This report is not found anywhere in the Exhibits. However, from the deposition alone it is clear that Weitzman described the rifle found in the Book Depository in considerable detail to the FBI. The metal was blue; the wood was dark oak brown. The description of the rifle in the Report *(WR 81 and 553-555)* does not include the color of the metal or the wood.

Above all, the 6.5 Mannlicher-Carcano which the Report asserts is the rifle found in the Book Depository *was not shown to Weitzman so that he could affirm or deny that it was the same rifle* that he discovered on the sixth floor of the Book Depository. This was an elementary and indispensable procedure which a thorough investigation would not have omitted. The failure to obtain such corroboration from Weitzman leaves open the possibility that a substitution of rifles took place, or that a second rifle may have been found at the Book Depository but kept secret. In evaluating that possibility, it should be noted that Lieutenant Day testified that when he took the rifle to the police headquarters on Friday afternoon he dictated a detailed description of the weapon to his secretary *(4H 260)* but that that document is not included in the Exhibits.[3] A second police officer wrote a description of the rifle at about 9 p.m. on the same day *(CE 2003*, p. 195), but his report is also omitted from the official documents. Consequently, we do not know the contents of either of those two contemporaneous descriptions of the rifle. It is difficult to understand why those documents were not exhibited in support of the assertions in the Report, since the Warren Commission was certainly aware of widespread suspicion that a Carcano had been substituted for a Mauser actually found in the Book Depository.

When the Warren Report appeared, its explanation for the announcements that the rifle was a Mauser—carried by all the news media for about 24 hours after the assassination—seemed facile. It is surprising that although Weitzman received the blame for the error, the Report did not explain how his mistake led to universal misidentification of the rifle by high officials and by the news media, since Weitzman—a deputy constable—was neither a spokesman for the police nor the source to whom the district attorney went for his information.

Two months later the Hearings and Exhibits were released. After studying testimony and documents, I have no confidence in the official account of how the confusion about a Mauser originated. The facts have been misrepresented. The investigation has been incomplete and unsatisfactory, by objective standards. Relevant documents have been withheld. The question of the identity of the rifle found in the Book Depository still awaits a conclusive determination.

The Guilty Carcano

The testimony and documents provide illuminating information on the quality of the Mannlicher-Carcano rifle as a category and about the condition of the particular weapon found on the sixth floor of the Book Depository and alleged to be the source of the shots that killed the President. Little of this information has found its way into the Warren Report.

---

3 Day also testified that he had never experienced doubt about the identity of the rifle because "it was stamped right on there, 6.5, and when en route to the office with Mr. Odum, the FBI agent who drove me in, he radioed it in, he radioed in what it was to the FBI over the air." *(4H 264)* Here was another source of corroboration: a witness who had seen and described the weapon very soon after it was found. However, the Warren Commission did not question FBI Agent Odum about this or check the FBI radio log, which may have contained important information about the events which took place immediately after the shooting of the President.

In his testimony when Sebastian Latona—one of the FBI experts on whom the Warren Commission relied—described the murder rifle as a "cheap old weapon" *(4H 29)*, Commissioner Boggs seemed taken aback. "A what?" asked Boggs. "A cheap old weapon," replied Latona. The Commissioners should have been forewarned by other reports in its possession. Among these was an FBI report stating that the rifle in question was part of a shipment of rifles that was the subject of "a legal proceeding by the Carlo Riva Machine Shop to collect payment for the shipment of the rifles which Adam Consolidated Industries, Inc., claims were defective." *(CE 1977)* John Brinegar, owner of The Gun Shop in Dallas, told the FBI in March 1964 that the Carcano was "a very cheap rifle and could have been purchased for $3.00 each in lots of 25." *(CE 2694, p. 11)* Dial Ryder of the Irving Sports Shop testified that the rifle was "real cheap, common, real flimsy looking . . . very easily knocked out of adjustment." *(11H 203)* And Edward Voebel, a former schoolmate of Oswald's, told the Secret Service four days after the assassination that he had: ". . . an Italian rifle of the same type as the one allegedly used to shoot the President; that he shot this rifle several times, but it is so poorly constructed he decided that it was best not to shoot it any more for the reason he was afraid it would explode." *(CE 3119)*

Small wonder, then, that in the Second World War among Italian soldiers the Mannlicher-Carcano was known as "the humanitarian rifle"—on the grounds that it could not hurt anyone *on purpose*.[4]

It is clear from these widely varying sources that, as a class of weapons, the Mannlicher-Carcano is cheap and old. A would-be assassin who selected this rifle would have to be hopelessly uninformed about firearms or desperately reluctant to hit his victim. What of the specific rifle found in the Book Depository? Perhaps it was in exceptionally good condition, a superior model or one reconditioned to a high level of efficiency? Army expert Ronald Simmons fully disabused the Warren Commission of any such notion in his testimony of March 31, 1964 concerning the tests conducted by three master riflemen with the same Carcano rifle.

> Yes, there were several comments made—particularly with respect to the amount of effort required to open the bolt. As a matter of fact, Mr. Staley had difficulty in opening the bolt in his first firing exercise. He thought it was completely up and it was not. . . . There was also comment made about the trigger pull, which is different as far as these firers are concerned. It is in effect a two-stage operation . . . in the first stage the trigger is relatively free, and it suddenly required a greater pull to actually fire the weapon.
> *(3H 447)*

Simmons explained that in order to achieve high accuracy even a highly skilled marksman would have to have had considerable experience with guns and . . .

also considerable experience with this weapon, because of the amount of effort required to work the bolt. . . . The pressure to open the bolt was so

---

4   John P. Conlon in a letter to the editor of *Analog,* June 1964.

great that we tended to move the rifle off the target, whereas with greater proficiency this might not have occurred.   *(3H 449)*

He explained that by "proficiency" he meant two things: (1) familiarity with the action of the bolt itself and the force required to open it, and (2) familiarity with the action of the trigger, which was a two-stage trigger. Asked if such familiarity could be acquired in dry runs, he said:

> Familiarity with the bolt can, probably as well as during live firing. But familiarity with the trigger would best be achieved with some firing. . . . There tends to be a reaction between the firer and the weapon at the time the weapon is fired, due to the recoil impulse. And I do not believe the action of the bolt going home would sufficiently simulate the action of the recoil of the weapon. . . .

Commissioner McCloy then asked: "If you were having a dry run with this, you could certainly make yourself used to the drag in the trigger without discharging the rifle, could you not?" Simmons replied:

> Yes. But there are two stages to the trigger. Our riflemen were all used to a trigger with a constant pull. When the slack was taken up, then they expected the round to fire. But actually when the slack is taken up, you tend to have a hair trigger here, which requires a bit of getting used to. . . .
> *(3H 450-451)*

Obviously, the Commission was able to extract from Simmons only the most lukewarm concurrence to the suggestion that it was possible for a rifleman to become accustomed to the drag in the trigger in dry runs and without actually discharging the weapon. His first response—that familiarity with the trigger pull could best be achieved by firing practice—creates an added obstacle to the credibility of the finding that Oswald fired three shots from this weapon without any difficulty, even though—by the Commission's own account—he had not used the rifle for at least two months. The Report delicately skirts the problem. *(WR 94)*

Besides the difficulties presented by the bolt and the trigger, the telescopic sight was defective. The Report acknowledges that the defect in the scope caused the shots fired by the three master riflemen in the marksmanship tests to land "a few inches high and to the right of the target." Did that new drawback of a defective scope cause any second thoughts about the feasibility of Oswald's alleged feat? On the contrary, the Report asserts that "the defect was one which would have *assisted the assassin* aiming at a target which was moving away." [Italics added] *(WR 194)*

The Report tells us furthermore that before the tests, the marksmen "had not even pulled the trigger because of concern about breaking the firing pin." *(WR 193-194)* Indeed, they had every cause for concern in the light of an FBI report of August 1964 informing the Warren Commission that:

> . . . the firing pin of this rifle has been used extensively as shown by wear on the nose or striking portion of the firing pin and, further, the presence of rust on the firing pin and its spring. . . .   *(CE 2974)*

In addition to the testimony quoted already, the Commission heard from several witnesses opinions similar to that of Charles Greener, owner of the Irving Sports Shop, regarding the scope.

> . . . with this frail mount . . . the possibility of it being real accurate would be pretty small, I think. . . . Even a fellow that was going to go deer hunting would want to take the gun out and shoot it before he went hunting, and I think that holds very true with this case. . . . I think the man would fire it before using it. . . . As far as your 6.5 Italian gun is concerned . . . it would be more important on that gun to shoot it than it would any other caliber or of an American make. . . .   *(11H 252-253)*

Dial Ryder, Greener's employee, said that the rifle scope "would be very easily knocked out of adjustment"; in his opinion, it was too light a mount and would easily "get jarred off on a high-powered rifle," throwing the accuracy off. *(11H 233)*

How has the Warren Commission dealt with the problems raised by all these witnesses? It discusses the difficulty of operating the bolt, but maintains that this could be overcome by dry runs. It does not mention the difficulty with the trigger, which can be overcome by familiarity acquired through firing the rifle. This omission may not be unrelated to the fact that persistent and arduous effort by the FBI failed to establish the smallest indication that Oswald had done any rifle practice with the Carcano at any time. *(CE 2694)*

Nor does the Report reflect the testimony of Greener and Ryder to the effect that anyone who intended to use this rifle with accuracy would first have fired it to zero in the scope or that the telescopic sight on the Carcano was particularly susceptible to being knocked out of adjustment. It does acknowledge that there was a defect in the scope, as mentioned earlier, but no attempt is made to account for behavior on Oswald's part which—in the context of the Commission's theory and conclusions—can only be called imbecilic. From his previous experience with firearms and his training in the Marine Corps, Oswald was aware that the rifle sight had to be zeroed in before shooting for record. *(11H 301-302)* Perhaps he was not aware of the Carcano's reputation as the world's worst shoulder weapon,[5] and purchased it because it was inexpensive. But surely if he was going to kill a President and wanted the maximum chance of finding his mark, he knew that the telescopic sight had to be zeroed in before he took aim and fired at the victim. He could not expect the aim to be accurate after the rifle had been transported to Dallas on the back seat of a car disassembled, and if it was not accurate, he might hit the wrong person or hit nothing at all but still forfeit his life in a rain of Secret Service bullets or risk disgrace and imprisonment.

Even assuming that Oswald disregarded all these considerations and stood at the window waiting for the motorcade—what happened when he pulled the trigger? If he had had no previous firing practice with the rifle (as everything suggests), how did he overcome the two-stage problem in working the trigger? With such a difficulty confronting him, it would be a wonder if he were able to complete the first shot, much less fire two more within little more than five seconds.

---

5 *Ibid.*

In the face of all those defects in a rifle of such low repute[6]—the Warren Report calmly contends that " . . . the assassination rifle was an accurate weapon . . . in fact, as accurate as current military rifles. . . . " *(WR 194-195)* So bland a perversion of reality is matched only in the pages of *1984*.

The Serial Number

According to the Warren Report

The Warren Commission describes the steps by which the rifle found on the sixth floor of the Book Depository was traced to Oswald by means of its serial number, C2766, and other evidence. The Report states:

> Information received from the Italian Armed Forces Intelligence Service has established that this particular rifle was the only rifle *of its type* bearing serial number C2766. [Italics added]   *(WR 119)*

A similar assurance given in Appendix X (Expert Testimony) states that: ". . . the number 'C2766' is the serial number of the rifle, and the rifle in question is the only one of its type bearing that serial number." *(WR 554)* Footnotes indicate that the basis for these assertions is the testimony of Robert Frazier, FBI weapons expert.

---

6   Renaud de la Taille wrote an authoritative critique of the alleged assassination rifle in *Science et Vie* in December 1964. According to an unofficial translation, De la Taille wrote that the 6.5 mm. Carcano is "the least precise of military rifles," with a bullet of poor penetration power and uncertain stability. The prototype M-91 rifle has a dispersion at 100 meters at 12 x 12 cms. "In other words," he wrote, "at 100 meters, the rifle being fixed to the ground, all shots fall into a rectangle of 12 x 12 cms.

"Obviously, then, the rifle has performed remarkably, considering its mediocrity. . . . An ordinary commercial weapon . . . does not exceed a rectangle 5 x 5 cms. at 100 meters. . . . The surface range of the Italian rifle, Model 1891, therefore was four times greater—less precise—than military rifles used by other nations.

"Moreover, those official figures are valid only for a new, perfectly well-adjusted rifle with choice ammunition. But Oswald's weapon was the M-91/38 rifle similar to the M-91 model but equipped with a shorter barrel, a fact which reduces the initial speed and consequently diminishes the precision. What is more, this is a used rifle, made in 1940 or in time of war, which further decreases its precision. One may therefore conclude that Oswald's rifle, at best, would have placed ten bullets in a rectangle of 20 x 20 cms. at 100 meters.

"One must consider also the dispersion range proper to the marksman and that of the ammunition. One then remains skeptical before the figures given by the Warren Commission, which specifies 13 cms. as maximum dispersion, identical to that achieved in two series by the same rifleman at 23 meters, or a distance four times smaller. When one realizes that the obtained dispersion increases at a faster rate than distance, the most serious doubt is justified.

"In effect, when one takes the best Warren Commission rifleman . . . one ends up with a dispersion of at least 50 cms. at 100 meters, which to us seems quite in conformity with the capacity of a 91/38 used rifle."

De la Taille asserts, on this basis, that "only a miraculous accident would have enabled Oswald to place his two bullets at only 10 cms. of dispersion. . . . Even Anderson, the world shooting champion, could not have done better with Oswald's rifle than to place the bullets in a circle of 20 cms. at 100 meters."

According to the Hearings and Exhibits

In his testimony on March 31, 1964, Frazier stated that the placement of a specific serial number on a weapon is generally confined to one weapon of a given type, and that:

> *Frazier:* The serial number consists of a series of numbers which normally will be repeated. However, a prefix is placed before the number, which actually must be part of the serial number, consisting of a letter.
> *Eisenberg:* Have you been able to confirm that the serial number on this weapon is the only such number on such a weapon?
> *Frazier:* Yes, it is.   *(3H 393)*

Subsequent to Frazier's testimony, the Warren Commission received a letter dated April 30, 1964 from the Director of the FBI, enclosing a 22-page report on the tracing of all documents relating to the C2766 rifle and to an "Italian carbine rifle, serial number 2766." The following information appears on page 15 of this report:

> . . . the Mannlicher-Carcano rifle was manufactured in Italy from 1891 until 1941; however, in the 1930's Mussolini ordered all arms factories to manufacture the Mannlicher-Carcano rifle. Since many concerns were manufacturing the same weapon, *the same serial number appears on weapons manufactured by more than one concern. Some bear a letter prefix and some do not.* [Italics added]   *(CE 2562)*

Appraisal of the Known Facts

It is not clear what is meant by the assertion in the Warren Report that the rifle is the only one "of its type" bearing serial number C2766. *(WR 119)* The Report does not specify whether "type" refers to the model, the year of manufacture, or the Mannlicher-Carcano category of rifles. The lack of an explicit explanation is unfortunate, in itself. However, the FBI communication of April 30, 1964 *(CE 2562)* exposes the insupportability of the Warren Commission's claim that the serial number on the rifle found on the sixth floor is exclusive. It suggests that there may be as many Mannlicher-Carcano rifles bearing the serial number C2766 in circulation as there were arms factories in Italy in the 1930's.

The evidence that the C2766 rifle found in the Book Depository is the rifle shipped by Klein's Sporting Goods to "A. Hidell" is therefore inconclusive, so far as the serial number is concerned. The Warren Commission nevertheless has attempted to link the rifle to Oswald by means of a serial number represented as being exclusive, despite information in its hands that it was *not*.

The fact that a considerable number of Mannlicher-Carcano rifles may bear serial number C2766 clearly weakens the case against Oswald. The Warren Commission has suppressed and misrepresented facts which it definitely ought to have acknowledged, in fairness to the accused assassin. Other evidence alleged to incriminate Oswald with respect to the rifle must be scrutinized in the light of this deception.

Scope, Shims, and Tests

Police Chief Jesse Curry held a small press conference on Sunday morning, November 24, before Lee Oswald was shot. The transcript includes the following passage:

> *Question:* Is Oswald right-handed?
> *Curry:* I don't know. I haven't seen him write. I mean, I haven't seen him do anything that would indicate whether he was right or left.   *(CE 2147)*

There is nothing to indicate why the reporter asked this question; surely it was not academic, but had some relation to the charges against Oswald. Was there reason to think that Oswald could not have committed the assassination if he was right-handed, or left-handed? In any case, the FBI also exhibited interest in the matter in an interview with Marina Oswald on December 3, 1963. She told the FBI that Oswald was right-handed. (*CE 1401*, p. 297)

Robert Oswald was interrogated at some length on this point when he appeared before the Commission on February 20, 1964. He asserted categorically that Oswald had been right-handed: "I would say without qualification . . . I have never known him to do anything left-handed. . . . He was instinctively a right-handed person. . . ." *(1H 293-294)* The immediate impetus for the close examination to which Robert was subjected may have been cryptic assertions by Marguerite Oswald, who had preceded him as a witness, that Oswald was left-handed, or that he might have been a left-handed rifleman. *(1H 163)* Even so, the significance of a determination one way or the other is never made clear and one can only wonder what inspired such interest and how it was relevant to Oswald's guilt or innocence. •

A clue may lie in a telephone message from the Aberdeen Proving Ground on April 6, 1964, addressed to a counsel for the Commission.

> There were three pieces in the scope examined by the BRL gunsmith. Two pieces were .015 inches thick, so placed as to elevate the scope with respect to the gun. One piece was .020 inches thick so placed as to point the scope leftward with respect to the gun. The gunsmith observed that the scope as we received it was installed as if for a left-handed man.   *(CE 2560)*

The Warren Commission, which was so preoccupied in February with Oswald's dominant hand, now had good reason to be concerned. If Oswald was right-handed—as Marina and Robert Oswald had insisted—and if the scope was mounted for a left-handed rifleman, on instruction, extremely serious doubt must arise with respect to the purchase and ownership of the Carcano rifle. This was not the only problem that arose with respect to the mounting of the scope, it will be recalled. As detailed in the Report *(WR 315-316)*, there was evidence that Oswald had had a scope mounted on a rifle in Irving; the matter was never resolved completely and, as discussed in a later chapter, has some earmarks of an impersonation designed to incriminate Oswald. With the message from Aberdeen, another dilemma arose. But now the Commission became silent on the subject of Oswald's right- or left-handedness; so far as can be seen, no step was taken to explore the implications of the left-handed mounting of the scope. It seems clear that the gunsmith who mounted the scope at Klein's Sporting Goods should have been interrogated and that it should have been established whether he did, in fact, mount the scope for a left-handed man and, if so, on whose instructions.

The impression that the scope was not suitable for use by a right-handed man is reinforced by the information that shims[7] had to be inserted to elevate it and move it to the left of the rifle before the weapon was utilized in tests to "determine the possibility of scoring hits with this weapon on a given target at a given distance under rapid-fire conditions." *(3H 444)*

It must be emphasized at once that these tests have not the slightest claim to being comparable with the performance credited to Oswald by the Warren Commission. The tests used three master riflemen whose skill was as superior to Oswald's as a chief surgeon's to an intern. In 1959 Oswald qualified as a marksman, the minimum classification used in the Marine Corps, scoring 191 on a scale of 190-250, after which he had had no target practice of significance and no proven practice with the Carcano rifle. This alone is sufficient to invalidate the tests as in any sense comparable with or indicative of the skill allegedly demonstrated by Oswald. In addition, the tests utilized stationary rather than moving targets. Each participant was told to take as much time as he wished with the first shot; it will occasion no surprise that they all hit the first target, but it should be borne in mind that the alleged assassin did not enjoy such an advantage.

In repudiating these tests a priori, it should be pointed out that experiments genuinely comparable to the feat ascribed to the accused assassin could easily have been conducted. It would have been necessary only to rope off the Book Depository area—as was done for the on-site tests—and to tow a car down Elm Street with dummies occupying the positions of the actual victims. Marksmen with the same general level of skill as Oswald's (when he last shot for record) could have been positioned at the sixth-floor window, and each one instructed to fire three shots at the dummies in the moving car. If no candidates with sufficiently mediocre ability as marksmen were available in the armed forces, surely volunteers would have flocked to Dallas to perform a service tó truth. Had that been done, the results of the tests would have been legitimate, and the scrupulousness which has been claimed by the Commission or on its behalf would have been demonstrated.

The tests actually conducted at Aberdeen remain supremely irrelevant as a measure of Oswald's rifle capability. The results are nevertheless significant in some respects.

The rifle tests are discussed in the Warren Report, in somewhat evasive terms *(WR 193-194)*, and in the testimony of Army Expert Ronald Simmons *(3H 441-451)*. Three master riflemen each fired two series of three shots, using the so-called assassination rifle with the telescopic sight. (One of the experts fired an extra series of three shots with iron sights.) Two of the master riflemen

---

7   A shim is a thin strip of metal, wood, or the like, for filling in, as for bringing one part in line with another.

completely failed to match the feat attributed to Oswald. The best of the three, Miller, got two hits out of three in each series, taking 4.6 and 5.15 seconds respectively. Staley got two hits out of three in 6.75 seconds, and then three out of three in 6.45 seconds. Hendrix got two hits out of three in each of his two series, taking 8.25 and 7.0 seconds respectively.

In the first series of 9 shots, the three experts missed a total of 3 shots or 33⅓ per cent. In the total of 18 shots, they missed 5 collectively, or more than 25 per cent.

RIFLE TEST RESULTS

	Alleged assassin November 22, 1963	*Army tests performed by three Master Riflemen on March 27, 1964*		
Markmanship rating	One point above the minimum to qualify as "marksman" on Marine Corps scale in 1959 with no known subsequent rifle practice	Rated as Masters by National Rifle Association (i.e., at top of scale extending above top Marine Corps marksmanship rank by two or more classes) and qualified for shooting competitions and Olympics		
Target	Moving car, receding from rifleman, moving on slight downgrade, from elevation of 60 feet	Three stationary silhouettes of upper body, on two-foot boards, aiming from 30-foot tower		
Range	180 to 265 feet	Targets at 175, 240, and 265 feet respectively		
Number of shots	Three	Two series of three shots each		
		First series		
		Hendrix	Staley	Miller
Firing time (in seconds)	Maximum of 5.6 seconds	8.25	6.75	4.60
		Second series		
		7.00	6.45	5.15
		Each of two series		
Results first shot	Hit upper back or neck	Hit / Hit	Hit / Hit	Hit / Hit
Results second shot	Missed, or hit Governor	Missed / Hit	Missed / Hit	Missed / Missed
Results third shot	Hit head	Hit / Missed	Hit / Hit	Hit / Hit

All three experts hit the first target (at a distance of 175 feet) on each of two series, after taking as much time as they wished to aim before firing. According to Simmons:

Simmons: We had to make an assumption here about the point of aim. It is quite likely that in fact each man was aiming at a different portion of the target—there were no markings on the target visible to the firer.

Eisenberg: Did I understand you just told the firers to aim at the target without referring to—

Simmons: Yes.

Eisenberg: There is an apparent crossline running darkly through that photograph.

Simmons: These lines were drawn in afterwards, in order for us to make some measurements from the actual impact point.   *(3H 445-446)*

Each of the experts missed the second target on their first try; Miller missed it on his second try as well. Each of them hit the third target on the first try; but one expert (Hendrix) missed it on the second attempt. Not one of the master riflemen got three-out-of-three in both series. Staley, who got three-out-of-three on his second attempt, took 6.45 seconds.

After testifying on the results achieved by the three master riflemen, Expert Simmons—virtually ignoring those results—told the Commission: "In order to achieve three hits, it would not be required that a man be an exceptional shot." *(3H 450)* A further basis for evaluating the expertise of this witness is found in the following passage of his testimony:

Eisenberg: Now, you have given us probabilities of hit with three variations of aiming error. You have selected these three variations in what manner, Mr. Simmons?

Simmons: These were actually the three values which were demonstrated in the experiment.

Eisenberg: But each of those values is associated with one target?

Simmons: Yes.

Eisenberg: However, you have applied them to all three targets?

Simmons: Yes.

Eisenberg: Did you have a special reason for doing that?

Simmons: No. We are victims of habit, and we tend to provide such information in parametric form.   *(3H 448)*

In other words, the "nil" error on the first target was applied in such a way as to reduce the probability of error on the second and third targets. By merging instead of separating three individual values, the fact that the probability of missing the second target ranged from 66 to 100 per cent is easily concealed.

The Commission did not take testimony from the three master riflemen but relied on the account of the tests given by Simmons on March 31, 1964. A month later, on May 1, 1964, Lieutenant-Colonel Allison G. Folsom of the U.S. Marine Corps was asked to testify, primarily to interpret and clarify abbreviations, test scores, and other entries on Oswald's Marine records. *(8H 304)* During the course of his deposition, Folsom evaluated Oswald's last recorded score of 191 in target shooting ("a low marksmanship rating") as that of a "rather poor shot." *(WR 191)*

Almost three months later, on July 24, 1964, testimony was taken from Major Eugene D. Anderson and Sergeant James A. Zahm, both of the U.S. Marine Corps. They reviewed Oswald's Marine marksmanship record (showing that he had last scored 191, or one point above the minimum to qualify for the lowest of three ratings) and the feat attributed to him on November 22.

Anderson and Zahm were informed of the details of the feat (distance from target, trajectory, speed of the car, etc.), but in soliciting their opinion, counsel did not include one piece of essential information: that the three shots were fired in only five and a half seconds. Even so, one marvels that they proceeded to opine that Oswald, whom for baffling reasons (and in contradiction of a Lieutenant-Colonel) they rated as "a good to excellent shot" and even an "excellent shot" *(WR 192)*, could easily have committed the assassination. I leave it to the reader to imagine the cross examination to which Anderson and Zahm or Simmons or the three master riflemen would have been subjected had Oswald been represented by a defense counsel.

The results of the tests all but rule out any possibility that Oswald fired all the shots at the Presidential car, but the Warren Commission has presented these results as an indication of the exact opposite conclusion. The Commission has solicited and relied upon opinions rendered by four government experts—FBI Expert Robert Frazier, Army Expert Simmons, and Marine Experts Anderson and Zahm. I am more impressed by the opinion of a civilian, Dean Andrews, which did not find its way into the Report. Andrews said:

> *I know good and well he did not* [kill the President]. *With that weapon, he couldn't have been capable of making three controlled shots in that short time.* [Italics added]   *(11H 330)*

A fuller account of Andrews' opinion will be found on page 376 of this book. His pragmatic assessment is more convincing than the irrelevant tests, the pronouncements belatedly solicited from government experts, and the abstruse mathematical calculations with their built-in errors. The conditions under which the rifle tests were conducted, the introduction of shims to correct the telescopic sight, and the unresolved questions related to the mounting of the scope—all these only reinforce the impression that the Commission indulged in self-deception in finding that Oswald had the capability to carry out the feat no less remote from his actual skill than a flight to the moon.[8]

---

8   De la Taille wrote in his article in *Science et Vie:* ". . . what was Oswald's rating as a marksman? Not very high, if one considers his military record. He was barely able to qualify as a sharpshooter once, by one point above the required minimum. Otherwise, he was always a marksman—the lowest class. . . . According to the National Rifle Association of America, shooters are classified into four groups: marksman, sharpshooter, expert, and master. Everyone is a marksman and with a little training any average rifleman manages frequently to be classified as a sharpshooter.

"Oswald was therefore in the low average . . . and if the precision of firing achieved on November 22 is already incompatible with the capacity of the Italian rifle, it is even more so with the capabilities of the shooter Oswald."

After discussing the adjustment of the scope on a rifle ("a long, delicate and, what is more, unstable operation") and the fact that the riflemen in the tests conducted for the Warren Commission placed the bullets too high and to the right of the target, De la Taille writes, "If it was already in that condition on November 22, Oswald is out of the question unless one conceives that extreme chance allowed him to fire precisely with a rifle that was shooting to the side of the target. . . . For Oswald, taking into account the angle at which he was shooting, there was a lateral displacement of the target of about 20 cms. Between the moment when Oswald pulled the trigger and the moment at which the bullet reached its goal, the target had moved 20 cms.

"One should therefore have pulled the trigger .13 seconds before President Kennedy's head reached the center of the scope. It amounts to a feat such as could be realized only by a crack shot with years of training behind him. . . . When one considers that military firing at mobile targets requires four-fold machine-gun mountings putting out tens of missiles a second, the firing being directed by automatic correctors, and this sometimes to place a bullet on the target, one will better assess Oswald's miracle."

The Peculiar Sling

Despite the superlatives with which the press greeted the Warren Report when it was finally released, the respect and wonder with which statistics were cited on the numbers of witnesses interviewed and exhibits collected and the like, and the general verdict that this investigation was unparalleled in scope and meticulous care, the fact remains that important mysteries remain unresolved. The problem of the sling on the rifle found in the Book Depository is a case in point.

The Report says that the sling consisted of two leather straps, one of which had a broad patch, which apparently had been inserted on the rifle and cut to length—not a standard rifle sling but a homemade one utilizing what appeared to be a musical instrument strap or the sling from a carrying case or camera bag. *(WR 553-554)*

Study of the Hearings and Exhibits yields only a little more information, mostly negative. We learn that Marina Oswald did not recognize the sling *(CE 1403)* and that Ruth Paine did not recall ever seeing a strap of that nature in her home or anywhere else: she could not identify the sling or suggest its source. *(3H 25)* FBI Expert Frazier testified that attempts to identify the sling had met with no success and that it probably would not be very helpful to a marksman using the rifle, since it was "too short, actually, to do more than put your arm through it. . . . It is rather awkward to wrap the forward hand into the sling in the normal fashion." *(3H 397)* Having said that much, Frazier then conceded to Commissioner McCloy that "the sling would tend to steady the aim, even in this crude form."

Little notice has been taken of the fact that in the notorious photographs of Oswald holding the rifle *(CE 133)* the rifle has a different sling. According to FBI Expert Shaneyfelt, the sling in the photograph:

> has the appearance of being a piece of rope that is tied at both ends, rather than a leather sling, and it is my opinion that it is a different sling than is presently on the rifle.   *(4H 289)*

One is led to assume, then, that Oswald improvised one sling and then another for this rifle and that he did so during a period of eight months. During at least three of those months (September 25 to November 22, 1963), according to the Warren Report, the rifle was not in Oswald's possession. At no time was he seen by *anyone* carrying the rifle from one place to another or using these slings which seemed clearly designed for carrying rather than as an aid in firing.

Is there a scrap of objective evidence to link the homemade leather sling with Oswald? The Commission has provided an avalanche of numbing detail on Oswald's life as a child and a man but has not told us where he obtained this rifle sling, or the rifle ammunition, or where he practiced shooting the rifle until he acquired supreme efficiency, or why this 40-inch rifle was dispatched by Klein's Sporting Goods to a customer who ordered a 36-inch rifle.

The person who made the sling did not go out and purchase the straps; he obtained them from some other articles and put them together as a substitute for a conventional rifle sling. If Oswald took the straps from articles such as a musical instrument (Oswald possessed none) or a camera or a carrying case, why are no straps missing from such articles in the possession of his widow or the authorities who have custody of them? Did he steal the straps from articles which belonged to someone else, at a place where he was employed or in the home of a friend or a relative? This should be easy enough to determine, since the theft would have taken place after the photograph was taken showing a different sling—March 31, 1963—and before the Oswalds left New Orleans on about September 25, 1963, after which the rifle was not in Oswald's possession.

Regrettably, the Warren Commission did not consider it necessary or worthwhile to seek more precise information about the rifle sling. It should not have been brushed aside as inconsequential, for it was a clue that might have opened a trail to a person or persons who had conspired with Oswald, or against him, in the assassination.

Ammunition for the Murder Rifle

Early press coverage from Dallas reported that police officials expected to trace the assassin's purchase of ammunition. According to a story in *The New York Times* on November 24, 1963:[9]

> Officers starting a canvass of . . . outlets observed that the odd-sized ammunition—a little smaller than ordinary .30-caliber—might provide an important clue. The assassination, they said, involved excellent marksmanship that could only have come from regular practice recently, and this in turn would have required sizable quantities of the special ammunition.

Later, serious objections were raised against the official theory of the crime · on the ground that ammunition for the alleged assassination rifle had not been manufactured since World War II and was notoriously unreliable and of poor quality.

When the Warren Report appeared, it presented no evidence that Oswald had purchased ammunition for this rifle (or for the revolver, for that matter), or evidence that Oswald had "excellent marksmanship," or evidence that he had engaged in "regular practice" with the rifle before the assassination. Yet it made certain assertions about the recency and reliability of the rifle ammunition:

> The ammunition used in the rifle was American ammunition *recently* made by the Western Cartridge Co., which manufactures such ammunition *currently*. In tests with the same kind of ammunition, experts fired Oswald's Mannlicher-Carcano rifle more than 100 times without any misfires. [Italics added]   *(WR 646)*

---

9 "Evidence Against Oswald Described As Conclusive," *The New York Times,* November 24, 1963, p. 2, col. 1.

The cartridge is readily available for purchase from mail-order houses, as well as *a few gun shops;* some 2 million rounds have been placed on sale in the United States. [Italics added]   *(WR 555)*

The information that the Western Cartridge Company ammunition was "recently made" and is being manufactured "currently" is not accompanied by a citation of its source, despite the fact that the claim of recency clashed with persistent, widespread objections that Carcano ammunition was old and unreliable.

Moreover, the claim stands in conflict with the Commission's own Exhibits, which include the following FBI report:

On March 23, 1964, Mr. R. W. Botts, District Manager, Winchester-Western Division, Olin Mathieson Chemical Corporation, Braniff Building, advised [that] the Western Cartridge Company, a division of Olin Industries, East Alton, Illinois, manufactured a quantity of 6.5 M/M Mannlicher-Carcano ammunition for the Italian Government during World War II. At the end of the war the Italian Carcano rifle, and no telling how much of this type ammunition, was sold to United States gun brokers and dealers and subsequently was distributed by direct sales to wholesalers, retailers, and individual purchasers.   *(CE 2694, p. 12)*

To investigate this startling contradiction between the Report and the FBI document, I wrote to the Western Cartridge Company on the chance that Mr. Botts was mistaken and the Report was accurate in its assertions.

An official of the Company replied in a letter of April 1965 that the ammunition had once been produced under a government contract but was no longer available. Further inquiry elicited a letter dated April 20, 1965 in which the manufacturer states frankly that the reliability of the ammunition still in circulation today is questionable.

I also attempted to obtain information from the Commission's legal staff about the basis for the assertion that the ammunition was recently and is still manufactured. The letter remains unanswered to this day.

From all this, it may be inferred that the statement in the Report is sheer fabrication, employed to rebut a serious criticism of the official theory when the evidence, in fact, sustains that criticism.

Clearly it is necessary to the Commission's conclusions to establish Oswald's purchase and possession of the ammunition. But the Report is silent. The Hearings, however, reveal that Marina Oswald told the FBI on December 16, 1963 that *"Oswald did not have any ammunition for the rifle* to her knowledge in either Dallas or New Orleans, and he did not speak of buying ammunition." [Italics added] *(CE 1403)* Yet when Marina Oswald was shown a 6.5 mm. cartridge during her testimony before the Commission on February 3, 1964, she then stated that it "seemed larger than Oswald's" and, on further questioning, that she had seen ammunition in a box "in New Orleans and on Neely Street." *(1H 119)* The Commission did not confront her with her earlier statement to the FBI or with other self-contradictions or inconsistencies which show a distinct and progressive tendency to incriminate Oswald.

That Oswald had possession of the alleged murder ammunition is, of course, implicit in the Report. But the evidence is preponderant against that inference because (1) Marina Oswald's testimony is unsupported and unreliable, and (2) the Commission has adduced no proof of purchase and omitted from its Report the negative evidence on that point.

Both the Dallas police and the FBI made unsuccessful attempts to establish Oswald's purchase of 6.5 rifle ammunition. Dallas Detective F. M. Turner made inquiries at the Irving Sports Shop and learned that ammunition of that type was not sold there. *(7H 226)* In March 1964 the FBI conducted a canvass of retail shops in the Dallas-Irving area without success. *(CE 2694)* The canvass turned up only two dealers who had ever handled Western Cartridge Company 6.5 mm. ammunition; both were certain that they had never seen Oswald or sold ammunition to him. One of the shops had moved into Dallas from another location (Carrollton, Texas) on November 1, 1963. Consequently, the other shop was the sole source from which Oswald could have purchased the ammunition in Dallas. The owner, Mr. Masen, had purchased "about ten boxes . . . early 1963," he told the FBI, and some of the cartridges had been reloaded with a soft hunting bullet. *(CE 2694)*

Since Masen did not sell ammunition to Oswald and since he did not purchase any by mail order, where did Oswald obtain the box of ammunition that his wife testified was in his possession when they lived on Neely Street?

Although the Report says nothing about Oswald's purchase and possession of the rifle ammunition, the Hearings manifest the Commission's anxiety about the abortive efforts to establish such a link. Questions put to FBI weapons expert Cortlandt Cunningham *(3H 479)* and to the owner of the Irving Sports Shop, Charles Greener *(11H 253),* indicate that the Commission even considered the possibility that Oswald had resorted to hand-loading his ammunition but had to abandon that notion as untenable because of the bulk and expense of the required equipment. FBI Expert Cunningham described hand-loading as "nothing more than taking components and by means of a press [making] your own cartridges." *(3H 479)* He confirmed that no evidence had been found in this case to suggest hand-loading and said, moreover, that the equipment needed for hand-loading was bulky and could not have been overlooked in the search of Oswald's personal effects. *(3H 479)*

Further devastating the Commission's conclusions is the fact that no rifle ammunition was found on Oswald's person at his arrest or among his possessions in Dallas or Irving, which were searched and seized the same day. *(CE 2003)* Ammunition is not sold by the dozen, like eggs, but in substantial quantity, generally in boxes of about a hundred. The same mail-order advertisement for Klein's Sporting Goods from which Oswald is said to have ordered the assassination rifle also offers Mauser ammunition in boxes of 130. (Curiously, that advertisement is not found anywhere in the 11 volumes of Exhibits, which include an abundance of documents far less germane to the crime.)

But only four 6.5 mm. cartridges enter into the Commission's case: three shells found at the sixth-floor window of the Book Depository, and one live bullet ejected from the rifle found on the same floor. The Commission insists that Oswald obtained, possessed, and loaded these four cartridges into the rifle and fired three at the President and the Governor, but it offers no evidence of such purchase or possession of the four cartridges or of the larger supply of ammunition in which they were presumably obtained.

The Commission's rationale seems to be that since Oswald used the bullets to shoot the President, it is entitled to assume that he obtained and possessed them. And since he obtained and possessed them, obviously he used them to shoot the President.

But this circular reasoning postulates an assassin who (1) obtained and exhausted a supply of ammunition, except for four cartridges which remained in his possession on the morning of the assassination; (2) covered his tracks so ingeniously that it was beyond the resources of the local and federal investigators to trace the source of the ammunition, or to trace expended shells from the largest part of the supply of cartridges; and (3) loaded the remaining four cartridges into a clip-fed rifle which can hold seven, firing three times with such phenomenal skill as to make the fourth cartridge superfluous.

The alternative is that this singular assassin squandered more than $20 of his meager earnings for a rifle but—unable or unwilling to spend a small additional sum for ammunition—stole, borrowed, or found on the street five cartridges that just happened to fit the weapon; and that those five cartridges sufficed, from March through November 1963, for dry runs, attempted murder, and successful assassination.

No one would entertain such notions seriously. Yet the Commission has strayed dangerously close to absurdity with its statement that:

> . . . examination of the cartridge cases found on the sixth floor of the Depository Building established that they had been previously loaded and ejected from the assassination rifle, which would indicate that Oswald practiced operating the bolt.　　　　　　　　　　　　　*(WR 192-193)*

The alleged practice with the bolt took place, according to Marina Oswald, some six months before the assassination, when the Oswalds were living in New Orleans. *(WR 192)* The Commission evidently does not shrink from elevating nonsense to the plane of logic by offering an explanation based on limiting Oswald's supply of ammunition to five cartridges.

Nor does the Commission shrink from misrepresentation. The examination did *not* establish that the shells had been loaded and ejected previously from the assassination rifle, as the Report asserts. The FBI informed the Commission in a letter signed by J. Edgar Hoover that:

> . . . the extractor and ejector marks on C6 as well as on C7, C8, and C38 did not possess sufficient characteristics for identifying the weapon which produced them. There are also three sets of marks on the base of this cartridge which were not found on C7, C8, C38, or any of the numerous tests obtained from the C14 rifle. It was not possible to determine what produced these marks. . . . Another set of follower marks were found on C8. . . . These marks were not identified with the C14 rifle. . . .　　　　　*(CE 2968)*

In its predisposition to prove one thesis, the Commission has refused to examine the real implications of the evidence and has (1) falsified the age of the ammunition and the period of its manufacture; (2) withheld the failure of attempts to establish the purchase and possession of ammunition by the accused; (3) misrepresented the nature of the markings on the cartridge shells; and (4) compromised the credibility of its conclusions and the impartiality of its motives.

The net result of an investigation advertised as unprecedented in diligence and scope is a great abundance of microscopic and often irrelevant detail but no fragment of independent, credible evidence to establish Oswald's purchase or possession of the ammunition used in the infamous crime of which he is accused.

The Commission's failure to incriminate him is a grave interruption in the so-called chain of evidence; it poses a serious dilemma which is only compounded by the Commission's resort to outright fabrication.

The Ammunition Clip

After the assassination, skepticism about the police case against Oswald rested in part on the rapidity of the shots. One critic wrote:[10]

How could the gun in question, a Model 1938, 6.5-mm. bolt-action rifle, be operated quickly enough to fire three shots into the President's car within five seconds? The rapidity of the shots led most observers at the scene of the assassination to assume that an automatic weapon had been used. A Mannlicher-Carcano must be laboriously loaded with one shell at a time into the chamber before firing, unless a charger, or clip, is first loaded with six cartridges and then inserted into the action of the rifle, thus permitting more rapid firing. *There is no indication from Dallas authorities that the alleged murder weapon was equipped with such a charger,* in which case it would have been impossible for the assassin to snap off three shots at the President and Governor Connally in such rapid succession. [Italics added]

This commentary seemed well-founded and suggested that a number of questions would have to be answered fully and precisely:

(1) Did the man who fired the Carcano rifle use an ammunition clip?

(2) If so, where was it found and by whom?

(3) The Dallas police and District Attorney Henry Wade were excoriated in editorials and by responsible leaders and organizations for their unrestrained public statements about the evidence against the accused, including inaccurate and invented evidence. How is it that police spokesmen and Wade never mentioned any ammunition clip?

(4) What is the evidence linking the ammunition clip, if one was found, to Lee Harvey Oswald?

10   Eric Norden, "The Death of a President," *The Minority of One,* January 1964, pp. 16-23.

In subsequent months, numerous articles appeared in news magazines purporting to put an end to "nagging rumors" and countering criticism of the official case on the basis of leaks and briefings from "authoritative sources," generally thought to include the FBI and the Warren Commission. In discussing the rapidity of the shots, not one of these articles mentioned any ammunition clip. They merely said that tests with the rifle had shown that it was possible to fire the weapon as rapidly as the accused assassin was said to have done.

It was only when the Warren Report was issued in September 1964 that we learned that "when the rifle was found in the Texas School Book Depository Building it contained a clip." *(WR 555)* A footnote cites the testimony of Captain Fritz *(4H 205)* and Lieutenant Day *(4H 258)* as authority for this assertion.

Yet there is not one word on those pages about an ammunition clip, nor is there anything elsewhere in the testimony of Fritz or Day or other witnesses which establishes that an ammunition clip was found at all. The assertion in the Report that the rifle found in the Book Depository contained a clip is absolutely unsupported by direct evidence or testimony.

Lieutenant Day stated elsewhere in his testimony that when he took the rifle to his office, he dictated to his secretary that:

> . . . when the bolt was opened one live round was in the barrel. No prints are on the live round. Captain Fritz and Lieutenant Day opened the barrel. Captain Fritz has the live round. Three spent hulls were found under the window. They were picked up by Detective Sims and witnessed by Lieutenant Day and Studebaker. The clip is stamped "SMI, 9 x 2." *(4H 260)*

This mention of the clip by Lieutenant Day is not sufficient to establish the implied discovery of the clip or its location when discovered, especially when the document purportedly dictated by Day on Friday afternoon, November 22, 1963 is not included among the Exhibits.[11] No witness who gave testimony about the search of the Book Depository or the discovery of the rifle mentioned an ammunition clip, either in the rifle or elsewhere on the sixth floor. Day testified only that the clip had certain letters and numbers stamped on it (his description differing from the official one, "SMI 952"). He was not asked and he did not volunteer any information about where the clip was found or that it was found at all.

Other references to an ammunition clip are found in the testimony of FBI Experts Latona and Frazier. Latona told the Commission that he did not succeed in developing "any prints at all on the weapon . . . the complete weapon, all parts. . . ." *(4H 23)* He added explicitly that he had found no prints on the ammunition clip. The same negative findings are recorded in an FBI report. *(CE 2003,* p. 135) It is noteworthy that no prints were found on the ammunition clip despite the statement in the Report that "there is no evidence that Oswald wore gloves or that he wiped prints off the rifle." *(WR 647)*

The Commission took little interest in the absence of prints on the clip, but

---

11 Detective C. N. Dhority reported that at about 9 p.m. Friday Lieutenant Day showed him the 6.5 rifle and that he "wrote a description from the rifle." *(CE 2003,* p. 195) Why should Dhority record a description when Day had already done so hours before, and why is Dhority's "description" also omitted from the Exhibits?

it cannot be assumed that the reason given for the lack of prints on the surface of the rifle—"poor quality of the metal and wooden parts" *(WR 647)*—applies automatically to the clip. It is not an integral part of the rifle but a separate accessory of different composition and manufacture. If Oswald did not wear gloves or wipe his prints off the rifle and its parts, the Commission must explain the absence of prints on the clip before it can prove that he handled or used it, as the Report implies.

FBI weapons expert Frazier testified at some length about the ammunition clip, explaining the bolt action and the clip-feed mechanism and describing the extraction and ejection mechanism by which the clip feeds bullets into the chamber of the rifle. *(3H 397-398)* However, neither counsel nor Frazier initiated any discussion of the mechanism which comes into play after the last cartridge moves from the clip into the chamber, leaving the clip empty. The significance of this is that the ammunition clip used in this kind of rifle—when it has fed the last cartridge into the chamber—is normally ejected automatically from the weapon and falls nearby, much like the shells ejected when the rifle is fired. I have seen this demonstrated on a replica of the Carcano. If an ammunition clip was used in firing the rifle found in the Book Depository, it must have been empty, since the single, live round was ejected from the chamber and no other unexpended ammunition was found in the Book Depository. The clip should therefore have been ejected, falling on the floor somewhere near the southeast corner window. If it was not ejected, it may have been defective or deformed in such a way that it remained stuck in the weapon—and that in itself should have been the subject of comment by Frazier or other witnesses. No such comment was made.

Another salient point arises in the following passage of Frazier's testimony:

Eisenberg: Could you pull out the clip and explain any markings you find on it?
Frazier: The only markings are the manufacturer's markings, "SMI," on the base of the clip, and a number, 952. The significance of that number I am not aware of. It could be a part number or a manufacturer's code number.   *(3H 398)*

Frazier's reply should be viewed together with the statement in the Report that "the rifle probably was sold without a clip; however, the clip is commonly available." *(WR 555)* The Commission—celebrated in a hundred different ways for leaving no stone unturned in its search for all the facts—tells us that the rifle *probably* was sold without a clip. Why should this information be indefinite? Mr. Waldman and Mr. Scibor of Klein's Sporting Goods testified well after Frazier. They should have been asked whether or not an ammunition clip had accompanied the mail-order rifle. If the answer was no, an attempt should have been made to trace the clip and to determine by whom, and to whom, it was sold. As will be seen in a moment, the clip was not a common size or style. That might have facilitated tracing. However, no attempt was made to determine the manufacturer, the meaning of the markings, or the retail purchase of the clip—information which might well have had relevance to the nature of the crime and the identity of the assassin.

That the clip ostensibly found in the rifle is not a standard one is seen in Frazier's reply to an enigmatic question.

Eisenberg: Is there any reason that you can think of why someone might call that a five-shot clip?

Frazier: No, sir, unless they were unfamiliar with it. There is an area of confusion in that a different type of rifle shooting larger ammunition, such as a 30.06 or a German Mauser rifle, uses five-shot clips, and the five-shot clip is the common style or size of clip, whereas this one actually holds six.

(3H 398)

Eisenberg's question surely was not academic. Someone must have described the clip as a five-shot clip, although nothing found in the testimony or exhibits provides a basis for his question. It is another coincidence, one supposes, that someone has mistaken a six-shot clip for a clip suitable to a Mauser, just as the Carcano rifle was mistaken for a Mauser.

Boggs: How many shots in the weapon? Five?

McCloy: The clip takes six itself. You can put a seventh in the chamber. It could hold seven, in other words. But the clip is only a six-shot clip.

Boggs: Was the weapon fully loaded at the time of the assassination?

McCloy: I don't know how many shells—three shells were picked up.

Eisenberg: Off the record.

(Discussion off the record)

McCloy: Back on the record.

Eisenberg: Mr. Frazier, turning back to the scope. . . .   *(3H 411)*

What was discussed here that could not be discussed *on* the record? Perhaps the peculiar fact that three shells and one live round were recovered but that no rifle ammunition was found on Oswald or among his possessions. This indicated that the rifle had *not* been fully loaded at the time of the assassination but had held only four cartridges instead of seven. Thus, it conjures up a picture of a most implausible assassin, who set out to kill the President armed with only four bullets, his last and only ones at that. Such an assassin would have had to be certain that he would hit his victim or victims without missing, and that his escape was guaranteed, so that there would be no need to shoot his way out of the Book Depository.

If Oswald entertained such sublime confidence in his own marksmanship, in spite of his record, he should have been placed into a straightjacket instead of handcuffs; and the chief of police and district attorney of Dallas should have been heralding his dementia instead of his unquestionable sanity.

Appraisal of the Known Facts

It is inescapable that if no ammunition clip was used neither Oswald nor the world's champion rifleman could have fired the Carcano three times in five and a half seconds. If there was no clip, Oswald was no lone assassin. The clip must therefore have impeccable credentials and absolute authenticity.

What is the status of the ammunition clip described in the Warren Report and pictured in the Exhibits? *(CE 574-575)* The assertion that the clip was in the rifle found in the Book Depository is completely unsupported by testimony or documents.[12] The citations in the footnote are specious. There are no contemporaneous references to any ammunition clip, or references at any time prior to the Warren Report. No link between the clip and Oswald has been established—by purchase, possession, fingerprints, or other methods.

Few people would be ready to convict a man of murder on the basis of such incomplete investigation or such a dishonest presentation of "evidence." Those who would not send a living man to his death on such a basis must ask themselves whether Oswald should be assigned to history stigmatized as an assassin on grounds that would be inadequate if he were still alive.

The Palmprint on the Rifle

We learn from the Warren Report *(WR 122-123)* that a few minutes after the discovery of the rifle in the Book Depository, Lieutenant J. C. Day examined it with a magnifying glass and later applied fingerprint powder to the side of the metal housing near the trigger, noticing traces of two prints. [Neither Day nor any other police officer seems to have checked the rifle when it was discovered for signs—such as traces of fresh gunpowder inside the barrel—indicating that the weapon had actually been fired that day; FBI Expert Robert Frazier, who examined the rifle early the next morning, when asked if there was metal fouling in the barrel, replied, "I did not examine it for that." *(3H 395)*] At 11:45 p.m. on Friday, November 22, the rifle was released to the FBI, and on Saturday morning it was examined at the FBI Laboratory in Washington, D.C., by FBI fingerprint expert Sebastian F. Latona. Latona told the Commission that when he

---

12   A former assistant counsel who asked that his name not be disclosed told me over the telephone that the footnote (to the Report's assertion that an ammunition clip was in the rifle when it was found) was indeed erroneous. He was unable to cite testimony or documents substantiating this assertion. But he was not perturbed: he believed it possible that three shots could have been fired in five and a half seconds even without a clip. If several cartridges were inserted in the space provided to house a clip, he suggested, the cartridges would still feed automatically into the chamber, because the rifle contained a spring while the clip did not.

Nothing in the literature suggests such an outlandish possibility. Cartridges must be inserted into the chamber manually, a time-consuming operation that would rule out three shots in only five and a half seconds, or they must be placed into an ammunition clip which would feed them automatically and rapidly into the chamber. Moreover, if the counsel's theory *was* viable, it would be all the more disturbing that the Warren Commission's evidence includes an unauthenticated ammunition clip which one had been led to believe was indispensable for the perpetration of the crime within the specified time period. It is no answer to say, when it is pointed out that the presence of the ammunition clip in the rifle found in the Book Depository is not supported by evidence, that the ammunition clip is not, after all, essential to the Commission's theory of the crime. The answer needed is whether the ammunition clip can be authenticated, and why the Commission has put the clip forward as verified evidence without first properly verifying its discovery and the chain of possession. This answer is needed all the more when the best available information indicates that an ammunition clip is indispensable to the alleged assassin's ability to fire three shots in about five and a half seconds, and that ability in turn is indispensable to the Commission's conclusion that Oswald was the lone assassin.

received the rifle, "the area where prints were visible was protected by cello-phane." He examined these prints "as well as photographs of them which the Dallas police had made" but concluded they were valueless. Latona then pro-cessed the complete weapon but developed no identifiable prints. "He stated that the poor quality of the wood and the metal would cause the rifle to absorb moisture from the skin, thereby making a clear print unlikely."

But, the Report next informs us, Lieutenant Day of the Dallas Police had lifted a palmprint from the underside of the gun barrel before surrendering the rifle to the FBI just before midnight. "The lifting had been so complete in this case that there was no trace of the print on the rifle itself when it was examined by Latona" nor was there "any indication that the lift had been performed." Nevertheless, "Day, on the other hand, believed that sufficient traces of the print had been left on the rifle barrel." Day therefore did not release the lifted print until November 26, when he was told to send everything to the FBI. The lifted print arrived at the FBI Laboratory on November 29, 1963 and was identified as that of Lee Harvey Oswald's right palm.

The Report then assures skeptics that they have no cause for suspecting the evidence was fabricated: "The print's positive identity as having been lifted from the rifle was confirmed by FBI Laboratory tests which established that the ad-hesive material bearing the print also bore impressions of the same irregularities that appeared on the barrel of the rifle."

This is very soothing, until one examines the testimony and documents. For such scrutiny raises considerable doubt about the actual authenticity of the palmprint, the role of the Dallas police and of Lieutenant Day in particular, and the purposes and competence of the Warren Commission; this evidence shows that if the palmprint is genuine, it is genuine against all the odds.

The Vanished Traces

The primary problem is how the traces of the lifted print disappeared between Dallas and Washington, although the print was under the wooden stock of the rifle and could not be disturbed unless the weapon was disassembled. Day testi-fied that when he released the rifle to the FBI at 11:45 p.m. on Friday, he thought that "the print on the gun . . . still remained on there. . . . There were traces of ridges still on the gun barrel." *(4H 261-262)* In fact, when the rifle arrived at the FBI Laboratory, there was no trace whatever of a print or of the lifting of a print.

The Warren Commission made no attempt to ascertain how the traces of the print could have vanished so completely. The need for such an inquiry should have been obvious from the testimony of FBI hair-and-fiber expert Paul Stombaugh. Stombaugh told the Commission on April 3, 1964 that he had examined the rifle when it arrived on Saturday morning, *before* it was examined for fingerprints:

> I noticed immediately upon receiving the gun that this gun had been dusted for latent fingerprints prior to my receiving it. Latent fingerprint powder was all over the gun. . . .   *(4H 81)*

If the fingerprint powder was "all over the gun" on its exterior—testifying
to the care with which it had been transported from Dallas to Washington—it
is almost impossible to understand how the same fingerprint powder and the
dried ridges could have disappeared from the gun barrel under the stock, which
provided secure protection against any disturbance.

Absence of Other Evidence

FBI Expert Latona testified that when he received the rifle he noted an area
where traces of prints had been protected by cellophane. He had also received
photographs of those same prints, located on the exterior of the rifle.

In the case of the latent palmprint under the stock, not only was there no
trace of the print or the fingerprint powder, there was no cellophane, no photograph, and no verbal or written notification by Lieutenant Day calling attention to it.

What explanation was given for these peculiar omissions? Lieutenant Day
explained that he had taken the rifle to the Dallas police building and had tried
to bring out the two prints he had seen on the side of the weapon at the Book
Depository.

> *Day:* They were still unclear. Due to the roughness of the metal, I photo-
> graphed them rather than try to lift them. I could also see a trace of a print
> on the side of the barrel that extended under the woodstock. I started to
> take the woodstock off and noted traces of a palmprint near the firing end
> of the barrel. . . . On the bottom side of the barrel which was covered by
> the wood, I found traces of a palmprint. I dusted these [traces] and tried
> lifting them, the prints, with scotch tape in the usual manner. A faint palm-
> print came off.
>
> I could still see traces of the print under the barrel and was going to
> try to use photography to bring off or bring out a better print. About this
> time I received instructions from the chief's office to go no further with the
> processing, it was to be released to the FBI for them to complete. . . .
>
> *Belin:* Did you do anything with the other prints or partial prints that you
> said you thought you saw?
>
> *Day:* I photographed them only. I did not try to lift them.   *(4H 260-261)*

In response to another question Day said that he had taken the photographs
of the partial prints on the exterior of the rifle at about 8 p.m. He had already
explained that he did not photograph the latent palmprint because of orders
from Chief Curry "to go no further with the processing." But in an FBI interview *(CE 3145)* Day said that he received those orders from Curry *shortly
before midnight.*

Apparently, then, Day had almost four hours available after taking photographs of the exterior prints and before receiving Curry's order to suspend his
work of examining the evidence, yet he did not photograph the palmprint.

Moreover, as already mentioned, he did not cover the latent print with cellophane, because, he said, he saw no reason for wrapping the print with any protective covering "since it was protected by the woodstock when fully assembled

and . . . it was not necessary to use . . . protective coating as it would have been on the exposed prints." *(CE 3145)*

The Cart Before the Horse

Here is the testimony of FBI Expert Latona on a pertinent question: Which usually comes first, the photograph or the lift?

> *Eisenberg:* Is it normal to take a photograph of a print before it is lifted?
> *Latona:* If it is fairly visible, yes. . . . The purpose of the lift is simply to insure the probability of getting a good record of the print, because a lot of times when you photograph a print, you have to go through the process of having it developed and then printed and at the same time by lifting it you may, that would be an additional security that you are getting the best results. Then you take your choice as to which result turns out best. . . . Primarily our recommendation in the FBI is simply every procedure to photograph and then lift.   *(4H 41)*

That the FBI recommendation in every procedure is first to photograph and then to lift becomes all the more interesting when we learn from Lieutenant Day that he attended "an advanced latent-print school conducted in Dallas by the Federal Bureau of Investigation." *(4H 250)* Day learned his lesson well so far as the exterior prints were concerned; those he photographed, then covered with protective cellophane. Indeed, Day admitted that "it was his customary practice to photograph fingerprints in most instances prior to lifting them." *(CE 3145)*

The evidence does not provide any satisfactory reason, from Day or any other source, for his failure to follow his customary practice in the case of the palmprint on the rifle barrel.

The Contemporaneous Record

Against all the odds, Lieutenant Day neglected every possible procedure by which proof would have been provided for the existence of the palmprint on the rifle barrel on the day that he claimed to have found and lifted the print. The rifle then went to the Washington FBI for scientific examination. It was returned to the Dallas police (the return was their precondition for releasing the weapon in the first instance) on November 24, 1963. Presumably the FBI notified the Dallas police on returning the rifle that the FBI had been unsuccessful in developing or identifying any print whatever on that weapon.

At that point, Day should have been spurred to action, for on Friday night he already believed that the latent palmprint he had lifted was that of Lee Harvey Oswald. Yet he did nothing further with the latent palmprint until November 26, 1963, when all the physical evidence was transferred—this time permanently—to the Washington FBI. (No one has explained why the lift of the palmprint did not arrive until November 29, whereas the other prints—from cartons in the Book Depository—arrived and were examined on November 27.)

After this list of frustrated opportunities to establish a contemporaneous record of the lifted palmprint, it will come as no surprise that no witness can corroborate the physical act of the lifting of the print. Day told the FBI that "he had no assistance when working with the prints on the rifle, and he and he alone did the examination and the lifting of the palmprint from the underside of the barrel." *(CE 3145)*

Did Day at least *tell* anyone that he had made the lift and had tentatively identified the print as matching that of Lee Harvey Oswald? He claimed that he told two people—Chief Curry and Captain Fritz. Day could not remember the exact time at which he had identified the print as Oswald's or the exact time at which he advised Curry and Fritz of his identification, but it *was* before 11:45 p.m., when he released the rifle to FBI Agent Vincent E. Drain. (It is hard to understand why Day—having neglected to photograph the print or place any protective covering on it—did not at least tell Drain verbally that he had found it and tentatively identified it as that of the prime suspect.)

Is there any indication that Fritz or Curry was aware of the existence or tentative identification of the latent palmprint sometime before midnight on Friday, or during the next two days? During that period, both Curry and Fritz were reeling off an abundance of information—whether true or false—to the television cameras and microphones,[13] yet neither ever mentioned the incriminating palmprint (see transcripts, *CEs 2141-2173*). It was as if Day had told them nothing of what he said (though much later) he *had* told them.

Oddly enough, the first public mention of Oswald's palmprint on the rifle came from District Attorney Henry Wade at his Sunday night press conference (of which Mark Lane has said that Wade was not guilty of a single accuracy).

The Chicken or the Egg?

The question is, where did Wade learn about the palmprint? When he testified on June 8, 1964 he said that Captain Fritz had told him on Friday night that "they had a palmprint or a fingerprint of Oswald on the underside of the rifle and I don't know whether it was on the trigger guard or where it was but I knew that was important, I mean, to put the gun in his possession." *(5H 220)* However, Wade did not mention the palmprint in his many television interviews on Friday night and Saturday *(CEs 2142, 2169-2173)*, even when he was asked by the reporters if fingerprints had been found on the rifle. He waited until the Sunday night press conference, of which the Warren Report states: "The police refused to furnish Wade with additional details of the case. Wade nonetheless proceeded to hold a lengthy formal press conference that evening." *(WR 236)*

If Wade, Fritz, and Curry knew about a palmprint on the underside of the rifle as early as Friday night, all three of them exercised extraordinary self-restraint in regard to this important clue, while liberally advertising other items of alleged evidence together with the conclusions they had already reached.

---

13 J. Edgar Hoover told the Commission *(5H 115)* that he had had to send a special emissary to Chief Curry to express concern about the incessant and promiscuous statements concerning the evidence being made by police spokesmen.

Nevertheless, the Commission made no serious effort to establish contemporaneous proof of the palmprint's existence.

The Authenticity of the Palmprint

The problem here is not whether the print was Oswald's but whether it was lifted from the rifle. Here is a passage from the testimony of FBI Expert Sebastian Latona.

Eisenberg: Now, Mr. Latona, as I understand it, on November 23, therefore, the FBI had not succeeded in making an identification of a fingerprint or palmprint on the rifle, but several days later by virtue of the receipt of this lift, which did not come with the weapon originally, the FBI did succeed in identifying a print on Exhibit 139?

Latona: That is right.

Eisenberg: Which may explain any inconsistent or apparently inconsistent statements, which I believe appeared in the press, as to an identification?

Latona: We had no personal knowledge of any palmprint having been developed on the rifle. The only prints that we knew of were the fragmentary prints which I previously pointed out had been indicated by the cellophane on the trigger guard. There was no indication on this rifle as to the existence of any other prints. The print which indicates it came from the underside of the gun barrel, evidently the lifting had been so complete that there was nothing left to show any marking on the gun itself as to the existence of such—even an attempt on the part of anyone to process the rifle.

(4H 24)

Eisenberg: So that you personally, Mr. Latona, did not know anything about a print being on the rifle which was identifiable until you received, actually received the lift, Exhibit 637?

Latona: On the twenty-ninth of November.

Eisenberg: Seven days after the assassination. And in the intervening period, correspondingly, the FBI had no such knowledge?

Latona: As far as I know.

Eisenberg: Mr. Latona, could you tell us what portion of the palm of Lee Harvey Oswald you identified that print as being?

Latona: Yes. Here again I have a photograph that will show the approximate area involved, which is the ulnar side of the lower portion of the palm . . . down near the base of the palm toward the wrist . . . the right palm.

Eisenberg: As it was in the case of the paper bag, Exhibit 142?

Latona: Yes, sir.

Eisenberg: Could you display that photograph, please? This is a photograph which you took of the inked print which was furnished to you by the Dallas office? . . . This photograph shows a red circle around the portion which you identified—

Latona: That is right.

Eisenberg: As being the latent found on the lift, is that right?

(Discussion off the record.)

Latona: Yes.

(4H 24-25)

Latona then proceeded to compare photographs of the latent print lifted from the rifle by Lieutenant Day and the inked print taken of Oswald's right palm—"made on purpose for purposes of recording the ridges." *(4H 26-27)* Latona enumerated no less than 12 points of identity between the lift and the inked print. No questions were asked. (I shall return to this matter soon.)

Latona gave that testimony on April 2, 1964. Lieutenant Day testified three weeks later, on April 22, 1964, at which time he recounted the sequence of events on the day of the assassination and his own actions—or non-actions—which had resulted improbably in the *de facto* concealment for seven days of the existence of the lifted palmprint. Lieutenant Day was not cross-examined nor was there any evidence that the Warren Commission entertained any skepticism about his strange story.

Moreover, the Commission made no attempt at that time to ascertain from Latona or any other source whether there was any way to authenticate the claim that the palmprint had been lifted from the rifle barrel. Of necessity, the Dallas police had come under *some* suspicion generally—after all, Oswald had been shot to death while in police custody, by a police hanger-on, and many aspects of the Dallas authorities' handling of the case appeared suspicious. And here, in Day's incredible account of the lifting of the palmprint, was a case of possible fabrication of prima-facie evidence against the accused by his custodians.

The Warren Commission knew that the rifle had been returned to the Dallas police on November 24, and had remained in their hands until November 26, 1963. The Commission knew that a palmprint identified as that of Oswald's right hand had been found on a carton in the Book Depository. The Commission knew that it had only Day's word and no corroboration from any source, in testimony or documents, of the authenticity of the lift of the palmprint from the rifle barrel. In his testimony, Latona volunteered no information to confirm that the print had been lifted from the rifle—he merely identified the lifted print as Oswald's. No witness volunteered or was asked to provide any theory to account for the disappearance of all traces of the lifted print between Dallas and Washington.

The salient problem for the Commission to resolve, then, was whether the palmprint could have been or was in fact faked. At no time before September 1, 1964 did the Commission appear even to consider that question—although all the so-called hard evidence against Oswald which came from or through the Dallas police would have had to be re-evaluated for evidence of fabrication had the Commission determined at any early stage that the lifted palmprint was indeed suspect.

On September 1, 1964, when the Commission first showed awareness of the delinquency apparent in the matter, its conclusions were long since formulated and its Report was almost ready to go to press. On that very late date the Commission wrote to the FBI requesting certain additional information about the lifted print (the actual letter does not appear in the Exhibits).

On September 4, 1964, J. Edgar Hoover replied, stating that the palmprint lift had been compared with the assassination rifle in the FBI Laboratory, and that the laboratory examiners had positively identified the lift as having come from the assassination rifle on the basis of a comparison of irregularities on the surface of the metal of the barrel with the impressions of those irregularities as shown in the lift. *(CE 2637)* The authentication was obtained not in sworn testimony, but in a letter, and no inquiries were made to determine whether those "irregularities" could have been imposed or superimposed on the lift.

Obviously, the authenticity of the lift cannot be taken as proved unless the possibility of the imposition of the rifle markings can be ruled out. The possibility of fabrication clearly still exists—and becomes all the more apparent on returning to Latona's testimony and his 12 points of identity between the lift and the inked palmprint.

An arrested person having his fingerprints and palmprints taken holds his inked hand flat, on a police record form. A person who handles a rifle curls his hand around the barrel. The curving of the hand would almost certainly, it seems to me, distort the lines and loops so that the resulting print would differ markedly from a print made by the flat of the hand.

Nothing in Latona's testimony suggests that the lifted palmprint had any characteristics indicating that the print was made by a curved hand. On the contrary, Latona found 12 points of identity between the lift and a palmprint made by a hand in flat position.

The photographs of the latent or inked palmprints in the Commission's Exhibits are practically useless to the researcher for the purpose of seeking differences, or similarities; they are dark, blurred, and unclear. *(CE 638-640)*

If answers to all the outstanding questions were supplied, they might remove the last cause for suspicion of fabrication and show beyond doubt that the lifted print was authentic. Be that as it may, how is it possible to justify the way in which the Warren Commission refused to ask the questions which demanded investigation, and then finally at the eleventh hour before the Report was issued accepted as conclusive proof a form of evidence which remains questionable?

Was the Commission concerned to rule out fabrication of evidence offered against the alleged assassin or concerned only to rule out the appearance of fabrication? To that question, at least, the answer is crystal clear.

It should be added that Burt Griffin, former assistant counsel to the Commission, recently was asked during a public discussion of the Warren Report whether, if the Dallas police or the FBI had forged evidence, it would have been possible to detect the forgery. Griffin replied haltingly, "It would be very, very difficult." (WBAI-New York, radio broadcast December 30, 1966 of the Theater for Ideas forum of September 30, 1966.)

The Rifle in the Closet

Of the hundreds of witnesses who gave testimony to the Warren Commission and the thousands who were interviewed by federal investigators, only one person other than Marina Oswald ever claimed to have seen the alleged assassination rifle under circumstances suggesting that Oswald possessed it. That person was Jeanne De Mohrenschildt.

Here is how the Warren Report describes the incident in question:

In connection with the relations between Oswald and De Mohrenschildt, the Commission has considered testimony concerning an event which occurred shortly after Oswald shot at General Walker.

The De Mohrenschildts came to Oswald's apartment on Neely Street for the first time on the evening of April 13, 1963, apparently to bring an Easter gift for the Oswald child. Mrs. De Mohrenschildt testified that while Marina Oswald was showing her the apartment, she saw a rifle with a scope in a closet. Mrs. De Mohrenschildt then told her husband, in the presence of the Oswalds, that there was a rifle in the closet.

Mrs. De Mohrenschildt testified that "George, of course, with his sense of humor—Walker was shot at a few days ago, within that time. He said, 'Did you take a pot shot at Walker by any chance?' "

At that point, Mr. De Mohrenschildt testified, Oswald "sort of shriveled, you see, when I asked this question . . . made a peculiar face . . . [and] changed the expression on his face" and remarked that he did target shooting.

Marina Oswald testified that the De Mohrenschildts came to visit a few days after the Walker incident and that when De Mohrenschildt made his reference to Oswald's possibly shooting at Walker, Oswald's "face changed . . . he almost became speechless."   (WR 282-283)

From those carefully selected bits of testimony no one would suspect that Marina Oswald and the De Mohrenschildts gave completely contradictory versions of the episode, nor that the account which the Commission chose to believe—that of the De Mohrenschildts—is flawed by enough faulty logic as to make their story highly suspect. However, their account may not be illogical after all if (as discussed in a later chapter) Marina Oswald's story of Oswald's implication in the attempted shooting of General Walker is nothing more than a crude and cruel fiction.

The first reference to the incident is found in a report of an FBI interview of Marina Oswald on December 11, 1963. (CE 1403, pp. 776-777) According to the FBI report, Marina Oswald said on that date that during Mrs. De Mohrenschildt's visit to the Neely Street apartment she had shown her "a rifle which Oswald had bought" and that "this rifle was standing in a corner or on a shelf in the house on Neely."

The FBI agents then questioned Marina Oswald further about the alleged attempt by Oswald to shoot General Walker on the night of Wednesday, April 10, 1963. According to the FBI report:

Marina said she had asked Oswald when he returned home on the night of the attempted assassination what he had done with the rifle because she was worried lest he had left it somewhere where it would be found. Oswald had said he had *buried the rifle in the ground* far from the actual spot of the shooting. . . .

She recalls Oswald returned to the Neely Street home with the rifle wrapped in a raincoat *on the Sunday following the night of the assassination attempt.*

> Marina said that a few days after the assassination attempt, George De Mohrenschildt was in their home at Neely Street and made a joking remark to Oswald to the effect, "How is it that you missed General Walker?" . . . Oswald . . . visibly paled. . . . She does not know why De Mohrenschildt made this remark other than that he had said it for a joke. [Italics added]
> *(CE 1403*, p. 777)

In this interview Marina Oswald appeared to be describing two visits by the De Mohrenschildts—one by the wife, apparently unaccompanied, and a second visit "a few days after the assassination attempt" of April 10, when the husband had twitted Oswald for missing General Walker.

But Mrs. De Mohrenschildt testified that her first and only visit to the Neely Street apartment was on the night of April 13, 1963, and the Warren Commission has accepted that date as accurate. *(9H 315-317, WR 282)* In fact, the visit had to take place after April 10, when someone tried to shoot General Walker, and before April 19, when the De Mohrenschildts left Dallas, never to see the Oswalds again. Both De Mohrenschildt and his wife were certain that the visit was within a day of Easter Sunday, which fell on April 14 that year; Mrs. De Mohrenschildt was definite in stating that the visit was on Saturday night, April 13, 1963.

On that date, however, the rifle was still "buried" in the ground at some undetermined location—in a field near a railroad track *(CE 1403*, p. 777)—and thus the incident described by George De Mohrenschildt *(9H 249)* and his wife Jeanne *(9H 315-317)* and the Warren Report *(WR 282)* could not possibly have occurred.

To digress for a moment, let us consider the allegation that after taking a shot at General Walker, Oswald had buried the rifle and then retrieved it some days later. In his book *The Oswald Affair*, Léo Sauvage has raised several serious questions which the Warren Commission completely ignored.

How did Oswald bury a rifle in the ground without using a spade and shovel or any implement other than his bare hands? How did he protect the rifle from corrosion and other damage to be expected if the rifle was buried in soil for some four days or more? If he used no protective wrappings, why did the microscopic examination of the rifle by FBI Expert Stombaugh on November 23, 1963 *(4H 81)* reveal no traces of soil? Since Oswald ostensibly buried the rifle in the dark of night, how did he locate the place of burial some four days later? And how did he dig it up without a shovel or any other implement?

To my colleague's questions, I will add one of my own: How is it that the many searches of Oswald's property and possessions by local officers and federal agents uncovered no rifle-cleaning equipment? According to the Commission, Oswald made active and frequent use of the rifle, even burying it in the ground for a few days. That he did so but failed to clean the weapon (which was "well-oiled" when discovered in the Book Depository, as mentioned earlier) is scarcely believable. Yet, the inventories of Oswald's belongings, which list such miscellany as "Label with King Oscar Kipper recipes" *(CE 3042)* and "One Texas flag —small" *(CE 2713)*, do not include any rifle-cleaning paraphernalia.

In any case, Marina Oswald told the FBI on December 11, 1963 that Oswald had retrieved the buried rifle on Sunday, April 14, 1963. In April 1964 Mrs. De Mohrenschildt testified that she had seen the rifle in the closet on Saturday night, April 13, 1963, when she and her husband had visited the Oswalds. Subsequently, on July 24, 1964, Marina Oswald was questioned again by Commission counsel. She now said, felicitously, that "it was the weekend—Saturday or Sunday when Lee brought the rifle back home." *(11H 293)* It should be noted that the modification was not a response to a challenge but was volunteered, apparently gratuitously, by Marina Oswald—and this was not the first time that she happened to change an earlier story after the Commission received testimony or evidence with which the earlier story was inconsistent.

On July 24, 1964 Marina Oswald went on to say that after Oswald had arrived home with the recovered rifle he showed her a notebook containing detailed plans and notes for the attack on General Walker. At her urging, he had burned the incriminating notebook within the hour. *(11H 294)* She had pointed out that it would be awfully dangerous to keep an object like that around the house. *(11H 293-294)*

Suppose that the recovery of the rifle and the burning of the notebook actually took place on Saturday, and not on Sunday as Marina Oswald told the FBI in the first instance. That would eliminate the anachronism that otherwise destroys the credibility of the De Mohrenschildts' story. But even if it is assumed that the rifle was returned to its place in the closet before the De Mohrenschildts arrived later that evening, is the story really plausible?

George De Mohrenschildt testified that he and his wife had driven over to the Oswald apartment:

> ... quite late in the evening.... I think they were asleep.... We knocked at the door and shouted, and Lee Oswald came down undressed, half undressed you see, maybe in shorts, and opened the door....   *(9H 249)*

Supposedly, only a few hours earlier Oswald had recovered the rifle with which he had attempted to shoot General Walker and had burned the tell-tale notebook. When Marina Oswald heard that knocking, surely her first thought must have been that it was the police coming to arrest her husband. And surely, relieved as she must have been to find that it was only the De Mohrenschildts on a social visit, the last thing in the world that she would have done that night would have been to call attention to that rifle or to remark casually that Oswald "just loves to shoot." *(9H 316)*

Psychologically, it is impossible that this incident occurred as it was described by George and Jeanne De Mohrenschildt (and in the Warren Report) unless Marina Oswald fabricated the whole story of the attack on General Walker—which is exactly what much other evidence suggests. Only if Oswald had nothing to do with that shooting does it become believable that Marina Oswald blithely opened a closet and switched on the light so that a visitor would see the rifle so clearly that she would be able to identify it a year later. *(9H 315)*

Even so, there is still a serious contradiction or two which makes it difficult to accept the De Mohrenschildts' story at face value.

Marina Oswald testified that the rifle was kept in a small storeroom in the Neely Street apartment, sometimes in the corner and sometimes up on a shelf, and that "Lee didn't like me to go into this room. That is why he kept it closed all the time and told me not to go into it." *(5H 396)* Since Oswald had instructed her not to go into the storeroom, it seems all the more unlikely that she would have displayed the room and its contents to a visitor, in Oswald's presence and against his express injunction. Indeed, in her first appearance before the Warren Commission, on February 3, 1964, there was the following peculiar passage of testimony:

> *Rankin:* Did you ever show that rifle to the De Mohrenschildts?
> *Marina Oswald:* I know that De Mohrenschildt had said that the rifle had been shown to him, but I don't remember that.   *(1H 14)*

A little later on the same day, after Marina Oswald described the alleged attack on General Walker, she volunteered the following information:

> By the way, several days after that, the De Mohrenschildts came to us, and *as soon as he opened the door* he said, "Lee, how is it possible that you missed?" I looked at Lee. I thought that he had told De Mohrenschildt about it. And Lee looked at me, and he apparently thought that I had told De Mohrenschildt about it. [Italics added]   *(1H 18)*

This account of the incident is, of course, completely inconsistent with the account given by De Mohrenschildt and his wife (and in the Warren Report). Both testified that they had been in the apartment for a while and that it was only when Mrs. De Mohrenschildt saw the rifle in the closet and called attention to it that De Mohrenschildt made his jest about Oswald having missed the General. De Mohrenschildt specifically denied Marina Oswald's allegation. *(9H 250)*

In spite of these unexplained contradictions and the inherent psychological implausibility of the story, the Warren Report makes a series of assertions— those quoted at the outset *(WR 282-283)*—which are arbitrary and highly questionable but which serve the dual purpose of (1) providing the sole outside corroboration of Oswald's possession of a rifle with a telescopic sight, and (2) providing, inferentially, corroboration of Oswald's alleged attack on General Walker.

The Warren Commission carefully emphasized that it did not conduct a trial but a fact-finding investigation. On what basis did the Commission decide that disputed allegations were "fact"? Why did the Commission conceal in its Report the very existence of contradictions among the witnesses?

Since the Commission and its lawyers have taken refuge in silence, we must supply our own answers in an attempt to approach a more accurate historical record.

Oswald's Rifle Practice

Chapter 4 discussed the reputation of the 6.5 Mannlicher-Carcano as the "humanitarian" rifle and the decrepitude of the specimen found in the Book Depository—its difficult bolt, eccentric trigger, maladjusted scope, and disintegrating firing-pin. Despite its impressive list of disabilities, the Warren Commission, undismayed, concluded that it was the rifle that felled the President and the Governor. The Commission concluded also that Oswald had acquired sufficient familiarity with the rifle to achieve accuracy and to eliminate the risk of malfunction. Is such an assumption justified?

The Commission's Exhibits reveal that in the course of four FBI or Secret Service interviews which took place between December 4 and 16, 1963, Marina Oswald was asked whether or not Oswald had engaged in rifle practice. On each occasion she replied that Oswald had never left or returned to their home carrying a rifle; that he had never mentioned that he intended to practice shooting; that he had never done so, to her knowledge; and that she had never seen him clean the rifle or hold it. (*CE 1785; CE 1401,* p. 286; *CE 1790; CE 1403,* p. 735) Apparently in response to suggestions from the interviewer, she agreed, however, that Oswald might have practiced shooting when he was supposed to be attending typing classes.

Two months later Marina Oswald told a different story. She said on February 17, 1964 that Oswald had told her after the General Walker shooting that he had practiced in a field near Dallas (*CE 2694,* p. 5); that one day in January 1963 Oswald was cleaning his rifle (which was mailed by Klein's Sporting Goods some two months later on March 20, 1963) and said that he had been practicing that day (*CE 2694,* p. 5); and that one evening in March 1963 Oswald had gone off at six o'clock carrying the rifle (wrapped in a raincoat),[14] boarded a Love Field bus, and returned at 9 p.m. to say that he had been practicing where no people were around to hear him. (*CE 2694,* p. 6) On February 18, 1964 she retracted her statement of the previous day about Oswald cleaning the rifle in January 1963—realizing, or perhaps being reminded, that the rifle was not yet ordered, much less received, in January. She now said that the incident had actually occurred shortly before the Walker incident in April 1963. (*CE 1404*)

Clearly, Marina Oswald misstated the facts, either in the December 1963 interviews or in the February 1964 statements. Whichever set of replies was false, the self-contradiction raises inescapable questions about her credibility (further discussed in Chaper 11).

If the later statements incriminating Oswald are the false statements, questions arise also about the possibility of coercion or improper influence exerted on the witness by government agents. But if the later statements are truthful, objective evidence in some form should exist in corroboration of her story.

Perhaps this was the line of reasoning that the FBI and Secret Service pursued when they conducted a thorough investigation at various locations in Dallas and Irving where Oswald might have engaged in rifle practice—an investigation that produced completely negative results. (*CE 2694, CE 2908*) The FBI collected many pounds of rifle shells from commercial ranges and from locations in the woods and the bed of the Trinity River, including 23 pounds of shells from the Sports Drome Rifle Range, at which witnesses claimed to have seen Oswald on several occasions. (*CE 2921*) Laboratory examination failed to turn up a

---

14   No raincoat is listed in the inventory of Oswald's possessions.

single shell that came from the Carcano alleged to belong to Oswald. *(CE 3049)*

No evidence of any kind was found in support of Marina Oswald's allegations that Oswald had engaged in rifle practice. This is apparent from the Warren Report, which makes no assertion that Oswald had practiced shooting the rifle but states that Marina Oswald said that he had. *(WR 192)* Of course, this creates the impression that Oswald *had* familiarized himself with the rifle by practice shooting. But the Report makes no comment about documents in the Commission's possession which strongly suggest the reverse—that is, (1) reports showing that Marina Oswald steadfastly maintained in interviews before February 1964 that Oswald had not engaged in rifle practice; and (2) reports showing that painstaking search by the FBI and Secret Service had failed to uncover the smallest indication of rifle practice by Oswald in the Dallas-Irving area.

The Commission is not relieved of moral responsibility for slanting the evidence against the accused by its device of citing Marina Oswald's statements but refraining from expressing a finding of its own with respect to Oswald's alleged rifle practice—especially when expert testimony made it clear that the defects and eccentricities of the weapon, in the hands of a man who had not familiarized himself with its operation by actual firing practice, virtually ruled out the possibility of accurate shooting.

Marina Oswald's self-contradictions and conflicting stories must be weighed against the lack of any objective evidence that Oswald had engaged in rifle practice or that he had purchased or possessed ammunition for that purpose. This leaves no ground for concluding that Oswald had practiced shooting the Carcano or that he performed an unparalleled feat of marksmanship with that decrepit weapon. Indeed, common sense suggests that if he *had* practiced with that rifle, he would have lost no time in dumping it for a bow and arrow.

Chapter 5
The Autopsy and Medical Findings

This chapter identifies (1) serious discrepancies between the objective evidence and the medical findings in the Warren Report, and (2) serious misrepresentation of the recorded testimony and withholding by the Warren Commission of important documentary evidence.

A wealth of discrepancies, distortions, and omissions impels one to conclude that the official autopsy report is unreliable; that the description of the President's wounds is inaccurate; that the single-missile theory (see Chapter 1) is wholly unsupported by and in conflict with the evidence; that this theory represents an attempt to salvage the case against Lee Harvey Oswald as a lone assassin; that the conclusions in the Warren Report on the source, number, and perpetration of the shots are completely invalid; and that the evidence in fact constitutes proof of conspiracy.

Press Descriptions of the President's Wounds

In the first days and weeks after the assassination a series of news stories constantly revised the number, location, and nature of the President's wounds. According to the doctors at Parkland Hospital, the President suffered an entrance wound at the Adam's apple and a massive wound in the head.[1] The official theory to account for those wounds was that the President had been

---

1 *New York World-Telegram and Sun*, November 23, 1963, p. 2; *The New York Times*, November 24, 1963, p. 2, col. 6; *New York Post*, November 24, 1963, p. 2, col. 3.

shot while his car was approaching the Book Depository building.[2] That was soon dropped in favor of a new theory: that he was shot on Elm Street while the car was moving away from the Book Depository, when he had turned backward to wave at the crowd.[3] That was dropped in turn when films of the assassination showed that the President was facing forward at the strategic time.

On-site tests were conducted on December 5, 1963 by the Secret Service—presumably with the autopsy report in hand (Commission Document No. 37 or 370 in the National Archives consists of a receipt for various items, including "one copy of autopsy report and notes of the examining doctor," turned over to Robert I. Bouck of the Secret Service Protective Research Section by the White House physician on November 26, 1963). The tests were conducted for the acknowledged purpose of determining how the President was shot in the front from behind.[4] The experiment was not successful.

About four weeks after the assassination, it became known that the Parkland Hospital doctors had been interviewed by the Secret Service and informed of the autopsy findings.[5] A new version of the wounds was made public, which mentioned for the first time that the President had been shot in the back.[6] Some of the stories also said that the bullet that struck the back "was found deep in his shoulder."[7] One story said that the bullet had entered "five to seven inches below the collar line";[8] others said "several inches below the collar line." (The *Washington Post* said on May 29, 1966 that the information had been confirmed by the FBI before publication.) It was reported that the Parkland doctors now agreed that the entrance wound at the Adam's apple in reality was an exit wound.[9]

Some reports of the autopsy findings leaked to the news media contradicted each other as well as the official autopsy report ultimately published. *The New York Times* stated on December 17, 1963 that the FBI Report of December 9, 1963 revealed that one bullet had struck Kennedy where the right shoulder joins the neck and another had struck his right temple.[10]

The next day *The New York Times* published another report, from a "source fully acquainted with the results of the autopsy."[11] Now there was a small neat wound in the back which had penetrated two or three inches, and according to "the pathologists at Bethesda," the wound at the Adam's apple had been caused by a metal or bone fragment from the fatal head shot.

Within 24 hours, *The New York Times* gave still another account, in which the pathologists were said to have found that the bullet in the back had lodged

2   *New York Herald-Tribune*, November 27, 1963, pp. 1 and 9.
3   Paul Mandel, "End to Nagging Rumors: The Six Critical Seconds," *Life*, December 6, 1963, p. 52F, col. 2.
4   *The New York Times*, December 6, 1963, p. 6.
5   *St. Louis Post-Dispatch*, December 18, 1963.
6   *The New York Times*, *Washington Post*, and *St. Louis Post-Dispatch*, December 18, 1963.
7   *Washington Post*, December 18, 1963 and May 29, 1966.
8   *Ibid.*
9   *St. Louis Post-Dispatch*, December 18, 1963.
10 *The New York Times*, December 17, 1963, p. 31, cols. 7-8.
11 *Ibid.*, December 18, 1963, p. 27, cols. 4-6.

in Kennedy's body and that a second bullet had hit the right rear of his head.[12] The story added that a fragment of the head bullet had passed out the front of the neck. More than a month later the *Times* was still reporting that a bullet had lodged in Kennedy's right shoulder.[13]

Thus, for more than two months after the assassination the press asserted repeatedly that the first bullet to strike the President had entered several inches below the collar line and had lodged in the body. The same stories gave a variety of versions of the head wound: that a bullet had gone in and out of the back of the head, according to Dr. Kemp Clark;[14] that a bullet struck the back of the head, to the right;[15] that a bullet struck the right temple;[16] the back of the skull;[17] and the right rear of the head.[18]

The autopsy report, with its presumably authoritative data, was not published; Dr. J. J. Humes, the chief autopsy surgeon, said that he had been forbidden to talk.[19]

As one version of the wounds succeeded another with dizzying speed and confusion, only one constant remained: Oswald was the lone assassin and had fired all the shots from the sixth floor of the Book Depository. When facts came into conflict with that thesis, the facts and not the thesis were changed. Critics of the already implausible case against Oswald concluded from this that the truth was being suppressed and perverted in order to persuade the public, at all costs, to accept his sole guilt. Nothing that came to light later presented grounds for altering that conclusion.

The Official Findings

In September 1964 the Warren Report provided the official version of the wounds and, at first glance, appeared to support its findings with full, detailed medical evidence. According to the Report:

> (1) President Kennedy was first struck by a bullet which entered at the back of his neck and exited through the lower front portion of his neck, causing a wound which would not necessarily have been lethal. The President was struck a second time by a bullet which entered the right-rear portion of his head, causing a massive and fatal wound.
>
> (2) Governor Connally was struck by a bullet which entered on the right side of his back and traveled downward through the right side of his chest,

---

12 *Ibid.*, December 19, 1963, p. 23, col. 1.
13 *Ibid.*, January 26, 1964, p. 58, col. 4.
14 *New York Post*, November 24, 1963, p. 2, col. 3.
15 *New York Herald-Tribune*, November 27, 1963, pp. 1 and 9.
16 *The New York Times*, December 17, 1963, p. 31, cols. 7-8.
17 *Ibid.*, December 18, 1963, p. 27, col. 5.
18 *Ibid.*, December 19, 1963, p. 23, col. 1.
19 *Ibid.*, December 6, 1963, p. 18, col. 7.

exiting below his right nipple. This bullet then passed through his right wrist and entered his left thigh where it caused a superficial wound.

(WR 19)

Elsewhere the Commission expressed the view that the bullet that struck the President first and exited through the front of his neck then struck the Governor and inflicted all of his wounds. *(WR 19)* The Commission acknowledged, however, that the Governor himself did not agree with that view but was convinced that he was hit by a second bullet fired after an earlier bullet struck the President.

The Autopsy Report

The first point to be made about the autopsy report *(CE 387)*, which appears in Appendix IX of the Warren Report, is that it is undated. Commander J. J. Humes, chief autopsy surgeon, testified on March 16, 1964:

> In [the] privacy of my own home, early in the morning of Sunday, November 24, I made a draft of this report which I later revised, and of which this [handwritten draft of autopsy report] represents the revision. That draft I personally burned in the fireplace of my recreation room.   *(2H 373)*

In a certificate dated November 24, 1963, Dr. Humes states that he burned certain "preliminary draft notes" relating to the autopsy and officially transmitted all other papers related to the autopsy report to "higher authority." *(CE 397, p. 47)* This certification is not consistent with Dr. Humes's testimony, which reveals that in reality he burned the first draft of the autopsy report. *(2H 373)* In a second certificate of the same date Dr. Humes states that all working papers related to the autopsy had remained in his personal custody at all times; that his notes and handwritten draft of the final report were handed over to the commanding officer of the U.S. Naval Medical School at 5 p.m. on November 24, 1963; and that no papers related to the case remained in his possession. *(CE 397, p. 48)* Again, there is a conflict between the certification and the testimony: Dr. Humes told the Commission that schematic drawings of the wounds had been prepared on the basis of his memory and notes of the autopsy. *(2H 349-350)*

These certificates suggest that the official autopsy report was completed and handed on to higher authority two days after the death of the President. The document begins with a description of the circumstances of the assassination, based, it is explained, on "available information" and newspaper reports. It includes the statement that three shots were fired and that a rifle barrel was seen to disappear into a window on an upper floor of the Book Depository.

Obviously the conclusions reached by the Warren Commission with respect to the President's wounds lean heavily on the results of the post-mortem examination. If we are to have confidence in the Commission's conclusions, we must feel certain of the authenticity and objectivity of the autopsy report. It is thus a matter of serious concern that there is no date to be found on the report and that the Commission has not explained the omission.

The absence of a date on the autopsy report is a strange and dramatic fact when viewed against the unauthorized release of its supported contents in December 1963—weeks after the report was completed and handed over, according to Dr. Humes. The findings leaked at that time are completely inconsistent with the actual contents of the autopsy report. Moreover, the on-site tests carried out by the Secret Service in December 1963 were based on findings different from those in the published autopsy report, which, it is now claimed, were recorded and known to the Secret Service before these on-site tests.

It is noteworthy that suspicions about the autopsy report that arose long before the official document was published are confirmed, at least to the extent that "certain preliminary draft notes" were burned by the autopsy surgeon. The surgeon has certified that he handed over his final report on November 24, the day he burned the notes—yet the certificates read as if they had been written after a passage of time, as if to account for the disposition of documents at an earlier date. But whether or not it is authentic, the evidence that the autopsy report was completed on November 24 fails to account for the leaking of different autopsy findings on December 17 and December 18, or for the conduct of on-site tests on December 5 on the basis of findings other than those in the final document.

The autopsy report is further compromised by internal evidence. The assumptions in the opening paragraphs about the number of shots fired and their source have no legitimate place in a scientific report of this nature. The autopsy findings should have served as a test of subjective testimony and other evidence. Instead, the post-mortem examination was performed on the basis of unproved assumptions about the circumstances of the crime. Small wonder that the findings appear to authenticate those very assumptions.

In the light of the questions which persist about the date of the autopsy report in its published form and in view of indications that the findings were governed by a predisposition to interpretations consistent with police theory, the autopsy report remains suspect.[20]

It is not only critics of the Warren Report who have raised questions about the autopsy report. It has come under fire from members of the medical profession, purely for its defects as a record in the field of forensic pathology, as may be seen in the pages of the *Journal of the American Medical Association*.[21] One doctor termed the autopsy report "a grossly incomplete record" and pointed out that it failed to mention gross findings with respect to "such obvious and

20   Those who dismiss as preposterous, if not sacrilegious, the very notion that an autopsy report might be adjusted to serve police or political imperatives should consult David M. Spain's article "Mississippi Autopsy" in *Rampart's* special issue "Mississippi Eyewitness" (December 1964, pp. 43-49). They will find incontrovertible proof of the falsification of autopsy findings in the case of James Chaney, who was murdered with Andrew Goodman and Michael Schwerner in the summer of 1964 in Philadelphia, Mississippi.

21   Letters to the Editor, *Journal of the American Medical Association,* February 15, 1965, p. 602; April 5, 1965, p. 63.

easily identifiable organs as the liver, spleen, kidneys, pancreas, thyroid, and adrenals." Another challenged the prerogative of unknown officials to "deny the right of the electorate to know whether the adrenals significantly altered the President's health or the nation's history."

Since a number of doctors raised questions about the post-mortem examination of the President's adrenals, the editor of the *AMA Journal* sent an inquiry to the Chief of the Bureau of Medicine and Surgery, U.S. Navy, on November 10, 1964. The editor reported in the April 5, 1965 issue:

> The request was forwarded to the White House Physician, Rear Admiral George G. Burkley, MC, USN, to whom complete protocol had been submitted by the Navy pathologists and from whose office the official report, lacking mention of the adrenals, had been released to the nation. The *Journal* waited three months for pertinent information regarding the adrenals; received none.[22]

These are additional grounds for questioning the completeness, competence, and strictly scientific character of the autopsy report, with respect to findings which have no bearing on the assassination as such but which do present political implications. The editors of the quarterly *Current Medicine for Attorneys* write:

> The question is, was President Kennedy "impaired for public life" when he ran for office—by reason of adrenal pathology. Certainly the absence of findings in the autopsy on this point suggest that he was.

Obviously an autopsy report which has been influenced by political considerations and about which officials responsible refuse to provide clarification requested by reputable sources[23] cannot be regarded as an authoritative document in the reconstruction of the crime.

The President's Wounds:
Entrance Wound in the Back

According to the Warren Report an entrance wound was found by the autopsy surgeons near the base of the back of the neck, about 5.5 inches (14 cm.) from the tip of the right shoulder joint and 5.5 inches below the tip of the right mastoid process. The corresponding holes in the coat and shirt were about 5.5 inches

---

22 "The Warren Report: How to Murder the Medical Evidence," *Current Medicine for Attorneys,* Vol. XII, No. 50, November 1965, pp. 1-12.

23 In a discussion of the Warren Report on a Philadelphia radio station on November 19, 1965 Charles Kramer, an attorney, indicated that he had contacted Commander Humes, chief autopsy surgeon, seeking clarifications with which he might rebut criticism of the autopsy findings. Commander Humes told Kramer that he was not permitted to discuss the autopsy.

below the top of the collar. The wound was relatively small, sharply delineated and with clean edges. The holes in the clothing were about the same size as the corresponding wound. This information can be found more precisely in the Report. *(WR 87-92)*

The Report explains in some detail why there was no public report on the existence of this wound for a month after the assassination and why Dr. Charles James Carrico and his medical colleagues at Parkland Hospital overlooked it. The explanation given by Dr. Carrico in his testimony *(3H 361)* and in the Report is generally plausible and might be readily accepted were it not for traces of evasiveness in the questioning of other witnesses. Two nurses who had assisted the team of doctors in the emergency room remained there with the President's body after he was pronounced dead. Both nurses testified that they undressed the body, cleaned it, and wrapped it in sheets. The natural question for counsel to pose was whether either of the nurses had seen a wound in the President's back while performing these procedures, but this was not asked. *(6H 136-137, 141)*

The discovery of the wound is described by Secret Service Agent Roy Kellerman in his testimony of March 9, 1964.

> While the President is in the morgue, he is lying flat. And with part of the skull removed, and the hole in the throat, nobody was aware until they lifted him up that there was a hole in his shoulder. That was the first concrete evidence that they knew that the man was hit in the back first.
>
> *(2H 103)*

But there is an earlier indication that the President was wounded in the back, according to the Report *(WR 111)*, in notes written by Secret Service Agent Glen A. Bennett. Bennett was riding in the follow-up car, directly behind the President's limousine, and he "saw that shot hit the President about four inches down from his right shoulder." The Warren Commission gives substantial weight to Bennett's corroboration of a bullet striking Kennedy's back, recorded in notes written by him "on the airplane en route back to Washington, prior to the autopsy, when it was not yet known that the President had been hit in the back." (Bennett's handwritten notes *(CE 2112)* and subsequent formal report *(CE 1024)* are included in the Exhibits.) Unfortunately, the Commission did not give as much weight to other elements in his reports; Bennett's observation that the wound was about four inches below the shoulder was disregarded completely.

The autopsy surgeon, Dr. Humes, testified, however, that this wound was "near the base of the back of President Kennedy's neck." He presented schematic drawings prepared under his supervision by a medical artist which show the wound in the lower neck. *(CEs 385, 386, 388)* But in his handwritten autopsy report, a diagram ("face sheet") shows the wound well below the neckline. *(CE 397)* True, notes in the margin give measurements consistent with the wound in the neck shown in the schematic drawings. But since the diagram purports to *show* the location of the wounds, it is hard to understand why those measurements were recorded in the margin—recorded only for this particular wound but not for other wounds, scars, or incisions, and written in heavier ink than the other notations found on the same diagram.[24]

The actual notation in the margin is "14 cm from rt Acromion 14 cm below rt mastoid process." (Fourteen centimeters are equivalent to five and a half inches.) As Harold Weisberg has pointed out in his book *Whitewash II* (privately published at Hyattstown, Md., 1966, p. 120), the autopsy surgeons oriented the back wound by reference to the mastoid and shoulder (acromion) joint, while in the Oswald autopsy *(CE 1981)* the gunshot wound is located by reference to the midline and the top of the head—less "flexible" points than the mastoid and the acromion. Dr. Cyril Wecht, Director of the Institute of Forensic Sciences at Duquesne University School of Law and Chief Forensic Pathologist, Allegheny County, states in a letter of February 10, 1967, that "the acromion process and/or the mastoid process are not customarily or routinely used by forensic pathologists as landmarks in pinpointing the location of bullet wounds on the body. Therefore, one must ask why these points were used by the pathologists who performed the autopsy on President Kennedy." The Warren Commission, lacking expertise in forensic medicine, not unnaturally raised no questions about the reference points or other such anomalies in the autopsy report and diagrams which, in an adversary procedure, would have been questioned, elaborated, and probably clarified, in cross-examination. Without that indispensable testing, we must apply at least the test of logic, in confronting the unresolved conflict between the autopsy diagram representation of the position of the back wound and the position specified in the written marginal measurements.

Those measurements situating the wound in the neck are in conflict not only with the accompanying diagram but with the testimony of several witnesses other than Glen Bennett. Roy Kellerman testified that the wound was in the "right shoulder . . . in that large muscle between the shoulder and the neck, just below it." *(2H 81)* Secret Service Agent William Greer said that the wound was in "the soft part of the shoulder," the upper right shoulder. *(2H 123)* Secret Service Agent Clinton Hill, who was summoned expressly to view the condition of the body, said that he saw "an opening in the back, about *six inches below the neckline.*" [Italics added] *(2H 143)*

The Commission appears to authenticate Hill's description. Discussing the on-site re-enactment tests of May 24, 1964, the Report states that "the back of

---

24 Dr. J. Thornton Boswell (Commander, U.S. Navy, Retired) said that he had marked the back wound on the autopsy diagram ("face sheet") and that the dot placed the wound incorrectly. "This was unfortunate. If I had known at the time that this sketch would become public record, I would have been more careful." (*The New York Times,* November 25, 1966.)

Still unexplained is the fact that when the document which includes the incorrectly marked autopsy diagram was admitted into evidence *(2H 373-374)* the autopsy surgeons did not call attention to the error and no questions about the low position of the dot were raised by examining counsel (Arlen Specter) or anyone else present (Chief Justice Warren, Senator Cooper, Representative Ford, Allen W. Dulles, J. Lee Rankin, Francis W. H. Adams, Norman Redlich, or Charles Murray, observer for the President of the American Bar Association, who was in attendance to ensure "fairness to the alleged assassin").

the stand-in for the President was marked with chalk *at the point where the bullet entered.*" [Italics added] *(WR 97)* One can see in one of the photographs of the on-site tests *(CE 886* Position A Frame)—and more dramatically in a photograph on the inside cover of the Bantam Books edition of the Warren Report—that, by the Commission's own admission, the bullet entered the President's back well below the neckline.

The holes in the President's coat and shirt are also powerful evidence of a wound well below the neckline.[25] The holes are about 5.5 inches below the top of the collar, while the wound is supposedly about 5.5 inches below the tip of the mastoid process. The discrepancy is substantial. Yet Dr. Humes testified that the holes and the wound "conform quite well." He conceded that they gave the appearance "when viewed separately . . . as being somewhat lower," and proceeded to belabor a hypothesis that the discrepancy resulted from the fact that "the President was extremely well-developed, an extremely well-developed muscular young man with a very well-developed set of muscles. . . . I believe this would have a tendency to push the portions of the coat which show the defects somewhat higher on the back of the President than on a man of less muscular development." *(2H 365)*

This explanation is singularly unconvincing and guaranteed to stir the wrath of Mr. Kennedy's tailor. The President's coat fit him with elegance, as photographs show. Governor Connally is also a large, well-developed, well-muscled man, but his wounds and the holes in his clothing correspond almost exactly. Was his tailor more gifted than Kennedy's?

The Warren Commission may accept Humes's implausible speculations but it does not dispose of reports by eyewitnesses that the wound was four or six inches below the neck.[26] Nor is it understandable that the Commission has failed to mention the discrepancy between the alleged location of the wound and the holes in the clothing in its Report, with or without the preposterous explanation from Humes.

It becomes all the more extraordinary, then, to learn from the testimony

---

25 Preoccupation with the discrepancy between the location of the wound and the corresponding bullet holes in the coat and shirt has distracted attention from other clothing holes and related evidence. The Warren Report claims that the bullet that entered the back of the neck exited from the throat, producing a ragged vertical slit in the front of the shirt under the collar button and a nick in the tie. *(WR 91-92)* The Commission admits that the "irregular nature of the slit precluded a positive determination that it was a bullet hole" but states that the slit "could have been caused by a round bullet." It does not acknowledge that FBI Expert Robert Frazier said also that it could have been caused by a bone fragment *(5H 61)* as it was "not specifically characteristic of a bullet hole."

Nor does the Report mention that the traces of copper found at the holes in back of the clothes were missing from the front of the shirt and the tie. *(5H 62)* This adds weight to the possibility that the slit in the front of the shirt and the defect in the tie were produced by a fragment of bone or metal. If one bullet caused all the holes in the President's clothes, it is hard to understand why it left traces of copper on entrance but no metallic traces on exit, since, according to the Commission, the bullet merely slid between the strap muscles without getting mutilated.

26 In July 1966 Paul Hoch and Vincent Salandria made available an important document which they had obtained from the Archives, consisting of the report of FBI Agents James W. Sibert and Francis X. O'Neill, Jr., on their observations during the autopsy on the President's body, throughout which they were in attendance. *(CD 7)* According to Sibert and O'Neill, the wound was situated below the shoulders.

that the Commission had at its disposal means by which it could have resolved the uncertainty about the exact location of the wound. According to Dr. Humes, 15 to 20 photographs[27] were taken of the body before and during the autopsy. However, those photographs were not developed. They were turned over to the Secret Service in their cassettes, unexposed, and Dr. Humes never saw them again. When he learned that he was to appear before the Commission, Dr. Humes decided to have drawings made on the basis of his records (as mentioned earlier, in his certificate of November 24, 1963, Humes had said that no papers related to the case remained in his possession) and recollections, in order to make his testimony more understandable. But these drawings were made on about March 14 and 15, more than three months after the autopsy, and the artist "had no photographs from which to work and had to work under our description, verbal description of what we had observed. . . ." *(2H 349-350)*

The Commission was fully aware that those drawings could not substitute for photographs or establish with precision the appearance or location of the wounds. It had merely to requisition those photographs made at the autopsy, which Roy Kellerman had handed over to the Special Agent-in-Charge, Mr. Robert Bouck, of the Secret Service. *(CE 1024)* That the Commission failed to do so, despite the importance of establishing the exact location of the wound, is incomprehensible.

The nature and location of the wound are factors central to the theory of the crime. The autopsy report states that the wound is "presumably of entry." *(CE 387)* Dr. Humes testified that he reached the conclusion that it was a point of entry because the characteristics of the wound were similar to those of the wound in the head, which was incontrovertibly an entrance wound. *(2H 364)* Lieutenant Colonel Pierre A. Finck, another of the autopsy surgeons, also testified that in his opinion this was a wound of entrance, because "this wound was relatively small with clean edges. It was not a jagged wound, and that is what we see in wound of entrance at a long range." *(2H 380)*

It is true that the wound in the back is similar to the entrance wound in the head, according to the descriptions of the autopsy surgeons. But it is also similar to the wound in the front of the neck as described by the doctors at Parkland Hospital, who did not see the entrance wound in the head or the wound in the back. These doctors repeatedly indicated verbally and in writing that the neck wound was an entry wound (as I shall discuss), until they were compelled to reverse their original opinion and agree that it was an exit wound, in the face of the autopsy and police findings as reported to them.

How did this transformation come about? It began with the conclusion of Dr. Humes that the wound in the back was a point of entry. Dr. Humes testified that he had searched for a missile in the body but had not found one. The search for the bullet during the autopsy was described by Roy Kellerman.

---

27 According to Sibert and O'Neill, 45 photographs were taken (22 4" x 5" color photographs, 18 4"x5" black-and-white photographs, and one roll of 120 film containing five exposures). Dr. Humes was therefore wide of the mark when he testified that 15 to 20 pictures were taken.

We couldn't determine what happened to it. They couldn't find it in the morgue; they couldn't find any leeway as to whatever happened to the shell when it hit the President's shoulder; where did it go. So our contention was that while he was on the stretcher in Dallas, and the neurosurgeon was working over him no doubt with pressure on the heart, this thing worked itself out. . . . Colonel Finck—during the examination of the President, from the hole that was in his shoulder, and with a probe, and we were standing right alongside of him, he is probing inside the shoulder with his instrument and I said, "Colonel, where did it go?" He said, "There are no lanes for an outlet of this entry in this man's shoulder."   *(2H 93)*

Dr. Humes, testifying on the same point, said:

Attempts to probe in the vicinity of this wound were unsuccessful without fear of making a false passage. . . . We were unable . . . to take probes and have them satisfactorily fall through any definite path at this point.
(2H 361)

At the stage when these probes for the path of the bullet were being performed, Dr. Humes and his colleagues presumably had formed the opinion, on the basis of the appearance of the wound, that it was a point of bullet entry. It was only afterwards, however, that Dr. Malcolm Perry received a telephone call from Dr. Humes, about which Dr. Perry said:

. . . he asked me at that time if we had made any wounds in the back. I told him that I had not examined the back nor had I knowledge of any wounds on the back.   *(6H 16-17)*

Dr. Humes also testified about his telephone conversations with Dr. Perry, during which he obtained information about the wound at the Adam's apple observed by the doctors at Parkland Hospital and about its appearance before it was obliterated by the tracheotomy incision. After describing in detail his examination of the body in the area of the neck and chest, Dr. Humes replied to questions put by Counsel Arlen Specter.

Specter: Now, Dr. Humes, at one point in your examination of the President, did you make an effort to probe the point of entry with your finger?

Dr. Humes: Yes, sir; I did.

Specter: And at or about that time when you were trying to ascertain, as you previously testified, whether there was any missile in the body of the President, did someone from the Secret Service call your attention to the fact that a bullet had been found on a stretcher at Parkland Hospital?

Dr. Humes: Yes, sir; they did.

Specter: And in that posture of your examination, having just learned of the presence of a bullet on a stretcher, did that call to your mind any tentative explanatory theory of the point of entry or exit of the bullet?

Dr. Humes: Yes, sir. We were able to ascertain with absolute certainty that the bullet had passed by the apical portion of the right lung producing the injury which we mentioned. I did not at that point have the information from Dr. Perry about the wound in the anterior neck, and while that was a possible explanation for the point of exit, we also had to consider the possibility that the missile in some rather inexplicable fashion had been stopped in its path through the President's body and, in fact, then had fallen from the body onto the stretcher.   *(2H 367)*

On the basis of that testimony, the Report explains that at one stage of the autopsy the surgeons were unable to find a path into any large muscle in the back of the neck and, when informed that a bullet had been found at Parkland Hospital, speculated that it might have penetrated a short distance into the back of the neck and then dropped out. *(WR 88)* Indeed, that is what was reported by all the non-medical witnesses present at the autopsy (Secret Service Agents Roy Kellerman and William Greer and FBI Agents James Sibert and Francis O'Neill).

But, the Report continues, "further exploration" had disproved that theory, the surgeons having determined that the bullet had passed between two large strap muscles and bruised them without leaving any channel.[28] The claim that further exploration had caused the autopsy surgeons to abandon the first assumption that the bullet had penetrated a short distance and dropped out is without the slightest corroboration from the four non-medical witnesses. On the contrary, their accounts of the autopsy implicitly indicate that the surgeons at no time suggested the missile had proceeded through the body to exit from the throat. One of the witnesses was explicit on that point.

Specter: Was anything said about any channel being present in the body for the bullet to have gone on through the back?

Greer: No, sir; I hadn't heard anything like that, any trace of it going on through.   *(2H 127)*

The unpublished report of FBI Agents Sibert and O'Neill dated November 26, 1963, which is included in Commission Document No. 7 in the National Archives, contains the following description:

During the latter stages of this autopsy, Dr. Humes located an opening which appeared to be a bullet hole which was below the shoulders. . . . This opening was probed by Dr. Humes with the finger, at which time it was determined that the trajectory of the missile entering at this point had entered at a downward position of 45 to 60 degrees. Further probing determined that the distance traveled by this missile was a short distance inasmuch as the end of the opening could be felt with the finger.

Inasmuch as no complete bullet of any size could be located in the brain area and likewise no bullet could be located in the back or any other area

---

28 In *Inquest* (p. 58), Edward Jay Epstein quotes Dr. Milton Helpern, Medical Examiner of New York, as insisting that it is impossible for a bullet to pass through a human body under such circumstances without leaving a discernible path.

of the body as determined by total body X rays and inspection revealing there was no point of exit, the individuals performing the autopsy were at a loss to explain why they could find no bullets.

The Sibert-O'Neill report then describes the receipt of information that a bullet had been recovered from a stretcher at Parkland Hospital and the delivery to Dr. Humes of a segment of the President's skull.

On the basis of the latter two developments, Dr. Humes stated that the pattern was clear that the one bullet had entered the President's back and had worked its way out of the body during external cardiac massage and that a second high velocity bullet had entered the rear of the skull and had fragmentized prior to exit through the top of the skull.

That is the last paragraph in the Sibert-O'Neill report which deals with the conduct of the autopsy or the findings of the surgeons. It is followed by a final paragraph detailing the disposition of the photographs, the segment of the skull, and metal fragments removed from the brain area. And there the report ends.

Clearly, the observers at the autopsy took away the impression that the bullet in the back had penetrated only a short distance, without exiting from the body, and that the surgeons believed that the missile had worked its way out of the body during external cardiac massage. Everything suggests that their impression was correct, and that Dr. Humes did not come to believe that the bullet had passed through and exited from the body until at least the next day, when he learned from Dr. Perry at Parkland Hospital that the President had arrived there with a bullet wound at the Adam's apple which had been obliterated during the tracheotomy.

Indeed, it is possible that Dr. Humes did not arrive at his new conclusions even after consulting with Dr. Perry, apparently on Saturday morning (although Dr. Perry himself believed that the telephone conversations with Humes had taken place on Friday, when the consultation logically should have taken place, in fact. *(6H 16; 3H 380)* After talking to Dr. Perry, Dr. Humes was apparently still not in a position to write a report on the autopsy; he did so only some 24 hours later, on Sunday morning, November 24, 1963, according to his testimony. Surely Dr. Humes realized how important the autopsy findings were to police investigation; he must have had a good reason for waiting.

In any case, the autopsy report said to have been written on Sunday morning was soon in the hands of the Secret Service and eventually of the FBI. If this autopsy report was identical to the one published as an appendix to the Warren Report, it is very difficult to understand the behavior of the two federal agencies. On December 5, 1963 the Secret Service proceeded to conduct re-enactment experiments in an attempt to discover how the President was hit in the front from behind.[29] And, as Vincent Salandria pointed out in an article in *The Minority of One* in April 1966[30] and Edward Jay Epstein noted at about the

29   Joseph Loftus in *The New York Times,* December 6, 1963, p. 18.
30   "The Separate Connally Shot," *The Minority of One,* April 1966, p. 13.

same time,[31] the *FBI claimed in its Summary Report of December 9, 1963 and its Supplemental Report of January 13, 1964 that the bullet which had struck the President's back had penetrated only a short distance and had not exited from the body.*

The Warren Commission maintained silence about these FBI reports and the conflicting descriptions of the entrance wound in the President's back. Even published statements in the Report and the Hearings and Exhibits that indicated that the wound was well below the neck were ignored by the Commission in its reasoning and conclusions. It appeared not to notice that witnesses referred constantly to a wound in the shoulder or a wound in the back—never to a wound in the neck or in the back of the neck. Inspector Thomas J. Kelley of the Secret Service called it a "wound in the shoulder" *(5H 175);* Kellerman called it "a hole in his shoulder" *(2H 103);* Greer said that the wound was "just in the soft part of the shoulder" *(2H 127);* and Hill called it "an opening in the shoulder." *(2H 143)*

The language used by the witnesses becomes significant when their descriptions are juxtaposed with the holes in the President's coat and shirt, which are supposed to correspond with the entrance wound in the back but which are irreconcilably lower than the position stated by Dr. Humes in his testimony and his autopsy report. Humes's attempt to account for the discrepancy was feeble and implausible. The photographs of the body which might resolve the conflict and indicate conclusively just where the wound was situated have been withheld.

The extent of the discrepancy between (1) the location of the entrance wound as described by Dr. Humes in his testimony and in schematic drawings executed under his instructions and (2) the location of the wound indicated by the clothing holes can best be appreciated by viewing together the schematic drawings *(CEs 385, 386)* and the FBI photographs of the shirt and coat which were first revealed publicly in Edward Jay Epstein's book *Inquest* but which were omitted from the Commission's exhibits.

The weight of the evidence irresistibly places the wound too low in the back for the bullet to exit at the Adam's apple unless it originated at a point lower than the car. The Commission has tried to demonstrate that the bullet was on a path of descent and that it struck the President at a point in the back higher than the so-called exit wound at the Adam's apple. In this, the Commission has failed. The testimony and evidence on which it relied is demolished by massive contrary testimony and evidence which is not nullified by virtue of the fact that the Commission concealed or ignored it.

Thanks to such researchers as Paul Hoch and Vincent Salandria, among others, vital information—in particular, the FBI reports of December 9, 1963 and January 13, 1964 and the report of FBI Agents Sibert and O'Neill of November 26, 1963—which appeared in neither the Warren Report nor the Hearings and Exhibits—has been placed before the public almost two years after the Report was issued. The FBI reports strongly reinforce the inferences

---

31 Op. cit., p. 48.

drawn by the critics from the Warren Report and the 26 volumes even before the documents were uncovered.[32]

Apologists who still insist, in the face of all the facts, that the Commission's assertions and conclusions are correct and honest say, in effect, that it is only innocent coincidence that:

(1) The bullet holes in the back of the clothes are too low.

(2) The entrance wound is shown well below the neckline on the autopsy diagram because of an error by Dr. J. Thornton Boswell which happens to correspond with the clothing holes and erroneous eyewitness descriptions.

(3) Federal Agents Sibert, O'Neill, Hill, and Bennett mistakenly describe the wound as too low and in a position corresponding with the clothing holes and the autopsy diagram.

(4) The chalk mark representing the site of entrance of a bullet is correspondingly low on the back of the stand-in for the President in photographs taken at the on-site re-enactment tests of May 24, 1964.

(5) The Commission did not question the autopsy surgeons about the low position of the wound when the autopsy diagram was admitted into evidence.

(6) FBI Agents Sibert and O'Neill were not asked to give testimony.

---

32 When the FBI Summary and Supplemental Reports came to light in May 1966 various unnamed FBI spokesmen gave the press a series of unofficial "explanations" that explained nothing. Generally they suggested that the Reports presented an accurate account of the "medical findings at that time" (*Washington Post*, May 29, 1966). It was only on November 26, 1966 that J. Edgar Hoover deigned to issue an official statement.

He said: "While there is a *difference* in the information reported by the FBI and the information contained in the autopsy report concerning the wounds, there is no *conflict*. . . . The FBI and the Warren Commission each received a copy of the official autopsy report on December 23, 1963. . . . Its contents were not repeated in an FBI report" (of January 13, 1964). [Italics added]

The statement was unfortunately published without a key to Mr. Hoover's secret code language; it fails to make clear the distinction between "difference" and "conflict." Nor does it explain why the FBI deliberately reiterated, in its report of January 13, 1964 an erroneous wound description given in its December 9, 1963 report which it knew by December 23 to be erroneous.

What Hoover seemed to say was that the Warren Commission would realize that the statement in the January 13, 1964 report that "the bullet which entered the back had penetrated to a distance of less than a finger length" was wrong, because the Commission now had in its possession the autopsy report which said that the bullet in fact had exited at the Adam's apple. Moreover, Hoover says, the January 13 report indicated that the clothing holes in the front of the shirt were "characteristic of an exit hole for a projectile" and that this "clearly indicated the examining physician's early observation that the bullet penetrated only a short distance . . . probably was in error."

Is it possible that Hoover was playing games with the Commission in his January 13 report, expecting the Commission to infer from one statement therein that a second statement was invalidated? In any case, the indication in that report that damage in the front of the shirt was characteristic of an exit hole of a projectile did not necessarily signify, then or now, that the FBI intended to "point up the probability" that the bullet that entered the back had penetrated the body and exited at the Adam's apple—on the contrary, it was the prevalent theory in December and January, as reported widely in the press, that a fragment of the head bullet or a piece of bone from the skull had exited from the front of the throat.

The Hoover statement of November 26, 1966 (reprinted in full in *The New York Times* of the same date) is a blatant exercise in doubletalk and obfuscation of the same kind that permeates the Warren Report. It only strengthens the impression that the autopsy report received by the FBI on December 23, 1963 was not the same autopsy report that was published as an appendix to the Warren Report or, if it was the same, that the FBI rejected the finding that the bullet in the back had exited at the Adam's apple. The alternative is that the FBI, on whose investigative work the Warren Report is largely based, is so confused, careless, and untrustworthy as to invalidate the whole official case.

(7) The description of the wound in the Sibert-O'Neill report of November 26, 1963 and in the FBI Summary and Supplemental Reports of December 9, 1963 and January 13, 1964 respectively is not mentioned in the Warren Report.

(8) All three FBI reports are excluded from the Hearings and Exhibits.

(9) The autopsy photographs and X rays were not examined by the Warren Commission and although they were deposited at the National Archives (on October 31, 1966) they remain unavailable for examination by independent experts, researchers, or any other individuals (including government agents and officials).[33]

(10) The Commission published photographs of the President's clothes which do not show the bullet holes in the back, although it had in its possession photographs which do show them.

One can believe in innocent coincidence but not when it reaches epidemic proportions and works persistently in favor of the Commission's fixed lone-assassin thesis. I can more readily accept as innocent coincidence some of the evidence which appears to incriminate the accused—a man who had no counsel or experts for his defense, in life or in death, while the Commission that convicted him had unlimited government resources at its command, yet stands incriminated by deceit and falsehood, in letter and spirit.

The Anterior Neck Wound

Anyone who took a serious interest in the news that issued from Dallas on the day of the assassination and thereafter will remember that for a month or so it was the general belief that the President had been shot by a bullet which entered the neck at the Adam's apple. This theme, with one or another variation, can be found in innumerable press and magazine stories.

The Warren Report nevertheless professes that (a) the doctors at Parkland Hospital did not in fact form an opinion as to the nature of the anterior neck wound; (b) the appearance of the wound was consistent with either entrance or exit of a missile; (c) the Parkland doctors considered the autopsy findings consistent with their observations; (d) they agreed, in the light of the autopsy report and other known facts, that the anterior neck wound was an exit wound; and (d) confusion about the nature of the wound had arisen because of the

---

33 At a public discussion of the Warren Report, Irving Howe said—after expressing disdain for the critics of the Warren Report—that he was shocked by the admission of former Commission Counsel Griffin and Liebeler that the autopsy photographs and X rays had not been examined by the Warren Commission and that their whereabouts (as of September 30, 1966) were unknown. Howe explained, "You've been saying, well, we can't be sure about Point A; Point B is circumstantial; Point C is probable; Point D we're not sure of. Now here is something that apparently is concrete and specific, but not available." (WBAI-New York, radio broadcast December 30, 1966)

misinterpretation of comments made by Dr. Malcolm Perry to the press, leading to erroneous beliefs about the wound and about the direction of the shots.
(WR 90-91)

Is it true that the doctors present during the treatment of the President at
Parkland Hospital did not form an opinion about the nature of this wound?
According to their written reports of the same day, it is not true. Dr. Charles J.
Carrico described a "small penetrating wound" of anterior neck in lower third.
(CE 392) Dr. Ronald C. Jones referred to "a small hole in anterior midline of
neck thought to be a bullet entrance wound." *(Jones, Dr. Ronald, Exhibit 1)*
Dr. Malcolm O. Perry, Dr. Charles R. Baxter, and Dr. William Kemp Clark
did not suggest in their written reports whether the wound was produced by
the entrance or the exit of a bullet. *(CE 392)*

The Parkland doctors gave testimony in depositions taken at the end of
March 1964, several of them on two occasions. They were asked by counsel to
indicate their original impression of the anterior neck wound, when they saw the
President in the emergency room. Their testimony on this point is paraphrased
from the transcripts.

> *Dr. Carrico*—He and Dr. Perry had talked on Friday afternoon, trying to
> determine exactly what had happened. As they were not then aware of the
> wound in the President's back, they had postulated a tangential wound from
> a fragment, or possibly another entrance wound in the anterior neck. The
> wound could have been an exit wound, but they were not aware of any
> corresponding entrance wound, and there were no characteristics within
> the neck area to indicate the direction of the bullet.   *(6H 5-6)*

> *Dr. Perry*—He did not have sufficient facts at the time to enable him to
> reach an opinion on the cause of the anterior neck wound. He could not
> determine how the wound had been inflicted, as such a determination would
> require tracing of the trajectory. *(6H 11)* As he did not have the autopsy
> findings initially, he was "somewhat confused about the nature of the
> wounds." He could not tell whether the President had been hit by one
> bullet or two.   *(6H 14)*

> *Dr. Clark*—He had not seen the anterior neck wound himself, as he had
> arrived in the emergency room after the tracheotomy had been started. He
> recalled that Dr. Perry had assumed from the findings (free blood and air
> in the neck) that a bullet might have entered the chest. Dr. Perry had
> therefore ordered the insertion of chest tubes to drain this material. *(6H 22)*

> *Dr. Robert N. McClelland*—He had assisted Dr. Perry in performing the
> tracheotomy but had not seen the original wound. Dr. Perry had described
> it as a very small wound, less than one-quarter inch in diameter, clear-cut
> although with somewhat irregular margins, with minimal tissue damage of
> the surrounding skin.

> He and the other doctors had discussed the President's wounds, in terms
> of their nature and source. At that time, they had had no information on
> the number of shots or their direction. Their impression was that the
> anterior neck wound was an entrance wound, and that if only one bullet
> had hit the President, it might have been deflected by the spine up through
> the skull. They had also speculated that two bullets were involved, which
> had seemed more plausible.   *(6H 33, 35)*

Dr. Baxter—The wound was not jagged, as one would expect with a very high velocity bullet. The doctors could not determine whether it was an exit or an entrance wound. Judging from the caliber of the rifle found later, the wound more resembled an entrance wound.   *(6H 42)*

Dr. Marion T. Jenkins—He had seen the wound before the tracheotomy commenced and had thought that it was an exit wound because it was not a clean wound. By "clean" he meant a clearly demarcated, round, punctate wound, as is usual with a missile of some velocity. The doctors had speculated that two bullets might have hit the President; they had also thought that one bullet had traversed the pleura and lodged in the chest. *(6H 48, 51)* [Dr. Jenkins did not mention the anterior neck wound explicitly in his written report—S.M.]

Dr. Jones—He had stated in his written report of November 22, 1963 that the wound in the anterior neck was thought to be an entrance wound because it was very small and relatively clean-cut, as would be seen in entry rather than exit. Not knowing the number of shots or the direction of the bullets, the doctors had speculated that the President had been hit by one bullet which had entered the neck, been deflected by the spine, and produced the massive head wound in its exit.   *(6H 55, 56)*

Dr. Gene Akin—The wound was a slightly ragged punctate hole. . . . "The thought flashed through my mind that this might have been an entrance wound, depending on the nature of the missile." He had not formed any opinion about the wounds until it was revealed later where the President was when he was shot and where the assassin was when he fired the weapon.   *(6H 65, 67)*

Dr. Paul C. Peters—". . . we speculated as to whether he had been shot once or twice, because we saw the wound of entry in the throat and noted the large occipital wound, and it is a known fact that high velocity missiles often have a small wound of entrance and a large wound of exit. . . ." Dr. Peters explained that by "we" he meant "all the doctors who were present." He himself had not seen the anterior neck wound before the tracheotomy.   *(6H 71)*

Nurse Margaret Henchliffe—She saw a small hole in the middle of the President's neck, about as big as the end of her little finger. It looked like an entrance bullet hole to her. She had never seen an exit wound that looked like that. It was small and not jagged like most exit wounds.   *(6H 143)*

Appraisal (Initial Medical Opinion): It is clear that the Parkland Hospital doctors did form an opinion of the anterior neck wound—they thought it was an entrance wound. Dr. Carrico and Dr. Jones reveal this, both in their reports and in their testimony. Dr. Perry acknowledges that he was "somewhat confused" about the nature of the wound until he became aware of the autopsy findings of an exit wound in the anterior neck—which justifies the inference that he regarded it initially as an entrance wound. Dr. Clark and Dr. McClelland corroborate that Dr. Perry, and the doctors as a group, had the impression that a bullet had entered the front of the neck and might have lodged in the chest, or been deflected by the spine into the head.

Dr. Baxter, on the other hand, says that it was not possible to determine whether the anterior neck wound was an entrance or an exit hole—but adds that it more resembled an entrance wound, judging from the caliber of the rifle.

Only Dr. Jenkins claims that he thought the wound was an exit wound when he saw it. Unfortunately, he did not say so in his written report of the same day.

The weight of the testimony discredits the claim in the Warren Report that the Parkland doctors did not form an opinion of the anterior neck wound, and demonstrates that they considered it an entrance wound.

News Conferences: Dr. Perry testified by deposition on March 23, 1964 that in press conferences immediately after the assassination reporters tried to get him to speculate on the number of bullets that had struck the President, the direction of the shots, and the exact cause of death. He had not been able to make any judgments on these matters or the nature of the anterior neck wound. He and Dr. Clark had both told the press that they could not say if one bullet or two, or more, were involved. He had said, however, that it was "conceivable or possible that a bullet could enter and strike the spinal column and be deviated superiorly to exit from the head," addressing himself solely to a hypothetical question. He believed that he had said the same thing, in essence, at later press conferences. *(6H 12-14)*

When he appeared before the Warren Commission on March 30, 1964 Dr. Perry again explained his statements to the press, giving the same account generally as in his previous testimony. He was then asked if any recording had been made at the first press conference, and replied:

> *Dr. Perry:* There were microphones, and cameras, and the whole bit, as you know, and during the course of it a lot of these hypothetical situations and questions that were asked to us would often be asked by someone on this side and recorded by someone on this, and I don't know who was recorded and whether they were broadcasting it directly.
>
> There were tape recorders there and there were television cameras with their microphones. I know there were recordings made but who made them I don't know and, of course, portions of it would be given to this group and questions answered here and, as a result, considerable questions were not answered in their entirety and even some of them that were asked, I am sure were misunderstood. It was bedlam.   *(3H 375)*
>
> *Dulles:* Was there any reasonably good account in any of the press of this interview?
>
> *Dr. Perry:* No, sir. . . . In general they were inaccurate. . . . I found none that portrayed it exactly as it happened. . . . They were frequently taken out of context. They were frequently mixed up. . . .   *(3H 376)*

Dulles, Counsel Specter, and Perry then discussed the feasibility of having Dr. Perry examine press clippings and indicate misquotation of his actual remarks in those news stories. Specter indicated that attempts were being made to obtain television tapes of the interviews. The networks had a huge backlog of transcriptions, but it was expected that the film clips and audio tapes would be made available in "a matter of a couple of weeks." *(3H 378)*

After discussion off the record, it was decided that the press stories should be checked against television and radio tapes by the staff of the Warren Commission, so as to secure "adequate information to deal with a great many of the false rumors that have been spread on the basis of false interpretation of these appearances before television, radio, and so forth and so on." *(3H 379)*

Although the Warren Report attributes the "confusion" solely to the misinterpretation of remarks by Dr. Perry, other doctors also made statements to the press and gave news interviews. Dr. Clark participated in the press conferences at Parkland Hospital after the President's death and gave television interviews during the ensuing two weeks to C.B.S., N.B.C., and B.B.C. He was questioned by the Warren Commission about a *New York Times* story[34] and an article in *L'Express*[35] which quoted him as saying that a bullet had hit the President in the front of the neck, entering the chest, and had not come out. He replied that these stories had quoted him incompletely and inaccurately. *(6H 21-30)*

Dr. McClelland was asked about a story in the *St. Louis Post-Dispatch*[36] by Richard Dudman. He acknowledged that he had told Dudman that the anterior neck wound was a small, undamaged punctate area which "had the appearance of the usual entrance wound of a bullet," and that he and his colleagues at Parkland Hospital were experienced and could usually tell the difference between entry and exit wounds. He suggested to the Warren Commission that the press had tended to interpret the findings of the Parkland doctors as conclusive, rather than as "educated guesses," which they in fact were. *(6H 36-37)*

Appraisal (News Stories): The Warren Report gives an incomplete, distorted, and misleading version of the origin and extent of the "erroneous beliefs" which resulted from news conferences at Parkland Hospital. The Report discusses only Dr. Perry's role, maintaining discreet silence about statements of at least two other doctors quoted in the press, after the first "bedlam" gave way to calm. As for Dr. Perry, who claims that the press accounts of his statements were generally inaccurate and that there was not even one reasonably good account of the first press conference, it is significant that he took no steps to correct the misleading reports of his remarks.

It is even more revealing that the Warren Commission has not furnished the transcripts of the television and radio tapes which were to be used to show how Dr. Perry's comments had been misinterpreted or distorted in the press. One might well assume that the transcripts are not helpful in this respect.

This assumption is borne out in the edited transcript of television broadcasts from November 22 to 26, 1963, issued by N.B.C. nearly two years after the Warren Report in the book *Seventy Hours and Thirty Minutes*.[37] The edited television log contains a telephone report from N.B.C. newsman Robert MacNeil at about 2:40 p.m. Dallas time on November 22.

Dr. Malcolm Perry reported that the President arrived at Parkland Hospital in critical condition with neck and head injuries. . . . *A bullet struck him in*

---

34 *The New York Times,* November 27, 1963.
35 *L'Express,* February 20, 1964.
36 *St. Louis Post-Dispatch,* December 1, 1963.
37 *N.B.C. News, Seventy Hours and Thirty Minutes* (New York: Random House, 1966).

front as he faced the assailant. He never regained consciousness. [Italics added]

Other television and radio networks and stations—and, indeed, the federal government—should be challenged to make verbatim transcripts of their broadcasts available, so that the public may know exactly what the Parkland doctors said about the anterior neck wound when they were fresh from the emergency room.[38] All available information indicates that the Warren Report has made grossly misleading statements on that question.

Secret Service and FBI Interviews

Dr. Humes supposedly completed the autopsy report on Sunday, November 24, 1963 and transmitted it to his superiors. An autopsy report was in the hands of the Secret Service within a few days. According to Dr. Carrico of Parkland Hospital, the Secret Service held a "fairly long interview" with the doctors at Parkland within a week of the assassination, the first of several such interviews. Describing that first interview, Dr. Carrico said:

> There was a meeting in Dr. Shires' office, Dr. Shires, Dr. Perry, Dr. Mc-Clelland and myself, and two representatives of the Secret Service in which we went over the treatment. They discussed the autopsy findings as I recall it, with Dr. Shires. . . . I don't recall any specific questions I was asked. In general, I was asked some questions pertaining to [the President's] treatment, to the wounds, what I thought they were. . . . I said that on the basis of our initial examination, this wound in his neck could have been either an entrance or exit wound, which is what they were most concerned about, and assuming there was a wound in the back, somewhere similar to what you have described that this certainly would be compatible with an exit wound.   *(3H 363-364)*

It will be recalled that in his written report prepared immediately after the President's death, Dr. Carrico described a small penetrating wound of the anterior neck. His written report did not suggest any doubt about the nature of the wound on the basis of its objective appearance. He modified his opinion after a "fairly long interview" with the Secret Service in which he was told about a wound in the back (not the back of the neck, it should be noted) but not shown an autopsy report. Dr. Carrico recalled that the autopsy findings had been discussed with Dr. Shires, but when Dr. Shires was deposed by Arlen Specter, he was not asked about discussion of the autopsy findings with the two Secret Service agents.

Referring to the same interview with the Secret Service, Dr. Perry said that he had been asked questions "essentially in regard to the treatment and once

---

38 I am indebted to Paul Hoch for the information that a Commission document in the National Archives *(CD 678)* consists of a two-page letter from the head of the Secret Service to the general counsel of the Warren Commission dated March 25, 1964, stating that the tapes of Dr. Perry's press interview could not be found. That is a singular disappearance. Dr. Perry said that there were microphones, cameras, tape recorders, and television cameras with their microphones at the press conference held after the President's death was announced. Is it possible that only one tape recording of the press conference was made? Or could none of the tapes be found?

again speculation as to where the bullets might have originated and what the nature of the wounds were. . . ." *(3H 387)*

Did those two Secret Service agents have in their possession during the interview with the doctors the same autopsy report that is reproduced in the Warren Report? If they did, the fact that the two agents were most concerned about the nature of the anterior neck wound is surprising. That wound supposedly had been postulated by Dr. Humes during the autopsy process on Friday night, corroborated in conversation with Dr. Perry on Saturday morning, and identified as an exit wound in the formal autopsy report on Sunday.

Subsequent to the first interview with Parkland Hospital doctors by two unnamed Secret Service agents sometime before November 29, 1963, additional interviews were conducted with the Parkland doctors, nurses, and orderlies by both the Secret Service and the FBI. There were known to be 24 Secret Service and 6 FBI interviews, or a total of at least 30 interviews. *(6H 7-139)*

Not one report on those 30 or more interviews has been included in the Hearings and Exhibits. Yet, it was a general practice for Commission counsel to give witnesses an opportunity to review and, if necessary, to correct FBI and Secret Service reports of interviews with them prior to their formal testimony, and then to enter the reports into the record for publication among the Exhibits.

That this was not done in a single instance in the case of Parkland Hospital personnel is striking. Like the failure to publish the transcripts of press conferences and statements, the failure to publish these reports deprives us of the opportunity to judge—from the questions as well as the replies—exactly what medical opinions or findings were under discussion at various time periods—in particular, what autopsy findings were in the hands of the Secret Service within a week of the assassination and prior to the re-enactment tests of December 5, 1963.

Final Medical Opinion: After relating their first impressions of the President's wounds, the Parkland doctors were asked to indicate whether they believed that the anterior neck wound could have been an exit wound, taking into account the autopsy findings and a hypothesis stated in the following terms:

> Assume first of all that the President was struck by a 6.5-mm. copper-jacketed bullet fired from a gun having a muzzle velocity of approximately 2,000 feet per second, with the weapon being approximately 160 to 250 feet from the President, with the bullet striking him at an angle of declination of approximately 45 degrees,
> striking the President on the upper right posterior thorax just above the upper border of the scapula, being 14 cm. from the tip of the right acromion process and 14 cm. below the tip of the right mastoid process,
> passing through the President's body striking no bones, traversing the neck and sliding between the large muscles in the posterior portion of the President's body through a fascia channel without violating the pleural cavity but bruising the apex of the right pleural cavity, and bruising the most apical portion of the right lung inflicting a hematoma to the right side of the larynx . . . striking the trachea . . . and then exiting from the hole . . . in the midline of the neck. Now, assuming those facts to be true, would the hole . . . in the neck of the President be consistent with an exit wound under those circumstances?   *(3H 373)*

According to the Warren Report, Dr. Carrico and Dr. Perry expressed the belief that, on those assumptions, it was an exit wound; other doctors (Baxter, McClelland, Jenkins, and Jones) agreed with Carrico and Perry. The Warren Report does not suggest that any of these witnesses expressed any reservations or that their agreement was conditional, as their testimony reveals.

> *Dr. McClelland*—testified on March 21, 1964 that his knowledge of the entrance wound (anterior neck wound) was based purely on Dr. Perry's description. His present opinion was colored by everything he had heard and read about the assassination, but if he saw a wound such as the one described by Dr. Perry and knew nothing of the circumstances, he would call it an entrance wound. However, under the assumptions specified and in the light of the autopsy findings, he agreed that the anterior neck wound might be consistent with exit, since a bullet traveling through soft tissues would have lost much of its initial velocity and kinetic strength and therefore, particularly if it was a fragment, would have made a small hole in exiting.
> *(6H 37-38)*

> *Dr. Baxter*—Under the assumptions specified, it is possible that the anterior neck wound was an exit wound, although it would be unusual for a high-velocity missile of the type described to cause such a wound. It would be unlikely because the missile would tend to strike tissues of greater density than this missile did; it would then begin to tumble and would do much more damage, ordinarily leaving a large jagged wound of exit. *(6H 42)*

> *Dr. Jenkins*—The anterior neck wound would not be inconsistent with an exit wound, under the assumptions specified. *(6H 51)*

> *Dr. Jones*—The anterior neck wound would be consistent with an exit wound "of very low velocity to the point that you might think that this bullet barely made it through the soft tissues and just enough to drop out of the skin on the opposite side." *(6H 55)*

> *Nurse Henchliffe*—(who had maintained firmly that the wound was an entrance wound) conceded that she had been told that a high-powered rifle could produce an exit wound that looked very much like an entrance wound, if the missile struck only soft tissues. *(6H 143)*

The crux of the matter is in Dr. McClelland's frank statement that his opinion was colored by everything he had heard and read about the assassination, but if he were to see a wound like the anterior neck wound without knowing anything about the circumstances of the shooting, he would call it an entrance wound. His candor is to be admired, and his statement is perhaps a more genuine reflection of the real opinion of the other Parkland doctors than they themselves ventured. They were hardly in a position to take a stand at variance with the elaborate hypothesis posed by Specter, which obviously represented the official view of the crime and to which their agreement was clearly desired. They had, after all, overlooked two of the President's four wounds, thus creating misunderstandings and problems in terms of the public. This had contributed to persistent skepticism about the number and nature of the wounds, the direction of the shots, and the identity of the assassin. It is small wonder if the Parkland doctors were willing to co-operate by authenticating the official conclusions, adjusting their initial impressions, modifying their statements to the press, in the retelling, and facilitating the metamorphosis of the entrance wound into an exit wound.

It is revealing that even after the metamorphosis Dr. McClelland committed the *faux pas* of referring to the wound as an entrance wound. *(6H 37)* He need not have been abashed: Arlen Specter, the counsel who was mainly responsible for the medical and ballistics evidence, made the same slip of the tongue while questioning another witness. *(2H 82)*

As discussed earlier, the autopsy findings were conditioned by external factors such as the number and direction of the shots and by "information received from Parkland Hospital." The Parkland doctors, conditioned by "everything heard and read," and by autopsy findings supporting and supported by an external version of the crime, reversed their original opinion. Can such conditioning produce medical findings of an independent, objective, or scientific standard? The answer is plain enough and is confirmed in the testimony.

In assessing the medical and autopsy findings, the Warren Commission has made no attempt to achieve precision, coherence, or plausibility. Parts of the testimony that introduced complications or heresy with respect to the official theory were brushed aside without mention in the Report. Useful passages of testimony were lifted out of context and used to support arguments to which the testimony was really antithetical. The Commission has not even troubled to explain how the 45-degree trajectory specified repeatedly by its counsel, Arlen Specter, became transformed in its final version into about 17 degrees. It has written a false version of events on and immediately after the day of the assassination, making a scapegoat of the press for alleged misrepresentation of statements made by the Parkland doctors about the President's wounds; however, it has not documented its charges against the news media by means of the transcripts of those statements and interviews which, according to available information, were obtained by or accessible to the Commission. There are legitimate grounds for castigating the press, not the least of which is its obeisance to the Warren Report. But from all indications, the newspapers reported what the Parkland doctors said, with reasonable fidelity. *The New York Times* did not invent the remarks published as an exact quotation from Dr. Kemp Clark. Richard Dudman reported in the *St. Louis Post-Dispatch* what Dr. McClelland actually said, as he himself acknowledged.

The Warren Commission has walked a thin line between distortion and misrepresentation in reporting the testimony on the anterior neck wound. A faithful account would have acknowledged that (1) the Parkland doctors originally thought it was an entrance wound and said so to the press; (2) they later concurred in the autopsy findings because those findings postulated relationships between wounds that they themselves had seen and wounds that they had overlooked, thus jeopardizing their ability to make an independent judgment or to challenge the conclusions; and (3) they now agree conditionally that the anterior neck wound was, or could have been, an exit wound, on the basis of assumptions posed to them which left no alternative.

The misrepresentation of the Parkland doctors' views by the Commission is reprehensible in itself. But the Commission becomes even more censurable when we take into account the suppressed FBI reports (dated November 26,

1963, December 9, 1963, and January 13, 1964 respectively), all of which assert without qualification that the missile which struck the President's back penetrated only to the length of a finger and did not exit from his body. If those FBI descriptions are correct, the anterior neck wound cannot be an exit wound caused by that same missile.

Then what caused the wound at the Adam's apple?

One of the early theories was that the wound was made by a fragment of metal or a piece of bone from the head shot. I regard this theory as untenable, for the simple reason that the President clutched at his throat at least four and one half seconds before a bullet struck his head.

If the bullet wound in the throat was made by neither the missile that struck the back nor the one that struck the head, and if the wound had the appearance of an entrance wound and was regarded as such by the Parkland doctors, the possibility becomes inescapable that a shot was fired from a position in front of the President (whose head was turned toward the grassy knoll to his right during the moments before shots were heard).

The Warren Commission completely suppressed the FBI descriptions of the back wound; it did not take testimony from Agents Sibert and O'Neill; it did not admit the existence of a conflict between the FBI reports and the autopsy report with respect to the back wound and, inferentially, the anterior neck wound; it did not resolve that conflict but arbitrarily chose to present the autopsy report as the correct and the only finding; and, some nine months after the FBI Summary and Supplemental Reports were finally made known to the press and the public in page-one stories and major articles in the most widely read mass circulation magazines, no one who served the Commission or who can speak today with official authority has been able to produce a single counter-argument to the charge that the autopsy report is spurious.

Such monumental default of responsibility must be considered prima-facie vindication of the critics of the Warren Report and the charges leveled against the autopsy report.

To accept the findings of the Warren Commission it is necessary now to accept as innocent coincidence not only the ten constraints listed on pages 148 and 149 but the following "innocent coincidences" as well:

(1) The Parkland Hospital doctors in reports written within hours of the President's death and in statements to the press described the wound at the Adam's apple as a wound of entrance.[39]

(2) The Warren Report mistakenly asserts that the Parkland doctors formed no opinion as to whether it was a wound of entrance *or* exit.

(3) The transcript or tape of the doctors' press conference on November 22 has been "lost."

---

39 Dr. Nathan Jacobs has pointed out that the doctors at Parkland Hospital described a laceration of the pharynx and trachea larger than the small wound at the anterior surface of the neck, indicating that the bullet had traveled from the front of the neck to the back. (Letters, *Ramparts,* January 1967, pp. 6-7)

(4) All Secret Service and FBI reports of interviews with the Parkland doctors and nurses are excluded from the published exhibits.

(5) There is no metallic residue at the holes in the front of the shirt.

(6) The Secret Service, with the autopsy report in hand, conducted on-site re-enactment tests on December 5, 1963 with the avowed purpose of determining how Kennedy was hit in the front from behind.

(7) The FBI confirmed to the *Washington Post* that the first bullet to hit Kennedy "was found deep in his shoulder" before that statement was published on December 18, 1963.

The Fatal Head Wound

Immediately after the assassination there were conflicting reports about the location of a wound or wounds in the President's head, the most frequent report being that a bullet had struck the right temple. Ten months later the Warren report asserted that a bullet had entered the right rear of the President's head, causing a massive and fatal wound. *(WR 86)* Nevertheless, the Hearings and Exhibits reveal unresolved questions: indications of a wound on the left side of the head, persistent suggestions that a bullet struck the right temple, the failure of a single doctor or nurse at Parkland Hospital to observe the alleged entry wound in the right-rear area of the head, the failure of two Secret Service agents and two FBI agents present at the autopsy examination to report an entry wound in the right rear of the head, the ambiguous description of the entry wound by a third Secret Service agent, and—perhaps the most significant of all—the President's reaction to the shot to the head as seen in the Zapruder film, already mentioned in Chapter 1, showing conclusively that the bullet sent the President sharply backward and to his left and that the bullet must have come not from the Book Depository window but from the front and to the right of the President.

The Left Side

Dr. Robert McClelland of Parkland Hospital stated in his written report of November 22, 1963, completed at 4:45 p.m. that day, that "The cause of death was . . . massive head and brain injury from a gunshot wound of the left temple." *(CE 392)* In his deposition of March 21, 1964 Dr. McClelland was questioned about that written report.

> Specter: Dr. McClelland, I show you now a statement or a report which . . . has been identified in a previous Commission hearing as Commission Exhibit No. 392 . . . and I would ask you first of all if this is your signature . . . and next, whether in fact you did make this report and submit it to the authorities at Parkland Hospital?

McClelland: Yes.

Specter: And are all the facts set forth true and correct to the best of your knowledge, information and belief?

McClelland: To the best of my knowledge, yes.   *(6H 35)*

Was Specter oblivious to the startling and contradictory report of a gunshot wound of the left temple when the autopsy report and the testimony of the autopsy surgeon, taken by Specter himself on March 15, 1964, placed that wound on the right side of the head? His failure to remark on the discrepancy evidences inexcusable inattention to detail and a degree of carelessness inappropriate to his responsibility—especially when he was somewhat preoccupied with allegations of a wound on the left side of the President's head at the time that he took Dr. McClelland's deposition. On the same day, March 21, 1964, Specter also examined Dr. Kemp Clark.

Specter: At any of the press conferences were you asked about a hole on the left side of the President's head?

Dr. Clark: Yes. . . I was asked about this at the C.B.S. conference and I stated that I personally saw no such wound.

Specter: And who asked you about it at that time, if you recall?

Dr. Clark: The man who was conducting the conference. This was brought up by one of the physicians, I think Dr. McClelland, that there was some discussion of such a wound.

Specter: Did Dr. McClelland say that he had seen such a wound?

Dr. Clark: No.

Specter: What was the origin, if you know, as to the inquiry on the wound, that is, who suggested that there might have been a wound on the left side?

Dr. Clark: I don't recall—I don't recall.

Specter: Had there been some comment that the priests made a comment that there was a wound on the left side of the head?

Dr. Clark: I heard this subsequently from one of the reporters who attended the press conference with N.B.C.   *(6H 25)*

In the light of this dialogue, Specter's failure to clarify the issue with Dr. McClelland on the same day or when McClelland returned to give further testimony on March 25, 1964 compounds the negligence of his performance. Also noteworthy is the failure of the Commission or its investigative agencies, particularly the FBI, even to interview the priests who administered the last rites. One of them, Father Oscar L. Huber, was quoted in the press as saying that he had seen a terrible wound over the President's left eye.[40]

Dr. Marion Jenkins, another Parkland Hospital doctor, introduced the subject of the location of the head wound during his testimony on March 25, 1964:

Dr. Jenkins: I don't know whether this is right or not, but I thought there was a wound on the left temporal area, right in the hairline and right above the zygomatic process.

Specter: The autopsy report discloses no such development, Dr. Jenkins.

(6H 48)

---

40 *Philadelphia Sunday Bulletin,* November 24, 1963.

Have you ever changed any of your original opinions in connection with the wounds received by President Kennedy?

Dr. Jenkins: I guess so. The first day I had thought because of his pneumothorax, that his wound must have gone—that the one bullet must have traversed his pleura, must have gotten into his lung cavity, his chest cavity, I mean, and from what you say now, I know it did not go that way. I thought it did. . . . I asked you a little bit ago if there was a wound in the left temporal area, right above the zygomatic bone in the hairline, because there was blood there and I thought there might have been a wound there . . . the left temporal area, which could have been a point of entrance . . . but you have answered that for me. *(6H 51)*

Dr. Adolph H. Giesecke, Jr. also testified on March 25, 1964, responding as follows:

Specter: What did you observe specifically as to the nature of the cranial wound?

Dr. Giesecke: It seemed that from the vertex to the left ear, and from the browline to the occiput on the left-hand side of the head the cranium was entirely missing.

Specter: Was that the left-hand side of the head, or the right-hand side of the head?

Dr. Giesecke: I would say the left, but this is just my memory of it—I was there a very short time, really. *(6H 74)*

The autopsy documents also provide some cryptic indications of damage to the left side of the head. The notorious face-sheet on which Dr. J. Thornton Boswell committed his unfortunate "diagram error" consists of front and back outlines of a male figure. On the front figure, the autopsy surgeons entered the tracheotomy incision (6.5 cm.), the four cut-downs made in the Parkland emergency room for administration of infusions (2 cms. each), and a small circle at the right eye, with the marginal notation "0.8 cm.," apparently representing damage produced by the two bullet fragments that lodged there. Dr. Humes testified that the fragments measured 7 by 2 mm. and 3 by 1 mm. respectively. *(2H 354)* Although he said nothing about damage at the left eye, the diagram shows a small dot at that site, labeled "0.4 cm." *(CE 397, Vol. XVII, p. 45)* Neither Arlen Specter, who conducted the questioning of the autopsy surgeons, nor the Commission members and lawyers present asked any questions about this indication on the diagram of damage at the left eye.

Turning to the back outline of the male figure—the one Dr. Boswell did not realize would become a public document even though it had to be assumed at the time of the autopsy that the findings would become evidence at the trial of the accused assassin—we find a small circle at the back of the head about equidistant from the ears and level with the tops of the ears. Apparently this represents the small entrance wound which the autopsy surgeons and the Warren Commission say entered the back of the head and exploded out through the right side, carrying large segments of the skull. But an arrow at the wound on the diagram points to the front *and left* and not to the front and right.

A forensic pathologist who was asked to interpret this feature said that it signified that a missile had entered the back of the head traveling to the left and front. And as if in confirmation, an autopsy diagram of the skull (*CE 397*, Vol. XVII, p. 46) shows a large rectangle marked "3 cm." at the site of the left eye, with a ragged lateral margin, seemingly to indicate fracture or missing bone.

The autopsy surgeons were not questioned about any of the three diagram indications of bullet damage at the left eye or left temple. Nevertheless, when Dr. Jenkins testified that he thought there was a wound in the left temporal area, Arlen Specter replied, "The autopsy report disclosed no such development."

The Right Temple

Seth Kantor of the White House Press Corps recorded his observations at Parkland Hospital in handwritten notes. When Press Secretary Malcolm Kilduff announced the death of the President, Kantor noted "voice shook failed wetness down face" and then he wrote a phrase which obviously refers to the fatal head shot: "entered right temple." (*Kantor Exhibit 3*, p. 353) Hurchel Jacks, Texas State Highway Patrolman who served as driver of the Vice-President's car in the motorcade, said in his written report of November 28, 1963, "Before the President's body was covered it appeared that the bullet had struck him above the right ear or near the temple." (*CE 1024*, p. 801) It was, in fact, the general impression that the bullet had struck the right temple. As memory alone testifies, news bulletins on the radio and television on the fatal day stated repeatedly that a shot had struck the right temple. (*The New York Times* reported this as late as December 17, 1963.)[41]

The impression originated with the doctors at Parkland Hospital, who had observed the massive damage to the right side of the head but failed to note or confirm the presence of a small, round entry wound in the back of the head. Every doctor testified that he had not seen such a wound: Dr. Carrico (*6H 6*), Dr. Perry (*6H 16*), Dr. Clark (*6H 25*), Dr. McClelland (*6H 35*), Dr. Baxter (*6H 42*), Dr. Jenkins (*6H 48, 51*), Dr. Jones (*6H 56*), Dr. Curtis (*6H 60*), Dr. Bashour (*6H 62*), Dr. Akin (*6H 67*), Dr. Peters (*6H 71*), Dr. Giesecke (*6H 74*), Dr. Salyer (*6H 81*), and Dr. White (*6H 82*).

The Entry Wound

In view of the indications that there was a bullet wound on the left side of the head and that a bullet entered the right temple, one hesitates to accept the Warren Report's assertion that the entry wound was in the back of the head. Secret Service Agent William Greer, who was present throughout the autopsy, testified that he did not see that wound. (*2H 128*) Secret Service Agent Clinton Hill, who was called in to witness the wounds, did not mention it. (*2H 143*) FBI Agents Sibert and O'Neill do not explicitly indicate the presence of such a wound in their report. Roy Kellerman of the Secret Service is, in fact, the only witness present as an observer at the autopsy who confirmed the existence of the entry wound in the head, but he described it as located in the hairline to the right of

---

41 *The New York Times*, December 17, 1963, p. 31.

the right ear. *(2H 81)* If Kellerman said what he actually meant, the entry wound would be situated in the hairline above the right cheek, which in turn would be consistent with the original reports of a shot to the right temple.

Corroboration for the existence of the entry wound in the back of the head (to which the autopsy surgeons certified) is strangely scarce. None of the medical personnel at Parkland Hospital saw this wound. Because Specter's interrogation of them was so imprecise, it is not clear whether the doctors failed to see the wound because they did not look at the part of the head where it was situated, or whether, having examined that area of the head, they simply failed to notice the wound. Dr. Clark, for example, testified that he had "examined the wound in the back of the President's head," and described it as "a large, gaping wound" *(6H 20)*; however, Specter did not pursue this with questions to determine whether the examination had been superficial, or sufficiently thorough to have revealed the presence of the wound if it was indeed present.

FBI Agents Sibert and O'Neill say that "X rays of the brain area . . . disclosed a path of a missile which appeared to enter the back of the skull," but nowhere in their detailed six-page report is there any mention of a small bullet wound in the back of the head. (*Commission Document No. 7*, pp. 280-286.) It seems singular that the two FBI agents should cite X rays to infer that a bullet had entered the back of the head but not a bullet entrance wound which, if it were there, would be "best evidence."

All the more baffling, then, is the crude skull diagram made during the autopsy (*CE 397*, Vol. XVII, p. 46) that discloses to the layman's eye nothing which seems identifiable with a small entrance wound in the skull. A forensic pathologist who was asked to interpret this diagram stated:

> "As far as I can see, the sketch on page 46, Volume XVII does not show the small round entrance wound that was described by the pathologist in the right occipital area of the skull."[42]

Needless to say, Specter did not raise any questions with the autopsy surgeons about this extraordinary feature of the skull diagram.

Consequently we have a so-called entrance wound in the back of the head that was not seen by witnesses who should have seen it; that was seen in the wrong place by the one autopsy witness who did see it; and that is not shown at all on the autopsy skull diagram on which it should have been a central feature.

The 313 Head Shot

In discussing the head wounds the Warren Report finds all the evidence consistent with shots fired from the Book Depository window. Here, too, as in the case of the anterior neck wound, a metamorphosis has taken place. Findings originally inconsistent with shots from the Book Depository have become compatible with that source in their final version. Uncertainties and contradictions

---

42   Letter to the author dated August 5, 1966 from Dr. Cyril H. Wecht, Director, Institute of Forensic Sciences, Duquesne University School of Law and Chief Forensic Pathologist, Allegheny County.

which create doubt about the pronouncements in the Warren Report have been ignored by the Commission.

But the most compelling evidence against the Commission's findings with respect to the head wounds is found in the Zapruder film, Frame 313 and the frames which follow. Not only Thomas Stamm (quoted on pages 33-34) but also other researchers who have viewed and analyzed the Zapruder film and its individual frames (including, for example, Vincent Salandria, Gaetano Fonzi, and Ray Marcus) consider—on the basis of mathematically precise measurements of the President's movement to the back and the left in reaction to the impact of the bullet which struck his head in Frame 313—that the Zapruder film proves conclusively that the bullet came from some point on the grassy knoll to the President's right, and that the bullet could not possibly have come from the Book Depository.

Chapter 1 presented some of the evidence that vitiates the single-missile hypothesis and this section has presented evidence that the bullet in the President's back did not exit from his body. To maintain that the Governor was a victim of the same bullet that hit the President has become impossible. But if he was hit by a different bullet, there had to be at least two riflemen, because, according to the Warren Report, the Governor was hit too soon after the President for the same rifleman to have operated the bolt (2.3 seconds is the minimum time, without including aiming time) and fired a second shot.

The President's reaction to the bullet that struck his head in Frame 313 of the Zapruder film provides another compelling indication of two or even three assassins, operating their weapons in a synchronized cross fire. The evidence of a conspiracy is ample and irresistible.

This is not to say categorically that the conclusions of the Warren Commission about the fatal head shot must be rejected. They may be accepted, so long as one is prepared to dismiss the following manifestations as random, innocent, and misleading coincidence:

(1) The Zapruder film shows that the impact of the head bullet in Frame 313 sent President Kennedy slamming back against the seat and to his left.

(2) The Warren Commission has neither mentioned nor investigated with forensic experts the significance of the President's body recoil to the back and left, which is prima-facie evidence of a shot from the front and right of the car.

(3) Frames 314 and 315 are transposed and misnumbered in the Commission's Exhibit No. 885.

(4) Not one of the sixteen medical personnel at Parkland Hospital confirms the presence of a small entrance wound in the back of the head, including the doctor or doctors who may have examined the back of the head.

(5) Four federal agents present at the autopsy do not corroborate the existence of the wound.

(6) One federal agent saw an apparent small entrance wound but at a location inconsistent with the schematic drawings and the autopsy findings.

(7) X rays of the skull have been withheld from the Exhibits.

(8) The autopsy skull diagram does not show the wound.

(9) The autopsy face sheet shows the wound, but traveling from right to left.

(10) The autopsy surgeons were asked no questions about any of these anomalies when they testified before the Warren Commission.

Adding these ten points to those previously listed makes a total of 27 incongruities. To accept the findings and conclusions of the Warren Commission of the President's wounds despite these constraints and contradictions requires an extravagant act of faith. But we are dealing with murder, not metaphysics; and the magic names of the Commission members are not sufficient to overcome the evidence against the Commission when that evidence is weighed impartially and without fear of committing heresy.

The Governor's Wounds, the Single-Missile Hypothesis, and the Stretcher Bullet

In this section I shall discuss still more instances in which prime data cited in the Warren Report proves to be unreliable as a result of the atrocious disorder, apathy, and capriciousness already encountered in the medical evidence regarding the President. In the Governor's case, basic information appears within the Warren Report in two different and irreconcilable versions; far worse, the Report utilizes testimony which was later retracted, without acknowledgment, thus resting its central conclusions in part upon expert opinion subsequently withdrawn, and doing so both consciously and deliberately. Finally, it will be shown that there is the most serious doubt about the legitimacy and source of the stretcher bullet and its assigned role as the missile which inflicted two of the President's wounds and all the Governor's.

The Wound in the Back

The Warren Report states that Governor Connally sustained bullet wounds of the back, chest, right wrist, and left thigh, and that "Because of the *small size and clean-cut edges* of the wound on the Governor's back, Dr. Robert Shaw con-concluded that it was an entry wound." [Italics added] *(WR 92)*

Only 17 pages later in the Report, in the exposition of the sequence of the shots and the trajectories of the bullets, the wound has changed its size as easily and imaginatively as a detail on canvas is swiftly enlarged at an artist's whim. Now we are told that:

> ... the *large wound* on the Governor's back would be explained by a bullet which was yawing, although that type of wound might also be accounted for by a tangential striking. [Italics added]   *(WR 109)*

Study of the testimony indicates that the contradictory descriptions of the Governor's back wound derived from the testimony of Dr. Robert Shaw, the surgeon who operated on Governor Connally for a gunshot wound of the chest with comminuted fracture of the fifth rib. First he had reported the dimensions of the wound as "three centimeters (1.2 inches) in its longest diameter." *(CE 392)* Later he had testified that the wound was "approximately a centimeter and a half (3/5 inch) in its longest diameter." *(6H 85; 4H 104)*

But Dr. Alfred Olivier, Army wound ballistics expert, relied not on Dr. Shaw's testimony but on his earlier report, in which the wound was twice as large. Olivier, on May 13, 1964, gave the following testimony:

> The surgeon's report described [the back wound] as about three centimeters long, its longest dimension, and it is hard for me to remember reading it or discussing it with him but I did both. Apparently it was a jagged wound. He said a wound like this consists of two things, usually a defect in the epidermis and a central hole which is small, and he could put his finger in it so it was a fairly large wound.   *(5H 79)*

Another Army ballistics expert, Dr. Arthur J. Dziemian, testified also on the same day as Dr. Olivier.

> *Specter:* Based on the description provided to you of the nature of the wound in the Governor's back, what is your opinion as to whether or not that was a pristine bullet or had yaw in it, just on the basis of the nature of the wound on the Governor's back?
> *Dr. Dziemian:* It could very well have yaw in it because of the rather large wound that was produced in the Governor's back. The wound from a non-yawing bullet could be considerably smaller.   *(5H 93)*

Specter was so eager to elicit expert opinion that the missile that hit the Governor in the back had yaw in it (and was not pristine and therefore had first traveled through the President's body) that he never even noticed that there were two radically different descriptions of a single wound. The opinion of Dr. Dziemian and his colleagues, said by the Report to suggest that "the same bullet probably passed through both President Kennedy and Governor Connally" *(WR 107)*, was based on data which may well be absolutely incorrect.[43] Even at this point in time, it is still impossible to be sure whether the wound was in fact large and jagged or small with clean-cut edges—whether it measured 1.2 inches or only .6 inch. The hole in the back of the Governor's coat (5/8" x 1/4") corresponds more with the smaller wound, but this in itself is not conclusive.

Such blundering can scarcely qualify as "fact finding." Perhaps some of the enormous errors and oversights in the Commission's investigation can be charged to the lack of co-ordination between the separate areas of inquiry, parceled out as they were among lawyers or pairs of lawyers who did not or could not maintain adequate liaison or transmit their findings to each other. But it is clear from the Hearings that Arlen Specter had the sole responsibility for the autopsy and

---

43   Epstein points out in *Inquest* (p. 121) that the wound ballistics experiments, moreover, employed an erroneous mathematical equation in measuring loss of bullet velocity.

medical evidence and was independent, for all practical purposes, in establishing the facts in that area. Specter handled all the testimony on the wounds, including the wounds ballistics experiments; presumably he also wrote the corresponding sections of the Warren Report. Since the conflicting versions of the entry wound in the Governor's back did not register with him, it must be asked whether the size of the wound was irrelevant to the elaboration of the official hypothesis—whether the conclusions would have been the same regardless of the actual size of the wound—and whether the official hypothesis was formulated gradually, as various items of evidence were collected, as it should have been, or had another origin.

If Specter and the Commission had embarked on a journey in faithful pursuit of the facts, wherever they might lead, it is incomprehensible that something as elementary as determining the size of a wound (on a victim who had survived his injuries and displayed his scars to the Commission) remained undone. It becomes understandable only if there were prefabricated conclusions to which the strict determination of facts was irrelevant—or even dangerous.

The Single-Missile Theory

If the Commission wished to demonstrate that a single bullet had wounded both the President and the Governor, it would have to establish first that all the Governor's wounds were, or could have been, inflicted by the same missile. The Warren Report claims that this indeed was accomplished. It states:

> In their testimony, the three doctors who attended Governor Connally at Parkland Hospital expressed independently their opinion that a single bullet had passed through his chest; tumbled through his wrist with very little exit velocity, leaving small metallic fragments from the rear portion of the bullet; punctured his left thigh after the bullet had lost virtually all of its velocity; and fallen out of the thigh wound. *(WR 95)*

The footnote at the end of that passage cites the depositions taken from Dr. Robert Shaw, Dr. Charles Gregory, and Dr. George Shires on March 23, 1964. *(6H 83-112)* Their testimony on that date is consistent with the statement in the Report.

But Dr. Shaw and Dr. Gregory testified a second time, on this occasion at a Commission hearing on April 21, 1964. Before they were examined by Arlen Specter, they were given the opportunity to view the Zapruder film, the stretcher bullet, and other physical evidence which they had never seen before.

Dr. Shaw proceeded, explicitly and unambiguously, to modify the opinion he had rendered when his deposition was taken a month earlier.

> *Dr. Shaw:* Mr. Dulles, I thought I knew just how the Governor was wounded until I saw the pictures [the Zapruder film—S.M.] today, and it becomes a little bit harder to explain. I felt that the wound had been caused by the same bullet that came out through the chest . . . and this is still a possibility. But I don't feel that it is the only possibility.
>
> *Senator Cooper:* Why do you say you don't think it is the only possibility? What causes you now to say that it is the location—

Dr. Shaw: This is again the testimony that I believe Dr. Gregory will be giving, too. It is a matter of whether the wrist wound could be caused by the same bullet, and we felt that it could but we had not seen the bullets until today, and we still do not know which bullet actually inflicted the wound on Governor Connally.

Dulles: Or whether it was one or two wounds?

Dr. Shaw: Yes.

Dulles: Or two bullets?

Dr. Shaw: Yes; or three. . . . He has three separate wounds. He had a wound in the chest, a wound of the wrist, a wound of the thigh.

McCloy: You have no firm opinion that all these wounds were caused by one bullet?

Dr. Shaw: I have no firm opinion. . . . If you had asked me a month ago I would have.

Dulles: Could they have been caused by one bullet, in your opinion?

Dr. Shaw: They could.

McCloy: I gather that what the witness is saying is that it is possible that they might have been caused by one bullet. But that he has no firm opinion now that they were.

Dulles: As I understand it too. Is our understanding correct?

Dr. Shaw: That is correct.   *(4H 109)*

Dr. Shaw: As far as the wounds of the chest are concerned, I feel that this bullet [the stretcher bullet—S.M.] could have inflicted those wounds. But the examination of the wrist both by X ray and at the time of surgery showed some fragments of metal that make it difficult to believe that the same missile could have caused these two wounds. There seems to be more than three grains of metal missing as far as the—I mean in the wrist. *(4H 113)*

I feel that there would be some difficulty in explaining all of the wounds as being inflicted by bullet Exhibit 399 [the stretcher bullet] without causing more in the way of loss of substance to the bullet or deformation of the bullet.   *(4H 114)*

Dr. Gregory's testimony in April 1964 suggested that he too had modified or developed reservations with respect to his earlier opinion.

Specter: What opinion, if any, do you have as to whether that bullet could have produced the wound on the Governor's right wrist and remained as intact as it is at the present time?

Dr. Gregory: The only way that this missile [the stretcher bullet] could have produced this wound in my view, was to have entered the wrist backward. . . . That is the only possible explanation I could offer to correlate this missile with this particular wound.   *(4H 121)*

Specter: Assume, if you will, another set of hypothetical circumstances: That the 6.5 millimeter bullet traveling at the same muzzle velocity, to wit, 2,000 feet per second, at approximately 165 feet between the weapon and the victim, struck the President in the back of the neck passing through the large strap muscles, going through a fascia channel, missing the pleural cavity, striking no bones and emerging from the lower anterior third of the neck, after striking the trachea. Could such a projectile have then passed into the Governor's back and inflicted all three or all of the wounds which have been described?

Dr. Gregory: I believe one would have to concede the possibility, but I believe firmly that the probability is much diminished.

Specter: Why do you say that, sir?

Dr. Gregory: I think that to pass through the soft tissues of the President would certainly have decelerated the missile to some extent. Having then struck the Governor and shattered a rib, it is further decelerated, yet it has presumably retained sufficient energy to smash a radius.

Moreover, it escaped the forearm to penetrate at least the skin and fascia of the thigh, and I am not persuaded that this is very probable. . . . *(4H 127)*

On March 16, 1964, a month before hearing that testimony from Dr. Gregory and Dr. Shaw, the Commission questioned two of the autopsy surgeons about the possibility that the stretcher bullet had inflicted the Governor's wounds.

Specter: . . . could that missile have made the wound on Governor Connally's right wrist?

Dr. Humes: I think that this is most unlikely. . . . This missile is basically intact; its jacket appears to me to be intact, and I do not understand how it could possibly have left fragments [in the Governor's wrist]. . . .
(2H 374-375)

Specter: Dr. Humes, under your opinion which you have just given us, what effect, if any, would that have on whether this bullet, 399, could have been the one to lodge in Governor Connally's thigh?

Dr. Humes: I think that extremely unlikely. The reports . . . from Parkland tell of an entrance wound on the lower midthigh . . . and X rays taken there are described as showing metallic fragments in the bone, which apparently by this report were not removed and are still present in Governor Connally's thigh. I can't conceive of where they came from this missile.   *(2H 376)*

Specter: And could it have been the bullet which inflicted the wound on Governor Connally's right wrist?

Dr. Finck: No; for the reason that there are too many fragments described in that wrist.
(2H 382)

Now that we have read the testimony of the expert medical witnesses, let us see how it is reflected in the Warren Report. The Report asserts:

All the evidence indicated that the bullet found on the Governor's stretcher could have caused all his wounds. The weight of the whole bullet prior to firing was approximately 160-161 grains. . . . An X ray of the Governor's wrist showed very minute metallic fragments, and two or three of these fragments were removed from his wrist. All these fragments were sufficiently small and light so that the nearly whole bullet found on the stretcher could have deposited those pieces of metal as it tumbled through his wrist.
(WR 95)

That passage is a tissue of misstatement and crude misrepresentation. We have already seen how the Commission, unabashed, cited the testimony of three doctors without adding that one of the doctors subsequently retracted his original opinion, a second doctor qualified his earlier testimony, and the third doctor was never recalled, never shown the Zapruder film or the stretcher bullet, or given the opportunity to reconsider his opinion in the light of physical evidence he had never seen or taken into account. The assertions about the stretcher bullet are no less deceptive in their deviation from the facts. Predictably, this author's letters to General Counsel J. Lee Rankin requesting a clarification of these misstatements have gone unanswered.

The Stretcher Bullet

The Report asserts that "all the evidence" indicates that the stretcher bullet could have caused all the Governor's wounds, despite the flat statements by Drs. Humes and Finck that it could not and the serious doubts of Drs. Shaw and Gregory. Next, the Report deals with the weight of the whole bullet prior to firing, approximately 160-161 grains, arguing that the stretcher bullet, 158.6 grains in weight, could have deposited the fragments in the Governor's wrist without greater depletion of its substance. The Report does not mention that FBI Expert Robert Frazier testified that the stretcher bullet had not necessarily lost any of its original weight, because there was a normal variation of at least two grains in the standard weight of the manufactured bullet. *(3H 430)* Contending that the fragments in the wrist were "sufficiently small and light" to have come from the stretcher bullet without decreasing its weight below 158.6 grains, the Report takes no account of the bullet fragment, miniscule though it is, that remained embedded in the Governor's thigh bone. *(6H 106)* And it does not mention or resolve a conflict in the testimony about bullet fragments in the chest.

Dr. Shaw testified that there was no metallic substance in the X ray of the Governor's chest, and that none was found during surgery. *(4H 105)* But Dr. George T. Shires had testified a month earlier as follows:

> *Specter:* Do you have any knowledge as to what fragments there were in the chest, bullet fragments, if any?
> *Dr. Shires:* No, again except from postoperative X rays, there is a small fragment remaining, but the initial fragments I think Dr. Shaw saw before I arrived.   *(6H 111)*

X rays of the Governor's chest taken on November 22 and November 29, 1963 *(CE 681-682)* do not resolve the issue for the layman. Because the Commission made no effort to reconcile the contradiction in the testimony, the possibility that Dr. Shires was correct remains open.[44]

Spectrography

Because only the wrist fragments were taken into account in the Report, the argument that they were so small and light that they could have been

---

44 W. David Slawson, Assistant Counsel to the Warren Commission, wrote recently that Dr. Shaw, ". . . who did the work on Connally's chest, was apparently not even aware that a bullet fragment was present there." (Letters to the Editor, *Commentary*, April 1967, page 14, column 3.)

deposited by the "nearly whole bullet" (which in fact may be whole) is scarcely scientific or conclusive. Yet there was open to the Commission a scientific and conclusive method for determining whether a metallic fragment recovered from Connally's wrist had originated in the stretcher bullet. That method was the neutron activation analysis—the same scientific test the Commission utilized in an abortive attempt to reverse the negative result of the paraffin test of Oswald's face.

On the night of November 22, Dallas police took a paraffin test of Oswald's hands and right cheek, to determine if there were traces on his skin indicating that he had fired a weapon; the test was positive for the hands, but negative for the cheek. *(WR 560)* The negative result for the face was generally regarded as evidence in Oswald's favor, but the Warren Report asserts that the paraffin test "is completely unreliable in determining either whether a person has recently fired a weapon or whether he has not." *(WR 561)* The Commission arranged for the paraffin casts of Oswald's hands and cheek to be examined by neutron activation analyses, but the results were inconclusive (if not indeed negative). *(WR 562)*

The Report also mentions the paraffin test in the appendix devoted to the debunking of speculations and rumors. Here, as was the case also with the "speculation" that the rifle found in the Depository had been identified by Seymour Weitzman as a 7.65 Mauser *(WR 645-646)*, the Report labels fact as fiction, and fiction as fact. It states as a "speculation" that "Gordon Shanklin, the special agent in charge of the Dallas office of the FBI, stated that the paraffin test of Oswald's face and hands was positive and proved that he had fired a rifle." The "finding" which follows is that the FBI denied that Shanklin or any other FBI representative had ever made such a statement, and that the Commission discovered no evidence that Shanklin "ever made this statement publicly." *(WR 647)* The Commission could not have searched hard, for it overlooked a story by Anthony Lewis in *The New York Times* of November 25, 1963 (p. 11, cols. 6-8) naming Shanklin as the source of information that a paraffin test "showed that particles of gunpowder from a weapon, probably a rifle, remained on Oswald's cheek and hands."

Neutron activation analysis can determine to the millionth of a part the composition of a metal fragment and establish whether or not it is identical with another sample. Such analysis would have eliminated all need for guesswork. But the Commission presented dubious and slanted arguments for insisting, despite contrary expert testimony, that the stretcher bullet had caused all of Connally's wounds, and declined the opportunity to prove its claim by neutron activation analysis.

Another scientific test—spectrographic analysis—*was* utilized to establish the composition of bullet fragments and metallic residue. The bullet fragments recovered from Kennedy and Connally, the fragments found in the car, and the residue found at the clothing holes, the curb, and the crack on the windshield were submitted to spectrography. The spectrographic analysis was performed by FBI Expert John Gallagher but no testimony was taken from him as to the results. The spectrographic report is missing from the Commission's Exhibits, as

Harold Weisberg pointed out in his book *Whitewash*,[45] and it is not among the documents available in the Archives—presumably it remains "classified" for unknown reasons.

The only information we have about the results of the spectrography is that, according to FBI weapons expert Robert Frazier, "the lead fragments were similar in composition" *(5H 67)*, and that comparison of the stretcher bullet, the various bullet fragments, and the lead scraped from the windshield showed that they were "similar in metallic composition." *(5H 74)* The similarity relates to the lead in these samples, but no information is given about the copper fragments or residue (on the stretcher bullet, on two of the fragments found in the car, and at the holes in the back of Kennedy's clothes). The fact that the lead in the samples was "similar in composition" in no way proves that it came from the same bullet or the same kind of bullet—on the contrary. To say that the metals were of "similar" composition, according to Lawrence R. Brown, historian and critic of the Warren Report:

> . . . means in fact that they were spectrographically dissimilar since spectrographic analysis—there are many kinds [and] that, or those, used is not specified in the record—can be made sufficiently refined to go on down to the number of parts per million where the two pieces of metal were shown to be either the same or different. When the tests failed to prove identity they automatically proved lack of identity.[46]

The physical evidence, including the metal fragments and scrapings, presumably still exists and can still be subjected to neutron activation analysis. Certainly it is not too late to produce the spectrographic report which has been excluded from the published exhibits and the testimony of the responsible FBI expert and which is not available in the Archives. Nor is it too late for spokesmen of the Warren Commission to explain why the spectrographic report was suppressed and why the neutron activation analysis was not performed despite weighty evidence against the unsupported conclusions in the Report.

Pending such a determination, we must continue to rely on the available evidence in evaluating the Commission's claim that the stretcher bullet, although virtually intact, could have left fragments in the Governor's body. The whole argument about the number of grains missing from the bullet in terms of its pristine weight is inconclusive so long as the pristine weight is unknown, and there is considerable evidence to suggest that the fragments exceeded the maximum depletion of the original weight of the stretcher bullet.

Perhaps the real issue, as Dr. Finck suggested in his testimony, is why the stretcher bullet was not completely mutilated and fragmented or deformed after the performance postulated by the Commission.

Dr. Alfred G. Olivier, U.S. Army wound ballistics expert, testified that 260 rounds of Western Cartridge Company 6.5 mm. ammunition were obtained for use in the wound ballistics tests carried out to determine the penetration charac-

---

45 *Op cit.*, p. 164.
46 In a letter to the author dated December 19, 1966.

teristics of the bullets. *(5H 75)* It is not known how many of the 260 cartridges were used in the experiments, but the Exhibits show only two. *(CE 853, 856)* One bullet, fired into a human cadaver wrist, emerged with the nose completely flattened *(CE 856)*, in startling contrast to the stretcher bullet *(CE 399)* which, according to the Commission, had penetrated the neck of one man and fractured a rib and wrist bone of a second man.

Two test bullets fired by the FBI for comparison purposes *(CE 572)* (probably into a bale of soft material to prevent mutilation or fragmentation), on the other hand, closely resemble the stretcher bullet.

Asked if it were typical for a bullet to fragment in the way that the bullet that struck the President's head did, Dr. Finck replied that it was; the pattern of the wound and the degree of fragmentation depended largely on the type of ammunition used. Asked if the President's other wounds could have been inflicted by the same kind of bullet that struck the head, Finck said yes, and explained that one bullet had fragmented and the other had not because the fragmented bullet had hit bony structures and the other had not. *(2H 384)*

But the Commission argues that the bullet that hit the President without striking bone then proceeded to hit Connally, shattering a rib and the wrist bone. According to Dr. Finck's expert testimony, the bullet should have been smashed and fragmented in the process. Logic alone suggests that the same kind of bullet, subjected to the same kind of dynamics, would manifest the same characteristics, and that therefore: (a) the stretcher bullet did not inflict the Governor's wounds; or (b) if the two men were struck by a single missile, then the President was hit by two different kinds of bullets fired by different weapons.

Another mortal blow to the Commission's single-missile–single-assassin conclusions is the surface condition of the stretcher bullet when it was delivered to FBI Expert Robert Frazier for examination within hours of its discovery. Frazier testified that the bullet was clean and had no blood or tissue on it. *(3H 428-429)* Yet, asked later about the bullet *fragments* which had been recovered from the Presidential car *(CEs 567, 569)*, Frazier indicated that "there was a very slight residue of blood or some other material adhering" which was wiped off to clean up the fragments for examination. *(3H 437)*

Even more extraordinary than the absence of blood and tissue on the stretcher bullet is the absence of fabric threads or impressions. This bullet, according to the Commission, penetrated and damaged the back of the President's coat and shirt and the front of the shirt, after which it penetrated the Governor's shirt and coat, in back and in front and at the end of the right sleeve in each garment. *(WR 94)* There was also a hole in the trousers, near the left knee. Not only did the bullet have searing contact with garments of four different fabrics, but it carried bits of thread and cloth into the wound in Connally's wrist from which Dr. Gregory was able to deduce the color and fabric of the Governor's suit. *(4H 119)*

Dr. Cyril H. Wecht, chief forensic pathologist of Allegheny County, has said that it is *tantamount to impossible that a bullet could have emerged from such contacts without readily apparent traces of threads*. Such an event was unknown in his experience. While it was possible that blood and tissue might have been shed from the stretcher bullet, leaving only microscopic traces, it was inconceivable that the missile should be barren of thread from the several fabrics it supposedly penetrated. Ballistics expert Joseph D. Nicol testified that he had examined the stretcher bullet to ascertain whether there was any evidence of contact with fabric but had found "nothing of such a nature that it would suggest a pattern, like a weave pattern or anything of that nature." *(3H 505)* This information, casting still more doubt on the stretcher bullet, was blandly disregarded by the Commission.

The Commission has told us that "all the evidence" supports what in actuality it demolishes.[47] It has cited an "independent opinion" but said nothing about its subsequent retraction. And the Commission has told us that there was only one assassin.

But we have seen from the Commission's own evidence that the first two assertions are dubious. Can the third assertion be credible, when the others are clearly distortions of fact?

Whose Stretcher?

Not to be overlooked is the Commission's bland statement that all the evidence indicated that the bullet "found on the Governor's stretcher" could have caused his wounds. *(WR 95)* Arlen Specter, who announced that he would develop evidence to show that the bullet came from the Governor's stretcher *(2H 368)*, nearly managed to prove that it did not—but that did not inhibit the authors of the Report from stating as a certainty what was demonstrated to be all but impossible.

We have already discussed the unscrupulous way in which the Warren Report misrepresented the testimony, both in asserting that the stretcher bullet could have caused all of Governor Connally's wounds, and in pretending that three Parkland Hospital doctors voiced the independent opinion that all of his wounds were caused by one missile. Although the Report is careful not to claim that the three doctors thought that the stretcher bullet was the missile that had caused all the Governor's wounds, that is, of course, what is implied.

Against that insupportable hypothesis, there is the testimony of the medical witnesses—testimony which virtually proves that the stretcher bullet could not have caused any one of Connally's wounds, or any combination of them. Even without such testimony, one would have to marvel at the fact that a bullet considered by the Warren Commission to have inflicted multiple injuries on two men, including the smashing of bones, had no blood or tissue on it. *(3H 429)*

How, then, did this bullet come to be found on a stretcher at Parkland Hospital?

---

47   Wesley J. Liebeler said in a public meeting on September 30, 1966, "The fact that the Report says that all the evidence supports the one-bullet theory is simply not correct. The Report is wrong in that respect, and there is no doubt about it." (WBAI-New York radio broadcast, December 30, 1966)

According to the Commission, the bullet could not have come from the President's stretcher. The Report asserts:

> . . . evidence . . . eliminated President Kennedy's stretcher as a source of the bullet. President Kennedy remained on the stretcher on which he was carried into the hospital while the doctors tried to save his life. He was never removed from the stretcher from the time he was taken into the emergency room until his body was placed in a casket in that same room. After the President's body was removed from that stretcher, the linen was taken off and placed in a hamper and the stretcher was pushed into trauma room No. 2, a completely different location from the site where the nearly whole bullet was found. *(WR 81)*

That is well and good. But the fact is that no attempt was made to determine what happened to the President's stretcher once it was placed in trauma room No. 2, and that it is impossible to account for one of the two stretchers involved in the discovery of the bullet.

Nevertheless, I am inclined to believe that the bullet cannot be attributed to the President's stretcher because of the lack of specific evidence. For the same reason, as well as for the reasons already discussed which suggest forcefully that the stretcher bullet was never in Connally's body, I cannot agree that it came from the Governor's stretcher.

Let us trace the history of that stretcher.

(1) Connally was removed from the Presidential limousine and placed on a stretcher. *(Price Exhibit No. 27)*

(2) He was wheeled to the emergency room *(Price Exhibit No. 27)* where he was disrobed completely by attendants and nurses while lying on the same stretcher. No bullet was seen or recovered. After all garments were removed, the Governor was covered with a sheet. *(6H 116, Price Exhibits No. 23 and 26)*

(3) Still on the same stretcher, the Governor was wheeled to the emergency area elevator and taken to the second-floor operating suite. *(6H 117-118, 121, 124)*

(4) The stretcher was wheeled to the entrance of operating room 5, where the Governor was transferred to an operating table. *(6H 121, 126)*

(5) The stretcher was wheeled part of the way back toward the elevator by a nurse who stopped midway to remove the paraphernalia on the stretcher (sponge, gauze, hypodermic syringe wrappers, roll of one-inch tape). She then rolled the two sheets on the stretcher, one inside the other, into a small tight package, which remained on the carrier. She did not see any bullet—the stretcher bullet is more than an inch long—or hear one fall. *(6H 121-123)*

(6) An orderly then rolled the stretcher onto the elevator and left it there, to be removed two floors below (on the ground level) and returned to the emergency room area by other personnel. *(6H 126-127)*

(7) The senior engineer, who was operating the elevator manually, removed a stretcher from the elevator and placed it next to another stretcher which was already standing there, the origin of which is unknown. He then made several trips up and down in the elevator, leaving the two stretchers unguarded on the ground floor. *(6H 129-131)*

(8) At some point before the Presidential party left the hospital a bullet was noticed on one of the two stretchers after it was jostled. The engineer recovered the bullet and gave it to the chief of personnel, who gave it, in turn, to a Secret Service agent. *(6H 130; CE 1024, p. 799)*

That is the outline of the movements of the Governor's stretcher. The testimony indicates that the stretcher removed from the elevator by the senior engineer corresponded in appearance with the condition of the Governor's stretcher at the time it was placed on the elevator. The second stretcher, which was already standing in the corridor, had on it various items of paraphernalia (including rubber gloves and a stethoscope) and was thought possibly to be the President's stretcher at the time that the stretcher bullet was turned over to the Secret Service agent. *(CE 1024, p. 799)* The engineer believed that the bullet had come from that stretcher and not from the stretcher he had removed from the elevator. According to the orderly, the Governor's stretcher was the only one placed on the elevator during the relevant period of time.

The nurses, the orderly, and the engineer who were involved in handling the Governor's stretcher were interviewed by the FBI at unspecified times before they were deposed by Commission counsel. The FBI reports on those interviews are not found in the published exhibits, although they exist and were referred to by counsel during examination of the witnesses.

The Secret Service agent who took custody of the stretcher bullet at the hospital returned to Washington with the Presidential party. He gave the bullet to his superior, Chief James J. Rowley; Rowley gave it to an FBI agent. In June 1964 the Commission requested the FBI to establish the chain of possession of the stretcher bullet; but the engineer, the chief of personnel at the hospital, the Secret Service agent, and Chief Rowley were unable to make a positive identification of the stretcher bullet *(CE 399)* as the bullet found on the day of the assassination. *(CE 2011)*

Appraisal

The Commission's conclusion that the stretcher bullet came from the Governor's stretcher contradicts the facts. If the autopsy surgeons and the Parkland doctors are not completely confused, the bullet was never in the Governor's body. The Commission has failed to establish on which stretcher the bullet was found or how it got there in the first place.

Several critics of the Warren Report, including Ray Marcus and Vincent J. Salandria, have argued that the stretcher bullet was deliberately planted in order to incriminate the alleged assassin. In the light of the persistent misrepresentation of fact in the Warren Report with respect to evidence which relates directly or indirectly to the stretcher bullet, one can find considerable force in that hypothesis.

Recapitulation

Partisans of the Warren Report will continue to argue that its conclusions are infallible, regardless of the existence and in some instances the concealment by the Warren Commission of fundamental and irreconcilable contradictions in the basic evidence. Some will defend the Report now, as before, out of the fierce faith that has little regard for facts. Others may take the position now, as before, that the Commission muddled through—that its Report is a sorry compilation of half-truths and sophomoric reasoning, that its methods were faulty, and its predisposition plain—but that somehow the illustrious Commission (and by analogy the FBI and the Dallas police) came up with the right answers: Oswald was the assassin, and he acted alone.

To contend with such sophistry is quixotic and perhaps demeaning. There is a film which indicates that the President was shot fatally by a bullet that came from his right front and not from the Book Depository. The Commission and its lawyers must have seen it just as certainly as their critics have seen it, but it maintains silence on this subject to this day. The three FBI descriptions of the back wound, supported by eyewitness testimony and material evidence, are irreconcilable with the autopsy report and the Commission's conclusions. The relevant FBI reports were put before the public for the first time in 1966 by Vincent J. Salandria and by Edward Jay Epstein, having been carefully excluded from mention in the Warren Report and in the Hearings and Exhibits. There are autopsy photographs and X rays which the Commission neglected to see and which were deposited belatedly in the National Archives but under restrictions which effectively debar their examination in the foreseeable future by competent interested persons.[48] (Drs. Humes and Boswell, who authenticated these docu-

---

48 Confused and contradictory accounts of the conditions imposed have appeared in the press. The authoritative statement of restrictions against access to the autopsy photographs and X rays appears in a letter dated January 6, 1967 from Robert H. Bahmer, Archivist of the United States, to Representative Theodore R. Kupferman of New York City, which the latter released to the press on April 13, 1967. Replying to Representative Kupferman's request for an opportunity to examine the X rays and photographs, accompanied by forensic pathologists Dr. Milton Helpern and Dr. Cyril H. Wecht and by me, the Archivist wrote: "As you may know, these materials were accepted for deposit in the National Archives under authority of 44 USC 397e. Conditions imposed by the Kennedy family pursuant to this authority provide that for a period of five years these items, unless otherwise determined by Mr. [Burke] Marshall [representing the Kennedy family in this matter], may be made available only to persons authorized to act for a committee of Congress or a committee or agency in the Executive Branch vested with authority to investigate matters relating to the death of President Kennedy."

Mr. Marshall subsequently denied Representative Kupferman's request.

ments for the Archives and then told a waiting world that the photographs confirmed their autopsy report and testimony, must have developed a curious sense of humor in this matter.)

The onus is on the authors of the Warren Report and its advocates; it cannot be shifted to those whose legitimate questions remain still unanswered.

PART II
THE ACCUSED

Chapter 6
Hidell

The first chapter of the Warren Report states the conclusions reached by the Commission. One conclusion is that "the shots which killed President Kennedy and wounded Governor Connally were fired by Lee Harvey Oswald." *(WR 19)* Another is that no one "assisted Oswald in planning or carrying out the assassination." *(WR 21)*

To sustain the finding that Oswald acted alone and not as part of a conspiracy, it was necessary to account for the recurrence of the name "Hidell" (with one or another preceding initials or name) on various papers and documents connected with Oswald. In some instances, "Hidell" appeared to be a pseudonym for Oswald himself; in others, the name appeared to be a designation for a person other than Oswald.

The Commission concluded that "Hidell was a completely fictitious person created by Oswald." *(WR 14)*

Despite this assertion, there are indications in the Hearings and Exhibits that Oswald acted (and not necessarily in the sense that the Commission used the word) not alone but with another person or other persons whose mysterious existence we can only glimpse from the documents published or infer from the documents withheld. One of these persons is "Hidell."

Although he is not mentioned in the text of the Warren Report, the Hearings reveal the existence of a real person who may be the Hidell in Oswald's life, or at least during one phase of his life. The Commission has ignored this man completely in its assertions that Oswald used the alias "Hidell." It has portrayed Oswald as a man who used false names habitually, when the evidence shows that he presented himself under a name other than his own on only one occasion and then for a plausible and understandable reason: to avoid eviction or job loss that he attributed to recognition of his real name. Oswald apparently did rent a

181

room in Dallas under the name "O. H. Lee" for reasons discussed later, but the evidence indicates no other instance in which he presented himself under a false name.[1]

The Commission was seemingly determined to reach a conclusion of "no conspiracy." Consequently, the "Hidell" who manifested himself in Oswald's activities some months before the assassination has been deemed to non-exist, merely a figment of Oswald's imagination. To that end, the actual evidence— and the implications to which it gives rise in terms of the commission of the crime, the role of the Dallas police, and the purposes of the authorities—has been reflected in the Warren Report incompletely, selectively, and inadequately.

In this chapter I shall show the profound contradictions between the propositions stated in the Report and the evidence in the Hearings and Exhibits. This evidence constitutes a prima-facie case for a real Hidell who was involved with Oswald in hidden activities, a Hidell who may be a key to the events in which Oswald became involved. I shall show that the assertions about Hidell in the Warren Report are dubious and in conflict with the known facts.

Let us look at those assertions as a body before we scrutinize them individually. The Commission tells us:

> The arresting officers found a forged selective service card with a picture of Oswald and the name "Alek J. Hidell" in Oswald's billfold. On November 22 and 23, Oswald refused to tell Fritz why this card was in his possession or to answer any questions concerning the card. . . . Captain Fritz produced the selective service card bearing the name "Alek J. Hidell." Oswald became angry and said, "No, I've told you all I'm going to tell you about that card in my billfold—you have the card yourself and you know as much about it as I do."
>
> . . . There is no evidence that an "A. J. Hidell" existed. . . . Investigations were conducted with regard to persons using the name Hidell or names similar to it. . . . Diligent search has failed to reveal any person in Dallas or New Orleans by that name. . . . Hidell was a favorite alias used by Oswald on a number of occasions. . . . It was merely a creation for his own purposes. . . . No doubt he purchased his weapons under the name of Hidell in an attempt to prevent their ownership from being traced. . . . Oswald's repeated use of false names is probably not to be disassociated from his antisocial and criminal inclinations.

The Fabrication of the Card

The Report makes no comment about the date and place of the fabrication of the forged selective service card, allegedly by Oswald. The Hearings and Exhibits, in turn, provide scanty information on that score.

---

1 On one occasion handbills calling for "Hands Off Cuba!" were ordered from a New Orleans printing company by a person understood by the secretary who accepted the order to have identified himself as "Osborne." The secretary may have confused "Oswald" with "Osborne"; in any event, she did not recognize Oswald as the person who ordered the handbills. (CE 1410) Because of those uncertainties, it is not possible to conclude that Oswald used the alias "Osborne" in connection with his pro-Castro activities.

Appendix X of the Report, "Expert Testimony," includes a section on questioned documents in which the spurious certificates and cards in the name "Hidell" are discussed in technical detail. *(WR 571-578)* The Report states that two typewriters were used to fabricate one of the cards (a selective service notice of classification, in the name "Alek James Hidell"). Oswald did not own a typewriter, and his known access to typewriters was restricted. In the spring of 1963 Oswald attended an evening class in typewriting at a Dallas high school, apparently irregularly; and during the same period of time, he was employed in a photography and graphic arts plant where typewriters were no doubt accessible. According to the description in Appendix X, the forgery required practice, on a typewriter in the case of one spurious card and with photographic printing plant equipment in another. Presumably the forger did his preparatory trials discreetly rather than in the public view. It seems unlikely that conditions at either the typewriting class or the graphic arts plant allowed Oswald the necessary unhurried privacy. To reduce speculation and assumption to the minimum, the Commission might have attempted to identify the typewriters used in the fabrication of the notice of classification by examining the typewriters to which Oswald had access during the probable time of the counterfeiting. It might also have attempted to make a determination as to his access to and use of the "very accurate camera" required for the forged selective service card during his tenure at the graphic arts plant.

Alwyn Cole, FBI expert in questioned documents, testified that the fabrication of the Hidell draft card required a very accurate camera "such as are found in photographic laboratory and printing plants." *(4H 388)* Although the Commission did not address itself to the question of when and where Oswald made the card, it may be assumed—in the context of the Commission's assertions—that he must have done so during his employment at Jaggars-Chiles-Stovall, a graphic arts company in Dallas, from October 1962 to April 1963. Oswald had no other known access to the necessary equipment.

If Oswald made that forged Hidell card sometime before April 1963, he must have had in mind a specific purpose or use. However, there is no trace of the existence or use of the card at any time up to and including the hour of Oswald's death. The Commission or its advocates might argue that Oswald fabricated and used the Hidell card in order to obtain from the post office the revolver and rifle ordered in that name; but the Commission makes no such argument. Indeed, the Report presents no evidence that Oswald personally obtained the parcels containing the weapons; it merely takes for granted that he did so. The Hearings and Exhibits indicate no attempt to ascertain from the post office personnel any information or records of the actual delivery of the packages. In the absence of such inquiries, it cannot be assumed that Oswald made the card or used it to gain possession of packages addressed to Hidell—or even that he obtained possession by any other means.

If Oswald fabricated the Hidell card sometime before April 1963, the card must have been in his possession during his stay in New Orleans, from the end of April to the end of September 1963.

Arrest in New Orleans

Yet when Oswald was arrested in New Orleans in August 1963 he had no Hidell card on his person. Lieutenant Francis Martello of the New Orleans police reported:

> I asked Oswald if he had any identification papers. At this time Oswald produced his wallet. Upon my request, he removed the papers and I examined them.
>
> He had in his wallet a number of miscellaneous papers, cards and identification items . . . (1) Social security card bearing #433-54-3937 in the name of Lee Harvey Oswald. (2) Selective service draft card in the name of Lee Harvey Oswald bearing #41-114-395-32. . . . (3) Card bearing name Lee Harvey Oswald reflecting he was a member of the FPCC [Fair Play for Cuba Committee] . . . signed by V. T. Lee . . . issued 5/28/63. . . . (4) Card for the New Orleans Chapter of the FPCC in the name of Lee Harvey Oswald signed by A. J. Hidell, Chapter President, issued June 6, 1963. . . .
> *(10H 52-54)*

Lieutenant Martello made that detailed record at the time of the arrest (one wishes that the Dallas police had followed such orderly practices). Clearly, Oswald did not have a forged Hidell card in his wallet. In the Commission's terms, then, it appears that Oswald was too cautious to carry the forged card when embarking on the dangerous mission of distributing political handbills on the streets of New Orleans, but imprudent enough to carry it when setting forth to assassinate the President with a weapon purchased under the false name.

The Forged Signature

As Lieutenant Martello reported, Oswald did carry a Fair Play for Cuba Committee membership card in his own name when he was arrested and also a New Orleans FPCC chapter card in his own name, signed by "A. J. Hidell, Chapter President."

The Commission's handwriting experts concluded that the Hidell signature on that card was not in Oswald's hand. Subsequently Marina Oswald testified that *she* had signed the name "Hidell" on the card, under duress. The experts then agreed that she could have written, or did write, the signature.[2] *(4H 399-400 and CE 2726)*

Marina Oswald testified *(5H 401)* that that was the only occasion on which her husband had asked her to sign the name "Hidell" on any document. The Commission has made no attempt to elucidate Oswald's rationale in coercing his wife to forge the name on an innocuous FPCC membership card, while

---

2 One of the Commission's experts was also an expert witness for the government in the Alger Hiss trial and gave testimony which some authorities regard as technically and morally dubious. *See* Fred Cook, *The Unfinished Story of Alger Hiss* (New York: William Morrow Company, 1958), p. 132.

writing the name in his own hand on other documents, including such incriminating papers as the mail orders for the revolver and the rifle.[3]

This act cannot be shrugged off as random and irrational when there is no evidence of any collateral instance of irrationality on Oswald's part during the same period of time. It was the Commission's responsibility to seek an understanding of Oswald's reason for such inconsistent and seemingly senseless actions and, if no logical reason could be uncovered, to re-examine the testimony and reconsider the premise that in one instance alone Oswald had forced his wife to forge the signature "Hidell." The more so when, as will be discussed, Marina Oswald's statements about Oswald's use of the name "Hidell" as an alias were self-contradictory and suspect.

Did the Arresting Officers Find a Forged Hidell Card?

With that background, and keeping in mind that there is no manifestation of the existence of the forged draft card in the name "Hidell" and bearing Oswald's likeness at any time before November 22, 1963, let us now test the Commission's assertion that the arresting officers in Dallas found such a card in Oswald's wallet while en route from the Texas Theater to the police station in a police car.

According to a footnote *(WR 181)*, this assertion relies on: (1) a series of FBI reports listing the contents of Oswald's wallet upon his arrest—in particular, a report that Detective Paul Bentley on June 11, 1964 had identified a photograph of the Hidell card as the one he had obtained from Oswald's wallet en route to the police building; and (2) the testimony of Police Officers Richard Stovall and Guy Rose.

The Report does not cite testimony from Bentley, who was not a Commission witness, or testimony on the alleged discovery of the Hidell card from other officers who were present in the car.

One of the officers, Sergeant Gerald Hill, testified on April 8, 1964 that when Oswald was asked his name, he made no reply. Hill said that he then suggested that Bentley should see if the suspect had identification on his person. Bentley put his right hand into Oswald's left hip pocket and took out a billfold.

> . . . the name Lee Oswald was then called out by Bentley from the back seat. . . . And he also made the statement that there was some more identification in this other name which I don't remember, but it was the same name that later came in the paper that he bought the gun under.   *(7H 58)*

Hill's story is open to the gravest doubt. First of all, we know that Oswald was wearing an identification bracelet on his left wrist at the time of his arrest.

---

3 I suspend judgment on the authenticity of the handwriting identification with respect to those documents. They may well be in Oswald's script, as the Commission maintains, but the identifications have not been tested by adversary experts (who in the courtroom often successfully challenge the prosecution findings). Other "hard evidence" against Oswald has been overstated or misrepresented. The block printing and handwriting in this instance was identified from microfilm rather than from the original documents, which in itself increases the possibility of error.

William Whaley, the taxi-driver who had been engaged by Oswald less than two hours before, had taken special notice of the bracelet (Whaley's hobby was collecting identification bracelets) as Oswald sat beside him in the cab. *(2H 256, 293)* Detective Richard Sims, who removed the bracelet from Oswald's wrist before taking a paraffin cast that evening, said explicitly that he had examined the bracelet and that it "had his name on it." *(7H 174)*

Second, and far more significant, is the stark contradiction between Sergeant Hill's testimony of April 8, 1964 and his description of the arrest on N.B.C. television on November 22, 1963, only a few hours after the event.

> *Hill:* The only way we found out what his name was to remove his billfold and check it ourselves; he wouldn't even tell us what his name was. . . .
> *Question:* What was the name on the billfold?
> *Hill:* Lee H. Oswald. O-S-W-A-L-D.   *(CE 2160)*

Hill said nothing about the identification card in the name "Hidell" bearing Oswald's photograph (which supposedly had been discovered in Oswald's wallet, in Hill's presence and as a result of his suggestion, short hours before Hill went before the television cameras). That Hill would have failed to mention such important and incriminating evidence, if the incident was authentic, is inconceivable.

Equally disquieting is *Bentley's* failure to mention the Hidell card in his report dated December 3, 1963 to Dallas Police Chief Curry. Bentley wrote:

> On the way to the city hall I removed the suspect's wallet and obtained his name. He made several remarks en route to the city hall about police brutality and denied shooting anybody. . . . I turned his identification over to Lieutenant Baker. I then went to Captain Westbrook's office to make a report of this arrest.   *(CE 2003, p. 78)*

It is certainly very peculiar that both Hill and Bentley in contemporaneous statements made absolutely no mention of the Hidell card or gave any hint that they had found evidence that Oswald was using an alias. Exactly the same silence about the Hidell card is seen in the reports submitted to the police chief during the first week of December 1963 by other arresting officers—Bob Carroll, K. E. Lyon, and C. T. Walker *(CE 2003,* pp. 81-82, 91, and 100-101 respectively).

And it is surely unnatural that—as I shall discuss later in this chapter—the Hidell card turned over by Bentley to Lieutenant Baker was seen elsewhere subsequently, by several police officers.

The Other Detectives

Richard Stovall testified on April 3, 1964 that he had talked to Oswald just after he was brought into the police station, before Captain Fritz began the formal interrogation.

> I went in and asked him for his identification, asked him who he was and he said his name was Lee Oswald, as well as I remember. Rose and I were

both in there at the time. He had his billfold and in it he had the identification of "A. Hidell," which was on a selective service card, as well as I remember . . . and at that time Captain Fritz opened the door to the office there and sent Rose and I to go out to this address in Irving. . . .

(7H 187-188)

But Guy Rose, who was also present, gave a different account of the incident when he testified five days later, on April 8, 1964:

Rose: In just a few minutes they brought in Lee Oswald and I talked to him for a few minutes. . . . The first thing I asked him was what his name was and he told me it was Hidell.

Ball: Did he tell you it was Hidell?

Rose: Yes; he did.

Ball: He didn't tell you it was Oswald?

Rose: No, he didn't; not right then—he did later. In a minute—I found two cards—I found a card that said "A. Hidell." And I found another card that said "Lee Oswald" on it, and I asked him which of the two was his correct name. He wouldn't tell me at the time, he just said, "You find out." And then in a few minutes Captain Fritz came in and he told me to get two men and go to Irving and search his house.

Ball: Now, when he first came in there—you said that he said his name was "Hidell"?

Rose: Yes.

Ball: Was that before you saw the two cards . . . before you saw the cards?

Rose: Yes; it was.

Ball: Did he give you his first name?

Rose: He just said "Hidell"; I remember he just gave me the last name of "Hidell."

Ball: And then you found two or three cards on him?

Rose: Yes; we did.

Ball: Did you search him?

Rose: He had already been searched and someone had his billfold. . . .

Ball: And the contents of the billfold supposedly were before you?

Rose: Yes.

(7H 228)

An unusual procedure, to say the least: the police confiscate a billfold but leave the contents with the suspect. Counsel Ball took that in his stride and although he had taken Stovall's testimony only five days before he examined Rose, he paid no attention to the gross discrepancies and conflicts between their stories. The Commission then proceeded to rely on the testimony of these two witnesses as authority for the claim that Oswald was carrying a forged Hidell card when he was arrested.

The Commission was too easily satisfied. It should have obtained sworn testimony from Paul Bentley, who was the primary witness, and it should have taken some notice of the absence of any reference to the Hidell card in the contemporaneous reports of the arresting officers. This was all the more necessary when the testimony of one of those officers, C. T. Walker, varied from that of both Stovall and Rose. Walker testified on April 3, 1964 that when the party arrived at the police station with Oswald:

> *Walker:* We took him up [to] the homicide and robbery bureau, and we went back there . . . and Oswald sat down, and he was handcuffed with his hands behind him. I sat down there, and I had his pistol, and he had a card in there with a picture of him and the name A. J. Hidell on it.
> *Belin:* Do you remember what kind of card it was?
> *Walker:* Just an identification card. I don't recall what it was. . . . And I told him, "That is your real name, isn't it?" . . . And he said, "No, that is not my real name."   *(7H 41)*

A fourth detective, Walter Potts, gave testimony on April 3, 1964 which, at first glance, also seems to corroborate the finding of the Hidell card. Potts testified that shortly after 2 p.m. he had been instructed that Captain Fritz wanted him to "go out to Oswald's or Hidell's or Oswald's room." Potts said: "On his person—he must have had—he did have identification with the name Alex Hidell and Oswald. . . . *(7H 197)*

Potts alleged that when he and other officers arrived at the rooming house they spoke to Earlene Roberts, the housekeeper, and to the Johnsons, the owners, and that they had said that they did not know "a Lee Harvey Oswald or an Alex Hidell either one." But Earlene Roberts *(6H 438; 7H 439)* and the Johnsons *(10H 295, 303)* said only that the police had come looking for Lee Harvey Oswald. They mentioned nothing about Hidell, or about any name other than Oswald. Thus, they in no way corroborated Potts's allegations.

The Contemporaneous Record

One of the officials who was present with Potts and the other police officers at the rooming house was Justice of the Peace David Johnston, who issued the search warrant. Johnston seems to have spent the next twelve hours at the police headquarters, fraternizing with the press and, by his own account *(15H 509-510),* "in conference" with police and prosecution officials until 3:45 a.m. Presumably Johnston was made familiar with the evidence against Oswald (he presided twice at the arraignment proceedings).

However, in his handwritten report *(Johnston Exhibit No. 1),* after listing Oswald's name and other particulars, Johnston wrote the following entry: *"Alias —O.H. Lee"*—an entry that suggests that Johnston, like the other witnesses, never heard a whisper of "Hidell" for at least some 24 hours after the arrest.

Similar evidence is found in the handwritten notes made by reporter Seth Kantor as events progressed at the police station after the assassination. The second notation after the swearing-in of President Johnson (which took place at 2:38 p.m.) is the encircled name "O. H. Lee" *(Kantor Exhibit No. 3,* p. 360). Fifteen pages later (p. 375) we find Kantor's first mention of "A. Hidell," under the notation, "FBI has March 20 letter to mail order gun house in Chicago." The discovery of the letter became known only on Saturday afternoon, November 23, 1963.

Meanwhile, from November 22 to December 2, 1963, four Secret Service agents were conducting an intensive investigation of Oswald at New Orleans. *(CE 3119)* They maintained a constant exchange of information with Dallas by long-distance telephone. Nevertheless, they showed no awareness on November 22, 23, or 24 that Oswald was known to have used the alias "Hidell" or that a forged card in that name had been found on his person—even though they encountered references to "Hidell" in their investigation of Oswald's activities in New Orleans (see, for example, *CE 3119*, pp. 5, 11, and 12).

If the Commission has found one contemporaneous mention of the name "Hidell" in the press or in police or federal records *before* the rifle was traced (apart from one FBI report to be discussed later), that record has not been included in the Exhibits. The Commission apparently was unwilling, or unable, to refute the suggestion of Mark Lane that evidence had been fabricated in order to link Oswald with the name "Hidell," and that that had been done only after the rifle was traced to Hidell. *(2H 46-49)*

The Interrogators

On November 22 and 23, Oswald refused to tell Fritz why this card was in his possession or to answer any questions concerning the card.   *(WR 181)*

The footnote to this statement in the Warren Report cites the testimony of Captain Fritz on April 22, 1964, notably the following passage:

Ball: Another thing, that day, at sometime during the twenty-second when you questioned Oswald, didn't you ask him about this card he had in his pocket with the name Alek Hidell?
Fritz: I did; yes, sir.   *(4H 221-222)*

Here we have a leading question and a misleading answer. Fritz, in his written report on the interrogation of Oswald, had stated explicitly:

During the second day interviews I asked Oswald about a card that he had in his purse showing that he belonged to the Fair Play for Cuba Committee. . . . I asked him about another identification card in his pocket bearing the name of Alex Hidell.   *(WR 602)*

According to that written report, then, Fritz did not mention the name "Hidell" until the Saturday interrogation, and, it will be noted, his reference to the card is imprecise. Fritz did not specify that the identification card bore Oswald's photograph, as one might have expected him to do. Indeed, he might almost have been referring to the membership card in the New Orleans chapter of the FPCC which was in Oswald's own name but signed by A. J. Hidell as chapter president.

In any case, the question remains whether Fritz questioned Oswald about a Hidell card on Saturday, as he wrote in his report, or on Friday, as he testified under oath. The reports of other investigators who were present at the Friday interrogations throw light on that question.

FBI Agents James Bookhout and James Hosty, in their reports on the

Friday interrogation sessions, do not mention a Hidell card or any questions put to Oswald about Hidell. *(WR 612-613, 619-620)* Bookhout mentions the Hidell card for the first time in his report on the Saturday interrogation session. *(WR 623)*

Two Secret Service officials were also present at a Friday interrogation. Forrest Sorrels, head of the Dallas office of the Secret Service, questioned Oswald in the presence of Winston Lawson of the White House detail. Both Sorrels and Lawson testified about the interrogation; neither mentioned any Hidell card or indicated any awareness on that day of Oswald's possession of such a card or use of such an alias. *(4H 356; 7H 353)*

Sorrels was also present at the Saturday interrogation. He testified on May 7, 1964 that Oswald was questioned about the rifle because at that time it had been learned that the weapon had been shipped to A. Hidell: "And he was questioned by Captain Fritz along those lines. And he denied that the rifle was his. He denied knowing or using the name of A. Hidell or Alek Hidell." *(7H 356)* Sorrels, it is seen, does not refer to a Hidell card but only to the information obtained from Klein's Sporting Goods about the sale of the rifle to a customer named Hidell.

Not one of the four witnesses corroborates the assertion that Fritz questioned Oswald about a Hidell card on Friday. Elsewhere I have pointed out that no reports have been provided on almost six hours of interrogation, in four sessions, on Friday between early evening and midnight. Theoretically it is possible that Fritz questioned Oswald about the Hidell card during one of those sessions on which no reports have been made available. But this is highly implausible, because at the very first session Fritz questioned Oswald about the "alias" O. H. Lee, the name under which Oswald was registered at the Beckley Street rooming house, as Fritz himself reported *(WR 602)* and FBI Agents Bookhout and Hosty corroborated in their report. *(WR 612)* The fact that Oswald was registered as O. H. Lee was discovered only when police officers went to search his room, but the Hidell card was supposedly found earlier, during the ride from the Texas Theater to the police building. That Fritz did not question Oswald about the Hidell card, if that card was really discovered first, is all but inconceivable. If he did question him about Hidell as well as O. H. Lee, it is incomprehensible that the reports of Fritz, Bookhout, and Hosty mention *only* O. H. Lee.

Thus far, the weight of the evidence suggests that the name "Hidell" entered the case only when the rifle was traced to a purchaser by that name. Consider Police Chief Curry's statements to the press on Saturday, for example.

Question: What was the name under which he ordered the gun?
Curry: The name—the return—the name on the return address was A. Hidell. A. Hidell.
Question: Is that the name under which the post office box was rented?
Curry: I don't know that.
Question: Had Oswald ever used the alias Hidell before?
Curry: I do not know.   *(CE 2145)*

Against the preponderance of evidence that there was no Hidell card known to the police on Friday, there is only one contemporaneous report that indicates the existence of the forged card on that day. That is a report by FBI Agent Manning Clements, dated November 23, 1963 and purporting to refer to an interrogation of Oswald on the preceding evening. Ironically, the Warren Report does not cite Clements' report in support of the claim that the Hidell card was found on Oswald's person when he was arrested, and, still more ironically, Clements allegedly questioned Oswald on Friday night in the absence of Captain Fritz and FBI or Secret Service witnesses.

Clements states in his report *(WR 614)* that he examined the contents of Oswald's wallet and put questions to him about the selective service card in the name "Hidell" which Oswald declined to answer. Is it possible that the wallet or its contents were still with Oswald at 10 p.m. when Clements supposedly questioned him, as they had been at 2 p.m. when Stovall, Rose, and Walker ostensibly saw the same items? Bentley, it will be recalled, said that he had turned that evidence over to Lieutenant Baker when the arresting party arrived with the suspect. Moreover, Detective Richard Sims testified on April 6, 1964 that he had searched Oswald at 4:05 p.m. on Friday and that he had not seen a wallet or identification cards, which he had assumed "had been taken off of him." *(7H 180)*

Clements' report cannot in itself be sufficient to override the massive contrary evidence—especially when, as discussed in a later chapter, Clements played a strange and ambiguous role in the investigation of another matter involving Oswald which came to light on Saturday.

John Rene Heindel

... there is no evidence that an "A. J. Hidell" existed. *(WR 292).* ... Investigations were conducted with regard to persons using the name "Hidell" or names similar to it *(WR 313).* ... Diligent search has failed to reveal any person in Dallas or New Orleans by that name.   *(WR 644-645)*

These are the categorical disclaimers which appear in the Warren Report. The Hearings and Exhibits tell a completely different story.

A short affidavit is found, in the fashion of a purloined letter, buried in the dense pages of the volumes of testimony. It is dated May 19, 1964 and signed by John Rene Heindel of New Orleans.

I served in the United States Marine Corps from July 15, 1957 until July 15, 1961. I was stationed at Atsugi, Japan, with Lee Harvey Oswald. ... While in the Marine Corps, I was often referred to as "Hidell"—pronounced so as to rhyme with "Rydell." ... This was a nickname and not merely an inadvertent mispronunciation. It is possible that Oswald might have heard me being called by this name; indeed he may himself have called me "Hidell." ...   *(8H 318)*

There is only one other mention of Heindel in the Hearings; it is found in the testimony on May 1, 1964 of Daniel Powers, another witness who had known Oswald in the Marines.

Jenner: Do you remember a Marine by the name of John Heindel?

Powers: No, sir.

Jenner: Sometimes called Hidell?

Powers: No. *(8H 288)*

From this we know at least that the affidavit is not a hoax, slipped into the Hearings volumes by a mischievous printer; it is an authentic document of which Counsel Jenner and the Commission itself must have been aware when they formulated the carefully phrased assertions in the Report which reiterate that Hidell was only a figment of Oswald's imagination. But the affidavit provides only the bare fact that there is a Heindel/Hidell. None of the questions which flow from this startling fact have been answered—although we may be sure that the FBI and/or the Secret Service investigated Heindel and reported the results to the Warren Commission, which has withheld the information from the public.

Surely the Commission does not believe, or expect the public to believe, that the existence of Heindel/Hidell, and his residing in New Orleans, has no connection with Oswald's use of the name Hidell to designate a real person, verbally and on FPCC documents, even though Oswald's first known public use of that name began during his residence in New Orleans. Surely no one is expected to believe that Oswald, by pure coincidence, invented an alias which corresponded with the real nickname of a fellow Marine whom Oswald himself may have addressed by that nickname. Surely the odds against such a coincidence would be so astronomical as virtually to rule it out.

One mention of Heindel also appears in the Exhibits (where it may be discovered with the aid of a magnifying glass). The document is a 24-page report by four Secret Service agents to their superiors, on investigations conducted in New Orleans from November 22 to December 2, 1963. *(CE 3119)* The agents had learned that "Lieut. J. Evans" and "Sgt. Robert Hidell" were listed as references on Oswald's application for employment with the William B. Reily Company *(WR 726)* and had instituted inquiries to trace those names.

At 1:30 a.m. on 11-24-63, Mr. David Kerr, Office of Naval Intelligence, contacted SAIC Rice by telephone, advising that a thorough search had been made of the Marine Corps records with the following results:

There are four persons on active duty by the name of J. Evans, and twelve on inactive duty. . . . He said that there was only one officer, Lieutenant John Stewart Evans . . . who might be associated with Oswald's reference.

He further advised that there is no record of a "Hidell" either on active duty or inactive; and that the only similar name is John R. Heindel, age thirty-eight, born in Louisiana, who is not active, his record being available at the Federal Records Center, St. Louis. *(CE 3119, p. 12)*

The Secret Service inquiry about "Hidell" related only to the application form; the report indicates no awareness of the alleged use of that name by Oswald as an alias. There is no further mention in the documents of Lieutenant

J. S. Evans, "who might be associated with Oswald's reference"; the Report says merely that the name was apparently fictitious.[4] *(WR 726)*

Considerable time elapsed between the Secret Service report of December 1963 and the Heindel affidavit of May 1964. During those months Heindel undoubtedly was investigated and interviewed by one or more of the federal investigative agencies, in accordance with the Commission's practice of calling witnesses on the basis of prior screening by the FBI or the Secret Service. However, there are no reports of those prior interviews among the Exhibits. The documents have been withheld. Should one infer that the results of the inquiry about Heindel or of interviews with him were negative, and that no evidence was uncovered of any association between Heindel and Oswald in pro-Castro activities, or other activities, in New Orleans in the summer of 1963? If that was the case, I fail to understand why the Commission did not say so in the Report and why the relevant documents were withheld from the Exhibits; and I certainly do not understand why the Commission did not obtain sworn testimony from Heindel, regardless of the nature of the information obtained by the investigative agencies.

The Mail Orders

The Warren Commission contends that Oswald "no doubt . . . purchased his weapons under the name of Hidell in an attempt to prevent their ownership from being traced." *(WR 315)* In its anxiety to create the impression of a solid argument where there was only a porous and dubious case against Oswald, the Commission has thus involved itself in reasoning that verges on absurdity. Its inference is entirely too facile.

Had Oswald intended to purchase weapons that could not be traced to him, a mail-order purchase should have been his last choice. A mail order was insurance that the transaction would be recorded in written form, preserving his handwriting, specifying his post office box number, and virtually guaranteeing that the weapon would be traced to him. If, instead, Oswald had merely walked into a gun shop or an H. L. Green chain store, he could have purchased a rifle or a pistol over the counter without leaving a trace of the transaction. The only risk would be that many months later a clerk might identify him as a customer, and such eyewitness identifications—standing alone and possibly demolished by a capable defense counsel—would leave a large margin of reasonable doubt and might well be chalked off (as so many other reports of incidents allegedly involving Oswald have been) as mistaken identity. There would be no record of a serial number, no handwriting to be identified, and no post office box number to incriminate Oswald.

But let us suppose for the sake of argument that Oswald did use the least

---

4 In concluding that the name "J. Evans" was "apparently fictitious," the Commission ignored the fact that at about the time Oswald obtained his job at the Reily Company, he had visited old friends of his mother—Julian Evans and his wife—in the hope that they could help him find an apartment in New Orleans. *(8H 58, 72)*

suitable method of purchase by which to evade identification as the purchaser, assuming for the occasion the alias "Hidell" (and not in a moment of folly, since he supposedly ordered weapons by mail on two occasions spanning several months). By what antithesis of logic, then, did he make sure to carry on his person a forged indentification card in the name of Hidell, bearing his own photograph—as if to eliminate any possible doubt? And, one might also ask, by what eccentric calculation had he earlier had himself photographed holding weapons purchased "in an attempt to prevent their ownership from being traced," by a camera evidently used solely for purposes of self-incrimination and (as will be discussed) never for snapshots of a child, a friend, or a landscape?

If Oswald intended to commit murder and to confess, such actions might make sense. If he were psychotic, such actions would not make sense but they would be plausible. Oswald did not confess, and there is no written or spoken word from any qualified witness—before Oswald was murdered—pointing to psychosis, mental aberration, or lack of adequate contact with reality (see page 244). In the Texas environment it is statistically normal for any adult male to own a firearm or two; most men in Texas own such weapons as a matter of course. Even in Oswald's immediate milieu, the possession of firearms was not at all unusual. Wesley Frazier, the young man who worked at the Book Depository and drove Oswald to Irving on the weekends, owned a rifle (CE 2003); Warren Caster, a book company executive who had an office in the Book Depository, only two days before the assassination had purchased rifles for himself and for his young son, which he displayed before various Book Depository workers (7H 386-388); and Dr. Malcolm Perry of Parkland Hospital owned firearms (6H 18). Indeed, when one Dallasite said at the end of his testimony that he did not own a rifle, a member of the Commission expressed incredulity at hearing such an admission from a Texan. (4H 129)

Since the purchase and possession of rifles and pistols are common in Dallas —with few if any restrictions imposed against the acquisition of firearms and their across-the-counter sale a mere routine transaction not only in gun shops but in drugstores and chain stores selling sundry articles—Oswald's purchase of a rifle and a revolver is hardly in itself incriminating. What is striking is that his method of purchase was one that a would-be assassin would have avoided at all costs, because a mail-order transaction would ultimately introduce a distinct and unnecessary risk for his life.

The very fact that Oswald elected to secure firearms by mail orders easily traceable to him might even suggest that he may have selected that method deliberately for a specific purpose—a purpose not at all incriminating to the purchaser. Students of the assassination have pointed to two related factors which may explain Oswald's otherwise inexplicable mail-order purchases of firearms: (1) some evidence indicates that Oswald may have been a petty operative for a federal investigative agency; and (2) if he was employed by a federal agency, he might have been involved in attempts by a Senate committee to introduce legislation curbing the mail-order sale of firearms.

The kind of hypothesis that arises from these considerations is scarcely less plausible than the interpretation which the Commission has placed on the same set of facts.

Marina's Stories

Much of the Commission's "evidence" that Oswald habitually employed false names derives from the testimony of Marina Oswald. The following passage is found in her testimony of February 4, 1964:

> *Rankin:* Have you ever heard that he used the fictitious name "Hidell"?
> *Mrs. Oswald:* Yes. . . . In New Orleans . . . when he was interviewed by some anti-Cubans, he used this name. . . . I knew there was no such organization. And I know that Hidell is merely an altered Fidel, and I laughed at such foolishness. . . . No one knew that Lee was Hidell.
> *Rankin:* How did you discover it, then?
> *Mrs. Oswald:* I already said that when I listened to the radio, they spoke of that name and I asked him who, and he said it was he. . . . *(1H 64)*

However, the records show that Marina Oswald told conflicting stories both before and after that testimony. In an interview with the Secret Service on December 10, 1963 she was asked if, to her knowledge, her husband used the name of Alek Hidell, and she replied in the negative. *(CE 1789)*

Scarcely two months later, in the testimony quoted above, she told the Commission that she had learned about the fictitious Hidell from Oswald's radio debate in New Orleans. But that story suffered from two defects: (1) the name "Hidell" does not appear in the transcript of the radio debate *(Stuckey Exhibit No. 3);* and (2) before the radio discussion took place, Lieutenant Martello had already seen and made a record of the New Orleans FPCC membership card on which the signature "Hidell," supposedly in Marina's handwriting, appeared.

The story that Marina Oswald had told under oath on February 4, 1964 was therefore inconsistent with known facts and had to be modified. When she returned to testify again on June 11, 1964, she was shown the FPCC membership card and she identified the signature "Hidell" as her own writing. She claimed that Oswald had threatened to beat her if she did not sign the card; she said that that was the only card he had ever asked her to sign with the name "Hidell"; she said that he had forced her to sign the card in order to create the impression that two people were involved in FPCC activities in New Orleans, not just one; and that the signing had taken place in the Oswald apartment one evening at about eight or nine o'clock.

> *Dulles:* Had you ever heard the name "Hidell" before?
> *Mrs. Oswald:* I don't remember whether this was before or after Lee spoke on the radio. I think it was after.
> *Dulles:* Did he use the name "Hidell" on the radio?
> *Mrs. Oswald:* I think that he might have when he was talking on the radio said that Hidell is the President of his organizaton but, of course, I don't understand English well and I don't know. He spoke on the radio using his

own name but might have mentioned the name Hidell. This is what he told me. When I tried to find out what he said on the radio.   *(5H 401-402)*

That felicitous modification of Marina's earlier account of how she first learned about Hidell is remarkable, considering that it took place not as a result of cross-examination in which her earlier testimony was challenged as being in conflict with the known facts, but seemingly in a spontaneous refinement of memory in which new facets appeared and old certainties became uncertainties. Perhaps it was pure coincidence that between Marina's appearances in February and June, the Commission heard testimony from FBI Agent John Quigley, on May 5, 1964 *(4H 434, 439)*, from which it emerged that he had seen the card with the Hidell signature (in Marina's handwriting) *before* the radio debate.

The widow's recall seemed to improve with the passage of time. The official version of her story came only in June, after a defective version in February and a denial in December that she even knew of any use of the name Hidell by her husband. Why did she disclaim knowledge of Hidell in December when she was freely providing incriminating information about Oswald—including the alleged attempt on General Walker's life? The Commission did not ask her why, or take any notice of her unqualified disclaimer in December, but merely relied on the most serviceable of her three stories.

O. H. Lee

The Commission also relied heavily on Marina Oswald's testimony in asserting that Oswald had used the name "O. H. Lee" as an alias. The Commission saw no inconsistency between Marina's "laughing at such foolishness" when she learned that Oswald was using "Hidell" as an alias *(1H 64)* and her account of the bitter quarrel with her husband when she discovered that he was living in Dallas under the name "O. H. Lee" because

> . . . he did not want his landlady to know his real name because she might read in the paper of the fact that he had been in Russia and that he had been questioned. . . . And also he did not want the FBI to know where he lived. . . . Because their visits were not very pleasant for him and he thought that he loses jobs because the FBI visits the place of his employment.
>
> *(1H 46)*

Again, Marina's testimony in February was inconsistent with her earlier statements. The FBI had questioned her about this matter on November 28, 1963.

> Mrs. Oswald was asked if Oswald had used any other names, and she replied that he had not to her knowledge. She was then asked if he had not used a different name in Dallas when he had rented a room upon his return to Dallas on October 3, 1963, and she said that she now recalled Oswald had used another name.
>
> She said that on one occasion Mrs. Paine had telephoned the place where Oswald was staying and had asked to speak to Mr. Oswald, and the man who answered the phone said there was no one by the name of Oswald at the place.

Mrs. Oswald said she herself had called this number and talked to Oswald, at which time he said he had been there the day before when someone had called and asked for Mr. Oswald, but that he was using another name at the house and had not answered to the name Oswald. He told Mrs. Oswald he was using another name because he did not want any questions asked about himself.   *(CE 1781)*

Despite the bitter quarrel to which she later testified, Marina Oswald did not remember without prompting from the FBI that the incident had even occurred, although less than two weeks had elapsed between the alleged telephone calls and the FBI interview. Which was correct: her statements to the FBI on November 28, 1963, or her testimony before the Commission in February 1964? The two stories are not mutually exclusive, but it is noteworthy that she failed to mention a quarrel in the first instance. Indeed, her flights from inherent plausibility and her pattern of alteration of earlier statements and testimony in later versions—later versions that served to strengthen the case against Oswald—leave little ground for confidence in her.

"Antisocial" and "Criminal"

The Commission has *not* established "Oswald's repeated use of false names" but has attributed that unproved practice to Oswald's "anti-social and criminal inclinations." There is no trace of anti-social or criminal behavior in Oswald's history (except for the alleged attempts on the lives of General Walker and Richard Nixon, for which we have only Marina Oswald's dubious evidence). If the Commission had studied Oswald's history and morals before he became an accused assassin, there would have been no finding of criminal or anti-social inclinations. In this and other instances of circular reasoning, the Commission has used a premise to justify conclusions, and then used those same conclusions to justify the premise.

The Reality of Hidell

The Dallas Police list of property seized on November 23, 1963 at the Paine residence contains the following item: "four 3 x 5 cards bearing respectively names G. Hall; A. J. Hidell; B. Davis; and V. T. Lee." (*CE 2003*, p. 269)

Gus Hall, Benjamin Davis, and Vincent T. Lee are real persons of some prominence in political movements on the Left. If A. J. Hidell is a spurious, invented personality, or an alias created by Oswald for his own purposes, his subtlety in preparing an index card for Hidell and introducing it among cards for known, genuine personalities is nothing less than brilliant. Anyone capable of such an inspired stroke in covering his tracks would, it seems to me, be temperamentally and intellectually incapable of leaving a trail of incriminating evidence such as that which, under the official pronouncements, led to Oswald and Oswald alone within a few hours.

The index card, the widely contradictory testimony, and the existence of a real Heindel/Hidell combine to cast the gravest doubt on the Commission's contentions concerning use of false names, and on the methods and probity of the Commission itself as well as those of the Dallas police.

Dallas police witnesses testified in April 1964 or later that a forged draft card in the name "Hidell" and bearing Oswald's photograph was found on his person when he was arrested. We have seen that their actions, statements, and reports at that time are completely at odds with the later testimony, which must raise the possibility of perjury and collusion.

We have also seen that the Warren Commission overlooked or deliberately ignored the serious contradictions in the evidence, and the implications of those contradictions with respect to the Dallas police. Mark Lane explicitly called the Commission's attention to the paradoxical fact that there was immediate publicity on November 22, 1963 about the alias "O. H. Lee," which became known after investigation, but not about Hidell, supposedly discovered at once in a search of Oswald's person. (2H 46) The Commission did not attack that apparent paradox as one of the "speculations" to which it devoted a separate appendix in its Report—perhaps because there is striking evidence that the paradox was real.

The Commission was duty-bound to seek and provide proof that the name "Hidell" was indeed known to the police at the hour of Oswald's arrest, as the Report claims, by examining radio and television tapes and other records to determine whether or not there was any reference to Hidell at any time before the FBI traced the rifle to a purchaser by that name. The newspapers of the time which I have searched do not mention Hidell. Is it credible that the police deliberately withheld public mention of Hidell or the forged Hidell card, and the palmprint discussed earlier, while announcing to the press with crude alacrity every other scrap of "incriminating" evidence, real or imagined? Significantly, the police themselves did not suggest that they had withheld information about the forged card. Even if they had done so, that would hardly explain their failure to question Oswald's wife or mother, or Ruth Paine, about Hidell on Friday night, when they were at the police station; or their failure to set into motion immediate inquiries to see if other police agencies had a record of Hidell; or their failure to institute investigation inside Dallas to determine what activities and associations could be traced to Hidell, or Oswald in the role of Hidell.

We have not received the accounting which was due—a complete and convincing explanation of why the Dallas police and the other official agencies acted for at least 24 hours as though there were no Hidell card and no Hidell.

Another issue that the Commission has evaded is that, according to its own account of events, Oswald used the name "Hidell" both as his own alias and as the designation of a second person, real or invented. Criminologists—who were conspicuous by their absence from the roster of the Commission's staff—perhaps could have enlightened us about the known patterns in the use of aliases by criminals. It would be interesting to know whether there is an established pattern, or even a single precedent, for the indiscriminate use of a false name both as the criminal's alias and the designation of a second person.

The Commission should also have addressed itself more seriously to the question of why Oswald should have taken pains to fabricate the Hidell card at all. It seems to have been an exercise in futility, if not in self-defeat. There is no indication that Oswald needed such a card for any purpose or that he ever used it for such purposes as cashing checks, obtaining retail credit, or verifying that he was old enough to be served alcoholic beverages. No one has come forward to this date with information that "Hidell" used the forged card to obtain an official license of any sort, to gain admission to a place of entertainment, to engage in commerce or theft, or to accomplish any other objective. I will not join the Commission in speculating about Oswald's motives for allegedly purchasing weapons under the name "Hidell" because I am by no means convinced that he did so.

Apart from those various derelictions, the Commission is guilty of omitting all mention of John Rene Heindel from its report. Few of its sins of omission are as astonishing and regrettable as this one.

Knowing, as we do, that Heindel was known by the nickname "Hidell"; that he and Oswald were acquainted with each other through service in the Marines; and that Heindel was a resident of New Orleans at the very time that Oswald began to use the name "Hidell" in public—not as an alias, but to designate a person other than himself—knowing these facts, who can in good conscience accept the assertions about Hidell in the Warren Report?

Chapter 7
Photograph of Oswald with Rifle

The Warren Report *(WR 125-128)* asserts that on Sunday, March 31, 1963 Marina Oswald took two photographs of Oswald holding a rifle, a pistol, and two newspapers. The Commission finds that the rifle in the photograph *(CE 133-A)* is the same as the rifle found on the sixth floor of the Book Depository. It finds the photograph authentic on the basis of expert testimony that links it with the Imperial Reflex camera *(CE 750)* with which Marina Oswald testified she took the pictures.

The account given in the Report appears to be straightforward, but close study of the Hearings and Exhibits discloses that there are a number of peculiar and unresolved features to the story, most of which are not mentioned in the Report. Others, which are mentioned as "facts," remain subject to some doubt.

The Taking of the Photograph

The Commission has carefully avoided any finding of mental disturbance or derangement in the alleged assassin, yet persists in attributing to him motives and actions which must be viewed as irrational. The Commission believes that Oswald made careful plans to shoot General Walker and attempted to do so on Wednesday, April 10, 1963, after which he carefully burned his "blueprint" for the crime and took other steps to escape suspicion. At the same time, we are asked to believe that ten days before Oswald attempted to commit this murder he asked his wife to take photographs of him holding the rifle with which he planned to shoot the General. This certainly was a reckless if not irrational act, as was his failure to destroy the incriminating photographs after the Walker attempt or before the assassination.

Sunday, March 31, 1963, the day on which the photographs are said to have

200

been taken, was a cloudy day with traces of rain, according to the Dallas office of the U.S. Weather Bureau. The photograph was taken in bright or brilliant sunlight, as can be seen from the darkness of the shadows and the contrasting lighted areas. Since the location in which the photo was taken was known to the Commission's investigators, it should have been possible to determine on the basis of direction of light and angle of shadows the hour at which the image was recorded, and then to check the weather records to see if it was sunny or cloudy at that time. This was not done.

The Commission states that two photographs were taken *(CE 133-A and 133-B),* apparently on the basis of Marina Oswald's testimony of February 3, 1964, when she said:

> I had even forgotten that I had taken two photographs. I thought there was only one. I thought that there were two identical pictures, but they turned out to be two different poses. *(1H 16)*

One pose shows the rifle in the left hand; the other shows the rifle in the right hand. But Marguerite Oswald's testimony suggests that there was a third photograph. She told the Commission that Marina had taken her into the bedroom in the Paine home on Friday night and that:

> *Mrs. Oswald:* She opened the closet. . . . And she came out with a picture— a picture of Lee, with a gun. It said, "To my daughter June"—written in English. I said, "Oh, Marina, police." I didn't think anything of the picture. Now, you must understand . . . I don't know all the circumstances, what evidence they had against my son by this time . . . anybody can own a rifle, to go hunting. . . . So I am not connecting this with the assassination. . . . No one is going to be foolish enough to take a picture of themselves with that rifle, and leave that there for evidence. . . .
> No, sir, that is not the picture. He was holding the rifle up. . . .
> *Rankin:* By holding the rifle up you mean—
> *Mrs. Oswald:* Like this.
> *Rankin:* Crosswise, with both hands on the rifle?
> *Mrs. Oswald:* With both hands on the rifle.
> *Rankin:* Above his head?
> *Mrs. Oswald:* That is right. *(1H 146 and 148)*

No notice was taken of this description of a third photograph and Marina Oswald was not questioned about it on her subsequent appearances before the Commission. It is not clear, consequently, why the Warren Report asserts that two pictures were taken when the allegation that there was a third photo has not been investigated.[1]

The Report does not comment on the question of the place where the photographs were developed. The Hearings and Exhibits provide no information on

---

1 The photograph seen by Oswald's mother, in which Oswald may have been holding the shotgun he owned there rather than a rifle, may have been one taken in the Soviet Union. Because the questions put to Marguerite and Marina Oswald were not searching, the available information about the third photograph is insufficient to warrant any conclusion about it.

this point except for a handwritten reminder in a reporter's notebook recording the events following Oswald's arrest:

Ask Fritz—
1—Who N.C. preacher who tipped them about the mail-order purchase?
2—501 Elm is place that processed photo. What are details of photo (showing gun & Daily Worker head: "Be Militant")
(*Kantor Exhibit No. 3,* Vol. XX, p. 376)

It is logical to assume that Kantor learned from the police that the photo of Oswald holding the rifle had been processed at 501 Elm. If so, the police have said nothing about this in reports or testimony, and neither the FBI nor the Warren Commission has shown any interest in the question. When were the photographs developed, and by whom, and how were they traced to 501 Elm Street—which is less than a block away from the Book Depository?

It should be recalled that on March 31, 1963, the day on which Marina Oswald is said to have taken the photographs, Oswald was still employed at Jaggers-Chiles-Stovall, in the photographic department. According to a co-worker:

. . . about one month after he started . . . he seemed interested in whether the company would allow him to reproduce his own pictures, and I told him that while they didn't sanction that sort of thing, that people do it now and then.   (*10H 201*)

One would think that Oswald—whose parsimony was often emphasized by witnesses who knew him—would have taken advantage of the opportunity to have the photographs developed at no cost to himself.[2] It is true that he was dismissed from this job at the end of the week. Once dismissed, presumably before an opportunity to print the photographs, why should Oswald have taken them to 501 Elm? He could easily have had them developed and printed near his apartment at Oak Cliff. Consequently, the date on which the films were left to be developed assumes some interest, and it is a pity that no inquiry was made by the Commission.

The Camera

We turn now to the camera with which the photographs are alleged to have been taken. On February 6, 1964 Marina Oswald was shown Commission Exhibit 136, a camera contained in a leather case. She said:

Mrs. Oswald: This is a Russian camera.
Rankin: Is that the camera you used to take the pictures you have referred to?
Mrs. Oswald: I don't remember exactly whether it was an American camera or this.   (*1H 118*)

---

2   According to Marina Oswald, Oswald did so on at least two occasions, once printing photographs of General Walker's house and once a name plate. (*CEs 1156, 1840*)

She was next shown another camera in a leather case, Exhibit 137, but she said that she had never seen it before. *(1H 119)*

The camera is next mentioned in the April 23 testimony of FBI photographic expert Lyndal L. Shaneyfelt, in the following passage:

Eisenberg: Mr. Shaneyfelt, I now hand you an Imperial Reflex Duo Lens camera. Let me state for the record, that this camera was turned over to the FBI by Robert Oswald, the brother of Lee Harvey Oswald, on February 24, 1964.

Robert Oswald identified the camera as having belonged to Lee Oswald and stated that he, Robert, had obtained it from the Paine residence in December 1963, several weeks after the assassination.

On February 25, 1964, Marina was given the camera and she identified it as the one which she had used to take the pictures. . . . When did you receive the camera, Mr. Shaneyfelt?

Shaneyfelt: It was—I can't pinpoint the date exactly, I don't have the notes here for that. It was, I would say, the latter part of February, not too long after it had been recovered on February 24.

Eisenberg: Was it in working order when you received it?

Shaneyfelt: No; it had been slightly damaged. . . . In order to be able to make a photograph with the camera, I had to make slight repairs to the shutter lever, which had been bent. I straightened it and cleaned the lens in order to remove the dirt which had accumulated. These are the only things that had to be done before it was usable to make pictures with.

(4H 284)

On June 11, 1964 Marina Oswald returned to testify again before the Commission. At this time she was shown the Imperial Reflex camera *(CE 750)*, and she identified it as the camera with which she had taken the photographs of Oswald holding the rifle. *(5H 405, 410)*

Study of the Exhibits yields further information on the camera. We find that Marina Oswald was interviewed by the FBI on January 29, 1964. She was shown photographs of a Russian camera and an American camera with a Realist trademark. She said that the cameras appeared to be the ones owned by her husband. *(CE 1155)* On February 17, 1964 she was interviewed again and shown the same photographs of the cameras. This time she said that the Realist camera was not Oswald's and that to her knowledge she had never seen that camera. *(CE 1156)* In a further FBI interview on the next day, February 18, she said that the American camera with which she had taken the photographs of Oswald with the rifle was grayish in color, a box-type camera, but that she did not know where the camera was. *(CE 1404,* p. 448)

The next document is a letter dated February 28, 1964 from J. Edgar Hoover to J. Lee Rankin, general counsel of the Warren Commission, stating:

On February 24, 1964, Mr. Robert Lee Oswald, brother of Lee, furnished to a Special Agent of the Dallas Office of this Bureau a Duo-lens Imperial Reflex camera which he stated was the property of Lee. . . . Robert advised that he obtained this camera from the residence of Mrs. Ruth Paine, Irving, Texas, in December, 1963. . . . On February 25, 1964, this camera was displayed to Marina Oswald and she immediately identified it as the American camera which belonged to her husband and the one which she used to take the photograph of him with the rifle and the pistol.   *(CE 2083)*

There is no record in the Exhibits of the February 24 interview with Robert Oswald; on that date, he had already completed his testimony before the Warren Commission, and he was not re-called later. Therefore, no independent testimony from Robert Oswald corroborates the statements made by the FBI and there is no identification by Robert Oswald of the camera which the FBI claims to have obtained from him.

Curiously enough, there is no record either of the February 25 interview with Marina Oswald, although the Exhibits include about 50 FBI reports of interviews with her.

There is an FBI report on an interview with Robert Oswald on March 15, 1964, in which he is alleged to have said that he obtained property belonging to Lee Oswald, including the small American-made camera, from the home of Ruth Paine on December 8, 1963. He said that he had not made the camera available to the authorities before February 24, 1964 because it had never occurred to him that anyone would be interested in the camera. *(CE 2466)*

The next document in this series is an FBI report dated March 26, 1964 summarizing the interviews with Robert Oswald and Marina Oswald between February 16 and 24, already discussed, and providing additional information which, in effect, accounted for the fact that the Imperial Reflex camera had been overlooked in the searches and seizures conducted at the Paine home on November 22, 23 and subsequent occasions. The report states that Detective John A. McCabe of the Irving Police Department had assisted Dallas police officers in a search of the Paine premises on November 23, 1963 and was certain that he had seen a light gray box camera in a box in the garage. McCabe said that he did not take the camera because he did not consider it to be of evidential value. He said that the Dallas police officers had not examined the box containing the camera, because he had already examined it, and he said that he did not point out the camera to them. *(CE 2557)* Indeed, none of the Dallas police officers who were present on that occasion could recall ever having seen the camera; but they all stated that if it had been discovered during the search, they would have taken it in.

Detective McCabe, the only person who can place the Imperial Reflex camera in the Paine garage on November 23, 1963, was not a witness before the Warren Commission. Robert Oswald, who is alleged to have taken the camera together with other belongings of Lee Harvey Oswald when he visited the Paine home on December 8, 1963, and who turned the camera over to the FBI on February 24, 1964, did not testify on these points and there is no record of the February 24 interview. In fact, from beginning to end we have only FBI reports as authority for this history of the chain of possession of the camera. According to this history, Detective McCabe saw the camera but did not attach importance to it or mention it to the other police officers present. It must be determined whether or not this is plausible under the circumstances which prevailed when McCabe ostensibly saw the camera.

Discovery of the Photographs

Dallas police officers had searched the Paine premises on Friday afternoon after the assassination and the arrest of Oswald. Michael Paine, who was present, testified that one of the plainclothesmen

> ... collected all the useless stuff in our house, he went around and collected all the files of Ruth, and a drawer of cameras, mostly belonging to me. I tried to tell him one of the files contained our music or something like that, and the more I suggested it, that he not bother taking those, the more insistent he was in taking those objects. ... Their [the Oswalds'] possessions were searched by various waves of succeeding policemen, Dallas, and Irving and FBI, and what not.   *(2H 428)*

The following afternoon Dallas Police Officers Adamcik, Moore, Stovall, and Rose together with McCabe of the Irving Police reappeared at the Paine residence. Mrs. Paine departed to do her marketing, leaving the policemen alone in her home. When she returned, they had departed. *(3H 85-87)* During the time that the officers were alone on the premises, they discovered the photographs of Oswald holding the rifle. The Dallas police officers were examined by counsel for the Warren Commission early in April 1964. Adamcik claimed that the photographs were found while he was in the back of the garage; he did not know who had found them. *(7H 209)* Moore, on the other hand, said that he had seen Detective Rose discover the pictures.

> *Belin:* Did Rose show it to you out there?
> *Moore:* Yes, he did; at the time he found it.
> *Belin:* Were you near him when he found it?
> *Moore:* Yes.
> *Belin:* How far away was he from you?
> *Moore:* This was a one-car garage, and it would have to be close. Four men searching in that garage. I would say a matter of three or four feet.
> *(7H 215)*

Stovall also testified that Rose had found the photographs. *(7H 194)* Rose himself said,

> I found two negatives[3] first that showed Lee Oswald holding a rifle in his hand, wearing a pistol at his hip, and right with those negatives I found a developed picture ... a picture that had been developed from the negative of him holding this rifle, and Detective McCabe was standing there and he found the other picture—of Oswald holding the rifle.   *(7H 231)*

Under these circumstances, it is hardly plausible that McCabe, having participated in the discovery of the photographs, would completely ignore any camera he saw nearby and say nothing to his companions about it. In any case, there is no direct testimony from McCabe, despite the importance of his role in relation to the photographs and the camera.

---

3 The Commission claims that only one negative was found. *(WR 127)*

Elsewhere I discuss the discovery of the undated note which led to the disclosure by Marina Oswald of the story that Oswald had made the attempt on the life of General Walker. Because the undated note had remained in a book in the Paine home, undiscovered in the various searches by the Dallas police, the FBI on December 4, 1963 carefully collected all remaining property of the Oswalds from Mrs. Paine. *(CE 1403)* But the Imperial Reflex camera was overlooked again, and was then collected by Robert Oswald on December 8, with various items of apparel and paraphernalia such as an extension cord and a pencil sharpener which had belonged to his dead brother.

Testifying on July 23, 1964, Ruth Paine was asked if she recalled what things Robert Oswald had taken on December 8, 1963. She replied:

> They took the clothes from the closet, boxes and things that I did not look into. I have heard from the police that it also included an old camera which they had to chase later and went up to Robert Oswald's to find it. *(11H 398)*

Again, a witness testifying under oath is unable to authenticate the whereabouts of this important item of evidence; again, we have only hearsay on which to rely.

In earlier testimony on March 21, 1964, Ruth Paine provided arresting information which must give us pause in contemplating the elusive Imperial Reflex camera.

> *Jenner:* Was there any picture-taking during the period, during the fall of 1963, either in New Orleans or in Irving or in Dallas?
> *Mrs. Paine:* Not by either Lee or Marina that I heard of.
> *Jenner:* And did you hear any conversation between them in your presence or with you with respect to his or they having a snapshot camera or other type of camera to take pictures?
> *Mrs. Paine:* No; the only reference to a camera was made by Lee when he held up and showed me a camera he had bought in the Soviet Union and said he couldn't buy film for it in this country, it was a different size.
> *Jenner:* Did they ever exhibit any snapshots to you?
> *Mrs. Paine:* Yes; a few snapshots taken in Minsk.
> *Jenner:* But no snapshots of any scenes in America that they had taken?
> *Mrs. Paine:* No.
> *Jenner:* Or people?
> *Mrs. Paine:* No.   *(9H 344)*

Indeed, included in a group of about 75 photographs obtained in searches and seizures which were identified by Marina Oswald in an FBI interview on January 31, 1964 are two photographs of the Oswalds with their daughter June which were taken in a photograph booth in a bus station in Dallas but no other photographs taken in the United States with the Imperial Reflex camera. We are therefore forced to conclude that Oswald used that camera *only to take two sets of incriminating photographs*—those of himself holding the rifle and the revolver alleged to have been used in the murder of the President and of Tippit, and those of General Walker's house alleged to have been taken preparatory to the attempt on his life. No one disputes that Oswald was a devoted, even a doting, father. It is a strain on credulity to believe that the Imperial Reflex camera was in his possession and that he used it only for those two sets of incriminating pictures but did not bother to photograph his little girl so that he would have a record of her babyhood and growth. It is a strain to believe that that same camera was overlooked time and again in police searches and that it was in fact seen, and ultimately recovered, by witnesses who did not testify or did not testify under oath on this specific matter. We are dependent entirely on the FBI, which in another context was considered by the Warren Commission itself to be a "questioned authority."

Clearly it is a dubious story and an unsatisfactory and wholly inadequate procedure of "fact finding," especially when weighed against the discovery of the incriminating photographs by police officers in the absence of any witness and Oswald's insistence that the photographs were fakes.

The Authenticity of the Photographs

According to Captain Fritz, Oswald was confronted by the photograph of himself holding the rifle at 6 p.m. on Saturday, less than 24 hours before he was shot to death, with the following response:

> He said the picture was not his, that the face was his face, but that this picture had been made by superimposing his face, the other part of the picture was not him at all and that he had never seen the picture before. . . . [He] said that he knew all about photography, that he had done a lot of work in photography himself, that the small picture was a reduced picture of the large picture, and had been made by some person unknown to him. He further stated that since he had been photographed here at City Hall and that people had been taking his picture while being transferred from my office to the jail door that someone had been able to get a picture of his face and that with that, they had made this picture. He told me . . . that in time, *he would be able to show that it was not his picture and that it had been made by someone else*. [Italics added]   *(WR 608-609)*

Only when the Warren Report was released in September 1964 did it become generally known that Oswald had charged that the photograph was a fabrication and that his face had been superimposed on someone else's body. For some six months before this information was published for the first time, Mark Lane and other critics had been voicing the very same view about the photograph on the basis of the shadows and other of its features.

As was true for the camera, one is wholly dependent on the FBI and the testimony of an FBI expert in evaluating the authenticity of the photograph which Oswald charged was a forgery. I do not feel in a position to state a conclusive opinion but would like to call attention to two features of the picture which are apparent to even the untrained eye.

One is the size relationship between Oswald and the rifle shown in the photograph. We know from various sources, including the autopsy report *(CE 1981)*, that Oswald was 5 feet 9 inches tall; we know from the Warren Report *(WR 81)* that the rifle found in the Book Depository is 40.2 inches long. If we add an inch to Oswald's height to account for his shoes, his height in the photograph is 70 inches. The 40.2-inch rifle would then be 57.4 per cent of Oswald's height.

In the full-page reproduction of the photograph which appeared on the cover of *Life* on February 21, 1964, Oswald's height measures 12.75 inches and the rifle measures 7.75 inches. It is 61 per cent instead of 57.4 per cent of Oswald's height.

Therefore, if the rifle in the photograph is actually the 40.2-inch Carcano, the man's height should be 13.5 inches instead of 12.75; however, if the man is actually 70 inches tall, the rifle should be 7.3 instead of 7.75 inches. Thus, (1) the man in the photograph is only 64 inches tall, or 5 inches shorter than Oswald in bare feet; or (2) the rifle in the photograph is actually 42.6 inches long, or 2.4 inches longer than the Carcano.

However, those calculations presuppose the absence of significant distortion in the photograph of the apparent height of the man or the apparent length of the rifle. The calculations may not be significant or valid if the picture gives a false perspective. Indeed, the discrepancy is important not so much in absolute terms as it is in terms of the failure of the investigators and experts to utilize comparative measurements of that sort in assessing the authenticity of the photograph.

The second feature of the photograph which is apparent to the casual eye is the seeming inconsistency in the direction of shadows. In the large print *(CE 746-A)* one sees clearly that the shadow of the man's body falls behind him and to his right, but the shadow under his nose falls in dead center and not to the right. In an enlarged section of the photograph *(CE 746-C)* the shadow under the nose is seen even more clearly as a triangle with the apex at the middle of the upper lip.

The FBI attempted to demonstrate that the rifle in the photograph was the 40.2-inch Carcano found in the Book Depository by having an agent pose with that rifle in the same posture as Oswald and with sunlight in the same direction. In the re-enactment photograph the shadow of the agent's body falls behind him and to his right (somewhat more sharply than in the original photograph). Consequently, we should be able to judge from the shadows under the agent's nose and left side of the face whether or not the corresponding shadows in the Oswald photograph are consistent with the shadow of the body. *But the agent's face and head have been blacked out completely. (CE 748)* This was discussed with FBI Expert Shaneyfelt in his testimony of April 23, 1964. Asked to explain why the head of the individual was blacked out, he said: "I blanked out the head because it was one of the employees of the FBI, and I felt it was desirable to blank out the head because it was not pertinent." *(4H 281)*

I must point out that in a re-enactment photograph taken in the backyard at the Neely Street address by the Dallas police crime lab, in the presence of Special Agent Sorrels of the Secret Service, the face of the stand-in has *not* been blacked out, although it has no greater pertinence than that of the FBI agent. *(CE 712)* But in that photograph, there is no attempt to duplicate the lighting, and the shadows on the stand-in's face do not help us at all in evaluating the original photograph.

The FBI's exercise in evasion is so blatant that I am tempted to consider it innocent, but it is a temptation I shall resist until the apparent conflict between the shadows in the original incriminating picture have been resolved in a satisfactory manner.

Recapitulation

It is impossible to understand why Oswald should have caused these damning photographs to be made, using a camera which was supposedly utilized only for incriminating pictures but never for conventional photography, or why he should have left this evidence to be found and used against him when it easily could have been destroyed. It is not adequate to shrug this off as an aberration; there is an obligation to discover a rational explanation, or a pattern of faulty logic into which this behavior fits, and that obligation has not been fulfilled.

The Commission has ignored completely the relevant questions of where and when the incriminating photographs were developed and printed, and has not followed up the clue in Seth Kantor's notes about 501 Elm Street.

The Commission has relied on hearsay evidence with respect to important facts relating to the discovery of the photographs and the chain of possession of the camera. There is no FBI report of the recovery of the camera from Robert Oswald on February 24, 1964 by the agent or agents who were present and took possession of the camera on that date; there is no sworn testimony from Robert Oswald corroborating the circumstances described in later FBI reports. In relying on the FBI for the authentication of the photographs, the Commission has relied—by its own criterion—on a questioned authority. No independent opinion from an outside expert has been obtained. The problem of the shadows on the face versus the shadow of the body in the original photograph has been "solved" by blacking out the face of the stand-in in the re-enactment picture, for reasons so lame as to be confounding.

In the light of all the anomalies discussed, it is not possible to determine whether the photograph is genuine or forged, but I do conclude that the Commission's procedures were so loose and its judgment so oblivious in considering this matter that it would have been possible to introduce spurious evidence and have it accepted as authentic.

Chapter 8
FBI Agent Hosty, Ruth Paine, and Oswald

Soon after the assassination, newspaper and magazine articles appeared which suggested that Oswald, the alleged assassin of the President, may have been an undercover operative for a federal agency and specifically for the Federal Bureau of Investigation. The articles called attention to various anomalies and uncertainties in Oswald's history which suggested his clandestine service in the FBI: his available funds, apparently in excess of his known income; allegations that he had received small sums of money from unknown sources via Western Union; his unhampered travel across the border in spite of his earlier defection and attempt to become a citizen of the Soviet Union; his request to see an FBI agent when he was arrested in New Orleans in August 1963, and the like.

Because of the "numerous rumors and allegations that Oswald may have been a paid informant or some type of undercover agent for a Federal agency" the Warren Commission included in Chapter VI of the Report ("Investigation of Possible Conspiracy") a section titled "Oswald Was Not an Agent for the U.S. Government." *(WR 325-327)* Neither in that section of the Report nor in the Hearings and Exhibits is there any mention of the secret emergency meetings held by the Commission in January 1964 as a result of allegations by high officials of the State of Texas. The officials claimed that Oswald was an undercover informant on the FBI payroll at $200 a month, with the number S-172, and their charges came to light only in 1965, in a book entitled *Portrait of the Assassin* by Congressman Gerald Ford.[1] The Commission's disposition of this

---

1 *Op. cit.*

matter is discussed in a later chapter of this book, indicating that the question was not resolved at all.

Another question which raises the issue of Oswald's real relationship with the FBI is the discovery in Oswald's notebook of the name, address, and telephone and auto license numbers of FBI Agent James P. Hosty, Jr. According to the Warren Report:

> The Commission also investigated the circumstances which led to the presence in Oswald's address book of the name of Agent Hosty together with his office address, telephone number, and license number. Hosty and Mrs. Paine testified that on November 1, 1963, Hosty left his name and phone number with Mrs. Paine so that she could advise Hosty when she learned where Oswald was living in Dallas. Mrs. Paine and Marina Oswald have testified that Mrs. Paine handed Oswald the slip of paper on which Hosty had written this information. In accordance with prior instructions from Oswald, Marina Oswald noted Hosty's license number which she gave to her husband. The address of the Dallas office of the FBI could have been obtained from many public sources. *(WR 327)*

Contrary to the assertions in the Report, the Hearings and Exhibits raise doubts about the means by which Hosty's license number found its way into Oswald's address book. The Exhibits indicate, moreover, a fact of which the Report discreetly makes no mention: that the FBI initially withheld from the Warren Commission the information that entries concerning Hosty were found in Oswald's papers. This comes to light in a letter of March 26, 1964 in which the Commission asked the FBI for a "reasoned response" to some thirty questions, including the following one.

> When and for what reason were pages 279 through 283 of the report of SA [Special Agent—S.M.] Gemberling of February 11, 1964, prepared [setting forth the entries in Oswald's address book which had not been included in the report of SA Gemberling of December 23, 1963]?

The FBI Director responded in a letter of April 6, 1964:

> Pages 279 through 283 of the report of SA Gemberling dated February 11, 1964, were prepared at the time such report was being typed by the Dallas Office during a few-day period immediately preceding submission of such report to FBI headquarters by the Dallas Office. In this connection, your attention is also directed to this Bureau's letter to the Commission dated February 27, 1964, enclosing an affidavit executed by SA Robert P. Gemberling explaining in detail his handling and reporting of data in Lee Harvey Oswald's address book. You will note that in his affidavit, SA Gemberling explains why certain data in Oswald's address book was reported in his December 23, 1963, report, whereas the remaining data . . . was reported in SA Gemberling's February 11, 1964, report. *(CE 833*, p. 15)

This "answer" does not give the requested explanation but suggests that the explanation is found in an affidavit executed by Special Agent Gemberling. But that affidavit is not included in the published Exhibits.

In his testimony before the Warren Commission on May 14, 1964, J. Edgar Hoover made some further remarks about the Gemberling report.

This report was not prepared for this Commission but rather for investigative purposes of the FBI, and therefore the information concerning Hosty's name, telephone number, and license number was not included in the report, as the circumstances under which Hosty's name, etc., appeared in Oswald's notebook were fully known to the FBI.

After our investigative report of December 23, 1963, was furnished . . . we noted that Agent Hosty's name did not appear in the report. In order that there would be a complete reporting of all items in Oswald's notebook, this information was incorporated in another investigative report . . . dated February 11, 1964. Both of the . . . reports were furnished to the Commission prior to any inquiry concerning this matter by the . . . Commission. *(5H 112)*

In fact, the Commission had questioned Marina Oswald about the Hosty entries on February 3, or eight days before the FBI report of February 11, 1964, presenting the information omitted, for still unknown reasons, from the report of December 23, 1963. The channel by which the Commission first became aware of the Hosty entries in Oswald's notebook remains unknown, although clearly it was from a source other than FBI reports. Also still unknown is why, as late as December 23, 1963, the FBI was preparing reports "for its own purposes," a practice which seems inconsistent with the fact that the FBI was designated as the investigative arm of the Warren Commission when the Commission was appointed on November 29, 1963. *(WR 471-472)* Since the FBI report of December 23, 1963 was submitted to, although "not prepared for," the Commission, why were the Hosty entries omitted? If the "circumstances were fully known" to the FBI, why did the December report not include an explanation, together with an account of the Hosty entries, which at face value implied a compromising relationship between Hosty and/or the FBI and Oswald?

One is led to wonder if in December 1963 the FBI found the Hosty entries inexplicable and highly embarrassing and if the information was not withheld from the Commission until some explanation was compelled by the Commission's discovery, from some other source, of the Hosty entries. At the least, it would seem that Gemberling protected Hosty; Hoover protected Gemberling; and the Commission protected the FBI by withholding from its Exhibits such documents as the Gemberling affidavit and reports.

What is more disconcerting is the fact that the testimony throws considerable doubt on the assertion that Marina Oswald copied the license number of Hosty's car and gave the number to Oswald. It is true that she testified that she did, as the Report carefully phrases it. During her hearing before the Commisson on February 3, 1964, Marina Oswald was questioned about Hosty's November 1, 1963 visit to the Paine home in Irving, Texas.

Rankin: After you received the telephone number, what did you do with it?
Mrs. Oswald: He gave the telephone number to Ruth, and she, in turn, passed it on to Lee. . . .
Rankin: Did the agent also give his license number for his car to Mrs. Paine or to you or to your husband?
Mrs. Oswald: No. But Lee had asked me that if an FBI agent were to call, that I note down his automobile license number, and I did that.

Rankin: Did you give the license number to him when you noted it down?
Mrs. Oswald: Yes ... the man who visited us, that man had never seen Lee. He was talking to me and to Mrs. Paine. But he had never met Lee. ...
(1H 48)

It is implicit in this testimony that Marina copied the license number on the first of Hosty's two visits, which took place on November 1 and 5. She said that Oswald had asked that "if an FBI agent were to call" she note down the agent's auto license number. Had she not done this on the November 1 visit, Oswald might have said, "if the FBI agent calls again, take down his license number," or he might have reproached her for forgetting his earlier instructions. She does not suggest that anything like that transpired. But if logic suggests that it was on the November 1 visit that Marina took down the license number, the facts indicate that she did not. According to Ruth Paine:

... the first time he had come on the first of November, he had parked down the street, and he made reference to the fact that they don't like to draw attention for the neighborhood to any interviews that they make, and in fact my neighbor also commented when she talked to him a few days previously [during a pretext interview] that his car was parked down the street and wasn't in front of my house. ... *(3H 100)*

Clearly, we must rule out the possibility that Marina took down the license number on that occasion, when Hosty's car was at some distance from the Paine house and there was no way for Marina to know that it was Hosty's car, even if it was within her range of vision.

If we put aside the implications of Marina's testimony and assume that she copied the license number on the November 5 visit, we still encounter major difficulties. This time Hosty parked his car in front of the Paine house; but Ruth Paine testified:

Mrs. Paine: My best judgment is that the license plate was not visible, however, while it was parked; not visible from my house. *(3H 100)*

Hosty and I, and a second agent was with him, I don't know the name, stood at the door of my home and talked briefly, as I have already described, about the address of Oswald in Dallas. Marina was in her room feeding the baby, or busy some way. She came in just as Hosty and I were closing the conversation, and I must say we were both surprised at her entering. He then took his leave immediately, and as he has told me later, drove to the end of my street which curves and then drove back down Fifth Street.

Jenner: Now you are reporting something Agent Hosty has told you?
Mrs. Paine: Yes.
Jenner: Were you aware of the fact that he drove to the end of the street?
Mrs. Paine: Not at that time, no. *(3H 99-100)*

Jenner continued to question Mrs. Paine in an attempt to determine whether or not it was physically possible for Marina Oswald to have seen and copied Hosty's license number on the second visit. Mrs. Paine said that Marina had been in her bedroom the entire time.

Jenner: Are you firm, reasonably firm that Marina, even if she desired to learn of the license number on Agent Hosty's car, that she could not have seen or detected it while remaining in the house?

Mrs. Paine: She might possibly—oh, I wouldn't say that. It is conceivable depending on where it was parked, it is conceivable that she could have seen it from the bedroom window.   *(3H 101)*

This testimony was taken on March 19, 1964. On March 23, Jenner and Secret Service Agent Joe Howlett accompanied Ruth Paine to the bedroom which Marina had occupied, to test the visibility of the license plate number on a car stationed where Hosty had parked on his second visit. Jenner said:

Jenner: It is impossible—at least impossible to see any license plate on either of the two automobiles parked at the curb. . . .

Howlett: Yes; that's correct. . . . I am shining a flashlight on the front and rear of both automobiles and you cannot even see the license plate, much less any of the numbers.   *(9H 398)*

At that moment, therefore, Jenner confronted the fact that (1) Marina could not have taken the license number on the November 1 visit because Hosty had parked his car down the street; (2) the license plate was not visible when the car was parked in front of the Paine house on the second visit because it was screened by another automobile standing there; (3) Hosty said that on the second visit he drove to the end of the street, turned, and drove past the Paine house —however, Ruth Paine did not see him do so, nor does she suggest that Marina might have seen him pass the house in his car at the end of the visit or that she might have copied the number from his moving vehicle at that time. On the contrary, she said on March 19 that it was conceivable that Marina might have seen the license plate from her bedroom window. The experiment on March 23 eliminated that possibility. Yet if Marina took the license number at all, she must have taken it covertly—Ruth Paine testified that the first she had heard anything about the license number was when Hosty told her, "well after the assassination," that a notation of his name, telephone number, and license number had been found in Oswald's room.

There was, then, strong reason on March 23, 1964 to discredit Marina's story that she had copied Hosty's license number and given it to Oswald. Marina testified before the Commission on at least three occasions after that date, but not one single question was asked about the license number, when investigation had made it clear that she could not have copied that number as she testified she did early in February. In the face of those findings and without re-opening the question with Marina, the Warren Commission asserts that Marina testified that she had copied the number. That is literally true, but fundamentally dishonest and misleading, because, as the Hearings indicate, she could not have copied the number on either of Hosty's two visits.[2]

---

2 On June 22 and July 3, 1965, the author wrote to Counsel Jenner requesting clarification of the Commission's reasoning, in view of the conflict between the evidence and the tacit assertion in the Warren Report that Marina was the agent by which Hosty's license plate number was conveyed to Oswald and placed by him in his notebook. On July 8, 1965 Mr. Jenner replied that he would provide the requested clarification when he returned to his office about July 19, 1965. He never honored his stated intention or replied to a follow-up letter of reminder.

Another assertion in Marina's February testimony was that FBI Agent Hosty had never seen or met Lee Harvey Oswald. *(1H 48)* That assertion appears to be no more trustworthy than her claim that she had copied the license number. Testifying on February 21, 1964, Robert Oswald described Marina's refusal to be interviewed by two FBI agents who wished to question her on November 26, 1963, only a few days after the assassination:

> *Oswald:* When the FBI agents arrived . . . when the two agents and Mr. Gopadze came in, Marina immediately identified or recognized one of the agents who she had talked to before, and it is my understanding now, at the Paines' home in Irving, Texas. . . .
>
> *Jenner:* Did she have an aversion to being interviewed by the FBI agent on this occasion?
>
> *Oswald:* Yes, sir, she did. . . . Marina had recognized this one FBI agent as a man who had come to the Paines' home in Irving, Texas, and perhaps at another location where they might have lived in Dallas or the surrounding territory, and had questioned Lee on these occasions. . . . In or outside of the home . . . within the immediate grounds of the home, at least. . . . She had an aversion to speaking to him because she was of the opinion that he had harassed Lee in his interviews. . . . I would say this was certainly so. His manner was very harsh, sir. . . . It was quite evident that there was a harshness there, and that Marina did not want to speak to the FBI at that time. . . . And they were insisting, sir. And they implied in so many words . . . they were implying that if she did not cooperate with the FBI agent there . . . that they would perhaps deport her from the United States and back to Russia. . . .   *(1H 409-410)*

> I went over to Mr. Brown, the agent I knew, who was sitting at the end of the coffee table . . . and I was shaking my finger at him . . . that I resented the implications that they were passing on to Marina, because of her apparent uncooperative attitude. . . . They attempted for another five or ten minutes to interview Marina Oswald at that time. . . . Mr. Brown—he left the immediate area of interviewing there, and came over and started speaking to me. . . . And the other FBI agent arose rather disgustedly to end the attempted interview, he walked to the door, opened the door, and spoke very harshly to Mr. Brown. . . . He said, "Just cut it off right there, Mr. Brown."

> Mr. Brown indicated he wanted to talk to me some more. He just motioned to him to cut it off right here. Mr. Brown left and went outside with him. . . .   *(1H 411-412)*

This FBI agent to whom Marina had an aversion because in her opinion he had harassed Oswald "in his interviews" is the same Hosty who, she testified some months later, had never seen or met her husband. *(CE 1780)* Indeed, she must have had a strong aversion to Hosty to refuse, only a few days after the assassination and vulnerable as she was, to answer his questions.[3] Her undisguised hostility and anger toward Hosty on that occasion, like that of Oswald himself when Hosty appeared at the interrogation session right after his arrest, is incomprehensible if Hosty's two visits to the Paine home were as pleasant and

---

[3] Although Robert Oswald told the Commission on February 21, 1964 that Hosty had threatened Marina with deportation if she did not co-operate, Hosty was not asked about this when he testified on May 5, 1964.

innocuous as he, Marina, and Ruth Paine all testified. But by the time they testified on the visits, several months had passed, and Marina told a story which had little in common with her earlier statements about and attitude toward Hosty, as recounted by Robert Oswald. A few days after the arrest and murder of her husband, Marina was accusing Hosty of having harassed Lee "in his interviews." Other hints of possible personal contact between Oswald and Hosty emerge from both Marina's and Ruth Paine's testimony.

> *Rankin:* Now, did you report to your husband the fact of this visit, November 1, with the FBI agent?
>
> *Mrs. Oswald:* I didn't report it to him at once, but as soon as he came for a weekend, I told him about it. . . . I told him that they had come, that they were interested in where he was working and where he lived, and he was, again, upset. He said that he would telephone them—I don't know whether he called or not—or that he would visit them. . . . Lee had told me that supposedly he had visited their office or their building. But I didn't believe him. I thought he was a brave rabbit.   *(1H 57)*

Ruth Paine told a similar story about Oswald's assertion that he had called at the FBI office and attempted to see Hosty:

> I perhaps should put in here that Lee told me, and I only reconstructed this a few weeks ago, that he went, after I gave him—from the first visit of the FBI agent I took down the agent's name and the number that is in the telephone book to call the FBI and I gave this to Lee the weekend he came . . . that would have been the weekend of the second, the next day. . . . Then he told me, it must have been the following weekend. . . . He told me that he had stopped at the downtown office of the FBI and tried to see the agents and left a note. . . . He was irritated and he said, "They are trying to inhibit my activities." . . . I learned only a few weeks ago that he never did go into the FBI office. Of course knowing, thinking that he had gone in, I thought that was sensible on his part. But it appears to have been another lie.   *(3H 18-19)*

Although Mrs. Paine did not say and counsel did not ask the source of her information, "most probably" it was Hosty himself. It would be most naïve to accept a denial from such a source. In the wake of the assassination, the FBI experienced shock waves of criticism for its handling of the Oswald case, after long immunity from disapproval. The FBI would hardly be willing to admit that the accused assassin had been pounding at its door for attention and still been permitted to go about his deadly business without interference.

The FBI may well deny that the visit took place, but it would have been quite characteristic of Oswald's aggressive insistence on his rights, his audacity in his dealings with the American Embassy in Moscow, and his passionate denunciation of Hosty and the FBI in general, when Hosty appeared in the police station after Oswald's arrest. If the charges confronting him at that moment did not silence him, one wonders what considerations would have restrained him from taking his protests to the FBI office after Hosty's first visit to the Paine home. The FBI office in Dallas is on Commerce Street, no great distance from the Book Depository, and Oswald could have gone there easily when work finished at 4:45 p.m. or even during his lunch hour.

It is not clear from the reports on the interrogation of Oswald after his arrest (Appendix XI of the Report) whether his outburst against Hosty indicated prior acquaintance or only recognition of his name. Certainly there is nothing to obviate a previous meeting between the two.

Two further comments are apropos: In the first place, Oswald was irritated by the renewal of interest in him on the part of the FBI and what he regarded as an attempt to inhibit his activities; for all he knew, he might have been under 24-hour surveillance. Therefore, it is hard to understand why that possibility did not inhibit his alleged actions only three weeks later, on the morning of the assassination. Secondly, the Warren Commission has made no attempt independently to ascertain whether or not Oswald visited the FBI office, as he told both his wife and Ruth Paine; it merely accepted the denial of such a visit by an unknown source to Mrs. Paine, as mentioned in her testimony. Oswald's assertion, juxtaposed with the unexplained puzzle of the Hosty license number and the FBI's delay in telling the Commission that Hosty's name and numbers were found in Oswald's notebook, certainly required more fact finding than was attempted. This is one of many matters that should be weighed in the context of the Commission's attitude toward the FBI and the other police agencies involved in the assassination—but that is another subject.

It is noteworthy that both Marina Oswald and Ruth Paine were willing to believe that Oswald had lied about his visit to the FBI. As discussed elsewhere, the presumption that Oswald was lying was wholly unjustified in several important instances. Ruth Paine, a major witness in the case, is a complex personality, despite her rather passive facade. Some examples from her testimony show a predisposition against Oswald and a real or pretended friendliness toward the FBI and other Establishment institutions which should not be overlooked in evaluating her role in the case. Her account of the birth of Oswald's second child, for example, betrays considerable ill will toward Oswald. She testified that she had taken Marina Oswald to the hospital in her car at the onset of labor on a Sunday night. Oswald, who was unable to drive, remained at her home to care for the children. As Mrs. Paine described it:

> He was already asleep when I got back—no; that is not right. He was not asleep . . . but he had gone to bed, and I stayed up and waited to call the hospital to hear what word there was. So, that I knew after he was already asleep that he had a baby girl. I told him in the morning before he went to work. . . . I did not awaken him. I thought about it and I decided if he was not interested in being awake, I would tell him in the morning. . . .
>
> (3H 39-40)

Despite the loftiness of her principles, Mrs. Paine had on occasion acted in contradiction to them. She testified on March 19, 1964 that on Saturday morning, November 9, 1963, Oswald had asked permission to use her typewriter and had concealed his papers when she came near. This, she admitted, aroused her curiosity.

> Sunday morning I was the first one up. I took a closer look at this, a folded sheet of paper. . . . The first sentence arrested me because I knew it to be false. . . . I then proceeded to read the whole note, wondering, knowing this

to be false, wondering why he was saying it. I was irritated to have him writing a falsehood on my typewriter, I may say, too. I felt I had some cause to look at it.   *(3H 13-14)*

Mrs. Paine proceeded to read Oswald's private paper, a draft of a letter dealing in part with the visits of FBI Agent Hosty, in which Oswald said that Hosty had tried to coerce him to refrain from pro-Castro activities and to press Marina to "defect" and place herself under FBI protection. According to Mrs. Paine, that was a completely false version of Hosty's visits. She was offended on her own behalf. She read the letter in the quiet of her living room on Sunday morning and decided that she

> *Mrs. Paine:* . . . should have a copy to give to an FBI agent coming again, or to call. I was undecided what to do. Meantime I made a copy. . . .
> *Jenner:* But you did have the instinct to report this to the FBI?
> *Mrs. Paine:* Yes . . . and after having made it, while the shower was running, I am not used to subterfuge in any way, but then I put it back where it had been and it lay the rest of Sunday on my desk top. . . .   *(3H 15)*

Whether or not Oswald was aware of Mrs. Paine's hostility toward him, he nevertheless turned to her for help—in the last hours of his life, as it turned out. Mrs. Paine told the Warren Commission that Oswald had telephoned from jail on Saturday afternoon and had asked her to try to reach John Abt, a New York lawyer, on his behalf. Asked to repeat everything about the conversation that she remembered, Mrs. Paine said:

> I can't give the specific words to this part but I carry a clear impression, too, that he sounded to me almost as if nothing out of the ordinary had happened. I would make this telephone call for him, would help him, as I had in other ways previously. He was, he expressed gratitude to me. I felt, but did not express, considerable irritation at his seeming to be so apart from the situation, so presuming of his own innocence, if you will. . . . I was quite stunned that he called at all or that he thought he could ask anything of me, appalled, really.   *(3H 85-86)*

Mrs. Paine said that she tried to telephone Abt on Saturday evening and perhaps also on Sunday morning (she was not sure), without reply, and that she had never reached him.

> *Jenner:* Did you ever attempt to report to Lee Oswald that you had been unable to reach Mr. Abt?
> *Mrs. Paine:* Not unless such transpired in our 9:30 conversation Saturday evening, but I made no effort to call the police station itself.
> *Jenner:* Excuse me?
> *Mrs. Paine:* I made no effort to call the police station.   *(3H 89)*

Mrs. Paine's conscience did not remind her that the accused must be considered innocent until proved guilty in a court of law, and Dallas officials, abetted by the news media, had Oswald convicted within hours of his arrest. And there is no precedent for Mrs. Paine's new principle: that the accused may not "presume" his own innocence. She was "considerably irritated," presumably that

Oswald did not grovel or disintegrate with fear and remorse. Apparently she did not consider the possibility that he might be innocent or that he was straining to exercise control and stave off panic at his predicament—and this was before there was "conclusive evidence" against him and before he could defend himself against the charges. Moreover, Mrs. Paine testified that before November 22 she had never considered Oswald potentially violent or had the slightest reason to think that he harbored any ill will toward the President.

Her failure to notify Oswald that she had been unable to reach Abt, so that he would realize the urgency of obtaining legal assistance elsewhere, is unforgivable. Rather she had expressed her "considerable irritation" frankly than let Oswald assume that she would help him. For all her modesty and self-abnegation, Mrs. Paine is sometimes a devious person, and her testimony must be evaluated in that light.

Hosty also played an unenviable role in the drama. Shortly after Oswald's arrest he became involved in a controversy with Lieutenant Revill of the Dallas Police about remarks made about the FBI's knowledge of the alleged assassin. Hosty did not tell Dallas Police Chief Curry or Captain Fritz that the FBI had a file on Oswald or that he was under active investigation. And, strangest of all, he absented himself completely from the police station after his brief participation in Oswald's first interrogation.

Returning to the point of departure—Hosty's name and numbers in Oswald's address book—we cannot be satisfied with the findings in the Report or the Commission's exercise in evasion and misrepresentation. The real relationship between Oswald and the FBI remains to be uncovered and the tactics used to conceal it merely increase suspicion of the nature of that relationship.

Chapter 9
The Post Office Boxes

Every FBI witness from James Hosty to J. Edgar Hoover emphasized and re-emphasized that there was no reason before November 22, 1963 to suspect that Oswald was potentially violent or dangerous. Consequently, the FBI had no reason to report Oswald to the Secret Service in connection with the President's security during the Dallas visit. Presumably, then, the FBI was not aware that Oswald had ordered and received firearms under an alias at his post office box, as the Warren Commission has asserted.

Was the FBI really unaware that Klein's Sporting Goods had shipped a rifle to "Hidell" at Post Office Box 2915, Dallas? Let us examine the replies provided by the FBI to a series of questions posed by the Warren Commission regarding the handling of the Oswald case before the assassination. This interrogation raised new questions which were neither explored nor resolved. The FBI communication to the Commission includes the following passage. (*CE 2718*, p. 5)

8. *QUESTION:* The report of SA Hosty of September 10, 1963 contains the following item:

> On April 21, 1963 Dallas confidential informant T-2 advised that LEE H. OSWALD of Dallas, Texas, was in contact with the Fair Play for Cuba Committee in New York City at which time he advised that he passed out pamphlets for the Fair Play for Cuba Committee. According to T-2, OSWALD had a placard around his neck reading, "Hands Off Cuba Viva Fidel."

Is this information correct as of the date indicated, and does it describe activities which occurred before Oswald's move to New Orleans?

ANSWER: Information from our informant, furnished to us on April 21, 1963, was based upon Oswald's own statement contained in an undated letter to the Fair Play for Cuba Committee (FPCC) headquarters in New York City. A copy of this letter is included as Exhibit 61 in our Supplemental Report dated January 13, 1964. . . .

Our informant did not know Oswald personally and could furnish no further information. Our investigation had not disclosed such activity on Oswald's part prior to this type of activity in New Orleans.

It is certainly clear that in April 1963 the FBI had access to the contents of letters written by Oswald, before those letters left Dallas, through an informer who was not personally acquainted with Oswald and who, it must be inferred, was able to intercept letters that he placed in the mails. In the case of the specific letter mentioned under Question 8, Oswald gave his return address as P.O. Box 2915 *(Vincent T. Lee Deposition Exhibit No. 1)*, the same box to which the Carcano rifle was sent. But the FBI probably knew about that post office box much earlier than April, from informers who transmitted information about Oswald's subscriptions to "subversive" publications like *The Worker* and the *Militant*.

During this period the FBI took an interest in Oswald, according to testimony and documents, because of the suspicion that he might have been recruited as a secret agent for a foreign government during his residence abroad. A post office box is a good vehicle for transmitting clandestine messages such as might be sent to a secret agent by his superiors. The FBI knew that Oswald maintained Post Office Box 2915, and the FBI enjoyed excellent co-operation with the post office officials in Dallas. Is it conceivable that the FBI did not keep a close and continuous watch on material delivered to that box, but did achieve the far more difficult feat of intercepting and reading Oswald's outgoing mail?

I shall not comment on this practice in the context of Oswald's constitutional and civil rights—and those of unknown numbers of citizens whose rights to privacy are violated by the FBI or other federal agencies—except to express surprise that the Warren Commission, presided over by the Chief Justice of the U.S. Supreme Court, did not see fit to mention, much less reprove, this invasion of privacy. But it is not possible to excuse the Commission's failure to ask the FBI whether or not a mail cover was maintained on Oswald's post office box. Common sense insists that the box was under surveillance and that every piece of mail delivered to that box was reported to the FBI.

On that assumption, the FBI must have known that a revolver and then a rifle were delivered to Oswald's box addressed to Hidell. Is it credible that the FBI—knowing that Oswald had purchased firearms under an alias and aware that he was manifesting pro-Castro and pro-Communist sentiments—considered him "harmless" and saw no reason to report him to the Secret Service? The moment Oswald accepted delivery of a revolver or a rifle, he *had* to be regarded as potentially violent and dangerous to the man who had taken personal responsibility for the Bay of Pigs.

The following possibilities arise: (1) that the FBI for its own inscrutable reasons neglected to maintain surveillance over mail delivered to Oswald's post office box, though it managed the more difficult feat of acquiring access to the contents of his outgoing letters; (2) that the FBI did maintain a watch on the post office box but that no weapons were delivered to Hidell or to Oswald; or (3) that the FBI maintained a watch on the post office box and was aware that

Oswald had received two weapons under an alias, and that—for whatever reason —they did nothing.

I do not suggest which theory is correct and which unfounded. I am suggesting only that it was a gigantic omission on the part of the Warren Commission not to ask the questions that should have been asked and not to obtain reliable answers.

Chapter 10
The Interrogation Sessions

Oswald was taken into custody on Friday at about 2 p.m. and murdered in the basement of the Dallas Police Department on Sunday shortly after 11 a.m. The Warren Report states that he was questioned intermittently for about 12 hours during that period. *(WR 180)* Throughout his detention, Oswald was without legal representation. The Report acknowledges that on Friday at midnight Oswald said to assembled reporters and television cameras "I do request someone to come forward to give me legal assistance." *(WR 201)* The Report acknowledges also that earlier on Friday evening representatives of the American Civil Liberties Union appeared at the police building to determine whether Oswald was being deprived of counsel and that they were told by police officials that Oswald was informed of his rights and free to seek a lawyer. *(WR 201)* The ACLU representatives were discouraged from seeking to consult the alleged assassin himself; Gregory Lee Olds, the president of the Dallas chapter of the ACLU, later reproached himself for having accepted those assurances so readily. *(7H 322-325)*

Not only was Oswald interrogated over a prolonged period of time during which he had no legal counsel but—as has been widely discussed with amazement, disbelief, and suspicion—no stenographic or taped record was made, and Captain Fritz "kept no notes." *(WR 180)* The sole source of information about the interrogations are reports, based in large part on memory, prepared by some of those present and covering some of the interrogation sessions. *(WR 598-636)* There are no reports on the interrogation sessions which began at about 4:20, 6:20, and 7:40 p.m. on Friday. There are no transcripts of Oswald's arraignments for either of the two homicides with which he was charged.

Consequently, the known facts or assertions about what transpired during the interrogation sessions must be scrutinized with particular care for what they reveal or what they omit, as a basis for evaluating the evidence against the accused.

In the following pages I have excerpted and presented in the form of a single paraphrased narrative the responses given by Oswald to questions put to him in the interrogation sessions during his detention by the Dallas police, as reported by Captain Fritz in Appendix XI of the Warren Report. (Oswald's narrative is not, of course, verbatim but an extrapolation from a summary report.)

Friday, November 22, 1963

"My full name is Lee Harvey Oswald. Yes, I work at the Texas School Book Depository. I usually work on the second floor but sometimes my work takes me to all the other floors. [Note: Oswald probably said, as other interrogation reports indicate, that he usually worked on the first floor, not the second floor as reported by Fritz.] At the time the President was shot I was having my lunch on the first floor. The police officer stopped me on the second floor while I was drinking a Coca-Cola.

"I left the building because there was so much excitement that I didn't think there would be any more work done that day; anyhow, the company is not particular about hours, I don't have to punch a clock, so I thought it would be all right to take the rest of the afternoon off.

"No, I do not own a rifle, but I saw one at the Depository a few days ago. Mr. Truly and some of the others were looking at it.

"When I left work, I went to my room on North Beckley and changed my trousers. I got my pistol and went to the picture show; why? you know how boys do when they have a gun, they just carry it.

"Yes, I was in the Soviet Union for three years; I have corresponded with the Soviet Embassy.

"[FBI Agent] Hosty mistreated my wife on two different occasions; he practically accosted her. No, I have not been to Mexico City. I attended school in New York and Fort Worth; then I went into the Marines, where I finished my high school education. I won the usual marksmanship medals while in the Marines.

"My political beliefs? I have none but I do belong to the Fair Play for Cuba Committee, the headquarters are in New York City. I was secretary of the New Orleans Fair Play for Cuba Committee when I lived there. I support the Castro revolution.

"I didn't rent the room on Beckley in the name of O. H. Lee. It was my landlady; she didn't understand my name correctly.

"Am I permitted to have an attorney? I would like to talk to Mr. Abt, an attorney in New York."

Commentary   I interrupt the narrative at this point in order to comment on certain of Oswald's statements, and on the Friday interrogation as a whole.

At the time the President was shot I was having my lunch on the first floor.

I have already discussed Oswald's known movements at the Book Depository on Friday morning before the assassination and the testimony of Eddie Piper and William Shelley, who stated that they had seen Oswald on the first floor at noon and ten minutes of noon respectively. The Warren Report does not mention that testimony, even with the usual remark that the witnesses were probably mistaken. I believe that the testimony given by Piper and Shelley has probative value with respect to Oswald's statement that he was having his lunch on the first floor. The Commission has determined that Oswald did not bring lunch to work on that day; however, it made no attempt to establish whether or not Oswald had purchased his lunch. Wesley Frazier testified *(2H 221)* that some of the men brought their lunch and some bought it at the Book Depository, from a caterer who came around about ten o'clock every morning. In a conscientious investigation, that caterer would have been interviewed, to see whether or not Oswald obtained lunch from him regularly, and whether or not he did so on that Friday.

It is true that at a later interrogation session, Oswald is alleged to have said that he had brought his lunch from Irving that morning. If he actually said that, it appears to be a falsehood. But there is no transcript of what he said and it would have done no harm to question the caterer and to establish whether Oswald purchased lunch that day. At the same interrogation, Oswald said—according to Fritz—that he ate lunch with some of the Negro fellows who worked with him, one who was called Junior and the other a short man whose name he did not know; according to FBI Agent Bookhout, he said that he ate lunch alone but recalled that two Negro employees had walked through the room, one called Junior and the other a short person whose name he could not recall but whom he would be able to recognize.

The two men described by Oswald appear to correspond with James Jarman, Jr., and Harold Norman. Norman testified that after he had eaten his lunch, he "got with James Jarman, he and I got together on the first floor"; he had eaten in the domino room on the first floor, and thought that "there was someone else in there," but he could not remember who. *(3H 189)* Therefore, if we assume that Oswald was lying and was not actually present on the first floor, we must acknowledge that by phenomenal luck or coincidence he described two men who were indeed there, although there was no known basis for his expecting or predicting that they would be.

In further corroboration of Oswald's presence on the first floor of the Book Depository is a document unearthed at the Archives early in 1967 by Harold Weisberg. *(CD 5,* p. 41) The document reveals that Mrs. R. E. (Carolyn) Arnold, a secretary employed in the Book Depository, told the FBI on November 26, 1963 that she believed that she had seen Oswald standing in the hallway between the front door and the double doors on the first floor a few minutes before 12:15 p.m. on the day of the assassination.

It was at 12:15 p.m. that Arnold Rowland noticed a man with a rifle whom he took to be a Secret Service agent, and about whom he commented to his wife, at the southwest corner window of the sixth floor. Unless Mrs. Arnold or Rowland, or both, are mistaken, a man *other* than Oswald was present on the sixth floor at 12:15 p.m., and that man had a rifle in his hands.

In March 1964, the FBI took a series of statements from all Book Depository personnel, responding to a request from the Warren Commission that the whereabouts of each person at the time of the shooting, and other stipulated items of information, be determined. The inquiry was so superficial and perfunctory that Mrs. Arnold's replies to the FBI's questions did not reflect the information she had given four days after the assassination. *(CE 1381,* p. 7) Nevertheless, the Commission had that information in an earlier FBI report, only to ignore and withhold it in a determined effort to damn Oswald as the lone assassin.

As mentioned in Chaper 3, motorcycle officer M. L. Baker executed an affidavit on September 23, 1964 in which he attested that he "saw a man standing in the lunch room drinking a coke" but then crossed out "drinking a coke," initialing the deletion. *(CE 3076)* Although the inclusion of the phrase in the first instance may not have legal force, we suggest that the deleted words, by their very presence, corroborate Oswald's assertion that he was drinking a coke when he was stopped by the police officer.

Baker is not the only person who, when off guard, restored to Oswald the bottle of coke which the Warren Report removed, thus depriving the alleged assassin of an even stronger alibi than the encounter itself provides. A former senior counsel to the Commission, Albert E. Jenner, Jr., said on WNYC-TV on December 23, 1966, " . . . the first man this policeman saw, was Oswald with a bottle of coke."

The Warren Report, discussing the statements made by Oswald during detention *(WR 180-183),* asserts that Oswald made statements known to be lies. Where the bottle of coke is concerned, the evidence suggests the contrary.

No, I do not own a rifle, but I saw one at the Depository a few days ago. Mr. Truly and some of the others were looking at it.

FBI Agent Hosty testified before the Commission on May 5, 1964. He was asked if he had questioned Roy Truly about Oswald's allegation that he had seen a rifle in Truly's possession. Hosty said that he had not questioned Truly about this and did not know if anyone else had done so. A discussion off the record then followed, after which General Counsel J. Lee Rankin stated that it had been reported to him that Truly had been questioned and that he had denied the incident. *(4H 472)* A short while later Mr. Rankin made a further statement: he admitted that he had been in error and that "there was a statement by Mr. Truly in regard to two rifles in which he explains it, as he says, innocently." *(4H 474)*

This incident suggests that both witness and counsel were predisposed to assume that Oswald had been guilty of falsehood when, in fact, he may well have been telling the truth. Hosty apparently did not think it worthwhile even to make inquiries, and counsel hastily assumed that Truly had denied a story which in fact he had corroborated.

We need not belabor this point or its implications.

Hosty mistreated my wife on two different occasions; he practically accosted her.

Fritz stated in his report on the interrogation of Oswald that he had become "very upset and arrogant with Agent Hosty. . . . When Agent Hosty attempted to talk to this man, he would hit his fist on the desk." *(WR 601)* Hosty himself and FBI Agent Bookhout, reporting on the same incident, said that Oswald was handcuffed with his hands behind him and that, on Oswald's request, Fritz had the handcuffs removed and refastened with Oswald's hands in front of him, *after* his outburst against the FBI in general and Hosty in particular. *(4H 467)*

It is true that Hosty saw Marina Oswald on two different occasions. She described these encounters to the Warren Commission as entirely amicable, as almost tantamount to a social call. However, she refused to be interviewed by the same Hosty on November 26, 1963, and at that time she indicated to Robert Oswald that she had an aversion to Hosty. Robert Oswald, who was present when this incident took place, testified that Hosty's manner was harsh and threatening. *(1H 409-410)*

Consequently, there are sufficient grounds to warrant the assumption that Marina Oswald's account to her husband of Hosty's two visits, whether truthful or not, sparked Oswald's outburst against the FBI agent. His bitterness and anger apparently were neither feigned nor irrational.

No, I have not been to Mexico City.

Captain Fritz reports that "Mr. Hosty also asked Oswald if he had been to Mexico City, which he denied." *(WR 601)* Hosty and Bookhout, in a joint report on the same interrogation session, stated that Oswald had said that "he had never been in Mexico except to Tijuana on one occasion." *(WR 612)*

When Hosty testified before the Warren Commission some six months later (May 5, 1964), he was questioned rather pointedly about his failure to tell Captain Fritz, at the interrogation session which took place right after Oswald was arrested, the contents of the FBI's dossier on Oswald. Hosty admitted that he had not told Fritz about Oswald's trip to Mexico, his previous residence in the Soviet Union, his arrest in New Orleans, and other particulars known to the FBI and to Hosty in particular as agent-in-charge of the Oswald case. Hosty justified his silence in these terms:

> But you see Oswald then proceeded to tell himself, he told the police *all this information,* so there was no point in me repeating it when he himself, Oswald, had furnished it directly to the police. [Italics added] *(4H 468-469)*

The literal meaning of this testimony is that, contrary to the written accounts of the interrogation session provided by Fritz, Hosty, and Bookhout, Oswald *did* volunteer full information about his trip to Mexico in September 1963. But since Hosty was attempting to justify his failure to disclose to Fritz the background and activities of the suspect, his testimony in itself is insufficient to resolve the question. Fortunately, the record provides corroboration for the inference that Oswald did not conceal his Mexico trip.

Harry D. Holmes, postal inspector and FBI confidential informant Dallas T-7 *(CE 1152)*, was present at the Sunday morning interrogation which took place before Oswald was shot to death in the police basement. When Holmes was asked if Oswald had said anything about going to Mexico, he replied:

> *Holmes:* Yes. To the extent that mostly about—well—he didn't spend, "Where did you get the money?" He didn't have much money and he said it didn't cost much money. He did say that where he stayed it cost $26 some odd, small ridiculous amount to eat, and another ridiculous small amount to stay all night, and that he went to the Mexican Embassy to try to get this permission to go to Russia by Cuba, but most of the talks that he wanted to talk about was how he got by with a little amount.
>
> They said, "Well, who furnished you the money to go to Mexico?" "Well, it didn't take much money." And it was along that angle, was the conversation.
>
> *Belin:* Did he admit that he went to Mexico?
>
> *Holmes:* Oh, yes.   *(7H 303)*
>
> *Belin:* Is this something that you think you might have picked up from just reading the papers, or is this something you remember hearing?
>
> *Holmes:* That is what he said in there.   *(7H 304)*

Four days later Counsel Belin questioned another witness, Dallas Police Detective L. C. Graves, on the same point.

> *Belin:* What about the interrogation? Do you remember any subjects that were covered?
>
> *Graves*: Well, I couldn't think of Mr. Kelley's name, the last time, but he questioned Oswald along the line of his activity in Mexico and in Russia.
>
> *Belin:* Do you remember whether or not Oswald admitted that he was in Mexico?
>
> *Graves:* I believe he did admit it.   *(7H 257)*

Holmes and Graves testified in April 1964. Some three months later the Commission solicited affidavits, from Thomas Kelley on July 30, 1964 and from Forrest Sorrels on August 6, 1964. Both of these Secret Service officials attested therein that they "did not recall" that Oswald was questioned or that he made statements about a trip to Mexico or about plans to travel to Cuba. *(7H 590, 592)*

In other words, the Warren Commission—which has accused Oswald of lying to the police—in May 1964 had received conflicting evidence on the issue of Oswald's statements to the police about his trip to Mexico. Fritz, Hosty, and Bookhout said in written reports that Oswald had denied the trip, but Hosty later gave testimony which justifies the inference that Oswald in fact had spoken freely about it. In contradiction to the written reports, the Commission had sworn testimony from Holmes, in which he said categorically that Oswald had volunteered detailed information about his trip to Mexico City, and sworn testimony from Graves which tended to support Holmes. The weight of evidence was clearly in favor of Oswald's candor rather than his prevarication.

What did the Commission do? It solicited affidavits from two newcomers who "did not recall" that Oswald had been questioned about a trip to Mexico and "did not recall" that he had made statements about travel to Mexico or Cuba. By thus contriving an apparent shift in the weight of the evidence, the Commission enabled itself to proclaim that Oswald had lied repeatedly to the police.

We leave it to common sense to decide which is the more convincing—the bald statements by Kelley and Sorrels that they did not remember that Oswald was even asked about his visit to Mexico at that interrogation session, or the testimony of Holmes and Graves. The FBI had received information from the CIA about Oswald's stay in Mexico City; it is hardly credible that he was not questioned repeatedly about his activities there. Oswald had done nothing illegal and he had no reason to deny his trip. Nevertheless, the Warren Commission has chosen to obtain affidavits which contradict the witnesses who gave answers favorable to Oswald, and then to pronounce solemnly that Oswald "repeatedly and blatantly lied to the police." *(WR 180)*

I didn't rent the room on Beckley in the name of O. H. Lee. It was my landlady; she didn't understand my name correctly.

According to the Report *(WR 182)* examination of the register at the rooming house revealed that the signature "O. H. Lee" was in Oswald's handwriting. It seems entirely credible that he registered under that assumed name. He had stayed at another rooming house for a week, and the landlady, Mary Bledsoe, had asked him to leave. Oswald felt, whether or not justifiably, that his history of residence in the Soviet Union and his unpopular political views had provoked his dismissal from jobs and perhaps his eviction from the rooming house. *(1H 46)* Thus it is understandable if he registered at the Beckley Street establishment under an assumed name; not even the Commission has seen this as criminal in motivation. Nor is it certain that he pretended that his landlady had misunderstood his name, as Fritz reported; Hosty and Bookhout, reporting on the same interrogation session, stated that "he further admitted that he was living at 1026 N. Beckley in Dallas, Texas, under the name of O. H. Lee." Hosty testified *(4H 467)* in the same vein.

The Commission has accepted the story that Oswald and his wife quarreled bitterly on November 18, 1963 when she learned for the first time that he was living in the rooming house under an assumed name. She had telephoned there on the preceding day and had been told that no one named Oswald was living there. It must be asked if we have been given a truthful or complete account of this episode by Marina Oswald and Ruth Paine, on whom the Commission has relied. When Oswald rented this room Marina was about to give birth to a second child and Oswald provided the telephone number of the rooming house so that he could be notified as soon as the birth seemed imminent. There would have been no point to giving that telephone number without specifying that the caller should ask for him as O. H. Lee if in fact he was living under an alias. Oswald *wanted* to be informed of the birth; it is obvious from his behavior when the event actually took place that it had great meaning for him and brought him much happiness. He "even wept a little." *(WR 738)* It is hardly plausible that he would have been so self-defeating as to make arrangements to be informed of the birth at a telephone where he could not be reached.

It is also somewhat implausible that Marina Oswald would have quarreled bitterly with Oswald merely because she discovered that he was living under an assumed name. According to her own testimony, she had kept silent about Oswald's supposed attempt to kill Walker and then his alleged intention to stalk and shoot Richard Nixon; she had also collaborated with Oswald in concealing his trip to Mexico City from Ruth Paine and others. Why, then, should she make a crisis of such a relatively unimportant matter as his living under an alias in order to avoid hostility and eviction? Indeed, she "laughed at such foolishness" when she learned he was using "Hidell" as an alias. *(1H 64)*

If we accept the story that the Commission has accepted, we must believe that Marina Oswald as well as Oswald himself manifested irrational feelings and behavior, when neither is considered irrational in the pathological sense.

Let us now give some thought to this Friday interrogation session as a whole. Now that some of Oswald's answers have been analyzed, let us also examine the questions that were put to him immediately after his arrest for the murder of Tippit and on suspicion of the assassination of the President. He was asked:

1. Did he work at the Book Depository, and on which floor?
2. Where was he when the President was shot?
3. Where was he when he was stopped by a policeman (Baker) and Truly?
4. Why did he leave the Book Depository and where did he go?
5. Did he own a rifle?
6. Why did he carry a pistol to the Texas Theater?
7. Had he been to Russia, and had he written to the Soviet Embassy?
8. Had he been to Mexico City?
9. What were his political beliefs?
10. Why did he rent a room on North Beckley in the name "O. H. Lee"?
11. Had he won medals for rifle shooting in the Marines?

It is noteworthy that not one question was asked which suggested suspicion by the police or the FBI that Oswald may have been a member of a conspiracy to assassinate the President, although when this interrogation took place (between about 2 and 4 p.m. Friday afternoon) many people throughout the country and throughout the world took it for granted that extremists had plotted and carried out the assassination.

It is also noteworthy that the name Tippit is not found once in the questions put to Oswald immediately after his arrest, ostensibly for the murder of Tippit. One may say that the police naturally were more preoccupied with the assassination; very well, but Fritz had just come from the Book Depository, where chicken remains were found which, for at least 24 hours, were thought to point to a sniper who had hidden in the building in preparation for his deed. Oswald was not asked about the chicken or the possibility that he had helped a fellow assassin conceal himself and later escape from the Book Depository. Strangest of all, at midnight Oswald himself did not appear to be aware that he was suspected of or charged with the assassination of the President. *(WR 201)* Posing this against the allegation that no transcript was made of the interrogation of a suspect in what was surely the most important crime ever committed in the city of Dallas, it becomes impossible to avoid some skepticism about the police version of the interrogation.

Furthermore, we have been left completely in the dark about the interrogation of Oswald which took place on Friday after the first session. The Warren Report *(WR 198)* informs us that he was questioned for five hours and fifty minutes between 4:20 and 11:25 p.m., but not one report on these interrogations is found anywhere except for a report by FBI Agent Manning C. Clements *(WR 614-617)* dealing mainly with the contents of Oswald's wallet.[1] Clements' report is the only one relating to the interrogations that took place on Friday, November 22 and mentions the name "Hidell." It is clear that Oswald was asked about the alias "O. H. Lee" that afternoon, when police officers sent to search his room on North Beckley Street learned that he was registered there under that name. But testimony from the officers who brought Oswald from the Texas Theater to the police station indicates that Detective Paul Bentley (who was not a witness before the Commission) had looked into Oswald's wallet en route from the theater and, presumably, had seen the forged draft card in the name "Hidell" which bore Oswald's photograph. It is astonishing, then, that he was asked nothing about the alias "Hidell," but was asked about O. H. Lee, at the first interrogation. As Mark Lane put it to the Commission on March 4, 1964:

> I think it is interesting that the name "Lee" as an alias was released immediately, although some investigation was required to secure that alias. But the name "A. Hidell" was not released as an alias, although that was present and obvious by mere search of Oswald's person when he was arrested. . . . The first release of the name "A. Hidell" came from the district attorney's office after the FBI had indicated that Oswald had purchased an Italian carbine under that name. *(2H 46)*

The complex matter of Hidell has been considered in detail in an earlier chapter. Let us turn now to the interrogations on Saturday. Again, Oswald's responses are presented in narrative form.

---

1 Although it is not included in the Commission's accounting of the interrogation sessions, we find in the testimony that Secret Service Agent Forrest Sorrels interrogated Oswald "early in the evening of November 22" in the presence of Winston Lawson of the White House Secret Service detail. Sorrels testified *(7H 353)* that Oswald "was arrogant and had a belligerent attitude about him" and that after he had answered a number of questions he said that he didn't care to answer any more. Lawson gave quite a different description of the same interrogation. *(4H 356)* He said that "Oswald just answered questions as asked to him. He didn't volunteer any information. He sat there quite stoically . . . he didn't seem to be belligerent at all. . . ." Lawson said further that he didn't believe that Oswald particularly resented the interrogation and that he believed that Oswald had answered all the questions put to him.

Saturday, November 23, 1963 (morning)

"I picked up the name Hidell in New Orleans while working in the Fair Play for Cuba Committee organization. Yes, I speak Russian and I correspond with people in Russia and receive newspapers from there.

"No, I do not own any rifle at all. I had a small rifle once, some years ago. You can't buy a rifle in Russia, only shotguns. I had one there and hunted once in a while, when I was living in the Soviet Union. No, I didn't bring any rifle from New Orleans. My personal possessions are stored in a garage at Mrs. Paine's home in Irving. I have a few other things in my room on Beckley.

"When I left the Depository I took a bus to a stop near my room and walked the rest of the way there. I got the bus transfer on that ride. Oh, yes— I did ride in a cab. The bus I took near the Depository got into heavy traffic and was going too slowly, so I got off and caught a cab. I remember when I got in the taxi a lady came up who also wanted it but the driver told her to take another cab.

"No, I never told Wesley Frazier that I was going to Irving for curtain rods.

"When I got home after the cab ride, I changed both my shirt and trousers before going to the show. The cab fare was about 85 cents. I put the soiled shirt and trousers in the clothes hamper.

"When the President was shot I was having lunch with some of the colored boys I work with, one called Junior and the other is a little short man whose name I don't know. For lunch I had a cheese sandwich and some fruit, which I brought to work with me. No, I did not bring any long package to work.

"The reason my wife lives with Mrs. Paine is that she is helping her to learn Russian, and Mrs. Paine helps my wife to care for our young baby. It is a nice arrangement for both of them. I don't know Michael Paine very well. He and his wife seem to be separated a lot of the time. No, I don't own a car but the Paines have two cars. I have some sea bags with a lot of my personal belongings in their garage; I left them there when I returned from New Orleans in September.

"I have a brother, Robert, who lives in Fort Worth. The Paines are close friends of mine. No, I have never belonged to the Communist Party or had a card . . . but I do belong to the ACLU; I paid $5.00 dues.

"I am not going to tell you anything about the pistol. I bought it several months ago in Fort Worth. Yes, I have been questioned before, once for a long time by the FBI, when I got back from the Soviet Union. They use various approaches—hard and soft, the buddy method, yes, I am very familiar with the techniques of interrogation. But I don't have to answer any questions, you know, until I talk to my lawyer. I don't have the money to phone Mr. Abt. No, I don't want another attorney; I want to talk to Abt first. I don't know him personally but I know about a case in which Abt defended some people who were accused of violating the Smith Act. If I don't get Abt, I feel sure that the ACLU will provide me with a lawyer—that is one of the services, ACLU helps people who need attorneys and are unable to get them.

"In New Orleans I lived at 4907 Magazine Street and I had a job at the William Reily Company near that address. I had a little trouble there as a result of my working with the Fair Play for Cuba Committee—a fight with some anti-Castro people. I had a debate on a radio station in New Orleans with some of those anti-Castroites.

"I haven't any views on the President. I like his family very well. I have my own views about national policy.

"No, I refused to take a lie detector test when the FBI asked me, and I certainly don't intend to take one now."

Commentary   A number of the answers attributed to Oswald by those present at this interrogation are questionable; others may or may not be false.

I picked up the name "Hidell" in New Orleans. . . .

As discussed elsewhere, there is considerable doubt that "Hidell" was an alias invented by Oswald. If the purchase documents for the revolver and the rifle are authentic, the name "Hidell" came into use in January 1963, some months before Oswald's stay in New Orleans.

Yes, I speak Russian and I correspond with people in Russia and receive newspapers from there.

These remarks, if actually made by Oswald, throw considerable light on his character. When he returned from the Soviet Union, Oswald wrote a number of essays and worked on a manuscript for a book in which he expressed bitter disillusion with the organization of society in the Soviet Union. He excoriated the bureaucracy and the monotony of life for the ordinary individual, and displayed unequivocal disappointment and even disgust with the results of the first great Socialist revolution. Now he found himself to be a suspect in two murders, imprisoned in the jail of a city notorious for its extreme anti-Communist passions—a city in which his political convictions were perhaps more damning than the crime of assassination. In his place, the temptation to denounce the Soviet Union and all its works must have been great. Yet he made no anti-Soviet remarks; on the contrary, he made no attempt to conceal his pro-Castro views and activities or his detestation of the FBI, and in a subsequent interrogation freely declared that he was a Marxist. This took courage, integrity, and idealism—especially in the setting in which Oswald found himself.

My personal possessions are stored in a garage at Mrs. Paine's home in Irving.

It must be asked why the man who never ceased to insist that he was innocent of the crimes with which he had been charged blithely directed the police to his stored possessions, among which they found the highly incriminating photographic evidence which he must have known would tighten the noose around his neck. The official theory is that Oswald sneaked into the garage the night before the assassination to get his rifle. Why, then, did he not take the opportunity to destroy the photographs of himself holding that rifle and the revolver, and the negatives which betrayed the forgery of the selective service and Marine Corps cards in the name of Hidell? To direct the police to that evidence, which he had not taken the trouble to destroy when he might easily have done so, and at the same time to maintain his innocence, is another irrational act by a man who was categorically pronounced rational throughout the period of his custody—however prompt the reversal of opinion once he was dead.

> I never told Wesley Frazier that I was going to Irving for curtain rods.

If Oswald made this statement, it appears to be untruthful. Wesley Frazier is a completely plausible witness, and there is every reason to believe all his testimony. He had no reason to lie and neither he nor his sister tried to incriminate Oswald (as discussed earlier), for while they testified about the long, bulky package that he carried to work, their patently truthful description of the package eliminated the possibility that it contained the assassination rifle. They did not retreat, despite the imposing and subtle pressure to do so.

> I haven't any views on the President. I like his family very well. I have my own views on national policy.

If there is one area in which all the testimony is consistent and unambiguous, it is Oswald's friendly and even admiring attitude toward President Kennedy. Witnesses of varying backgrounds and beliefs testified to Oswald's favorable feelings about the President—members of the Dallas and Fort Worth Russian-speaking community Samuel Ballen *(9H 48)*, George De Mohrenschildt *(9H 255)*, Peter Gregory *(9H 148-149)*, and Ilya Mamantov *(9H 124)*, among others; Michael Paine *(2H 399);* Lillian Murret and her daughter Marilyn Murret (Oswald's aunt and cousin respectively, and members of a devout middle-class family) *(8H 153, 173);* and Lieutenant Martello of the New Orleans police anti-subversive squad *(10H 60-61)*. No one who knew Oswald reported that he had ever said or done anything which suggested animus toward President Kennedy or his family. Consequently, Oswald's alleged reply that he had no views on the President was actually an understatement; he might have, but did not, protest that he had always entertained friendly feelings for the President: there were witnesses to corroborate this. His image here is difficult to reconcile with that of an assassin seeking to erect a facade of innocence and to evade the consequences of his crime by making false denials and utilizing a combination of truth and lies to counter the charges against him.

Viewing this interrogation session as a whole, we note the continued omission of questions about the chicken remains found on the sixth floor and the lack of any mention of J. D. Tippit. Nor was any question asked about the alleged encounter between Oswald and Charles Givens on the sixth floor 35 minutes before the assassination—despite the fact that police officers testified that they learned of the incident from Givens within about two hours of the assassination. The questions relating to the rifle are not discussed here, since the facts are reviewed in detail elsewhere in this book where it is demonstrated that there is reason to doubt Oswald's ownership of the Carcano found on the sixth floor. Finally, it should be noted that David B. Grant of the Secret Service and

Robert I. Nash, U. S. Marshal, were present at this interrogation *(WR 621),* but no report or testimony from either one is found in the Hearings and Exhibits. Apart from Grant, five other Secret Service agents and four FBI agents who were present at some interrogation sessions were never questioned. *(CE 2003,* p. 161)

Saturday, November 23, 1963 (afternoon)

Only two questions seem to have been put to Oswald at this short session: what were his previous addresses in Dallas (information presumably obtained the night before by FBI agent Manning C. Clements), and where were his personal belongings kept. Again the alleged master criminal unhesitatingly directed the police to Mrs. Paine's house and to his room on Beckley Street. The photographs of Oswald with a rifle, pistol, and two newspapers, supposedly discovered in the Paine garage that afternoon by four Dallas policemen and a detective from the Irving police force, formed the main subject of the next interrogation session, in which Oswald's replies are presented as a narrative.

Saturday, November 23, 1963 (evening)

"That is not a picture of me; it is my face, but my face has been superimposed— the rest of the picture is not me at all, I've never seen it before. No; I have never seen that picture before. I know all about photography, I've done a lot of photographic work myself. That small picture is a reduction of the large picture, that someone I don't know has made. I've been photographed repeatedly since you brought me here; someone took a picture of my face and faked that photograph. I understand photography real well and you'll see, I will prove that it is a fake. Now I don't wish to answer any more questions."

Commentary   The photograph of Oswald with a rifle is the subject of another section, which should be borne in mind in evaluating Oswald's statements when confronted with the photograph. A curious fact here, as mentioned earlier, is that critics of the lone-assassin thesis and Mark Lane in particular publicly and repeatedly questioned the authenticity of the photograph of Oswald holding a rifle, claiming that certain inconsistencies in the direction of various shadows might indicate that the photograph was a fabrication. Those assertions were made *before* the Warren Report was issued, revealing for the first time that Oswald himself apparently had charged that the photograph was a fabrication.

Sunday, November 24, 1963 (morning)

"That map? It has nothing to do with the shooting of the President. I used that map to locate addresses while I was job-hunting. I don't know anything about the President's shooting or about the shooting of Officer Tippit.

"I don't believe in any of the established religions; I don't care to discuss my beliefs in a deity. Will Cuba be better off with the President dead? Someone will take his place, Lyndon Johnson no doubt, and he will probably follow the same policy.

"I don't know anything about that photograph or the rifle and I never lived on Neely Street. If anyone says that they visited me there they are mistaken, because I have never lived there. I am a Marxist but not a Leninist-Marxist. The radio station in New Orleans where I was in a debate is the one that carries Bill Stuckey's program. No, I don't know any Alex Hidell in New Orleans. I believe in the Fair Play for Cuba Committee and what it stands for.

"I would like to have one of my own shirts to wear over this T-shirt; not that one, I'd rather wear something warmer, that black Ivy League sweater. No, I don't want to wear any hat, I don't want to camouflage my appearance."

Commentary From this last interrogation Oswald went to the police basement, manacled to a detective and surrounded by officers, to be shot to death. We are left only with an incomplete, sometimes contradictory, and somewhat suspect series of reports on the statements he made while undergoing about 12 hours of interrogation.

That map? It has nothing to do with the shooting of the President. I used that map to locate addresses while I was job-hunting.

Oswald's alleged reply to questions about the map is now acknowledged to be the simple truth. But on the day of his death, the map was heralded by the police and the district attorney as damning evidence of his guilt, in public statements perhaps unparalleled for irresponsibility and unfairness. It is questionable whether the finding that the map was used for the very purpose that Oswald indicated has yet caught up with the many people who were persuaded by this and other misrepresentations of evidence that Oswald had committed the crimes of which he was accused.

Will Cuba be better off with the President dead? Someone will take his place, Lyndon Johnson, no doubt, and he will probably follow the same policy.

Time has confirmed Oswald's prognostication. The radical right, which has been enamored of the theory that Oswald assassinated the President on instructions from Castro or for pro-Castro reasons, has not taken into consideration the elementary facts that Oswald recognized at once: that the substitution of Lyndon Johnson for John F. Kennedy offered no advantage to Castro or to any socialist or leftist faction, whether national or external. Can the same thing be said in regard to the conservatives or adherents of the radical right? As this is written, Lyndon Johnson is receiving support in his foreign policy from Barry Goldwater and his faction, while the Kennedy wing of his own party is silently or forthrightly dismayed. The end results of the assassination have not profited and could not have been expected to profit any Marxist or the causes in which a Marxist believed. Oswald was no simpleton and it is clear that he harbored no illusions about the political implications of Kennedy's death. He was without political or personal motive for the assassination, as this statement indicates.

I never lived on Neely Street.

There is no question but that Oswald with his wife and child did live in the apartment on Neely Street for some months in the spring of 1963. If in fact Oswald denied this during the interrogation, his motives were absolutely baffling. He would have known that there was irrefutable proof from a variety of sources that he had indeed lived on Neely Street. What purpose was served by denying it? The report of Manning C. Clements on the Friday night interview provides information on Oswald's former places of residence but does not mention Neely Street; presumably Oswald omitted that address in answering Clements' questions, and later denied to Fritz that he had lived there. If he actually pretended that he had not rented or resided in an apartment on that street, his reasons are baffling.

I don't want to camouflage my appearance.

From his arrest on Friday to his death on Sunday, Oswald declined to conceal his face; he never appeared cowed or ashamed but maintained his personal pride and dignity and seemingly full confidence in his ultimate vindication. He charged on a number of occasions that he was being railroaded, that he was "a patsy," and that he was the victim of a frame-up. He was pitifully unsuspecting of the fate that he was to meet in the police basement. Some police officers and Dallas officials saw this as arrogance and resented his failure to panic or grovel. Was his behavior characteristic of guilt, or of innocence? There is no objective test which can be applied, and the answer will depend on one's personal predisposition toward Oswald and one's private attitudes toward the nightmarish events that transpired in Dallas. What can be said without uncertainty is that the Warren Commission did not at any stage of its work appear to regard seriously the possibility that Oswald was the victim of a frame-up. The Commission has calmly accepted the explanation that no transcript of the interrogation was made. Fritz testified that he had no tape recorder, his past requests to his superiors for one having been denied. He was not asked why he had not borrowed a tape recorder; the FBI and Secret Service agents who were present at the interrogations were not asked why they had not offered one to Fritz. It is not necessary to belabor this issue: the point is that the Commission was uncritical, unskeptical, and complacent in dealing with the Dallas police—not on this question alone but also on other aspects of the case, including flagrant discrepancies or contradictions in the testimony and the suspect conduct or explanations of certain officials.

Chapter 11

The Scorpion's Lash:
Testimonies of Marina Oswald

Marina Oswald testified before the Warren Commission on four occasions between February and September 1964, answering questions for a total of seven days. She made her debut as a witness on Monday, February 3, 1964—the first witness to be heard by the Commission, and perhaps the most indulged. In her third hour of testimony, Marina Oswald admitted that she had made false statements to federal agents.

Rankin: Did you ever see him clean the rifle?

Mrs. Oswald: Yes. I said before I never had seen it before. But I think you understand. I want to help you, and that is why there is no reason for concealing anything. I will not be charged with anything.

Gopadze (Secret Service interperter): She says she was not sworn in before. But now inasmuch as she is sworn in, she is going to tell the truth.
(1H 14)

Only two hours later Marina Oswald prevaricated again, this time under the oath which was supposedly to guarantee her truthfulness.

Rankin: When you were asked before about the trip to Mexico, you did not say that you knew anything about it. Do you want to explain to the Commission how that happened?

Mrs. Oswald: Most of these questions were put to me by the FBI. I do not like them too much. I didn't want to be too sincere with them. Though I was quite sincere and answered most of their questions. They questioned me a great deal, and I was very tired of them, and I thought that, well, whether I knew or didn't know about it didn't change matters at all, it didn't help anything, because the fact that Lee had been there was already known, and whether or not I knew about it didn't make any difference. *(1H 28)*

The documents tell an entirely different story, as will be seen from the report of FBI Agents Wallace Heitman and Anatole Boguslav on an interview with Marina Oswald on November 28, 1963.

> Mrs. Oswald advised that upon her departure from New Orleans with Mrs. Paine, it was agreed by her and her husband that Oswald would remain in New Orleans to find work and if he could not find work, he would return to Dallas. Oswald also made the statement that he had a friend in another city and that he might contact this friend to see if he could find work. Mrs. Oswald said she did not think that this was true—she did not believe Oswald had a friend anywhere. She said that it is possible that Mrs. Paine would know who this friend was and what the name of the city was. She said she could not remember.
>
> When asked what the arrangements were at the time she left New Orleans, Mrs. Oswald said that her husband was to remain there in New Orleans or to return to Dallas, *but no arrangements were made for him to go to Mexico City.*
>
> Inasmuch as Mexico City had not been mentioned, she was asked why she had said no arrangements had been made for Oswald to go to Mexico City. She replied that she had been looking at television the past few days and had seen or heard that Oswald had been in Mexico City. *She said she was only trying to be helpful and that is the reason she had mentioned Mexico City as she did.*
>
> Mrs. Oswald said that she did not know anything about any trip that Oswald may have made to Mexico City. She said that upon Oswald's return to Dallas, which was in early October 1963, she had not asked him where he had been or what he had done because she knew that he had not found work and that it would only embarrass him to ask. She said that Oswald had not volunteered any information about where he had been or what he had done. [Italics added]   *(CE 1781)*

This FBI report exposes the dishonesty of Marina Oswald's "explanation" to the Commission. Contrary to her testimony, she did not merely fail to mention her prior knowledge of Oswald's trip to Mexico City, nor did she merely deny her knowledge, upon incessant questioning. The fact is that Marina Oswald herself introduced the question of the Mexican trip on her own initiative; she volunteered false information, knowing that it was false; and she pretended that she was "only trying to be helpful."

This is not the whole story. Earlier on the same day (November 28, 1963) Marina Oswald had been interviewed by Secret Service Agent Leon Gopadze. Gopadze's report states:

> She was asked whether she had any knowledge of Lee's trips to Mexico or Washington, D.C. She replied in the negative. . . . Apparently Marina was very much concerned that Mr. Gregory [present at the interview as interpreter] and I had any doubts as to her sincerity and truthfulness in her answers to our questions. She repeatedly would remark "I hope you believe me, as I swear by God, this is the truth." . . .
>
> After the reporting agent's return to the U.S. Secret Service Office, Dallas, Texas, Marina Oswald had one of the Secret Service agents phone the office and asked for the reporting agent. She apologized for not giving the following information . . . [that] on her departure from New Orleans with Mrs.

Paine, Lee told her and Mrs. Paine that he might go to some other cities to look for work, and particularly to a city where one of his friends was living; that the names of both cities were furnished by Lee to Mrs. Paine who no doubt will remember the names and may remember the name of his friend he mentioned.   (*CE 1792*, pp. 6-8)

To the Warren Commission, Marina Oswald implied that she had lied to the FBI agents because she disliked the FBI, but she suggested in no way that she bore any animosity toward the Secret Service—on the contrary, she had only praise and appreciation for its protection. Yet she not only gave false information about the Mexican trip to Secret Service Agent Gopadze but proceeded to "swear by God" that she was telling the truth. Then she exceeded herself by telephoning Gopadze at his office to supplement her false denial with a new untruth.

Marina Oswald's false statements to both the FBI and the Secret Service were seemingly gratuitous and not a manifestation of panic after a "third degree."

J. Lee Rankin must have been aware of the contents of the FBI and Secret Service reports which have been quoted, when he invited Marina Oswald to explain why she had concealed her foreknowledge of Oswald's trip to Mexico City. He put his questions with sympathy, using euphemistic language, and readily accepted an "explanation" delivered under oath which he must have known to be deceitful and a compounding of the earlier untruths.

The incident occurred during the first day of Marina Oswald's hearing. Rankin permitted her statements to stand unchallenged. He did not alert the Commission (nor the public that eventually might read the transcript) to the conflict between Marina Oswald's sworn statements and the actual facts as recorded in the FBI and Secret Service reports, nor to the danger of taking her testimony at face value. Why?

Because Rankin was silent, the Commission was apparently seduced into believing that Marina Oswald might lie to the FBI, but never to the Chief Justice and his colleagues. Marina Oswald herself later provided ample reason for the Commission to question her veracity and good faith, but as a whole the Commission seems to have been determined to believe and trust her. That, in any case, is the impression one receives from the Warren Report. The way in which Marina Oswald's statements were automatically accepted by the Chairman and his colleagues influenced their findings to a degree which can scarcely be overestimated.

Marina Oswald, whose testimony would have been inadmissible if Oswald had come to trial, was given free rein. She proceeded to give testimony which was self-contradictory or in conflict with the testimony of credible and disinterested witnesses and told stories that were internally incoherent and implausible, if not impossible.

Everything passed the scrutiny of the indulgent members of the Commission (i.e., the majority), who seemed at times to regard Marina Oswald with the fondness reserved for a protégé. Even when Marina belatedly came forward with a preposterous story—that Oswald had planned to shoot Richard Nixon at a time when Nixon was nowhere near Dallas, and that she had restrained Oswald by physical force—the Commission said merely:

> Marina Oswald might have misunderstood her husband. . . . In the absence of other evidence that Oswald actually intended to shoot someone at this time, the Commission concluded that the incident, as described by Marina Oswald, was of no probative value in the Commission's decision concerning the identity of the assassin. . . .   *(WR 189)*

In other words, the Commission concluded, mainly or exclusively on the basis of Marina Oswald's testimony, that Oswald had (a) made a prior attempt to kill, in an attack on General Walker, (b) purchased and possessed a rifle, (c) stored that rifle in the Paine garage, and (d) removed it in order to assassinate the President; yet the Commission also concluded that the incredible story of the thwarted attempt on Nixon, which fell apart at every point, in no way raised the issue of Marina Oswald's credibility. The same Commission unhesitatingly concluded that there was reason to suspect, or reject as untruthful, reasonable allegations made by other witnesses—disinterested persons who were, so to speak, innocent bystanders—even when the allegations were coherent, plausible, and corroborated.

It appears that the Commission did not dare to confront the issue of Marina Oswald's reliability and good faith, however much provocation she gave. Elsewhere in this study I have indicated her numerous revisions of statements on such specific questions as Oswald's use of aliases, his target practice with the alleged assassination rifle, and his possession of ammunition. I have discussed also the inherent lack of credibility in her account of the notation of FBI Agent Hosty's license number. A more detailed analysis of Marina Oswald's suspect statements or testimony would require a book in itself.

In stating that much of her testimony is suspect, I do not refer to the natural variations which are to be expected when a witness is asked to go over the same ground repeatedly over a span of many months. Rather, I have in mind the constancy of basic elements in a truthful story, however often it is repeated. In the case of Marina Oswald, radical changes in her story would be understandable if the dividing line were November 24, 1963—the date on which her husband was murdered. Had she concealed incriminating evidence while Oswald was alive, out of loyalty, and then reavealed the truth once he was beyond the reach of trial and punishment, it would be understandable. But that was not the case: her self-contradictions were indiscriminate, continuing into September 1964, when she was questioned by Senator Richard Russell (rather critically in comparison to her earlier hearings).

Marina Oswald admitted to the Warren Commission at the outset that she had not told the truth to federal agents. None of her allegations should be accepted as necessarily truthful unless supported by convincing independent evidence.

By that criterion, what would remain of the Commission's case against Oswald?

Chapter 12
Motive and Mind

The "motiveless" murder is a recurrent theme in detective fiction, but in this respect life seldom imitates art. Many murders appear at first to be unrelated to motives of passion or gain, the classic case being that of Leopold and Loeb. Ultimately they are shown to be the work of a calculating murderer who has covered his tracks well, or the expression of a diseased mind. Each year in New York City alone, several ghastly and meaningless slaughters are committed by released mental patients yielding to the compulsions of their derangement.

Assassination of the head of government has in modern times been an instrument in ruthless struggles for political power or a manifestation of fanaticism in which the victim was conceived by the assassin to be the author of injustice, guilty of the abuse of power. There have also been attempted and successful assassinations by psychotics whose obsessions centered specifically on a President. Attempts on the lives of American Presidents have been made by political conspirators, anarchists, or individuals judged to be insane—manifestly demented and requiring institutionalization. We have not had the spectacle of an assassin who is merely neurotic but without a political or personal grudge.

The assassination of President Kennedy is the first which appears to have a "motiveless" motive. The Warren Commission has concluded that Oswald was guilty but has not made a definite determination of his reasons. The Report throws out various suggestions—that his Marxist beliefs were a contributing factor, that personal failure had embittered him, that he was developing a persecution syndrome, and other halfhearted offerings—without committing the Warren Commission to a conclusive finding which it might have to defend.

Admiration of Kennedy

The complete absence of any motive was a main factor in the doubt of Oswald's guilt that flourished all over the world after the assassination. The Warren Commission has not resolved this problem despite its microscopic research into Oswald's life. On the contrary: its biographical labors uncovered material that suggests that Oswald would not have wished to see Kennedy eliminated. There are many indications that he voiced favorable if not warm views about Kennedy, and Oswald was not a man to be silent for reasons of discretion. He made no secret of his antipathy toward General Walker and the John Birch Society. Only a month before the assassination Oswald was aroused about the indignity done to Adlai Stevenson by the ultra right-wing. He attended a meeting of the Dallas Civil Liberties Union and took the floor to warn the audience not to underestimate the viciousness of the John Birch Society. Michael Paine, who had accompanied Oswald to the meeting, described the incident when he appeared before the Warren Commission on March 18, 1964.

> One of the things said was that the Birchers must not be considered anti-Semitic, anti-Semites because they are also Birchers. Lee at this point got up, speaking loud and clear and coherently, saying that, reporting that, he had been to this meeting of the right-wing group the night before or two nights before and he refuted this statement, saying names and saying how that people on the platform speaking for the Birch Society had said anti-Semitic things and also anti-Catholic statements or spoke against the Pope. . . . He said something very similar to, "I can't agree with what had just been said," and I do remember that it contained both some corroboration of his points of view. There had been some kind of anti-Semitic statement and criticism of the Pope. . . . That was good speaking . . . it made sense. . . .   *(2H 408)*

It is an affront to logic to suggest that Oswald, holding such views, would attempt to kill President Kennedy four weeks later—unless one is prepared to show that he was insane.

Mental Stability

The Warren Commission has avoided any categorical conclusions on Oswald's sanity, although not by any means discouraging an impression that he was alienated and maladjusted in the extreme. The Commission did not obtain a posthumous analysis, as it could have done. This is an accepted technique of psychiatry. A number of individuals who have approved of the Report have nevertheless criticized the Commission for failing to seek expert testimony from psychiatrists and for indulging in unqualified pronouncements about Oswald's mental balance and emotional problems.

It is easy to overlook the availability of *qualified* psychiatric findings on Oswald. In addition to the New York City Youth House report on Oswald at age thirteen, the following facts should be given due weight: (1) The Marine Corps medical records on Oswald for 1956-1959 *(Donabedian Exhibit No. 1)* consistently show no sign of emotional problems, mental abnormality, or psychosis. (2) Oswald was the subject of psychiatric evaluation in the Soviet Union after his effort to avoid deportation by feigning an attempt at suicide. Soviet records *(CE 985)* show that he was found to be "not dangerous to other people ... clear mind ... no sign of psychotic phenomena ... no psychotic symptoms."

Though relatively recent, neither the Marine Corps medical records nor the Soviet psychiatric evaluation support the facile finding that Oswald was "irrational"—all too frequently the response to objections that Oswald's actions were inconsistent with guilt. Nor does the Youth House report really justify the inference that he was unbalanced or deranged. Irresponsible statements purporting to be based on the Youth House report were published and given great prominence in the period immediately after the assassination. They created an exaggerated or erroneous impression, as the Report acknowledges. *(WR 379)* The Youth House psychiatric report *(Hartogs Exhibit 1)* actually found

> no indication of psychotic changes; superior mental endowment; no retardation despite truancy; no psychotic mental changes. Disturbed youngster who suffers under the impact of really existing emotional isolation and deprivation.

Dr. Renatus Hartogs, chief psychiatrist of Youth House, wrote that report on April 16, 1953 and did not see it again for eleven years. He testified on April 16, 1964 that the thirteen-year-old Oswald had "definite traits of dangerousness ... a potential for explosive, aggressive, assaultive acting out. . . ." *(8H 217)*[1] Hartogs was then asked to review his 1953 report. He conceded that it failed to mention any potential violence, assaultive or homicidal potential, or incipient schizophrenia. He conceded also that if he had found such traits in the boy, he would have said so in his report. He did not agree, however, with Liebeler's logical suggestion that his categorical comments before re-reading his report might have been based on mistaken identity, and that he had no personal recollection of Oswald at all. *(8H 221)*

Not a very professional performance.

There is, then, no basis in any of the available medical or psychiatric histories for allegations that Oswald was psychotic, aberrant, or mentally unsound in any degree. His life history is consistent with the conclusion that he was a rational and stable personality (which is not to say that he was appealing, admirable, or untroubled). He was capable of marriage and fatherhood, with responsibility and devotion, particularly to his two children. He was conscientious in his punctuality and work, completed military service satisfactorily, paid his bills and repaid his debts promptly, and managed his practical affairs capably.

---

[1]   Hartogs apparently described Oswald in similar blood-curdling but mistaken terms in an FBI interview on an unspecified date. The FBI report on that interview was mentioned during Hartogs' testimony but is not included among the Exhibits.

Since there has been unrestrained "psychoanalysis" of Oswald by amateurs who never heard of Oswald before November 22, it is apropos to examine the judgments of those who knew him, on the two key questions of (a) motivation and (b) capacity for violence.

His wife, star witness for the prosecution, considered Oswald "mentally sound, smart and capable, not deprived of reason." *(1H 123)*

Most members of the Russian-speaking community in Dallas, including those who were not fond of Oswald, were astounded by the news of his arrest. Sam Ballen, for example, was unable to conceive of Oswald harboring any hostility toward the President; it was his impression that, on the contrary, Oswald had warm feelings for him. Oswald was dogmatic but not mentally ill. Ballen, like George De Mohrenschildt, considered Oswald a man "with no hatred in him." When he heard of Oswald's arrest, Ballen felt that there must have been a mistake. He did not believe Oswald capable of such a crime, in spite of the force of the circumstantial evidence. *(9H 48-54)*

George Bouhe was not an admirer of Oswald's. He regarded Oswald as "crazy," a mental case. But it had never entered Bouhe's mind, he testified, that Oswald was capable of such an act. *(8H 370)* Everett Glover said that he had never questioned Oswald's mental stability and did not consider him capable of violence. *(10H 29)*

Anna Meller was "completely shocked" at the news of Oswald's arrest and could not believe that he had done such a thing. *(8H 386-390)* Elena Hall had never regarded Oswald as dangerous or mentally unstable; she was incredulous when he was arrested. *(8H 405)*

Michael Paine *(2H 399)*, Paul Gregory *(9H 148)* and George De Mohrenschildt *(9H 255)* testified that Oswald was an admirer of President Kennedy and had praised him. Lillian Murret, Oswald's aunt, said that he had liked the President and admired his wife. *(8H 153)* Marilyn Murret, her daughter, confirmed that Oswald had spoken favorably of the President. She felt strongly that Oswald was not capable of having committed the assassination and that he had no motive for such an act; and she disagreed completely with theories that Oswald resented authority or craved a place in history. *(8H 176-177)*

None of Oswald's fellow Marines suggested that he was psychotic, violent, or homicidal. Lieutenant Donovan saw no signs of any mental instability (although he found it unusual for anyone to be so interested in foreign affairs). *(8H 299)* Kerry Thornley said that Oswald had never shown any tendency toward violence; on the contrary, he was a "talker." *(Thornley Exhibit No. 1)*

Adrian Alba, who knew Oswald in New Orleans in 1963, said that he "certainly didn't impress me as anyone capable or anyone burdened with a charge of assassinating the President . . . let alone any individual, for that matter." *(10H 227)* Tommy Bargas, Oswald's former employer at the Leslie Welding Company, said that he had been a good employee, with potential, and had shown no sign of temper or violence. *(10H 165)* Helen P. Cunningham, an employment counselor, had found no indication of emotional problems in her contacts with Oswald. *(10H 128)*

FBI Agent Quigley, who had interviewed Oswald after his arrest in New

Orleans for disturbing the peace, found absolutely no indication that he was dangerous or potentially violent. *(4H 438)*

And the comments of Lieutenant Francis Martello, intelligence division (anti-subversion) of the New Orleans Police Department, are especially memorable. He had interviewed Oswald at length in August 1963 and had formed the impression that he liked President Kennedy. He considered Oswald not to be potentially violent.

> " . . . not at all. Not in any way, shape, or form violent . . . as far as ever dreaming or thinking that Oswald would do what it is alleged that he has done, I would bet my head on a chopping block that he wouldn't do it.
> *(10H 60-61)*

J. Edgar Hoover suggested to the Warren Commission that Oswald had a "twisted mind"; then, realizing his *faux pas,* he hastened to emphasize that until the assassination there had been "no indication at all that Oswald was a man addicted to violence" or that he had any mental abnormality. *(5H 105)* Police Chief Curry assured the television audience (while Oswald was still alive) that he was "mentally right" and not "off his rocker." *(CE 2146)* District Attorney Wade said repeatedly, before Oswald was murdered, that he was "not a nut," and that "he was sane." Police Captain Glen King said on Dallas television station WFAA-TV on November 23 that Oswald was mentally competent and not deranged. *(CE 2162)* The President of the Dallas Bar Association, H. Louis Nichols, emerged from an interview with Oswald on Saturday saying that he "did not appear to be irrational." *(7H 330)*

Detective L. C. Graves of the Dallas Police expressed the view that Oswald was "an eight ball . . . in any vernacular." *(7H 259)* Somehow we sense his meaning, mixed as his metaphors may be: In Dallas, Oswald was an oddity, poised directly behind the eight ball.

But he was without a personal or political motive for assassinating the President, and he was not irrational, disturbed, or psychotic. If he had no sane reason for killing Kennedy, and if he was not insane, how are we to understand his alleged crime?

Plea of Innocence

One aspect of the Oswald case that has remained constant throughout is that the accused assassin steadfastly maintained that he was innocent, from the moment of his arrest until he was shot to death. The Report records this fact but does not evaluate Oswald's posture of innocence in relation to the apparent wealth of incriminating evidence, both on his person and at locations to which he unhesitatingly directed the police. Nor does the Report reflect significant elements of Oswald's behavior on arrest or in detention, reported in documents and in the testimony of witnesses.

This material suggests, for example, that even as Oswald was being subdued and placed under arrest, he was extremely apprehensive. Johnny Calvin Brewer testified:

> As they were taking him out, he stopped and turned around and hollered, "I am not resisting arrest," about twice. "I am not resisting arrest." And they took him on outside.   *(7H 6)*

The same report is found in written statements of police officers Bob Carroll (*CE 2003*, p. 81) and K. E. Lyon (*CE 2003*, p. 91). If Oswald was genuinely apprehensive of death at the hands of the police, on the pretext that he was attempting to escape, he must have believed that he was marked for a frame-up, as he later charged explicitly.

Sergeant Gerald L. Hill was in the car with Oswald and other policemen on the way from the Texas Theater to the police station. Hill testified:

> We got the suspect to the city hall as rapidly as possible . . . and we explained to him this—I did, before we got into the basement, that there would probably be some reporters and photographers and cameramen waiting . . . and that if he so desired . . . he could hide his face. . . . As we pulled into the basement . . . [I] told the suspect again he could hide his face if he wanted to. And he said, "Why should I hide my face. I haven't done anything to be ashamed of."   *(7H 59)*

A similar report is found in the testimony of John G. McCullough, a Philadelphia reporter.

> He at one time, when he was walking along the corridor . . . he held his hands high so that the handcuffs he was wearing would be seen on camera. And this struck me as a little unusual, because having had many, many years as a police reporter, I have seen people who were charged with crimes try to cover their faces. He made no such movement. . . .   *(15H 382)*

Finally, the Warren Commission has omitted from its Report this next testimony, and it is really very difficult to excuse this omission. Detective B. H. Combest, who was at Oswald's left side when he was shot by Ruby, related what happened afterward.

> *Combest:* I didn't hear him say a word hardly, after he had been shot. He was moaning at the time Jimmy Leavelle, Graves, and I laid him down on the floor and removed the handcuffs that he had on him. . . . At the time I asked him and talked to him trying to get him to make a statement to me at the time. Especially, after I realized how serious the wound was. When we first asked him he appeared to comprehend what I was saying. . . .
>
> I told him was there anything that he wanted me to tell anybody or was there anything he wanted to say right now before it was too late . . . trying to let him know if he was ever going to say anything he was going to have to say it then.
>
> *Hubert:* You thought he was dying?
>
> *Combest:* Yes, sir; I did.
>
> *Hubert:* And do you think you used language to him to convey to him your idea that he was dying?
>
> *Combest:* Yes, sir.
>
> *Hubert:* Did you get any indication that he actually understood what you were trying to convey to him?

Combest: When I first started asking him he did. He looked up at me, seemed to recognize that I—who was talking to him. . . .

Hubert: But, he didn't say anything?

Combest: No sir, just shook his head and I said, "Do you have anything you want to tell us now," and he shook his head. . . . I kept talking to him as long as I thought he would try to answer me, hoping that he would give a dying declaration on the shooting.   *(12H 185)*

It is perfectly clear, then, that we are confronted not only by Oswald's insistence of his innocence during the interrogations and in the police corridors, but also as he lay dying, knowing that he was dying. Did the significance of Combest's testimony escape the Warren Commission? Their "assassin" indicated even as he was being arrested fear of a frame-up; he said explicitly that he was a patsy; he implied that the "overwhelming evidence" was fraudulent; and he had no word or gesture of confession even when he knew that he was fatally wounded. It was the Commission's duty to weigh these facts—even if it remained convinced after weighing them that Oswald nevertheless was guilty—and to defend that conclusion. This was not done. Little of the relevant testimony was included in the Report. We, then, must evaluate these matters, and decide for ourselves what they reveal, about the Commission as well as Oswald.

Men have killed Presidents and felt no need for shame, regarding their deed as righteous and confessing it freely and with pride. Oswald does not fall into that category. He insisted that he was innocent and that he had done nothing— by society's standards—for which he needed to feel shame. It is interesting that at the same time Oswald made no attempt to conceal his Marxist convictions, which in Texas might arouse far more fury than the murder of a President unpopular there. It seems strikingly inconsistent in psychological terms that Oswald should reveal and defend highly unpopular political commitments but exercise secrecy and cunning about deeds presumably inspired by those commitments and therefore, in his own mind, justified by high motives.

The records indicate that Oswald repeatedly claimed that he was the victim of a frame-up. Seth Kantor's handwritten notes show that Oswald told reporters at 7:55 p.m. on Friday, "I'm just a patsy." (*Kantor Exhibit 3,* p. 366)

William Whaley, the taxi-driver, gives a vivid picture of Oswald in the line-up held on Saturday afternoon.

He showed no respect for the policemen, he told them what he thought about them. They knew what they were doing and they were trying to railroad him and he wanted his lawyer.   *(2H 261)*

On Saturday Oswald had visits from his wife, his mother, and his brother Robert. Robert testified that he had tried to point out that the evidence against him was overwhelming, and that Oswald replied, "Do not form any opinion on the so-called evidence." *(1H 468)* Robert's diary adds the following graphic details:

All the time we were talking I searched his eyes for any sign of guilt or whatever you call it. There was nothing there—no guilt, no shame, no nothing. Lee finally aware of my looking into his eyes, he stated, "You will not find anything there."   *(CE 323,* p. 13)

Later on the same day Oswald was interviewed in his cell by H. Louis Nichols of the Dallas Bar Association, whom he told:

> . . . if I can find a lawyer here who believes in anything I believe in, and believes as I believe, and believes in my innocence as much as he can, I might let him represent me.   *(7H 329)*

PART III
OTHER CRIMES

Chapter 13
Tippit

The Murder of Tippit

Although the Warren Report inundates the reader with biographical material on Oswald, the so-called lone assassin remains essentially a mysterious personality, motivated by commitments or convictions which in the last analysis leave even the Warren Commission in fumbling uncertainty. Indeed, the Commission's preoccupation with Oswald's history is out of balance with its somewhat cursory attention to the crimes of which he was accused. If Oswald did not commit those crimes, his life history has very limited relevance. Although the Commission did not quite succeed in inadvertently proving his outright innocence, it certainly failed to prove his guilt. This might be more obvious if Oswald's biography, distracting attention from the evidence and scarcely calculated to arouse sympathy, did not appear three times—in capsule form, then expanded, and finally in an appendix in full detail—between the covers of the Warren Report.

The Report also gives generous attention to the biography of Jack Ruby.

When we turn to J. D. Tippit, we find no biographical excesses but extreme reticence. Tippit, the policeman and the man, is a one-dimensional and insubstantial figure—unknown and unknowable. The Commission was not interested in Tippit's life, and apparently interested in his death only to the extent that it could be ascribed to Oswald, despite massive defects in the evidence against him.

The Commission's profound lack of interest in Tippit may be measured by its failure to take testimony from his widow, who probably saw him less than two hours before his death *(CE 2985)*, or from his brothers and sisters (their names appeared in the obituary columns of the Dallas newspapers), or from any of his friends or neighbors. We know strangely little about Tippit. According to an FBI report *(CE 2985)*, he led the most ordinary of lives. He had been on the Dallas police force ten years (without promotion), and at the time of his death he had a weekend job at Austin's Barbecue, to supplement his salary. The owner, Austin Cook, said that he and Tippit never discussed politics. (Yet as

253

a self-proclaimed member of the John Birch Society, wouldn't Cook have had an occasional impulse to proselytize?) Tippit's bank balance was very modest; his standard of living was consistent with his station in life and his known income. He was a devoted family man and church-goer.

There are only a few tiny discordant notes in that exemplary record—fragmentary hints which rouse curiosity. One wonders, for example, why Tippit needed an unlisted telephone. An FBI report states that the Tippits obtained unlisted service "because J. D. Tippit, many times, would be working at night and disgruntled people to whom he had given traffic citations would call and complain to Mrs. Tippit about her husband having given them a ticket." (CE 2985, p. 5)

Another fragment—a question to Chief of Police Jesse Curry from Commissioner Allen Dulles: Is there any truth to the rumor that Tippit was involved in narcotics? No, Curry never heard such a rumor, knew nothing about anything like that. (4H 177-178) Where did the Commission hear that rumor? Was Curry's disclaimer sufficient to dispose of it or was it investigated as it should have been? The documents do not disclose these answers.

Missing also from the documents is an autopsy report on Tippit. The ambulance attendants who removed him to the hospital were never questioned; the doctor who performed the post-mortem examination was not a Commission witness. A Dallas police captain told the American Society of Newspaper Editors, months after the murder, that Tippit had been shot three times (King Exhibit 4); the Commission says four times. (WR 165)

Nor are we on firm ground when we come to the one segment of Tippit's life to which the Commission devoted such energies as it reserved for him: the hour of his death.

As I shall show later, the Commission's version of the circumstances that took Tippit to the street where he died is completely at odds with the evidence, which the Commission has examined hastily, superficially, and incompletely in its anxiety to determine an "innocent" reason for his presence in a strange district of Dallas where nothing was happening—until he himself was murdered.

The time of the shooting remains uncertain. The key witness, Helen Louise Markham, said in her affidavit of November 22 that the shooting took place at 1:06 p.m.; when she testified in March 1964, she reiterated the time as 1:06 or 1:07 p.m. (CE 2003, p. 37; 3H 306) But as her testimony reveals, she is not a person in whom reasonable men would place implicit trust—for she appears to be given to extreme confusion or even, at times, estrangement from reality.

Another citizen, a Mr. T. F. Bowley, also put the time of the shooting earlier than the Commission, which claims it was at approximately 1:15 p.m. (WR 165) Bowley was in his car on his way to call for his wife when he saw Tippit's body lying on the street; he got out of the car and looked at his watch, which said 1:10 p.m. (CE 2003, p. 11) Of course, Bowley's watch may have been slow, or fast. He was never interviewed by the Commission or its servant agencies.

Bowley is the only known witness who deliberately checked the time. Other witnesses on whom the Commission relied were not certain of the exact time, or were not asked about it. Three said that it was about one o'clock; one said that it was shortly after; one said that it was about 1:20 p.m.; and one said 1:30 p.m.

The exact time of the shooting is of great importance in the context of Oswald's alleged timetable after the shooting of the President. If the shooting of Tippit took place at 1:06 or 1:10 p.m., Oswald would have to be exonerated on the grounds that he could not possibly have walked the nine-tenths of a mile from his rooming house, from which he departed a few minutes after 1 p.m., in time to reach the scene. The Commission has estimated Oswald's other walks (from the Book Depository to the bus and from the bus to the taxi) at one minute per block. At that rate, Oswald would have required 18 minutes to walk from his rooming house to the spot where Tippit was shot.[2] Therefore, if Tippit was shot at 1:15 p.m. as the Commission asserts, Oswald should have left his rooming house a few minutes before, not after 1 p.m.—and that does not even allow for the fact that he was last seen by Earlene Roberts standing motionless at a bus stop near the rooming house. Not one witness has come forward who saw Oswald walking from the house to the Tippit scene. The Commission assumes that he took the shortest route (after all, didn't he get there in time to shoot Tippit at 1:15?) but offers no evidence. Indeed, the Commission has ignored the question of where Oswald was heading—if it *was* Oswald—when he was stopped by Tippit. He had no known social or business contacts in that immediate area, but, as many critics of the Report have pointed out, Jack Ruby's apartment was in the direction in which "Oswald" was walking and only a few short blocks from the scene of the Tippit shooting. Another "irrelevancy" in this "most exacting and detailed investigation in the history of crime."

Oswald did not have time to reach the Tippit scene on foot even if the shooting took place at 1:15 p.m.; if it was earlier by seven or ten minutes Oswald must be ruled out.

But, the Commission points out, two eyewitnesses to the shooting identified Oswald as the killer, and seven eyewitnesses identified him as the man who was seen fleeing the scene holding a revolver *(WR 157);* at least 12 persons, the Commission says, saw the man with the revolver immediately after the shooting. *(WR 166)* The Commission also provides a photo/chart showing "the location of eyewitnesses to the movements of Lee Harvey Oswald in the vicinity of the Tippit killing" *(WR 164)* which mixes indiscriminately the names of those who did *not* identify Oswald with those who did.

The two eyewitnesses to the shooting who identified Oswald as the killer were, according to the Commission, Helen Markham and William Scoggins. Scoggins, a taxi-driver, was not really an eyewitness because a bush obstructed his view of the actual shooting. The second eyewitness to the shooting was really Domingo Benavides, a truck-driver, who was in fact the closest person to the policeman and the killer at the moment of the murder—he was about 15 feet

---

2   Commission Counsel David Belin reenacted the walk, stopwatch in hand, in 17 minutes, 45 seconds. *(6H 434)*

away, according to his testimony *(6H 447)*, although the report says 25 feet. *(WR 166)* He told the police that he did not feel able to identify the killer. The police evidently took him at his word and did not take him to view Oswald in a line-up.

Benavides, the man who had the closest view of the murder, did not identify Oswald at that time or even when he was shown a photograph of Oswald months later during his testimony for the Commission. This should be borne in mind when the other identifications are evaluated, whether on the basis of a line-up or photographs.

The testimony of Helen Markham, the other eyewitness to the shooting, has been denounced sufficiently by critics of the Warren Report. I do not wish to further belabor the point that she lacks any semblance of credibility. She said that she was alone with Tippit for 20 minutes before an ambulance arrived, and that Tippit—who is said to have died instantaneously—tried to talk to her; she was in hysterics and somehow managed to leave her shoes on top of Tippit's car *(CE 1974);* sedatives had to be administered before she was taken to view the line-up at about 4:30 p.m. on Friday.

Mrs. Markham identified Oswald as the man who shot Tippit, just as the Commission claims, but here is how she described it in her testimony, which the Commission contends has "probative value."

Ball: Now when you went into the room you looked these people over, these four men?
Mrs. Markham: Yes, sir.
Ball: Did you recognize anyone in the line-up?
Mrs. Markham: No, sir.
Ball: You did not? Did you see anybody—I have asked you that question before—did you recognize anybody from their face?
Mrs. Markham: From their face, no.
Ball: Did you identify anybody in these four people?
Mrs. Markham: I didn't know nobody . . . I had never seen none of them, none of these men.
Ball: No one of the four?
Mrs. Markham: No one of them.
Ball: No one of all four?
Mrs. Markham: No, sir.
Ball: Was there a number two man in there?
Mrs. Markham: Number two is the one I picked. . . . Number two was the man I saw shoot the policeman. . . . I looked at him. When I saw this man I wasn't sure, but I had cold chills just run all over me. . . . *(3H 310-311)*

Reading this testimony about the "identification" on which the Commission relied, I feel a few cold chills too.

But the Commission has a third witness—the taxi-driver, Scoggins, whom it classifies as an eyewitness to the shooting although there was a bush which obstructed his view of the gunman in the act of firing. But Scoggins identified Oswald as the man who came toward him right after the shots, gun in hand, escaping from the scene. The identification took place at a line-up on Saturday at about midday. William Whaley, another taxi-driver, came with Scoggins to view the line-up. Whaley testified:

> . . . me and this other taxi-driver who was with me, sir, we sat in the room awhile and directly they brought in six men, young teen-agers, and they were all handcuffed together . . . you could have picked [Oswald] out without identifying him by just listening to him because he was bawling out the policeman, telling them it wasn't right to put him in line with these teen-agers. . . . He showed no respect for the policemen, he told them what he thought about them . . . they were trying to railroad him and he wanted his lawyer. . . . Anybody who wasn't sure could have picked out the right one just for that. . . .   *(2H 260-261)*

If Scoggins or the other witnesses who picked Oswald out of the line-up could not tag him by his protests of a frame-up, or by his conspicuous bruises and black eye, they had the added advantage of hearing him state his name and place of work—the Book Depository, which the whole country believed to be the site of the assassination. The three men who appeared in the line-ups with Oswald on Friday were all Dallas police employees—W. E. Perry and Richard Clark, detectives, and Don Ables, jail clerk. Each of those men testified that he was asked his name and occupation and that he gave fictitious answers. Oswald also responded when he was asked his name and occupation—information which was saturating all the news media—but his replies were factual, not fictitious. *(7H 234, 237-239, 241-242)* The same question-and-answer routine was followed at the Saturday line-up, according to one of the participants. *(7H 245-246)* How, then, could anyone fail to "identify" Oswald?

The Warren Commission saw nothing wrong with the composition or management of the line-ups. It was "satisfied that the line-ups were conducted fairly." *(WR 169)* In my view neither the line-ups nor the Commission were "fair," and I would insist that all the identifications of Oswald by witnesses to the Tippit murder be discarded as utterly valueless.

The witnesses who saw a man fleeing the scene are numerous.[3] Four of

---

3 There have been reports of at least four more eyewitnesses who are never mentioned in the Warren Report. A B.B.C. broadcast includes an interview with a Mrs. Ann McCravey (phonetic spelling), who witnessed the shooting from her window. George and Patricia Nash, in an article "The Other Witnesses" in the *New Leader* of October 12, 1964, revealed the existence of three additional witnesses—Frank Wright and his wife, and Acquilla Clemons. None of those four witnesses was summoned by the Warren Commission or, apparently, even interviewed by its servant agencies.

Still another witness at the Tippit scene comes to light in the testimony of a Dallas Police Reserve, Kenneth Hudson Croy. *(12H 186-206)* Croy told Commission Counsel Burt Griffin (the same Griffin as the one who cited as evidence for Oswald's presence in the Book Depository window the fact that Oswald had shot Tippit) that he had been driving to a restaurant where he had a lunch date when he came to the Tippit scene, just as the body was being loaded into the ambulance. He had talked to several of the known eyewitnesses and also to "a man that was standing there in the yard." *(12H 202)* The man had seen "Oswald" walk up the street "some blocks to where he got to before he got to Tippit's car."

Croy testified that he had turned this witness over to some other officers "and they talked to him"; he did not remember the man's name. Nor is there anything in the record about this man, without or with a name, although he had witnessed the Tippit killer's walk along East Tenth Street and might well have had important information and at least a description to contribute. The fact that the Dallas police (other than Reserve Officer Croy) have mentioned nothing about this unnamed man cannot justify the assumption that his observations were unimportant or unnecessary; they may in fact justify the opposite inference.

Mr. Griffin seems not to have followed up Croy's interesting testimony about a hitherto unknown Tippit witness.

them (Barbara Jeanette Davis, Virginia Davis, Ted Callaway, and Sam Guinyard) identified Oswald after viewing a line-up on Friday. I discount those four
identifications for the reasons already given. Moreover, there is reason to question whether Callaway really saw a man fleeing the scene, as he claimed, as may
be seen from the testimony of Domingo Benavides (Callaway's employee).

> . . . when Ted Callaway got around there, he opened the car door and picked
> up the phone and called in and told them there was an officer that had been
> killed. . . . Then he jumped out and ran around and asked me did I see what
> happened, and I said yes. And he said let's chase him, and I said no. . . . So
> he then turned around and went to the cab that was sitting on the corner. . . .
> And so Ted then got in the taxicab and the taxicab came to a halt and he
> asked me which way [the killer] went. I told him he went down Patton
> Street toward the office, and come to find out later Ted had already seen
> him go by there.   *(6H 452)*

Indeed, it is paradoxical that Callaway, who supposedly had seen the killer
after he turned the corner and was out of Benavides' range of vision, should have
asked him "which way he went." The lawyers for the Commission seem to have
been immune to discrepancies of this kind; predictably, they did not pay attention to this contradiction.

Other witnesses who saw a man fleeing the scene were never contacted
until the end of January 1964, two months after their fleeting glimpse of an
unknown man. Several of them identified Oswald from a photograph as the man
they had seen two months before—however, they did not select his photograph
from a group, according to standard practice, because they were shown only
Oswald's picture. That such "identifications" are worthless is, of course, self-
evident. The Commission makes itself ridiculous by asking us to regard them
as serious evidence.

Some of the witnesses who were contacted at the end of January did not
identify Oswald. One of them, Warren Reynolds, was shot in the head the next
day. (This will be discussed in a later chapter.) He recovered and conveniently
reversed himself, in July 1964, and at that time identified Oswald from a photograph shown him during his Commission testimony. L. J. Lewis, on the other
hand, maintained that he had been too distant from the man to identify him—
an obstacle that did not deter two witnesses in the same location as Lewis from
identifying Oswald from a photograph, on January 22, 1964.

The eyewitness identifications are highly vulnerable and would have been
torn to shreds in a courtroom. What other evidence, then, remains to incriminate
Oswald? A jacket discarded near the Tippit scene, which will be discussed in
detail later, and the fact that four discarded shells matched the revolver which
Oswald is said to have had on his person when he was arrested in the Texas
Theater. As we shall see, the four shells do not correspond exactly with the four
bullets recovered from Tippit's body, and the bullets themselves were too
mangled to be identified as having been fired from any specific weapon. Consequently, the ballistics evidence does not provide conclusive proof of Oswald's
culpability.

Finally, one more point must be taken into account. It involves a signed,

first-person story by Dallas Police Officer N. M. McDonald, in which he gives an
account of the arrest of Oswald in the Texas Theater. The story appeared in the
Dallas Morning News of November 24, 1963.[4] McDonald wrote that while he
was cruising toward Oak Cliff the police got a tip that a "man acting funny was
holed up in the balcony of the Texas Theater. . . . The cashier at the picture
show was the one who called in to say this guy was acting suspicious and hidden
out in the balcony." There were ten to fifteen people in the theater, "spread out
good" (only two of whom gave evidence, the others remaining unknown to this
day). "A man sitting near the front, and I still don't know who it was, tipped me
the man I wanted was sitting in the third row from the rear, not in the balcony"
(this is not the story as told in the Warren Report or in the testimony of Johnny
Calvin Brewer, the shoe salesman who supposedly pointed Oswald out).

"I went up the aisle, and talked to two people sitting about in the middle. I
was crouching low and *holding my gun* in case any trouble came." McDonald,
according to his published story, then approached Oswald, who muttered that it
was all over now and hit him a "pretty good one" in the face with his fist. "I saw
him going for his gun and I grabbed him around the waist." They struggled;
McDonald got his hand on the butt of the pistol but Oswald had his hand on the
trigger. McDonald pulled the gun toward him and heard the hammer click. "The
primer was dented and it didn't fire."

There are many discrepancies between McDonald's newspaper story and
the final version of the arrest. For example, here is a passage from the testimony
of FBI firearms expert Cortlandt Cunningham.

> *Eisenberg:* Now, Officer McDonald's statement that the primer of one
> round was dented on misfire: as far as you can tell, could this statement be
> confirmed?
> *Cunningham:* No, sir; we found nothing to indicate that this weapon's firing
> pin had struck the primer of any of these cartridges.   *(3H 463)*

Did an experienced police officer really make so gross an error as to see a
dent where there was none?

Even more intriguing is McDonald's statement that he was crouching low
and *holding his gun* as he approached Oswald. Here is a truly sensational admission, one which undermines the whole official version of the arrest—for no one
of sound mind can possibly believe that Oswald punched McDonald, or tried
to draw his own gun, while the policeman's gun was already pointing at him.

After the story of November 24, McDonald never suggested in his testimony or reports that he had his revolver in his hand as he approached Oswald,
but that is what he wrote right after the event, when the predispositions of the
case were not yet clear.

The Warren Commission undoubtedly studied the contents of the Dallas
newspapers which appeared both before and after the assassination. Surely the
Commission did not overlook McDonald's signed story, with its startling implications. Yet when McDonald testified before the Commission, he was not

---

4 N. M. McDonald, "Officer Recalls Oswald Capture," *Dallas Morning News,* November
24, 1963, p. 13.

questioned about or confronted with his published statement and its crucial discrepancies.

A question of such importance must not be allowed to remain unresolved, for historians to grapple with many years from now. It is not too late: McDonald should be allowed to speak now—to the American people, if the Warren Commission has not the dignity to clarify this and a host of similiar defects in its case against Oswald.

Tippit's Movements

First news flashes out of Dallas on the Tippit shooting said that he had been shot to death when he and another policeman pursued a suspect in the assassination into the Texas Theater following a tip. The suspect—Lee Harvey Oswald—had shot Tippit. He was subdued and arrested by other policemen.

By the next day, newspapers reported that Tippit actually had been shot and killed some blocks away from the theater and that Oswald had been arrested for Tippit's murder, not for the assassination of the President. The new version of the Tippit shooting raised a puzzling question: What was Tippit doing outside of his assigned district, at the locaton where he was shot? This remained a mystery until the Warren Report was published, leading to the various conspiracy theories predicated on Tippit's complicity in the assassination.

The Warren Report seemed to dispose of the question, telling us that at 12:45 p.m. the police dispatcher had ordered No. 78 (Tippit) to "move into central Oak Cliff area" *(WR 165)* and assuring us that that instruction appeared on the police radio log. *(WR 651)* But study of the radio log and scrutiny of the testimony of various police witnesses suggest that the pronouncements in the Warren Report, far from clearing up the mystery of Tippit's whereabouts, are untenable and illusory.

The Warren Commission received three different transcripts of the police radio log. The first transcript was an edited one prepared by the Dallas police on December 3, 1963. *(Sawyer Exhibits No. A and No. B)* An explanatory covering note indicated that it covered only messages relating to the assassination and to the shooting of Tippit but not routine police business. But this transcript did not include an instruction to Tippit at 12:45 to move into central Oak Cliff, although such an instruction was indisputably relevant to the Tippit murder and could not be classified as "routine police business." If the instruction was on the tape record, it should have been transcribed in the edited transcript.

In early April 1964, the Warren Commission was still seeking to determine the reason for Tippit's presence on the street where he was shot. A number of Dallas police officers were asked why, in their opinion, Tippit had left his assigned district and moved to the scene of the shooting.

Sergeant Calvin Bud Owens *(7H 81)*, Lieutenant Rio S. Pierce *(7H 77)*, and Sergeant James A. Putnam *(7H 75)* speculated about what Tippit's reasoning might have been under the circumstances that prevailed immediately after the police broadcast that shots had been fired at the President at Dealey Plaza. They postulated that Tippit, exercising proper discretion in the light of the prevailing emergency, had started in the direction of the downtown area where the attack on the motorcade had occurred, and that his route to that destination had taken him to the vicinity where his body was found. Not one of the witnesses suggested that Tippit had been sent out of his own district by the police dispatcher. Apparently talk and speculation within the Dallas Police Department during the five months which had elapsed since the Tippit murder had not elicited any reference to the alleged 12:45 instruction to Tippit, at least in the hearing of Owens, Pierce, or Putnam.

The suggestion which they had put forward—that Tippit had proceeded on his own initiative to the district where he was killed—is weak. Had Tippit decided by himself to move to the scene of the assassination, he would have arrived there within 15 or 20 minutes at most (the Commission asserts that it took Oswald only six minutes to make a somewhat shorter trip in reverse). But Tippit was cruising slowly on East Tenth Street at 1:15 p.m., that location being some four miles from Dealey Plaza. Obviously he was not en route to the Book Depository area, as the three witnesses speculated. The lawyer who had solicited their opinions did not pose this self-evident objection to their rationalization.

At the end of April, the Warren Commission—still without an acceptable explanation of Tippit's movements—requested and received a verbatim transcript of the radio log, again prepared by the Dallas police, in which the personnel reporting to the dispatcher were designated by number and not by name. *(CE 705)* (Still later, the Commission requested the FBI to prepare a transcript in verbatim form, setting forth the names as well as the numbers of the personnel *(CE 1974);* the FBI verbatim transcript was completed in August 1964.)

Although a number of police witnesses had suggested that Tippit's departure from his own district was a normal procedure under the existing circumstances, the Dallas police verbatim transcript of the radio log *(CE 705)* now included an instruction—issued simultaneously to No. 78 (Tippit) and No. 87 (Nelson)—to move into central Oak Cliff, transmitted at 12:45 p.m.

This was the first indication of the alleged instruction, and it immediately raised the question of why it had not appeared in the edited transcript of December 1963. That question was posed to Police Chief Jesse Curry when he appeared before the Commission on April 22, 1964. His reply was confused and incoherent. Curry, one of the key officials responsible for the President's safety in Dallas, was distraught and seemed merely to improvise his answers—at one point seeming to suggest that Tippit had moved out of his assigned district to search for his own murderer. *(4H 192)*

Curry said first that the 12:45 instruction to Tippit had been omitted from the December edited transcript because it was difficult to hear everything clearly; his men had spent many hours replaying the recording and copying down the conversations; he himself had heard the recording and could vouch for the correctness of the verbatim transcript. *(4H 186)* A dubious reply, for if the instruction to Tippit was audible when the verbatim transcript was prepared, it must have been equally audible when the edited transcript was made.

J. Lee Rankin vindicated Curry by asking if the instruction might not have been omitted from the first transcript for reasons of brevity, as other routine messages had been omitted. Curry hastened to agree. *(4H 185-186)* But it has already been pointed out that the instruction to Tippit was fundamental to the events leading to his murder and could not be regarded as "routine" by any standard.

The omission of the message in the first transcript of the radio log, its sudden appearance in the second transcript, and the lame or absurd explanations given by Curry and other police witnesses inevitably raise suspicion about the authenticity of the message. That suspicion is intensified by further study of the radio log.

If the instruction to Tippit—and Nelson—is authentic, we must ask why the dispatcher singled out those two officers for special and quite curious treatment. They were the *only* officers contacted by the dispatcher with instructions unrelated to the assassination and lacking any other apparent purpose. During the half-hour after the President was shot there was no breach of law and order in central Oak Cliff, and no strategic reason for sending reinforcements there. The assassination took place at a point some four or more miles from central Oak Cliff. As it turned out, a Book Depository employee who was missing and under suspicion was en route to his furnished room in Oak Cliff at 12:45 p.m.— but there was no way for the dispatcher or Tippit to know that. Oswald's absence had not yet been noticed at 12:45; his Oak Cliff address was not known to his wife or his employers, much less to the Dallas police. If the dispatcher nonetheless sent two policemen closer to the vicinity of Oswald's rooming house, at random, or if Tippit went there on his initiative, it would have been an incredible coincidence.

The order to Tippit and Nelson was given 15 minutes after the President was shot, in a setting of unprecedented emergency. A frenzy of police activity centered at the Book Depository and at Parkland Hospital. So much traffic jammed police communications lines that officers had to wait their turn to get through with urgent information.

The dispatcher had sent out a general order for all downtown squads to proceed to the Book Depository. Aside from Tippit and Nelson, the dispatcher did not contact any specific squad cars, nor did he give any general order to men in the outlying districts to move elsewhere. We are asked to believe that, in the midst of this consternation, the dispatcher took the time to call Tippit and Nelson and give them instructions which make no sense.

The Warren Commission saw nothing curious in this. The Commission did not question the dispatcher about his reason for giving the alleged instruction, although there was already a peculiar aura about the radio log. Such questioning was all the more necessary because, according to the transcript, policemen from the outermost districts of Dallas who called the dispatcher to ask if there was anything they could do in the emergency were told to report to the Book Depository—even though in some instances they were far more distant from that location than Tippit or Nelson.

Even stranger is the fact that Nelson, supposedly told simultaneously with Tippit to move in to central Oak Cliff, is not heard from until 45 minutes later, at about 1:30 p.m., *at the Book Depository,* as if he had never received or acknowledged the 12:45 instruction. When Nelson reported from the Book Depository, the dispatcher raised no question about his seeming disregard for an explicit order to proceed to a different location. In itself this suggests that Nelson never received such an order, nor did Tippit; the force of this inference is strengthened by a police report on a different matter *(CE 2645),* stating that after the assassination, Nelson was dispatched to the Book Depository, where he remained on guard in front of the building for the remainder of the afternoon!

If the 12:45 instruction to Nelson to proceed to central Oak Cliff was fabricated, as his actions at the time and the later report *(CE 2645)* suggest, was the 12:45 instruction to Tippit—never mentioned until some five months later—authentic?

According to the radio log, Tippit not only was sent to central Oak Cliff, but he remained the subject of extraordinary solicitude. At 12:54, nine minutes after the alleged instruction, the dispatcher signaled Tippit again and asked his location. Tippit replied that he was in Oak Cliff, as instructed, at Lancaster and Eighth Streets. The dispatcher then told Tippit to "be at large for any emergency that comes in." In the prevailing atmosphere of crisis and intense police activity, such an axiomatic reminder is certainly bizarre.

The next relevant entry in the radio log creates still more confusion and perplexity. At 1 p.m. the same dispatcher who supposedly heard Tippit report at 12:54 that he was at Lancaster and Eighth signaled Tippit again—this time, it would appear, in search of a squad car to pick up blood and rush it to Parkland Hospital. The exchange of messages between the dispatcher and various cruising policemen indicates that the dispatcher was seeking the squad car nearest to the blood bank.

But the blood bank was located in the 2000 block of Commerce Street, about five miles distant from Lancaster and Eighth. If the 12:45 and 12:54 messages were authentic, the dispatcher would have known that Tippit was nowhere near the blood bank. If he did not signal Tippit at 1 p.m. in connection with the delivery of blood to the hospital, what else was he calling about? This question, too, remained unasked by the Warren Commission and unanswered by the dispatcher.

Tippit did not reply to the 1 p.m. signal. Where was he? Why didn't he answer?

Let us look at the testimony of Dallas policeman Harry Olsen, who was a casual friend of Jack Ruby and boy friend of Kay Coleman, a stripper at Ruby's Carousel Club. Olsen's account of his whereabouts at the time of the assassination is extremely interesting. He told Commission Counsel Arlen Specter, who deposed him on August 6, 1964, that he had been off duty on the day of the assassination and had agreed to substitute on a moonlighting job for a motorcycle policeman assigned to the motorcade. The job was to guard an estate in the absence of its owners. Olsen did not remember the name of the motorcycle policeman; there is no indication that the Commission attempted to establish his identity. Where was the estate? Olsen said it was on Eighth Street in Oak Cliff, about two blocks from the freeway—that is, at or very near Lancaster and Eighth, the location from which Tippit supposedly had reported at 12:54.

Where was Olsen at that hour? He testified that he had learned that the President had been shot when he answered a phone call for the absent owner of the estate; he had then gone outside and exchanged comments about the tragedy with passersby. *(14H 629)*

Olsen, then, was in the right place at the right time to encounter Tippit—with whom he admittedly was acquainted—if Tippit was actually at Lancaster and Eighth. Arlen Specter seemed unaware of the import of Olsen's testimony. He did not ask Olsen if he had seen or spoken to Tippit, perhaps at one o'clock (when Tippit failed to answer the dispatcher's signal).

But perhaps Olsen never saw Tippit; there seems to have been another reason for Tippit's silence at 1 p.m. At that very time, a police car pulled up to the rooming house on North Beckley Street where Oswald was a tenant, sounded its horn, and slowly drove away, according to Earlene Roberts, the housekeeper there. *(6H 443-444)* Mrs. Roberts said that there were two police officers in the car; she was confused about the number on the vehicle and gave several different versions. In some of the three-digit combinations she suggested, the first two figures were a 1 and a 0; Tippit's car was "No. 10."

Investigation failed to turn up any squad car that stopped in front of Oswald's boarding house at 1 p.m. or any officer who admitted stopping there. Tippit, who did not reply to a one-o'clock signal, cannot be questioned, of course.

According to the police verbatim transcript of the radio log *(CE 705)*, Tippit twice signaled the dispatcher at 1:08 p.m., but the dispatcher did not acknowledge or reply to the signal. In the corresponding part of the FBI verbatim transcript *(CE 1974, p. 48)* Tippit's call number ("No. 78") is missing, and the signal is attributed to "No. 488," with a notation that the sound was garbled. No. 488 is not identified by name, and no other listing for No. 488 appears anywhere in the radio log.

Between 12:45 and 1:08 p.m. there was a total of four signals involving Tippit—three calls by the dispatcher in a 15-minute interval, the last call unanswered, and an unanswered call from Tippit to the dispatcher at 1:08 p.m. The Warren Commission sees nothing strange in the fact that an inconsequential patrolman, stationed far from the scene of the assassination, is called repeatedly by the dispatcher for no apparent reason, at a time of unparalleled traffic on the police radio.

Finally we come to the most extraordinary of the Tippit signals to be found in the radio log. At about 1:16 p.m. a citizen broke in on the police radio, to report the shooting of a policeman at 404 East Tenth Street (which lies in District 91). According to all three transcripts of the radio log, the dispatcher's immediate reaction was to call No. 78 (Tippit) again—and, according to two of the transcripts, before there was any reason for the dispatcher to link the officer who was shot with Tippit.

The police verbatim transcript interpolates a parenthetical reference to background noises in which No. 78 and Car No. 10 could be heard, giving the impression that the dispatcher heard Tippit's code number and car number before signaling him. (*CE 705*, p. 408) But the indication of background noises is *not* found in the FBI verbatim transcript, which, like the edited transcript (*Sawyer Exhibit A,* p. 394), indicates that the dispatcher began to signal Tippit immediately after the citizen's intrusion and before the mention of any numbers by which Tippit might be identified. (*CE 1974,* p. 858) The reference to background noises, which is found only in the police verbatim transcript, is all the more suspect for the fact that no one at the scene of the shooting could have known that the murdered policeman was No. 78.

Tippit, ostensibly pulled out of his own district, No. 78, reported at 12:54 from a location inside District 109.[5] Some 20 minutes later he was shot to death on a street inside District 91, where the assigned officer, No. 91 (Mentzel), was present on duty in his squad car. The dispatcher, on receiving a citizen's report of a shooting on East Tenth Street, did not signal No. 91 (Mentzel)—he signaled Tippit, without any reason to believe that Tippit was the victim of the shooting or that he was the closest officer to the scene. Only after calling Tippit did the dispatcher signal and reach Mentzel, who, according to an FBI report: "Was eating lunch at 430 West Jefferson at time of assassination. Left restaurant to answer shooting call in 400 block East Tenth Street, Oak Cliff." (*CE 2645*)

The transcripts of the radio log are studded with aberrations and inconsistencies, both in absolute terms and in divergence from each other. None of the many warning signals in the transcripts indicating that something more than meets the eye was transpiring in the hour of Tippit's death has been acknowledged or investigated by the Warren Commission. The assurances in the Warren Report that everything was innocent and routine are misleading. The radio log suggests irresistibly that Tippit was on something other than routine business, on his own behalf or under instructions, and that the truth of the circumstances which led him to the quiet street where he was shot to death has either not been ferreted out, or has been carefully concealed.

I cannot accept the assertion in the Warren Report that Tippit was instructed as a matter of normal police routine to move into central Oak Cliff, for the following reasons:

(1) The first transcript of the radio log did not include the 12:45 instruction to Tippit, and five months later police witnesses were still unaware of such a transaction and were venturing the opinion that Tippit must have acted on his own initiative in leaving his assigned district.

(2) Officers from the outermost districts were sent to the Book Depository.

(3) No other districts received orders such as those allegedly given to No. 78 (Tippit) and No. 87 (Nelson).

(4) Nelson's actual movements suggest that he never received a 12:45 instruction to move into central Oak Cliff; another Commission exhibit establishes the fact that Nelson was actually assigned to the Book Depository.

---

5 Identification of district numbers is based on the official Dallas Police Radio Patrol District Map (*Putnam Exhibit No. 1*) and on a street map of Dallas.

(5) The dispatcher tried to contact Tippit at 1 p.m. for an apparent purpose which is completely inconsistent with the authenticity of the 12:45 and 12:54 messages.

(6) Tippit's failure to respond to signals at 1 p.m. remains unexplained; his 1:08 call to the dispatcher comes after too long an interval to be regarded as a response to the 1 p.m. signal, if Tippit was merely cruising at a leisurely speed on quiet streets where there was no incident requiring police action until he himself was shot.

(7) The dispatcher's signals to Tippit after a citizen's report of a shooting—without reason to believe that Tippit was in the district and before any indication that Tippit was the victim—remain unexplained and may point to clandestine activities on Tippit's part which would nullify the official theory of his murder.

Tippit and the Pedestrian

In the early days of the case police spokesmen maintained that Tippit had heard the police radio description of the suspect in the assassination and on that basis had halted the pedestrian who shot him. Skeptics ridiculed this as being utterly inconsistent with the facts and with an eyewitness description of the encounter. Rumors circulated that Tippit and Oswald were known to each other, and published speculations suggested that the two men were involved in a plot to assassinate the President.

The Warren Report later asserted that there was no evidence that Oswald and Tippit were acquainted, had ever seen each other, or had any mutual acquaintances. There was no way to determine with certainty whether Tippit had recognized Oswald from the description broadcast on the police radio, but it was "conceivable, even probable," that Tippit had done so. (WR 651)

Information in the Hearings and Exhibits provides cause for serious reservations about the Commission's assertions and reasoning. I have already pointed out that the radio log throws grave doubt on the official explanation of Tippit's movements and that at 1 p.m. he was mysteriously absent from his car, or refused for other reasons to reply to the dispatcher's signal. We do not know what Tippit was doing between 12:54 p.m. and the time he was shot, but there is nothing to suggest that he was stopping pedestrians who fit the description of the assassination suspect, an "unknown white male, approximately thirty, slender build, height five feet ten inches, weight 165 pounds, reported to be armed with a .30 caliber rifle." (CE 705) It would be amazing if Tippit saw no male pedestrian on the streets of Oak Cliff between 12:45 and the time he was shot who fit that vague description. Did Oswald, viewed from behind, fit the description? He was younger than thirty by six years; was not armed with a rifle. It would be even more remarkable, then, if Tippit stopped him and no one else.

Were the actions of Tippit and the pedestrian whom he stopped consistent with the theory that the man was stopped because he resembled the description broadcast on the police radio? Only one witness claims to have seen what happened: Mrs. Helen Markham.

Ball: Where was the police car when you first saw it?

Mrs. Markham: He was driving real slow, almost up to this man, well, say this man, and he kept, this man kept walking, you know, and the police car going real slow now, real slow, and they just kept coming into the curb, and finally they got way up there a little ways up, well, it stopped.

Ball: The police car stopped?

Mrs. Markham: Yes, sir.

Ball: What about the man? Was he still walking?

Mrs. Markham: The man stopped. . . . I saw the man come over to the car very slow, leaned and put his arms just like this, he leaned over in this window and looked in this window. . . . The window was down. . . . Well, I didn't think nothing about it; you know, the police are nice and friendly and I thought friendly conversation. Well, I looked, and there were cars coming, so I had to wait. . . . This man, like I told you, put his arms up, leaned over, he—just a minute, and he drew back and he stepped back about two steps. . . . The policeman calmly opened the door, very slowly, wasn't angry or nothing, he calmly crawled out of this car, and I still just thought a friendly conversation. . . .   *(3H 307)*

The encounter as Mrs. Markham has described it is compatible with any number of causes. Tippit might have stopped the man to ask for a match, and they might have exchanged comments about the shooting of the President less than an hour before. Tippit might have stopped an acquaintance and stopped to ask how his sick mother was feeling. The scene sketched by Mrs. Markham suggests that the pedestrian made no attempt to avoid the policeman and that he exhibited no signs of alarm or tension. This hardly suggests a man unnerved by fear and guilt or a man who had spent the preceding 45 minutes darting about on foot and by vehicle in an "escape." Tippit's behavior is even less compatible with the Commission's theory. He should have known better than to leave the car had he been suspicious of the man he stopped. He should have summoned reinforcements on the police radio, just as another officer did who was working alone and found a man whom he wished to arrest, as shown in the radio log. (*CE 1974*, pp. 48-51) He might have told the man to get into the car to be taken to the police station for questioning. But why should Tippit leave the car under the circumstances which the Commission considers "conceivable, even probable"? He did not leave the car in order to search the pedestrian for a concealed rifle. He did not leave the car to subdue by force a suspect who had made no gesture of resistance and didn't try to run away. If Tippit had stopped the pedestrian—whether Oswald or someone else—on suspicion that he was the Presidential assassin, it was reckless and probably against regulations for him to leave his car. It seems to me that a solitary policeman seeking to apprehend a dangerous criminal would first have called on the police radio to give information, ask instructions, and seek help.[6] That is what was done by other officers.

---

6 Perhaps that was the purpose of Tippit's unanswered signal at 1:08 p.m. If so, the suspect could not have been Oswald, who could not have walked from his rooming house to the scene of the shooting in time.

Unfortunately the Commission did not inquire into the rules that were applicable in the "conceivable, even probable" circumstances which it postulated. Unfortunately the Commission did not ponder the strangeness of Tippit's actions under such a hypothesis.

These considerations suggest that it was not probable, perhaps not even conceivable, that Tippit stopped the pedestrian who shot him because of the description broadcast on the police radio. The facts indicate that Tippit was up to something different which, if uncovered, might place his death and the other events of those three days in a completely new perspective. We do not know what was in Tippit's mind during his last hours. There was a clue, but the Commission did not follow it up, as seen in the testimony of Sergeant W. E. Barnes of the police laboratory. Barnes, who had taken photographs at the scene of the Tippit shooting, was questioned about those photographs on April 7, 1964.

> *Belin:* Inside the window there appears to be some kind of paper or document. Do you remember what that is at all, or not?
> *Barnes:* That is a board, a clipboard that is installed on the dash of all squad cars for the officers to take notes on and to keep their wanted persons names on.
> *Belin:* Were there any notes on there that you saw that had been made on this clipboard?
> *Barnes:* Yes; we never read his clipboard. . . . I couldn't tell you what was on the clipboard. *(7H 274)*

Perhaps the Commission found it plausible that the Dallas police did not bother to examine the clipboard of a murdered officer, seeking a clue to his murder. Be that as it may, why did the Commission not obtain and examine it? There might have been notations on the clipboard which might have cast light on Tippit's activities before he was shot—notations which might have strengthened the basis for the Commission's speculations, or shown them to be mistaken.

If neither the police nor the Commission took the trouble to examine Tippit's clipboard, they were poorly qualified to undertake a murder investigation. If the clipboard was examined, the findings have been concealed and must be assumed to be incompatible with the official theory.

We revert now to the Commission's assertion that there was no evidence that Oswald and Tippit were acquainted or had ever seen each other.

In the early days there was considerable speculation, some of which was irresponsible, that Oswald and Tippit might have been fellow conspirators in a plot with other unknown persons to assassinate the President. The theory of a clandestine or criminal association between Oswald and Tippit was unaccompanied by serious evidence. Apparently it sprang from an effort of the imagination to invest logic and credibility in the implausible and naïve version of the Tippit murder which issued from official sources. The proposition that Tippit had stopped an unknown pedestrian on the strength of a vague description on the police radio satisfies few students of the case and offends those who seek meaning in human affairs and do not conceive of history as governed by random, irrational, and incessant coincidence.

The theorists and their theories of sinister links between Oswald and Tippit

were coldly dismissed by the Warren Commission. The Commission said flatly
that there was "no evidence that Oswald and Tippit were acquainted, had ever
seen each other, or had any mutual acquaintances." *(WR 651)*

Like many other assertions in the Report, this pronouncement collides head-
on with the Commission's own exhibits. In this case, the exhibit concerns an FBI
investigation of possible links between Oswald and Ruby which led the FBI to
Dobbs House, a restaurant reputedly patronized by both men. According to the
FBI report, one of the waitresses who was interviewed, Mary Dowling, said
that she

> . . . recalled the person now recognized as Oswald was last seen by her in the
> restaurant at about 10 a.m. Wednesday, November 20, at which time he was
> "nasty" and used curse words in connection with his order. She went on to
> relate that Officer *J. D. Tippit was in the restaurant, as was his habit at
> about that time each morning, and "shot a glance at Oswald."* She said there
> was no indication, however, that they knew each other. [Italics added]
>
> *(CE 3001)*

The interview with Mary Dowling took place in December 1963. Her report
of a link between Oswald and Tippit, however tenuous and impersonal the link
might be, obviously was of potential importance and demanded further investigation.

For unknown reasons, the FBI did not immediately inform the Warren
Commission of the results of the interview with Mary Dowling in December.
For equally inscrutable reasons, the FBI waited some six months before interviewing another waitress at Dobbs House, Mrs. Dolores Harrison, who was a
party to the incident reported by Mary Dowling. The FBI report on the interview with Mrs. Harrison indicates:

> Mrs. Dolores Harrison advised she had been employed as a waitress at the
> Dobbs House for approximately six years.
>
> She stated that during the latter months of 1963, specific dates unrecalled,
> Lee Harvey Oswald came into the Dobbs House numerous times. Mrs.
> Harrison related that on November 21, 1963 she recalls Oswald having
> been in the Dobbs House for breakfast, specific time unrecalled. She stated
> she recalls this particular occasion, inasmuch as Oswald had ordered "eggs
> over light" and, when served, made a complaint that the eggs were "cooked
> too hard."
>
> Mrs. Harrison advised [that] she prepared Oswald's eggs and Mary Dow-
> ling, a waitress, served same to him. She related that, although Oswald
> complained of the eggs, he accepted them.
>
> She related [that] although she saw Oswald at the Dobbs House a number
> of times, she did not know his identity until seeing his picture in the news-
> paper as being the accused assassin of President Kennedy. Mrs. Harrison
> advised she has never seen Jack L. Ruby at the Dobbs House at any other
> location; she has no knowledge of the assassination of President John F.
> Kennedy, or of any connections between Ruby and Oswald.   *(CE 3001)*

Surely Mrs. Harrison was describing the same incident as Mary Dowling. Nevertheless, the FBI did not ask her if J. D. Tippit had been present during the episode of Oswald's eggs. The information that Tippit had regularly patronized the

same restaurant that Oswald had visited numerous times during the months preceding the assassination only stirred further questions addressed to possible contacts between Oswald and *Ruby,* not Oswald and Tippit and certainly not Tippit and Ruby.

The FBI reported the results of these interviews with the two waitresses in a letter to the Warren Commission dated July 31, 1963 *(CE 3001),* apparently for the first time, more than seven months after receiving a report that Oswald and Tippit were both present in the same restaurant two days at most before the assassination. After reporting the interview with Mary Dowling, the FBI letter explains why her information was ignored: information previously obtained from the Book Depository indicated that Oswald had worked from 8 a.m. to 4:45 p.m. daily, with a lunch period at noon. The record indicated that he had worked eight hours on Wednesday, November 20; therefore, the reasoning seems to go, Oswald could not have been in Dobbs House at 10 a.m. as Mary Dowling claimed.[7]

Apparently the possibility that Mary Dowling might have been mistaken about the hour, or that time-keeping at the Book Depository was lax (as Oswald claimed), seemed to the Commission as well as the FBI to merit no inquiry. The possibility that Oswald and Tippit may have patronized the restaurant at the same time on other occasions was not investigated. Against this background of indifference to evidence of potential importance, the Report suavely asserts that Oswald and Tippit had never seen each other before the fatal encounter on the streets of Oak Cliff.

The treatment of this matter is part of a well-defined pattern in the Commission's "fact finding"; first, to discount information inimical to the thesis that Oswald was the lone assassin, and, second, to proclaim that such information does not even exist. Time and again, the Commission's own documents give the lie to its Report and outrage the handful of students who have ventured into the neglected pages of exhibits and testimony. In the light of Mary Dowling's report and the total deafness with which it was greeted, the Commission's disclaimer of any link between Oswald and Tippit and its apocryphal version of the encounter in which Tippit was shot to death can hardly be regarded as the last word.

Description of the Killer

The Warren Report informs us that at 1:22 p.m. the Dallas Police radio broadcast a description of the man wanted for the murder of Tippit, and that "according to Patrolman Poe this description came from Mrs. Markham and Mrs. Barbara Jeanette Davis." *(WR 175)* According to the Report, Mrs. Markham told

---

7   By that token, it is nonsense to believe that Oswald was arrested and incarcerated by the police on the afternoon of the assassination. According to Book Depository records, he worked a full eight-hour day on November 22. *(CE 1949,* p. 6)

patrolman J. M. Poe that the killer was a white male, about twenty-five, about five feet eight inches tall, brown hair, wearing a white jacket; Mrs. Davis gave Poe the same general description, also saying that the killer was wearing a white jacket. *(WR 175)*

This passage in the Report is almost wholly inaccurate and misleading. First, let us examine the statement that Poe obtained the description from the two women and then broadcast it over the police radio (the Report does not say that explicitly but it is the only possible inference which can be drawn). Poe did testify that when he arrived at the scene of the Tippit murder Mrs. Markham gave him a description of the killer, but he added:

Poe: We gave the description to several of the officers at the scene. You couldn't get on the radio . . . and then I talked to several more witnesses around there.
Ball: Did you ever put that description on the radio?
Poe: I believe we did. But I couldn't swear to it. . . . *(7H 68)*

Ball: At 1:22 p.m. on the transcript of the radio log, I note it says, "Have a description of suspect on Jefferson. Last seen about 300 block of East Jefferson. White male, thirties, five feet eight inches, black hair, slender built, wearing white shirt black slacks." Do you know whether you gave Walker that description?
Poe: I remember giving Walker a description. My partner got in the car with Walker.
Ball: Did you give Walker a description similar to that?
Poe: Yes, sir. *(7H 69)*

No wonder the Commission carefully avoided stating that Poe put the description on the police radio, but left the reader to infer just that: Poe was not at all certain that he had broadcast the description and "couldn't swear to it." Hence, Mr. Ball proceeded to ask if Poe had given the description to his fellow officer, C. T. Walker—for, according to the verbatim transcript of the police radio log, it was "85 (Walker)" who called in the description of the Tippit suspect at 1:22 p.m. *(CE 1974,* p. 59) But this is what C. T. Walker testified:

Belin: You were not the one that put out the first description of the suspect they sought?
C. T. Walker: I didn't. *(7H 36)*

If Ball and Belin had examined the radio log with greater care, they would have seen that it was not C. T. Walker who called in the description at 1:22 p.m., but R. W. Walker, a patrolman who was not a witness before the Commission. Indeed, they would have seen that immediately after R. W. Walker phoned in the description, Officer Poe reported to the police radio dispatcher that he and his partner, Patrolman L. E. Jez, had just arrived at the Tippit scene. *(CE 1974,* p. 59)

The Commission has labored to create the impression that the 1:22 p.m. description originated with Mrs. Markham and Mrs. Barbara Jeanette Davis, via officer Poe. That description actually originated with patrolman R. W. Walker, who called in saying:

> *R. W. Walker:* We have a description on this suspect over here on Jefferson. Last seen about the 300 East Jefferson. He's a white male, about thirty, five feet eight inches, black hair, slender, wearing a white jacket and dark slacks.
> *Dispatcher:* Armed with what?
> *R. W. Walker:* Unknown.   (*CE 1974*, p. 59)

Walker had no known contact with Mrs. Markham and Mrs. Davis and it is obvious from the contents of his message that he obtained the description from a person whose identity has never been established.

Not only is there no known contact between R. W. Walker and the two women, but the description he transmitted does not correspond with the description attributed to the women in the Report. *(WR 175)* The age is thirty, not twenty-five; the hair is black, not brown; and while the two women saw the suspect with a revolver in his hand, R. W. Walker did not know if the man was armed, or with what.

Moreover, there is reason to question the description that is said to have been given to Poe by Mrs. Markham and Mrs. Davis. FBI Agent Odum reported that on the afternoon of the Tippit murder Mrs. Markham told him that the killer was a white male, about eighteen, black hair, red complexion, wearing black shoes, tan jacket, and dark trousers *(3H 319)*—a description seriously in conflict with the one she is said to have given to Poe.

Mrs. Davis is said to have given Poe the same general description (of a man wearing a white jacket) as the one given by Mrs. Markham; but here is what Mrs. Davis told the Warren Commission:

> *Ball:* Was he dressed the same in the line-up as he was when you saw him running across the lawn?
> *Mrs. Davis:* All except he didn't have a black coat on when I saw him in the line-up.
> *Ball:* Did he have a coat on when you saw him?
> *Mrs. Davis:* Yes, sir . . . a dark coat.   (*3H 347*)

Despite all this contrary evidence, the Report tries to persuade the reader that the 1:22 p.m. description came from the two women and that Poe called it in over the police radio—assertions which are absolutely false and misleading. As if that were not enough, the Report then suppresses completely the important fact that between 1:33 and 1:40 p.m. the dispatcher received the following message from "221 (H. W. Summers)":

> Might can give you some additional information. I got an eyeball witness to the getaway man; that suspect in this shooting. He is a white male, twenty-seven, five feet eleven inches, 165, black wavy hair, fair complected, wearing light gray Eisenhower-type jacket, dark trousers and a white shirt and but last seen running on the north side of the street from Patton on Jefferson, and was apparently armed with a .32, dark finish, automatic pistol which he had in his right hand.   (*CE 1974*, p. 74)

There are a number of elements in Summers' message which should have occasioned careful investigation by the Commission. The identity of the "eyeball witness to the getaway man" should have been determined, and his testimony obtained and evaluated, since his observations as transmitted by Summers seem clearly incompatible with the Commission's conclusion that Oswald was the "getaway man." That any witness should have described Oswald as having "black wavy hair" is inconceivable.

Even more startling is the report, presumably by the same unknown "eyeball" witness, that the suspect was armed with a .32 automatic pistol, when the Tippit murder weapon is said to have been a .38 Smith & Wesson revolver—the ancestor, so to speak, of the automatic pistol. Anyone who was sufficiently familiar with firearms to describe a weapon as a .32 automatic pistol almost certainly would be too knowledgable to make such an error if the weapon were really a .38 revolver. That inference, in itself, is hardly sufficient to warrant a conclusion that the suspect actually was holding a .32 automatic pistol, but there is strong supporting evidence from another source.

Only a few minutes after Summers transmitted the description of the suspect, Sergeant Gerald Hill signaled the dispatcher with the following message: "The shell at the scene indicates that the suspect is armed with an automatic .38 rather than a pistol." (*CE 1974*, p. 78)

Sergeant Hill testified on April 8, 1964 that when he returned to the Tippit scene after an abortive search of two vacant houses toward which the killer had run, according to a citizen's report, he encountered officer Poe. Hill said:

> And Poe showed me a Winston cigarette package that contained three spent jackets from shells that he said a citizen had pointed out to him where the suspect had reloaded his gun and dropped these in the grass, and the citizen had picked them up and put them in the Winston package.   *(7H 48-49)*

Here is still more surprising news: not only did this trained police officer identify a shell at the scene as that of an automatic rather than a revolver, but he testified that there were three cartridge cases in the empty cigarette box, instead of two. Domingo Benavides testified that he had picked up and placed two shells in a cigarette box, which he then turned over to a policeman. *(6H 450)* Did the policeman then find or receive from someone else a third shell, as Hill's testimony suggests? Or did Hill mistake the number of shells as well as the type?

When we deal with the ammunition for the revolver in the Tippit shooting, discussed later in this chapter, we will find new discrepancies—involving the number and brand of the shells and the bullets—which the Commission was unable to resolve. Those discrepancies made it all the more important for the Commission to investigate the radio log messages from Summers and Hill, which create grave new doubt about the identity of the killer and the weapon. Instead, the Commission ignored the Summers description and turned a deaf ear to the startling discrepancy in Hill's testimony.

The passage in the Warren Report purporting to explain the origin of the 1:22 p.m. description of the Tippit suspect *(WR 175)* consists of sentences each of which is literally true, but which in the aggregate are completely misleading.

Misrepresentation piled on misrepresentation cannot be ascribed to inadequate work alone since it manifests a constant and premediated motif: the incrimination of a man who received even less justice and mercy from the Warren Commission after his death than he got from the Dallas police when he was alive.

The Abandoned Jacket

Commission Exhibit 162 is a light-weight gray zipper jacket. In the view of the Warren Commission, it is a key item of evidence in the Tippit murder. The Commission contends that the gray jacket (1) belonged to Lee Harvey Oswald, (2) was worn by Oswald at the time of the Tippit shooting, (3) was described and identified by eyewitnesses at or near the scene, and (4) was discarded by Oswald during his flight and discovered minutes later under a parked car by Captain W. R. Westbrook of the Dallas Police. These, in substance, are the explicit or implicit claims made in the Warren Report. (WR 175-176, 653)

A close examination of the testimony and documents discloses (1) that the ownership of the jacket is not established beyond reasonable doubt, (2) that the eyewitnesses' descriptions of the killer's jacket do not match the gray jacket and in some cases are completely inconsistent with it, (3) that some of those eyewitnesses were unable to identify the gray jacket when it was displayed to them, and (4) that the jacket was not found by Captain Westbrook, as the Report asserts, but by a man whose identity the Commission did not even try to establish.

If the evidence is evaluated objectively in its entirety, the only facts that remain solid are (a) that at about one o'clock Oswald donned a zipper jacket which did not correspond with the gray zipper jacket (CE 162), according to the only person who saw him at the time; and (b) that when Oswald was arrested inside the Texas Theater less than an hour later, he no longer wore any jacket nor, apparently, had a jacket in his possession. This, by itself, hardly incriminates Oswald in the Tippit murder. (The radio log and other documents reveal that a jacket was found during the same general time period on Industrial Boulevard; apparently an unidentified man discarded it there, yet he did not come under suspicion as a result.)

In the preceding pages, I have discussed the origin of the 1:22 p.m. description of the Tippit suspect in which he was said to be dressed in a white jacket, and Poe's testimony that both Helen Markham and Barbara Jeanette Davis had told him at the scene that the killer wore a white jacket. More significantly, the jacket discovered under a parked car near the Tippit scene was called a white jacket by the finder when he told the dispatcher over the police radio of the discovery. The Commission, on the other hand, tells us that the jacket under the car was the gray zipper jacket pictured in Commission Exhibit 162.

Are we to assume that the witnesses, including a police officer trained in accurate observation, saw a gray jacket but mistakenly called it white? Or did they call it white because it was in fact white?

The Commission does not offer any guidance—perhaps wisely, for while a weathered white garment might well be described as light gray or ivory, the reverse is far less likely.

That Mrs. Markham actually said that the killer wore a white jacket is doubtful, since she is a generally unreliable witness. That Mrs. Davis did so is even more doubtful, since she testified that the suspect wore a black or dark jacket. But if we eliminate those two references to a white jacket, we must still account for the fact that the unknown police officer who found the jacket and picked it up called it a *white* jacket; in addition, we must still account for the white jacket mentioned in the 1:22 p.m. description called in by Officer R. W. Walker on the basis of a report by a witness whose identity has not been established.

How did the known eyewitnesses describe the jacket worn by Tippit's killer? Mrs. Markham, when she testified before the Warren Commission, said that "it was a short jacket, open in the front, kind of grayish tan" *(3H 311);* however, when the light gray zipper jacket was displayed *(CE 162)* she said that she had never seen it before, that it was too light to be the jacket worn by the killer. *(3H 312)*

Domingo Benavides, the second if not the sole eyewitness to the shooting, testified that the killer wore a light beige zipper-type jacket. *(6H 450)* A few minutes later, Mr. Belin excused himself in order to obtain some exhibits for identification. He returned with a jacket which Benavides promptly identified as the jacket worn by Tippit's killer. But in his haste Belin had brought the wrong jacket—not the gray one *(CE 162),* but a blue zipper jacket *(CE 163),* also said to belong to Oswald, which had been discovered in the Book Depository about ten days after the assassination. *(6H 453)* Obviously, Mr. Benavides, much as he wished to be of assistance, was anything but helpful to the Committee.

William Scoggins, whom the Commission inaccurately designates as an eyewitness to the shooting, did not give an independent description of the killer's jacket; he wasn't asked for it by the lawyer who took his testimony. But when the gray zipper jacket was displayed *(CE 162),* Scoggins failed to identify it, saying, "I thought it was a little darker" *(3H 328);* he did not remember whether the killer's jacket had a zipper or buttons.

Barbara Jeanette Davis said, as mentioned already, that the suspect wore "a dark coat. . . . It was dark and to me it looked like it was maybe a wool fabric, it looked sort of rough. Like more of a sporting jacket." *(3H 347)* Shown the gray zipper jacket *(CE 162)* and asked if it was the one worn by Tippit's killer, Mrs. Davis said, "No." *(3H 347)*

William Arthur Smith, like Mrs. Davis, thought that the killer wore "a sport coat of some kind. . . . I can't really remember very well." Shown the gray zipper jacket *(CE 162),* Smith said, "Yes, sir; that looks like what he had on. A jacket." *(7H 85)*

The Commission paid no attention to the fact that two witnesses remembered a light gray zipper jacket as a sport coat or sport jacket, although for anyone to confuse the one with the other despite wide differences in style, fabric, and general appearance seems almost impossible.

Virginia Davis testified that the killer "had on a light-brown-tan jacket" *(6H 457)*, but no jacket was displayed to her for identification—not even the wrong one—perhaps because she nearly disoriented Mr. Belin by swinging like a pendulum between two versions of the time at which she first saw the killer.

Ted Callaway said that the man he saw wore "a light tannish gray windbreaker jacket"; when he was shown the gray zipper jacket *(CE 162)*, he said that it was the same *type* jacket but "actually, I thought it had a little more tan to it." *(3H 356)*

Sam Guinyard was the only witness who described the gray zipper jacket accurately and then identified it without qualification. Guinyard testified that the suspect "had on a pair of black britches and a brown shirt and a little sort of light-gray-looking jacket . . . and a white T-shirt"; when he was shown the gray jacket *(CE 162)*, he said, "That's the jacket." *(7H 401)*

The other seven witnesses either did not describe the gray zipper jacket accurately, or failed to identify it as the one worn by the suspect, or identified the wrong jacket. Because of the witnesses' wildly divergent and inconsistent testimony, the Commission was forced to acknowledge that "the eyewitnesses vary in their identification of the jacket." *(WR 175-176)* Mentioning some of the less glaring variations (but not of course the sport jackets, or the rough fabric, or the dark color described by some of the witnesses), the Commission salvages what it can and asserts that "there is no doubt, however . . . that the man who killed Tippit was wearing a light-colored jacket." *(WR 176)*

Needless to say, the Report does not call attention to the fact that the same group of witnesses failed to identify the brown long-sleeved shirt *(CE 150)* which Oswald supposedly was wearing under his jacket—not because they could not see the shirt but because they did not recognize it.

Three witnesses who were not present at the Tippit scene were also asked to identify the gray zipper jacket. *(CE 162)* Taxi-driver William Whaley identified it as the jacket Oswald was wearing in his taxi *before* visiting his furnished room and, according to the Commission, putting the jacket on. *(2H 260)* The Report considers that Whaley was mistaken, since, according to the Commission's reconstruction, Oswald was without any jacket during the taxi-ride. *(WR 163)*

Earlene Roberts, housekeeper at the rooming house, failed to identify the gray zipper jacket *(CE 162)* as the one Oswald wore when he left the premises a few minutes before the Tippit murder. Shown the jacket, Mrs. Roberts said, "I don't remember it," adding that Oswald's jacket was darker. *(6H 439)*

Finally, Wesley Frazier, who worked with Oswald and chauffeured him between Dallas and Irving on weekends, was unable to recognize the gray zipper jacket. *(2H 238)*

Turning to the discovery of the gray zipper jacket, we find again a wide gulf between the facts and the corresponding assertions in the Report. According to the Report:

Police Captain W. R. Westbrook . . . walked through the parking lot behind the service station and found a light-colored jacket lying under the rear of one of the cars. Westbrook identified Commission Exhibit No. 162 as the light-colored jacket which he discovered underneath the automobile.

(WR 175)

But Westbrook himself denied that he had discovered the jacket, as may be seen from his testimony.

Ball: Did you ever find some clothing?

Westbrook: Actually, I didn't find it—it was pointed out to me by either some officer that—that was while we were going over the scene in the close area where the shooting was concerned, someone pointed out a jacket to me that was lying under a car and I got the jacket and told the officer to take the license number.

Ball: Was that before you went to the scene of the Tippit shooting?

Westbrook: Yes, sir. . . . I got out of the car and walked through the parking lot.

Ball: What parking lot?

Westbrook: I don't know—it may have been a used car lot. . . .

Ball: Why did you get out of the car at that time?

Westbrook: Just more or less searching—just no particular reason—just searching the area— . . . Some officer, I feel sure it was an officer, I still can't be positive—pointed this jacket out to me. . . .

Ball: What was the name of the officer?

Westbrook: I couldn't tell you that, sir.   *(7H 115-117)*

No wonder Westbrook could not identify the policeman who pointed the jacket out to him—no wonder he was vague about the location of the parking lot, and at such a loss to explain why he had even left his car: according to the verbatim transcript of the police radio log, Westbrook set out to search for the jacket said to have been discarded by the suspect *about fifteen minutes after the jacket had already been found and reported.* The radio log contains the following entries, logged at about 1:25 p.m.

Caller	Conversation
279 (Unknown):	279 . . . 279 (Unknown)
Dispatcher:	279 (Unknown)
279 (Unknown):	We believe we've got that suspect on shooting this officer out here. Got his white jacket. Believe he dumped it on this parking lot behind this service station at 400 block East Jefferson, across from Dudley Hughes [funeral parlor], and he had a white jacket on. We believe this is it.
Dispatcher:	You do not have the suspect, is that correct?
279 (Unknown):	No, just the jacket laying on the ground.
	(About 1:39 p.m.)
550 (Capt. W. R. Westbrook):	We got a witness that saw him go up North Jefferson and he shed his jacket—let's check that vicinity, toward Tyler. *(CE 1974*, pp. 62-77)

Westbrook, then, was *not* present when the jacket was discovered by the mysterious "279 (Unknown)" and Westbrook cannot be used, as the Commission uses him, to authenticate the jacket or the circumstances in which it was found. The witness misrepresented the facts, and the Report then misrepresented his misrepresentation.

The Report does not mention another police officer, T. A. Hutson, who testified also that he witnessed the discovery of the jacket. Hutson said:

> . . . while we were searching the rear of the house in the 400 block of East Jefferson . . . a white jacket was picked up by another officer. I observed him as he picked it up, and it was stated that this is probably the suspect's jacket. . . .
> Belin: Do you know the name of the officer that found it?
> Hutson: No, sir; I don't know. (7H 30-33)

I am not prepared to consider Hutson's account sufficient to authenticate the jacket, since his testimony, like Westbrook's, has defects. In his written report to his superiors dated December 3, 1963, Hutson described his activities in connection with the Tippit murder but failed to mention anything about the discovery of a gray zipper jacket (which he termed white in his testimony) (CE 2003, pp. 89-90); Westbrook, in his similar report (CE 2003, pp. 102-103) also failed to mention the jacket. There is no report from any police officer who claims to have been present when the jacket was found or claims that he found it.

"No. 279 (Unknown)" obviously made no written report of the discovery which, the radio log indicates, was made by him. In an investigation that was merely adequate, it would have been elementary to establish the identity of No. 279, to take evidence from him, and to determine the chain of possession of the jacket from the moment it came under police custody. The Warren Commission did none of those things, although it is easy enough, simply by studying its own exhibits, to determine that No. 279 was J. T. Griffin of the second platoon, Traffic Division, Dallas Police. (Lawrence Exhibit 2, p. 2; Batchelor Exhibit 5002, p. 14)

The second platoon consists of 12 three-wheel motorcycle officers, including not only J. T. Griffin but also T. A. Hutson, who testified that he could not identify the officer who picked up the jacket. How could Hutson fail to recognize a fellow officer assigned to the same 12-man platoon, if Hutson was really present when the jacket was found?

If the Warren Commission had been interested in finding the truth, it should have conducted an inquiry to determine:

(a) the identity of No. 279, who was not recognized by his fellow officer Hutson or by Captain Westbrook;

(b) whether Westbrook was actually present when the jacket was found, despite the entries in the radio log, and if he was not present, why he lied, and in complicity with whom;

(c) why both Griffin (No. 279) and Hutson described a gray jacket as white, if it was in fact the gray jacket (CE 162) that Griffin found; and

(d) whether a gray zipper garment was really found near the Tippit scene, or any jacket—or whether evidence was fabricated to strengthen the case against Oswald.

If the gray zipper jacket *(CE 162)* is legitimate, it was in the hands of the police before Oswald was arrested. The police never confronted him with the jacket or gave him the opportunity to confirm or deny that it was his property. That singular omission becomes even stranger when we read that "Oswald complained of a line-up wherein he had not been granted a request to put on a jacket" like the other men in the line-up. *(WR 625)* If the police really had in their hands a gray zipper jacket which they believed to belong to Oswald and which they thought he had worn at the Tippit scene, why didn't they let him wear that jacket in the sight of witnesses for whose benefit Oswald was being displayed in the line-ups? Clearly it would have been to their own advantage and would have facilitated the identification of their suspect. Conversely, Oswald seemed not to realize that wearing a jacket might make it easier for the Tippit witnesses to identify him, although he had a fine appreciation of what was or was not incriminating, and complained loudly for a jacket to wear in the line-up.

When Captain Fritz interrogated Oswald about his visit to his rented room at one o'clock, Oswald stated that he had "changed both his shirt and trousers before going to the show." *(WR 604-605)* Fritz, with the gray zipper jacket (or a white jacket) presumably in his possession, did not even ask Oswald if he had put on any garment over his shirt. In short, both at the line-ups and the interrogations, the police acted as though there were no jacket, gray or white.

The claim that the gray zipper jacket was the property of Lee Harvey Oswald rests solely on the word of his wife. The Report says:

> This jacket belonged to Lee Harvey Oswald. Marina Oswald stated that her husband owned only two jackets, one blue and the other gray. The blue jacket was found in the Texas School Book Depository and was identified by Marina Oswald as her husband's. Marina Oswald also identified Commission Exhibit No. 162, the jacket found by Captain Westbrook, as her husband's second jacket.   *(WR 175)*

I have already shown that the jacket was not found by Westbrook; now, let us determine whether the whole of this passage from the Report is more reliable than one of its parts, which indisputably is false.

According to the list of items of evidence turned over to the FBI by the Dallas police on November 28, 1963, the gray zipper jacket bore a laundry tag with the number "B 9738." *(CE 2003,* p. 117) There is no indication of any attempt by the police or the FBI to trace the laundry tag, in accordance with what seems to be standard police procedure. An unsupported identification by Marina Oswald, who changed her testimony on other matters, is scarcely enough to establish ownership. Moreover, Marina Oswald told the FBI in an interview on April 1, 1964 that:

> . . . she cannot recall that Oswald ever sent either of these jackets to any laundry or cleaners anywhere. She said she can recall washing them herself. She advised to her knowledge Oswald possessed both of these jackets at Dallas on November 22, 1963.   *(CE 1843)*

The FBI, which might have traced the laundry tag as a matter of routine when it received the gray zipper jacket on November 28, 1963, heard from

Marina Oswald on the first of April that Oswald had never sent the jacket to any laundry or cleaners anywhere. How, then, did his jacket acquire a laundry tag? At this point, if not before, the FBI was obliged to trace the laundry tag and to determine whether Oswald, *or some other person,* had taken that jacket to be laundered or cleaned.

Why didn't the FBI trace that tag, and why didn't the Warren Commission ask the FBI to trace it? The reason seems obvious, for each serious probe into the so-called evidence against Oswald diminishes it, or destroys it outright.

The Revolver Ammunition

According to the Warren Report

The Report *(WR 559-560)* states that when Oswald was arrested, 6 live cartridges were found in the revolver—3 Western .38 Specials and 3 Remington-Peters .38 Specials. Five live cartridges were found in his pocket, all Western .38s. Four expended cartridge cases were found near the Tippit scene—2 Western .38s and 2 Remington-Peters .38s. Four bullets were recovered from Tippit's body—3 Western-Winchesters and 1 Remington-Peters.

The Report offers several possible explanations for the discrepancy between the shells (2 Westerns and 2 Remington-Peters) and the corresponding bullets (3 Westerns and 1 Remington-Peters):

(a) The killer fired 5 bullets—3 Westerns and 2 Remington-Peters; 1 Remington-Peters bullet missed Tippit; that bullet and one Western cartridge case were "simply not found."
(b) The killer fired only 4 bullets—3 Westerns and 1 Remington-Peters—but prior to shooting Tippit he had an expended Remington-Peters shell in the revolver which was ejected with the other 4 shells, including a Western shell which "was not found."
(c) That he used hand-loaded bullets to save money; this is extremely unlikely because there is no evidence that the 4 recovered shells have been resized.

Appraisal

In one respect, the ammunition for the revolver presents the same kind of problem as that presented by the ammunition for the rifle. Although two different brands of .38 Specials are found (11 Westerns and 4 Remington-Peters bullets, live or expended, and 2 shells of each brand), no bullets of either kind were found in Oswald's room in Dallas or in the Paine home at Irving. Presumably at some point in time Oswald purchased at least one box of Western .38s and one box of Remington-Peters .38s. His purchase of such ammunition has not, however, been established. Again we are presented with the paradox that Oswald must have exhausted his supply of both brands of ammunition except for 11 bullets of one brand and 4 of the other at the time of the Tippit killing.

How could he have used up most of two boxes of ammunition? There is nothing whatever to suggest that he ever fired the .38 Smith & Wesson revolver at any time before November 22. If he did *not* purchase two boxes of ammunition, how did he acquire the 11 Western and the 4 Remington-Peters .38s? If he *did* purchase supplies of each brand, there is no evidence of the transaction, no evidence of use, and no left-over ammunition among his possessions.

The Warren Commission has offered no answers to these questions in attempting to explain why the bullets recovered from Tippit's body failed to match the corresponding shells. Explanation (c) is a mere space-filler. The Commission had ruled out hand-loading long before, on the basis of the cost and bulk of the required equipment. Explanation (b) fails to present the slightest evidence that Oswald had ever fired a Remington-Peters bullet, leaving the shell in the gun, and is on the same level of probability as hand-loading. Explanation (a) requires the killer to fire five shots at point-blank range and miss one—inconsistent with the marksmanship of the sniper who hit Kennedy and Connally under vastly more difficult circumstances. Moreover, (a) ignores the fact that most of the Tippit witnesses heard only two to four shots. Even if one shot had missed, it is difficult to believe a claim that it went unnoticed and that the shell remained undiscovered.

The Commission's "explanations" explain nothing. The problem of reconciling 2 Brand A and 2 Brand B shells with 3 Brand A and 1 Brand B bullets awaits a serious and credible solution.

A related puzzle which the Commission has not acknowledged is the arresting fact that Captain Glen King—in an address in April 1964 to the American Society of Newspaper Editors—said that Tippit had been shot *three* times. (*King Exhibit No. 5*, Vol. XX, p. 465) It is surely strange that a senior police official should have made such an error six months after the murder, if error it was. We cannot be certain because the autopsy report on Tippit is not to be found in the 26 volumes of Hearings and Exhibits—a strange and unexplained omission.

To compound the puzzle, there is the peculiar manner in which three of the four bullets allegedly recovered from Tippit's body were presented to the FBI laboratory for examination *four months* after the murder. According to the testimony of FBI Expert Cunningham *(3H 474)*, the FBI originally received only one bullet, on November 23, 1963. The Dallas police said it was the only bullet recovered or obtained. The matter rested there until March 1964, when the Warren Commission (to its credit) asked the FBI to determine where the other three bullets were. They were discovered in the dead files of the Dallas Police!

It was only at that stage that the mismatching of bullets and shells became apparent, presumably too late to undertake a search for a missing bullet or a missing shell under explanation (a). The Report does not even mention the belated debut of the three bullets ostensibly recovered from Tippit's body, perhaps in order to spare us uneasiness about their authenticity.

But misgivings are unavoidable when one is confronted by an alleged assassin who shot the President when he was down to his last four rifle bullets, and the police officer when he was down to his last 15 revolver bullets out of a supply of two boxes. Misgivings are inevitable when bullets fail to match their shells and only contrived and irresponsible "explanations" are suggested. The Warren Commission, despite the unparalleled investigatory resources at its disposal, has left the case cluttered with mysteries like this—neither acknowledging their existence nor offering acceptable explanations.

These lacunae undermine the Commission's conclusions about the Tippit murder and, in turn, about Oswald's role during the fateful weekend of the assassination.

Chapter 14
General Walker

The Warren Commission concluded that Oswald made a "prior attempt to kill" General Edwin A. Walker. This conclusion is based primarily on (1) an undated note written by Oswald; (2) the testimony of firearms experts; and (3) the testimony of Marina Oswald. *(WR 183-187)*

The Walker incident is familiar from press stories after the assassination. On the night of April 10, 1963, as Walker sat in his study, an unknown assailant fired one shot from a rifle, missing him narrowly. Two nights before, two men had been observed lurking about the Walker house and had fled in an unmarked car. This had been reported to the Dallas police before the shot at Walker on April 10. When the shot was heard, a young neighbor saw two men leave the scene in cars. The bullet was recovered by the Dallas police. An Associated Press story in *The New York Times* on April 12, 1963 said that the bullet was a 30.06.[1]

Walker engaged private detectives to investigate a former employee whom he suspected of having tried to shoot him. The results of that investigation were inconclusive. The crime remained unsolved on the books of the Dallas Police until December 1963, when it was leaked to the press that Oswald had shot at General Walker and missed, using the same Carcano rifle as the one used in the assassination. Headlining this startling news, the press ignored the facts that the recovered bullet had been identified as a 30.06 and not a 6.5 and that two men, using a car or cars, had been observed under suspicious circumstances at the Walker residence before and after the shooting.

The first known suggestion of a possible link between Oswald and the attack on Walker came on the night of Oswald's arrest, when a reporter asked Police

---

1 "Walker Escapes Assassin's Bullet," *The New York Times,* April 12, 1963, p. 12, cols. 2-3.

Chief Curry if Oswald was implicated in that shooting. Curry replied that he did not know. *(CE 2146)*

The following morning, November 23, 1963, General Walker had a transatlantic telephone conversation with a representative of a right-wing West German newspaper. *(11H 425)* About three days later the November 29 issue of that paper went to press with a sensational story alleging that Oswald and Ruby were known by the Dallas police to have made the attack on Walker but that they had not been arrested on request of the Department of Justice. Substantially the same lurid story was published in the United States in May 1964 in the *National Enquirer. (CE 837)*

A week after the West German newspaper went to press in Munich, an undated letter handwritten in Russian was discovered in a book sent to Marina Oswald by Ruth Paine. When she was confronted with the letter on December 3, 1963, Marina informed the Secret Service that Oswald had written the letter before his attempt to shoot General Walker. She said that she had had no knowledge whatever that Oswald intended to commit this crime. When he left their apartment on the night of the Walker incident she had assumed that he was going to a typing class. She became worried when he did not return at the usual hour; she then discovered the undated note. When he returned late that night she demanded an explanation of the note; he then confessed that he had tried to kill Walker.

The Undated Note

Discovery of the Note Ruth Paine testified at great length on March 20 and 21, 1964. As Counsel Jenner was about to conclude his interrogation, Mrs. Paine reminded him,

> *Mrs. Paine:* . . . you have not yet asked me if I had seen anything of a note purported to be written by Lee at the time of the attempt on Walker. And I might just recount for you that, if it is of any importance.
>
> *Jenner:* Yes; I wish you would. . . . Tell me all you know about it. . . .
>
> *Mrs. Paine:* I knew absolutely nothing about it up to and including November 22. . . . I was shown a portion of a note by two Secret Service men . . . perhaps a week later. I had sent Marina one of these small collections of letters . . . notes to her and donations, and left such with the Irving police. And on one occasion left also a couple of books which were hers. . . .
>
> I believe it was probably the next day I got a call from the Secret Service saying something important had come up in this case, could they come out and see me. . . . They arrived. . . . Mr. Gopadze showed me a piece of paper with writing on it, a small piece of paper such as might have come from a telephone notepad.
>
> He asked me not to read it through carefully, but simply to look at it enough to tell whether I could identify the handwriting and whether I had ever seen it before. I said I could not identify the handwriting. . . . Mr. Gopadze indicated that it was his impression that I had sent this note to Marina. And this

surprised me. . . . It astounded me. . . . We went on for some time with Mr.
Gopadze—this in Russian—saying that "Mrs. Paine, it would be well for
you to be absolutely frank and tell us exactly what happened" and my saying
in turn . . . "I am. What more can I do than what I have said." And finally
we went over to English . . . and he volunteered this note had been in a book.
Then I realized what must have happened is that I did send Marina Oswald
a book and described my having sent this to the Irving police and the Secret
Service. And that seemed to clear up the mystery for all of us. And they
left.   *(9H 393-394)*

Mr. Jenner, who had been assigned general responsibility for the investigation of possible conspiracy,[2] proceeded to a different subject. Apparently the
mystery, if any, was cleared up for him also. He paid no attention to testimony
which Ruth Paine had given on the previous day, when she had described the
events of Saturday, November 23, 1963.

Mrs. Paine: . . . In the afternoon I was the only one there and I felt I had
better get some grocery shopping done. . . . I was just preparing to go to the
grocery store when several officers arrived again from the Dallas Police
Office and asked if they could search.

This time I was in the yard, the front yard on the grass, and [they] asked
if they could search and held up their warrant and I said, yes, they could
search. They said they were looking for something specific and I said, "I
want to go to the grocery store, I'll just go and you go ahead and do your
searching."

I then went to the grocery store and when I came back they had finished and
left, locking my door which necessitated my getting out my key, I don't
normally lock my door when I go shopping.   *(3H 85)*

Ford: While you were shopping and after the officers had come with a
warrant, they went in the house, no one was in the house?

Mrs. Paine: For a portion of the time they were looking, no one was in the
house.

Ford: They were there alone?

Mrs. Paine: That is right.

McCloy: Did they indicate—were they still there when you got back?

Mrs. Paine: No; they were not. Remember the door was locked.

McCloy: Yes; the door was locked, that is what I gather. Do you know what
they took on this occasion, or did they tell you what they were coming for?

Mrs. Paine: No; I do not. Before I left they were leafing through books to
see if anything fell out but that is all I saw.

McCloy: All right.   *(3H 86-87)*

Is it, indeed, "all right"? The Dallas police came there looking "for something specific" and were seen "leafing through books to see if anything fell out."
If that undated note was actually hidden in a book which Mrs. Paine later sent
to Marina Oswald, they did not find it. That in itself should have alerted Jenner
and caused a more searching inquiry into the discovery of the note ten days
later—not by the Irving police, to whom Ruth Paine had delivered the book to

---

2 Albert E. Jenner, Jr., "Your Right to Say It," WNYC-TV, December 23, 1966.

be delivered in turn to Marina Oswald, but by an unnamed Secret Service agent. (*CE 1403*, pp. 718-719) The Warren Commission made no attempt to determine the identity of that agent and the exact circumstances under which he found the note; nor did the Commission take the elementary step of asking the Dallas police officers what specific evidence they were seeking at the Paine house, why they were leafing through books to see if anything fell out, and how they had overlooked the undated note which ostensibly was then hidden in one of those books. The officers who conducted the search were John Adamcik, Henry Moore, Guy Rose, and Richard Stovall. Each of them gave testimony on April 3 or April 8, 1964 *(7H   186-195, 202-211, 212-217, and 227-232),* but not one of them was asked questions on these points.

It is impossible to tell from this vantage point whether Jenner and his colleagues Ball and Belin (who took depositions from the four Dallas police officers) failed to appreciate the implications of Ruth Paine's testimony or just what it was that caused them to omit the questions that should have been asked. The Commission accepts as authentic the account of the discovery of the undated note without having inquired into the strange circumstances related by Ruth Paine, in the same way that it has ignored other anomalies, discussed next.

Contents of the Note   I share the view that the note "appeared to be the work of a man expecting to be killed, or imprisoned, or to disappear." *(WR 184)* But the contents are not entirely consistent with Marina Oswald's story that the note was written on the occasion of an attempt by Oswald to murder General Walker.

The note reads:

1. This is the key to the mailbox which is located in the main post office in the city on Ervay Street. This is the same street where the drugstore, in which you always waited is located. You will find the mailbox in the post office which is located 4 blocks from the drugstore on that street. I paid for the box last month so don't worry about it.

2. Send the information as to what has happened to me to the Embassy and include newspaper clippings (should there be anything about me in the newspapers). I believe that the Embassy will come quickly to your assistance on learning everything.

3. I paid the house rent on the 2d so don't worry about it.

4. Recently I also paid for water and gas.

5. The money from work will possibly be coming. The money will be sent to our post office box. Go to the bank and cash the check.

6. You can either throw out or give my clothing, etc. away. Do not keep these. However, I prefer that you hold on to my personal papers (military, civil, etc.).

7. Certain of my documents are in the small blue valise.

8. The address book can be found on my table in the study should need same.

9. We have friends here. The Red Cross also will help you. (Red Cross in English). [*sic*]

10. I left you as much money as I could, $60 on the second of the month. You and the baby [apparently] can live for another 2 months using $10 per week.

11. If I am alive and taken prisoner, the city jail is located at the end of the bridge through which we always passed on going to the city (right in the beginning of the city after crossing the bridge).   *(CE 1)*

The second paragraph of the undated note is particularly interesting, because it suggests clearly that Oswald assumed that Marina Oswald would know what happened to him even if there were no newspaper stories in which he was named. This suggests that Marina Oswald was not, as she claims, ignorant of what it was that Oswald intended to do when he wrote the letter of instructions. The paragraph as worded indicates also that Oswald foresaw that the action he was about to take might *or might not* result in newspaper publicity. That, too, appears to be somewhat inconsistent with an attempt to shoot General Walker. There was every reason to believe that such an attempt, whether or not it succeeded, would produce headlines in Dallas and publicity nationwide—as was the case in reality—since General Walker was newsworthy, if not notorious, in the national political and civil rights arena. In any event, newspaper stories reporting an attempt on Walker's life by an unknown sniper would have left Marina Oswald in the dark—unless she knew in advance that Oswald planned to commit the crime.

Finally, this paragraph suggests that Oswald assumed that "the Embassy" (undoubtedly the Soviet Embassy, with which he and Marina Oswald were in regular communication) would come quickly to Marina Oswald's rescue "on learning everything." If he wrote that planning to shoot General Walker, he was naïve. It is unlikely that the Soviet Embassy would willingly become involved in what it would regard officially as the murder of one private individual by another, knowing very well the political implications and risks which might flow from giving aid and comfort to Oswald or his wife. Oswald was sophisticated enough to expect that the Soviet Embassy would be at pains to disassociate itself from the whole affair.

I suggest that Oswald wrote the undated letter in relation to a project other than an attack on General Walker—one that also involved risk of arrest or death—and that Marina Oswald was informed about her husband's plans in advance. The key lies in the clear meaning of Oswald's letter—that he intended to disappear and perhaps disappear out of the country, if he did escape arrest or death. Yet if he shot at Walker and escaped, he was not likely to come under suspicion (indeed, he did not, in the wake of the Walker shooting) and he had no need to go into hiding. He had no hideout in which to take refuge; no passport with which to go abroad; and little or no money. For these reasons, the undated note seems inconsistent with the alleged attempt on General Walker's life as Marina Oswald described it.

The Commission has failed to recognize that part of the undated letter is irreconcilable with Marina Oswald's story. She seems to have convinced a willing audience.

Marina's Testimony

Marina Oswald revealed for the first time during an FBI interview on December 3, 1963 that Oswald had taken a shot at General Walker—about a week after the Munich newspaper had gone to press with a similar story. According to the Warren Report, the newspaper story was "fabricated by an editor of the newspaper" and was a work of pure fiction. *(WR 662)*

Was it only a coincidence that within a week that fabrication proved to be true, at least in part? Or is it possible that existing channels of communication were used both to plant a story in a Munich newspaper and to inspire Marina Oswald's explanation?

The Commission has taken no notice of the peculiar sequence of "revelations" from seemingly unconnected sources.

The Walker Bullet

The *Dallas Morning News* of April 11, 1963 carried a page-one story by Eddie Hughes stating that the bullet that crashed through the rear window and into the wall of the Walker house was "identified as a 30.06," and citing other police findings on the authority of Detective Ira Van Cleave.[3] The April 12 issue carried the same statement[4] as did *The New York Times* of the same date.[5]

However, the Warren Report and the Hearings and Exhibits contain no reference to those press reports or to the contemporaneous identification of the Walker bullet. Surely the Commission and its investigating agencies should have been professional enough to check the original newspaper stories about the Walker shooting and ought to have been aware that the bullet was described as a 30.06 by the Dallas police. The more so when Mrs. Katherine Ford, a close friend of Marina Oswald in the months after the assassination, testified on March 13, 1964, that:

> Marina was saying that Lee had laughed about the attempt to kill General Walker, that he said that they were even too stupid to find out what gun was used to kill him because it was written up a different type of gun was used other than the one really used by Lee. . . . Lee had commented on that they were not even smart enough to identify the gun by a bullet. . . . I think right after that it was in the papers that a different type of gun was used, and to shoot the President was different again, there were supposedly two guns, you see, so maybe that is why he [McKenzie, Marina Oswald's lawyer] advised her [to say] that he had only one gun.   *(2H 322)*

It does not require great imagination to wonder if the lawyer did not also prompt Marina Oswald to "remember" and repeat to a witness to be called before the Commission a story that appears to explain the discrepancy between a 30.06 bullet and a 6.5 rifle. Even if the Commission chose to believe that the police were "too stupid" to identify the bullet correctly, it was a duty to at least report the original 30.06 identification and to explain why they had nevertheless con-

---

3   *Dallas Morning News,* April 11, 1963, p. 1.
4   *Ibid.,* April 12, 1963, p. 5.
5   *The New York Times,* April 12, 1963, p. 12, cols. 2-3.

cluded that the bullet actually came from the Carcano. The omission of historical fact in 1964 is not far, in chronological or moral terms, from the transgres-
sions of the society George Orwell has warned us about in *1984*.

Walker's Telephone Number

The Report devotes pages 183 to 187 to the Walker affair. It is not until page
663, however, that we learn that Oswald's notebook contained not only notations relating to FBI Agent Hosty but also General Walker's name and telephone
number. This curious fact emerges because the Commission deals with the
speculation that Oswald and Walker may have had some hidden relationship,
suggested by the notation in Oswald's notebook.

The Commission nevertheless finds that "there was no evidence that the two
knew each other" and that Oswald probably made the notations when he was
planning to shoot Walker. General Walker, the Commission points out, testified
that he never heard of Oswald before November 22.

But General Walker was not told that his name and number were found in
Oswald's notebook, or asked to comment on that specific circumstance, when
he gave his testimony. If he did know Oswald, Walker would not necessarily
have had an irresistible desire to admit it. On the other hand, he or his aides
might have been able to suggest a reason for the notations in Oswald's notebook
had they been asked to do so. They were not asked.

The Dog Next Door

Robert Surrey, General Walker's aide, testified before the Warren Commission
on June 9, 1964 about various matters, including the shot fired at the General on
the night of April 10. Surrey was asked about a house next to Walker's, owned
by Dr. Ruth Jackson.

> *Jenner:* Does she have a dog that is sometimes obstreperous, does a lot of
> barking?
> *Surrey:* Yes; she does. . . . Anyone approaching the house, generally her
> house or General Walker's house, would be barked at, in the middle of the
> night noises.
> *Jenner:* And you have approached General Walker's house, I assume, at
> night, have you?
> *Surrey:* Yes.
> *Jenner:* If the dog is out in Dr. Jackson's yard, the dog is alerted and barks?
> *Surrey:* Not so much any more. Evidently he knows who I am now.
> *Jenner:* I see. But before the dog became familiar with you, he did bark?

Surrey: Yes, sir. . . .

Jenner: Do you recall whether or not at or about the time of the attempt on General Walker's life that dog became or was ill?

Surrey: Yes; it was. This was reported to me. I do not know of firsthand knowledge.

Jenner: I would prefer not to have your hearsay. You have no knowledge firsthand, however?

Surrey: No; I do not.

Jenner: Unless, Mr. Chairman, you desire to pursue the hearsay—

The Chairman (Justice Warren): No, no.   (5H 433)

Those who are not surprised by this sudden legalistic scrupulousness might take the time to count up instances in which hearsay evidence was warmly welcomed, if not solicited, during the examination of witnesses. The exercise certainly strengthens the impression that the Warren Commisson shied away from pursuing relevant and even crucial information offered on a platter, with a lack of curiosity that would be startling in a trainee, to say nothing of an illustrious group of fact-finders. Despite the unwillingness of the Commission to receive more information about the infirmity of the dog next door, some details emerge from an FBI report of June 10, 1964, of an interview with the dog's owner, Mrs. Ross Bouve. According to the FBI report,

> She advised her dog "Toby" became very sick on April 11 and 12, 1963. She stated she was of the opinion someone had given him something to quiet him or drug him or poison him, because he did become sick and vomited extensively on April 11 and 12, 1963. . . . She based her belief that the dog had been given something because of the shooting incident and the dog's habit of barking at anyone or anything in the alley area. . . . This was only opinion on her part.   (*CE 1953*, p. 22)

Did Oswald poison Toby, in addition to his other crimes, or is it more likely that someone familiar with the Walker household and its environs silenced the dog? Or was it only another in the devastating series of "coincidences" that plague the Oswald case to a degree that is increasingly unnatural? Unnatural, not for their numbers alone, but for the persistence with which these "coincidences" seem to point away from Oswald and toward some unknown agent or agents of the crimes with which he is charged, and for the regularity with which they are dismissed and discounted by the Warren Commission.

The Boy Next Door

Walter Kirk Coleman, a teen-aged boy who lives next door to General Walker, saw two men leave the scene by car after the shot was fired. He was not asked to testify before the Warren Commission. (*CE 2958, 3114*) General Walker testified that his own attempts to question the boy had been frustrated because the boy had been silenced. He had been told not to talk, by unspecified officials who investigated the Walker affair. (*11H 416-417*)

The Warren Commission heard of Walker's charge that the boy had been told not to talk. There is no indication that the Commission paid the slightest attention or took any step to find out why Coleman had been given such instructions or what he had to say.

There the matter rests.

Marina Tidies Up

Mrs. Katherine Ford testified before the Warren Commission (as already mentioned) on March 13, 1963. She was questioned about her knowledge of the Walker incident, and said:

> *Mrs. Ford:* . . . the only thing I remember about Marina was saying that Lee had laughed about the attempt to kill General Walker, that he said that they were even too stupid to find out what gun was used to kill him because it was written up a different type of gun was used other than the one really used by Lee.
> *Representative Ford:* Marina said that?
> *Mrs. Ford:* That is right. Lee had commented on that they were not even smart enough to identify the gun by a bullet.   *(2H 322)*

This is a doubly interesting revelation. First, it demonstrates that the bullet was indeed identified at the time of the Walker shooting as something other than one that could have come from the 6.5 Carcano, and thus, if the Commission did not know that already, there was no excuse for failing to establish the facts after hearing Mrs. Ford. The Commission nevertheless asserts that the Walker bullet was too mangled to be identified when it was recovered and in effect pretends that it was not identified to the press as coming from a 30.06 rifle.

The other interesting aspect of Mrs. Ford's testimony is that Marina made these remarks some time after she first revealed that Oswald was implicated in the Walker shooting, as though to dispose of the very criticism and skepticism generated by the original identification of the bullet. The other weaknesses in Marina's story and in her fanciful account of Oswald's alleged plan to shoot Richard Nixon—although he did not enter Nixon's telephone number in his notebook and this even the Warren Commission did not accept—certainly justify such an interpretation of Marina's remarks to Mrs. Ford.

Offering more fascinating information to the Commission, Mrs. Ford described a meeting which she and Marina attended in the office of Mr. William McKenzie, Marina's attorney at one period.

> *Representative Ford:* This meeting with Mr. McKenzie, when Marina and you were discussing matters—
> *Mrs. Ford:* That was about General Walker. . . . He advised her "They will ask you if there were two guns, you tell them there was one gun that was used," he told her.

Representative Ford: One gun used where?

Mrs. Ford: For Walker, I mean the same one they had at the house. . . .
(2H 321)

Mrs. Ford's husband, Declan Ford, confirmed the incident in his testimony before the Commission, also on March 13, 1964.

Liebeler: Do you remember anything else about the Walker incident that you and your wife may have talked about?

Ford: Yes; we have discussed it some after, I believe, Marina came to stay with us, and I expressed the doubt that Lee Oswald was the one who took a shot at Walker.

Liebeler: Did you have any basis for expressing that doubt?

Ford: The only basis for it was that there was a story in one of the newspapers that they could not identify the bullet taken out of the wood in Walker's home as having come from a gun that Lee Oswald owned. . . .

Liebeler: Mr. Ford, were you at any time present in Mr. McKenzie's office, William McKenzie, when there was a discussion with Marina Oswald concerning guns and the gun that was used to or presumably used to attack Walker and the gun that was subsequently presumably used to attack the President? . . . Did you hear McKenzie at any time advise Marina if she were asked about these guns she should say there was only one gun?

Ford: I think I did hear him say that once or something to that effect. . . . But I don't think it was any discussion about the gun used in shooting General Walker. . . . As nearly as I can remember it, the whole discussion was, he was telling her, he had asked her if there was anything else but this one rifle and she said no, and he said, "Be sure you always say that there was just this one gun," but I thought he was referring to the gun used only in the case of the assassination. . . . I just had the impression they were talking about the possibility that more than one gun was used in the assassination. . . .
(2H 332, 336-337)

This hearsay evidence was not interrupted or refused by Chairman Warren, but, having heard the account given by Declan Ford and his wife, the Commission did not follow up the matter with Marina Oswald in any of her subsequent appearances.

Appraisal

The evidence suggests that two men committed the attack on Walker using a 30.06 rifle; that Marina Oswald was encouraged to improvise the story that Oswald had tried to shoot Walker so as to increase the credibility of his guilt in the assassination and to conceal the actual circumstances in which the undated note was written as well as her own foreknowledge of Oswald's unknown plans at that time; and that the Warren Commission disregarded numerous indications that Oswald was not responsible for the attack on Walker, concluding that he was guilty without adequate investigation or critical evaluation of the evidence.

Chapter 15
Betty MacDonald: Another Prisoner Lost

Warren Reynolds, a witness in the Tippit shooting *(WR 169, 175, 652)* was ignored by all the police agencies until he was interviewed by the FBI on January 21, 1964, two months after the assassination *(11H 435)*. At that time he was shown photographs of Oswald but failed to make a positive identification, although he believed there was a resemblance to the man he had seen leaving the scene of the Tippit murder. *(CE 2523)*

Two days later, on January 23, 1964, Warren Reynolds himself was shot in the head by an unknown assailant. Although FBI agents had interviewed Reynolds only two days before he was shot, the FBI took no notice of the attempted murder of the witness and did not initiate any inquiry into the new crime. The Dallas police, by the same token, did not notify the FBI of the shooting of Reynolds or seek FBI cooperation in the investigation of the shooting. Neither the FBI nor the Dallas police called the attention of the Warren Commission to the attack on Reynolds.

On February 5, 1964, a former strip-tease dancer named Betty Mooney MacDonald (also known as Nancy Mooney) provided an alibi for Darrell Wayne Garner, a suspect in the attempted murder of Reynolds. Garner was released by the Dallas police on the strength of her statement and the polygraph test to which she submitted. On the same day, Betty MacDonald told Detective Ramsey of the Dallas Police that she had worked as a stripper at Jack Ruby's club when she was very young. *(CE 2589)*

On February 13, 1964, Betty MacDonald was arrested for breach of the peace after an altercation with her roommate, Patsy Swope Moore. After being placed in a cell at the Dallas City Jail, she hanged herself "with her toreador trousers, causing death by asphyxiation." *(WR 663; CE 2589)* At this time the FBI was actively investigating the assassination and the murders of Tippit and Oswald, on the scene at Dallas and elsewhere. The suicide of Betty MacDonald, less than a month after the shooting of Reynolds, still aroused no interest on the part of the FBI. The Dallas police even now did not inform the FBI or the Warren Commission of the Reynolds or MacDonald cases.

The police obtained an affidavit dated February 13, 1964 from an acquaintance of Betty MacDonald's named William Grady Goode. Goode attested that he had known the victim for about six weeks and that she had attempted suicide twice during that time—once by turning on the gas in her apartment at 319 North Windmere and once by cutting her wrists. The police also learned from Patsy Swope Moore, who "had shared Apt. 4 at 5400 Live Oak" with Betty MacDonald, that she had known Betty for about six weeks; that Betty had advised her that she had four children who had been taken away from her, "causing her to be very despondent at times"; and that Betty had stated that "she had been a former strip-tease girl working at various bars . . . but the only one Patsy can specifically recall is Jack Ruby's Carousel Club." The police thereafter interviewed George Senator, but he failed to identify Betty MacDonald as a former employee of the Carousel Club. *(CE 2589)*

Writing in the *New York Journal-American* on February 23, 1964, Bob Considine broke the story of the attempted murder of Reynolds and the suicide of Betty MacDonald, hinting clearly that these new episodes of violence in Dallas might be connected to the assassination and the Oswald case. *(CE 342)* This publicity prompted neither the FBI nor the Warren Commission into action; each continued to ignore the shooting of Reynolds and the suicide of Betty MacDonald as if those events could have no possible connection with the assassination.

When Mark Lane testified before the Commission on March 3, 1964, he called attention to the Considine story and said:

> I would request the Commission to investigate into these series of most unusual coincidences, to see if they have any bearing upon the basic matter pending before the Commission. *(2H 38)*

The next known development was an FBI interview on March 17, 1964 with Captain Jones of the Dallas Police, who had been in charge of the Reynolds and MacDonald cases as well as the attempt earlier on the life of General Walker. The FBI transmitted to the Warren Commission the information obtained from Captain Jones in a report dated March 23, 1964 *(CE 2589)*, but the FBI did not undertake on its own initiative, nor did the Warren Commission request, any independent investigation of the shooting or the suicide. The uncorroborated Dallas Police version of the attempted murder of Reynolds and the death of a prisoner by hanging, while in police custody, was accepted without a murmur.

The Commission did make a halfhearted inquiry to determine whether or not Betty MacDonald had worked at Ruby's Carousel Club. Andrew Armstrong, general factotum at the Carousel Club, was questioned by counsel for the

Warren Commission on April 14, 1964, but did not remember a stripper named Betty MacDonald or Nancy Mooney; he did recall a "Nancy" who had worked at the Club for a few nights or a few weeks, but he could not remember her second name. *(13H 351-352)*

After Warren Reynolds recovered from the bullet wound in his head, he testified on July 22, 1964 that he believed there was a sinister link between the attempt on his life and the fact that he had been a witness against Oswald. Persistent attempts by counsel to persuade him that there could not have been any connection were not entirely successful; however, Reynolds did agree that the suicide of Betty MacDonald was only a coincidence.

> *Liebeler:* Did the police department tell you that she had worked for Jack Ruby?
> *Reynolds:* No. . . .
> *Liebeler:* . . . Did you ever hear that she tried to commit suicide prior to the time she hung herself in the Dallas Police Station? . . . Or that she had four children that had been taken away from her because of her conduct? . . . Considine was trying to create an impression that some girl had worked for Jack Ruby and was connected with Garner, and hung herself in the police department?
> *Reynolds:* Yes. *(11H 440)*

Anyone who wishes to read the full testimony given by Reynolds will find an abundance of leading questions, designed not so much to elicit information as to convince the witness that neither the attack on him nor the grotesque suicide had any connection with the assassination: they were only random coincidence. This kind of "questioning" would never have been permitted in a courtroom, of course, and there seems to be no reason to condone such improprieties in the conduct of the Commission's investigation. Since improprieties have been mentioned, it might be added that when Reynolds testified on July 22, 1964—exactly eight months to the day after the Tippit shooting—he was again shown photographs of Oswald. This time Reynolds identified him as the man he had seen leaving the Tippit scene. *(11H 435-437)* The inadmissibility of such an identification need not be belabored.

The Warren Report was made public at the end of September 1964. In two paragraphs it dismissed, in effect, speculation that there was a connection between the Reynolds shooting and the assassination, and explicitly denied that there was any link between Betty MacDonald and Jack Ruby:

> Investigation revealed no evidence that she had ever worked at the Carousel Club. Employees of the club had no recollection that she had ever worked there. *(WR 663)*

This is the chronology of events in the Reynolds/MacDonald affair. I shall now analyze and evaluate the known facts and determine whether or not the investigation justifies the conclusions stated by the Warren Commission or satisfies the demands posed by an incredible sequence of misadventures.

One is struck immediately by the incomprehensible failure of the Dallas police and the FBI to suspect or investigate a possible connection between the

Reynolds and MacDonald incidents and the earlier crimes which were under investigation; one is impressed equally by the passivity of the Warren Commission, its inaction until publicity and a frontal assault by Mark Lane forced the issue, and its strange complacency later. I question the indifference to occurrences which should have aroused suspicion, and I question the assumption at all stages that the new episodes of violence had no connection with the assassination.

Next it must be pointed out that the Warren Commission accepted without question the information in the FBI report of March 23, 1964 *(CE 2589)*, even though the FBI did not query Captain Jones of the Dallas Police about the circumstances of Betty MacDonald's suicide. When Captain Jones gave testimony for the Warren Commission on March 24, 1964 (after the preparation of the FBI report), he was not asked one question about Reynolds or MacDonald (or about the attack on General Walker, for that matter).

The Commission was convinced on the strength of information obtained by the FBI from the Dallas police that Betty MacDonald had a history of suicide attempts which cleared her actual self-destruction of other implications. This much seems apparent from the questions put to Reynolds by counsel. But the only evidence for this assumption is the affidavit from William Grady Goode, and although both he and the roommate, Patsy Swope Moore, had been acquainted with Betty MacDonald for about six weeks, the alleged suicide attempts seemed to be unknown to Patsy Moore, who referred only to periods of despondency but not to suicide attempts. She and Goode gave different addresses for Betty MacDonald even though both had known her for the same length and period of time. Even if the suicide attempts had occurred before the two girls decided to share the same apartment, Patsy Moore should still have known about them because she and Betty MacDonald also worked at the same place, Mickey's Bar. *(CE 2589)* Betty MacDonald would have great difficulty concealing the slashing of her wrists from a person with whom she lived and worked. Under these circumstances, Miss Moore's mention only of despondency but no suicide attempts raises the question of whether they actually took place. If they did not, is it as easy to assume that Betty MacDonald really hanged herself in the Dallas jail in a sudden wave of despair at her arrest or at separation from her children?

According to the FBI report, Betty MacDonald was arrested at 2:45 a.m. on February 13, 1964, after a quarrel with Patsy Swope Moore, her roommate. Why was Betty MacDonald arrested and not Patsy Moore as well? None of the persons who might have clarified these questions (Patsy Moore, William Goode, and Detective Ramsey, among others) were called as witnesses by the Commission. Those who did appear and might have provided valuable information (Captain Jones, for example) were not asked any questions on these matters.

If the circumstances of Betty MacDonald's death remain unclear, the allegation that she was linked with Jack Ruby assumes greater significance. Are there sufficient grounds for concluding that such a link did not exist? Andrew Armstrong and George Senator said that they did not know of her or remember her as a former employee of the Carousel Club. This is not an adequate basis for the conclusion that Betty MacDonald had not worked there, even though she told a Dallas police officer and her roommate that she had. The Commission had a duty to go beyond the formality of questions to Armstrong and Senator by checking records—the payroll of the Carousel Club, social security records, and the records of AGVA (American Guild of Variety Artists). Entertainers at Ruby's Club were obliged to be members of AGVA and to pay dues. Numerous disputes between Ruby and his entertainers had been brought to AGVA by Ruby or the other party involved. This is clear from the testimony on July 24, 1964 of AGVA branch manager Thomas Palmer, who was questioned extensively about his dealings with Ruby and Ruby's employees. He was obviously familiar with the affairs of the Carousel Club, yet he was not asked one question about Betty MacDonald or Nancy Mooney, whose name would have appeared in AGVA records because she had been a stripper in various Dallas night clubs, whether or not she had danced at the Carousel Club or any other Ruby establishment. A reading of his testimony *(15H 206-218)* makes it all the more incomprehensible that the Commission failed to ask him about Betty MacDonald. In the absence of so routine a check of the records Betty MacDonald's claim that she worked for Ruby remains to be dealt with.

The investigation cited by the Warren Commission as the basis for its findings in the Betty MacDonald affair is so sketchy and deficient that it leaves matters where they were when Bob Considine's story was published and adds a few new mysteries as well.

Chapter 16
Death and Misadventure

During the three-year period that followed the assassination and the murders of Tippit and Oswald in a single Dallas weekend, some 17 witnesses involved directly or peripherally in the original events have also died, and one witness was the victim of attempted murder but survived a bullet in the head. For statistical purposes, the attempted murder of Warren Reynolds will be treated here as an actual murder.* The manner in which the Warren Commission reacted to the attempted murder and a connected suicide, both of which occurred during the Commission's active investigatory phase, was discussed in the preceding chapter. Here, the deaths will be considered only collectively, in the context of their classifiable elements.

Omitted from consideration, of necessity, are certain deaths mentioned in the Hearings but about which information is inadequate for statistical analysis. For example, two deaths from unnatural causes were mentioned during the questioning of Jack Ruby in June 1964 by the Chairman of the Warren Commission:

Ruby: There was one Lane that was killed in a taxicab. I thought he was an attorney in Dallas.
Warren: That was a Dave Lane.
Ruby: . . . And there was a McClain.
Warren: Alfred was killed in a taxi in New York.   (5H 205-206)

The passage has a certain Shakespearean tragic ring, but the information is too sketchy to permit inclusion of the late Dave Lane and Alfred McClain in the tally. Omitted also is the death of Jack Ruby himself, discussed in Chapter 27.

A list of the deceased witnesses included in this survey—by name, connection with events or principals, cause of death, and date of death—appears in Table I following.

TABLE I.

Name	Connection with the Case	Cause of Death	Date
Eddy Benavides	Brother of eyewitness to Tippit shooting	Shot in back of head	February 1964
Lee Bowers, Jr.	Eyewitness to the assassination	Motor vehicle accident	August 9, 1966
Bill Chesher	Believed to have information about a Ruby/Oswald link	Heart attack	March 1964
David Ferrie	Alleged acquaintance of Oswald's and alleged assassination suspect	Apparent suicide	February 22, '67
David Goldstein	Helped FBI trace revolver used to shoot Tippit	Natural causes	1965
Tom Howard	One of Ruby's lawyers, was in police basement just before Oswald was shot	Heart attack	March 27, 1965
Bill Hunter	Reporter who was in Ruby's apartment 11/24/63	Gunshot wound	April 23, 1964
Hank Killam	Husband of Ruby employee; friend of fellow-roomer of Oswald's	Throat cut	March 1964
Jim Koethe	Reporter who was in Ruby's apartment 11/24/63 with Hunter	Karate chop to neck	September 21, '64
Levens (first name unknown)	Operator of Fort Worth strip joint employed some Ruby entertainers	Natural causes	November 5, '66
Betty M. MacDonald	Ex-Ruby entertainer; alibied suspect in the Reynolds shooting	Suicide by hanging in the Dallas Police jail	February 1964
Teresa Norton	Dancer employed by Ruby	Shot to death in motel	August 1964
Warren Reynolds*	Witnessed escape of Tippit killer	Shot in head (recovered)	January 1964
Earlene Roberts	Housekeeper, rooming house where Oswald lived	Heart attack	January 9, 1966
Harold Russell	Witnessed escape of Tippit killer	Killed by a policeman in brawl in bar	February 1967
Marilyn Moone Walle ("Delilah")	Dancer employed by Ruby 11/22/63	Shot by husband after one month of marriage	September 1, '66
William Whaley	Taxi-driver who took Oswald to Oak Cliff	Motor vehicle accident	December 1965
James Worrell, Jr.	Eyewitness to assassination; saw man escape from Book Depository	Motor vehicle accident	November 5, '66

The chronology of the deaths is given below.

1964

January	Reynolds* shot in head (recovered)
February	MacDonald committed suicide
February	Benavides shot in head
March	Killam died of cut throat
March	Chesher died of heart attack
April	Hunter shot in police station (Long Beach, California)
August	Norton shot
September	Koethe killed by karate chop

1965

March	Howard died of heart attack
December	Whaley died in collision with car
Unknown date	Goldstein died of natural causes

1966

January	Roberts died of heart attack
August	Bowers died in motor vehicle accident
September	Walle shot to death by husband
November	Levens died of natural causes
November	Worrell died in motor vehicle accident

1967

February	Russell killed by a policeman in brawl (Oklahoma)
February	Ferrie died in apparent suicide after being identified as a suspect in a conspiracy which led to the assassination of President Kennedy

Of the 18 witnesses (one of whom survived attempted murder) 5 died of natural causes, and 13 were the victims of accident, suicide, or murder. The unnatural deaths constitute 71.5 per cent of the total.[1] There were 6 murders, 1 manslaughter, 2 suicides, 3 motor vehicle accidents, and 1 presumed accident (or suicide) by a fall through a plate-glass window. Of the unnatural deaths, 53.9 per cent were murders. The natural deaths constitute 27.5 per cent of the total deaths; the murders, 38.5 per cent of the total.

Two of the 18 who died were eyewitnesses to the assassination whose testimony was inconsistent with the lone-assassin thesis. Both died in motor vehicle accidents not involving another car; both drove their own vehicles into an abutment, within three months of each other.

Two of the 18 had had contact or conversation with Oswald during the 40 minutes after the assassination. One died in an auto collision; the other, of a heart attack. The deaths took place within a period of about a month.

Three had direct or indirect connection with the Tippit shooting; two were shot in the head (one recovered), and the third was killed by a policeman in a brawl in an Oklahoma bar.

One was an alleged associate of Oswald's in New Orleans and was identified

---

[1] Mortality statistics for 1962 established a U.S. death rate per 100,000 population of 950. The unnatural deaths (males) per 100,000 population came to 96.2 or 10.12 per cent of the deaths from all causes. (*Statistics Annual 1962: Volume 1, Vital Statistics and Causes of Death,* World Health Organization, Geneva, Switzerland, 1965, pp. 24, 462.)

in the press as a suspect in a conspiracy to assassinate President Kennedy. He was an apparent suicide.

The remaining 10 had a known or probable connection with Ruby. They constitute from 44 to 55 per cent of the total deaths.

The strippers, drifters, and other birds of passage who are associated with the seamier parts of the entertainment world (sometimes linked with prostitution and other illegal activities) generally have a shorter life expectancy and a higher death rate involving acts of violence than the population as a whole. However, the Ruby-connected witnesses included 2 reporters, 1 lawyer, 1 housepainter, and 1 merchant. The preponderance of Ruby-connected witnesses who died cannot be assumed to be consistent with the mortality rate among itinerants employed in carnivals and cheap night clubs.

Of the 10 Ruby-connected deaths, 6 resulted from unnatural causes—1 suicide, 4 murders, and 1 accidental fall or suicide. Of the 13 unnatural deaths, at least 61.6 per cent were witnesses connected with Ruby.

Of the deaths in which the age of the witness is known or can be approximated, 82.5 per cent were under sixty; 71.5 per cent were under fifty; and 44 per cent were under forty years of age.

Seven of the 18 deaths involved "primary" witnesses—primary in the sense that their testimony is found in the 15 volumes of Hearings published by the Warren Commission. Six were "secondary" witnesses—they were interviewed by the FBI or the Dallas police and are mentioned in the Hearings or Exhibits. Five are not mentioned in the records published by the Commission but are known from stories in the press.

Eight of the deaths occurred between January and September 1964, while the Warren Commission was engaged in investigating the assassination and the murder of Oswald. Seven of those 8 deaths were unnatural (4 shootings, 1 karate chop, 1 suicide by hanging, and 1 throat cut in a fall or suicide). The Commission did not investigate any of the deaths. Testimony was taken, but not at the Commission's initiative, from Warren Reynolds, the man who survived a bullet in the head. After another witness forced the Commission to take note of the suicide of Betty MacDonald, the FBI was asked to inquire into the matter. The FBI transmitted the Dallas Police account of the detention and suicide of the victim, but neither the FBI nor the Commission carried out any independent evaluation of the facts obtained from the Dallas police.

Ten of the deaths occurred after the Warren Commission had dissolved, and where investigation was required, they were investigated by the local police authorities. Thirteen of the 18 deaths occurred in Texas—11 in Dallas, 1 in Fort Worth, and 1 in Houston. The other 5 died respectively in Oklahoma; Long Beach, California; Pensacola, Florida; Omaha, Nebraska; and New Orleans, Louisiana. Of the Dallas cases, the shooting of Reynolds and the murders of Benavides and Koethe apparently remain unsolved since September 1964 or earlier.

Viewed subjectively, the witnesses appear to be dying like flies. But an authoritative opinion on the mortality rate of those involved directly or marginally in the assassination and attendant events remains to be rendered by some actuarial expert.[2] It may be that the deaths are within the normal rates, despite the appearance of an epidemic; or it may be that they are radically out of line. Pending a more authoritative pronouncement, it can only be hoped that surviving witnesses will be on guard against misadventure.

---

2   An actuary who was asked by a London newspaper to compute the life expectancy of 15 of the deceased witnesses concluded that on November 22, 1963 the odds against all 15 being dead by February 1967 were 100,000 trillion to one. *(The (London) Sunday Times, February 26, 1967)*

This actuarial projection did not take into account the death of Albert Guy Bogard in February 1966, allegedly by suicide (asphyxiation in a parked car), which was brought to light in July 1967 by Penn Jones, Jr., too late for inclusion in the statistics presented in this chapter (which was already on the press). The deaths of many of the witnesses discussed here might also have remained unknown but for the indefatigable Penn Jones.

PART IV
THE INVESTIGATION

Chapter 17
The Distorting Mirror
(A Sampler of Discrepancies and Incongruities)

A Strange Arraignment

In his book *Oswald: Assassin or Fall-Guy?*[1] Joachim Joesten hurled many charges at the Dallas Police and other official agencies that investigated the assassination. One of his accusations was that Police Chief Jesse Curry and District Attorney Henry Wade had tricked the public by concealing the fact that Oswald had never been formally advised of the charges against him for the murder of the President. Joesten must have been chastened to learn from the Warren Report, published some six months after his book, that:

> . . . shortly after 1:30 a.m. [on November 22, 1963] Oswald was brought to the identification bureau on the fourth floor and arraigned before Justice of the Peace [David] Johnston . . . for the murder of President Kennedy.
> *(WR 198)*

According to a footnote, that statement rests on the testimony of Curry, Fritz, and Johnston. Examining the testimony of these and other witnesses and examining the Commission's documents provides even greater basis for skepticism.

A somewhat unconventional hour seems to have been selected for the arraignment. According to the official chronology of events on November 22, 1963 *(WR 198)*, Captain Fritz signed a complaint "shortly after 7 p.m." charging Oswald with the murder of Tippit, and at 7:10 p.m. in the office of Captain Fritz Oswald was formally arraigned for the Tippit murder.

At 11:26 p.m. Captain Fritz signed a second complaint against Oswald,

---

1 *Oswald: Assassin or Fall-Guy* (New York: Marzani & Munsell, 1964).

charging him this time with the murder of President Kennedy. At 11:26 p.m. Oswald was in Captain Fritz's office, and Judge Johnston was still in the building.

But this time the signing of the complaint was not followed immediately by formal arraignment. There was a delay of more than two hours, on which the Report does not comment.

At midnight Oswald was taken to the basement for a press conference. When a reporter asked, "Did you kill the President?" Oswald replied:

No. I have not been charged with that. In fact nobody has said that to me yet. The first thing I heard about it was when the newspaper reporters in the hall asked me that question.   *(WR 201)*

Oswald's seeming ignorance of his predicament is baffling. If one relies on Captain Fritz's report on the interrogation of Oswald during the preceding ten hours, it appears that all of the questions were directed to the assassination and that the murder of Tippit was scarcely mentioned. However (it cannot be repeated too often), there is no transcript of the interrogation sessions. Because Oswald's reply to the reporters is completely inconsistent with the interrogation as reconstructed from memory by Captain Fritz (he "kept" no notes) and because one can find no motive for Oswald to feign ignorance, one wonders if the official summaries of the interrogations faithfully reflect the proceedings.

The Report states that Oswald was removed to his cell at 12:20 a.m. The day had been eventful. Innocent or guilty, Oswald must have been overcome with exhaustion. But if he slept, he did not sleep long. "Shortly after 1:30 a.m." Oswald was removed from his cell and taken to the identification bureau to be arraigned for the murder of the President.

Surprisingly, when Oswald complained to the press the next day that he had been deprived of his "sanitary right" to take a shower *(WR 200)*, he did not throw in a few words about his right to undisturbed rest after a ten-hour stretch of questioning and line-ups. No one will deny that Oswald was jealous of his rights, to a fault.

Was it so urgent to arraign Oswald for the assassination that he had to be taken out of his cell in the middle of the night? If so, why was no proper record made of the arraignment?

The question of a record was raised with Curry when he testified before the Commission on April 22, 1964.

Warren: I suppose they make a stenographic record of that, do they not?

Curry: Yes, sir; I am sure they do.

Warren: That is all I have.

Rankin: Chief, our people made an inquiry to determine whether there was a stenographic record. They don't believe there was any.

Curry: I am not sure of that. I know at the time he was arraigned for the assassination of the President, I was present at the time. . . . . We were inside the offices of the criminal identification section . . . the identification bureau. . . . There was only about a half dozen of us altogether there, I don't recall who all was there.   *(4H 156)*

Without further ado, the Commission dropped the matter of a transcript of the arraignment—in a spirit of remarkable equanimity, considering its censurious attitude toward witnesses who failed to produce scrap paper on which they themselves had jotted the name "Oswald."[2] The Commission's equanimity becomes even more remarkable when one discovers the following passage in testimony taken two weeks before Curry's, from J. B. Hicks of the Dallas police laboratory.

Ball: Were you present when Oswald was arraigned in the identification bureau?

Hicks: No, sir; I left just a few minutes before that, I understand.

Ball: What time did you leave; do you know?

Hicks: I left shortly after 2. I don't know the exact time, maybe 2:15.

Ball: You think he was arraigned after you left?

Hicks: I am rather certain that he was because I believe I would have known about it had he been arraigned before I left because there is only one door in our office to go out and had any other group been there, I would have noticed it, I believe.   *(7H 289)*

Yes, Hicks undoubtedly would have noticed if half a dozen people came into the room and started arraignment procedures. The unacknowledged contradictions raise some doubt as to the alleged post-midnight arraignment. Unless it took place elsewhere or considerably later than the Report indicates, it seems unlikely for Hicks to have remained unaware of all the proceedings.

A possible reason for fabricating an arraignment is suggested in another passage of Curry's testimony.

Rankin: In regard to arrangements [*sic*], do you know the Texas law as to how soon after an arrest an arraignment is required?

Curry: Excuse me now; I am not an attorney.

Rankin: Yes.

Curry: It is my understanding that, so far in Texas, being brought immediately before a magistrate would be during the normal course of that court's business.

Rankin: Your law—

Curry: When they are in session.

Rankin: Your law says he shall be brought immediately.

Curry: Immediately, but it has been—

Rankin: But in interpretation you ordinarily follow a practice of—

Curry: During the normal course of the court's business. This was actually unusual because this type of arraignment—because usually it would have been later than this, but we were trying to take whatever precautions we could to see that he was given his—we were not violating his civil rights. That is the reason we did arraign him in the city hall. Ordinarily we would have taken him before a court.   *(4H 200)*

"Ordinarily" Oswald might not have been arraigned until court opened on Monday, the twenty-fifth of November, 1963—the date of his funeral, as it hap-

---

2 Discussed in Chapter 21.

pened. The Dallas police might have looked even less professional (if that is possible) had their prisoner been executed for a crime with which he had not been formally charged but of which the police and the Dallas district attorney had repeatedly announced his guilt, in complete violation of the rights of an accused, and while denying him legal representation—as Oswald himself charged.

Captain Fritz's testimony provides added fuel for speculation that something was amiss.

> *Ball:* You had an arraignment charging him with the assassination of President Kennedy, murder of President Kennedy.
> *Fritz:* Yes, sir; I went to that arraignment. . . .
> *Ball:* . . . That is one, 1:35 a.m., shortly after midnight was the arraignment.
> *Fritz:* Yes, sir.
> *Ball:* Now, your records show that he was checked in the jail at 1:10 a.m. and it doesn't show a check-out when he was taken to the arraignment.
> *Fritz:* To the arraignment. It probably wouldn't show that. Sometimes those cards, I don't usually make cards if the man is still in the custody of the jailers, and sometimes, of course, they might miss a card anyway because we use a lot of civilian employees up there.
> *Ball:* And the jailer was there with him, wasn't he?
> *Fritz:* Yes, sir. He brought him out.   *(4H 221)*

The Report has told us that Oswald was returned to his cell at 12:20 a.m. *(WR 198)* What is this about his being checked in at 1:10 a.m.?

> *Ball:* There is one problem here in your records that we asked about. Where was Oswald between 12:35 a.m. and 1:10 a.m. on Saturday, November 23, that is, right after midnight? . . . The jailer's records show he was checked out.
> *Fritz:* I think I know where he was right after midnight. I think he went to the identification bureau to be fingerprinted and have his picture made. . . . I think that, if it is the time that I am thinking about, if it is the time that after he was, after he had his arraignment, I think from what we found out since then that he went there for picture and fingerprints. . . . Maybe you should ask Lieutenant Baker here something that I don't know anything about, that he knows, that might help to clarify that question you asked me just then. I thought he went for the picture, but tell him.   *(4H 247)*

At that point, Lieutenant Baker intervened and rescued the English language from Captain Fritz.

> *Baker:* Yes, sir; at 12:35 a.m. Lieutenant Knight[3] of the I D bureau took him out of the jail on the fifth floor and with the assistance of Sergeant Warren[3] and one of the jailers[3] brought him to the fourth floor where the I D bureau was located. . . .
> There in the presence of Sergeant Warren and this jailer, one of his assistants, he was processed through the I D bureau, which consists of taking his pictures and fingerprints and making up the different circulars that go to the FBI, and so forth. . . . He was placed back in jail at 1:10.

---

3 Not a witness before the Warren Commission.

Approximately 1:30 Sergeant Warren received a call from Chief Curry, advising him to bring him back to the identification bureau the same place for arraignment. Sergeant Warren and the same jailer returned him to the I D bureau, where he was arraigned by Judge Johnston at approximately 1:35 a.m. This arraignment took approximately 10 minutes, and he was returned to the fifth floor jail by Sergeant Warren at approximately 1:45 a.m.

Ball: That is all.   *(4H 248)*

Obviously the assumption that Oswald was resting from 12:20 to 1:30 a.m. was premature. Now it appears that he was checked out at 12:35 a.m. for 35 minutes, checked in again at 1:10 a.m., checked out again at 1:30 a.m., and checked in at 1:45 a.m. The checkout at 12:35 a.m. and the return at 1:10 are recorded on a standard form *(CE 2003,* p. 141), but although he was subsequently checked out by the same personnel, ostensibly for arraignment, there is no record of departure or return.

Lieutenant Baker is precise, unhesitating, and coherent. However, we have it on the authority of Mr. Ball himself that the Dallas Police records showed that Oswald was fingerprinted at 8:55 p.m. on Friday *(4H 218),* and there is testimony from W. E. Barnes of the police laboratory, who said that he took Oswald's fingerprints and palmprints in Captain Fritz's office shortly after administering the paraffin test at about six o'clock that same day. *(7H 284-285)* Much as we admire Lieutenant Baker's precision, the matter becomes even more confused.

What is *not* unclear is the fact that in its Report the Warren Commission has withheld the information that Oswald was removed from his cell from 12:35 to 1:10 a.m., before being removed again at 1:35 a.m., allegedly for arraignment. The first absence is omitted from the Report but documented by a check-out slip *(CE 2003,* p. 141); the second absence is asserted in the Report but there is no corresponding check-out slip, and, moreover, the police officer who was present at the right time and place saw nothing of the ceremony at 1:35 a.m. or at any time before he departed at 2 or 2:15 a.m.

Rather than disposing of charges that have been called irresponsible and unfounded, the Commission's exercise in simplification tends to revive and enhance them. Certainly nothing on the face of the legal instrument charging Oswald with "killing John F. Kennedy by shooting him with a gun" *(Johnston Exhibit 4)* excludes the possibility of its retroactive completion.

Perhaps the authenticity of the arraignment is only an academic question at this point in history. The veracity of the Warren Report is not.

Listening with a Third Ear

Another example of the Commission's obliviousness to conspicuous contradictions arises, again from the testimony of Police Chief Curry.

Rankin: Do you know whether it is possible to monitor conversations between the prisoner and the visitor on the intercom?

> *Curry:* Not by intercom. It would be—they are brought into—when a prisoner is brought in to visit with an attorney or relative he is placed on one side of a wall and the prisoner—I mean the visitor—on the other side, but we don't have any means of recording this. They talk through by telephone. There is a glass that separates them.
>
> *Rankin:* Did you monitor any conversations between Lee Oswald and his brother Robert, or Lee Oswald and Marina at any time?
>
> *Curry:* I did not, and I don't know of any. We don't have any way of doing it. I mean we have no setup for doing this.   *(4H 200)*

An FBI report dated November 25, 1963, contradicts Chief Curry by implying the presence of monitoring equipment.

> Jack Ruby was observed by Special Agent Joseph M. Myers[4] at the Dallas City Jail, Fifth Floor, from 5:06 p.m. November 24, 1963 to 1:20 a.m. November 25.... He was allowed to talk to two visitors through the visitors' room on a communication system and the permit allowing these visitors was signed by Will Fritz, 5:55 p.m. The visitors were Pauline Hall[5] and Eva L. Grant.
>
> Ruby kept talking to his sister, Eva Grant, about all of his attorneys, naming Fred Bruner, Tom Howard, George Sanders, Jim Martin, and another named Kaufman. He made the following remarks to his sister:
>
> "Bruner is my man. I have friends here so don't worry about me. Something happens inside of you and then you crack and then it happens. Fred Bruner will come down in the morning and arrange bonds and have a hearing. I have nothing else to say and I've got the strength to stand up. I got lots of friends here so don't make a scene and get hysterical. Jack[6] came up and said 'we don't care how much the bonds are we'll make them.' You can't live forever so they will let any of my relatives come up to see me any time. The judge is real nice and they don't bother me here."   *(CE 2080)*

Or did the FBI introduce its own technology between Saturday (when Oswald was visited by members of his family) and Sunday?

If Rankin had seen the FBI report giving Ruby's verbatim remarks to his sister, his questions to Curry four months later seem excessively polite and indifferent to the contradiction between his replies and the contents of the FBI document.

If the FBI report of November 25, 1963 was transmitted to the Warren Commission after Curry testified in April 1964, the report did not provoke the Commission to reopen the question of monitoring, or to consider the implications of possible perjury and misrepresentation by an important witness.

A Watchful Neighbor

As indicated in the Warren Report *(WR 730)*, Eric Rogers, a neighbor of the Oswalds in New Orleans, was the only person to witness Oswald's departure from his apartment carrying two suitcases on the eve of his trip to Mexico City.

---

4   Not a witness before the Warren Commission.
5   Not a witness before the Warren Commission.
6   Identity unknown.

Rogers also witnessed Marina Oswald's departure from New Orleans on the preceding day.

According to the Report, "Marina and June departed with Mrs. Ruth Paine for Irving on the morning of September 23." *(WR 730)* Although the Commission relied solely on testimony from Marina Oswald and Ruth Paine on that event, Eric Rogers' description of the departure should not be overlooked. He told the Secret Service on January 14, 1964 that:

> . . . he was at home on the occasion when Mrs. Oswald and her child left in a light brown Ford or Chevrolet station wagon with *a man and a woman.* He said the man was about in his forties and was short and stocky. In reply to questioning, *Mr. Rogers stated that he is certain there was a man present on this occasion.* [Italics added]   *(CE 1154)*

Mr. Rogers' statement to the Secret Service in January 1964 is completely inconsistent with the testimony of Marina Oswald and Ruth Paine, who said that they were accompanied on the trip from New Orleans to Irving only by their children.

When Rogers gave formal testimony to the Warren Commission, six months after his interview by the Secret Service, his description of the departure now conformed exactly to that of Marina Oswald and Ruth Paine. The "short and stocky" man in his forties vanished completely.

The transcript of Rogers' testimony opens with the following lines:

> *Liebeler:* Mr. Rogers, I am an attorney on the staff of the President's Commission. I think I met you one day.
> *Rogers:* I remember you; yes sir.   *(11H 460)*

Further on in the transcript, Liebeler remarks:

> We talked to you previously at the apartment, and my recollection is that you told us . . . that a station wagon came and picked up Mrs. Oswald.
> *(11H 462)*

Rogers agreed and proceeded to discuss the departure of the two women and their children without the slightest allusion to the man, of whose presence on that occasion he had been "certain."

During the six months that elapsed between Rogers' Secret Service interview and his Commission testimony something must have happened to him that produced a partial amnesia. He still remembered the women and the children but the mysterious man had disappeared.

Perhaps the amnesia was contagious. Mr. Liebeler, who presumably had access to the Secret Service report, did not ask Rogers a single question about the man in the station wagon, who, if he existed, deserved serious attention from the Commission.

Presidential Protectors

Describing the advance preparations for the President's trip to Dallas, the Warren Report explains:

> The Protective Research Section [PRS] of the Secret Service maintains records of people who have threatened the President or so conducted them-

selves as to be deemed a potential danger to him. On November 8, 1963, after undertaking the responsibility for advance preparations for the visit to Dallas, Agent [Winston G.] Lawson went to the PRS offices in Washington.

A check of the geographic indexes there revealed no listing for any individual deemed to be a potential danger to the President in the territory of the the Secret Service regional office which includes Dallas and Fort Worth.
(WR 29-30)

Editorial columns after the assassination have discussed at sufficient length the astonishing revelation that the indexes listed no one in Dallas "deemed to be a potential danger to the President" despite the world-wide attention given to the ugly manifestations and physical assault and indignity suffered by Adlai Stevenson on his visit in October 1963. As Secret Service Agent Roy Kellerman testified:

> . . . it did seem strange that here we are hitting five cities in one State and— and from the apparent trouble that Ambassador Stevenson had down there one evening, we certainly should have had some information on somebody.
> *(2H 109-110)*

Without belaboring the baffling aspects of Secret Service practices, attention should be called to the curious procedures of the Commission.

When Secret Service Agent Lawson testified before the Commission, he described not only the advance preparations for the trip but also the events which took place at the police station on Friday evening, when Oswald was under interrogation. Lawson, who was present, told the Commission that he had been

> . . . called out for a phone call a couple of times. We were given information from Mr. Max Phillips, who was in our PRS section, and I believe it was during this time that someone, an agent, was wanted on the phone, and I went out and answered this, and *they gave us some information on people that it might have been—a case* [sic] *that wasn't Oswald.* [Italics added]
> *(4H 356)*

Neither counsel nor Commission members present paid the slightest attention to Lawson's startling remark. Had Lawson testified in the framework of the adversary procedure, some lively cross-examination might have followed, and we might not have been left with an additional unresolved question.

. . . and the Carriers of the Mail

A macabre postscript to the arrest and murder of Oswald was the letter delivered to Arnold Johnson, an official of the Communist Party, a week after the assassination.

The letter was from Oswald. It was postmarked November 1, 1963—exactly four weeks before it arrived at Johnson's address in New York City. Oswald wrote in the letter that he had attended a right-wing meeting at which General

Walker made a speech, and then a meeting of the American Civil Liberties Union, which he seemed to be planning to "infiltrate" in order to correct its moderate position.

Johnson, quite justifiably, considered the four-week delay in the delivery of the letter to be "beyond all normal procedure." The lateness, it should be noted, covered a period of three weeks before Oswald's arrest and cannot be attributed to his sudden notoriety on November 22.

Johnson testified further that there was

> . . . something odd about the whole letter. . . . For instance, you have a dif-
> ferent kind of ink in two places here. It seems that way to me. But that's
> pretty hard to say with modern pens. The way he signs his name and the
> way—that could be a problem, because he didn't always sign it the same.
> . . . I would just as soon leave that to a handwriting expert. . . . It may be
> worthwhile to check it with a handwriting expert. . . .   *(10H 103-105)*

Rankin, who deposed the witness, was not taking advice from so tainted a source. There is no indication that the letter was submitted to handwriting analysis or that any inquiry was made into the four-week delay in its transit.

. . . and the Guardians of the Border

Another apparent manifestation of official interest in Oswald was reported in the press a few days after the assassination. The *New York Post* reported on November 25, 1963[7] that William Kline, chief of U.S. Customs at Laredo, had said on the same date that Oswald's movements had been watched at the request of a "federal agency at Washington." The *New York Herald-Tribune* reported on November 26, 1963[8] that U.S. Customs official Oran Pugh had said that Oswald had been checked by U.S. Immigration officials on entering and leaving Mexico; Pugh had admitted that that was not the usual procedure but that "U.S. Immigration has a folder on Oswald's trip."

So far as is known, those press reports were not followed by denials from Kline or Pugh of the statements attributed to them.

The Warren Report does not mention the newspaper stories in the sections which deal with Oswald's trip to Mexico City or even among the "speculations and rumors" of which the Commission briskly disposed. *(WR Appendix XII)* Kline and Pugh appear nowhere in the text except on the List of Witnesses *(WR Appendix V);* in that list a symbol indicates that they provided affidavits rather than testimony involving examination by Commission counsel.

Since the names "Kline" and "Pugh" appear in the List of Witnesses, the Commission was aware of their existence and of the speculations provoked by remarks attributed to them by newspapers. Those who had awaited the publica-

---

7   Eric Norden, "The Death of a President," *The Minority of One,* January 1964, p. 18.
8   *Ibid.*

tion of the Warren Report in the anticipation that it would shed light on this affair had to resign themselves to waiting longer, until the publication of the Hearings and Exhibits, for illumination. It was hard to understand why the rumors generated by Kline and Pugh were not debunked by the Commission in Appendix XII of the Report, as was, for example, the rumor that a detachment of the U.S. Army "began to rehearse for the funeral more than a week before the assassination." *(WR 668)* The rumor that Oswald was being watched at the request of "an official agency in Washington" seemed no less consequential than the funeral rehearsal.

The impression that the Commission wished to avoid confronting the issue was borne out when the Hearings and Exhibits finally became available. Mr. Kline's affidavit (*15H 640*) states tersely:

> I do not recall being interviewed by Harold Feldman [*sic*] who I am informed represented the *New York Post*. . . . With respect to Lee Harvey Oswald, I have no personal knowledge whatsoever of any check made on him by the United States Public Health Service, Laredo, Texas, either upon his entry into or exit from Mexico in 1963. I have no personal knowledge whatsoever that any agency of the United States Government maintained a surveillance of Oswald's movements, and I have never indicated to the contrary to any news reporters.   *(15H 640)*

Pugh's affidavit (*15H 640-641*) follows along the same lines. He "did not recall" being interviewed by the *New York Post,* and "in any event" all information he had given to reporters had been supplied by his assistant, Kline, and did not derive from personal knowledge.

Kline's affidavit was executed on July 31, 1964; Pugh's, on August 26, 1964. If there are any intermediate reports, interviews, or documents, they are not evident in the Exhibits.

The affidavits do not dispose of the matter. They repudiate the story in the *New York Post* (attributing it erroneously to Harold Feldman, who merely referred to the story in the *Post* in an article in *The Nation*),[9] but the reporter who wrote the story was not questioned and we do not know whether, if he were questioned, he would retract, modify, or maintain it. The belated *pro forma* disclaimers from Pugh and Kline, his alleged sources, cannot by themselves resolve the conflict. And what about the story in the *New York Herald-Tribune?* That newspaper is not mentioned in the affidavits. Since the *Herald-Tribune* story of November 23, 1963 remains unchallenged, may we regard it as accurate?

The evidence suggests that there may be much more to this affair beneath the surface, but that it may be 75 years before it is excavated. It brings to mind a passage from the testimony of Revilo Oliver, professor of classical philology at the University of Illinois and student of the assassination, in colloquy with Counsel Albert Jenner on September 9, 1964.

> *Oliver:* The exact quotation is, "I do not know whether Oswald was paid by the CIA but I hear there was testimony before the Warren Commission that he was."

---

9 "Oswald and the FBI," *The Nation,* January 27, 1964, pp. 86-89.

Jenner: And from what source, on what source did you base the statement that you heard there was testimony before the Warren Commission that he was?

Oliver: Principally, although not exclusively, an article . . . by Henshaw in the *National Enquirer* at about the time that Earl Warren made his statement that the findings would not be released during the lifetime of the people then living.

Jenner: If you will pardon my correcting you, even that newspaper account didn't say that the Chief Justice said that the findings of the Commission would not be released.

Oliver: That the "full truth," wasn't that it?

Jenner: I think not. *It will be quoted in the report.* This occurred a long time ago, and I have forgotten just what it was. [Italics added]

(15H 736-737)

Let it suffice to say that it is not quoted in the Report.

To correct this deficiency, I quote the reply of the Chief Justice on February 4, 1964 to a reporter who asked whether testimony taken by the Commission would be made public:

Yes, there will come a time. But it might not be in your lifetime. I am not referring to anything especially, but there may be some things that would involve security. This would be preserved but not made public.[10]

10   "Warren Commission Will Ask Mrs. Oswald to Identify Rifle Used in the Kennedy Assassination," *The New York Times,* February 5, 1964, p. 19, col. 7.

Chapter 18
The Feebees

"That's what we call the Federal guys. . . . They are on you like the plague. They never leave. They are like cancer. Eternal."—Dean Adams Andrews *(11H 334)*

When shots were fired at John F. Kennedy on Elm Street at 12:30 p.m. the Secret Service and the Dallas police were in trouble. They were responsible for his safety in a city known to be hazardous to any man of Kennedy's liberal political persuasions. Almost a year was to pass before the public learned that in spite of the world-wide scandal of the behavior of Dallasites toward Adlai Stevenson, the Secret Service Protective Research Section "had no listing for any individual deemed to be a potential danger to the President" in Dallas *(WR 29-30);* the public learned also that some members of the Secret Service White House detail on the night before the assassination had violated rules by visiting The Cellar, a Fort Worth bistro, until the early hours. *(WR 449-452)* The agents had escaped disciplinary action because such action "might have given rise to an inference that the violation of the regulation had contributed to the tragic events." *(WR 451)* The Warren Commission joined with the Chief of the Secret Sevice in absolving the guilty agents, even though the Report concedes that the agents in question "might have been more alert" but for their late hours and in some cases their consumption of alcohol. The Commission was generous. One would not suspect from its Report that Senator Ralph Yarborough had been appalled by the sluggish reactions of the agents in the motorcade at the time of the shooting. *(7H 439)*

Even before those facts become known, the Secret Service was in trouble. (See Chapter 3, footnote 8.) They had lost a President. The FBI was in the clear, but only for two hours. Shortly before the new President took off for Washington, as the first interrogation of Oswald was getting under way, it became known to the Dallas police that the suspect had a thick FBI dossier and was under the immediate jurisdiction of FBI Agent James P. Hosty, Jr., of the FBI Dallas office. It became known that the FBI had not informed the Dallas police or the Secret Service of Oswald's presence in Dallas and his employment at the Book Depository.

Suddenly the FBI became an interested party with huge stakes in the investigation of the assassination—stakes no less than reputation, trust, authority, and continued autonomy.

The same FBI became the chief investigative agency for the Warren Commission, the main source of the Commission's expert findings on technical evidence such as fingerprints, handwriting, and ballistics, and the channel of eyewitness reports and background investigations into the lives of principals. The FBI carried out about 25,000 interviews on behalf of the Commission, submitting more than 2,300 reports totaling some 25,400 pages.

No one can deny that the possibility of a conflict of interests arose when the same agency which had kept Oswald under investigation and observation from June 1962 to the day of the assassination became the chief investigatory arm of the Commission charged with establishing the truth as far as it could be known. The question arises: Are there any indications that such a conflict of interests (or any other considerations) compromised the performance of the FBI as the central servant agency of the Warren Commission?

Study of the Hearings and Exhibits reveals examples of FBI interviews with witnesses, in which no interest was taken in significant statements made; instances of alleged intimidation; and numerous allegations by witnesses when they were questioned by the Warren Commission that the FBI reports of preceding interviews misrepresented their actual statements to the agents. It is left to the individual to judge whether such performance, as exemplified by the instances described below, merits confidence in the FBI's impartiality or efficiency; and whether the Warren Commission, in neglecting to discuss allegations of FBI intimidation of witnesses—indeed, in failing even to look into those charges of intimidation—and in excluding from its Report mention of the numerous allegations of FBI misreporting, has fulfilled its obligation to the public.

Investigative Work

An earlier chapter discussed the strange affair of the FBI Summary and Supplemental Reports of December 9, 1963 and January 13, 1964 respectively, in which a supposedly erroneous description of one of the President's wounds was given, even though in the interval between the two reports the FBI had received a copy of the autopsy report with its conflicting description of the same wound. Many commentators have raised the quite legitimate question of whether an agency capable of such superficial and careless work on what is perhaps the most important evidence in the whole investigation can have carried out its other investigations at a high level of accuracy, thoroughness, or skill.

Chapter 8 discussed the FBI's lack of candor with the Commission about the still-cryptic presence in Oswald's notebook of the telephone and auto license numbers of FBI Agent James P. Hosty, Jr. Nothing in the Warren Report provides the reader with a clue to that lack of candor, nor to the FBI's self-protectiveness about its handling of the Oswald dossier, as reflected in the following passage of Hosty's testimony:

> *Stern:* Did you tell Captain Fritz at this time any of the information you had about Oswald, about his trip to Mexico, for example?
> *Hosty:* No.
> *Stern:* About his being in touch with the Russian authorities seeking a visa?
> *Hosty:* No.
> *Stern:* About his previous residence in the Soviet Union?
> *Hosty:* Oswald himself told Captain Fritz about this. I didn't have to. Oswald came right out and told him.
> *Stern:* About the affair in New Orleans and his arrest there?
> *Hosty:* No.
> *Stern:* Did you subsequently tell Captain Fritz?
> *Hosty:* No; I didn't tell Captain Fritz; no.
> *Stern:* Was any of this information provided to the Dallas police as far as you know?
> *Hosty:* I provided it to Lieutenant Revill earlier, as I pointed out. . . .
> *Stern:* Wouldn't it be difficult for Lieutenant Revill to have gotten the information from you under the conditions that you described, running up the stairway and the rest of it? Do you think he heard enough of this?
> *Hosty:* Well, that is true, he might not have. But you see Oswald then proceeded to tell himself. He told the police all this information, so there was no point in me repeating it when he himself, Oswald, had furnished it directly to the police.
> *McCloy:* But you did tell Revill that you had a file on Oswald?
> *Hosty:* No; I didn't tell him I had a file; no, sir. (4H 468-469)
>
> *McCloy:* Did you notice that Oswald said in the course of his interview by Captain Fritz that he had not had a rifle but he had seen a rifle in the possession of Mr. Truly?
> *Hosty:* Right.
> *McCloy:* Did you interrogate Mr. Truly about that?
> *Hosty:* No, I didn't.
> *McCloy:* Do you know whether anyone else did?
> *Hosty:* I can't say for certain, no. (4H 472)

Other Commission witnesses gave descriptions of encounters with FBI agents which serve to throw new light on their methods, attitudes, and efficiency.

Ira Walker, one of several television technicians who stated that they saw Jack Ruby outside the police station on Sunday morning considerably before Ruby is supposed to have been there, testified on April 15, 1964.

Hubert: You have already testified that you recall the interview of you on December 4, by FBI Agents Earle Haley and Robley Madland. At the time you were interviewed, were you interviewed by those agents alone?

Walker: No. . . . The two agents, myself, Warren Richey, Johnny Smith, and there might have been some others, Jimmy Turner was there part of the time—of course, he introduced us to the FBI men, and I think he had already talked to him previously.

Hubert: All of you were interviewed as a group rather than individually, is that right?

Walker: That's right. . . .

Hubert: During the interview, did the FBI agents ask each of you to speak alone, or was it a composite sort of interview?

Walker: It was composite. We spoke as we remembered the situation. I mean, everybody described the whole thing as it progressed along as best he could.

Hubert: Do you remember what the FBI did by way of segregating the identification of each of you?

Walker: No, sir; I don't know. (13H 295-296)

Kenneth L. Dowe, KLIF radio announcer, provided information that Jack Ruby had telephoned the station on November 23, 1963, asking when Oswald was to be transferred. Dowe testified on July 25, 1964:

I talked with the FBI first, and they weren't too interested. I am sure it was the FBI that I talked with. . . . I wasn't in there more than five or six or seven minutes, and he didn't seem like it was too pertinent at the time. . . .
(15H 436)

Alfred Hodge, proprietor of a gun shop and a bar-and-grill, had known Jack Ruby for about fifteen years. He testified that he had met Ruby on an elevator in the police station late Friday night.

[Lieutenant Baker] come back to the elevator and he got off, I think, on the—I'm not positive about that, but he could have gotten off on the third floor, and this FBI agent and I want to say his name is Wilson, but I'm not positive, who I had called that day and he had been down to the store and checked the books with me—he was on the elevator too and I spoke to him. . . .

. . . I think I got to the store approximately 12:15. There was two FBI agents waiting there for me when I got there, and so they told me they wanted to see me, and we walked on into the bar, I mean, into the gun shop and they said, "Mr. Hodge," and they showed me their badges and all that . . . and they said, "There's an operator in Fort Smith, Arkansas that got an anonymous call this afternoon stating 'If you want to know who killed the President, check with the manager of the Buckhorn Bar.'" I said, "That could be one of my bartenders or it could be he probably throwed some drunk out and he just wanted to be important and wanted to get back at the bartender," and they said, "Well, don't think nothing about it. . . . We got one call this afternoon, Mr. Hodge, from a woman that told us that her husband just confessed to killing the President," and so that was that.
(15H 498-499)

Stanley Kaufman, Ruby's lawyer and friend for many years, testified on June 27, 1964:

About the Anti-Defamation League, although I do say I talked to the agents about it, but not in connection with a conversation with Jack. I do admit that the agents and I, in talking about that, they were very kind and they stayed there and they related to me how they had Jewish agents in the FBI, Bob Strauss of Dallas had been an agent, and I mean that they spent a lot of time discussing this matter with me, and I'm sure they had a lot of things on their mind, Mr. Hubert, and they were not sitting down taking notes although I think they did take names down maybe on the back of an envelope or a scratch pad. . . . In other words . . . I do want the record to be correct, because I don't think that Jack Ruby and I ever discussed the Anti-Defamation League. . . . (15H 522)

Arnold Rowland, an important eyewitness to the assassination, testified before the Commission on March 10, 1964.

Specter: Did you tell the police officials at the time you made this statement that there was a Negro gentleman in the window on the southwest corner of the Texas School Book Depository Building which you have marked with a circle "A"—pardon me, southeast?

Rowland: At that time, no. However, the next day on Saturday there were a pair of FBI officers, agents out at my home, and they took another hand-written statement from me which I signed again, and this was basically the same. At that time I told them I did see the Negro man there, and they told me it didn't have any bearing or such on the case right then. In fact, they just the same as told me to forget it now. (2H 183)

Specter: Did you ask them at that time to include the information in the statement which they took from you?

Rowland: No. I think I told them about it after the statement, as an afterthought, an afterthought came up, it came into my mind. I also told the agents that took a statement from me on Sunday. They didn't seem very interested, so I just forgot about it for a while. . . . They just didn't seem interested at all. They didn't pursue the point. . . . I mean, I just mentioned that I saw him in that window. They didn't ask me, you know, if was this at the same time or such. They just didn't seem very interested in that at all. (2H 184-185)

Alleged Intimidation

Marina Oswald, the Commission's star witness, testified on February 4, 1964:

In the police station there was a routine regular questioning, as always happens. And then after I was with the agents of the Secret Service and the FBI, they asked me many questions, of course—many questions. Sometimes the FBI agents asked me questions which had no bearing or relationship, and if I didn't want to answer they told me that if I wanted to live in this country, I would have to help in this matter, even though they were often irrele-

vant. That is the FBI. . . . Mr. Heitman and Bogoslav. . . . I have a very
good opinion about the Secret Service, and the people in the police department treated me very well. But the FBI agents were somehow polite and
gruff. Sometimes they would mask a gruff question in a polite form. . . .

I think that the FBI agents knew that I was afraid that after everything
that had happened I could not remain to live in this country, and they somewhat exploited that for their own purposes, in a very polite form, so that
you could not say anything after that. They cannot be accused of anything.
They approached it in a very clever, contrived way.   *(1H 79-80)*

Robert Oswald described the attempts of FBI agents to interview Marina
Oswald while she was in Secret Service custody, informing the Commission:

Oswald: Marina had recognized this one FBI agent as a man who had come
to the Paines' home in Irving, Texas, and perhaps at another location where
they might have lived in Dallas, or the surrounding territory, and had questioned Lee on these occasions.

Jenner: In the home?

Oswald: In or outside of the home. I do not know whether it took place on
the inside—but within the immediate grounds of the home, at least.

Dulles: And this was early in 1963? Prior, anyway, to November 22, 1963,
was it not?

Oswald: Yes, sir, that is correct. And that this particular one agent—not
the Mr. Brown I have referred to, but the other gentleman that I do not
recall his name—she had an aversion to speaking to him because she was of
the opinion that he had harassed Lee in his interviews, and my observation
of this at this time, at this particular interview, was attempting to start—
I would say this was certainly so. His manner was very harsh, sir. . . . It was
quite evident there was a harshness there, and that Marina did not want to
speak to the FBI at that time. And she was refusing to. And they were
insisting, sir. And they implied in so many words, as I sat there—if I might
state—with Secret Service Agent Gary Seals, of Mobile, Alabama—we were
opening the first batch of mail . . . and we were perhaps just four or five feet
away from where they were attempting this interview, and it came to my
ears that they were implying that if she did not co-operate with the FBI
agent there, that this would perhaps . . . in so many words, that they would
perhaps deport her from the United States and back to Russia.   *(1H 410)*

Nelson Delgado, Oswald's friend and fellow Marine, testified that he had
been interviewed repeatedly by FBI agents. His testimony, which is too lengthy
to quote *in extenso,* should be read in full. *(8H 228-265)* It uncovers a campaign of apparent intimidation by the FBI, during which Delgado was subjected
to a written examination in the Spanish language and attacks on his credibility
about various matters, including Oswald's poor marksmanship. Delgado testified:

Delgado: . . . I was upset because this guy kept on badgering me. . . . The
Spanish agent. . . . I couldn't concentrate on what he was saying because he
kept staring at me, and he was giving me a case of jitters, you know. . . .
(8H 239) . . . I told him basically the same thing I told you, only then this
fellow came out, this other agent came out with this test he gave me . . . a
written thing. . . .   *(8H 245)*

Liebeler: Did you teach anybody else Spanish while you were in the
Marines?

Delgado: Just one fellow, but he denied that I taught him any Spanish . . . Don Murray. He took Spanish in college, and we were stationed in Biloxi, Mississippi, together, and he would ask me for the same thing. . . .

Liebeler: What makes you say he denied that you taught him any Spanish?

Delgado: That is what the [FBI] agent interviewing me told me. . . .

Liebeler: Did you get the impression that the FBI agent was trying to get you to change your story?

Delgado: Yes.

Liebeler: He was trying to get you to back away from the proposition that Oswald understood Spanish?

Delgado: Well, am I allowed to say what I want to say?

Liebeler: Yes; I want you to say exactly what you want to say.

Delgado: I had the impression, now, wholeheartedly, I want to believe that Oswald did what he was supposed to have done, but I had the impression they weren't satisfied with my testimony of him not being an expert shot. His Spanish wasn't proficient where he would be at a tie with the Cuban government. *(8H 248-249)*

Liebeler: You mentioned this fellow by the name of Call . . . Richard Call. . . . Was he a friend of Oswald?

Delgado: Semi-friendly. I know personally that he used to call Oswald "Oswaldovich" or "Comrade." We all called him "Comrade," which is German for friend. We didn't put no communistic influence [*sic*] whatsoever. But then he made the statement saying, no, he never called Oswald "Comrade," or anything else like that, you know. . . .

Liebeler: How do you know?

Delgado: The FBI agent told me. . . . Call said he didn't. Well, that's his prerogative. He didn't want to get mixed up in it. *(8H 257)*

Orest Pena, owner of a New Orleans bar, reported that on one occasion Oswald and two companions had visited his establishment and that Oswald had ordered a lemonade. Pena, testifying about his participation in an anti-Castro organization in New Orleans, said:

Pena: Then De Brueys came to the organization . . . he didn't join it, but he was sticking with the organization very, very close. . . . We knew he was an FBI agent. So from time to time he called me at my place . . . asking me about this guy and that guy. . . . I told him about people that I am for sure they are for Castro here in New Orleans. So one way or the other, he was interfering with me somehow, Mr. De Brueys. . . . So one day I went to the FBI. They called me to the FBI. . . . I told the agency there I don't talk to De Brueys. I don't trust him as an American. . . . We got in a little bit of argument there. . . . So two days later he went to my place of business. . . . He said not to talk about him any more because what he could do is get me in big trouble. He said, "I am an FBI man. I can get you in big trouble." But he made a mistake. I had a girl that was with me that was here when he was discussing me. . . .

Liebeler: So your complaints about the FBI here in New Orleans relate basically to the anti-Castro proposition and not to the investigation of the assassination; is that correct?

Pena: No, no. That was way before.

Liebeler: You don't have any criticism of the FBI as far as the investigation of the Kennedy assassination was concerned except that you just don't like to talk to the FBI any more; is that right?

Pena: You mean after the assassination?

Liebeler: Yes.

Pena: After the assassination, they came and asked me so many times about the same thing, lemonade, it just looked silly to me. They came over so many times. . . . I got in an argument with one of the men there, the same thing I told you about the printing and propaganda. . . . He told me that the United States is a big country and it was hard to find. . . . I said, "It doesn't matter. Each printing has their own type or letter that can be found somehow."

Liebeler: So you told this FBI agent that they should find where the propaganda literature had been printed?

Pena: The propaganda that Oswald was giving away. They put that on television about four or five days after the assassination—Oswald giving that propaganda. They knew that Oswald was giving that propaganda away before Mr. Kennedy was killed. They got all of that propaganda and all of that film of Oswald. . . . If they went all the way from that propaganda, from where it was printed, maybe they can put Oswald in jail. Maybe the President not be killed. . . .

I will stand a lie-detector test . . . and I invite De Brueys, too, to ask De Brueys if that's true or not true he went to my place and tried to intimidate me.   *(11H 361-363)*

W. W. Litchfield, explaining why he had weakened in his conviction that he had seen Oswald in the Carousel Club, said:

. . . when the federal agents talked to me, they said, "You know, if you say you are positive and it wasn't him, it's a federal charge," and I said, "Well, I'm not that positive." . . . They said, "If you give false information as to an exact statement—" not an opinion, but if I say I'm positive, that's a statement.   *(14H 107)*

Alleged Misreporting

Bonnie Ray Williams, Book Depository employee who lunched on chicken on the sixth floor and then with two companions watched the motorcade from a fifth-floor window, testified on March 24, 1964:

Ball: Now, I want to call your attention to another report I have here. On the twenty-third of November 1963, the report of Mr. Odum and Mr. Griffin, FBI agents, is that you told them that you went from the sixth floor to the fifth floor using the stairs at the west end of the building. Did you tell them that?

Williams: I didn't tell them I was using the stairs. I came back down to the fifth floor in the same elevator I came up to the sixth floor on. *(3H 171-172)*

Ball: Well, now, when you talked to the FBI on the twenty-third day of November, you said that you went up to the sixth floor about 12 noon with your lunch, and you stayed only about 3 minutes, and seeing no one you came down to the fifth floor. . . . Now, do you think you stayed longer than 3 minutes up there?

Williams: I am sure I stayed longer than 3 minutes. . . . I finished the chicken sandwich maybe 10 or 15 minutes after 12. . . . Approximately 12:20, maybe. . . . I do not remember telling them I only stayed 3 minutes. . . .

Ball: And then on this fourteenth of January 1964, when you talked to Carter and Griffin, they reported you told them you went down to the fifth floor around 12:05 p.m., and that around 12:30 p.m. you were watching the Presidential parade. Now, do you remember telling them you went down there about 12:05 p.m.?

Williams: I remember telling the fellows that—they asked me first, they said, "How long did it take you to finish the sandwich?" I said, "Maybe 5 to 10 minutes, maybe 15 minutes." Just like I said here. I don't remember saying for a definite answer that it was 5 minutes.   (3H 173)

Ball: They reported that you told them on the twenty-third of November that you and . . . Hank Norman . . . and Junior Jarman were standing where they would have seen anyone coming down from the sixth floor by way of the stairs. Did you tell them that?

Williams: I could not possibly have told him that, because you cannot see anything coming down from that position. . . . An elephant could walk by there, and you could not see him.   (3H 180)

Harold Norman, one of Bonnie Ray Williams' companions at the fifth-floor window, testified also on March 24, 1964.

Ball: . . . On the twenty-sixth of November, an FBI agent named Kreutzer advises us in a report that he talked to you. Do you remember that? . . . He reports that you told him that you heard a shot and that you stuck your head from the window and looked upward toward the roof but could see nothing because small particles of dirt were falling from above you. Did you tell him that?

Norman: I don't recall telling him that.

Ball: Did you ever put your head out the window?

Norman: No, sir; I don't remember ever putting my head out the window.

Ball: And he reports that you stated that two additional shots were fired after you pulled your head back in from the window. Do you remember telling him that?

Norman: No, sir; I don't.

Jack Dougherty, a Book Depository employee, gave testimony in the form of a deposition on April 8, 1964.

Ball: On the day that this happened, on the twenty-second of November, you told the FBI Agents Ellington and Anderton that you heard "a loud explosion which sounded like a rifle shot coming from the next floor above me." Now, did you tell them that it sounded like a rifle shot, coming from the next floor above you, or didn't you?

Dougherty: Well, I believe I told them it sounded like a car backfiring.

Ball: Well, did you tell them it sounded like it was from the floor above you, or didn't you tell them that?

Dougherty: No.
Ball: You did not tell them that?
Dougherty: No. *(6H 380)*

Nelson Delgado, some of whose testimony has already been quoted with respect to alleged intimidation by the FBI, also indicated the misrepresentation or omission of his statements during FBI interviews. He denied that he had told the FBI that he himself had not come close to winning a jackpot for marksmanship, emphasizing that he was one of the highest scorers and always had an expert badge on him. *(8H 238)* He denied that he had told the FBI that Oswald was so proficient in Spanish that he would discuss his ideas on socialism in Spanish, as the FBI apparently reported he had said. *(8H 246)* He denied that he had told the FBI that he had transferred to another hut in order to avoid Oswald's company *(8H 256)* or that Oswald had accompanied him regularly on visits to Los Angeles. *(8H 263)*

Detective Leavelle, who was handcuffed to Oswald as he was being led through the police basement, testified on March 24, 1964. Counsel questioned him about a report that he had dictated two or three days after Oswald was shot to death.

Hubert: Now, I notice . . . you state that you had suggested the transfer be via the first floor of the Main Street door. . . . Did you state that fact to the FBI, sir?
Leavelle: I don't recall whether I did or not. . . . To the best of my knowledge it seems as though I might have made that suggestion, made the reference to that, but whether whoever was taking it said that they didn't need it in their report . . . I can't swear to this, but I think that is correct because I know . . . I am not able to recall at this time exactly what the conversation was between myself and the agent—I—in this, in its entirety, I do know there was one or two things I told them about, which they did say that they didn't think was necessary for their report, so, they did not put it in there. Now, whether that was one of them or not, I do not recall. *(13H 18)*

Alfred Hodge, the gun shop and bar proprietor who has been mentioned earlier, provided the following testimony:

Hubert: Now, you say that you did say to the FBI people when they interviewed you on the twenty-fourth that you had gone down on the elevator with two detectives and with Ruby? You told them that, although it doesn't appear in this exhibit [report]?
Hodge: Yes; I told them that Sunday afternoon. . . . I told them the whole story. . . . *(15H 501)*

Richard Saunders of the *Dallas Morning News,* who handled Jack Ruby's advertisements for his night clubs, testified on June 26, 1964.

Hubert: Your comment, therefore, is that this report indicating that you had said to the FBI people that he was more shook up or probably more shook up than any of the other people, is not an accurate statement of what you expressed?
Saunders: I feel not.

> *Hubert:* And the accurate statement is that he was shook up like everybody else?
>
> *Saunders:* Right.
>
> *Hubert:* But not more so?
>
> *Saunders:* Right.   *(15H 581)*

Referring to the manner in which the FBI reported his statements about Ruby's credit standing with the paper, Saunders said:

> I will not say I never doubted Jack Ruby's word at any time. I think that is a misquote. It is a fact that he did do what he told me he would do on each instance, but any time in any business when you are dealing with someone who is on a credit basis where there is no credit that has been established, you can't help but take a tongue-in-cheek attitude, and certainly the state- ment makes it sound like I am trying to whitewash him, which I certainly do not mean to do.   *(15H 581)*

Appraisal of the Known Facts

The testimony provides considerable insight into James P. Hosty Jr., one of the most important FBI witnesses in the case. He is seen in squirming disarray, seek- ing to explain away his failure to tell Captain Fritz what the FBI knew about Oswald. He told the Commission that he did not tell Fritz about Oswald's trip to Mexico or other peregrinations because Oswald himself was providing all the information directly to the police. Yet in his report on the interrogation at which he was present *(WR 612),* Hosty stated that Oswald told Fritz that he had never been in Mexico except to Tijuana on one occasion. The Commission did not con- front Hosty with this discrepancy or criticize him directly for his performance before or after the assassination.

There are many examples of omission and distortion in the reports pro- vided by FBI agents. In the case of Rowland and Williams, the errors are serious and suggest an attempt to make the case against Oswald look as strong as pos- sible. In other cases, the witnesses report a lack of interest in relevant informa- tion by the FBI agents who interviewed them which at the least reflects poor judgment.

But the most serious manifestations are the attempts to intimidate Marina Oswald, Nelson Delgado, and William Litchfield. It seems that the FBI did not like what Delgado said about Oswald's poor marksmanship, or the apparent evidence from Litchfield that Oswald and Ruby were not unknown to each other before the assassination. Apparently the Commission did not like that testimony either, and has ignored or discredited the witnesses. There is no indi- cation that the Commission was perturbed by the reports of intimidation—they are not mentioned in the Warren Report, nor is there any indication that the reports led to any inquiry or action by the Commission. On the contrary, the Commission's case rests heavily on FBI evidence and investigation. As we shall see, the Commission had compelling reasons, in addition to inaccuracies and intimidation, to regard the FBI as a "questioned authority."

Chapter 19
Oswald and the State Department

Chronological Summary[1]

Lee Harvey Oswald, aged twenty and newly discharged from the Marine Corps, appeared without warning at the American Embassy in Moscow at the end of October 1959. He handed to Consul Richard E. Snyder his passport and a written statement to the effect that he wished to renounce his U.S. citizenship and that he affirmed his allegiance to the Soviet Union. He informed Snyder that his application for Soviet citizenship was pending before the Presidium and that he had offered Soviet authorities all information on radar operation that he had acquired in the Marine Corps.

Snyder told Oswald that he would have to return to the Embassy on a regular working day to complete the formal act of renunciation. A few days later Oswald sent an angry letter to the Embassy, protesting the frustration of his act of renunciation and reiterating his wish to dissolve his U.S. citizenship. He did not reappear in person to carry out the necessary formalities.

Early in January 1960 Oswald was sent to Minsk. He had been issued a Soviet identification document designating him as a stateless person ("without citizenship"). Later Oswald was to assert that he had never in fact applied for Soviet citizenship, but according to a spokesman for the Soviet government Oswald's application had been submitted but rejected by the Presidium. *(5H 311)*

After little more than a year at Minsk, Oswald wrote to the Embassy in February 1961 indicating that he had become disillusioned and now wished to return to the U.S., provided that he received guarantees against prosecution under any circumstances on repatriation.

---

1   Based on Chapter VII, Appendix XIII, and Appendix XV of the Warren Report.

While Oswald's request was under consideration by the State Department, Oswald met Marina Nikolaevna Prusakova and in April 1961 married her. He notified the Embassy of his marriage and of his wife's wish to accompany him to the U.S., requesting that the necessary procedures for her entry be set into motion.

After interviewing the Oswalds in Moscow in July 1961, the Embassy recommended that the State Department rule that Oswald had not expatriated himself and that Marina Oswald's application for a visa to enter the U.S. should be approved.

The State Department ultimately adjudicated Oswald's legal status and determined that he had not expatriated himself. The Department also took action to approve Marina Oswald's papers, placing strong pressure on the Immigration and Naturalization Service (INS) to reconsider its denial of sanctions. As a result of representations by the State Department, INS eventually agreed to waive sanctions against Marina Oswald's admittance.

When Oswald came to the Embassy in July 1961, he told Consul Snyder that he had learned his lesson and was a loyal American. He said that he had never given classified information to the Russians, as he had said he would: the Russians had not questioned him or asked him for such information and he doubted if he would have complied if they had.

Marina Oswald, for her part, told the Embassy that she had never been a member of Komsomol (the Communist youth organization), membership in which might have disqualified her from receiving a visa. Her denial was later found to be false.

At the end of 1961 the Oswalds received exit visas from the Soviet authorities, permitting them to leave the U.S.S.R. Oswald now told the Embassy that he needed financial assistance to cover travel costs to the U.S. for his wife and himself (and later for their infant daughter). After futile attempts by Oswald to obtain the needed funds from private sources in the U.S., the State Department authorized the Embassy to make a loan to Oswald. He signed a promissory note for $435 in June 1962, and his passport was returned to him, renewed for 30 days and good only for travel to the U.S. The Oswalds departed the Soviet Union en route to Fort Worth, Texas.

One year later Oswald applied for a new passport at the New Orleans passport office. His application was dated June 24, 1963. His new passport was granted 24 hours later, on June 25, 1963.

Critical Evaluation

The Warren Commission reviewed the transactions between the State Department and Oswald from September 1959 to November 1963 and concluded that the decisions taken by the Department in its transactions with Oswald and his wife were innocent and proper. The Oswalds were treated just like anyone else. (WR 746)

A review of the testimony and the documents suggests that the Commission's inquiry was incomplete and at times uncritical and that its conclusions are highly questionable. There is a consistent pattern of unusual and favorable treatment of Oswald by the State Department. Decision after decision, the Department removed every obstacle before Oswald—a defector and would-be expatriate, self-declared enemy of his native country, self-proclaimed discloser of classified military information, and later self-appointed propagandist for Fidel Castro—on his path from Minsk to Dallas.

The State Department's extraordinary and unorthodox decisions and the decisions taken by other U.S. official agencies in regard to Oswald fall into several general categories: (1) repeated failure to prepare a "lookout card"[2] to check Oswald's movement outside the U.S.; (2) grant and renewal of Oswald's passport despite cause for negative action; (3) apparent inaction and indifference to Oswald's possible disclosure of classified military data; and (4) pressure exerted and exceptional measures taken on behalf of Marina Oswald's entry into the U.S.

In referring to measures taken by the State Department and other U.S. agencies as unusual or extraordinary, I speak in the context of official policies, practices, and attitudes, without intending to suggest a personal view on the constitutional or moral validity of the policies and procedures involved.

By dealing with specific instances, I will now try to show that the record of Oswald's transactions with the State Department is replete with anomalies, ambiguities, lacunae, and simply preposterous actions.

The Defection

At the outset, questions arise about Oswald's journey to the Soviet Union: how did he acquire money for the trip, when and how did he travel from London to Helsinki, and what was the exact date of his first contact with the U.S. Embassy at Moscow?

Oswald sailed for Europe on September 20, 1959, nine days after he completed 34 months of service in the Marine Corps and obtained a discharge on the grounds of hardship arising from his mother's illness. *(WR 688-689)* When his history was detailed in the press after the assassination, many people wondered how Oswald had acquired the substantial sum of money needed for his trip to the Soviet Union, and some suggested that his travel must have been subsidized by a U.S. Government intelligence agency. The Warren Report appeared to resolve this mystery:

> During his service in the Marines Oswald had saved a comparatively large sum of money, possibly as much as $1,500, which would appear to have

---

2   Under the procedures in effect in 1960 a "refusal sheet" was prepared in the State Department Passport Office whenever circumstances created the possibility that a prospective applicant would not be entitled to receive an American passport. On the basis of the refusal sheet, the records section would prepare a "lookout card" and file it in the "lookout file." Whenever anyone applied for a passport from any city in the world, his application was checked against the lookout file. If a lookout card for the applicant was found, appropriate action, including the possible refusal of a passport, was taken. *(WR 750)*

been accomplished by considerable frugality and apparently for a specific purpose. *(WR 12)* There is no evidence that Oswald received outside assistance in financing his trip to the Soviet Union. After he arrived in Moscow, Oswald told a newspaper correspondent, Aline Mosby, that he had saved $1,500 out of his Marine Corps salary. . . . During his two years and ten months of service, he received $3,452.20, after all taxes, allotments and other deductions.   *(WR 256-257)*

While the suggestion that Oswald had managed to save about $1,500 out of a total income of $3,400 over a period of 34 months is reasonable, given his frugal habits, the Report does not indicate where the accumulated money was kept physically—in a money-belt, stuffed in a locker or a duffel bag, or sent elsewhere for safekeeping.

In a later section of the Report, we learn:

No bank account or safe deposit boxes were located which could be identified with Oswald during this period of his life (i.e., June 1962–November 1963), although evidence was developed of a bank account which he had used prior to his trip to the Soviet Union in 1959.   *(WR 328)*

At first this seems to explain where he kept the fifteen hundred dollars. But then we encounter the following document in the Exhibits:

Records of the West Side State Bank reflect a savings account in the name of Lee H. Oswald, mailing address U. S. Marine Corps Air Station, El Toro, Santa Ana, California, was opened December 8, 1958, with a cash deposit of $200. On June 3, 1959, interest of $3.00 was credited to the account. The account was closed September 14, 1959, when the total amount on deposit, $203, was withdrawn.   *(CE 1150)*

Apparently, then, Oswald had saved only $200 in the account during his two years in the Marines. Did he save the remaining $1,300 or a large part of that amount in the ten months that remained after he opened the savings account and before he sailed for Europe on September 20, 1959? If the Commission believes that he did, it must bear the burden of proof. If the Commission argues that Oswald had accumulated much more than $200 at the end of two years but chose to place only a small part of the total in the bank, again it must prove it.

The Report conceals the very existence of the problem, by separating the assertion that Oswald saved as much as $1,500 from the evidence that he had maintained a savings accounts in an unspecified amount, which turns out to be $200.

It may be, as the Commission concludes, that Oswald did not receive outside assistance in financing his travel to the Soviet Union. But is the Commission entitled to offer that conclusion without first acknowledging and then confronting the paradox of the $200 savings account?

Turning to Oswald's travel route, the Report indicates that he entered the Soviet Union from Helsinki. The only firm information about his visit to that city seems to be the record of his hotel stay (in two different hotels), from October 10 to 15, 1959. This information is contained in a CIA report of September

18, 1964. *(CE 2676)* But the same CIA report indicates that there was no flight leaving London on October 10, 1959 that would have arrived at Helsinki in time for Oswald to register at the hotel, as he did, before midnight on the same day.

The Commission solves that problem by stating arbitrarily that Oswald left London on October 9, 1959 *(WR 690),* untroubled by the fact that Oswald's passport contains a stamp of the immigration officer, London Airport, and the words "Embarked 10 Oct 1959." *(CE 946,* p. 7) This is typical of the repeated misrepresentation of simple fact in the Warren Report, in spite of contradictory documentary evidence in the accompanying exhibits. Because the Commission did not establish the exact means by which Oswald traveled from London to Helsinki, there is reason to wonder if he went on a commercial flight at all.

Next, there is some uncertainty about the exact date of Oswald's first contact with the U.S. Embassy at Moscow. According to the Warren Report, Oswald appeared at the Embassy on Saturday, October 31, 1959, some two weeks after he entered the Soviet Union. *(WR 747)* But a cablegram sent by the naval attaché in the Embassy to the Navy Department in Washington refers to a previous Embassy dispatch *dated "26 October"* dealing with Oswald's renunciation of U.S. citizenship and his offer to furnish Soviet authorities with information on U.S. radar operation. *(CE 917)*

Curiously enough, Consul Snyder sent a confidential letter on October 28, 1959 to Gene Boster, Officer in Charge of U.S.S.R. Affairs at the State Department, in which Snyder requested advice on how to handle an attempted renunciation of American citizenship. *(CE 914)* Snyder testified that the letter "wasn't directed at any particular case" *(5H 271);* indeed, if Oswald first contacted the Embassy on October 31, he could not have inspired Snyder's request for advice. Snyder also testified that he had encountered only one case of renunciation of citizenship prior to Oswald's appearance, and that case was already resolved when Snyder wrote his letter of the 28th. *(5H 279)*

If Oswald really came to the Embassy earlier than October 31, Snyder's confidential letter to Boster would take on a different hue—as would his effort to discourage or delay Oswald's act of renunciation.

The Disappearance

Another mystery and perhaps a much more serious one involves Oswald's whereabouts for a period of some six weeks after his visit to the Embassy at the end of October 1959 and before his departure for Minsk early in January 1960. According to the Report, Oswald was interviewed at the Hotel Metropole in Moscow by news correspondent Priscilla Johnson on November 16, 1959 and "for the rest of the year, Oswald seldom left his hotel room." *(WR 696)* The Report indicates elsewhere *(WR 750)* that the Embassy notified the State Department at the end of November 1959 that "Oswald had departed from the Hotel Metropole within the last few days" for an unknown destination *(CE*

921); but the Commission says that Oswald "probably" did not in fact leave Moscow for Minsk until about January 4, 1960,[3] basing itself on Oswald's diary and on "other records available to the Commission." *(WR 750)*

But the diary has an entry dated "Nov 17–Dec 30" rather than daily entries. It would be an arresting paradox if Oswald had found time before November 17 to write daily entries, although he was busy with official interviews and sightseeing during that period, but no longer found time to record his meals or his emotions daily during a six-week period of being holed up in his hotel room.

The "other records" to which the Commission refers as providing evidence for Oswald's presence in Moscow until about January 4, 1960 consist of documents from the U.S.S.R. file on Oswald. *(CE 985)* Those documents merely establish his presence on December 29, 1959 and on January 4 and 5, 1960.

Six weeks of Oswald's life (November 16 to December 29, 1959) therefore remain unaccounted for and wrapped in mystery, and this has been completely glossed over in the Report.

The Lookout Cards

The peculiar business of the lookout cards which were never prepared brings us closer to the heart of the matter. Oswald's attempt to renounce his citizenship at the end of October 1959 provided the State Department with reasonable grounds for preparing a lookout card, as the Department later acknowedged. *(WR 751)* The card was not prepared, apparently as the result of the exercise of discretion by the responsible officers of the Department. No explanation is offered in the Report.

On two subsequent occasions, however, the preparation of a lookout card was mandatory rather than discretionary, but no card was prepared either time.

The first instance was in March 1960. The Embassy had lost all contact with Oswald and it was not known whether or not he had expatriated himself by an act of allegiance to the Soviet Union. Because Oswald's status was in doubt, an official of the Passport Office in the State Department (Bernice Waterman) made up a "refusal sheet" for Oswald on March 25, 1960. *(CE 929)*

The automatic consequence should have been the preparation and filing of a lookout card, so that the Department would be alerted in the event that Oswald applied for documentation at a location other than the Embassy at Moscow, where he was known. Yet no lookout card was ever "prepared, modified, or removed from the file" according to the Report. *(WR 751)* The reason for the failure has not been determined; the Report merely cites conjectures by the Passport Office that there may have been a clerical error or misunderstanding.

The second occasion for the mandatory and automatic preparation of a

---

3   Commission lawyer William T. Coleman gives the date of Oswald's departure for Minsk as "January 7" *(5H 277),* which is probably more accurate than the date mentioned in the Report.

lookout card was in June 1962, as a consequence of the advance of $435 to Oswald for his travel to the U.S. Lookout cards are prepared routinely when such loans are made as a protection against default by the borrower, who is not entitled to travel abroad until full repayment is made.

Again, no lookout card was prepared for Oswald. *(WR 772)* Again, the Commission failed to determine the explicit responsibility for that violation of the rules and merely cites a State Department memorandum filled with conjectures about possible administrative or clerical errors which may have produced this second lapse. *(WR 772)*

The Money

Before contracting for a State Department loan, Oswald had made attempts to obtain a grant or loan of funds to meet the costs of repatriation travel from nongovernmental agencies in the U.S. One of the agencies to which Oswald appealed was the International Rescue Committee, Inc., which describes itself as a "strongly anti-Communist organization." *(CE 2766)* In a letter dated May 1, 1964 to J. Lee Rankin, General Counsel of the Warren Commission, the program director of the International Rescue Committee, Inc., stated that the Committee first heard of Oswald in a telephone call from the State Department's Special Consular Service recommending assistance to Oswald. The letter continues:

> A few days later we received a letter from Mrs. Harwell of the Wilberger County Chapter, Vernon, Texas [Red Cross], dated January 14, 1962, to which, to the best of my recollection were attached copies of a letter written by Consul Norbury, American Embassy, Moscow, to Lee Harvey Oswald, dated December 14, 1961, and of a letter addressed to the International Rescue Committee, dated January 13, 1961 [*sic*], and ostensibly written by Oswald. . . . To a layman's eye it would appear that both copies were typed on the same typewriter. I do not know who added the handwritten words, "Mrs. Helen Harwell, Executive Secretary, American Red Cross," to the Norbury copy. *What is most puzzling,* although it did not then attract my attention, *is that the letter from Oswald, dated January 13, could have reached the United States by January 14, and that it reached us via Texas. . . . On or about February 5, 1962 we did receive a handwritten letter directly from Oswald, dated January 26, which makes no reference to a previous communication of his. . . .* [Italics added] *(CE 2766)*

This "minor" mystery among many has not been probed by the Warren Commission; Consul Norbury of the American Embassy, Moscow, was not among the Commission's witnesses, and the State Department officials who gave testimony *after* Rankin presumably had received the letter quoted above were not questioned about this strange episode. Was it possible that the Embassy and the State Department, in their ardor to repatriate Oswald, had gone so far as to write letters in his name? The Warren Report tacitly, and perhaps inadvertently, acknowledges the counterfeit nature of the January 13 letter, purportedly written by Oswald in the U.S.S.R. and received in the U.S. the next day; it states that "between February 6, 1962, and May 1, 1962, Oswald attempted to secure a loan from the Red Cross and the International Rescue Committee." *(WR 770)* The citation does not include the exhibit which reproduces the letter quoted above.*

A Perfect Record

The average reader may be nonplused by the State Department's perfect record of oversight and error in the matter of lookout cards for Oswald, but the Commission takes it in stride. It presents a dead-pan account, without editorializing, which is really only a paraphrase of the testimony of the spokesmen for the Department. By way of mitigation of what was rather uncommon carelessness and, at best, unreliability, the Commission points out that even if the lookout cards had been prepared, everything would have happened just as it did.

The lookout card that should have been prepared in March 1960 but was not, would have been removed from the file in August 1961, when the Passport Office determined that Oswald had not expatriated himself. *(CE 939)* The lookout card that should have been prepared in June 1962 but was not, would have been removed from the file when Oswald liquidated his debt to the State Department in January 1963.

This pat rationalization will not do. The real point is that a lookout card for Oswald should have been prepared and retained in the file primarily on the ground that Oswald's presence abroad was not in the interests of the United States. That was the obvious inference to be drawn from his defection and disloyalty when he arrived in the Soviet Union in 1959. That was also the ostensible justification for the Department's loan to Oswald, despite his inability to qualify for the loan by "loyalty to the United States Government beyond question." *(WR 771)*

The Freedom of Oswald's Travel

The State Department had an established procedure for preventing certain categories of persons from traveling abroad, one category being persons whose travel was judged not to be in the interests of the United States. Moreover, as Abram Chayes, the Department's legal advisor, testified, other federal agencies had the same privilege.

> The Federal Bureau of Investigation, for example, requests the addition of several hundred [lookout] cards each year. Similarly, the National Security Agency, the Office of Naval Intelligence and the Central Intelligence

---

* I am indebted to Peter Dale Scott for calling to my attention testimony of Marguerite Oswald which indicates that she mailed the January 13th letter to Vernon, Texas, from Fort Worth. This clears up the illusory problem of a one-day transit of mail from the Soviet Union to Texas.

Agency each request the addition of cards. In all cases, these requests are complied with, and the agencies concerned are notified when any of the individuals in question apply for a passport.   (*CE 950,* pp. 3-4)

In Oswald's case, however, neither the State Department's security branch nor the CIA, FBI, or Office of Naval Intelligence set in motion the procedure under which they would be informed if Oswald planned to leave the U.S. again. Those agencies did not request notification despite the fact that Oswald had affirmed his allegiance to the Soviet Union, proudly declared himself to be a Marxist, and even offered classified radar data to the Soviet authorities.

To appreciate fully the bizarre and incomprehensible nature of that universal lack of interest in Oswald, one need only refer to a case described in *The New York Times* of March 23, 1966.[4] A front-page story reveals that messages bearing the name of Miss Frances Knight, Director of the Passport Office, had been sent to the American Embassies in Paris and Moscow asking them to keep an eye on a Harvard professor who intended to go abroad in the fall. Sent at the request of the FBI, the messages alleged that the professor had strong pro-Communist convictions and that the State Department was to be notified of pertinent information on his activities.

The Harvard professor who unwittingly triggered the uproar had not even applied for a passport when the *Times* story was published, but according to Miss Knight, the practice of sending such messages was "somewhat routine," going back at least two decades.

The FBI was really on its toes when confronted with a Harvard professor who seems to be guilty of nothing more than advocacy of a sane nuclear policy and disarmament. Why didn't a Marxist defector rate as much vigilance? Replying to a query on that very point from the Commission, the FBI explained:

We did not request the State Department to include Oswald on a list which would have resulted in advising us of any application for a passport inasmuch as the facts relating to Oswald's activities at that time did not warrant such action. Our investigation of Oswald had disclosed no evidence that Oswald was acting under the instructions or on behalf of any foreign government or instrumentality thereof.   (*CE 833,* question 24)

If Oswald did not warrant such action, one can only wonder what frightful deeds caused the FBI to ask for several hundred lookout cards each year, as Abram Chayes had told the Commission.

And why was the State Department's Passport Office not worried about Oswald? Its arbitrary restriction of the right to travel has become the subject of a whole body of jurisprudence. Henry Steele Commager said in an article in *The New York Times Magazine,*[5] for example:

Beginning in the forties, and feeding on the crises, real and alleged, of the fifties, the State Department took the position that travel was not a right to

---

4   "Miss Knight Given Rebuke for Action Sought by F.B.I.," *The New York Times,* March 23, 1966, p. 1, col. 5.

5   Henry Steele Commager, "Passport Barrier: It Must Come Down," *The New York Times Magazine,* October 20, 1963, pp. 12, 109-116.

be exercised at the discretion of the citizens, but a privilege to be exercised at the discretion of the State Department. . . . Again and again, it has denied passports to American citizens. . . . Yet even when forced by the Court to acknowledge that travel was a "natural and constitutional right," the Department has persisted in using its power to withhold or reclaim passports. . . . With a stubbornness and arrogance characteristic of the bureaucratic mind, it still insists on the right to decide what is best for the United States. . . . For the past 15 years, the Department has attempted to deny passports to many Americans on the ground that their travel might be embarrassing.

But not Oswald's passport, which was issued to him 24 hours after he made application on June 24, 1963.

Clearly, on every occasion on which the State Department or other agencies should, by their normal practice, have set up a lookout card for Oswald, they did not do so. The Department did not withhold or reclaim Oswald's passport, although his presence abroad had already proved "embarrassing." The radical deviation from orthodox practice where Oswald was involved cannot be dismissed as random, inadvertent, or innocent—it is too consistent and uniform to be attributed to recurrent clerical error. It is a pattern that makes sense only in the context of a secret arrangement which placed Oswald outside the scope of normal measures of precaution.

The Passport Application

Oswald certainly did his best to compensate for the persistent negligence which left him without a lookout card. When he applied in July 1961 for the renewal of his 1959 passport, he was thoughtful enough to indicate on the application form that he had committed an act or acts which might expatriate him or make him ineligible to receive the renewal.

The application form contained a printed statement which set forth, in the disjunctive, a series of such acts, preceded by the two phrases "Have" and "Have Not." In filling out the form, Oswald struck out the words "have not."

The Commission acknowledges that one existing carbon copy of the application shows that "Have not" has been typed over and that, in effect, Oswald had thus admitted that he might be ineligible for an American passport.

Snyder, who had handled Oswald when he came to the Embassy and filled in the application form, was questioned, but he did not remember to which of the proscribed acts Oswald had admitted: it may have been "swearing allegiance to a foreign state." On the other hand, Snyder suggested, the blocking-out of "have not" may have been a mere typographical error! *(WR 755-757)*

The Commission next states that there is an "actual signed copy of the application" in the Embassy files at Moscow "which is not a carbon copy of the copy sent to the Department." On this the obliteration is slightly above the "Have," which appears on the line above the "Have not." The Commission infers from this that the strike-out may have been intended to obliterate "Have."

What is an "actual signed copy of the application . . . which is not a carbon copy of the copy sent to the Department"? Where is the original application form that Oswald filled in?

There is "one existing carbon copy," location unknown. There is an "actual signed copy" in the Embassy files—but it is not a "carbon copy of the copy sent to the Department."

Is it a carbon copy of *any* document? Is it the original of the carbon copy sent to the Department?

Only when the testimony is searched does it emerge that on July 10, 1961, Oswald filled in not one, but two separate applications.

Coleman: Do you have an explanation of why on July 10, two separate typings were made of the application for renewal?

Snyder: No, sir; I do not.   (5H 286)

The Warren Report obfuscates the whole baffling situation by employing a plethora of "copies" and "carbon copies" from which no sense can be made. The technique only heightens the appearance of subterfuge and deception, by all concerned.

In spite of Oswald's strike-out of the phrase "Have not," his application for passport renewal was approved on the basis of an accompanying questionnaire detailing specific acts which the State Department evaluated as non-expatriative.

Two years later Oswald applied for a passport at New Orleans. In the absence of a lookout card, his passport was granted within 24 hours. But Oswald was generous enough to provide a substitute for the missing lookout card: he specified on his application for a passport that his previous passport had been cancelled. (*CE 950,* p. 7)

This in itself should have alerted the Passport Office to check his past file, yet apparently it did not delay his passport by an hour.

What light does this shed on the reasoning presented in the Warren Report? The Commission takes the position that even if the required lookout cards had been prepared in March 1960 and June 1962, no card would have remained in the file in June 1963 and Oswald's new passport would still have been issued. As for the issue of the passport in 24 hours, the Commission explains that Oswald was one of 25 applicants, all of whom received the same fast service. The "NO" alongside Oswald's name on the teletype list of the applicants meant "New Orleans" and the contiguity was purely coincidental.

But the Commission did not inquire why the Passport Office paid no attention to the cancellation of Oswald's previous passport.

Oswald went even further than inserting information on his passport application to call attention to himself. According to the testimony of Lieutenant Martello of the New Orleans police, Oswald forthrightly told him after his arrest in August 1963 that he intended to redefect to the Soviet Union and had already applied to the State Department for the necessary documents. (*10H 56*) Oswald's interview by Martello was followed by an interview conducted by FBI Agent John Quigley. Quigley surely could have elicited the information that

Oswald intended to return to the Soviet Union, from Martello if not from Oswald himself. Had he done so, would the FBI not have taken steps immediately to prevent a second defection by Oswald, with its consequent embarrassment to the U.S. Government? Yes, *if* Oswald's relationship with the Government—and with the FBI in particular—was nothing more than met the eye.

Quigley's interview notwithstanding, Oswald proceeded from New Orleans to Mexico City, where his activities were logged by the CIA. About the middle of October 1963, the State Department received a CIA report which stated that Oswald had visited the Soviet Embassy in Mexico City. The CIA memorandum resulted in a review of Oswald's complete file by two Passport Office lawyers, neither of whom saw any need for action.

James L. Ritchie, attorney advisor in the Passport Office, testified that he read the CIA telegram noting Oswald's visit to the Soviet Embassy at Mexico City, which had been left on his desk together with the Oswald file, on October 22, 1963—exactly one month before the assassination. He said that he then reviewed the entire Oswald file.

Coleman: What did you then do?

Ritchie: I made a judgment there was no passport action to be taken, and marked the file to be filed.   *(11H 192)*

Ritchie's immediate superior, Carroll Hamilton Seeley, Jr., also read the CIA telegram and reviewed the Oswald file.

Coleman: Did you after you looked at it say to yourself "Can we revoke this passport?"

Seeley: I am sure that is why I looked at it. I am sure of that, Mr. Coleman, that I looked at it with that view in mind, if there was any action to be taken of that sort. . . .

Coleman: . . . Did you know he had defected or attempted to defect in 1959? . . . That he was going to pass some radar information to the Russians if they gave him citizenship?

Seeley: Yes, sir.

Coleman: Did you know that the Soviet desk had indicated in 1961 or 1962 that it would be to the interest of the United States to get him out of Russia and back to the United States? . . . Did you note in his passport application for his 1963 passport that he indicated that one of the countries that he intended to travel to was Russia? . . . And you are saying with all that information that you would look at that file . . . read it and just put it back and did nothing about it?

Seeley: I did nothing about it other than to note the fact that I had read the telegram. . . . There was no particular passport significance to the fact that a man shows up down at the Soviet Embassy in Mexico City. . . . *(11H 203)*

Abram Chayes was questioned also about the State Department's indifference to the prospect of Oswald's redefection to the Soviet Union.

Dulles: Is it not correct though that when you were trying to get the visa for Mrs. Oswald, you made a very strong case that his continued residence in the Soviet Union was harmful to the foreign policy of the United States, or words to that effect?

Chayes: Well, we were very anxious to get him back. . . . We had him on our hands then. . . . He was very directly our responsibility, so that anything he did or that went wrong during that period, he was under our protection and we were necessarily involved. If he went back as a tourist and got into some trouble of some kind or another, we would then have the choice I think to get involved, and we might or might not. *(5H 332)*

The Department had the same choice in 1959, 1961, and 1962, when it elected not only to "get involved" but to move mountains on behalf of Oswald and his Russian wife.

Military Secrets, Anyone?

The most forceful indication that there was more to the Oswald "defection" than met the eye is the Government's dumbfounding inertia in the face of Oswald's proclaimed intention when he arrived in the U.S.S.R. to give classified data to the Russians. As Embassy official John McVickar described it,

> . . . it was almost as though he was trying to bait the consul into taking an adverse action against him. He mentioned that he knew certain classified things in connection with having been I think a radar operator in the Marine Corps and that he was going to turn this information over to the Soviet authorities. And, of course, we didn't know how much he knew or anything like that. . . . *(5H 301)*

Snyder testified that Oswald had "volunteered this statement. It was rather peculiar." *(5H 265)*

The first question that arises is, what kind of information did Oswald possess? John Donovan, former lieutenant in the Marine Corps, testified:

> . . . shortly before I got out of the Marine Corps, which was mid-December 1959, we received word that he had showed up in Moscow. This necessitated a lot of change of aircraft call signs, codes, radio frequencies, radar frequencies.
>
> He had access to the location of all bases in the West Coast area, all radio frequencies for all squadrons, all tactical call signs, and the relative strength of all squadrons, number and type of aircraft in a squadron, who was the commanding officer, the authentication code of entering and exiting the ADIZ, which stands for Air Defense Identification Zone. He knew the range of our radar. He knew the range of our radio. And he knew the range of the surrounding units' radio and radar. *(8H 298)*

At the time of the first contact with the would-be defector, the Embassy had no way of evaluating how much sensitive information Oswald had, yet there is no record that any attempt was made to dissuade Oswald from disclosing what he knew to a hostile foreign government. However, a dispatch was sent to the Office of Naval Intelligence as well as to the State Department reporting that Oswald intended to furnish the Soviet authorities with information on U.S.

radar. *(CE 917)* The Office of Naval Intelligence in its reply to the Embassy (copies of which went to the FBI, CIA, INS, Air Force, and Army) asked to be informed of "significant developments in view of continuing interest of HQ, Marine Corps, and U.S. intelligence agencies." *(CE 918)* On these and other cablegrams and dispatches which appear in the Commission's exhibits, lines and parts of lines have been obliterated by strips of what appears to be white paper superimposed before the photocopy was made.

It may be inferred that the Office of Naval Intelligence ordered the change of codes and frequencies described by Lieutenant Donovan, and took steps which led to Oswald's discharge from the Marine Corps Reserves as undesirable. There is no indication of any other activity on the part of the Office of Naval Intelligence, which, as already indicated, did not at any time use its right to request a lookout card on Oswald from the State Department.

FBI replies dated April 6, 1964 to a series of written questions posed by the Warren Commission about the handling of the Oswald case between the defection in October 1959 and the assassination in November 1963 provide some additional curious information. The FBI states that it was determined on November 2, 1959 (only three days after Oswald's appearance at the Embassy) that "no derogatory information was contained in the USMC files concerning Oswald" (U.S. Marine Corps, where Oswald supposedly was known for his political deviation, study of the Russian language, and other heresies) and that "ONI (Office of Naval Intelligence) advised that no action against him was contemplated in this matter." *(CE 2718,* question 1)

Despite the quick decision by Naval Intelligence that no action would be taken, the Marine Corps acted in 1960 to give Oswald an undesirable discharge. Oswald was indignant, if not incensed, at the "injustice" of that action. He filed an application for review of the unsatisfactory discharge, appending a "brief" and a four-page statement. He also attached two letters addressed to him by the American Embassy in Moscow, commenting with respect to one of those letters that "the tone of the letter . . . hardly reflects the opinion of the American Embassy that I am undeserving, through some sort of breach of loyalty, of their attentions." *(CE 2661)*

The brief and the accompanying four-page statement were written by Oswald in Minsk, the brief being dated April 18, 1962 under that address. Yet the documents not only manifest a correct style and surprising familiarity with legal form and substance but cite specific sections of the U.S. Code!* Did Oswald memorize a body of law in advance of his defection? Did he carry the U.S. Code around with him on his travels and consult it in Minsk? Or did he have expert advice and assistance in writing his legal brief and accompanying statement?

Oswald not only appealed for nullification of the unsatisfactory discharge but also *requested recommendation of his re-enlistment,* on the following grounds:

> In accordance with par. 15(e) (5) I request that the Board consider my sincere desire to use my former training at the aviation fundamentals school, Jacksonville, Florida, and radar operators school, Biloxi, Miss., as well as the special knowledge I have accumulated through my experience

---

* The author learned in 1975 that Oswald's references to the U.S. Code (Title 18, section 1544) related to the illegal use of passports. He had access to the relevant title and section of the Code in his own passport, which was in his possession when the "brief" was written.

since my release from active duty in the Naval Service. [Emphasis in original]　　　　　　　　　　　　　　　　　　　　　　　*(CE 2661)*

Apparently neither the Marine Corps nor the Office of Naval Intelligence nor the FBI felt the smallest interest in any "special knowledge" which Oswald may have acquired in the Soviet Union; nothing in the Report or the Hearings and Exhibits indicates that the offer was followed up with Oswald upon his return to the U.S. It would seem that the American intelligence agencies are no less self-denying than their Soviet counterparts.

The Commission did not take testimony from anyone representing the Office of Naval Intelligence, nor do the Exhibits include interviews with such persons by the Commission's servant agencies. Consequently, we have no firm information on the actions taken by the Office of Naval Intelligence other than those inferred here and no explanation whatever of the apparent decision not to prosecute Oswald on his return to the U.S.

Did the Office of Naval Intelligence conduct an investigation which led to the conclusion that there was insufficient evidence to launch proceedings against Oswald? Did the Office conclude that Oswald had not carried out his threat to betray classified information? Did the Office even interview Oswald at any time?

These are some of the questions that the Commission should have answered but did not.

We know only that Oswald reappeared at the Embassy in July 1961, almost two years after his announced offer to give radar information to the Russians. He was somewhat chastened. He now said that he had not carried out his threat and that the Soviet authorities had never in fact questioned him to elicit what he knew about radar and related matters. *(CE 977)* He reiterated the demands he had made by letter, in February 1961 and thereafter, for full guarantees that he would not be prosecuted under any circumstances upon his return to the U.S. *(WR 752, 754)*

The State Department had instructed the Embassy not to give Oswald any assurances, one way or the other, about prosecution. *(WR 753)* In his report on Oswald's return visit to the Embassy, Snyder wrote that Oswald "indicated some anxiety as to whether he would face possible lengthy imprisonment." *(CE 977)* According to his report, Snyder told Oswald "informally" that he did not perceive on what grounds Oswald might be subject to conviction leading to any severe punishment. However, Snyder emphasized, he told him that the Embassy could give him no assurances of immunity.

If we accept the Commission's evaluation of those transactions, we must accept one implausible inference, and another that is incredible. First, that despite repeated demands for guarantees which the Embassy and the State Department refused to give, Oswald decided to return to the U.S. where he faced the risk of prosecution and a long jail sentence. Everything suggests that, on the contrary, he returned knowing full well that he would not be prosecuted.

Second, we must believe Oswald's statement that the Russians had not been interested in his offer of radar information and that they had not solicited and he had not given that information. Collaterally, we must believe—and this is even more difficult—that the State Department and the other intelligence agencies accepted Oswald's disclaimer as sufficient to close the book on the question.

If the FBI, the CIA, and the State Department really believed that the Soviet Union had abjured the classified military information which Oswald of his own volition had offered them, they are not staffed by the mentally competent and vigilant individuals we are told about. It is more plausible to interpret their serenity about the disclosure of classified data as an indication that they knew there was nothing to get excited about.

Even the Commission could not bring itself to suffer in silence these agencies' bland pose of naïveté. Although J. Edgar Hoover and his confreres were not questioned directly about this particular phase of the Oswald affair, Hoover himself absolved the FBI of error by stating that "the Embassy gave him a clean bill." *(5H 104)*

Abram Chayes of the State Department had different ideas about where the buck should be passed.

Ford: What about Oswald's statements to either Mr. Snyder or Mr. Mc-Vickar that he as a former Marine was going to give information he had acquired as a former Marine to the Soviet authorities?

Chayes: That is, of course, a more difficult one. Of course we know he didn't have very much information.

Ford: No, but he was a Marine and he had been trained as an electronics radar specialist. He said he was going to give this information. . . . This is a question of giving away government secrets. . . . Was any investigation of that aspect made at the time?

Chayes: Yes.

Ford: When he came back and asked for the renewal of his passport?

Chayes: No; but what happened was when he returned to the United States —first of all the FBI was kept constantly informed, and as you know kept looking into the Oswald situation periodically from the time he came back.

Coleman: And those reports were in the passport file.

Chayes: They were in the passport file, and immediately after he came back, he was interviewed very fully by the FBI, and I think as I recall the file—I haven't reviewed it recently—I think he was questioned on this very point by the FBI and he said he hadn't given any and they weren't very much interested in it. *And the FBI apparently was satisfied with that.* They made no further move against him on that basis. [Italics added] *(5H 333)*

State Department passport lawyer Carroll Seeley was also examined on the matter of Oswald's disclosure of radar secrets.

Coleman: Did the fact that he had originally stated that he had information as a radar operator in the Marine Corps which he would make available to the Soviet Union—did that in any way raise in your mind a security problem?

Seeley: Yes, sir; I thought that this certainly raised a doubt. . . . [The witness then referred to Oswald's disclaimer of disclosure of information to the Russians, as reported by Snyder in *CE 977.*]

Coleman: Merely because a person who had attempted to defect now says when he is trying to get back into the country, "I really didn't tell the Soviets anything," that wouldn't completely satisfy you that maybe he hadn't, would it?

Seeley: No, sir; but I had no information that he had in fact done so. He had just made a statement that he would. . . .

Coleman: But you didn't do anything other than read Seeley Exhibit No. 5? [the report on Oswald's disclaimer referred to above]

Seeley: That is right, sir.   *(11H 200)*

And here the Commission let the matter rest. An FBI content with the "clean bill" purportedly given Oswald by the Embassy, a Passport Office prepared to accept Oswald's verbal assurance that he had not given away classified data as he threatened to do, a State Department and CIA ready to believe that the Russians were not even interested in Oswald's radar secrets—those are certainly not the agencies we are familiar with.

Nevertheless, the Commission managed to digest a gargantuan serving of clerical error, persistent coincidence, and official solicitude for a man who seemingly had forfeited all claim to protection from his government. The Commission concluded that the cuisine was delicious, and nourishing too.

The burden of evidence in fact lends considerable credence to Marguerite Oswald's constant thesis that her son had gone to the Soviet Union on clandestine assignment by his own government. She made that suggestion, it should be remembered, in January 1961 *(CE 2681)*—almost three years before the assassination of President Kennedy at the hands of unknown murderers. The record of Oswald's relations with the State Department and other federal agencies, particularly the FBI, despite many blanks and missing links, goes a long distance toward vindicating the intuition and inferences of Oswald's mother.

The Americanization of Marina

The State Department's transactions with respect to Marina Oswald are discussed in Appendix XV of the Report. *(WR 761-769)*

The Commission indicates that Marina falsely denied membership in Komsomol when she applied for admittance to the U.S. Her testimony reveals that she was a member of Komsomol until she was expelled in 1961 as a result of her intention to emigrate to the U.S. *(5H 608-609)* The Embassy and the State Department accepted Marina's affidavit of non-membership in Komsomol, apparently without any attempt at independent verification.

The Commission, for its part, points out that neither Marina's membership in Komsomol, nor her false denial of membership, had it become known, need necessarily have resulted in her exclusion from the U.S. *That* I am entirely prepared to believe.

Marina's application for a non-quota visa was recommended favorably by the Embassy in August 1961 and approved by the State Department in October. At that time the State Department transmitted Marina's papers to the INS (Immigration and Naturalization Service) for the necessary action.

The law required that the INS should agree to a waiver of sanctions before a Soviet national could enter the United States. The purpose and effect of the sanction is described in the testimony of Virginia James, of the State Department's Soviet desk.

> *Coleman:* Could you explain for the record just what the sanction is under Section 243 (g)?
>
> *Miss James:* Yes; the sanction is that the United States will not issue an immigration visa to a citizen of a country which refuses to accept a deportee from the United States based on the reasoning that if you can't deport to that country, if a person turns out to be an unsatisfactory immigrant, you are stuck with that immigrant.
>
> *Coleman:* Does that mean that the person cannot come into the United States?
>
> *Miss James:* No; it means that Mrs. Oswald could have gone to Belgium, France, England, any other country that accepts deportees, and applied for an immigration visa and have been admitted without any question on a Section 243 (g) waiver.   *(11H 186)*

In the case of Marina Oswald, the INS decided after a field investigation at Dallas to deny a waiver of sanctions, on the ground that Oswald did not meet the requirement as a "meritorious case" and that there was doubt about his loyalty to the U.S., in the opinion of INS, despite his recantation.

That evaluation by INS was in conflict with the view of the State Department and the Embassy that Oswald had purged himself and was entitled to the help and protection of the U.S. Government. The position taken by the INS, which was consistent with prevailing official attitudes and practices, did not inspire the State Department to reconsider its own assessment of Oswald. Instead, the Department proceeded to seek ways to circumvent or reverse the refusal of INS to waive sanctions.

INS informed the State Department of its decision to deny waiver of sanctions for Marina Oswald by a letter dated January 31, 1962, and also by a telegram sent a few days later and probably received before the letter, because the Department had been manifesting impatience for action by INS.

On February 12, 1962 the State Department Visa Office told the INS by telephone that the political desk believed that "We're better off with subject in U.S. than in Russia." *(WR 764)*

On March 9, 1962 the Department informed the Embassy that INS had declined to waive sanctions and suggested that the Embassy might advise Marina Oswald to proceed to a third country where the sanctions issue did not arise and request a U.S. visa.

On March 16, 1962 the Embassy contacted the American Embassy in Brussels, which indicated that if Marina came there she would receive a visa in two or three days.

That same day the Embassy removed another obstacle to Marina's entry into the U.S. by accepting Oswald's unsubstantiated affidavit of support as "sufficient assurance that she would not become a public charge." *(WR 762)* The Embassy explained that Oswald's affidavit had been accepted because he had been unable to find anyone in the U.S. to execute such an affidavit and despite the fact that Oswald had no concrete prospect of a job on his return.

Meanwhile, the State Department was exerting pressure on INS to reverse its denial of waiver. A high official of the Department wrote to INS on March 27, 1962 formally urging that its decision be reconsidered.

On May 8, 1962 the Department's Soviet desk learned by telephone that INS had capitulated. The good news was cabled immediately to the Embassy. The next day the INS by letter formally communicated its agreement to waive sanctions on behalf of Marina, stipulating that its action was based on "strong representations" by the Department.

Thus, Marina Oswald was spared the inconvenience of going to Brussels and was able to proceed from the Soviet Union directly to the United States. One wonders if she appreciates the prodigious efforts made on her behalf.

When the Oswalds opened negotiations at the Embassy in Moscow for Marina's admittance into the United States, they faced four requirements:

(1) That Oswald had not expatriated himself and had remained an American citizen. This determination was made by an adjudicator in the Passport Office of the State Department about one month later.

(2) That Marina Oswald was not a voluntary member of any Communist organization. As discussed already, Marina's false denial of membership in Komsomol was not uncovered until well after the assassination.

(3) That an affidavit of support was provided against the possibility that Marina might become a public charge. The Embassy, after prolonged correspondence with Oswald and the State Department on that problem, took the unusual step of accepting an affidavit from Oswald himself. (Subsequently Marguerite Oswald persuaded an employer to sign an affidavit of support, as the Report points out, but that is irrelevant to the evaluation of the actions taken by the State Department when it appeared that no such affidavit would be forthcoming.)

(4) That the INS would agree to waive sanctions, which it first refused to do but later granted on the basis of "strong representations."

"Best" Interests

All of the actions and decisions were predicated on the State Department's view that it was in the best interests of the U.S. for Oswald to return.

What would have happened if the State Department had not been ready to take such pains on Oswald's behalf? Presumably he and his wife would have remained in Minsk, leading their family life in more or less the same fashion as before. They might have suffered some temporary disapproval or hostility from the community because of their attempt to defect to the U.S., but that would have passed in time. There was no likelihood that the Soviet Government, or the American public, would make a *cause célèbre* of Oswald: the Russians obviously were leery of Oswald from the beginning, and the American public would have given Oswald no sympathy whatever after his disloyal behavior.

In what way, then, would the interests of the United States have suffered if Oswald had been left to fend for himself in Minsk? At worst, the Russians might have said self-righteously—if and when it suited them—that it was the Americans, not the Soviets, who were preventing the departure of the Oswalds. Didn't the State Department have a few cases in reserve of Soviet denial of exit visas? When Chayes was questioned about the average waiting time between a request for an exit visa and its approval in cases similar to Marina's, Chayes replied that some of the applicants had never received permission to leave the Soviet Union. *(5H 340)* There was probably a wealth of material with which to rebut possible Soviet accusations, if and when they were made.

The whole self-justification by the State Department for its decisions and its transactions with Oswald is "the interest of the United States." The Department has not provided the smallest substantiation for its claim that such a principle was relevant or decisive in Oswald's case. It has defended its actions on the grounds of scrupulous care for the rights of the citizen, human compassion, trust, and political tolerance. Those criteria are wholly absent from the Department's known practices and policies in passport cases and manifestations of political unorthodoxy or suspected unorthodoxy.

But the Warren Commission has conveniently concluded that there was no irregularity, no illegal action, and no impropriety on the part of the officials involved in the transactions with the Oswalds. *(WR 777)*

My only rejoinder, after reviewing the undeviating record of clerical errors and administrative decisions to the benefit of the undeserving Oswald, is that no agency is *that* perfect.

Chapter 20
Truth Was Their Only Client

The 26 volumes of Hearings and Exhibits provide little material that offers an insight into the Warren Commission's process of reasoning or evaluation of testimony and evidence which ultimately produced the official conclusions. We are therefore indebted to Representative Gerald R. Ford, not only for the piquant information that the unofficial motto of the Commission on which he served was "truth is our only client here," but for the whole first chapter of his book *Portrait of the Assassin,*[1] which provides a brief glimpse behind the Commission's closed doors. (The remainder of Ford's work consists mainly of excerpts from the Hearings.) Here we learn for the first time the dramatic story of the Commission's reaction to the rumors that Oswald was an undercover agent for the FBI, and of its efforts to deal with that delicate matter that had been placed into its hands.

According to Ford, the Commission held an emergency meeting on January 22, 1964, after a telephone call from Waggoner Carr, Attorney-General of the State of Texas, alleging that Oswald was an FBI undercover operative. The Commission heard in secret what Carr and Dallas District Attorney Henry Wade had to say about this potentially explosive allegation, and then reconvened on January 27 to consider what steps to take on the report from the Texas officials and the similar allegations that had appeared in the press. It had been claimed at the secret meeting with Carr and Wade that Oswald was on the FBI payroll as undercover agent No. 179 at $200 a month, from September 1962 to the day of the assassination. Rumors to that effect had appeared in stories by

---

[1] *Portrait of the Assassin,* pp. 13-25.

Joe Goulden in the *Philadelphia Inquirer* of December 8, 1963,[2] Lonnie Hudkins in the *Houston Post* of January 1, 1964,[3] and Harold Feldman in *The Nation* of January 26, 1964.[4]

At the January 27 meeting, General Counsel J. Lee Rankin suggested that the Commission should take the story to J. Edgar Hoover with a request that he produce facts to put an end to the speculations, but making it clear that the Commission would feel free to take any necessary steps in order to satisfy the American people that Oswald had not been an FBI undercover agent. (Rankin seems to have assumed from the first that there would be no substance to the rumors.)

Chairman Warren, on the other hand, considered that the Commission should first find out from "these people" if there was any substance to the allegations or if "just plain rumor" was at work. Warren felt that Hudkins should be questioned; if he claimed privilege and refused to reveal the source for his story, the Commission could go to his publisher and enlist his services to "have this man tell us where he got his information." Warren said, according to the transcript quoted in Ford's book, that he was not in favor of going to any agency and saying, "We would like to do this." He believed that "We ought to know what we are going to do, and do it, and take our chances one way or the other. I don't believe we should apologize or make it look that we are in any way reticent about making any investigation that comes to the Commission."

No one will deny that the Commission was confronted with a painful and delicate problem when it appeared that the very investigative agency on which it had to rely for its detective work was itself the subject of allegations of a most compromising nature. The situation was all the more difficult because the head of that agency, J. Edgar Hoover, has long been immune to criticism from any quarter. Warren's position was therefore courageous and faithful to the high responsibility with which the Commission was charged. Apparently he had a decisive influence on the other Commissioners. According to Ford, the discussion resulted in a consensus of all seven men that the only way to proceed was to conduct "extensive and thorough hearings of as many witnesses as was necessary. . . . Where doubts were cast on any United States agency, independent experts would be hired and the investigation conducted in such a way as to avoid reliance on a questioned authority."[5]

With this preface, I searched the Hearings and Exhibits for the "extensive and thorough hearings" of Lonnie Hudkins, Joe Goulden, Harold Feldman and others who had published speculations or made allegations that Oswald was on the FBI payroll. None of the three writers was a witness before the Commission. An undated, unsigned interview with Lonnie Hudkins is included in one exhibit (*CE 2003*, p. 327), but it deals with the events of Sunday, November 24, 1963 and not with the possibility that Oswald was an FBI undercover man.

2   Joe Goulden, *Philadelphia Inquirer,* December 8, 1963, Section A, p. 22.
3   Lonnie Hudkins, "Oswald Rumored as Informant for U.S.," *Houston Post,* January 1, 1964.
4   Harold Feldman, "Oswald and the FBI," *The Nation,* January 27, 1964, pp. 86-89.
5   *Portrait of the Assassin,* p. 25.

There is no trace of Goulden or Feldman at all. The Hearings and Exhibits contain no testimony from or interview with Waggoner Carr on this subject, or with Dallas Assistant District Attorney William Alexander, who appears to be the principal advocate of the hypothesis that there was a clandestine relationship between Oswald and the FBI. Alexander's views are reflected in the testimony of District Attorney Henry Wade; although Wade's testimony suggests that Alexander continued to hold that opinion long after the first rumblings which caused the emergency meetings in January, Alexander himself was not asked to testify before the Commission or interviewed on the question.

J. Edgar Hoover did appear before the Warren Commission on May 14, 1964. In the light of the Commission's consensus less than four months earlier to conduct its investigation in such a way "as to avoid reliance on a questioned authority," it is surprising to find the following passage in Hoover's testimony.

> I think a Houston reporter was the first one who wrote that Oswald was an informant of the FBI. We went to the newspaper reporter. He refused to tell us his source. He said he had also heard it from other persons. We asked him the names of these persons and we interviewed them but none of them would provide the source. In other words, I was trying to nail down where this lie started. *(5H 116)*

Despite what the Commission had professed earlier, the questioned authority was permitted to investigate the charges against itself and to find itself not guilty. The questioned authority, not the Commission itself or independent experts engaged by it, went to Hudkins "to nail down where this lie started." Who would expect Hudkins to reveal his sources under such circumstances?

An indication of Hudkins' source came to light in Edward Jay Epstein's book, *Inquest,* which referred to a Secret Service report of an interview with Hudkins in which the reporter stated that his information that Oswald was on the FBI payroll came from Allan Sweatt, Chief of the Criminal Division of the Dallas Sheriff's Office.[6] In July 1966, researcher Paul Hoch turned up this Secret Service report, Commission Document 320, at the National Archives. The report is dated January 3, 1964, and contains an account of an interview with Alonso H. Hudkins III of the *Houston Post* which includes the following passage:

> On December 17, Mr. Hudkins advised that he had just returned from a weekend in Dallas, during which time he talked to Allan Sweatt, Chief Criminal Division, Sheriff's Office, Dallas; Chief Sweatt mentioned that it was his opinion tht Lee Harvey Oswald was being paid $200 a month by the FBI as an informant in connection with their subversive investigations. He furnished the alleged informant number assigned to Oswald by the FBI as "S172."

This Secret Service report as well as other documents dealing with the allegation that Oswald was on the FBI payroll were withheld from the Report and the Exhibits. Allan Sweatt, like Hudkins and the other reporters, was not called before the Commission to give testimony.

---

6   *Op. cit.,* p. 39.

On the basis of this "investigation" the Warren Commission "found" that Oswald was not an agent for the FBI. In support of its conclusion, the Commission cites affidavits from J. Edgar Hoover and his assistant, Alan H. Belmont, and from FBI Agents Fain, Hosty, and Quigley, and an "independent review of the FBI files on the Oswald investigation." *(WR 327)* But no such independent review took place. Chairman Warren refused to accept the FBI files on the grounds that if the Commission looked at it, claims would be made that everyone should have the same right, even if prohibited security matters were included in the dossier. *(5H 13)* According to Edward Jay Epstein, Counsel Samuel Stern said that Oswald's files were returned to the FBI without examination and no independent check was ever made of the contents.[7]

Compelling questions must arise. What moved the Commission to reverse its original position? Were pressures exerted? Who had sufficient power to force a Presidential Commission of unparalleled prestige and broad authority to nullify its previous unanimous decision? What considerations exerted greater force than the dictates of the Commission's conscience?

It is not possible to accept a "finding" based on procedures which violate the Commission's own criteria. The possibility of a clandestine link between Oswald and the FBI has not been eliminated. The Commission has disposed of neither the allegations which originated with Hudkins nor the Hosty entries in Oswald's notebook. They are two pieces in a single puzzle.

It comes as comic relief after tracing this travesty of the investigative process to read in Ford's book that "the Commission labored . . . with soul-searching thoroughness" and that its unofficial motto was "Truth is our only client here."[8] One must laugh, lest one weep, at his self-satisfied pronouncement that "the monumental record of the President's Commission will stand like a Gibraltar of factual literature through the ages to come."

History inevitably will pronounce a ruder verdict on the report of an investigation tainted at every crucial point by the hopeless reliance of the authors on a questioned authority.

---

7 *Op. cit.,* p. 38.
8 *Op. cit.,* pp. 491-492.

Chapter 21
No Conspiracy?

Note: In the analysis of the "auto demonstration" episode and others which follow, it is not the writer's intention to suggest that Oswald was the instrument of a conspiracy. The known facts are subject to several different interpretations, including the practice of deliberate impersonation. The analysis seeks only to raise legitimate questions about the performance of FBI agents who investigated the assassination and about the competence and good faith with which the Warren Commission pursued, evaluated, and reported the evidence.

The Auto Demonstration

The Warren Report devotes little more than a page to the incident reported by Albert Guy Bogard, a car salesman. His allegations and the manner in which they were handled are more important than suggested by the space they receive in the 888-page volume.

The Report states that Bogard's testimony "has been carefully evaluated be-cause it suggests the possibility that Oswald may have been a proficient automobile driver and, during November 1963, might have been expecting funds with which to purchase a car." *(WR 320)* The facts, as presented in the Report *(WR 320-321)*, are that Bogard claimed that he had a customer on Saturday, November 9, 1963 whom he identified as Lee Harvey Oswald. Oswald had tested a car by driving over the Stemmons Freeway at high speed and had said that he would

have the money to buy the car in several weeks. He gave his name as Lee Oswald. Bogard said he wrote the name on the back of a business card, but asserted that when he heard on the radio that Oswald had been arrested, he threw
the card away, commenting to his fellow employees that he had lost his prospective customer.

The Report indicates that Bogard's story received corroboration from
Frank Pizzo, assistant sales manger, and from salesmen Oran Brown and Eugene
Wilson. Brown also wrote the name "Oswald" on a paper which both he and his
wife remembered as being in his possession before the assassination.

However, the Report says, "doubts exist about the accuracy of Bogard's
testimony." He, Pizzo, and Wilson "differed on important details of what is
supposed to have occurred when the customer was in the showroom." Bogard
said that he (the customer) wanted to pay cash while Pizzo and Wilson said that
he wanted credit. Wilson claimed that the customer made a sarcastic remark
about going back to Russia. "While it is possible that Oswald would have made
such a remark," the statement was not consistent with Bogard's story; Bogard did
not mention that the customer had ever conversed with Wilson. "More important," the Report emphasizes, "on November 23, a search through the showroom's refuse was made, but no paper bearing Oswald's name was found. The
paper on which Brown reportedly wrote Oswald's name also has never been
found."

Apart from these differences in detail, the Report points out that (a) Pizzo
developed serious doubts about the customer's identity after examining photographs of Oswald, whose hairline did not seem to match the customer's; (b)
Wilson said that the customer was only about five feet tall; and (c) Oswald was
unable to drive, "although Mrs. Paine, who was giving him driving lessons,
stated that Oswald was showing some improvement by November." Moreover,
according to Marina Oswald and Ruth Paine, "Oswald's whereabouts on November 9 would have made it impossible for him to have visited the automobile
showroom as Mr. Bogard claims."

Finally, a footnote *(WR 840)* indicates that Bogard took an FBI polygraph
(lie-detector) test. His responses were those normally expected of a person telling the truth. However, because of the uncertain reliability of polygraph tests,
the Commission placed no reliance on the results of Bogard's test.

The Commission does not state any explicit conclusion which it may have
reached after its "careful evaluation" of Bogard's testimony. On the basis of the
Report alone, one might form the impression that the Commission believed
Bogard to be a liar but was too polite to say so. Indeed, one might conclude that
his story in fact was a fabrication.

It is only when the relevant Hearings and Exhibits are examined carefully
that we begin to see that there is more reason to doubt the Commission, and the
Commission's FBI investigators, than to doubt Bogard. The picture which
emerges from the documents, especially when they are considered in terms of
the chronological sequence of events—which is not even suggested in the Report
—is considerably different from the picture drawn in the official text. Only after
mastering the substance and sequence of the raw material is it possible to recog-

nize the incomplete and misleading nature of the final product and to appreciate the Commission's sophisticated technique and careful phraseology. Consequently, the section in which the Report discusses the auto demonstration is composed of literally truthful sentences which, in sum, misrepresent the facts in essence and detail and evade the real meaning of the evidence.

The Commission's dexterity of language and its selectivity in reporting the facts are manifest in its treatment of the Bogard story. For example, the Report makes much of Oswald's inability to drive, while conceding that he was "showing some improvement by November." *(WR 321)* It does not mention here that on the very day of the auto demonstration, November 9, 1963, "Mrs. Paine took him to the Texas Drivers' License Examining Station" *(WR 740)* or that the station was situated in Oak Cliff *(2H 515),* not far from the showroom where Bogard worked. Presumably Oswald's driving ability had improved sufficiently for him to attempt a driver's test on November 9—more improvement than one might suspect from the Report. As it happened, Oswald was unable to take the driver's test on November 9 because the station was closed that day. He must have been impatient and disappointed. He had tried to take the wheel of Mrs. Paine's car some weeks before, but she had been unwilling to let him drive her car on the street. *(2H 505-506)* Psychologically, it seems plausible that Oswald might have visited the showroom pretending to be interested in a new car, for the opportunity of testing himself as a driver rather than testing the car, and if he had, that he might have said without any basis in fact that he expected to receive money soon, as a pretext to extricate himself from high-pressure salesmanship. Physically, his whereabouts on November 9 brought him into relative proximity to the showroom, and he could have gone there had he absented himself from Mrs. Paine's car for about an hour. Mrs. Paine, in an affidavit dated June 24, 1964, denies that Oswald left her presence during the trip to take a driver's test. *(11H 154)* She may be mistaken.

Several other factors add credibility to Bogard's allegations but are not mentioned in the section of the Report that deals with him. Oswald was serious about obtaining a driver's license and made a second attempt to take the driver's test on Saturday, November 16 *(WR 740);* he even started to fill in the application form *(CE 426).* He told Wesley Frazier that he wanted to get a cheap used car. *(2H 221)* And the agency where Bogard worked was "right under the triple underpass" *(10H 345),* in sight of the Book Depository, and therefore a logical place for a novice like Oswald to look at new cars.

Arguing against such a visit by Oswald, the Report points out that Eugene Wilson stated that Bogard's customer was only about five feet tall, without mentioning that cataracts had left Wilson without vision in one eye and defective sight in the other. *(CE 3078)* The Report emphasizes the discrepancies between Wilson's story and Bogard's, without mentioning that Wilson did not enter the scene until an FBI interview on September 8, 1964, having failed to come forward with his valuable information during the ten preceding months when Bogard's story was under investigation. The Commission discredited a previous witness on just such a time lapse: "Mrs. Helmick's reliability is undermined by her failure to report her information to any investigative official until June 9,

1964." *(WR 359)* Apparently they did not see fit to apply the same standard to Wilson.

The Report implies that it is strange that Bogard didn't mention any contact between his customer and Wilson, as if that automatically casts doubt upon Bogard. Bogard had told a consistent story from his first FBI interview on November 23, 1963 until the last, on September 17, 1964. In his second FBI interview, on December 9, 1963, he had been warned ostentatiously that his statement could be used against him in a court of law, but he proceeded to give a written statement maintaining the same story he had told before and told on all subsequent occasions *(CE 2969)*; later he submitted to an FBI polygraph test which indicated that he was telling the truth *(WR 840)*; and he reiterated his assertions and his identification of Oswald under oath in his Commission testimony. *(10H 352-356)*

Bogard was never confronted with Wilson's allegations or given an opportunity to defend his testimony where it differed from Wilson's. When Bogard was interviewed by the FBI after Wilson's report, he was merely asked to name those with whom he had discussed the prospective customer on the day of the encounter. Bogard replied that he had discussed the customer with Frank Pizzo and Oran Brown before going out of town the same evening. Indeed, Pizzo testified that after the assassination he "could have sworn" that the customer Bogard brought to his office on or about November 9, 1963 was Oswald. *(10H 347)* (Pizzo's testimony is too lengthy to reproduce here but should be read in its entirety for an appreciation of the subtlety with which he was encouraged to doubt his original and spontaneous identification of Oswald.) Oran Brown also corroborated Bogard's story, in an FBI interview on December 10, 1963 *(CEs 3078, 3091)*, while his wife independently corroborated Brown's story *(CEs 3078, 3092)*

It is Wilson, not Bogard, whose story is uncorroborated. The Report has no business insinuating that their stories enjoy parity. If Wilson's allegations were really credible to the Commission, it has certainly minimized his report that the customer made a sarcastic remark about going back to Russia. If the customer actually made such a remark, it greatly strengthens the probability that he was Oswald, an inference which is obviously unattractive to the Commission, or that the customer was engaged in a deliberate impersonation—an unavoidable inference which the Report manages to avoid completely.

The Commission attaches considerable significance to the failure of the search for the card on which Bogard had written the name "Oswald" and the paper on which Oran Brown had made the same notation. Apparently the members of the Commission and their lawyers have never experienced the peculiar torment and frustration of hunting for a mislaid scrap of paper. The authorities in Dallas were not immune to that failing, as the district attorney tactlessly revealed in his testimony *(5H 242)*; nevertheless, the Commission that was so skeptical about the mysterious disappearance of Bogard's card and Brown's bit of paper was quite nonchalant about the disappearance of a writ of habeas corpus from the files of Dallas officialdom.

There is some ambiguity about the diligence of the search for Bogard's card.

Pizzo is really the only authority for the assertion in the Report that a search took place. Bogard himself was never questioned by the Commission about an attempt to find the card or given an opportunity to comment on the fact that it was not found. *(10H 352-356)* The FBI agents who interviewed Bogard on November 23 and who were said by Pizzo to have made a thorough search for the card reported merely that they had asked Bogard to locate the card and that "he stated trash had been picked up by the janitor and placed in a large receptacle to the rear of the building, somewhat inaccessible for a thorough search. He did not locate the card." *(CE 3071)* This hardly suggests that the FBI agents had made a search, or that Bogard did so.

Pizzo's account of the search for the card was given in his testimony, on March 31, 1964. *(10H 340-351)* His earlier statements on the subject as well as his earlier identification of the customer are beyond our reach, because the reports on his FBI interviews on November 25 or 26 and on January 8 *(10H 350)* have been withheld and are not among the Exhibits.

Why should the Commission attach such importance to the lost card anyway? That Bogard had a customer who gave his name as Oswald on November 9, 1963 is confirmed both by Pizzo and Oran Brown. That he took out a card and threw it away upon hearing of Oswald's arrest is corroborated directly by Brown *(CE 3078)* and indirectly by Pizzo himself. According to Pizzo's testimony, he first learned of the card at about four or five o'clock on the day of the assassination, when he overheard some salesmen who were talking about the incident. When Pizzo made inquiries, they told him that a few minutes earlier Bogard had thrown a card away on hearing of Oswald's arrest on the radio. The next morning, "one of the boys" also told Pizzo of the same incident, saying that Bogard had lost his prospective customer with Oswald's arrest. *(10H 345-346)*

The failure to find the card surely fades into relative insignificance in the face of such strong corroboration, both for the original visit by Bogard's customer and for the subsequent episode in which Bogard assumed from the news of Oswald's apprehension that he had lost the prospective sale.

If it is strange that the Commission exaggerates the loss of the card, it is stranger still that the FBI reacted to Bogard's story on the day after the assassination by focusing on a discarded bit of paper as if it were the only significant element. The really significant element was the report that a man who identified himself as "Lee Oswald," and whom Bogard firmly believed to be Oswald after seeing his likeness on television and in the newspapers, had indicated on November 9 that he expected to receive enough money soon to buy a car that cost from $3,000 to $3,500.

The FBI received that information within 24 hours after the assassination by means of a telephone call at 11 a.m. on Saturday. *(CE 3093)* At that time, suspicion of conspiracy or attempted *coup d'état* was virtually universal. Oswald had been formally charged with the assassination of the President. He was under interrogation by Captain Fritz of the Dallas Police, in the presence of FBI and Secret Service agents.

The 11 o'clock telephone call caused FBI agents Manning Clements and Warren De Brueys to go immediately to the auto agency and interview Bogard.

They had Bogard drive them over the same route as "Oswald," noting in their report that it coincided closely with the route of the President's motorcade. *(CE 3071)* The re-enactment drive took Bogard and the two FBI agents within relative proximity to the police building, where Oswald was being questioned and appearing in identification line-ups.

FBI Agent Clements had interviewed Oswald on Friday night, according to his report *(WR 614-618);* the interview had been interrupted twice when Oswald had been taken to appear in the line-up. *(7H 320)* Clements was a seasoned FBI agent with 23 years of service. De Brueys, for his part, was aware of Oswald before the assassination. An FBI report indicates that De Brueys had given information on Oswald's activities in New Orleans in a report dated October 25, 1963.[1] *(CE 833,* question 13)

Yet Clements and De Brueys did not take the elementary and logical step of bringing Bogard to the police building to see Oswald in a line-up and determine whether or not he was in fact the customer of November 9 who had called himself "Oswald." Nor did they inform Captain Fritz, as they should have done at once, of the information obtained from Bogard—information which not only incriminated the suspect but might have been a distinct lead to the source of the money that Bogard's customer was going to receive, the possible conspirators.

Clements, like Bogard, was deposed by Commission counsel, on the same date in the same building and within the same hour *(7H 318-322);* he was asked no questions about Bogard's story and he volunteered no information on the subject.

The very fact that two experienced FBI agents, both already active and knowledgable in the Oswald case, avoided taking these steps is incomprehensible. The agents' failure to take the necessary and expected action upon interviewing Bogard must be regarded in the larger context of the over-all ambiguity of the relationship between Oswald and the FBI, as well as in terms of the specific prior contacts between each of the agents and Oswald.

The reports on the interrogation of Oswald *(WR Appendix XI)* are remarkable in that they reflect no intensive questioning directed to uncovering his fellow assassins, if he had any. The very circumstances as they existed on November 23 inevitably should have made that line of questioning central to the interrogation. Yet it is difficult to find one direct question to Oswald based on the possibility of conspiracy. One might almost think that FBI Agents Clements and De Brueys were intent upon concealing rather than investigating evidence of a plot to assassinate the President.

A Second Rifle

Another instance of inadequate investigation by the Commission occurs with Robert Adrian Taylor, a mechanic in an Irving service station. Some three weeks after the assassination Taylor reported to the FBI that he believed that Lee

---

1 Not found in the Exhibits.

Harvey Oswald was the man who had sold him a U.S. Army rifle in lieu of payment for repairs to a car in which Oswald was a passenger. The incident had occurred in March or April 1963. (That was just about the time when Oswald supposedly received the "humane" Carcano from Klein's of Chicago; leave it to the inscrutable Oswald to discard a U.S. Army rifle, the lethal efficiency of which is famous, in favor of a piece of Italian junk.)

According to the Report, another employee at the service station, Curtis Crowder, recalled the incident but believed that although the man resembled Oswald slightly he was not Oswald. "Upon reflection," the Report concludes, "Taylor himself stated that he is very doubtful that the man was Oswald." *(WR 318)*

Having disposed of Taylor in some twelve lines, the Commission goes on to other matters. If we proceed more cautiously, several interesting discoveries can be made in the documents cited in the footnotes. *(WR 839)*

The first discovery waiting in the Exhibits is that the statement in the Report that Taylor became very doubtful, after reflection, that the man was Oswald, is false. Before documenting that charge, I shall examine the evidence and evaluate the investigation on a chronological basis.

(1) "Some three weeks" after the assassination Taylor made his report to the FBI and was interviewed by an FBI agent or agents at the service station where he worked. The report on that interview has been withheld and does not appear among the exhibits. However, as we shall see in a moment, Taylor was shown a photograph of Oswald and identified him to the FBI as the man who had sold him the rifle.

(2) On December 18, 1963 FBI Agent Maurice White interviewed Curtis Crowder, who said that he recalled the incident but believed that the man who sold the rifle to Taylor was not Oswald. *(CE 2975)*

(3) On April 1, 1964 Commission Counsel Wesley Liebeler took testimony from Glenn Emmett Smith, who worked at the same service station. *(10H 399-405)* Smith had no direct knowledge of the sale of the rifle but he was present when the FBI interviewed Robert Adrian Taylor at the service station "about two or three months ago." *(10H 401)* Smith testified that the FBI had shown a photograph of Oswald to him as well as to Taylor.

Liebeler: He showed both of you the picture?
Smith: Yes.
Liebeler: And Taylor told you after the FBI agent left that the picture the FBI agent showed you was a picture of the man from whom Taylor had purchased the rifle, is that correct?
Smith: He told the FBI man that. He didn't tell me that after he left, but he definitely told him that in my presence. I heard him.   *(10H 401)*

Liebeler: Have you ever formed any opinion as to Taylor's truthfulness or his reliability?
Smith: I think he is truthful, and I think he is reliable.
Liebeler: You don't think he would tell the FBI agent that he got a rifle from this fellow if he didn't in fact get a rifle from this fellow?
Smith: I don't. I sure don't.   *(10H 402)*

Smith's testimony suggests why the FBI report on that interview with Taylor does not appear among the Commission's exhibits. Taylor did not merely believe that the man was Oswald, as the Report states, he made a positive identification from a photograph. Indeed, the inference becomes irresistible when we notice that there is no reference to Smith's testimony in the Report, in the paragraph which deals with Taylor's story, or in the footnotes.

Yet Taylor's positive identification of Oswald from a photograph, on the basis of a transaction some nine months earlier that involved conversation and relatively prolonged contact, surely is no less persuasive than identifications by other witnesses which the Commission has accepted—specifically, identifications on the basis of a photograph by witnesses who had seen a man "running south on Patton" on November 22, 1963, exactly two months before they identified that man as Oswald. *(WR 171)*

After hearing Smith's testimony that Taylor had made a firm identification of Oswald and that Smith had a high opinion of Taylor's truthfulness and reliability, the Commission still did not call Taylor himself to give testimony. In fact, the Commission never called him as a witness at any time.

(4) On April 30, 1964 the Commission requested the FBI to reinterview Taylor. *(CE 2977)*

(5) The reinterview, which is our only source of direct information from Taylor, took place on May 13, 1964. Taylor obligingly told his story again, describing the rifle he had purchased as a Springfield Bolt Action, .30-06 caliber, bearing the markings "U.S. Rock Island Arsenal, Model 1903," and the serial number 66091. *(CE 2977)* He told the FBI that:

> ... on November 23, 1963, he was watching television and, upon viewing Lee Harvey Oswald, commented to his wife, "Say, that looks like the guy I bought the .30-06 from." He stated, however, he cannot be positively sure the man who sold him the rifle was Oswald. He stated that *he feels that it was Oswald* since, upon viewing Oswald on television, he immediately thought of this rifle and, at that instant, thought Oswald was the man who sold the weapon to him. [Italics added] *(CE 2977)*

Continuing, Taylor said that there was a possibility that the man who had sold him the rifle had returned to the service station a second time, about a month later, but that he was

> ... very doubtful that this actually was Lee Harvey Oswald because, on reflection, he recalls the person from whom he purchased this rifle promised to give him two boxes of ammunition for the rifle. He said he is almost sure that, if Oswald had been this person in the station at that time [i.e., about a month after the barter of the rifle], he would have remembered him because of the promised ammunition. *(CE 2977)*

This perfectly clear statement that Taylor was very doubtful, after reflection, that a second customer at the station was the same man who had sold him a rifle a month earlier and whom he had identified as Oswald and still believed to be Oswald—this has been converted by the Commission into the completely misleading assertion in the Report that Taylor, upon reflection, became very doubtful that the man who sold him the rifle was Oswald.

Naturally, the Commission doesn't explain why it failed to take the necessary and feasible step that would remove Taylor's assertions from the area of speculation and uncertainty and establish whether or not it was Oswald who sold Taylor the rifle. What was needed was to ask the FBI, who had traced an Italian rifle to Oswald within 24 hours, to trace Taylor's rifle.

Instead of producing that evidence, the Commission has rendered a misleading account of Taylor's statements to the FBI, neglected the opportunity to take his testimony under oath, and, after misrepresenting his story, airily dismissed it.

Two Oswalds

Albert Guy Bogard's story of the auto demonstration was dismissed by the Warren Commission mainly on the grounds that Oswald was unable to drive a car and that he was elsewhere when the incident occurred. Robert Adrian Taylor's story was dismissed on the spurious ground that Taylor became very doubtful of his own assertion that Oswald was the man who had sold him a rifle.

Other witnesses also came forward with information that collided head-on with the lone-assassin thesis. Some of the allegations were inconsistent with evidence regarding Oswald's whereabouts at particular times and, if those allegations were accepted, posed the logical absurdity that Oswald on various occasions had been in two places at the same time. Some of the allegations also suggested that Oswald had been engaged in activities or associations fatal to the lone-assassin thesis.

Yet the stories tend, for the most part, to be convincing. Several were corroborated by other witnesses. The person described was indeed Oswaldian in physical appearance and behavior. The witnesses were plausible and seemingly objective.

In each case, the story was susceptible to one of several possible explanations. (1) The alleged Oswald was the real Oswald, despite apparently conclusive evidence to the contrary. (2) It was a case of mistaken identity in which the witness had been misled by a physical resemblance to Oswald. (3) It was a fabrication. (4) It was a case of deliberate impersonation.

The Warren Commission must have faced a painful dilemma. If the allegations were accepted as truthful and accurate, they would demolish the Commission's preconceived image of the loner who, because of fissures deep in his psyche, had committed a horrible but non-political assassination. They would jeopardize the laborious official reconstruction of Oswald's movements, activities, and associations. They would destroy the credibility of Marina Oswald and other principal witnesses who had provided the foundation for the official findings.

Understandably, then, the Commission subjected this "two-Oswalds" group of witnesses to very severe tests, in marked contrast to its display of indulgence toward the witnesses whose testimony posed no compelling problems.

Ultimately, the Commission concluded that Oswald was not the "Oswald" identified in the problematic testimony. That is indicated, at least implicitly, in the Report. *(WR 315-333)* So much for possibility (1).

While the Commission generally abjured an explicit evaluation of a particular story, the Report implies that about half of the "two-Oswalds" stories were cases of mistaken identity, and insinuates that the other half were mischievous inventions. So much for possibilities (2) and (3).

As to possibility (4), deliberate impersonation, the Commission nowhere in its Report even acknowledges that such a possibility exists, much less evaluates the evidence for or against such an explanation.

But it remains open to serious question whether the Commission, in selecting certain possible explanations and rejecting or ignoring others, first evaluated the full facts in an impartial and reasonable spirit.

In the "mistaken identity" cases, the Commission is open to criticism for overlooking, or pretending to overlook, the arresting fact that the pseudo-Oswald abruptly ended his appearances at various establishments such as a supermarket, a barber shop, and a rifle range, and that the cut-off point in each instance preceded the arrest and murder of Oswald. This phenomenon seriously undermines the possibility of mistaken identity, unless one finds it credible that an innocent party or parties, resembling Oswald in appearance and behavior, discontinued certain innocent activities at a fixed point in time by innocent coincidence. Moreover, the genuineness of the Commission's belief that particular allegations were based on mistaken identity is open to question, for the simple reason that the Commission made no public appeal for the pseudo-Oswald to come forward and identify himself as the person wrongly identified as Oswald in perfectly innocent transactions. Nor did the Commission seek by investigation to establish that mistaken identity had occurred, except in one case (discussed below).

A public appeal or normal investigative processes might have yielded results which would have enabled the Commission to present evidence of mistaken identity instead of guesswork. Because the Commission stopped short of exhausting many avenues of inquiry, and because other possibilities were not effectively excluded, it becomes difficult to dismiss as mistaken identity the "Oswald" reported by seemingly dependable witnesses.

In the cases of implied fabrication the Commission in some instances has demonstrated a shocking readiness to impeach the character of a witness on very slender grounds, not hesitating to go out of their way to find derogatory information about a witness whose testimony could not be dismissed by other methods.

The other methods included tests of credibility which were nothing less than unreasonable, and the exaggeration of essentially minor discrepancies.

The Commission seizes upon the unfavorable opinion of a witness voiced by his employers as grounds for dismissing his story as a figment of his imagination; in a parallel case, the employer gave the witness the highest character reference and voiced his confidence in the man's veracity, yet the Commission found him untrustworthy.

In one case the Commission expressed skepticism of a witness because a piece of documentary evidence could not be found; in another, the documentary evidence is produced only to have the Commission suspect its authenticity.

One witness is impeached because a woman acquaintance disparaged her as having a "strange obsession for injecting herself into any big event," but the fact that the witness did not inject herself into *this* event, as she might well have done (indeed, should have done, by reporting an encounter with "Oswald") even in the absence of the alleged obsession, is ignored.

That readiness of the Commission to impeach character on flimsy grounds has been deplored by eminent members of the legal profession.[2] It stands in startling contrast to the Commission's complacent finding of credibility, or probative value, in the testimony of self-interested, self-contradictory, confused persons or those with dubious motives—including a convicted murderer as well as lesser criminals—so long as those witnesses gave testimony compatible with the lone-assassin thesis. To determine the impact on the individuals who were subjected to innuendos and discredit in the pages of the Report, and who may have suffered in their personal associations or in their work, is beyond our reach.[3]

The Commission's failure to use its full powers of investigation is to be regretted, not only to establish that the allegations resulted from mistaken identity, if indeed they did, but, more importantly, to rule out the possibility of deliberate impersonation. Several of the stories evoke the almost irresistible suspicion of impersonation because of the flamboyant and gratuitous care "Oswald" took to call attention to himself in a way that later appeared to incriminate the real Oswald and to implicate the alleged murder rifle. For the Commission to pursue the evidence of impersonation was of great importance if it meant to evaluate the inferences that would flow from proof of an imposter-Oswald: that there was a plot to kill the President, planned carefully long before the event; that the conspirators were familiar with Oswald's background and circumstances and had selected him as their fall guy; that Oswald had to be murdered to prevent him from presenting evidence of his innocence, or evidence implicating others; and that the killers of the President were still at large.

While the Warren Report is silent on the matter of impersonation, the Commission in reality was not so unaware of the matter as the silence suggests. The Hearings suggest that the Commission actively entertained the suspicion that Larry Crafard, an associate of Jack Ruby, might have impersonated Oswald at the auto sales agency and the rifle range. This impression derives from the fact that photographs of Crafard were displayed to several of the witnesses concerned by Commission counsel. In each case, the witness stated that Crafard was not the man and later, having been shown a photograph of Oswald, identified him.

---

2   Freese, *op. cit.*

3   In one instance, a witness who entered the scene as a reputable and employed member of the community and whose story was the subject of open skepticism by the authorities who interviewed and reinterviewed him was last questioned at the county jail, where he was held on charges of passing fraudulent checks. A cause-and-effect relationship is not at all fantastic, although it is purely conjectural; and, to give credit where it is due, although the Commission did reject his story, the Report does not allude to the man's downfall.

The Commission seems to do itself an injustice by omitting from the Report any indication that the possibilty of impersonation *had* been considered, but perhaps it was wise to avoid the subject. Discussion would have exposed the superficial and fragmentary attention given to this crucial area of investigation in which Crafard alone was the subject of somewhat fitful suspicion.

But Crafard was not the only witness who resembled Oswald.

The Man in the Doorway

The Warren Report states, as a "speculation":

> A picture published widely in newspapers and magazines after the assassination showed Lee Harvey Oswald standing on the front steps of the Texas School Book Depository Building shortly before the President's motorcade passed by.   *(WR 644)*

But the Commission's "finding" was that:

> The man on the front steps of the building, thought or alleged by some to be Lee Harvey Oswald, is actually Billy Lovelady, an employee of the Depository, who somewhat resembles Oswald.   *(WR 644)*

If one looks at the photograph, the "Altgens photo" *(CEs 203, 900, 1407-1408)* taken by press photographer James W. Altgens during the shooting (at the point in time that corresponds with Frame 255 of the Zapruder film), it becomes clear that the man in the doorway might be Oswald's identical twin. Is the man nevertheless really Billy Lovelady?

Neither the Report nor the Hearings and Exhibits provides any visual means of judgment since no photograph of Lovelady is found in any of the volumes. Merely asserting that it is Lovelady and not Oswald in the doorway, the Commission presents no supporting visual evidence by which one can appraise the resemblance between Lovelady and the man in the doorway, or Lovelady and Oswald, although nothing less hangs on the accurate identification of the doorway man than Oswald's possible total innocence of the assassination.

Moreover, the members of the Warren Commission never saw Lovelady personally, nor is it certain that they even saw photographs of him. The assertion that it is Lovelady in the doorway rests on Lovelady's own statement and on testimony by Wesley Frazier and William Shelley that Lovelady was present on the steps of the Book Depository. But Shelley told the FBI on March 18, 1964:

> I recall that as the Presidential Motorcade passed I was standing just outside the glass doors of the entrance. At the time President John F. Kennedy was shot I was standing at this same place. Billy N. Lovelady who works under my supervision for the Texas School Book Depository was seated on the entrance steps just in front of me.   *(CE 1381, p. 84)*

When Shelley was deposed by Commission Counsel Ball only three weeks after his FBI statement he was not asked to describe Lovelady's exact position on the steps nor was he shown the doorway photograph and asked to indicate Lovelady. When Frazier and Lovelady testified, they were asked to look at the photo and to place an arrow on the picture to identify which figure was Lovelady. *(2H 242; 6H 338)* Both were presented with the same print of the Altgens photo *(CE 369)* and both supposedly placed an arrow on it. Yet the photograph shows only one arrow, not two. It points to the man who looks like Oswald's double. Who put that arrow there—Lovelady himself, or Frazier? Can that single arrow constitute sufficient identification and corroboration, and does it really rule out the possibility that the man standing in the doorway is Oswald?

Documents and photographs discovered in the National Archives in the summer of 1966 revive this possibility. The documents indicate that Lovelady told the FBI within a few days of the assassination that as he stood watching the motorcade, he had worn a short-sleeved shirt with vertical, alternating, broad red and white stripes, buttoned at the neck. The face in the doorway could be Lovelady's face (as it could be Oswald's) but the photographs show Lovelady wearing that short-sleeved striped shirt in a series of poses. By no stretch of the imagination can that shirt be thought to correspond with the shirt on the man in the doorway. He is wearing a long-sleeved reddish-brown shirt, opened half-way to the waist—a shirt that looks exactly like the one Oswald wore on the day of the assassination. *(CE 150)* No wonder the FBI, in its re-enactment photograph of the Altgens photo *(CE 900),* did not pose Lovelady in the doorway wearing his striped short-sleeved shirt, as one might have expected would be done in support of a significant claim of identity.

The Commission's nonchalance about the man in the doorway and its failure to present in full the evidence at its disposal (inconclusive as it is) is astonishing. Even more astonishing is the Commission's request to the FBI to carry out comparisons between Oswald's shirt, the physical object pictured in *CE 150,* and the shirt worn by Oswald in the police station after his arrest as shown in photographs taken in the police corridors or elevators. *(CEs 1996-1997)* This shirt was taken from Oswald by the police and a chain of possession was maintained as it went to the FBI and to the Commission itself. No one challenged its legitimacy or identity. Why, then, was this laborious comparison undertaken and why was FBI photographic expert Lyndal Shaneyfelt called to testify at length to his findings? *(15H 694-695; Shaneyfelt Exhibits No. 24A-24D)* The record does not offer any explanation.

The comparison that *had* to be made, in a fact-finding investigation worth the name, was a comparison between Oswald's shirt and the shirt worn by the man in the doorway. The comparison that *was* made, at the Commission's request, was unnecessary and irrelevant, serving no known purpose except to inflate the official record and pad the evidence.

The man in the doorway presents us with this paradox: The Commission received, on the one hand, many allegations by objective witnesses of encounters with Oswald or his identical twin; on the other hand, it received a photograph which appeared to be one of Oswald or his double but which is said to be a man who is a fellow employee at the Book Depository. If the Commission had any genuine conviction that the man was Lovelady, why was he not a better candidate than Larry Crafard for the Oswald impersonator? Lovelady was directly linked with Oswald, while no link between Crafard and Oswald was established, and—if it is Lovelady in the doorway—he resembles Oswald far more than Crafard does *(see CEs 451, 453-456, photographs of Crafard in several poses).*

Some of the other "two-Oswald" episodes should be examined, to see if the Commission has disposed of them in a manner that satisfies objective criteria.

The Grocer

Leonard Hutchison, proprietor of a supermarket in Irving, Texas, testified that Oswald had made purchases in his store from time to time early on weekday mornings: once he had come on a Wednesday evening, accompanied by a woman believed to be Marina Oswald and a second, elderly woman, and during the first week of November 1963, Oswald had tried to cash a personal check made out to him for $189. *(WR 331-332)*

Having considered this testimony, the Commission concluded that there were "strong reasons for doubting the correctness of Hutchison's testimony." Oswald was not known to have received a check for $189 from any source; he was actually in Dallas at the times Hutchison claimed he was in his store at Irving; both Marina and Marguerite Oswald denied ever having been in Hutchison's market.

The reasoning appears to be valid and to justify the assumption that Hutchison had confused a different customer with Oswald.

But one difficulty is that the customer stopped coming into the store after the assassination and has not reappeared to this day or come forward to assert his identity. Another difficulty is that Hutchison's story received corroboration from a man who did not rate mention in the Warren Report: Clifton Shasteen.

Shasteen is the proprietor of a barber shop in Irving, situated not far from Hutchison's supermarket. Shasteen testified that Oswald had come to the barber shop several times to have his hair cut. On some occasions he had been accompanied by a boy about fourteen years of age. One time the boy had criticized American policy, voicing pacifist and socialist views. As for Oswald, Shasteen testified:

> The only time I remember seeing him, you know, other than just going in the grocery store across the street, Mr. Hutchison's food market, and I was down at the drugstore one night, down at Williamsburg's and he was in there. . . . And, why I remembered seeing him in there, I knew I couldn't understand his wife, and that was before—I believe it was before she had her baby. The best I remember she was pregnant. . . . That's the only time I had ever saw her, that I remember. You know, she may have come to the grocery store with him but I didn't pay any attention. Sometimes there were two women with him. . . .   *(10H 311)*

No wonder Shasteen is not mentioned in the Report. Not only did he corroborate Oswald's visits to Hutchison's store but he also volunteered that "sometimes there were two women with him," just as Hutchison had testified. Shasteen recognized Oswald as his customer as soon as he saw him on television on November 22; he had cut the man's hair and acquired more than casual familiarity with his face. Moreover, on one occasion Shasteen had admired his customer's lounging slippers, and the customer had volunteered that he bought them for $1.50 in Mexico *(10H 311)*—a further point of identity with Oswald, who had visited Mexico City at the end of September that year.

Was it the real Oswald who was seen by Shasteen and Hutchison, once together with a pregnant wife whom they believed to be Marina Oswald? Or was it a different man with a different wife, both of whom resembled their Oswald counterparts? Or was it a man impersonating Oswald, accompanied by a woman impersonating Marina? If it *was* the real Oswald, who was the source of the check for $189?

Western Union

Another indication that Oswald may have received mysterious funds came from C. A. Hamblen, early night manager at Western Union in Dallas. Hamblen reported that Oswald had collected money orders for small amounts of money on several occasions, and about ten days before the assassination he had come in to send a telegram to Washington, D. C., possibly to the Secretary of the Navy. *(WR 332)*

The Commission proceeds to point out that during his testimony (on July 23, 1964, many months after the initial report) Hamblen "did not recall with clarity the statements he had previously made, and was unable to state whether the person he reportedly had seen in the Western Union office was or was not Lee Harvey Oswald." (This is hardly surprising, considering the manner in which Counsel Liebeler launched his cross-examination, confusing the witness and concentrating on what Hamblen had told a newspaper reporter, not on his contacts with a customer he believed to be Oswald. The three pages of Hamblen's testimony *(11H 311-314)* have to be read in full to appreciate the fashion in which counsel conducted the examination.)

The Commission next states that Hamblen's fellow employees did not corroborate his story or identify Oswald as a customer; that neither the money orders nor the telegram to Washington could be found in a complete search of Western Union records; and that Hamblen's superiors have concluded that the whole thing was a figment of his imagination, "and the Commission accepts this assessment." *(WR 333)*

A reading of the documents raises some questions about the Commission's evaluation of Hamblen's story. Hamblen had first reported his encounters with a customer he believed to be Oswald to his superior, Laurance Wilcox, on November 26, 1963, and a few days later to Bob Fenley, a reporter for the *Dallas Times-Herald*. Another Western Union employee, Aubrey Lewis, had corroborated one part of Hamblen's story, involving a money order addressed to a person at the Dallas YMCA. *(Wilcox Exhibit 3015)* Wilcox, Fenley, Lewis, and another of Hamblen's superiors, W. W. Semingsen, were all deposed by counsel for the Warren Commission before Hamblen himself (as early as March 1964, in two cases). Another Western Union employee, Mrs. D. J. McClure—who denied having had anything to do with the customer—was not asked to give testimony at all though Hamblen had named her as being involved in one of the incidents with the man he alleged to be Oswald. *(10H 412)*

It seems curious that although Hamblen's allegations were publicized on November 30, 1963, he was not examined by the Commission until July 23, 1964, after four other witnesses had already testified on the matter. It seems curious also that Aubrey Lewis as well as Hamblen himself testified to the delivery of a money order to a payee at the YMCA, where Oswald in fact stayed for a few days upon his return from Mexico City early in October, and that both witnesses said that the payee had identified himself by exhibiting a "Navy ID card and a library card." *(Wilcox Exhibit 3005-3006)* Oswald, of course, was an ex-Marine and did carry a library card. *(WR 616)* Lewis recalled that the customer was effeminate and was accompanied by another man, of Spanish descent— a description strikingly like that given by Dean Andrews, a New Orleans attorney, who also alleged contacts with Oswald. *(WR 325)*

Hamblen recalled that the man he believed to be Oswald had sent a telegram to Washington, to the Secretary of the Navy; Oswald, in fact, had communicated with the Secretary of the Navy on earlier dates attempting to reverse his "unsatisfactory" discharge from the Marines. *(CE 2663)* Was Hamblen in a position to know that as early as November 26, 1963 and to invent the alleged telegram?

True, the employee named by Hamblen as having handled the payment for the alleged telegram denied it; true, a search of the records was made and no such telegram was found. That is unfavorable to Hamblen.

But Aubrey Lewis supported part of Hamblen's story. Was Lewis sharing a figment of Hamblen's imagination?

Mr. Hamblen's written statement refers to a money order made payable to Oswald several weeks ago on which Mr. A. L. Lewis, Relief Clerk, had difficulty in paying. Mr. Lewis has stated he does not recall the payee's name and that the transaction in question was a money order addressed to someone at the YMCA . . . and that the date of the occurrence was Tuesday, October 29, 1963. We have searched the paid money orders and extracted all money orders payable to anyone at the YMCA during October and November in an effort to locate the money order which both Messrs. Hamblen and Lewis say Mr. Lewis had difficulty in paying. Mr. Lewis does not recognize any of the several money orders that were extracted as covering the particular case he and Mr. Hamblen alluded to.

(Wilcox Exhibit 3015)

The Commission, with its usual *élan,* has been quick to conclude that the "whole thing" was a figment of Hamblen's imagination, but has not assessed the testimony of Lewis. Was his story also a fabrication? If not, why was the money

House, also helped produce the atmosphere of a political honeymoon.

Foreign problems brought this first phase to an end by early summer. An attempt to aid Cuban *émigrés* to invade Cuba and overthrow its dictator, Fidel Castro, ended in failure when the administration declined to back the invasion with full military support. Communist and guerrilla forces in Laos and Vietnam intensified their operations without major counteraction by the United States. The Berlin crisis came close to explosion when the East German communist regime sealed off West Berlin with a wall; hostilities were averted but the deadlock over the city tightened. On the other hand, the president launched a well received Alliance for Progress to promote economic development and social reform in Latin America; increased economic aid to other underdeveloped areas; created a Peace Corps (*q.v.*); and gave to the armed forces greater power and versatility. He won a major legislative victory when congress gave its approval to a program to reduce tariffs and stimulate international trade.

The administration's domestic efforts also brought mixed results. Forthright executive action along a broad front helped produce an economic revival in 1961 but it lost momentum in 1962. The president made vigorous use of his executive authority and influence in opposing a rise in steel prices in April 1962. He won the approval of congress for legislation to expand federal housing activities, raise minimum wages and broaden welfare programs. On most of his major new proposals, however, the president was defeated. In spite of its Democratic majority, congress refused to support a general aid-to-education bill, tax reform, medical care for the aged under social security, a new farm program, creation of a new cabinet-level department of urban affairs and authority to finance long-term loans to underdeveloped nations by borrowing from the treasury.

President Kennedy entered into the 1962 election campaign in behalf of congressional candidates who were likely to support the policies of his administration, but his speaking tour was abruptly cut off two weeks before the election when intelligence reports revealed that Soviet long-range missiles and other offensive weapons were being installed on the island of Cuba. The president immediately returned to Washington, addressed the nation by radio and television to explain the nature of the threat to the nation's security, and announced a naval "quarantine" of Cuba to prevent the arrival of additional weapons. He called upon the Cuban government and the Soviet Union to remove all offensive weapons from the island at once. After a brief period of tension the Soviet ships carrying additional weapons turned back and Premier Nikita Khrushchev announced that rockets and missiles already in Cuba would be withdrawn. Negotiations in which U Thant, acting secretary-general of the United Nations, took part, continued for some time in an effort to work out details for the verification of the removal of the weapons, and the administration was subjected to continuing criticism on the ground that large numbers of Soviet troops remained in Cuba months later.

In Jan. 1963 President Kennedy sent a budget message to congress calling for a total of $98,800,000,000 in expenditures during the fiscal year beginning July 1, 1963, and anticipating a large deficit. The president proposed a substantial reduction in income tax rates to stimulate the economy, and that reforms be made in the tax laws. He also called for federal aid for dealing with the problem of mental health and for a medical care program for the aged financed through social security taxes. All of these proposals were received with some coolness in a congress dominated by a coalition of conservative Democrats and Republicans. Some Democratic leaders urged the president to challenge the conservative coalition, but he clung to the traditional presidential methods of ... advancing congress, partly because he wanted to keep the na... ...as possible on foreign policy... ...successf...

tensions and eliminating the harmful effects of radioactive fallout.

President Kennedy visited Texas on a speaking tour in November, arriving in Dallas on Nov. 22. At about 12:30 P.M., as the presidential motorcade proceeded from the airport to a luncheon, three shots rang out. Two bullets struck and killed the president and another wounded Texas Gov. John B. Connally, who was riding with his wife, with Mrs. Kennedy and the president in an open car. The president's death was officially announced at about 1:30 P.M., whereupon Vice-Pres. Lyndon Johnson, who had been riding in

JOHN F. KENNEDY AT A PRESS CONFERENCE, 1961
WIDE WORLD

another car of the motorcade, took the presidential oath of office and returned to Washington. Meanwhile, Dallas police apprehended Lee Harvey Oswald, 24 years old, a self-styled Marxist, and charged him with the murder. There was evidence that he had fired the fatal shots from a sixth-floor window of a building overlooking the assassination scene. On Nov. 24, as Oswald was being transferred to the Dallas county jail, a man identified as Jack Ruby (born Rubenstein), a night-club operator, shot and fatally wounded him. The shooting took place in the basement of the Dallas police department building in full view of a nationwide television audience.

President Kennedy's body, after lying in state for one day beneath the Capitol rotunda, was buried in Arlington National cemetery on Nov. 25.

Warren Commission.—On Nov. 29, President Johnson ap-pointed a commission to investigate the circumstances surrounding the assassination of Kennedy and the shooting of Oswald. The chairman of the commission was the chief justice of the United States, Earl Warren; the other members were two U.S. senators, Richard B. Russell of Georgia and John Sherman Cooper of Kentucky; two members of the house of representatives, Hale Boggs of Louisiana and Gerald R. Ford of Michigan; and two men from private life, Allen W. Dulles, former director of the Central Intelligence agency, and John J. McCloy, former president of the International Bank for Reconstruction and Development. After months of investigation the commission submitted its findings to President Johnson in Sept. 1964, and they were immediately made public. The commission reported that the bullets that had killed President Kennedy were fired by Lee Harvey Oswald from a rifle pointed out a sixth-floor window of the Texas School Book Depository. The commission also reported that it had found no evidence that either Oswald or Ruby was part of any conspiracy, foreign or domestic, to assassinate President Kennedy. The commission described in detail its investigation of Oswald's life to provide a basis for determining his motives but did not itself attempt to analyze Oswald's motives. The commission also proposed strengthening the Secret Service organization; adopting improved procedures for protecting the president; and enacting legislation to make killing the president or vice-president a federal offense. The report was published by the U.S. Government Printing office under the title *Report of the President's Commission on the Assassination of President John F. Kennedy* (1964).

BIBLIOGRAPHY.—Most of Kennedy's speeches will be found in the *Congressional Record* (1947–60). Allan Nevins (ed.), *The Strategy of Peace* (1960) is a collection of his major foreign-policy pronounc... ...s, James M. Burns, *John Kennedy; a Political Profile* (1960)... ...Joseph McCarthy, *The Remarkable Ke...*

Melisa (new)

5 868-699 5

Kim { 410-0613 }

order addressed to the YMCA missing from the records of Western Union? Is it possible that that money order, and the telegram to Washington as well, was quickly removed and destroyed when the story broke in the papers and before the search was made?

The Commission had a duty to examine that possibility carefully since it was important to determine whether Oswald was receiving money from a mysterious source.

It would be interesting to know also why Hamblen said on November 26 or 28, 1963 that a photograph of Oswald was the "spit image" of the customer who had given him a hard time on several occasions *(Wilcox Exhibit 3005)* and why he said on July 23, 1964 when shown a photograph of Oswald that there was "no resemblance" to the trouble-making patron. *(11H 313)* What happened in the intervening eight months to cause such a complete reversal?

The Gunsmith and the Furniture Store Ladies

The Warren Commission, having quickly concurred with the opinion of Hamblen's employers that his story was a sheer invention, also solicited the opinion of the employer of another witness, gunsmith Dial Ryder.

Ryder had become known to the Dallas police on Sunday, November 24, 1963 (a few hours after Oswald was shot to death) as the result of an anonymous telephone call to a television newscaster informing him that Oswald had had a rifle sighted on Thursday, November 21, at a gun shop at 211 or 212 Irving Boulevard in Irving, Texas. The police had located the owner, Charles Greener, and his employee Ryder. According to Detective F. M. Turner's report:

> He [Greener] states that he and Ryder have talked about this and have seen photos of Oswald and photos of the gun in the paper and neither can remember doing any work for this man, or any work on this gun. He will check his files for names and call back if he finds anything. He states that another reason that both of them think that they never worked on this gun is that in the photo the screws that hold the clamp that holds the scope on the rifle look like they are on top of the gun, and he thinks that neither of them ever saw a gun with a scope mounted with these screws on top.
>
> On November 28, 1963, I talked to Mr. Greener again. He states they found a work ticket back in the rear of the shop. This ticket has no date on it, but the best they can figure out this work probably came in November 4 to November 8, 1963. This ticket has the name Oswald on it. . . . Neither he nor Ryder can remember the face, or doing any work for this man. . . .
>
> We talked to Mr. Dial D. Ryder. . . . He states that he wrote the work ticket up with the name Oswald on it. We showed him a new mug shot of Oswald, and he states that he cannot identify the man as the one who left a rifle with him.   *(CE 2003, pp. 252-254)*

Not a word of this appears in the Warren Report, nor is the police report even cited in the footnotes. Instead, the Report tells us:

> ... the authenticity of the repair tag bearing Oswald's name is indeed subject to grave doubts. Ryder testified that he found the repair tag while cleaning his workbench on November 23, 1963. However, Ryder spoke with Greener repeatedly during the period between November 22-28 and, sometime prior to November 25, he discussed with him the possibility that Oswald had been in the store. Neither he nor Greener could remember that he had been. But despite these conversations with Greener, it is significant that Ryder never called the repair tag to his employer's attention. Greener did not learn about the tag until November 28, when he was called by TV reporters. . . .
> Subsequent events also reflect on Ryder's credibility.   *(WR 315-316)*

That is a slanted account of what had happened. On Sunday, November 24 Greener himself had promised "to check his files" for any record of Oswald. Neither he nor Ryder remembered or identified Oswald. And Greener didn't believe for a minute that Ryder had fabricated the repair tag. He said:

> *Greener:* I have confidence in the boy, or I wouldn't have him working for me.
> *Liebeler:* You don't think he would make this tag up to cause a lot of commotion?
> *Greener:* I don't think so. He doesn't seem like that type boy. I have lots of confidence in him or I wouldn't have him working for me and handling money. Especially times I am going off. He—if he wasn't the right kind of boy, and he pretty well proved that he is by dependability and in all relations that we have together, and I just don't figure that is possible.
> *(11H 249)*

The Commission nevertheless decided to impeach Ryder's character on the basis of inconsequential discrepancies in what Ryder said to a reporter and an investigator—as well as the character of one of the two witnesses acknowledged by the Report to provide "possible corroboration" for his story. *(WR 316)*

Mrs. Gertrude Hunter and Mrs. Edith Whitworth testified that Oswald, with his wife and two daughters, had come into Mrs. Whitworth's furniture shop in Irving looking for a gunsmith who had formerly occupied those premises and whose sign "Guns" had not yet been removed. Oswald stayed to look at furniture, calling his wife in from the car in which they had arrived. In chatting with Mrs. Whitworth about his infant daughter Rachel, Oswald mentioned that she was born on October 20. He was carrying an object about 15 inches long, wrapped in paper. He indicated that he wanted to have the plunger (firing-pin) of his rifle repaired, and Mrs. Whitworth believes that she may have directed him to the Irving Sports Shop, where Ryder worked. *(11H 262-275)*

Mrs. Hunter, who was visiting Mrs. Whitworth when the incident occurred, gave the same account in her testimony. *(11H 253-261)*

The Commission made an elaborate investigation of the alleged visit to the furniture shop. A confrontation was held between Marina Oswald and her two children, and the two ladies. Both Mrs. Whitworth and Mrs. Hunter positively identified Marina Oswald and her daughter June. While Marina Oswald denied the whole incident, she acknowledged that she did possess a short coat like the one said by Mrs. Hunter to have been worn by the woman who had accompanied Oswald. *(11H 282)*

Nevertheless, the Commission concluded that Mrs. Hunter was not a credible witness, on the basis of disparaging remarks made about her by an acquaintance *(WR 317-318)* and without any other grounds for impeaching her character. Mrs. Hunter is accused of "attempting to inject herself into any big event that comes to her attention," although neither she nor Mrs. Whitworth had tried to inject themselves into the Oswald case. On the contrary, they had recognized Oswald as the man who visited the furniture shop as soon as they saw him on television on the day of the assassination, but they did not go to the police or to the newspapers. The incident came to light when a reporter for the *London Evening Standard* decided to canvass all the gun shops in Irving, looking for a trace of Oswald, and seeing the sign "Guns" outside the furniture shop, questioned Mrs. Whitworth. *(CE 1335)*

Why, then, does the Commission malign Mrs. Hunter for attempting to inject herself into the case? She did no such thing, nor has the Commission provided any evidence that she did so at any other time. In any event, Mrs. Hunter's alleged lack of credibility hardly disposes of Mrs. Whitworth, against whom the Commission has made no accusation.

Because the testimony of the two ladies strongly supported the authenticity of Dial Ryder's repair ticket, the Commission went to extraordinary lengths in investigating their story. In an attempt to determine whether some other family group paralleling the Oswalds might have visited the shop, the Commission asked the FBI to investigate all female births in the Dallas-Irving area on October 20, 1963. No family was found. *(CE 1338)* It was only after that futile inquiry (June 1964), which in itself suggests that the Commission initially believed the Whitworth-Hunter story, that Mrs. Hunter's acquaintance was interviewed (August 1964) and provided a basis *(CE 2976)* for the Commission to discredit Mrs. Hunter for seeking to inject herself into events.

In the furniture store affair, the Commission at least attempted to ascertain whether it might have been an innocent case of mistaken identity—although not going so far as a public appeal to those concerned to come forward. Having failed to establish mistaken identity, the Commission deemed the story a fabrication—without justification impeaching Mrs. Whitworth, by implication, as well as Mrs. Hunter.

Had the Commission continued to consider the story credible, as the search for a parallel family implies, it would have raised very serious difficulties. (1) It would have placed Oswald in Irving on a weekday afternoon, when he was supposedly at work in Dallas. (2) It would have destroyed the credibility of Marina Oswald, who denied the whole incident. (3) Moreover, it would have suggested culpability if not complicity on her part in a crime which Oswald planned to commit, had she knowingly accompanied him on an expedition to repair a rifle, after the alleged attempts on General Walker and Richard Nixon and her alleged threat to turn Oswald in if he ever showed signs of repeating such adventures. (4) Worst of all, acceptance of the Whitworth-Hunter story would go a long way to exonerate Dial Ryder from suspicion of fabricating the repair ticket.

If that ticket was authentic, Oswald must have had a second rifle, which Marina Oswald denied and which has not been found. That is one possibility.

Another possibility is that Oswald was impersonated, at both the gun shop and the furniture store.

No wonder the Commission declined to open such a Pandora's box and preferred to believe that both Ryder and Mrs. Hunter (and, implicitly, Mrs. Whitworth) had invented tales in order to inject themselves into a "big event." That these witnesses fabricated stories or misrepresented the facts remains, of course, within the realm of possibility; that the authors of the Report misrepresented facts is a certainty.

The Rifle Range

The illusion of two Oswalds is nowhere more pronounced than in the reports of numerous witnesses who placed him at the Sports Drome Rifle Range in Dallas on various occasions in September, October, and November 1963 when Oswald was actually in Mexico City or at the Paine home at Irving. (WR 318-320) The witnesses included a thirteen-year-old boy, Sterling Wood, and his father, Dr. Homer Wood, a dentist.

The Commission explains in considerable detail why it rejected all those reports and concluded that Oswald was not the man at the rifle range. Not only was it geographically impossible for Oswald to have been present on some of the reported occasions, but one witness said that the man at the rifle range had blond hair, and another said that he chewed bubble gum or tobacco and wore a huge, Texas-style hat. None of those characteristics corresponded with Oswald. Oswald could not drive a car, as one witness said the pseudo-Oswald had done. None of the witnesses' descriptions of the pseudo-Oswald's rifle corresponded exactly with the assassination rifle. For these and similar reasons, the Commission concludes that Oswald was not the man at the rifle range and that all the witnesses were mistaken.

By treating these witnesses as a group, the Commission has obscured the fact that the testimony of Sterling Wood and his father is not subject to serious objections. Sterling and his father went to the rifle range on Saturday afternoon, November 16, 1963, when Oswald was not in Irving as usual. He had remained in Dallas, at Marina Oswald's suggestion that he might be *de trop* at the birthday party for one of Mrs. Paine's children that weekend. It was therefore physically possible for Oswald to be at the rifle range, as the Woods testified he was.

Dr. Wood reported that his son was shooting next to a man who had an unusual rifle that expelled a "ball of fire" when he shot. (10H 386) Wood jocularly warned his son to watch out for the "105 howitzer," but the boy said it was all right, it was only an Italian carbine. He told his father that the man with the

Italian carbine was a good shot; when Dr. Wood himself looked at the target, he saw that most of the man's shots were inside, with a few of them an inch or two outside. He noticed his son exchange a few words with the owner of the Italian carbine.

Dr. Wood testified *(10H 387)* that when he saw Oswald on the television screen on the day of the assassination, he immediately told his wife that Oswald looked like the man at the rifle range. He decided to say nothing to his son and to see if the boy independently recognized Oswald.

About half an hour later the boy came in and as soon as he saw Oswald on the TV screen, he said, "Daddy, that is the fellow that was sitting next to me out on the rifle range."

During his testimony Dr. Wood was shown photographs, first of Larry Crafard, whom he failed to identify. Next he was shown photographs of Oswald on the street, with other men in the background. He unhesitatingly pointed to Oswald as the man at the rifle range.

Despite his youth Sterling Wood was also a Commission witness. *(10H 390-398)* He told the same story as his father but added an account of his brief conversation with the adjacent marksman whom he believed to be Oswald. He had asked the man if his rifle was a 6.5 Italian carbine with a four-power scope, the man had replied "yes," and that was the extent of the conversation. Later, he had seen the man leave the rifle range "with a man in a newer model car," the other man driving. *(10H 393)*

Sterling, like his father, was shown photographs of Larry Crafard, whom he failed to recognize. When he was shown a picture of Oswald and other men on a street, he immediately pointed to Oswald as the man he had seen at the rifle range. He also identified a photograph of the rifle found in the Book Depository as the weapon he had seen at the rifle range, but said that the telescopic sight was not the same. *(10H 396)* Finally, he volunteered that he had looked at his neighbor's target at the rifle range and that the man was "the most accurate of all." *(10H 397)*

There is no reason to question the credibility of this thirteen-year-old boy, and it is gratifying that the Commission did not do so. What the Commssion did was to obfuscate his story, lumping him together with the other witnesses, and then dismissing them all. Only when the full testimony is examined does it become obvious that the Woods' story does not suffer from the same weakness as the others and that the man they saw must have been Oswald's double if not Oswald himself.

If the Commission had accepted the Woods' testimony, it would have helped to corroborate its thesis of Oswald's marksmanship—a thesis which, as it stands, has been the subject of much justified criticism. On the other hand, it would have introduced an unknown friend who was driving Oswald to target practice.

If the Commission had accepted the Woods' testimony, it might have lengthened the shadow of an unknown accomplice or of a man deliberately engaged in impersonating Oswald.

The Bartender

The noncommittal Commission "noted" the testimony of Evaristo Rodriguez, a bartender in the Habana Bar in New Orleans, that he saw Oswald in the bar in August 1963 in the company of a man with a Latin appearance. However, the Report adds:

> Rodriguez' identification of Oswald was uncorroborated except for the testimony of the owner, Orest Pena; according to Rodriguez, Pena was not in a position to observe the man he thought later to have been Oswald. Although Pena has testified that he did observe the same person as did Rodriguez, and that this person was Oswald, an FBI interview report indicated that a month earlier Pena had stated that he "could not at this time or at any time say whether or not the person was identical with Lee Harvey Oswald."
> *(WR 325)*

Obviously the Commission rejects rather than "notes" the story, largely because Pena's identification of Oswald was uncertain and fluctuating. Assuming for the sake of argument that Pena did waver and contradict himself about the identity of the man in the bar, let us see how the Commission dealt with another witness who did some wavering and self-contradiction: Howard Brennan. The Report states:

> During the evening of November 22, Brennan . . . said he was unable to make a positive identification. Prior to the line-up, Brennan had seen Oswald's picture on television. . . . In an interview with FBI agents on December 17, 1963, Brennan stated that he was sure that the person firing the rifle was Oswald. In another interview with FBI agents on January 7, 1964, Brennan appeared to revert to his earlier inability to make a positive identification, but, in his testimony before the Commssion, Brennan stated that his remarks of January 7 were intended by him merely as an accurate report of what he said on November 22.
>
> Brennan told the Commission that he could have made a positive identification in the line-up on November 22. . . . Brennan stated, "I could at that time—I could, with all sincerity, identify him as being the same man."
>
> Although the record indicates that Brennan was an accurate observer, he declined to make a positive identification of Oswald when he first saw him in the police line-up. The Commission, therefore, does not base its conclusion . . . on Brennan's subsequent certain identification of Lee Harvey Oswald. . . . Immediately after the assassination, however, Brennan described to the police the man he saw in the window and then identified Oswald as the person who most nearly resembled the man he saw.
>
> The Commission is satisfied that, at the least, Brennan saw a man in the window who closely resembled Lee Harvey Oswald, and that Brennan believes the man he saw was in fact Lee Harvey Oswald.   *(WR 145-146)*

If Pena contradicted himself as the Commission claims, what can be said for Brennan? And why should Pena's alleged self-contradiction automatically discredit Rodriguez' testimony?

In fact, Pena contradicted the FBI rather than himself. During his testimony he denied that he had made the statements attributed to him by the FBI agents who interviewed him a month earlier *(11H 353);* moreover, he charged one of the agents with attempted intimidation *(11H 363).* That agent was the same one already encountered in the case of the auto demonstration, Warren C. De Brueys, who apparently shifted his theater of operations from Dallas to New Orleans sometime between November 23, 1963, when he and Manning Clements interviewed Albert Guy Bogard, and June 9, 1964, when he interviewed Orest Pena. How were Pena's allegations of FBI intimidation received?

> *Liebeler:* So your complaints about the FBI here in New Orleans relate basically to the anti-Castro proposition and not to the investigation of the assassination; is that correct?
>
> *Pena:* No, no. That was way before.
>
> *Liebeler:* You don't have any criticism of the FBI as far as the investigation of the Kennedy assassination was concerned . . . ; is that right?
>
> *Pena:* You mean after the assassination?
>
> *Liebeler:* Yes.
>
> *Pena:* After the assassination, they came and asked me so many times about the same thing, lemonade, it just looked silly to me. They came over so many times, I said, I better do something about it. I called my lawyer and I said, "Look! I don't know anything else about this. I want you to go with me there and put it clear that that's what I know about it and I don't want no more part of that." *(11H 362)*

The badgering alone would explain Pena's statement to the FBI, if he really made such a statement, that he could not say then or at any time if the man in the bar was identical with Oswald.

Pena's reference to "lemonade" arises from the fact that besides ordering tequila, the pseudo-Oswald and his companion ordered lemonade as well—to the consternation of the bartender, who did not know how to make it. Rodriguez testified:

> . . . the one who spoke Spanish ordered the tequila. . . . Then the man who I later learned was Oswald ordered a lemonade. Now I didn't know what to give him because we don't have lemonades in the bar. So I asked Orest Pena how I should fix a lemonade. Orest told me to take a little of this lemon flavoring, squirt in some water, and charge him 25 cents. . . . *(11H 341)*

No wonder the occasion was engraved on the memory of the witnesses. The Report does mention the lemonade but asserts:

> When present at Pena's bar, Oswald was supposed to have been intoxicated to the extent that he became ill, which is inconsistent with other evidence that Oswald did not drink alcoholic beverages to excess. *(WR 325)*

To the contrary, the ordering of lemonade *is* consistent with the evidence that Oswald did not drink alcohol to excess.

The Lawyer

The association between Oswald or the pseudo-Oswald and effeminate and/or Latin companions, suggested in the testimony of Aubrey Lewis of Western Union and Rodriguez and Pena of the Habana Bar, is reported by other witnesses too.

> The Commission has also noted the testimony of Dean Andrews, an attorney in New Orleans. Andrews stated that Oswald came to his office several times in the summer of 1963 to seek advice on a less than honorable discharge from the Armed Forces, the citizenship status of his wife, and his own citizenship status.
>
> Andrews, who believed that he was contacted on November 23 to represent Oswald, testified that Oswald was always accompanied by a Mexican and was at times accompanied by apparent homosexuals.
>
> Andrews was able to locate no records of any of Oswald's alleged visits, and investigation has failed to locate the person who supposedly called Andrews on November 23, at a time when Andrews was under heavy sedation. While one of Andrews' employees felt that Oswald might have been at his office, his secretary has no recollection of Oswald being there.
>
> *(WR 325)*

Again, "noted" seems to be a euphemism for "rejected." Andrews' story should not be dismissed too hastily, however, for if he really received a telephone call from a person who wanted him to defend Oswald, it would be interesting to know who was so concerned about our infamous "loner," and why.

The Report suggests that Andrews was under heavy sedation at the time that he allegedly received the phone call and that the whole thing was a hallucination. It is true that Andrews was hospitalized and under sedation for pneumonia *(CE 2899)* but doubtful that any hallucination could have induced him to take the actions he took, which are consistent with a real rather than an imagined experience.

Andrews telephoned his secretary, Eva Springer, on the same day as he allegedly received the phone call. *(CE 2901)* While the secretary corroborated the fact that Andrews had called and had told her that he had been hired to represent Oswald at Dallas, she herself had no recollection of Oswald as a client. But Andrews testified that Oswald had visited his office after hours *(11H 327)*, so the secretary's failure to remember Oswald in no way diminishes his credibility. Nor does the failure to locate a record of Oswald's visits diminish Andrews' credibility; as his testimony shows, Andrews made no record.[4]

> I figured that this was another one of what we call in my office "free alley clients," so we didn't maintain the normalcy with the file that—might have scratched a few notes on a piece of pad, and two days later threw the whole thing away. Didn't pay too much attention to him.   *(11M 328)*

---

4 Andrews testified that his office was rifled shortly after he got out of the hospital *(11H 331)*—perhaps by someone who was not familiar with Andrews' usual practice of making no files on "free alley" clients.

After the phone call, Andrews also called a fellow attorney, as he testified.

I called Monk Zelden on Sunday at the N.O.A.C. [New Orleans Athletic Club] and asked Monk if he would go over—be interested in a retainer and go over to Dallas and see about that boy. . . . While I was talking with Monk, he said, "Don't worry about it. Your client just got shot."   *(11H 337)*

The next day, November 25, 1963, Andrews notified the Secret Service of Oswald's visits to his office on several occasions in June and July 1963 and of the phone call on November 23, 1963 in which he was asked to represent Oswald. He said that he believed that the man who called him was Clay Bertrand, a "lawyer without a brief case" who had contacted him on various occasions on behalf of other "free alley" clients.

After Andrews notified the Secret Service, he was interviewed repeatedly by various agents. His testimony on this and other points is amusing and enlightening.

Andrews: I remember that pretty good because I called the Feebees, and the guy says to put the phone, you know, and nothing happened.
Liebeler: The Feebees?
Andrews: That's what we call the Federal guys. All of a sudden, like a big hurricane, here they come.
Liebeler: Do you remember telling him at that time that you thought that Clay Bertrand had come into the office with Oswald when Oswald had been in the office earlier last spring?
Andrews: No; I don't remember.
Liebeler: Was Bertrand ever in the office with Oswald?
Andrews: Not that I remember.
Liebeler: Let me ask you this: When I was down here in April, before I talked to you about this thing, and I was going to take your deposition at that time, but we didn't make arrangements, in your continuing discussions with the FBI, you finally came to the conclusion that Clay Bertrand was a figment of your imagination?
Andrews: That's what the Feebees put on. I know that the two Feebees are going to put these people on the street looking [for Clay Bertrand], and I can't find the guy, and I am not going to tie up all the agents on something that isn't that solid. I told them, "Write what you want, that I am nuts. I don't care." They were running on the time factor, and the hills were shook up plenty to get it, get it, get it. I couldn't give it to them. I have been playing cops and robbers with them. You can tell when the steam is on. They are on you like the plague. They never leave. They are like cancer. Eternal.
Liebeler: That was the description of the situation?
Andrews: It was my decision if they were to stay there. If I decide yes, they stay. If I decide no, they go. So I told them, "Close your file and go some place else." That's the real reason why it was done. I don't know what they wrote in the report, but that's the real reason.   *(11H 334)*

This is an interesting segment of testimony for what it reveals about witnesses who change their stories, or appear to change their stories, after the "Feebees" enter the scene. Andrews never retracted any part of his story, and his assertions about Oswald's visits to his office are borne out by the following facts: (1) that his secretary recalled that Andrews had talked to her about a client

who wished to change his Marine discharge *(CE 2901);* that another employee
in Andrews' office, R. M. Davis, recalled discussing with Andrews in June 1963
the procedure for reversing a discharge from the Marines and remembered that
Andrews had mentioned Oswald on various occasions *(CE 2900);* and (3) that
on November 25, 1963, Andrews gave the Secret Service information on Oswald's circumstances, and those of his wife, that would have been unknown to
him had he not been visited by and conversed with the real Oswald, as he
claimed.

The Report does not do justice to Andrews' testimony about his contacts
with Oswald and his phone call from a man, thought to be Clay Bertrand, who
asked him to defend Oswald. Needless to say, it does not mention the following
fascinating passage of Andrews' testimony.

> *Andrews:* There's three people I am going to find: one of them is the real
> guy that killed the President; the Mexican; and Clay Bertrand.
>
> *Liebeler:* Do you mean to suggest by that statement that you have consider-
> able doubt in your mind that Oswald killed the President?
>
> *Andrews:* I know good and well he did not, With that weapon, he couldn't
> have been capable of making three controlled shots in that short time.
>
> *Liebeler:* You are basing your opinion on reports that you have received
> over news media as to how many shots were fired in what period of time;
> is that correct?
>
> *Andrews:* I am basing my opinion on five years as an ordnanceman in the
> Navy. You can lean into those things, and with throwing the bolts—if
> I couldn't do it myself, eight hours a day, doing this for a living, constantly
> on the range, I know this civilian couldn't do it. He might have been a sharp
> marksman at one time, but if you don't lean into that rifle and don't squeeze
> and control constantly, your brain can tell you how to do it, but you don't
> have the capability. . . . You have to stay with it. You just don't pick up a
> rifle or pistol or whatever weapon you are using and stay proficient with it.
> You have to know what you are doing. You have to be a conniver. This boy
> could have connived the deal, but I think he is a patsy. Somebody else pulled
> the trigger. . . . It's just taking the five years and thinking about it a bit. I
> have fired as much as 40,000 rounds of ammo a day for seven days a week.
> You get pretty good with it as long as you keep firing. Then I have gone back
> after two weeks. I used to be able to take a shotgun, go on a skeet, and pop
> 100 out of 100. After two weeks, I could only pop 60 of them. I would have
> to start shooting again, same way with the rifle and machine guns. Every
> other person I knew, same thing happened to them. You just have to stay at
> it.
>
> *Liebeler:* Now, did you see Oswald at any time subsequent to that time you
> saw him in the street. . . .   *(11H 330)*

The defense rests.

The Proof of the Plot

When the radio flashed the news that the President had been shot while riding
in a motorcade in Dallas, a young woman who heard the bulletin fainted and
had to be removed by ambulance to a hospital in Irving.

She was Sylvia Odio, a twenty-six-year-old Cuban *émigrée* who was active in the anti-Castro movement. The shock that sent her into unconsciousness was the recollection of three men who had visited her apartment in Dallas at the end of September 1963 and the realization that it was "very possible that they might have been responsible, as one had mentioned that night that President Kennedy should have been killed by the Cubans." *(CE 3147)*

The three men who had called on Mrs. Odio on or about the twenty-sixth or twenty-seventh of September 1963 had identified themselves as members of an anti-Castro organization and as friends of Mrs. Odio's father, a political prisoner in Cuba, with whom they displayed personal familiarity. Two of the men appeared to be Cuban or Mexican. One called himself "Leopoldo" and the other had a name "something like Angelo." *(11H 370)* The third man was an American who was introduced as "Leon Oswald." *(11H 369)*

When Mrs. Odio saw Lee Harvey Oswald on television after his arrest, she recognized him immediately as "Leon Oswald." Her sister, Annie Laurie Odio, who had seen the three visitors briefly, independently recognized Oswald as one of the three men as soon as she saw him on television. *(11H 382)*

Mrs. Odio did not inform the authorities of her encounter with "Oswald" in September, perhaps because she "feared that the Cuban exiles might be accused of the President's death" *(CE 3147);* but a woman friend in whom Mrs. Odio had confided notified the FBI, on or before November 29, 1963 *(11H 379, CE 3108)*.

In reporting Mrs. Odio's experience *(WR 321-324)*, the Warren Commission does not question that three men visited her, as she alleged, but gives apparently forceful reasons for concluding that Oswald was not one of those men. The main argument is that Oswald's known movements ruled out his presence in Dallas at the time of the visit, on Thursday, September 26 or Friday, September 27, 1963.

The Commission points out that Oswald crossed the border into Mexico between 6 a.m. and 2 p.m. on Thursday, September 26. On Wednesday, he had cashed an unemployment check at a store in New Orleans which did not open until 8 a.m.; "therefore, it appeared that Oswald's presence in New Orleans until sometime between 8 a.m. and 1 p.m. on September 25 was quite firmly established." *(WR 323)*

The Commission acknowledges that there is no firm evidence of the means by which Oswald traveled to Houston on the first leg of his trip from New Orleans to Mexico but claims that his only time which is unaccounted for was between the morning of Wednesday the twenty-fifth (when his presence in New Orleans was "quite firmly established") and 2:35 a.m. on Thursday the twenty-sixth, when he boarded a bus in Houston headed for Laredo. The only way Oswald could have gone to Dallas, visited Mrs. Odio, and still arrived in Houston in time to catch the 2:35 bus to Laredo on Thursday the twenty-sixth was to fly, and investigation disclosed no indication that Oswald had traveled between those points by air.

Important Problems

In the Commission's own words:

> In spite of the fact that it appeared almost certain that Oswald could not have been in Dallas at the time Mrs. Odio thought he was, the Commission requested the FBI to conduct further investigation to determine the validity of Mrs. Odio's testimony. The Commission considered the problems raised by that testimony as important in view of the possibility it raised that Oswald may have had companions on his trip to Mexico. *(WR 324)*

Note should be taken of the stipulation that Mrs. Odio's testimony was important, although the Commission somewhat understates the reasons. If Oswald had companions on his trip to Mexico, it would point to an organized, covert activity almost certainly related in some way to the Castro regime. Such mysterious associations and activities in September would demolish any November proposition that Oswald was a *lone* assassin and would pose overwhelmingly the outlines of a plot, implicating Cubans of some denomination, perhaps with non-Cuban backers, joined in a conspiracy against the life of the President of the United States.

If any aspect of the investigation was more crucial in its implications, it is not readily apparent. The Commisson itself recognized the importance of Mrs. Odio's testimony. It is to be expected, then, that her story was the subject of extremely thorough and exacting scrutiny—scrutiny that enabled the Commission to satisfy itself and to assure the American people that there was no "Cuban plot" behind the assassination of President Kennedy but only a lone deranged assassin without political motive.

Just how thorough and exacting was the Commission's investigation?

Unfinished Business

The answer is that the Commission sent its Report to press without even completing the investigation into Mrs. Odio's story. This unbelievable denouement is acknowledged in the Report.

> The Commssion specifically requested the FBI to attempt to locate and identify the two men who Mrs. Odio stated were with the man she thought was Oswald.[5]
>
> On September 16, 1964, the FBI located Loran Eugene Hall in Johnsandale, Calif. Hall has been identified as a participant in numerous anti-Castro activities. He told the FBI that in September 1963 he was in Dallas, soliciting aid in connection with anti-Castro activities. He said he had visited Mrs. Odio. He was accompanied by Lawrence Howard, a Mexican-American from East Los Angeles, and one William Seymour from Arizona. He stated that Seymour is similar in appearance to Lee Harvey Oswald; he speaks only a few words of Spanish, as Mrs. Odio had testified one of the men who visited her did.

---

5   In a letter to J. Edgar Hoover dated August 28, 1964. *(CE 3045)*

> *While the FBI had not yet completed its investigation into this matter at the time the report went to press, he Commission has concluded that Lee Harvey Oswald was not at Mrs. Odio's apartment in September 1963.*
> [Italics added] *(WR 324)*

Considerable complacency is necessary to join the Warren Commission in assuming, on the basis of an unfinished investigation and an incomplete record, that William Seymour was the "Oswald" at Mrs. Odio's door. We are entitled to proof, not supposition. We are entitled to sworn testimony from Seymour, Hall, and Howard and to further testimony from Mrs. Odio and her sister after they are confronted with those three men.

However, even if the Commission had made a thorough investigation to prove that Hall, Howard, and Seymour were the three men who visited Mrs. Odio and that she and her sister mistakenly had identified Seymour as Oswald, the episode would still constitute strong evidence of conspiracy—but one directed against Oswald as well as the President.

Is there any other way to explain Seymour's introduction as "Leon Oswald"[6] or the telephone call that Mrs. Odio received from "Leopoldo" the next day *(11H 377)* when he carefully told her (1) that "Leon Oswald" was a former Marine; (2) that "Oswald" was a crack marksman; (3) that "Oswald" felt that President Kennedy should have been assassinated after the Bay of Pigs; and (4) that "Oswald" was "loco" and the kind of man who could do anything, like "getting" the Cuban underground or killing Castro.

Whether the visitor was Oswald himself, or Seymour impersonating Oswald, "Leopoldo" took pains to plant seeds which inevitably would incriminate Oswald in the assassination carried out on November 22, so that an anonymous phone call would be enough to send the police straight after him even if he had not been arrested within the hour.[7] In itself, this setting-the-stage made it imperative for the Commission to press the investigation to the limits and to consider Loran Hall, Lawrence Howard, and William Seymour as prime suspects in the assassination, if they proved to be the men who had visited Mrs. Odio, unless an innocent and incontrovertible explanation for their antics was established.

The Commission's failure to get to the bottom of this affair, with its inescapable implications, is inexcusable. If the Commission could leave such business unfinished, we are entitled to ask whether its members were ever determined to uncover the truth. Indeed, the Commission did not even give an honest account of such facts as *were* established. Its own Exhibits expose the "evidence" presented in the Report as a tissue of evasion and deception which discredits more than it justifies the conclusion that Oswald could not have visited Mrs. Odio.

---

6 The FBI was not unaware of this stumbling block, but it seems unnecessary to take seriously its suggestion that "the name Loran Hall bears some phonetic resemblance to the name Leon Oswald" *(CE 3146),* an "explanation" that the Commission prudently omitted from the Report—without, however, offering a better one, or, for that matter, confronting the difficulty at all.

7 See Chapter 3, footnote 8.

A Credible Witness

Before documenting the charge of deception by the Commission, we should examine the possibility of deception by Mrs. Odio in her testimony about a visit at the end of September 1963 by three men who represented themselves as members of the anti-Castro underground. Several points speak in favor of her credibility, including the fact that the Commission itself concedes the reality of the visit and questions only the identity of one member of the trio.

Mrs. Odio's sister corroborates the visit and recognizes Oswald as one of the men. A letter from Mrs. Odio's father (Odio Exhibit 1) corroborates her testimony (11H 368) that she had written to him to inquire whether the three men were his friends, as they claimed.

Moreover, Mrs. Odio related the incident to her psychiatrist a few days after the event (11H 373, 381); representatives of the Warren Commission had a discussion lasting more than an hour with the psychiatrist, Dr. Einspruch, which apparently satisfied them that Mrs. Odio was trustworthy (11H 381). (The official record does not include a transcript or summary of that discussion, perhaps in deference to the confidential nature of the doctor/patient relationship.)

Finally, Mrs. Odio's collapse upon hearing the news of the assassination adds force to her story.[8]

An Accurate Witness?

The accuracy of Mrs. Odio's identification of "Oswald" must be evaluated also. The following facts suggest that it is very unlikely that this was a case of mistaken identity:

(1) The use of the name "Leon Oswald";

(2) The immediate recognition of Oswald on television;

(3) The assertion by the three men that they had just come to Dallas from New Orleans (11H 372), the city which Oswald is said to have left on September 25;

(4) The assertion by the three men that they were "leaving for a trip" (11H 372), just as Oswald embarked on a trip to Mexico City; and

(5) "Leopoldo's" statement that he might attempt to introduce "Leon Oswald" into the underground in Cuba, shortly before Oswald actually attempted to obtain a visa for travel to Cuba.

This series of parallels may not constitute conclusive evidence that Mrs. Odio's identification of "Oswald" was correct, but if they are not in the realm of the supernatural, they are persuasive manifestations of the authentic Oswald. If the Commission nevertheless wishes to substitute William Seymour, it might at least explain the means by which the image of Oswald was projected with such fidelity—and why.

---

8   Edward Jay Epstein's book *Inquest* (p. 102) throws additional light on Mrs. Odio's credibility, revealing that Counsel Wesley J. Liebeler "found that a number of details in the woman's story coincided with facts she could not possibly have known."

The Wayward Bus-Rider

Although the prima-facie evidence for Mrs. Odio's encounter with the real Oswald is strong, the constraints postulated by the Commission against Oswald's presence in Dallas at the appropriate time cannot be ignored. According to the Report, Mrs. Odio fixed the time of the visit as Thursday the twenty-sixth or Friday the twenty-seventh of September. Mrs. Odio actually told the FBI that the visit might have been on Wednesday the twenty-fifth, "although she considered the Thursday date to be the most probable." *(CE 3147)*

While the Report does not make it clear that the visit *might* have taken place on Wednesday the twenty-fifth, it does concede the absence of firm evidence as to the means by which Oswald traveled on that date from New Orleans to Houston. Somewhat murkily, the Commission then suggests that Oswald's presence on a Continental Trailways bus that left New Orleans at 12:30 p.m. on Wednesday the twenty-fifth "would be consistent with other evidence." *(WR 323)* In Appendix XIII, the Commission becomes bolder, and asserts that "he left New Orleans by bus, probably on Continental Trailways Bus No. 5121, departing New Orleans at 12:20 p.m. on September 25 and scheduled to arrive in Houston at 10:50 p.m." *(WR 731)*

That assertion is arbitrary, lacking positive evidence and overcoming negative evidence by the simple expedient of disregarding it. As will be shown, the Commission did not even convince itself that Oswald left New Orleans on that bus. There is no documentary trace of his presence; the driver did not remember "ever seeing Oswald in person at any time" *(CE 2134);* and not one passenger has turned up who recalled seeing Oswald on Bus No. 5121. Since the bus ride from New Orleans to Houston takes almost 12 hours *(CE 2962),* the lack of witnesses to Oswald's presence on a bus between those two points is evidence of a sort against the Commission's supposition. Other dates or other modes of travel must therefore be considered.

Mrs. Odio's callers were traveling in a car, with "Leopoldo" driving *(11H 372),* a detail which the Report neglects to mention. The authors, arguing against a stopover in Dallas en route to Houston, say laconically that "automobile travel in the time available, though perhaps possible, would have been difficult." *(WR 323)*

Even under the Commission's restrictions on "the time available," and in the admitted absence of firm evidence of the way in which Oswald traveled the 358 miles from New Orleans to Houston *(CE 3090),* it appears that he *could* have traveled from New Orleans to Dallas (503 miles) in "Leopoldo's" car, and from Dallas to Houston (244 miles) in the same vehicle, or by private airplane for all we know.

Under the Commission's constraints, Oswald had to cover those distances between 8 a.m. Wednesday, September 25, and 2:35 a.m. Thursday, September 26. But if the basic facts are disentangled from the Report, extracted from the Hearings and Exhibits, and reassembled, the constraints begin to appear dubious, if not artificial. The evidence that Oswald boarded "Bus No. 5133 in

Houston and departed at 2:35 a.m." on Thursday, September 26 *(WR 732)* is unclear. A ticket agent in the Houston bus terminal sold a ticket to Laredo to a man who could have been Oswald *(WR 323);* but the man's clothes (brown and white sweater, white dungarees, and white canvas shoes) did not correspond with any of Oswald's garments, and none of the other 11 employees on duty in the bus terminal at the time had any recollection of seeing Oswald *(CE 2191).* A married couple who were passengers on Bus No. 5133 stated, in a brief affidavit, that they believed that they first saw Oswald on the bus shortly after they awoke at 6 a.m. *(11H 214);* however, they were not pressed to be more precise, and it cannot be said that their testimony is sufficient to place Oswald on the bus at 2:35 a.m. at Houston.

The other constraint imposed by the Commission is even shakier. Oswald was seen leaving his apartment in New Orleans, carrying two suitcases, on Tuesday evening, September 24, according to a neighbor. *(WR 730)* After that time, there is no definite trace of him in that city. But the Report insists that Oswald was in New Orleans at least until 8 a.m. on Wednesday because he cashed a check at a New Orleans store sometime after 8 a.m. that day. The citation for that statement is an FBI memorandum dated April 7, 1964, which reports:

> The Winn-Dixie Store, #1425, 4303 Magazine Street, New Orleans, Louisiana, the place where the warrant dated September 23, 1963 was cashed, was not open to the public on September 25, 1963 until 8 a.m. J. D. Fuchs, Manager . . . approved the warrant for cashing. . . . Mrs. Thelma F. Fisher, Cashier #3 . . . actually cashed the warrant. . . .   *(CE 2131)*

Usually, when the Commission discusses a specific check issued to and cashed by Oswald, the footnotes refer to reports of interviews with the cashiers *(see, for example, CE 1165, 1167)* and photocopies of the face and back of the check *(see CE 1173-1175, 3121).* But when the Commission discusses the $33 check which is claimed to fix Oswald's presence in New Orleans until a specific hour on a specific day, only the FBI memorandum *(CE 2131)* is cited—no interviews with Mr. Fuchs or Mrs. Fisher and no photocopy of the specific check.

In this instance the Commission itself was not satisfied with the evidence. The direction of the Commission's thinking less than a month before its Report was released is graphically revealed in a letter signed by J. Lee Rankin, addressed to J. Edgar Hoover, dated August 28, 1964. Rankin states:

> We are also concerned about the possibility that *Oswald may have left New Orleans on September 24, 1963 instead of September 25, 1963 as has been previously thought.* In that connection, Marina Oswald has recently advised us that her husband told her he intended to leave New Orleans the very next day following her departure on September 23, 1963. She has also indicated that he told her an unemployment check would be forwarded to Mrs. Ruth Paine's address in Irving from his post office box in New Orleans. We also have testimony that Oswald left his apartment on the evening of September 24, 1963 carrying two suitcases.
>
>   It also seems *impossible to us that Oswald would have gone all the way back to the Winn-Dixie Store at 4303 Magazine Street to cash the unemployment check* which he supposedly picked up at the Lafayette Branch of the Post Office when he could have cashed it at Martin's Restaurant, where

he had previously cashed many of his Reily checks and one unemployment
check. That is particularly true if he received the check on September 25,
1963, as previously thought, and had left his apartment with his suitcases
the evening before. [Italics added]   *(CE 3045)*

No new evidence on these points was turned up after Rankin's letter to
the FBI on August 28, 1964; the possibility that Oswald had left New Orleans
on Tuesday, September 24 instead of Wednesday, September 25 was not ruled
out. Nonetheless, when the Warren Report was published less than a month
later, the very same allegations which Rankin had questioned sharply were now
incorporated as "facts."

It is imprudent to overlook the alacrity with which the FBI produced Loran
Eugene Hall on September 16, 1964 following on Rankin's request of August 28
to "determine who it was that Mrs. Odio saw in or about late September."
(CE 3045) The FBI had been investigating Mrs. Odio's story without locating
the three men since December 18, 1963, when she was interviewed by FBI
agents James Hosty and Bardwell Odum. *(11H 369)* For reasons unknown, the
FBI report on that interview has been omitted from the exhibits; also missing
are about ten FBI reports mentioned in Rankin's letter to Hoover *(CE 3045)*.[9]

It's amazing how efficiently the FBI found Loran Hall after Rankin's letter,
following an unsuccessful investigation during the preceding nine months; unfortunately, there is no interview report on Loran Hall, no address, no physical
description, no indication of his age, nor any details which might permit a
comparison with "Leopoldo."

Another footnote to Rankin's letter of August 28, 1964, in which he suggested that Oswald might have left New Orleans a day earlier than believed
previously, is the press leak that appeared a few days later. The *New York Post*
of August 31, 1964 reported:[10]

Investigative agencies have spent many hours and interviewed hundreds of
witnesses since the Nov. 22 assassination trying to trace Oswald's steps on
the Mexico trip.

It is known, for instance, that *he was seen in a Dallas bus station at
6 p.m. Sept. 25* and that he crossed the border at Nuevo Laredo next day.
[Italics added]

That is the first and last we hear of witnesses who saw Oswald in a Dallas bus
station at six o'clock Wednesday; the Report does not dignify that rumor with a
refutation.

At the end of this trail of uncertain and shifting evidence, there seem to be
strong but not conclusive grounds for believing that Mrs. Odio's identification
of Oswald was correct. However, the Commission's failure to press its investigation to completion leaves open at least a possibility that "Leon Oswald" was

---

9 Reports of Gemberling, December 23, 1963; O'Connor, December 31, 1963; Clements,
December 14, 1963; Callendar, December 24, 1963, April 16, 1964; Kemmy, December 23,
1963; letterhead memorandum, April 15, 1964. The reports covered investigations in Dallas,
Miami, New Orleans, Houston, and San Antonio.

10 "Bus Stub Traces Oswald in Mexico," *New York Post*, August 31, 1964, p. 4.

really William Seymour; and that—in complicity with Loran Hall and Lawrence Howard—Seymour was possibly engaged in a deliberate impersonation of Oswald.

But such a hypothesis requires a link between Oswald and his impersonator through which the latter acquired sufficient familiarity with Oswald's history and circumstances to permit successful impersonation.

The Ingredients of Conspiracy

In the vein of pure speculation, it is possible to postulate a series of threads connecting persons known and unknown which would satisfy the conditions for successful impersonation. The starting point is the summer of 1963, when Oswald came into contact with Carlos Bringuier and others who were active in the organized anti-Castro movement at New Orleans. *(WR 407-408, 728-729)*

Oswald sought out Bringuier under circumstances which suggest a calculated attempt to infiltrate the anti-Castro movement, perhaps in the hope of acquiring "credentials" for a future defection to Cuba. That is how Bringuier regarded the incident. *(10H 32-43)*

Bringuier alerted other anti-Castroites against Oswald. One of Bringuier's cohorts went on an infiltration mission of his own, after consulting Bringuier. He went to Oswald's house "posing as a pro-Castro" to "try to get as much information as possible from Oswald." *(10H 41)* Bringuier also informed Edward Butler, an anti-Communist propagandist *(10H 42; 11H 166, 168)*, who tried "to contact some person, somebody in Washington, to get more the background of Oswald" *(10H 42)*, and apparently did obtain information on Oswald from the House Un-American Activities Committee *(11H 168)*.

It is a reasonable assumption that a warning against Oswald went out also to the right wing of the anti-Castro movement in other cities, Dallas included, and to their American sponsors and supporters, both official (CIA and perhaps FBI) and unofficial (various ultra-reactionary groups). The anti-Castro movement is composed of many competing factions, ranging from the Batistianos and far-rightists (DRF, for example[11]) who seek the restoration of a regime like Batista's (under which Cuba was an American colony in everything but name), to liberal and reform groups (like Manolo Ray's MRP or later his JURE,[12] which is considered leftist and tantamount to "Castroism without Castro"). The reactionary wing of the movement and the CIA have cordial and close relations, whereas the moderate and progressive factions do not enjoy the CIA's confidence and were systematically excluded from the CIA's planning of the Bay of Pigs adventure (see, for example, *Bay of Pigs* by Haynes Johnson,[13] or *A Thousand Days* by Arthur M. Schlesinger, Jr.[14]).

The right-wing Cuban *émigrés* were bitter and infuriated by the humiliating defeat at the Bay of Pigs, blaming President Kennedy for refusing to permit direct American military participation in the invasion. The CIA, whose conduct

---

11   DRF [*Frente Revolucionario Democratico*]
12   MRP [*Movimiento Revolucionario del Pueblo*]; JURE [*Junta Revolutionary*]
13   *The Bay of Pigs* (Dell Books, New York, 1964).
14   *A Thousand Days* (Houghton Mifflin, Boston, 1965).

of the whole affair brought the agency into disgrace and jeopardy, had made arrangements to overrule President Kennedy if he canceled the invasion at the last minute, so that the landing at the Bay of Pigs would go ahead regardless of Presidential orders. The revelation that the CIA had contemplated countermanding the White House, on top of its incredible bungling of the invasion from beginning to end, suggested an early end to what has been called "the invisible government,"[15] and a threat to their Cuban protégés.

Dallas, with its hospitable political climate and its plentiful money, inevitably was an outpost of the anti-Castro right wing. Mrs. Odio testified that the Crestwood Apartments, where she lived at the time of the visit by "Leon Oswald," was "full of Cubans." *(11H 374)* Fund-raising meetings were held in a Dallas bank, by Cuban exiles and their American sympathizers. *(CE 2390)* Mrs. Odio said that all the Cubans knew that she was a member of JURE, "but it did not have a lot of sympathy in Dallas and I was criticized because of that." *(11H 370)*

Father Walter J. McChann, who was active in a Cuban Catholic committee concerned with the welfare and relief of Cuban refugees in Dallas, told the Secret Service about a Colonel Caster who was associated with the committee. Father McChann said that Colonel Caster was a retired Army officer who seemed to be "playing the role of an intelligence officer in his contacts with the Cubans" and that he seemed to be "more interested in their political beliefs than in their economic plight or their social problems in the new country." *(CE 2943)*

Mrs. C. L. Connell, a volunteer worker in the committee, also mentioned the Colonel. She told the FBI on November 29, 1963 that "General Walker and Colonel (FNU) Caster, a close acquaintance of Walker, have been trying to arouse the feelings of the Cuban refugees in Dallas against the Kennedy administration" in speeches before Cuban groups in the Dallas area "in recent months." *(CE 3108)* (Neither the FBI nor the Warren Commission found that news of sufficient interest to warrant an interview with the Colonel.)

At this point, a hypothetical series of links connects Oswald to Bringuier— Bringuier to the anti-Castro movement in Dallas—the anti-Castro movement to Colonel Caster—and Colonel Caster to General Walker. Walker's right-hand man is Robert Allan Surrey.[16] According to Surrey's own statement in the *Midlothian* (Tex.) *Mirror*, he and FBI Agent James Hosty are bridge-playing companions.[17]

Another thread leads from the Walker establishment to Jack Ruby. A former employee of the General's, William McEwan Duff, believed that he had seen Ruby visiting the Walker residence. *(CE 2981)* There is strong evidence from Robert McKeown *(CE 1688-1689, CE 3066)* and testimony from Nancy Perrin Rich *(14H 345-353)* that Ruby was involved in the illegal supply of arms to the Cuban underground.

---

15 According to *The New York Times* of April 25, 1966 (p. 20, col. 3), President Kennedy told one of the highest officials of his Administration after the Bay of Pigs disaster that he wanted "to splinter the C.I.A. in a thousand pieces and scatter it to the winds."
16 Surrey, apparently, "closely resembled" Oswald *(CEs 1836, 2473)*.
17 "Reopen the Warren Commission," *Midlothian* (Tex.) *Mirror*, March 31, 1966, p. 2, col. 3.

Mrs. Rich testified that she had attended a meeting in Dallas to discuss an offer to her husband of a large sum of money for running guns to Cuba and bringing refugees out to Miami. The head of the group that tried to enlist her husband was an army colonel; another member present at the meeting was Jack Ruby, whom Mrs. Rich recognized at once as her former employer at the Carousel Club, where she had worked briefly as a cocktail waitress.

Ruby, of course, had close links to the Dallas police, some of whom had independent links to the ultra-right in Dallas. J. D. Tippit, for example, had a moonlighting job at Austin's Barbecue; the man who was his boss, Austin Cook, is an acknowledged member of the John Birch Society. *(CE 2985)*

All these threads can be combined in a web that covers the terrible and unfathomed events of November 22-24, 1963. The nucleus consists of reactionary Cuban exiles who have compiled a record of violence in their new country, ranging from attacks with bicycle chains and Molotov cocktails on peacefully assembled American citizens, to a bazooka attack on the United Nations building; these Cuban counter-revolutionaries are linked to the American ultra-right by many mutual interests, not the least of which was a hatred for President Kennedy, kept at the boiling point by systematic propaganda from, among others, former American army officers.

Is it farfetched to postulate the formation of a plot among members of those circles to revenge themselves not only against the President whom they considered a Communist and a traitor but also against a Marxist and suspected double-agent who had tried to infiltrate the anti-Castro movement?

This hypothesis is, of course, purely theoretical, a mere exercise in speculation attempting to explain the possible rationale for an impersonation of Oswald, in the context of Mrs. Odio's experience and of other stories that pose the possibility of deliberate and informed impersonation.

I am not arguing that such a plot existed, but I do suggest that the Warren Commission's job was to consider and check out all possible theories, however far-out, and not to dispose of disturbing evidence like that lingering in the Odio story by illusory "facts."

Congressman Gerald Ford, one of the members of the Commission, has said that "the monumental record of the President's Commission will stand like a Gibraltar of factual literature through the ages to come."[18] The Commission's unfinished business may not disturb the Commission's self-satisfaction or its self-imposed silence; but for those who are haunted by sentience of a frightful miscarriage of justice, and troubled by the loose ends in the "monumental record," that complacency remains incomprehensible.

Epilogue to the Odio Story

Senator John Sherman Cooper never replied to this author's letter of January 21, 1966, requesting information on the results of the investigation of Loran

---

18   *Portrait of the Assassin,* pp. 451-452.

Eugene Hall and his friends, which was still in progress when the Warren Report was published.

In July 1966 researcher Paul Hoch was kind enough to make available excerpts from Commission Document 1553 which he had obtained at the National Archives, consisting of an FBI report dated October 2, 1964. That FBI report indicates that only two days after the original locating of Loran Eugene Hall on September 16, 1964, an interview with William Seymour (the FBI did not say whether Seymour in fact resembled Lee Harvey Oswald) elicited a denial that he was even in Dallas in September 1963 or had ever had any contacts with Sylvia Odio. Subsequent interviews with Loran Hall, Lawrence Howard, Sylvia Odio, and Annie Laurie Odio resulted in the collapse of the assumption that Hall, Howard, and Seymour were the men who had visited Mrs. Odio, representing one of their number as "Leon Oswald."

The FBI report of October 2, 1964 was transmitted to the allegedly disbanded Warren Commission well before the release of the Hearings and Exhibits at the end of November 1964. The document was not included among the Exhibits, and if it ever came to the attention of Senator Cooper, he was not prepared to communicate the fact that the possibility of an innocent mistake in identity had disintegrated.

That denouement throws wide open again the whole Odio story with all its implications. We know from Warren Commission Counsel Liebeler that details in Mrs. Odio's story coincided with facts to which she had no access and that the possibility of fabrication is thus virtually destroyed. That leaves two possibilities open: that the real Oswald visited Mrs. Odio with two companions, one of whom deliberately planted highly incriminating information about him without his knowledge; or that a mock-Oswald visited her, to accomplish the same purpose.

If there is a re-investigation of the assassination—as there must be if we are not to become the permanent accomplices in the degradation of justice which has taken place—the Odio affair should be high on the agenda.

PART V
MURDER ON TELEVISION

Chapter 22
The Essential Ruby

The Warren Commission had the unenviable task of authenticating a Marxist as the lone assassin of the President in a city notorious for the excesses and physical violence of its lunatic right-wing fringe. That had to be accomplished in the face of evidence that the so-called lone assassin had no motive, no means, and no opportunity to commit the crime.

By the sheer prestige of its names, the Commission might have succeeded better had it not become necessary to pronounce the murderer of the alleged assassin *also* a soloist. Jack Ruby was without any single identifiable overpowering motive. A variety of alleged or possible reasons for his act were suggested at one time or another, by Ruby himself or those who spoke on his behalf. None achieved credibility or conclusiveness.

Those who might have accepted *one* random unpredictable motiveless assassin could not easily accept *two*, within the context of the events in Dallas. As the Warren Report puts it, when Ruby shot Oswald, "almost immediately, speculation arose that Ruby had acted on behalf of members of a conspiracy who had planned the killing of President Kennedy and wanted to silence Oswald." *(WR 333)*

Nothing in the Commission's voluminous records serves to eliminate that hypothesis, despite the Commission's effort to remodel the Ruby who emerges from a highly unsavory background into the relatively antiseptic portrait rendered in the Report. Muted in the Report, but revealed in the Exhibits, are Ruby's ties with the underworld, gamblers and hoods, narcotics traffic, and his "sudden and extreme displays of temper and violence." *(CE 2980)*

That the man was brutal is apparent from his readiness to inflict savage

391

beatings on other men and to knock around the girls who worked in his Carousel Club *(CE 1502, 1543)* and even his sister and business associate, Eva Grant. *(CE 1448)* He had "brutally beaten at least 25 different persons either as a result of a personal encounter or because they were causing disturbances in his club; the normal pattern is for Ruby to attack his victim without warning." *(CE 2980)* Attempts by the victims to prosecute Ruby for assault were coldly discouraged by the Dallas Police Department, where Ruby had protectors and friends. *(CE 1513, 1515, 1517)*

The Commission dismissed allegations that he was implicated in narcotics traffic. *(WR 370)* It downgraded his involvement in Cuban exile affairs *(Rich Exhibits 1-4; CEs 1688, 1689, 3066)* and his travel to Havana, which was judged to be innocuous. *(WR 370)* The Commission conceded "some uncertainty about Ruby's trip to Havana, Cuba, in 1959" but appeared to accept Ruby's testimony that "he went to Havana for eight days in August 1959" to visit a friend. *(WR 802)* Unmentioned in the Report are two exhibits that prove that in addition to the "purely social" eight-day visit, Ruby made at least one other trip to Havana—an overnight trip, departing September 12, 1959 and returning September 13—surely *not* for purely social purposes. *(CEs 1442-1443)*

Manifestations of a Ruby who was not a mere coarse stereotype but a man of ugly, purposeful, mysterious activities are minimized in the Report. On the basis of Ruby's testimony and selected evidence, the Commission concluded that in murdering Oswald, Ruby had acted on his own initiative and without collusion, inspiration, or involvement of any other party or parties. His motive was sometimes said to be the desire to spare the President's widow the ordeal of testifying at Oswald's trial; a wish to avenge himself for the death of the President he loved and revered; or the expectation that he would become a hero instead of a nonentity. At his trial the defense argued that Ruby was afflicted by psychomotor epilepsy and not responsible for his act, but that plea was rejected by the jury and ultimately proved unfounded when an autopsy surgeon found no sign of the disease in the body. As for the thesis of Ruby's overpowering grief at the death of President Kennedy, it seems unlikely that a love too slight to inspire Ruby to watch the motorcade should have led him to risk the death chamber.

The grief, whether of greater or lesser degree, that Ruby later claimed to have experienced was largely invisible at the time. Ruby spent most of Friday and Saturday in a state approaching euphoria—exhilarated, running from scene to scene of activity, and taking the occasion to drum up business for his strip-joint. He passed out cards to every stranger in the police headquarters, button-holing reporters to recommend the good times in store at his Carousel Club; sometime during that bitter weekend, he demonstrated a "twist-board" with suggestive gyrations for the general hilarity. He exhibited no animus toward the accused assassin, whom he compared to a movie star of the moment. *(15H 257)* He was everywhere in evidence—except at the ten-o'clock transfer of Oswald which, in the event, was delayed by an hour and twenty minutes. By that time, Ruby *was,* after all, on the scene.

The Warren Commission was long disbanded when the first of a series of letters written by Ruby and smuggled out of the Dallas county jail, in which Ruby (with varying degrees of coherence) charged that a conspiracy had executed the assassination of President Kennedy, came to light. We cannot reproach the Commission with failure to take account of *those* allusions to conspiracy, but we can scrutinize the manner in which it disposed of the evidence that did come before it, to judge the accuracy of its assertions and the validity of its conclusions.

Chapter 23
Ruby at Parkland Hospital

Seth Kantor, a member of the White House Press Corps, reported in the Scripps-Howard Alliance newspapers on November 25, 1963 that he met Jack Ruby at Parkland Hospital about an hour after the President was shot. Kantor had worked for the *Dallas Times-Herald* until 1962 and had become well acquainted with Ruby. He wrote that at about 1:30 p.m. he chatted briefly with Ruby, who had asked his opinion about closing his night clubs for the next three days. According to the story that Kantor filed, "Ruby shook hands numbly, having minutes earlier witnessed the tragic events of the President's assassination." *(Kantor Exhibit 7)*

The Warren Commission does not accept Kantor's account of his meeting with Ruby at Parkland Hospital and suggests that the incident really took place at the Dallas police assembly room at about midnight Friday. *(WR 335-337)* The Report describes Kantor as a newspaperman "who had previously met Ruby in Dallas," though in fact Kantor was clearly on terms of familiarity with him. Moreover, corroboration of Ruby's presence at the hospital came from a second witness, but her story has been rejected too, partly because she had never seen Ruby before. The Commission dismisses one witness because she had not seen Ruby before, and another although he had seen and known Ruby well, while each independently corroborates the testimony of the other. It will be remembered that this is the same Commission which accepted the testimony of witnesses who identified Oswald, although they had never seen him before and did not see him under circumstances comparable to those described by Kantor and Mrs. Wilma Tice.

Another reason for the Commission's skepticism is that "Ruby has firmly denied going to Parkland." *(WR 336)* Kantor, a man of high personal and professional reputation, has firmly and consistently maintained that he met Ruby at the hospital. Neither his sanity nor his morals can be impeached (obviously it is not possible to say as much for Ruby). The Commission does not attempt to do so but suggests that Kantor is mistaken.

The reasoning behind the contention that Kantor met Ruby at midnight is so careless that one wonders how it got into print. At 1:30 p.m. Ruby might have asked Kantor's advice about closing his clubs, but it would have been incongruous to do so at midnight, when he had long since made the decision and changed his newspaper ads accordingly. Kantor wrote, "Friday I saw tears brimming in Jack Ruby's eyes when he searched my face for news of the President's condition." *(Kantor Exhibit 8)* The President's condition was not in doubt at midnight, and according to many witnesses, Ruby was exhilarated at that hour. Kantor's reference to Ruby's tears was ignored, as was his comment that minutes before the encounter at the hospital, Ruby "had witnessed" the assassination.

When Ruby "firmly denied" being at Parkland Hospital, the Commission should have asked whether or not he met Kantor at all that day and, if so, where and at what hour. The untenable hypothesis offered in the Report is not an acceptable substitute for explicit information from a witness who was alive and accessible. Kantor and Ruby could even have been confronted with each other, as in the conflict of testimony between Marina Oswald and Mrs. Hunter and Mrs. Whitworth.

The investigators apparently were more concerned with disposing of Kantor's story than with establishing the facts. The FBI hastened to interview him on December 3, 1963 and again on January 2, 1964 and reported:

Kantor was pointedly told by interviewing agents that Ruby has emphatically denied he was at Parkland Hospital at any time November 22, 1963, or subsequent. Kantor was specifically asked whether he might be mistaken about seeing Ruby there. . . . Kantor reiterated he is absolutely certain he saw and spoke with Ruby at the Parkland Hospital on November 22. Kantor was told that he might be called upon to testify in this case. He was asked what he would say if under oath and on the witness stand in a court of law to the question, "Did you see and talk with Ruby at the Parkland Hospital on November 22, 1963?" Kantor stated that he would answer, "Yes," because he is absolutely certain he did. *(Kantor Exhibit 8)*

Months later, when Kantor testified for the Warren Commission, he maintained his story:

I was indelibly sure at the time and have continued to be so that the man who stopped me and with whom I talked was Jack Ruby. I feel strongly about it because I had known Jack Ruby and he did call me by my first name as he came up behind me, and at that moment under the circumstances it was a fairly normal conversation. *(15H 88)*

Kantor's testimony is convincing and the character described sounds very much like Ruby. It is curious, indeed, that the Commission went to such pains to dismiss the story—despite its reliable source and inherent plausibility—while giving scant attention to other information Kantor acquired as a passenger in the motorcade and keen observer at the police department.

Nevertheless, the Commission attempted to rule out Kantor's story on material grounds. It stated that it is unlikely that Ruby could have made the trip from Parkland Hospital to the Carousel Club within the 10 or 15 minutes available, "because of traffic conditions after the assassination." *(WR 336)* (The drive normally requires only 9 or 10 minutes.) As noted elsewhere, the Commission made no allowance for abnormal traffic conditions in fixing the time required for Oswald's taxi ride from the Greyhound Bus Terminal to North Beckley Street; on the contrary, the estimated time was reduced from 9 to 6 minutes. Apparently traffic conditions which delayed Ruby only facilitated Oswald's rapid transit. Yet Nancy Powell, one of Ruby's entertainers, also drove to Parkland Hospital from the Book Depository area after the assassination, and when asked how long the trip had taken her she said, "Well, I don't recall that it took any longer than it normally would . . . they were keeping traffic moving. . . ." *(15H 419)*

A second unwelcome witness to Ruby's presence at the hospital was Mrs. Wilma Tice. Her testimony suggests that at the time she did not realize the importance of having seen Ruby at the hospital. Not long afterward, she was injured in an auto accident and, as a result, was bedridden until April 1964. Despite certain derogatory implications in the Report, the record reveals no evidence that she had withheld information deliberately or that she had imagined the incident. According to an FBI report, Mrs. Tice went to the hospital at about 1:30 p.m. and

> . . . stopped beside a man who was at the time unknown to her, but whom she later believed to be Jack Ruby. . . . He had a hat . . . in his left hand, hitting it against his leg. . . . He wore a dark suit, white shirt, and possibly a tie. He was heavily built. She thought by hitting his hat against his leg he would ruin it. He was alone. She stood about three to four feet from this man when he was approached by another man who stated, "How are you going there, Jack?"
>
> Mrs. Tice said that some other individual in the crowd had made the remark that Governor Connally had been shot in the kidney . . . the man identified as Ruby then stated, "Couldn't someone give him a kidney?" The man who approached Ruby then stated, "Who the hell would give him a kidney?" to which Ruby replied that he would. *(CE 2290)*

The FBI report indicates that Mrs. Tice later recognized pictures of Ruby on television and in the papers as the man she had seen at the hospital but that she said nothing about it and "did not think any more about it at the time."

The Report states that she had an obstructed view of the man, yet she testified:

> . . . I was being nosey and listening. . . . I could only see the right side of this other man's face that walked up to him. Jack was standing right there, see, this man that is called Jack. . . . He turned around when this man walked up. . . . At the time, he was facing right toward me. . . . *(15H 392-394)*

The Report states that Mrs. Tice had never seen Ruby before and saw him only briefly. The same authors lean heavily on eyewitness identifications by such witnesses as Howard Brennan and Helen Markham in concluding that Oswald had murdered the President and Tippit. Brennan had never seen Oswald before, his view of the man in the window was substantially more distant, brief, and obstructed than Mrs. Tice's view of the man at the hospital, and Brennan did not overhear a conversation in which the man he saw was addressed by name; moreover, he failed to make a positive identification when he saw Oswald later that day. Yet his story is endorsed and Mrs. Tice's is rejected.

As for Mrs. Markham, she varied wildly in her accounts of the shooting of Tippit, gave false testimony about a telephone conversation with Mark Lane, and identified Oswald, whom she had never seen before, while under sedation for hysteria; yet the Commission finds her testimony of "probative value" but dismisses the testimony given by Mrs. Tice—testimony that provides a somewhat better impression of the witness than does the Report.

> *Griffin:* Mrs. Tice, did you know that Jack himself has denied very vehemently that he was out at the hospital?
> *Mrs. Tice:* Yes, I know he denied that, and I hated to say that I saw him out there. . . . Eva told me, "Well, I asked Jack and Jack said no, he wasn't out there." And I said, "Well, anybody can make a mistake." . . . She said, "Yes, because there are many Jacks" . . . and if it wasn't him it was his twin brother.
> *Griffin:* Do you think you could have been mistaken about the man you saw?
> *Mrs. Tice:* It could have been somebody else that looked just like Jack, named Jack; yes. *(15H 391)*

Mrs. Grant, Ruby's sister, had told the FBI that Mrs. Tice was "balmy"; she said also, however, that Mrs. Tice "had rather accurately described the clothing Ruby was wearing." *(CE 2343)* This point seems to have escaped the authors of the Report. If the man whom Mrs. Tice saw at the hospital was not Ruby, then it must have been somebody else that looked just like him, presumably named Jack, and wearing the same kind of clothes. Of course, triple coincidences are not foreign to this case, but there is still another obstacle to credibility: Mrs. Tice was "advised" not to talk about having seen Ruby at Parkland Hospital and received threatening anonymous phone calls warning her to keep her mouth shut. *(CE 2293)* According to an FBI report *(CE 2293),* there even seems to have been an attempt to terrorize her by a breaking into her home during the night, while her husband was at his job. Can that, too, be put aside as "coincidence"?

Why was it so urgent to repress reports that Ruby was at Parkland Hospital shortly after the assassination? A clue may lie in the title of the Report chapter dealing with the Kantor-Tice testimony—"Investigation of Possible Conspiracy, Involving Jack Ruby."

Chapter 24

Homicide in the Police Basement

The Anonymous Threats

During the night, between 2:30 and 3 a.m., the local office of the FBI and the sheriff's office received telephone calls from an unidentified man who warned that a committee had decided "to kill the man that killed the President." Shortly after, an FBI agent notified the Dallas police of the anonymous threat. The police department and ultimately Chief Curry were informed of both threats. *(WR 209)*

This paragraph from the Warren Report is a highly compressed summary of the facts, scarcely conveying the curious flavor of the events surrounding the anonymous telephone threats against Oswald's life. The statement that "ultimately" Chief Curry was informed of the threats stems from rather an odd circumstance which is not spelled out in the Report. A more substantial picture of the night's activities is found in the Hearings and Exhibits, including the report of Sheriff's Officer Perry McCoy, dated November 24, 1963 and addressed to Sheriff Decker.

When you called the office at 2:00 a.m. I had not received any threats on the life of Oswald but at that time you mentioned the fact that you thought that *Oswald should be transferred from the city jail while it was still dark* . . . and you asked me to call you at 6:00 a.m. and you would see about getting Oswald transferred while it was still dark.

At approximately 2:15 a.m. I received a call from a person that talked like a W/M and he stated that he was a member of a group of one hundred and that he wanted the sheriff's office to know that they had voted one hundred per cent to kill Oswald while he was in the process of being transferred to the county jail and that he wanted this department to have the information so that none of the deputies would get hurt. The voice was deep and course [*sic*] and sounded very sincere and talked with ease. The person did not seem excited like some of the calls that we had received running down this department, the police department, and the State of Texas and he seemed very calm about the whole matter.

A short time later, Mr. Newsome from the FBI office called and wanted to know if we had received any calls on the life of Oswald and I passed on the above information and he asked me to call the police department and give them the same information. I called the city hall and talked to someone in Captain Fritz's office. I did not get his name, the officer made some slight remark and said that they had not received any such calls as yet.

I received one other call regarding the transfer of Oswald and when I answered the telephone, a male voice asked if this is the sheriff's office and I said it was, he said just a minute and then another male voice stated that *Oswald would never make the trip to the county jail.* I could not determine whether or not this was the same voice that had called earlier.

As you know, when I called you at 6:00 a.m. . . . you asked me if I thought that Kennedy and I could transfer Oswald from the city jail without causing much of a scene by handcuffing Oswald to me and by keeping Oswald on the floor board of the car so that he could not be seen. I told you that we would give it a try and you advised to hold up until you talked to Fritz. A short time later, an officer called from the police department. I believe he was Captain Tolbert, and he wanted to talk to you and I told him that you could be reached at home and I gave him your number.

A short time later you called back and told me that you had been unable to reach Fritz but to hold up and also to hold the late night squads at the office for a while. A short time later Captain Frazier called, from the police department, and stated that he had been *trying to contact Chief Curry but could not get an answer on the telephone* and I believe he stated that he was going to send a squad by the chief's home.

I asked Captain Frazier to call you at home and give that information to you. All of the late night shift stayed at the station and was there when you called back at about 7:50 a.m. and you stated that they were not to go for making the transfer at this time [from the city jail to the county jail] and told us to go home and get some sleep. [Italics added]

(*Decker Exhibit 5323,* pp. 537-539)

The irony of the information in this report is evident. If Decker had been able to carry out his plan, Oswald would have been transferred secretly during darkness and might well have lived to come to trial. Decker was concerned about Oswald's safety even before the anonymous calls were received, but he could not proceed with the transfer because it was not possible to reach the chief of police, whose knowledge and consent were needed.

Chief Curry had made a commitment to the reporters that they would not "miss" anything if they showed up at police headquarters by ten o'clock on Sunday morning. Perhaps if Curry had been reached during the night, he would have refused to "double-cross" the press, even after anonymous telephone threats against the prisoner's life. The Report indicates that on Saturday night Curry and Fritz had discussed the possibility of a secret transfer during darkness, and that later each had tried to blame the other for the negative decision. As the Commission saw the situation,

. . . the basic decision to move Oswald at an announced time and in the presence of the news media was never carefully thought through by either man. Curry and Fritz had agreed Saturday evening that Oswald should not be moved at night, but their discussion apparently went little further.

(WR 229)

The Commission, too, "went little further" and did not indicate in its Report that Curry was incommunicado in the early hours of Sunday, or explain why.

Although the memorandum to Sheriff Decker suggests that Captain Fritz, too, could not be reached, Fritz himself testified:

Fritz: During the night on Saturday night, I had a call at my home from uniformed captain, Captain Frazier, I believe is his name, he called me out at home and they told me *they had had some threats and he had to transfer Oswald.*

And I said, well, I don't know. I said there has been no security setup, and the chief having something to do with this transfer and you had better call him, because—so he told me he would. . . .

He called me back then in a few minues and he told me *he couldn't get the chief* and told me to leave him where he was. I don't think that transferring him at night would have been any safer than . . . during the day. I have always felt that that was Ruby who made that call, I may be wrong, but he was out late that night and I have always felt he might have made that call. . . . If two or three of those officers had started out with him they may have had the same trouble they had the next morning. I don't know whether we had been transferring him ourselves, I don't know that we would have used this same method but we certainly would have used security of some kind.

Ball: Now weren't you transferring him?

Fritz: Sir, yes, sir.

Ball: What do you mean if we were transferring him ourselves?

Fritz: I mean transferring like I was told to transfer him.

Ball: I beg your pardon?

Fritz: I was transferring him like the chief told me to transfer him. [Italics added]

(4H 233)

Fritz reveals a great deal about himself in this passage of testimony, and he also raises an interesting point: Was it Ruby who made the anonymous threats, or was there an organized lynch mob that would have attempted to kill Oswald if he had not been murdered before he left the police basement? The anonymous calls were to the sheriff's office and to the FBI, but the police themselves received no telephone threats despite the fact that Oswald was in police custody. That is surely curious. In favor of Fritz's suspicion that it was Ruby who made the anonymous telephone threats is the fact that Ruby was on familiar terms with most of the police force and that his voice might have been recognized by an officer who answered the telephone. On the other hand, if Ruby was the person who called, there would be a clear evidence of premeditation as well as a suggestion of an organized conspiracy against the life of Oswald. Such inferences are inimical to the Commission's conclusions about the random and solitary nature of Ruby's act of murder. Still, it would have been instructive if it had been possible to have the sheriff's officer and the FBI agent who received the anonymous calls listen to Ruby's voice on the telephone, to see if it was possible to identify or to exclude him as the anonymous caller. Such an experiment was probably incompatible with the constitutional protection against self-incrimination, but certainly it was not rejected for *that* reason.

The anonymous caller specifically and prophetically warned that Oswald would "never make the trip to the county jail." Despite that explicit warning, the police failed to prevent the murder of the prisoner. That the tragedy might have been avoided if Sheriff Decker had been able to contact Curry is problematical; yet surely a secret transfer in darkness would have presented far less danger than the circus of the next morning, in which security measures were worse than haphazard.

The Warren Commission knew on March 25, 1964—if not earlier—that it had not been possible to reach Curry by telephone early Sunday morning, according to Chief Batchelor's testimony *(12H 4-7)*, but when Curry himself was deposed on April 15, 1964 he was not asked about it. The next day, April 16, Sheriff Decker also testified that his proposal for a secret transfer had been dropped because the police officers with whom he spoke had been unable to reach their superiors and obtain the necessary authorization. *(12H 48-49)* When Curry testified again, on April 22, 1964—this time before the Commission— again, no questions were asked about his seclusion from contact with the police department. One might almost say, as the Commission said in mild criticism of the Dallas police, that there was an "inadequacy of co-ordination" within the Commission.

It was only on July 13, 1964 that the Commission, through Counsel Leon Hubert, finally manifested some curiosity about this episode.

> *Hubert:* I think there has been some testimony by other people prior that an attempt had been made to reach you early Sunday morning but that the line was reported busy.
>
> *Curry:* The FBI asked me about that a few days ago,[1] and I recall that the squad that came out, or that they actually called me and said they had been trying to get me and the squad was on the way out there; and discussing this with my wife, she said that she had taken the phone off the hook sometime during the night, and that the telephone company had made some kind of noise over the phone that woke her up and told her that something was wrong with the line, and the phone was off the hook, and she replaced it on the hook.
>
> But when I was talking to the FBI Agent Vince Drain, about this, I didn't remember just what was wrong with the telephone.
>
> At the time, I had been up for quite a while, and it was not my instructions to her to take it off the hook. She took it off sometime on her own initiative, she said, so we could get some sleep. That was the trouble with the phone.
>
> *(15H 127)*

Counsel Hubert, apparently satisfied, went on to other matters. The Commission was not so bold as to question Mrs. Curry directly, to determine whether

---

1 The FBI interview report is not included in the Exhibits.

it was her custom to isolate her husband from contact with the police department, without his knowledge, and whether on this specific occasion there had been telephone calls which disturbed their sleep and caused her to remove the telephone from the hook.

Perhaps the Commission regarded the matter as just another of the ironic coincidences that plagued the whole case and appeared to lead inexorably from murder to murder. Not everyone is prepared to share the Commission's faith in the Dallas police—or in relentless coincidence.

Protecting Oswald

The anonymous telephone threats, if nothing else, should have impressed the Dallas police with the need for special precautions to protect Oswald during the scheduled transfer. Discussing the adequacy of the security measures instituted by the police, the Commission states that "Many newsmen reported that they were checked on more than one occasion while they waited in the basement. A small number did not recall that their credentials were ever checked." *(WR 212)*

Having seen what lay behind the word "ultimately" in the Commission's account of the anonymous threats, we might now examine the phrase "a small number."

The Commission estimates that 40 to 50 newsmen were present in the police basement when Oswald was shot. Twenty-seven press representatives are listed as present in the police report on the so-called abortive transfer *(CE 2002, pp. 54-55)*; the FBI interviewed at least another 17 reporters, which brings the number to 44.[2]

Stephen Alexander, a television cameraman, told the FBI that he was present in various parts of the police basement from 7:30 in the morning until Oswald was shot, at about 11:30 a.m.; "at no time was he asked for identification by any police officer," and he doubted that any other newsmen were asked to show their credentials. *(CE 2037)*

Ed Haddad, a radio newscaster, said that there was "no security set up as far as he could notice" and that "Oswald could easily have been slain on Friday or Saturday, for anyone could move freely throughout the building." *(CE 2044)*

William Lord, A.B.C. news correspondent, told the FBI that he had entered the police basement at about 9 a.m. on Sunday morning by public elevator from the third floor and that no one had asked him to identify himself; he did not observe that anyone was responsible for identifying those who entered the basement. *(CE 2047)*

---

2   Personal conversation with Philippe Labro of *France-Soir* and Lawrence Schiller, then with the *Saturday Evening Post*, revealed that these two reporters were within a few feet of Oswald when he was shot, although their names do not appear on the police list of those present and they were never questioned about the shooting by any authority.

Jimmy Turner, television director, testified that "up until the following morning after the shooting of Oswald, there was no checking of passes that we ran into." *(13H 131)*

Jerry O'Leary of the *Washington Evening Star (CE 2052),* Henry Rabun of United Press International *(CE 2054),* Seth Kantor of Scripps-Howard *(Kantor Exhibits),* Ike Pappas *(Pappas Exhibit),* Ira Beers of the *Dallas Morning News (Beers Exhibit),* and others made similar reports.

According to my count, 14 newsmen reported that their credentials had not been checked, or not checked on some occasions.[3] Fourteen is almost one-third of the total of 44 newsmen—something over 31 per cent. I suggest that 14 is not a "small number" but a large proportion, and that the Warren Report has minimized what was clearly inexcusable recklessness and irresponsibility on the part of the Dallas police in protecting a prisoner whose life had been threatened by unknown men.

Nothing in the Report suggests that something might have been involved other than the most colossal example of mismanagement in the history of organized police work. Suggestions do arise when we examine the question of how Ruby gained access to the police basement, at just the right moment to murder a handcuffed man "guarded" by about 75 police officers.

The Perfect Timing of Jack Ruby

Under the heading "possible assistance to Jack Ruby in entering the basement," the Commission indicates at the outset that it "found no evidence that Ruby received assistance from any person in entering the basement" but that "his means of entry is significant in evaluating the adequacy of the precautions taken to protect Oswald." (To which the Commission might have added, "in the wake of anonymous threats against his life.")

> Although more than a hundred policemen and newsmen were present in the basement . . . during the ten minutes before the shooting of Oswald, none has been found who definitely observed Jack Ruby's entry into the basement. After considering all the evidence, the Commission has concluded that Ruby entered the basement unaided, probably via the Main Street ramp, and no more than three minutes before the shooting of Oswald. *(WR 219)*

The Commission claims that it considered "all the evidence," but there is no indication that it dismissed or even evaluated accusations of perjury made by its assistant counsel, Burt Griffin, against two police witnesses whose testimony he took (discussed later in this section). If even two of the police witnesses were "damned liars" (as Griffin charged), one must have reservations about the Commission's conclusion that Ruby did not receive assistance from anyone in entering the basement and shooting Oswald to death.

---

3   A Dallas police report states, on the other hand, that "all members of the press who were interviewed stated their credentials were checked upon entering the basement, or that they knew the officers personally that admitted them to the basement." *(CE 2002,* p. 53)

The Commission's main arguments for concluding that Ruby acted alone *(WR 219-225)* are: (a) his transaction at Western Union only four minutes before the shooting, indicating a random accidental synchronization of his arrival in the basement and Oswald's—but here the Commission overlooks or deliberately ignores Ruby's stated intention to be present ("you know I'll be there") at the transfer *(15H 491);* (b) Ruby's assertion that he had entered by the Main Street ramp while the guard was distracted by a departing police car; and (c) the lack of credible evidence to support any other entry route.

The Dallas police force is housed in Dallas City Hall, which adjoins the Municipal Building. There are two ramps leading into the police basement—one on Main Street, normally reserved for entering vehicles, and one on Commerce Street, for departing vehicles.

On the morning of the transfer, the Commerce Street ramp was blocked by an armored car which was to serve as a decoy while Oswald was on his way to the county jail in an unmarked police car. Therefore, a police car driven by Lieutenant Rio Pierce, which was to serve as an escort, had to leave the basement by way of the Main Street ramp, about a minute or two before the shooting.

Apart from the two ramps, access to the basement is possible through five doors, reached by entering City Hall or the Municipal Building in the first instance. While police witnesses testified that all five doors to the basement were secure against unauthorized persons, the Commission believes that there is some doubt about one of the doors.

Despite the wealth of witnesses present in the basement before and during the shooting and the availability of films and photographs, the Commission was unable to reach a definite conclusion about Ruby's means of entry and could only assert that he probably used the Main Street ramp. The Commission acknowledges that Officer R. E. Vaughn, who was stationed at the top of the ramp, denied that Ruby had slipped past him while Lieutenant Pierce and two other policemen, Sergeants Maxey and Putnam, drove out of the ramp on to Main Street. It acknowledges also that the three officers in the car did not see Ruby and denied that he had entered the basement while they drove out. Nevertheless, the Commission says, Vaughn's denial is not sufficient to overcome the evidence that Ruby entered surreptitiously while Vaughn was distracted by the departing police car.

The Commission does not suggest that there are obstacles other than the denial of Vaughn and the other three officers; in fact, there *was* additional evidence against Ruby's use of the Main Street ramp which has not been overcome.

One obstacle, unmentioned in the Report, is a statement by UPI reporter Terrance McGarry. McGarry told the FBI that at least five minutes before Oswald was shot, he had stationed himself at the middle of the basement end of the Main Street ramp and that no one came down the ramp during that time. *(CE 2050)*

Another obstacle is a report by Harry Tasker, a taxi-driver, who had been hired by a reporter to stand by outside the police station. Tasker had positioned himself opposite the Main Street ramp and had kept the ramp entrance under constant observation, so that he would see the reporter as soon as he emerged and be ready to race to the county jail. Tasker told the FBI on December 6, 1963 that he had been standing at the ramp entrance for about five minutes before the shot and that no one resembling Ruby entered the basement while he was there. Tasker believed that he would have remembered Ruby if he had entered during those five minutes. *(CE 2063)* Tasker told the same story in an FBI interview on December 9, 1963 and in his Commission deposition, somewhat later, on August 24, 1964.

> *Hubert:* Do you know Jack Ruby at all?
> *Tasker:* No—no, sir.
> *Hubert:* You've seen his pictures, of course, since?
> *Tasker:* Oh, I've seen his pictures.
> *Hubert:* Did you see him around in the crowd that morning?
> *Tasker:* No, sir; I never have remembered seeing that man coming up, walking, riding, or anything else.
> *Hubert:* You didn't see him coming up Main Street from the Western Union office?
> *Tasker:* No.
> *Hubert:* You didn't see him walking along Main Street?
> *Tasker:* No.   *(15H 682-683)*

Tasker, like McGarry, is not mentioned in the Report. In fairness, the Commission should have indicated that Vaughn's claim that Ruby did not slip past him was corroborated not only by the three police officers in the car but also by the reporter and the taxi-driver—both disinterested witnesses.

Whereas Tasker did not know Ruby before he murdered Oswald, Officer Vaughn was acquainted with Ruby *(12H 359)*, but Ruby apparently did not know Vaughn, despite at least two encounters with him and despite his penchant for policemen. After refusing for four weeks to discuss his means of entry, Ruby told FBI Agent C. Ray Hall on December 21, 1963 that as he approached the police building after leaving Western Union, "he noticed a police officer standing at the entrance to the ramp . . . but he did not know the police officer." *(C. Ray Hall Exhibit 3, p. 11)* Lieutenant Pierce, who drove the police car off the ramp, had known Ruby for 12 or 13 years *(12H 340);* Sergeant Maxey, one of the officers in the car, also knew Ruby, at least "by sight" *(CE 2002, p. 130)*

Therefore, of the five witnesses who should have seen Ruby if he had entered by the ramp but did not see him, three knew Ruby well enough to recognize him. This is not without significance, as an indication that Ruby was not there or as an indication that Ruby was permitted to enter by his officer "friends."

Sergeant Putnam, who was in the car with Lieutenant Pierce and Maxey, did not know Ruby. But an FBI report on an interview with him states:

> Sergeant Putnam said he is positive no one entered the basement from the Main Street exit as Lieutenant Pierce's car was going up the ramp at approximately 11:20 a.m. He pointed out that the Main Street ramp exit is somewhat narrow and anyone walking down the ramp, as a car departed, would most certainly step close to the wall to avoid being hit.
>
> *(Putnam Exhibit 5073)*

Captain Talbert of the Dallas Police provided a vivid account of Lieutenant Pierce's reaction when Pierce learned that Ruby claimed to have entered the basement through the Main Street ramp.

> *Hubert:* Did you talk to Pierce, Lieutenant Pierce about how Ruby came into the basement, if you recall?
> *Talbert:* Many times. . . .
> *Hubert:* . . . did he seem to know about it?
> *Talbert:* No, sir. He was quite vociferous, in fact.
> *Hubert:* Vociferous in what way?
> *Talbert:* Language. We wouldn't want to put it in this deposition, sir. By that I mean he was alleging that he had entered that Main Street entrance. Lieutenant Pierce said he couldn't have. And then the vociferousness. . . .
> *Hubert:* In other words, Pierce's reaction was that it was not true, so far as he knew?
> *Talbert:* His reaction was startled . . . and that it couldn't possibly have been true. . . . Sam [Pierce] can be rather positive in his views. He is positive in his views, not "can be." And he was very positive in that. *(15H 189)*

Captain Talbert also contributed his opinion of the unfortunate Officer Vaughn, who was blamed by the Dallas police and, by implication, by the Warren Commission for the breach of security that enabled Ruby to enter the basement and shoot to death a helpless and handcuffed man.

> . . . the individual officer on Main Street was one of, if not the best patrolman I have. He is the type person that you can depend on thoroughly, and quite sizable physically. I don't know whether you have met Vaughn or not, but if we went into physical combat, I would want an edge on him of some sort. *(15H 189-190)*

Vaughn's testimony suggests that Talbert's high opinion of him was not undeserved. Vaughn consistently and unreservedly asserted that Ruby had not slipped by him and that he could not possibly have done so. He did not testify before the Commission but was deposed by counsel.

> *Hubert:* Did any of your superior officers question you about whether Jack could have gotten by you?
> *Vaughn:* Yes, they questioned me quite extensively about it . . . on Tuesday morning around nine o'clock they called me at home and told me to come in and write a report so I got up and went down there and wrote a report Tuesday . . . and Wednesday night they called me at home . . . and told me to come in and go to work Thursday morning, that Chief Fisher wanted to talk to me. . . .
> . . . so when I went up there, Chief Fisher, Captain Talbert, and Lieutenant Pierce, I believe, was all sitting in this little assembly room and they were talking. . . . Within a few minutes . . . we went on up to Chief Fisher's office which is up on the third floor. . . . Chief Fisher questioned me about it quite extensively, and I told him the exact story that I had in my report and [that] I have told you, and . . . he said he didn't doubt my integrity, but would I take a lie detector test and I told him—yes, I would take a lie detector test and I went in and Detective Bentley, who was operating the polygraph, and so I went in and took the test. *(12H 368-369)*

A report on Vaughn's polygraph test, in which he denied that he saw Ruby or permitted him to enter the basement, states that in the opinion of the examiner Vaughn answered every question truthfully. (*CE 2002*, p. 180)

Although Vaughn's superior, Police Chief Curry, blamed the breach of security on Vaughn's carelessness *(4H 190),* no action against Vaughn seems to have been taken on that account.

> *Hubert:* Tell me this, after the conversation and the examination by Fisher and the lie detector test, and so forth, was there any kind of disciplinary action taken against you by the police department?
> *Vaughn:* No; I had my efficiency cut.
> *Hubert:* That's one thing I am interested in—tell us about that.
> *Vaughn:* Well, I got cut four points.
> *Hubert:* Is that a drastic cut?
> *Vaughn:* Well, for me it was . . . normally for the last three or four years I have always carried a 90 efficiency, which is a fairly high efficiency, and I got cut four points on one certain thing. . . . It was cut from a 90 to an 86 and on one particular phase of how they grade you—on dependability.
> *Hubert:* Did you ascertain that that efficiency cut was done because of the Ruby incident?
> *Vaughn:* . . . I thought possibly it was over the Ruby incident and I went and talked to one of my supervisors. . . . I didn't feel that I should have had a cut on my efficiency under the circumstances. . . . They have never actually proved that Jack came in that way . . . and my understanding I got from him [Lieutenant Pierce] was that Chief Fisher said it was for letting Tom Chabot in the basement.   *(12H 369-370)*

Tom Chabot, a police mechanic married to a policewoman, was well known to Vaughn for years. *(12H 364)* Vaughn had admitted Chabot to the police basement about an hour and a half before the shooting in order for Chabot to check on the parking situation. Chabot had talked to Sergeant Dean at the foot of the ramp for two or three minutes and then had returned to the street.

That Vaughn was penalized for permitting Chabot to enter hardly suggests a genuine belief by his superiors that he had dragged the whole police force into disaster. Equally striking is the indication that Vaughn intended to contest the cut in his efficiency rating if that cut was linked to Ruby, but accepted with good grace a penalty imposed for the purely technical "infraction" of admitting a police mechanic to the basement. Since at least 14 newsmen had come and gone freely without having their credentials checked, presumably because of the negligence of many or most of the policemen on duty, the singling out of Vaughn for disciplinary action on the specious grounds that he had permitted a civilian employee to enter the building seems grossly unfair.

In spite of Vaughn's protestations, corroborated by other witnesses, the Commission concluded that Ruby "probably" did enter by the Main Street ramp, pointing out:

> Ruby's account of how he entered the basement by the Main Street ramp merits consideration in determining his means of entry. Three Dallas policemen testified that approximately 30 minutes after his arrest, Ruby told them

that he had walked to the top of the Main Street ramp from the nearby Western Union office and that he had walked down the ramp at the time the police car driven by Lieutenant Pierce emerged into Main Street. *This information did not come to light immediately because the policemen did not report it to their superiors until some days later.* Ruby refused to discuss his means of entry in interrogations with other investigators later on the day of his arrest. Thereafter, in a lengthy interview *on December 21* and in a sworn deposition taken after his trial, *Ruby gave the same explanation he had given to the three policemen.* [Italics added]　　　　　　　　　 *(WR 219)*

The Commission does not evaluate the strange failure of the three policemen to report "until some days later" that Ruby had told them that he had entered via the Main Street ramp. Indeed, the Report does not even name the three officers involved. The footnotes indicate that they were Sergeant Patrick Dean and Detectives B. S. Clardy and T. D. McMillon. But study of the testimony and documents reveals that there were *four*, not three, officers involved. Detective Don Ray Archer also reported "some days later" that Ruby had told him and the other officers that he had entered the basement by the Main Street ramp. All four officers also testified that Ruby had made remarks betraying premeditation. Some or all of these policemen were present when Ruby was interviewed, first by Secret Service Agent Forrest Sorrels, for about ten minutes, and subsequently by FBI Agent C. Ray Hall, for about five hours.

Within 30 minutes of his act of murder, Ruby chose, by astounding coincidence, to tell four officers that he had entered through the Main Street ramp, but not one of those officers reported what Ruby had said "until some days later." Having told the four policemen how he got in, Ruby then became uncooperative. When FBI Agent Hall began to interrogate him at 12:40 p.m., Ruby refused to reveal his means of entry *(15H 64, 67)*, even though Clardy and McMillon—to whom supposedly Ruby had already admitted using the Main Street ramp—were present with FBI Agent Hall. And, incredible though it is, neither of those experienced detectives informed the FBI agent that Ruby had given him the information he was withholding from the FBI.

At about three o'clock Ruby was removed to the Homicide Bureau, where he was questioned by Captain Fritz in the presence of FBI Agent Hall for about an hour. In his undated report of that interrogation *(CE 2003, p. 271)*, Fritz states, "Claimed he came in off of Main Street down ramp to basement of City Hall"; C. Ray Hall, however, describing the same interrogation, testified that "Ruby did not wish to say how he got into the basement or at what time he entered." *(15H 64, 68)* The Commission accepts Hall's version, and for once agreement is possible. Indeed, on December 6, 1963 Fritz was still attempting to determine how Ruby had entered the basement and how long he had been there before shooting Oswald, judging from his questions to one of Ruby's lawyers. *(CE 2025)*

The Warren Commission appears to accept and rely upon the assertions of the three policemen—Clardy, Dean, and McMillon—regarding Ruby's means of entry, but in its Report does not attempt to explain their failure to report Ruby's alleged statements "until some days later." Clardy, for example, did not report Ruby's remarks until November 30. *(CE 2002, p. 73)* Clardy gave testimony to Commission Counsel Leon Hubert on March 24, 1964. *(12H 403-414)* Hubert never confronted Clardy with a direct question about his failure to report Ruby's remarks until almost a week had passed, nor did he tax Clardy with his failure to brief FBI Agent Hall when he heard Ruby refuse to tell Hall how he had managed to enter the basement.

> *Hubert:* Did you ask Ruby, or did anyone ask Ruby in your presence how he had gotten into the basement?
>
> *Clardy:* I asked Ruby.
>
> *Hubert:* You did by yourself?
>
> *Clardy:* I asked him myself, and I am sure there were several others who did. . . .
>
> *Hubert:* What did you ask him, and what did he reply? What did you ask him first?
>
> *Clardy:* I asked him how he got into the basement and how long he had been there. I don't know whether that is the exact words I asked him in or not, and he said that Lieutenant Pierce, or he called him Rio Pierce—I believe [Ruby] said Rio Pierce, Lieutenant Rio Pierce drove out in the car and the officer stepped out from the ramp momentarily to talk to Lieutenant Pierce, or said something to him, and I come in behind him right on down the ramp, and says, "When I got approximately halfway down the ramp I heard somebody holler, 'Hey, you,' but I don't know whether he was hollering at me or not, but I just ducked my head and kept coming."   *(12H 412)*

Hubert proceeded to quiz Clardy, offering again and again the opportunity to add the same information to the reports *(Clardy Exhibits 5061 and 5062)* in which Clardy had failed to mention Ruby's alleged explanation. Clardy apparently didn't understand, and neither took advantage of the chance to claim that the information had been omitted from those reports by a third person's error, or volunteered any reasons for the omissions. Hubert, for unknown reasons, refrained from an explicit question. Consequently, we are left without any explanation of Clardy's belated report of Ruby's supposed remarks.

When Detective McMillon was examined by Commission Counsel Griffin on March 25, 1964 *(13H 37-55)*, he *was* asked direct questions about his failure to indicate in his written report of November 24, 1963 *(McMillon Exhibit 5018)* Ruby's alleged admissions about his means of entry.[4]

> *Griffin:* . . . on the date of the twenty-fourth, when these things were fresh in your mind at 3:30, you didn't mention anything in your report, did you, about how Ruby got down the ramp?
>
> *McMillon:* Just a second. No, sir; I didn't mention it then.
>
> *Griffin:* Why was that?

---

4 The transcript of McMillon's testimony as a prosecution witness at the Ruby trial appears in *CE 2409*. McMillon was cross-examined for a whole day by defense counsel about his failure to report until later statements allegedly made by Ruby in his hearing, indicating premeditation and specifying his means of entry into the police basement. McMillon gave no explanation other than that he had not remembered Ruby's admissions when he wrote his report a few hours afterwards. (Archer and Dean also testified for the prosecution at Ruby's trial but the transcripts of their testimony are not included in the Commission's Exhibits.)

McMillon: Well, I couldn't possibly have mentioned everything that I knew about the deal here. I just didn't mention it.

Griffin: But you knew that was important, didn't you?

McMillon: No, sir; I didn't think anything about it being important at all at the time. I gave that information, I believe—this report was written on Sunday—I gave it to them on Saturday, I believe, during the departmental investigation. . . .

Griffin: There came a time, didn't there, when Dean was under a lot of pressure from the people in the police department?

McMillon: I don't know anything about that. Probably no more than the rest of us. I don't know. I think that Dean got misquoted or something in the paper. . . .

Griffin: Didn't you know somewhere along the line that Dean might possibly be in trouble?

McMillon: No, sir; this article in the paper, I had heard all different kinds of rumors. . . .   (13H 52)

Griffin: Do you recall Hall asking Ruby how he got down the ramp?

McMillon: I don't recall.

Griffin: Or how Ruby got in the basement?

McMillon: I don't recall Hall asking him that. . . .

Griffin: I believe you stated before that you heard Ruby tell Dean that he came down the ramp?

McMillon: Yes, I heard Jack say that he came down the ramp.

Griffin: All right. Now, at the time that you signed this report on November the twenty-seventh [the typewritten copy of the report drafted by hand on the twenty-fourth], did you realize that such a statement from Ruby was a matter of concern to the police department?

McMillon: At the time that I signed those reports was just like all of the rest of them. I realized that anything that I might know or that I can remember might be of some value or of some significance to anybody who was investigating it.

Griffin: You certainly knew that any statement that Ruby made about how he got down into the basement would be something that somebody might want to know?

McMillon: Yes.

Griffin: You read that report over?

McMillon: Yes.

Griffin: And there is nothing in that report about Ruby having made such a statement, is there?

McMillon: No, sir; I don't see anything.   (13H 53-54)

Sergeant Dean, the third member of the tardy trio, reported Ruby's alleged statements for the first time on November 25, 1963. *(12H 439; Dean Exhibit 5009)* Dean gave testimony three times: first by deposition to Counsel Griffin, on March 24, 1964; then on April 1, 1964, this time accompanied by an attorney, Dean resumed his deposition with Counsel Hubert; and finally, at his own request, Dean testified before the Warren Commission on June 8, 1964, to place on the record the fact that during an "off-the-record" interruption of his deposition, Counsel Griffin had accused him of perjury and threatened him with the loss of his job.

In his first round of testimony, Dean had stated that shortly after Oswald was shot, he had escorted Secret Service Agent Sorrels to the jail so that Sorrels might question Ruby. Dean himself had remained there for a short time, and then had departed for Parkland Hospital, where Oswald had been taken in an ambulance.

Griffin questioned Dean about the brief period of time that he had spent with Ruby immediately after the shooting.

Griffin: What else did you talk with Ruby about, after Sorrels finished talking to him?

Dean: After Sorrels finished, I said, "Ruby, I want to ask you a couple of questions myself." And he said, "All right." I said, "How did you get in the basement?" And he said, "I walked in the Main Street ramp." And he told me, he said, "I have just been to the Western Union to mail a money order to Fort Worth." And he said, "I walked from the Western Union to the ramp." And he said, "I saw Sam Pierce—" and he referred to him as Sam Pierce—"drive out of the basement. At that time, at the time the car drove out is when I walked in." *(12H 432-433)*

Dean said that Sorrels had not asked Ruby how he had entered the police premises; while Dean was sure that others were present when he himself asked Ruby about his means of entry, he was not certain who they were. He said that on his way down from Ruby's cell, he had stopped at Chief Curry's office to return some keys, and then had proceeded to Parkland Hospital.

Griffin: Did you tell Chief Curry what Ruby had told you?

Dean: At the time; no. *(12H 433)*

Griffin: Did somebody assign you to go out to Parkland Hospital?

Dean: No, sir.

Griffin: How did you happen to go out there?

Dean: To check on the condition of Oswald. . . . I knew that I would probably be needed out there. . . .

Griffin: When you got to Parkland Hospital . . . did you talk with any police officers?

Dean: Well, I am sure I talked to some. . . .

Griffin: And did you tell them about the conversation you had with Ruby?

Dean: No, sir.

Griffin: Why not?

Dean: I just didn't tell anyone about it. *(12H 434)*

Dean testified that sometime later on the same day, when he returned to the police station, he told Lieutenant Pierce about Ruby's claim that he had entered by way of the Main Street ramp, and that Pierce relayed this to Captain Talbert. (As we have seen already, Captain Talbert's testimony suggests that he was the first one to tell Lieutenant Pierce about Ruby's statement, and had thus provoked Pierce to "language.") But Dean conceded that no one had questioned Vaughn about Ruby's allegations that day. (Vaughn was not questioned formally until the following Thursday, and was asked to write a report only on Tuesday, as previously discussed.)

At the end of his deposition, Dean did not offer any reason more explicit than "I just didn't tell anyone about it" in explanation of his failure to make an official report of Ruby's alleged statements until November 25.

Before proceeding to Dean's appearance before the Commission, it may be well to recapitulate the facts thus far elicited:

(1) Shortly after Ruby shot Oswald, he is alleged by Clardy, Dean, and McMillon to have said in their presence, or in direct reply to their questions, that he had entered the basement via the Main Street ramp while the officer on guard was distracted by the departure of Lieutenant Pierce's car.

(2) After 12:40 p.m. on the same day, Ruby refused to tell FBI Agent Hall his time or means of entry, and neither Clardy nor McMillon, who were present with Hall, told the FBI agent of Ruby's supposed admissions to them before Hall's arrival—McMillon, because he did not hear Hall ask Ruby about his means of entry, according to his testimony, and Clardy, for unknown reasons, about which he was not questioned by counsel.

(3) None of the three officers reported Ruby's alleged admissions on the same day he made them. Two of them could not give any explicit explanation for their delay; the third was not questioned on that point.

To those facts, we should add:

(4) Clardy, Dean, and McMillon had all known Ruby for some years. (*CE 2002,* pp. 74, 88, and 136) Although Ruby ultimately "gave the same explanation" that he had allegedly given to the three policemen, he never said that he had given them that story within half an hour of his arrest, as they claimed.

Dean appeared before the Commission at his own request in June 1964, with Chairman Warren presiding and Mr. Dulles present, explaining:

> . . . the main reason I wanted to appear before the Commission was about the 20 or 25 minutes that was off the record that I feel I would like the Commission to have on the record, and this is between Mr. Griffin and I. . . . Mr. Griffin had questioned me about two hours, or maybe a little longer. There was no problems at all, no difficulties. And after that length of time, a little over two hours, Mr. Griffin desired to get off the record and he advised the court reporter that he would be off the record and he could go smoke a cigarette or get a coke, and he would let him know when he wanted him to get back on the record.
>
> Well, after the court reporter left, Mr. Griffin started talking to me in the manner of gaining my confidence in that he would help me and that he felt I would probably need help in the future. My not knowing what he was building up to, I asked Mr. Griffin to go ahead and ask me what he was going to ask me . . . if I knew I would tell him the truth or if I didn't know I would tell him I didn't know.
>
> Mr. Griffin took my reports, one dated February 18, the subject of which was an interview with Jack Ruby, and one dated November 26, which was my assignment in the basement. *He said there were things in these statements which were not true,* and, in fact, he said both these statements, he said there were particular things in there that were not true, and I asked him what portions did he consider not true, and then very dogmatically he said that, "Jack Ruby didn't tell you that he entered the basement via the Main Street ramp."

And, of course, I was shocked at this. This is what I testified to, in fact, I was cross-examined on this, and he, Mr. Griffin, further said, "Jack Ruby did not tell you that he had thought or planned to kill Oswald two nights prior."

And he said, *"Your testimony was false, and these reports to your chief of police are false."*

So this, of course, all this was off the record. I told Mr. Griffin then this shocked me, and I told him it shocked me; that I couldn't imagine what he was getting at or why he would accuse me of this, and I asked him, and Mr. Griffin replied that he didn't or he wasn't at liberty to discuss that particular part of it with me, and that he wasn't trying to cross-examine me here, but that under cross-examination *he could prove that my testimony was false,* and that is when I told Mr. Griffin that these are the facts and I can't change them. This is what I know about it. [Italics added]

(5H 255-256)

To interrupt Dean's dramatic narrative for a moment, I should like to underline that if Dean had not taken the initiative in placing the dialogue on record, Griffin's accusations would have remained completely hidden. The stenographer had been sent out of the room. No one was present except the witness and Commission counsel. Counsel made an accusation of perjury, but he might have made any imaginable statement or proposition to the witness, and it would have remained secret, unless one of the two parties chose to make a disclosure.

The significance of Dean's experience must be weighed in the light of the numerous "off-the-record" interruptions in the testimony, which total more than 230. Of that total, about 128 "off-the-record" interruptions took place during depositions (the examination of a witness by counsel without the presence of members of the Commission).

The complete suppression of the Dean/Griffin affair from the Warren Report, the "authoritative" source of information for the overwhelming mass of the public, is a matter for disquiet. Only the handful of people who purchased the Hearings and Exhibits (perhaps .0000005 per cent of the U.S. population) are in a position to discover from the testimony how unusual the ways of the Commission were and how lively the private suspicions of some of its personnel.

To resume Dean's testimony before the Commission, we come to some direct remarks by Chief Justice Warren.

Rankin: Did you ask Mr. Griffin to ever put this part that was off the record on the record?

Dean: No, sir; I didn't.

Rankin: Why didn't you at that time?

Dean: Well, now the discussion was, I said, "Mr. Griffin, I have waived my rights for an attorney, of which I don't feel like I need one." I still don't feel like I need one.

Chairman Warren: And you do not need one either, Sergeant.

Dean: True.

Warren: You will get along all right.

Dean: Thank you.

(5H 256)

Truly, it is hard to disentangle the judge from the jury from the defense from the prosecution.

To denounce Griffin for his off-the-record dialogue with the witness would be unfair. The Commission took a decision at the beginning of its term that the preparation of witnesses by counsel—a technique fundamental and proper to the adversary procedure—was permissible, while denying explicit petition from a defense counsel designated by the mother of the accused and refusing to permit the adversary procedure. The Commission did not hesitate to utilize advantages properly enjoyed by an adversary while eschewing the corresponding obligations, all on the pretext of "impartial fact finding."

Griffin, then, can scarcely be reproached for taking his dry run with Dean during the testimony rather than before the deposition began. His secret talk with Dean may be considered as attempted coercion, as Dean himself considered it, but it can just as easily be regarded as "preparation" of the witness and entirely permissible under the Commission's *modus operandi*. Even so, questions remain unanswered.

Was Griffin bluffing or was he really able to prove that Dean was not telling the truth? If Dean was making false statements, what about the other police witnesses who gave the same or corroborating testimony? Did the Commission satisfy itself that Griffin's charges of false testimony were unfounded? If so, how did it reach that finding? If not, how in conscience could the Commission limit itself to the statement in the Report that three policemen had testified that Ruby had made explanations about his means of entry, in terms which clearly imply that that testimony was bona fide?

After the exchange of compliments between the Chairman and the witness, there was an attempt to elicit from Dean an explanation of why he had not included in his first reports the statements allegedly made by Ruby.

> *Rankin:* Yes; did you explain to Mr. Griffin in your prior testimony why you didn't put it in?
> *Dean:* I believe that I did; I am not sure. . . .
> *Warren:* Do you recall whether you were asked that specific question or not, Sergeant? May I ask, Mr. Rankin, was he asked that question, and did he answer it?
> *Rankin:* I have to look at the record to be sure. Mr. Chief Justice, in answer to your question . . . he was not asked for any explanation as to why he didn't give it at any earlier time.
> *Warren:* Then we can't blame him if he didn't answer why.   *(5H 257)*

Dean then volunteered that he had experienced great concern because somehow the newspapers had got hold of the information that he had been accused of making false statements, and because he had not been able to tell his side of the story.

> *Rankin:* What I was asking, Sergeant, was whether there is anything that you would like to tell the Commission or add to your testimony about why it wasn't in the earlier statement prior to February 18 that you haven't already told us.

Dean: Well, I don't think I would like—if I could, I would like to know why Mr. Griffin had accused me of perjury. Of course, this is something for you people to know, but I just—he wouldn't discuss it with me. *(5H 258)*

Either obtuse or skillful, the witness continued to evade giving a reason for his belated reports of Ruby's alleged remarks, managing to regain the offensive each time it appeared to be slipping away. To Dean's request for the reasons behind Griffin's charge of perjury, Chairman Warren replied that he had never discussed the matter with Griffin, as he had not known previously about the off-the-record conversation, but no member of the staff had a right to tell any witness he was lying. It was for the Commission to appraise testimony, and no staff member had any power to help or to injure any witness. *(5H 258)*

After a further exchange of pleasantries, Dean departed. The public is still waiting for the Commission's appraisal of his testimony.

Detective Archer, the fourth witness to Ruby's alleged admission of premeditation, gave his testimony to Counsel Hubert on March 25, 1964. *(12H 401-402)* He was questioned about various reports he had written and statements he had made to the FBI *(Archer Exhibits)*, and finally it emerged that Archer had said nothing to anyone about Ruby's statements until three weeks before the opening of Ruby's trial.

Hubert: It never occurred to you that it was your duty to tell your superior officer, or somebody, that you had heard this man said, "I meant to kill him"?

Archer: No, sir; it didn't. Had they inquired about it, I certainly would have told them. *(12H 403)*

It is difficult to believe Archer, as well as the others. District Attorney Henry Wade, however, saw nothing wrong with their stories. The Commission questioned Wade at some length about the preparation of the police officers who had served as prosecution witnesses at the Ruby trial. *(5H 245-250)*

Wade's testimony further depletes confidence in the legal process in Dallas. Wade not only glosses over the afterthoughts of the police witnesses but also reveals that the Dallas police "lost" or "misplaced" important documentary evidence in the Ruby case. *(5H 242)*

All of this disturbing information has been "reduced" to a single terse paragraph in the Warren Report *(WR 219)*, so worded as to create the impression that the testimony of three police officers corroborates the evidence that Ruby entered by the Main Street ramp. In the last analysis, their testimony does the opposite—and it is unmistakable that the Commission, or its counsel at least, suspected that the testimony was false.

However, the Commission claims to have still more supporting evidence for the Main Street ramp.

The testimony of two witnesses partially corroborates Ruby's claim that he entered by the Main Street ramp. James Turner, an employee of WBAP-TV Fort Worth, testified that while he was standing near the railing on the east side of the Main Street ramp, perhaps 30 seconds before the shooting, he observed a man he is confident was Jack Ruby moving slowly down the

Main Street ramp about ten feet away from the bottom. Two other witnesses testified that they thought they had seen Ruby on the Main Street side of the ramp before the shooting. *(WR 221)*

The Commission's unorthodox arithmetic of "partial corroboration" finds that one witness plus two other witnesses totals not three but two. One witness, Turner, is named; the "two others" are mentioned in a footnote, Police Reserve Officers Kenneth Croy and William Newman. But a reading of the testimony and documents shows that none of these witnesses actually provided corroboration of Ruby's story.

"James" Turner, who said explicitly that his name was not James but Jimmy, testified on March 25, 1964 that:

Turner: . . . I happened to glance up and this was at the same time the car drove out of the . . . level part. I saw Mr. Ruby coming in. . . .
Hubert: Now, you say you saw Jack Ruby. You had not known him to be Jack Ruby at that time?
Turner: No; what set him off from other men was the hat he was wearing.
Hubert: What sort of hat was it?
Turner: I don't know the technical name. . . . It was a felt hat, had a pretty large brim on it, and it was a—round on top, which you seldom see. . . . it wasn't a snap brim. It was just a wide brim. . . .
Hubert: Do you know what color it was?
Turner: It seemed to be gray. . . . he was dressed in an overcoat, or long— it could have been a suit coat, but I didn't notice. *(13H 135-136)*

Hubert: You did not see him come over the rail?
Turner: No, sir; I did not. I did not come in contact with the man until he was in the position—he was nearly in the center of it when I came in contact, and the man—the hat was the most obvious facial—I mean just glancing at a man you take something that you can pick a man out by and remember his name by it. That is the way I remember people is something they ordinarily wear, and he had the hat on, but I thought he was a—much larger than—by just glancing at him.
Hubert: . . . Is there any doubt in your mind that the man that you saw . . . was the man you later saw step forward and shoot Oswald?
Turner: No, sir; and without a doubt in my mind, sir.
Hubert: Off the record.
(Discussion off the record.) *(13H 141)*

What did Turner mean by his statement, "I thought he was a—much larger than—by just glancing at him"? Were the dashes in that sentence inserted to indicate hesitation or to represent words which the stenographer missed? Clarification might have been helpful, but perhaps counsel obtained clarification off the record. In any case, Turner's description of the hat is completely inconsistent with the hat Ruby was wearing when he shot Oswald, immortalized in many widely-published photographs and in the Commission's Exhibits. *(CE 2635,* for example) That hat has a narrow brim, not a "pretty large" one, and an ordinary top, not a "round" one.

Turner's testimony does not really do much to advance the Commission's

Main Street ramp thesis. What about the "two other witnesses" who thought "they had seen Ruby on the Main Street side of the ramp"?

Croy, the reserve sergeant, described a man who was standing near the railing on the Main Street ramp, where Croy was stationed, but he didn't know "whether it was (Ruby) or not." *(12H 193)* Croy, like his colleagues Archer, Dean, Clardy, and McMillon, failed to report this man in his written report after the shooting. That occasioned quite a grilling of Croy by Counsel Griffin.

> *Griffin:* Well, Mr. Croy, why didn't you mention in this report, dated November 26, your seeing this man you believe to be Ruby?
> *Croy:* Because at that time Captain Solomon told me that there would be another report made and I would have to go downtown to the city hall before a stenographer, and he told me just to leave that out for the time being . . . that this [report] right here was just basically to find out where we were in the city hall.

Griffin then elicited from Croy the information that the first time that he had reported seeing "Ruby" was on December 1, 1963, in a statement taken by Lieutenant Revill at the police department. *(Croy Exhibit 5053)*

> *Griffin:* . . . Did Revill indicate that he had heard about this before, about your having been a witness to this?
> *Croy:* Not that I recall.
> *Griffin:* Was anybody else there?
> *Croy:* Yes; Lieutenant, I think his name is Cornwall, he was present.
> *Griffin:* Did either of them indicate surprise by having seen this?
> *Croy:* No . . . they didn't act surprised. They didn't act like they didn't know about it. It kind of tied in with the other reports they had gotten, I presume, from the way they acted. . . .
> *Griffin:* . . . How would you describe their general attitude in this interview?
> *Croy:* They were very interested.
> *Griffin:* Well, can you tell me more about that?
> *Croy:* No; well, I will put it this way, that it took us eight hours to get that up. That is how interested they were. . . . The stenographer took it, and then she typed it up. Then the next day I went back down there and they re-read it to me and went over and over and over and over the same thing over and over again. And then I . . . signed it and had it notarized. *(12H 198-199)*

Griffin might have saved himself and Croy the trouble of this interrogation, if he had bothered to read the Commission's documents. A report directed to Police Chief Curry on December 19, 1963 by three senior police officers who were conducting an internal investigation of the events leading up to the murder of Oswald, referring to Croy's description of a man he believed to be Ruby who was at the foot of the Main Street ramp awhile before the shooting, states that,

> Investigating officers have determined that Robert Huffaker, KRLD-TV newsman was in this area at the time, and his clothes were identical to the clothing described by this officer.   *(CE 2002, p. 52)*

Since the clothing described by Croy included a maroon coat, we accept the finding that Croy's man was Huffaker and not Ruby. The Commission may be technically correct in saying that Croy was one of "two other witnesses" who thought they had seen Ruby, but in omitting from the Report the information that Croy had actually seen Huffaker, the Commission misleads the reader.

Finally, there is Reserve Officer William J. Newman. Newman testified that he had seen a man come down the ramp immediately after the shout, "Here he comes!" However, he had not realized that his information was significant until he was interviewed by Lieutenant Revill "the following Sunday" *(12H 327),* which was December 1, 1963. That, as others than the authors of the Warren Report will calculate, makes six out of six officers who reported *belatedly* "facts" that supported the Main Street ramp theory—Archer, Clardy, Croy, Dean, McMillon, and Newman.

Newman's deposition ended with the following passage, in which Counsel Griffin stated his mind bluntly, this time on the record.

(Pause)

Griffin: You are a d—— l——. I want you to come back tomorrow night and I want you—I want to question you some more.

Newman: I certainly don't appreciate that accusation. I have given you all I can, to best of my memory, for four months.

Griffin: I want you to regard yourself as still under the obligation to appear . . . and I would like to recess to continue this deposition until four o'clock tomorrow afternoon in this office. If you would care to consult with an attorney at that time, or anything like that, and would like to come in here with one, I would be most happy for you to do so.

Newman: May I ask: What are you getting at?

Griffin: Well, frankly, after having sat here for an hour and having listened to this testimony, my own personal opinion, either you are absolutely not telling the truth or plenty of other people who have been in here aren't telling the truth. Somehow I am going to see how the devil we can reconcile these differences.   *(12H 329-330)*

But when Newman returned, it was Hubert and not Griffin who resumed the deposition. Hubert said that he wished to mark for identification certain papers and letters and reports. *(Newman Exhibits 5037-5038-E)* During the process of identification, it emerged that Newman had not only seen a man come down the ramp but he had seen a second man "jumping over the rail" within ten minutes of the shooting. *(12H 330-334)*

But Newman could not identify either of the two men and was unable to say that Ruby was or was not the man on the ramp or the man who jumped over the rail.

By what reasoning, then, does the Commission offer us Newman as a witness who thought he had seen Ruby?

What really remains of the whole Main Street ramp thesis except discredited and misrepresented testimony which is riddled with collusion?

The question remains, how *did* Ruby enter the police basement? There were many rumors and speculations, one of which was that Ruby had used a press badge to gain admittance on the pretext that he was a reporter on legitimate business. This premise is logical, since Ruby actually told a detective friend on Friday night that he was serving as an interpreter for some Israeli reporters.

(Eberhardt Exhibit 5026) There was also a specific identification that "one of the reserves had let him in, and he had a lapel pass on."

Police Reserve Officer Harold Holly reported on November 29, 1963 that he had reported for duty on Sunday about ten minutes after Oswald was shot and that:

> . . . then he was sent to Parkland Hospital. While at Parkland, he engaged in conversation with another reserve officer whose name is unknown to him. This reserve officer told Mr. Holly that prior to the shooting, he either observed, or himself admitted Jack Ruby to the basement. That Mr. Ruby was wearing a press identification card on his jacket.
>
> Mr. Holly states he could recognize this reserve officer if he could see him again.   *(Holly Exhibit 5111)*

Subsequently, Captain Solomon of the Reserves showed Holly photographs of reserve officers in an effort to identify the man with whom Holly had conversed at Parkland Hospital. Holly selected the photograph of William J. Newman, the witness whom Griffin had called a "d—— l——." Solomon testified on March 26, 1964 that he was not satisfied with Holly's story because the man he had identified, William Newman, "wasn't out at Parkland Hospital where he [Holly] told them he saw him [Newman]." *(12H 89)*

But Newman *was* at Parkland Hospital, as he himself testified on March 25, 1964. He stated that he had arrived at the hospital shortly after noon and had remained on duty there until he was relieved. *(12H 326)*

Here is the way Holly described the incident when he testified on March 26, 1964:

> *Hubert:* Now, do you remember that during the time that you were out at Parkland Hospital another reserve officer approached you and stated that he had seen the man who shot Oswald coming down the ramp?
>
> *Holly:* No; he didn't approach me, because I approached him. I went over to find where I could get some water. I was stationed where the entrance is where the Governor was, and he told me there was some coffee and water if I wanted, and I went in and when I came back I struck up a conversation with the man . . . he was a reserve. And in the conversation he said that he either knew or he saw Ruby down in the city hall, knew of him getting down in there. . . . The conversation went like, well, how in the world could they ever let him in. Everybody knew him, which most reserves do know him.
>
> *Hubert:* You knew him?
>
> *Holly:* Oh, yes; I knew him. I did business with him. And I would know him if I saw him. But I wasn't stationed down there, so therefore, I don't know. And he said he saw him down there, or did see of him, or he in some way, one of the reserves had let him in, and he had a lapel pass on.
>
> *Hubert:* Now, do you know who he was, this reserve?
>
> *Holly:* No. I tried to go through the photographs of who I thought it was. I never have learned if it was him. . . . I haven't seen him since. I didn't know him and never had seen him before that. But I am pretty positive I picked out the right man, the one that I did see and talk to.
>
> *Hubert:* Let me see if I can get you straight. You say that you are pretty positive that you did pick out the right man, but a little while before you said that you weren't quite sure? There is a little difference between the two?

Holly: I went over several photographs with Captain Solomon and he is the only one that resembles him. The photographs he showed me were old photographs, so there was a little doubt there, and that is the only part I can be doubted on. I think he said the photographs he showed me were maybe three years old.

Hubert: But he didn't get the man and confront you with him?

Holly: No.   *(12H 262-263)*

Captain Solomon failed to confront Holly with Newman on the specious ground that Newman had not been assigned to Parkland Hospital, and the Commission, by oversight or indifference, did not confront the two men with each other, or notice Solomon's inaccurate (or false) testimony, or mention this matter in its Report.

Another allegation was that Ruby had entered the basement with a camera. That story appeared in the *Dallas Times-Herald* of November 25, 1963 under the by-line of Joe Sherman, who quoted Sergeant Roland Cox as his source.[5]

Cox was questioned about the newspaper report when he testified on July 13, 1964.

Hubert: Now there was a publication by a man named Joe Sherman of the *Dallas Times-Herald* on November the twenty-fifth which indicated that you had seen [Ruby], which of course is contrary to what you have just told us. Could you explain anything about that?

Cox: Yes; I will explain to you. I was talking to a reserve captain in the basement. Let me think of his name. Captain Kris [*sic*], I believe. We were talking about the thing happening, and also what people had said, and this news reporter went from there. In other words, that is the way he got it.

Hubert: Did you talk to this man, Joe Sherman?

Cox: Yes. He came into the conversation. Asked me if I knew Jack Ruby, and I said I once worked for him at that night club, the Vegas Club, and that is how the thing got in the paper. As far as me saying he had been in the basement, or how he had been in there, that was just strictly his say.

Hubert: For the record so we get it straight, let me read to you what he said, and then I am going to ask you if that is the truth or not. Police Sergeant R. A. Cox said he once worked for Jack Ruby as a special officer in the night club he once operated on Oak Lawn. He said that Ruby had a camera with him or when he entered the basement in the Dallas police station Sunday morning. Did you tell that to Joe Sherman?

Cox: No . . . I told Kris somebody said, "he even had a camera." This is how that happened. I didn't say that he had one. I said "someone said he had one."

Hubert: Now at what time did this conversation with Kris occur which was overheard by Mr. Sherman?

Cox: . . . About 20 minutes after [the shooting]; that's right. . . .

Hubert: So that your point is, you did not say this to Kris, but this reporter just picked it up? . . . The police reporter just heard you saying something about a camera, but did not hear you say that the people or somebody was saying that he had a camera?

Cox: That's right.   *(15H 157)*

---

5 *Dallas Times-Herald,* November 25, 1963, p. A9.

Hubert: This may be repeating the point, but this second apparent interview which is on page A-35 makes the flat statement that one police sergeant who worked for Ruby, and you are later identified as being that one, said that Ruby had a camera with him, indicating that you had seen him, and is it your opinion that this could only have come from the overhearing of your conversation with Kris by this writer called Sherman?

Cox: Definitely.

Hubert: In any case, to get the record straight on it, you never saw Ruby enter with a camera? . . . Nor did you in fact say that he did?

Cox: No, sir.

Hubert: All right, Sergeant Cox. . . .   *(15H 159)*

But Joe Sherman was not permitted to give *his* account of the conversation which had led him to publish the flat statements attributed to Sergeant Cox; nor was Captain Kriss questioned to see if he corroborated Cox's explanation of the erroneous press story. Obviously Cox's disclaimer by itself has little value.

The question remains as to how Ruby managed to enter the police basement at just the right moment to silence Lee Harvey Oswald with a single shot. Perhaps Ruby himself has offered the best clue to the still-unknown answer:

. . . I am certain—I don't recall definitely, but I know in my right mind, because I know my motive for doing it, and certainly to gain publicity to take a chance of being mortally wounded, as I said before, and who else could have timed it so perfectly by seconds. If it were timed that way, then someone in the police department is guilty of giving the information as to when Lee Harvey Oswald was coming down.   *(5H 206)*

At the very least, the Dallas police were guilty of alarming negligence in protecting Lee Harvey Oswald. If the Commission's "investigation" had been thorough instead of superficial, disinterested instead of predisposed to a specific theory, the role of the Dallas police might be less uncertain than it has been left. That the police were not lacking in gall is shown in a routine police department form filled out sometime after Oswald was murdered. The form is a "jail card" indicating that Oswald was kept in cell No. F-2, that the charge was "inv. murder," and that he was permitted to use the telephone three times on Saturday, November 23. One line on the form is preceded by the words, "Released by." On that line, someone had printed the words, "DECEASED 11-24-63," but those words had been crossed out by a series of horizontal lines, and the following words inserted in their place, "TRAN TO CO 11-24/11.20 am." Transferred to the county jail. Transferred! The Warren Commission, improving on this euphemism, refers constantly to the "abortive transfer," delicately avoiding such words as "murdered" or "shot to death." Euphemisms used by those who carry moral responsibility for Oswald's fate, before and after he was murdered, in no way mitigate the cruel and cowardly act by which he was slain.

Chapter 25
Ruby the Buff

" . . . starting with Sunday afternoon, you could no longer find a policeman in town who said that he knew Ruby. . . . "
                                              (Seth Kantor Exhibit 4, p. 417)

If a perfect stranger had slipped into the basement to shoot Oswald, the Dallas police would have been in disgrace for the failure of their security measures. The man who shot Oswald was not a stranger. He was a crony of the police and a habitué of the police station. Under the extraordinary circumstances which prevailed after the assassination, he came and went freely, circulating at will throughout the building. On one occasion, he even obtained an officer's service in paging a television station employee.

This same man, Jack Ruby, had been arrested by the Dallas police eight times since 1949. Two of the arrests were for carrying a concealed weapon. On both occasions, no charges were filed and Ruby was released on the same day. Less than a year before November 24, Ruby was arrested for simple assault (and found not guilty). With his record of violence and habit of carrying concealed weapons, Ruby enjoyed complete access to the police premises for two days, and on the third day he shot to death the most important prisoner in the country.

Ruby's known intimacy with the police force, more than any other single factor, generated a miasma of the conspiratorial—a miasma which persists, despite intense official and press denials.

To counter the universal distrust of the Dallas police, the Warren Commission states that the police department conducted an extensive investigation that revealed no complicity between any police officer and Jack Ruby. *(WR 224)* Moreover, the Commission says, Ruby denied that he had received any form of assistance. As for his friendship with the police, the Commission reports that Ruby gave free coffee and similar favors to policemen at his clubs but finds no wrongdoing. *(WR 224)* Much later, in an appendix to the Report, the Commission describes Ruby's record of arrests by the Dallas police. *(WR 800)* By separating the two issues, the Commission discourages any tendency to weigh the innocence of Ruby's friendship with the police on the scales of his repeated immunity from prosecution and other evidence of a mutual solicitude.

If the Commission's qualitative appraisal of Ruby's relations with the police is sympathetic, its quantitative appraisal is truly marked by delicacy.

> Although Chief Curry's estimate that approximately 25 to 50 of the 1,175 men in the Dallas Police Department knew Ruby may be too conservative, the Commission found no evidence of any suspicious relationships between Ruby and any police officer. *(WR 224)*

Twenty-five to 50 men! The Commission knew just how "conservative" that estimate really was. Of the 75 or so policemen who were present when Oswald was killed, at least 40 knew Ruby. If the same proportion—over 50 per cent—is applied to the total police force, Ruby must have known more than 500 of the men.

Ruby's friend, boxer Reagan Turman, told the FBI that "Ruby was acquainted with at least 75 per cent, and probably 80 per cent, of the police officers on the Dallas Police Department." *(CE 1467)*

But statistics by themselves cannot give an adequate picture of Ruby's links with the police. In investigating possible collusion between Ruby and his police friends in carrying out the murder of Oswald, one should examine Ruby's friendship with officers who were present and who were involved in the security measures for Oswald's protection.

Oswald was brought into the basement handcuffed to Detective Leavelle on the right, with Detective Graves at his left arm, preceded by Captain Fritz and Lieutenant Swain and followed by Detective Montgomery. Every one of those men except Captain Fritz "knew" Ruby and had known him for periods of ten to twelve years. Thirty-six other officers present knew Ruby. No one saw him until it was too late.

Although one would have thought the Commission would examine every one of the 40 policemen who were acquainted with Ruby, 17 of them were not asked to testify. Some of the omissions are surprising, and one is absolutely incomprehensible: Lieutenant George Butler, who had "known Jack Ruby for years." *(CE 2002,* p. 69)

Lieutenant Butler is mentioned only once in the whole of the Warren Report, in connection with allegations that Ruby was linked to various rackets, including gambling and narcotics.

The Report informs us:

> Steve Guthrie, former sheriff of Dallas . . . reported that shortly after his election as sheriff in July 1946, Paul Roland Jones, representing other Chicago criminals, offered him a substantial amount of money to permit them to move in and manage illegal activities in Dallas. Although he never met Ruby, Guthrie asserted that these criminals frequently mentioned that

Ruby would operate a "fabulous" restaurant as a front for gambling activities.

Despite its source, the Commission finds it difficult to accept this report. A member of the Dallas Police Department, Lieutenant George E. Butler, who was present during virtually all the conversations between Guthrie and Jones and who performed considerable investigative work on the case, stated that Ruby was not involved in the bribery attempt and that he had not heard of Ruby until the investigation and trial of Jones had been completed. . . . And 22 recordings of the conversations between Guthrie, Butler, and Jones not only fail to mention Ruby, but indicate that Jones was to bring from outside the Dallas area only one confederate, who was not to be Jewish.   (WR 793)

Butler's information on these matters and his contradiction of the former sheriff's allegations about Ruby warranted sworn testimony before the Commission from Butler and from former Sheriff Guthrie as well. That the Commission failed to take testimony from Butler, who was no less accessible than the other police witnesses, is baffling.

The Commission has been entirely too ready to accept Butler's version of the "negotiations." While Butler told an FBI agent on December 9, 1963 that Ruby had not been mentioned in those negotiations, as the Report indicates, Butler earlier told a Chicago newspaperman, Morton William Newman, that "Jack Ruby came to Dallas from San Francisco or Chicago in the late 1940's and was involved in an attempt to bribe Sheriff Steve Guthrie." (CE 2887) Butler is therefore in conflict not only with Guthrie but with Newman as well. The Commission, without even questioning Butler directly, arbitrarily accepts his story.

The 22 recordings scarcely obviate the need for closer scrutiny of Butler's assertions to the FBI. Those recordings were obtained from Butler himself, who had stored them at his residence. One disc (recordings 8 and 17, on opposite sides of a single record) was missing, and the remaining ones were monitored by an FBI agent working by himself, who prepared no transcript but merely reported on a standard FBI report form that Jack Ruby's name was not mentioned on any of the recordings. (CE 2416) This kind of evidence does not resolve an issue conclusively, as the lawyers on the Commission must have known full well.

On December 9, 1963, the day of Butler's FBI interview about the Guthrie-Jones affair, Butler had another interview. On his own initiative, Butler contacted two police officers who were conducting an investigation of Ruby's background and his possible links with Oswald. Butler told those officers (1) that he had information that Oswald was the illegitimate son of Jack Ruby; and (2) that he had information that Ruby had applied for a visa to Mexico at about the time of Oswald's visit to Mexico City, and that the Mexican Consul should be contacted to confirm this. (CE 2249, p. 41)

Both of Butler's tips seem to have been ignored. His allegation that Ruby was Oswald's father is fanciful, if not irresponsible, and scarcely suggests that other assertions by Butler should be taken at face value.

Butler works in the Criminal Investigation Division, Juvenile Bureau, under

Captain Martin. His colleagues include Detectives Cutchshaw, Lowery, and "Blackie" Harrison. All five men knew Ruby, and some knew him long and well. All five men were present in the police basement when Ruby shot Oswald. All of them except Butler were Commission witnesses.

That the Commission neglected to call Butler despite the facts mentioned already is all the more reprehensible in the light of the following testimony from reporter Thayer Waldo of the *Fort Worth Star-Telegram*.

Waldo: We had arrived some time earlier and had seen the preparations. I had gone upstairs and checked Chief Curry's office and had been told that it would be half to three-quarters of an hour yet before the prisoner would be removed . . . and that everybody would be notified before there was any movement. . . .

Hubert: Were you told it was going to be by elevator down into the basement and then through the basement ramps out Commerce Street?

Waldo: Yes, sir.

Hubert: Who told you that, sir?

Waldo: As I recall it, it was Lieutenant Butler himself, who was on the third floor at the time I went up, and I would like to for whatever it's worth add something at this point. Lieutenant Butler was since, oh, probably 2:30 on the afternoon of the twenty-second of November, the man whom I had sought out on every occasion that I wanted to learn something about developments, whenever I could find him, because he was a man of remarkable equanimity, poise, and very co-operative within the authorization that he had, and the first thing—

Hubert: You mean he would give you more news than anybody else?

Waldo: He was more able to understand what was wanted and he was always in on, apparently, on high-level information, and if it was for release, he would be the one who would have it and be most willing apparently to give it. This is a thing that happens in circumstances like this. A reporter picks out a man, tries him out, and if he finds that he's co-operative the first time he tries to stick to him, because by that time the official recognizes his face. . . .

What I wanted to say about Lieutenant Butler was that this almost stolid poise, or perhaps phlegmatic poise is a better word, that I had noticed all through even the most hectic times of the twenty-second and the twenty-third, appeared to have deserted him completely on the morning of the twenty-fourth. He was an extremely nervous man, so nervous that when I was standing asking him a question after I had entered the ramp and gotten down to the basement area, just moments before Oswald was brought down, he was standing profile to me and I noticed his lips trembling as he listened and waited for my answer. It was simply a physical characteristic. I had by then spent enough hours talking to this man so that it struck me as something totally out of character. *(15H 593-595)*

What had changed Butler's "phlegmatic poise" into extreme jitters and trembling of the lips? The Commission did not inquire.

Another curious omission from the list of the Commission's witnesses is Detective H. L. McGee, another of Ruby's acquaintances, who made the following report on November 24, 1963:

I had stationed myself in the general area in front of the information desk to await the transfer. While I was in this area, the only person I noticed come into the building from either the Commerce Street or Harwood Street doors was Attorney Tom Howard. He came in through the Harwood Street entrance and walked up to the jail office window.

At this time Oswald was brought off the jail elevator and Tom Howard turned away from the window and went back toward the Harwood Street door. He waved at me as he went by and said, "That's all I wanted to see." Shortly after that I heard a shot and someone said, "Oh." I did not see the shooting.   (CE 2002, p. 135)

Not only McGee but Tom Howard, who was Ruby's lawyer, should have been asked to testify about this curious incident. Now it is too late to ask Tom Howard why he was at the jail office just as his client was about to commit murder—Howard died in the spring of 1965.

Lieutenant R. E. Swain, who was in Oswald's escort party and who knew Ruby, is the man who gave Fritz the okay to come ahead with the prisoner. Swain's report of December 4, 1963 (CE 2002, p. 171) indicates that security, far from being "okay," was in disarray, even in the immediate area into which Oswald was being taken. Swain was not called before the Commission.

Several police officers who were said to be particular friends of Ruby are not listed among those present in the basement or responsible for security during the transfer. Even so, they should have been questioned by the Commission.

Lieutenant J. R. Gilmore, for example, seems to have known Ruby well and long. Joseph Cavagnaro, front office manager of the Sheraton-Hilton Hotel in Dallas, told the FBI that Ruby was a close friend of Lieutenant Gilmore (CE 1592); and Robert Larkin, former manager of a night club adjoining Ruby's Vegas Club, also told the FBI that Gilmore was "particularly friendly with Ruby" (CE 2329). Although Gilmore is not listed among the police personnel involved in the transfer, apparently he was in the building, and an unknown visitor asking to see Ruby soon after he was arrested was sent to see Gilmore. (12H 76, 78) Neither the Commission nor the FBI questioned Gilmore about the unidentified visitor, much less about Gilmore's own activities on the morning that Ruby murdered Oswald.

D. L. Blankenship, who worked under Gilmore, also is said to have "known Ruby over the years," according to Assistant District Attorney William Alexander. (CE 1628) Blankenship was interviewed by the FBI about his part in Ruby's arrest in 1954 (CE 1611) but not about his contacts with Ruby at the time of the assassination.

E. E. Carlson, who was also involved in Ruby's 1954 arrest, told the FBI that he was off duty on the morning of November 24 (CE 1612) Later that day, according to an FBI report of the same date, Carlson encountered Ruby in the identification bureau, where he was taken to be fingerprinted and photographed.

Ruby appeared very cordial toward Edward E. Carlson. . . . They greeted each other warmly and exchanged pleasantries. . . . Carlson . . . advised that he still had a liking for Ruby and would shake hands with him at any time.
                                                    (CE 2080)

Lieutenant George Arnett, said to be "quite good friends" with Ruby (CE 1467), told the FBI that he was not on duty when Oswald was shot (CE 1615).

Lieutenant Erich Kaminski, who worked with Lieutenant Gilmore, had known Ruby since 1953; he told the FBI that he was in his office from 9 a.m. to 9:30 p.m. on Sunday the twenty-fourth but that he took no part in the security arrangements. *(CE 1549)* Kaminski was said to be "a close friend" of Ruby. *(CE 1592)*

Officers Truett Walton and Glen Neal were mentioned as frequenters of the Carousel Club and on friendly terms with Ruby *(CE 1542);* neither Walton nor Neal was questioned about his relations with Ruby or his whereabouts on the twenty-fourth.

These seven police officers, like the 17 officers acquainted with Ruby who were on duty in the basement, were not called to testify before the Warren Commission.

Captain Fritz, who led Oswald into the basement without assigning a single man to walk directly in front of the prisoner and shield him from attack, was questioned about Ruby.

Dulles: Have you discovered any connection between any of your officers and Ruby?

Fritz: Well, I think a lot of the officers knew Ruby. I think about two or three officers in my office knew him, and I think practically all of the special service officers who handle the vice and the clubs and the liquor violations, I think nearly all of them knew him and, of course, the officer knew him who had arrested him carrying pistols a time or two, two or three times, uniformed officer mostly. He seemed to be well known. It seems a lot of people in town knew him.

But I was never in his place and I didn't know him.   *(4H 240)*

A different view was expressed by a former Dallasite who was interviewed by the FBI at San Francisco on December 6, 1963. Unfortunately, the FBI report on that interview is not presented in its entirety by the Commission but ends abruptly in the middle of a sentence.

Mr. Travis Kirk, former attorney at Dallas, Texas, for 23 years and who has been residing in San Francisco since August 1963, was interviewed near his place of employment . . . the Bank of California. . . .

Mr. Kirk stated he has been greatly disturbed regarding the recent Dallas murders of President John F. Kennedy and . . . Lee Harvey Oswald. He has formulated rather definite opinions regarding the circumstances surrounding the killing of Oswald, these based on his personal contacts over the years with law enforcement officials, attorneys, and judges in Dallas. He stated he also has had some association with individuals considered by him to be at least in the fringe of the Dallas underworld. He pointed out that he has defended persons in Dallas courts charged with felonies and involving cases investigated by the Dallas Police Department.

Mr. Kirk states he is acquainted with Captain Will Fritz of the Homicide Bureau. . . . He states he also knows Jack Ruby by reputation and has been in Dallas night clubs operated by this individual. He does not recall ever having engaged in conversation with Ruby. Mr. Kirk was asked specifically if he knows of any instance that would dramatize a close friendship or association between Ruby and Fritz.

Mr. Kirk could not recall any specific occasion when he has seen these persons together. He could not recall any occasion when he, Kirk, has seen Ruby in the Dallas Police Department. However, Mr. Kirk states it is inconceivable that Fritz did not know Ruby. He described Fritz as a domineering, dictatorial officer possessing a photographic memory and a thorough knowledge of the Dallas underworld. In light of Ruby's reputation and notoriety in Dallas prior to the murder of Oswald, and Fritz's long-time control of the most important segment of the Dallas Police Department, Mr. Kirk considers it utterly ridiculous that [the report ends at this word]

(*CE 3006*, p. 529)

Whether or not he knew Fritz, Ruby apparently tried to enter the Homicide Bureau (where Fritz's office is located and where Oswald was under interrogation) on Friday evening after the assassination. Victor Robertson, Jr., Dallas WFAA radio and television reporter, told the FBI on January 17, 1964 that he had

. . . known Ruby for approximately two years as operator of the Carousel Club on Commerce Street, Dallas. He met Ruby through Murphy Martin, a former reporter with WFAA who, at that time, was dating a girl employed at the Carousel Club. . . . He recalls seeing Jack Ruby in the third floor hallway of the Police Building sometime possibly between 5 and 7 p.m. on November 22, 1963. Ruby had started in the door of the Robbery and Homicide Division and two police officers pulled him back and did not allow him to enter.   (*Robertson Exhibit 1*)

In a later FBI interview, Robertson said:

Ruby appeared to be anything but under stress or strain. He seemed happy, jovial, was joking and laughing and more like—oh, any exuberant, interested person, a curious person who just had to see what was going on in his normal, extroverted self.   (*Robertson Exhibit 2*)

Robertson's report that he had seen Ruby trying to enter Fritz's office while Oswald was under questioning troubled the Commission, as became apparent when Robertson was deposed by counsel on July 24, 1964.

Griffin: We have asked you to come here today because in particular you provided some very helpful information to the FBI. . . . After February of 1963, did you have occasions to see Jack Ruby?

Robertson: Yes. Not frequently. I would see him on the street or up at the city hall or something like that.

Griffin: Is there anybody that you have confused with Jack Ruby?

Robertson: No.   (*15H 348*)

Griffin: You indicated when you talked to the FBI that you saw Jack Ruby sometime on November 22.

Robertson: That's correct. . . . It was before the police department changed for the first time their shift on guard at Captain Fritz's door. It was, I am reasonably certain, during the first shift of the two officers. . . . I believe it was after the first session of interrogation.

Griffin: Well, is there any question in your mind about that man that you did see was Jack Ruby up there on the floor?

Robertson: No; I have no doubts.

Griffin: Suppose I told you that we interviewed the police officers who were on guard, and one of them says he recalls a man, who says he recognized Ruby, that he recalls a man who looks like Ruby, but it wasn't Ruby, come up and do what you have previously described to the FBI, and go on. Would that shake your judgment in any way?

Robertson: No. I don't, of course, claim that I cannot make a mistake. In my judgment, the man I saw was Jack Ruby. I know no one else who looks like that. Obviously, I could have been mistaken, but I don't believe so.

Griffin: Tell us what you think Jack Ruby, the man you think was Jack Ruby, what you recall him doing.

Robertson: He walked up to the door of Captain Fritz's office and put his hand on the knob and started to open it. He had the door open a few inches and began to step into the room, and the two officers stopped him. I was reasonably certain one of them, or some voice at that time had said, "You can't go in there, Jack." And the man in question, if it was not Jack Ruby, turned around and passed some joking remarks with a couple of people who were there, I don't know who, and went back down the hall toward the elevator.   *(15H 348-351)*

Griffin: Did you see him; did you get a full front face view of him?

Robertson: No. He was in profile.

Griffin: Where were you standing in relationship to the homicide door and the main elevator, public elevator?

Robertson: I was standing almost immediately opposite Captain Fritz's door. Perhaps a matter of two feet beyond it toward the pressroom. . . .
                                                                      (12H 352)

Griffin: Now on Sunday, November 24, after Ruby shot Oswald, did you report to anybody in your station that you had seen Ruby?

Robertson: Yes.

Griffin: Who did you tell that to?

Robertson: To Walter Evans.   *(15H 353)*

Corroboration of Ruby's presence on the third floor of the police building on Friday evening came from several witnesses, including Dallas KBOX radio newsman Ronald L. Jenkins, who reported on December 10, 1963 that:

After seeing Ruby on November 24, 1963 and the photographs, he recalled that on the evening of November 22, 1963 between approximately 5:30 to 7:30 p.m. he saw a man believed to be Ruby on the third floor of the police station. Ruby was milling around in the crowd of press representatives and was alone.   *(Jenkins Exhibit 1)*

Jenkins was also asked to testify; counsel who took his deposition on July 14, 1964 did his best to shake Jenkins' identification of Ruby.

Hubert: Now you state in Exhibit 1 that you saw Jack Ruby, I believe, on November 22 on the third floor of the Dallas police station between the hours of 5:30 to 7:30 p.m. Did you know Ruby prior to November 22, 1963?

Jenkins: No; I did not.

Hubert: Had you ever seen him at all?

Jenkins: No; I hadn't.

Hubert: Did you know of his existence?

Jenkins: No.

Hubert: Now apparently later you identified Ruby as a man that you had seen on the third floor on November 22, and I ask you now how you identified the man that you saw on the twenty-second as Jack Ruby whom you did not know on the twenty-second?

(Anyone remember such questions being put to Howard Brennan, Helen Markham, the Davis girls, Scoggins, or any other witnesses who identified Oswald as a killer but who had not known Oswald prior to November 22, or seen him at all, or known of his existence?)

Jenkins: I don't think I ever have said that I saw him for sure and could identify him for sure. It was strictly by recall. I was able to see him in person, I believe it was on the afternoon of the Oswald shooting . . . the twenty-fourth. . . . He passed within a few feet of me. . . . The face was familiar, and it just seemed to me that I had seen the man on the Friday night previous. This was the first thing that struck me when I did see him. . . .   *(15H 602)*

I was trying to think where I had seen him before, and then it occurred to me that I had seen him in the hallway near the elevator shaft of the third floor on the evening of the assassination.

Hubert: I think you said also that you saw him later that Friday night at the time in the assembly room?

Jenkins: Yes, sir. . . . I am quite sure it seemed to me it was the same man. . . .

Hubert: Do you think that the man you saw earlier in the evening on the third floor was the same man that you saw in the assembly room?

Jenkins: Yes; I think so.

Hubert: And you think that Jack Ruby was that man on both occasions?

Jenkins: In my opinion, *it was the same man.*

Hubert: It might have been?

Jenkins: In my opinion, *it was the same man; yes, sir.* [Italics added]
(15H 603)

The Commission and its counsel could be very persistent when they wished a witness to back away from a categorical identification or statement; as we shall see, refusal by the witness or witnesses to be influenced and failure to accommodate the Commission by modifying prior testimony had little ultimate effect on the Commission's findings.

The testimony of reporters Robertson and Jenkins in some ways parallels the testimony of Seth Kantor and Wilma Tice, who reported seeing Ruby at Parkland Hospital while President Kennedy was still in the emergency room. In each case, one of the two witnesses knew Ruby, and the other, who did not know Ruby, provided credible corroboration. Another common factor among these witnesses is that they are private citizens who were not personally involved except as spectators in the events of November 22-24, and therefore perhaps more objective and trustworthy than witnesses from the police or other agencies whose reputations and more were at stake for their performance in the protection of the President and later of his accused assassin.

Robertson's and Jenkins' testimony was corroborated by three additional witnesses: a reporter from the *Dallas Morning News,* and two police detectives who knew Ruby and actually conversed with him on the third floor on Friday evening.

John Rutledge of the *Dallas Morning News* was interviewed on December 5, 1963 by Captain O. A. Jones, who reported:

> He remembers that before 6:00 p.m. on November 22, 1963 that he was standing by the door leading into the Burglary and Theft Bureau and that he saw Jack Ruby standing real close to some newsmen. Captain Fritz was being interviewed by a group of newsmen. Some newsmen asked who was being interviewed and Rutledge said Ruby answered thusly: "Will— W-I-L-L, Fritz—F-R-I-T-Z." Mr. Rutledge saw about four officers speak to Ruby during the time of the interview. He also saw Ruby at another time standing near newsmen just outside the door leading to the Forgery Bureau.
>
> (*CE 2249,* p. 14)

Worst of all (from the Commission's point of view) was the testimony of Detectives Eberhardt and Standifer, who had known Ruby for five years and 13 years respectively. Eberhardt told the FBI on December 20, 1963 that he had known Ruby and his sister for five or six years but had not seen Ruby for about three weeks before the assassination.

> On November 22, 1963, Eberhardt was on duty from 3 p.m. to 11 p.m. . . . He recalled seeing Jack Ruby in the hallway on the third floor at about 6 or 7 p.m. and asked him what he was doing there. . . . Ruby told him that he had brought some sandwiches over and was acting as interpreter for some Israeli reporters. Ruby was carrying a note book and he thinks he had on some kind of a lapel badge such as reporters were wearing. . . .
>
> (*Eberhardt Exhibit 5026*)

When Eberhardt was deposed by Commission Counsel Griffin on March 25, 1964 he repeated that he had seen Ruby on November 22 between 6 and 7 p.m., probably at 7 p.m. (*13H 187*), and that Ruby had come into the Burglary and Theft office where Eberhardt was at work, staying for about fifteen minutes.

Standifer, who worked in the same office as Eberhardt, testified on July 14, 1964 that he had seen Ruby on the third floor on Friday and had exchanged greetings with him, at about 7:30 p.m.

> *Hubert:* How do you fix it? Because it would helpful for us to have in the record what that estimate is based on.
>
> *Standifer:* I know that it was after dark, and I believe along about then darkness set in about 6 or 6:30 that time of year, and I know it was possibly an hour after dark.
>
> *Hubert:* . . . Do you remember what time you had supper that night?
>
> *Standifer:* 6:30 . . . I always eat at 5:30. I bring my sack and I eat right in my own office. I never leave the office. . . . Fixed habit. You could set your clock.
>
> *Hubert:* Are you willing to state that you did eat this day at 6:30?
>
> *Standifer:* Yes, sir.
>
> *Hubert:* How long after you had eaten did you see Ruby?

Standifer: Probably thirty minutes after. . . .

Hubert: All this was on the third floor, as a matter of fact, just outside your office, which is the Burglary and Theft division?

Standifer: Yes.

Hubert: Is that office near Captain Fritz's office?

Standifer: Directly across the hall.   (15H 617)

All this is a rather impressive, watertight body of evidence that Ruby was on the third floor of the police building early on Friday evening. Robertson, a reporter who had known Ruby for two years, saw him attempt to enter the Homicide office; two other reporters, Jenkins and Rutledge, corroborated Ruby's presence on the third floor, the location of the Homicide office; and two police detectives who had known Ruby for many years talked to him when he came to their office, directly across the hall from Homicide. Every one of those five witnesses placed Ruby on the third floor between 5 and 7:30 p.m. on Friday.

How does the Commission deal with that unassailable body of evidence? Here are the relevant passages from the Report, with comments interpolated.

At least five witnesses recall seeing a man they believe was Ruby . . .

The five were Robertson, Jenkins, Rutledge, Eberhardt, and Standifer. The last two conversed with Ruby, which eliminates any element of "belief."

on the third floor of police headquarters at times they have estimated between 6 and 9 p.m.;

The correct time interval is from 5 to 7:30 p.m.

however, it is not clear that Ruby was present at the Police and Courts Building before 11 p.m. With respect to three of the witnesses, it is doubtful that the man observed was Ruby. Two of those persons had not known Ruby previously . . .

Jenkins was the only one of the five witnesses who had not known Ruby previously. Robertson, Eberhardt, and Standifer knew Ruby well. Rutledge was not asked whether or not he knew Ruby, but his remarks to cameraman Jimmy Darnell (*CE 2249*, p. 13) indicate that Rutledge knew Ruby at least by sight and was familiar with his background and history.

and described wearing apparel which differed both from Ruby's known dress that night and from his known wardrobe.

The Commission's double standard again is manifest. It accepted Jimmy Turner's identification of Ruby despite Turner's lack of previous acquaintance with Ruby and despite the fact that Turner's description of the clothing did not match Ruby's actual apparel, particularly his hat. The very same failings are invoked by the Commission to cast doubt on two of the present witnesses, while Turner's dubious and uncorroborated testimony is accepted with enthusiasm.

The third man, who viewed from the rear the person he believed was Ruby . . .

Robertson saw Ruby in profile. He felt no uncertainty about the identity of the man he saw and reported having seen Ruby (describing the circumstances to which he later testified) at the television station where he was employed, immediately after Ruby murdered Oswald.

. . . said the man unsuccessfully attempted to enter the Homicide office. Of the police officers on duty near Homicide at the time of the alleged event, only one (Clyde Goodson) remembered the episode, and he said the man in question definitely was not Ruby. The remaining witnesses knew or talked with Ruby, and their testimony leaves little doubt that they did see him on the third floor at some point on Friday night; however, the possibility remains that they observed Ruby later in the evening, when his presence is conclusively established.

Eberhardt and Standifer said unequivocally that they had seen and talked with Ruby at about six or seven o'clock, which is consistent with the testimony of three other witnesses. To conclude that they were all "mistaken" is to depart from all semblance of objectivity.

Ruby has denied being at the police department Friday night before approximately 11:15 p.m.   (WR 338)

Oswald denied that he had killed anyone, and he was not a convicted murderer or known to any of the witnesses who identified and incriminated him. *That* didn't seem to matter to the Warren Commission.

The Commission has rejected the testimony of five witnesses on the basis of (a) Ruby's denial, and (b) statements by Officer Clyde Goodson in June and July 1964, many months after the event, that a man resembling Ruby but not Ruby himself attempted to enter the Homicide office.

The FBI interviewed Goodson on June 19, 1964 and reported:

Goodson . . . advised that he and Robert B. Counts relieved Officer H. L. Henley at 5:30 p.m. on November 22, 1963, to guard the door to the entrance of the Homicide Bureau. . . . Goodson related that he knew Jack Ruby and he did not see Ruby at any time while he was on duty, nor did Ruby attempt to enter the Homicide Bureau while he was on guard at the entrance. . . .

Goodson related that shortly before 6 p.m. as he recalls, a man fitting the description of Jack Ruby came to the door of the Homicide Bureau and wanted to enter. He told him that only authorized law-enforcement officers could enter and asked him for his identification. He stated the man said he was not a law-enforcement officer and turned and went back down the hall.   (Goodson Exhibit 1)

The evidence suggests that Goodson—assuming his good faith—was mistaken. In a series of FBI interviews, a number of photographs showing Ruby among the crowd at the police station after the assassination were displayed to a group of witnesses—including Victor Robertson and Officer Goodson as well as intimates of Ruby like his bartender, Andrew Armstrong, his roommate, George Senator, and Bruce W. McLean, the man who gave him scalp treatments. Of those persons, Officer Goodson was the only one who was unable to identify Ruby in any of the photographs, saying that "he does not feel that he knew

Ruby well enough to make an unqualified identification"; Robertson, on the contrary, immediately identified Ruby in some of the photos. (*CE 2439*, p. 567) This is an added reason for accepting Robertson's testimony rather than Goodson's.

As for Ruby's denial, what value should be attached to his testimony on any issue? Ruby was not a disinterested observer, but a convicted murderer who was appealing his death sentence and whose interests lay in maintaining the defense of "no premeditation" and "no conspiracy." Where *was* Ruby between 5 and 7:30 p.m. on Friday, if not at the police building as five witnesses testified? According to the Warren Report,

> Ruby probably arrived a second time at his sister's home close to 5:30 p.m. and remained for about two hours.   (*WR 337*)

Ruby had no alibi for the hours between about 5 and 7:30 p.m. on Friday. There is strong evidence that he was at the police building, added to which there might be included the following testimony from Bell Herndon, FBI polygraph operator:

> On question No. 2, Mr. Ruby did show a significant drop in the relative blood pressure. This question pertained to: "Did you go to the Dallas police station at any time on Friday November 22, 1963, before you went to the synagogue?"
>
> I asked him about this question later when he responded "No," and I noticed a physiological change. . . . Due to the nature of this change, however, it is possible that it was caused by a body motion that I failed to detect during the actual response.   (*14H 594*)

Many witnesses, including various experts like Herndon, seemed to know intuitively what the Commission wished to hear, and often that is what they told the Commission, not necessarily out of intentional dishonesty but probably as a result of subconscious influence on conscious judgment. Thus Herndon was ready to suggest that he had missed "a body motion," that he had not performed the test with full efficiency, rather than make the judgment that Ruby had lied.

If the actual evidence rather than the Commission's distorted presentation is weighed, it is perfectly plain that Ruby was at the police building early Friday evening and that he attempted to enter the office where Oswald was under interrogation. What is not plain is whether Ruby did so as "a curious person who just had to see what was going on in his normal, extroverted self," or whether he had some other purpose.

That Ruby's visit was intentional is demonstrated by his presence at Dealey Plaza near the county jail on Saturday afternoon, when it was thought that Oswald might be transferred (*CE 2407*), and by his telephone conversations with newsmen, including Ken Dowe of KBOX radio in Dallas, as heard by garage manager Claud Hallmark.

> *Hubert:* Now, you make the statement here that one of the remarks he made was "You know I'll be there." Do you recall in what context that was . . . what had immediately preceded that, so that we might be able to gain some light as to where he said he would be?
>
> *Hallmark:* He planned to be on the scene of the transfer.   (*15H 491*)

With this statement that Ruby was determined to be present when Oswald was transferred to the county jail, how could the Warren Commission be so complacent as to suggest that Ruby's presence in the police basement at just the moment when Oswald was left vulnerable to assault by his police escort was no more than a random, unpredictable coincidence? Indeed, the Commission's practice of reading opposite meanings into unwelcome testimony is prominent throughout the Ruby case. There was, for example, persuasive testimony from several witnesses that Ruby was at the police station on Saturday afternoon. One of those witnesses was Thayer Waldo, reporter for a Fort Worth newspaper.

Hubert: . . . I think you saw the man that you ultimately identified as Ruby on the third floor or in the police building on Saturday?

Waldo: That is correct, sir.

Hubert: When did you first see him?

Waldo: I would say five or ten minutes before he came up and gave me a card. I noticed he was passing out cards and saying something to people . . . as he gave out the card, giving the man a hearty slap on the arm. . . . I could catch the rather strident tone of his voice, and when he came up to me, although he did not behave in as gratuitously familiar a way in the sense of either clutching at my clothing or patting me, there was still a sort of over-done ingratiating manner as he gave out this card and said . . . "You're one of the boys, aren't you? Here's my card. . . . Ask anybody who Jack Ruby is. . . . I want all of you boys to come over to my place . . . and have a drink on me. . . ." That's approximately it.

Hubert: About what time was that?

Waldo: Approximately four o'clock, I would say. . . .

Hubert: . . . And you are quite certain that the man who did hand you this card and the man you ultimately came to know as Jack Ruby were the same person?

Waldo: To the very best of my belief and knowledge. . . . As I have stated, when he handed me the card, he identified himself verbally as Jack Ruby.

(15H 588-589)

How does the Warren Commission overcome such responsible testimony? It reverts to the now familiar "None of the persons who believed they saw Ruby at the police department on Saturday had known him previously. . . . " Is the Commission suggesting that someone had obtained a supply of Ruby's cards and, after studying his manner and behavior carefully, was deliberately impersonating Ruby for the benefit of bystanders like Thayer Waldo?

. . . Ruby has not mentioned such a visit.

Whereas in other instances it has rejected the convincing testimony of such witnesses as Seth Kantor on the ground of Ruby's denial, now the Commission is willing to disregard Waldo's account merely because Ruby didn't mention it and without even asking Ruby.

The Commission, therefore, reached no firm conclusion as to whether or not Ruby visited the Dallas Police Department on Saturday. *(WR 347)*

The record, on the other hand, suggests that Waldo is both honest and accurate, and that his testimony warrants the firm conclusion that Ruby did visit the Police Department on Saturday.

The Commission has repeatedly questioned or repudiated evidence that Ruby was at the police building on Friday evening and Saturday afternoon. As will be discussed, testimony suggested also that Ruby was at the police station on Friday morning before the assassination. Before we come to that, we should return to the testimony of one of the witnesses who corroborated Ruby's presence on Friday evening, Detective Augustus Eberhardt.

Eberhardt's testimony contributed important information on a matter other than Ruby's presence near Fritz's office early Friday evening: it shows that Ruby was an occasional police informer and a man with definite underworld links.

Griffin: Now, you and I talked for some time just prior to taking this deposition, is that right?

Eberhardt: That is right.

Griffin: . . . I made some notes during our interview and I want to dictate these for the record. I wish you would listen to them carefully. . . .

. . . to continue dictating what Detective Eberhardt told me, he stated that he regarded Jack Ruby as a source of information in connection with his investigatory activities. I asked him in particular whether he remembered any instances when Jack had been a source of such information, and he stated that at one time Jack reported to him a female employee of his whom he believed had been forging checks and also thought might be a source of narcotics or drugs of some sort, and as a result of the information which Ruby provided a charge was filed against this girl.

Now, do you remember the name of the girl?

Eberhardt: Not her true name. We handed her over to the forgery bureau. She had some dangerous drugs. She was up under the name of [deletion]. She never came back. We arrested her out of the club.

Griffin: How long ago was that?

Eberhardt: That was when I was working vice. Three years.

Griffin: And you also stated that he informed on a fellow by the name of [deleted], who was wanted in connection with a white slavery charge. Did you ever prosecute that?

Eberhardt: No. . . . He was already under indictment. [Ruby] told us that he was in town and where he was staying, which we like to know. . . .

(13H 181-184)

Griffin: I also asked Detective Eberhardt if he knew of anyone else whom he knew from the police department, and he mentioned that his partner on the vice squad, R. L. Clark, also got some useful information, but that Eberhardt hasn't worked with Clark since early 1962. . . . Now, is there anything else that you would want to add to what I have just dictated?

Eberhardt: No.

(13H 186)

Two weeks later R. L. Clark was questioned, but solely about the police line-ups *(7H 235-239);* nor does the Report mention Ruby's role as an informer, speaking merely of his "keen interest in policemen and their work" and his "personal attachment to police officers." *(WR 800-801)*

An allegation similar to Robertson's report that Ruby had tried to enter Fritz's office came from another newsman, N.B.C. news producer-director Frederic Rheinstein. Rheinstein testified that on Saturday, November 23, sometime before 5 p.m.,

> Ruby was seen on the third floor going into an office in which District Attorney Henry Wade was purportedly working. The reason this was significant was that reporters had not been permitted inside that office, and this man . . . had gained access where newsmen had been unable to gain access. . . .
> I saw the man who I am reasonably certain was Ruby go into a door where Henry Wade purportedly was. I did not see him come out. . . . He was later reported to have come out and he was followed in about ten minutes by District Attorney Wade, who then became available for questioning by newsmen.   *(15H 356-357)*

The Commission didn't place any stock in Rheinstein either; the Report says only that a news reporter "believed he saw Ruby enter an office in which Henry Wade was working, but no one else reported a similar event." *(WR 347)* That no one else reported a similar event seems beside the point. Why didn't the Commission ask Henry Wade himself, or Ruby?

Wade was not questioned about this specific incident but he was asked whether he knew any members of Ruby's family. Wade said:

> I knew none of them, none of the Ruby family, and didn't know Jack Ruby. I think he claims that he had known me or something or other but if he had, it is one of those things where you see somebody and I didn't know his name or anything when I saw him that night or didn't know who he was. I thought he was a member of the press, actually.   *(5H 242)*

Some members of the press who were present at Wade's famous news conference on Sunday night, after Oswald was murdered, seemed skeptical of Wade's disclaimer of acquaintance with Ruby. Russ Knight, Dallas KLIF radio announcer, testified:

> Wade said that he didn't know Ruby, but I guess Ruby could have seen him other places. But he did point him out. He said, "This is Henry Wade. This is the Weird Beard." But he seemed to know Wade.   *(15H 268)*

Seth Kantor, Scripps-Howard reporter, during his testimony read a section from his notes and then explained them.

> "Sunday afternoon District Attorney Henry Wade was to say to the press that Jack Ruby was present Friday night during that strange press conference, I understand or I am told. A New York City radio reporter, Ike Pappas, corrected Henry and said that he, Pappas, had been talking with Ruby in the assembly room and . . . that he brought Ruby over to the District Attorney and that the D. A. seemed to know Mr. Ruby. Henry smiled but gave no answer, after first saying that Ruby was mistaken for a reporter. . . ."
> The time which I referred to here that Mr. Wade smiled was when Ike Pappas reminded Henry Wade on Sunday that he had talked to Ruby on Friday night. . . . This was an announcement made by Wade Sunday . . . to

a gathering of reporters among whom I was present, in which he said that he understood that Ruby had been present Friday night, and then Ike Pappas said, "You know that he was present because the three of us were talking."   *(15H 91)*

Maybe Wade did not know Ruby, as he said, but there is testimony that Ruby was in the district attorney's office on Thursday, November 21, one day before the assassination, talking with Wade's assistant, William Alexander, "about insufficient fund checks which a friend had passed." *(WR 334)* It *is* a small world, in Dallas.

The Commission also discounted, and omitted from the Report, testimony indicating that Ruby was outside the police building on Friday morning, before the assassination, at about nine o'clock. The Report ostensibly details Ruby's activities from November 21 to November 24, 1963. *(WR 333-359)* Friday morning falls within this period. But the Report leaps from the night of the twenty-first to the hour of about 11 a.m. on the twenty-second without mentioning testimony that placed Ruby outside the police building earlier that morning.

The source of the information was T. M. Hansen, Jr., of the Dallas Police. He was interviewed in the first instance on December 11, 1963, by the FBI. The FBI report on that interview provides the following information:

> During the last four years or so he has socially visited Ruby's Carousel Club but has never been there on an assignment while on duty. . . .
>
> As best he could recall the last time he saw Ruby was on November 22, 1963, between 9 and 9:30 a.m. He was entering the City Hall Building from the Harwood Street entrance, and Ruby was standing on the north side of the entrance directly to the side of the stairway which leads to the basement. He said there were four or five individuals standing with Ruby but he could not recall their identity and at this time was not certain whether or not they were police officers. He felt the crowd was apparently gathering at that time in anticipation of the fact that President Kennedy would be driving through the downtown section of Dallas later in the morning. As he walked by Ruby he shook his hand and said good morning but did not engage in conversation with him.   *(Hansen Exhibit 1)*

The Commission did not get around to taking testimony from Hansen until July 24, 1964, more than seven months after the event, when his recollection was no longer perfect.

> *Griffin:* I now direct your attention to the activities of November 22. . . . Do you recall seeing Jack Ruby at any time on that day?
>
> *Hansen:* I am not positive. When I say I am not positive, I either saw Ruby the morning before the President came in from Love Field down Harwood to Main—I either saw him the morning that—I was going to the city hall that morning before we went to the corner, or the morning previous to that, I just don't recall which. I have tried—in fact I talked to an FBI man about it that interviewed me, and told him the same thing I am telling you. I don't remember whether it was the day before or the morning of the parade.
>
> And Jack spoke to me. He was beside the city hall on Harwood Street, and I started to go down the steps in the basement, and he hollered, "Hi, Hans," and I hollered, "Hi, Jack." It wasn't much of a conversation.   *(15H 442)*

Griffin: How long did you speak with Jack?

Hansen: Oh, I never stopped. I just kept moving. . . .

Griffin: Is it possible that it could have been even two or three days before the President arrived?

Hansen: No; I don't think so. I think it was either the day before he arrived or the morning that he did arrive. Now, I can't remember. I would give anything if I could, because I know it would help you folks, and I have thought about it since I talked to this FBI man ten thousand times. I am not going to say definitely what day it was. I can't say it and be right in here [pointing at self]. *(15H 443)*

Griffin: The fact that there were four or five people, that makes you think it was the day of the motorcade?

Hansen: Well, a normal day, like I said, Monday through Friday, there wouldn't be anybody sitting on there unless it was a day that the old men come down to get their paychecks.

Griffin: Would that have been on Thursday?

Hansen: It would have been more than four or five, because I can't help but remember because they blocked the whole sidewalk and spit snuff.

Griffin: Is there anything that makes you think it was the day of the President's motorcade?

Hansen: Nothing else that I can remember outside I do remember there was several people sitting on that, which is unusual unless there is something going on.

Griffin: Would you be willing to say positively that it was the day of the President's motorcade?

Hansen: No; I wouldn't just make a flat statement, because I don't feel like I can. I am not that positive. But like I say, an ordinary day, unless there is something going on, ordinarily there wouldn't be anybody sitting on that little stone railing around there.

Griffin: In your mind, is there just as much chance that it could have been the day of the motorcade or is there just as much chance it could have been the day before the motorcade, as the day of the motorcade?

Hansen: No. The fact that there were some people sitting on the rail around there would indicate, it would make me lean toward the day of the parade. *(15H 449)*

Griffin seemed to do everything possible to dilute Hansen's report that Ruby was outside the police building a few hours before the assassination, but he did not succeed. Would it be so much less noteworthy if Ruby was there on Thursday instead of Friday? And why does the Report say nothing about Hansen's testimony instead of indicating, at least, that Hansen encountered Ruby on an undetermined morning near the day, or on the day, of the motorcade?

The Commission prefers to avoid such incidents as Hansen reported, and equally peculiar happenings such as reported to the FBI on December 1, 1963 by N.B.C. cameraman Gene Barnes.

Barnes . . . heard a shot but continued on to his rented car parked nearby in order to be ready to follow the armored truck. Dallas Police Department Officer Spears was standing by the rented car and was to serve as driver. He had obtained three days off from duty and had been employed by Barnes to act as driver for Barnes for the first two of those days.

Barnes saw Sergeant Putnam, Dallas Police Department, run up to a . . . Lieutenant stationed at the armored truck and heard him say, "I got me a nigger." Upon seeing a microphone close by, he said, "I'm sorry. I have me a Negro." He then explained to the Lieutenant that the Negro had been climbing over the tops of the cars in the city hall basement.

Oswald was brought out very shortly thereafter and taken in an ambulance to a nearby hospital at a speed approximating 90 miles per hour, with Barnes and Spears following closely in the rented car, which had no radio.

Barnes was the first newsman to arrive at the hospital from the city hall, although other newsmen were there as they had been stationed previously at the hospital. As Barnes started setting up his equipment, Officer Spears came up to him and whispered, "Do you want the name of the guy who shot Oswald?" Barnes answered, "Sure." Spears said, "You'll have to grease his palm." Because of Spears's accent, Barnes asked him to repeat what he had said and Spears did so. Barnes asked, "What does he want —$5.00?"

Spears answered, "You're the newsman—you ought to know." Barnes asked, "How good is your source?" Spears answered, "He's only the guy who was handcuffed to him." Barnes understood this to refer to an officer who was handcuffed to Oswald.

Barnes answered, "I'll have to check my office," and just as he was receiving information on the telephone from his "office," N.B.C. colleagues in WBAP-TV in Fort Worth, Texas, that Jack Ruby had shot Oswald, Spears, who had stood guard for him at the telephone booth, stuck his head in the booth and said, "It's Jack Ruby." . . .

Barnes is at a loss to understand how Officer Spears knew so quickly who had shot Oswald or what officer was handcuffed to Oswald or why he believed that officer would give out any information. Barnes noted that when he telephoned his colleagues as to paying for information as to who shot Oswald, he was advised that they had learned less than three minutes before from their technicians on the mobile truck that it was Jack Ruby; that the technicians had recognized Ruby immediately when his picture was telecast at the very moment Oswald was shot, and before Ruby's name had been announced over the air. . . .

Barnes heard rumors but cannot pinpoint any source that the man who let Ruby into the Dallas City Hall basement just before Oswald was shot was in a Dallas Police Department Reserve uniform. Barnes recalled seeing this man on guard duty at elevators in Dallas City Hall basement at some time on the day Oswald was shot and described him as being in his sixties, having white hair and a slender build. Barnes believes it possible that he might have heard this through Clyde Goodson or Godson, an off-duty Dallas Police Department officer who drove for Barnes on November 26, 27, and 28, 1963.   (CE 2038)

The Commission's investigation of this odd incident might be called oblique. Instead of questioning Barnes and Spears (neither of whom was asked to testify for the Commission), other officers who had gone to Parkland Hospital behind the ambulance were interrogated by Commission counsel in what seems an attempt to establish that one of them had spread the word that Jack Ruby was the man who had shot the prisoner. Detective Montgomery, for example, maintained and reiterated that he had not told anyone that Ruby was the killer; finally, Counsel Griffin said in despair:

> *Griffin:* I might explain to you what I am getting at. We know that somewhere along the line somebody was out at Parkland Hospital who was a newspaperman . . . learned that Ruby was the person. This started a rumor to the effect that his informant must have had something to do with it, and I am really asking you this question to see if it isn't possible that you guys, as you guys got out to Parkland, somebody had said Ruby was the guy and just by dropping the words, you know, that would spread like wildfire out there.
>
> *Montgomery:* No; I didn't say anything about who it was that done the shooting, out there.   *(13H 32)*

A valiant effort, but it failed to produce an "innocent" explanation for Officer Spears's premature knowledge of the identity of the man who shot Oswald. At that stage, at least, the Commission should have questioned Spears himself about his source of information. The Commission also ignored the last paragraph of the FBI interview with Barnes, where Barnes referred to the rumor that a reserve officer "let Ruby in the basement just before Oswald was shot." Although Barnes specified that he may have heard that rumor from Clyde Goodson, when Goodson was deposed *(15H 596-600)* he was questioned solely on the allegation that Ruby had attempted to enter the Homicide Bureau on Friday evening. Moreover, Spears had suggested that he obtained Ruby's name from "the guy who was handcuffed to him," i.e., Detective Leavelle. Leavelle was a deposition witness, not once but twice, well after Barnes had given his information to the FBI, but he was never questioned about the allegation that Spears had obtained Ruby's name from him.

Chapter 26
Pendent Rubies

In its investigation of Ruby and the so-called abortive transfer, the Warren Commission has left the scene littered with mysteries and puzzles. Never in American history has such a highly praised enterprise been characterized by such carelessness and insensibility. Even on a simple matter like the address of Ruby's apartment, the documents are confused or mistaken. That Ruby and his roommate George Senator were residing in an apartment at 233 South Ewing Street at the time of the assassination seems to be clearly established, in the testimony of Senator and from various other sources. Yet, in one exhibit after another dated on or after November 24, 1963 Ruby's address is given as 3929 Rawlins Street, where his sister, Eva Grant, resided (*see,* for example, *CE 2003,* pp. 331, 346). Rawlins is located to the east of, and midway between, Love Field and Parkland Hospital. South Ewing Street is in Oak Cliff, only a short distance from the scene of Tippit's murder and from the Marsalis Zoo.

How is it possible, then, to make sense of the testimony of William Crowe, an entertainer at Ruby's Carousel Club under the stage name of "Bill DeMar," speaking of the hours immediately after Ruby shot Oswald:

> *Crowe:* . . . a newspaperman drove up front, and television drove up across the street, and the newspaperman, I think, and somebody else, and they started to ask the garage attendant if he knew where Jack Ruby lived, and I came forward and I said I knew where he lived, at least I thought I did, but I didn't know he had moved, so I didn't know actually.
> *Hubert:* But in any case you gave them an address?
> *Crowe:* Well, I didn't know the address but I knew how to get there. . . . And I went out with some newspaper reporter in his Volkswagen and drove out to the apartment out by the zoo where he used to stay.

Hubert: Then you found he was not there?
Crowe: Not there, he had moved. *(15H 105)*

What is the meaning of this bizarre report? Who told Crowe that Ruby had "moved" from the building where he was actually living? Hubert apparently was not even aware that Crowe's experience required further inquiry, and proceeded to other matters.

Then there is the mystery of Mrs. Tippit's mail. Patrolman Gerald Springer told the FBI on December 10, 1963 that on Sunday morning, before the transfer, he had been cruising in a police car in the downtown area when he received radio instructions to come to the police chief's office for assignment.

> . . . this was at approximately 10:30 a.m. as nearly as he can recall. . . . When he arrived on the third floor, Patrolman Art Hammett advised him to pick up some telegrams and other mail and deliver it to Mrs. Tippit, the wife of the slain policeman.
>
> . . . He left the third floor . . . got in his car, pulled out of the police station, and was in the vicinity of Ervay and Jackson Streets when he received a call on the radio to report back to the Central Police Station. . . . He went back to the third floor and Patrolman Hammett told him to disregard his assignment, that they would take the mail and so forth out to Mrs. Tippit later on.
>
> He went back to the basement, contacted Sergeant Putnam and asked if there was anything he wanted him to do. Sergeant Putnam told him there was nothing for him to do. . . . *(CE 2030)*

Why was Springer called back and prevented from delivering the mail to Mrs. Tippit, when there was nothing else for him to do? One might shrug one's shoulders and ask what difference that made, were it not for the similar experience of Sgt. Don Steele.

> *Steele:* I came to the city hall, came to the police station downtown early that morning to pick up some correspondence, telegrams, and things like that, to take to Officer Tippit's widow.
> *Hubert:* And what time was that?
> *Steele:* That was approximately 9:15.
> *Hubert:* What happened after that?
> *Steele:* . . . I asked Lieutenant Pierce if there was anything he needed me to do before I left, and he said . . . I'd better stick around a while. He might need me. . . . *(12H 354)*

Was there something more going on than meets the eye? Hubert, apparently unaware of Springer's report, did not pursue the matter; neither Springer nor Hammett—one of Chief Curry's assistants and the officer who had first called Springer in and then called him back without any apparent reason—was called to testify. Is it possible that there was some ulterior motive for bringing Springer's car into the basement, having the car depart, and then return again?

An investigative lead that was also neglected was the appearance of various men whose identities remain unknown. Police Reserve Officer Mayo reported that about 15 minutes after Oswald was shot, a large gentleman who was slightly bald and walked with a limp attempted to enter the building for the purpose of visiting Ruby. The man said that he was Ruby's roommate. He explained that Ruby had a large sum of money on his person and that he wanted to see if Ruby wished him to handle the money for him. The unknown man was quite right, for Ruby did have several thousand dollars in cash with him when he was arrested. But how did this man know about it? Although he said that he was Ruby's roommate, he was not George Senator. Senator had gone to the home of lawyer Jim Martin as soon as he heard the news about Ruby and did not come to the police building until later in the afternoon.

Mayo referred the large gentleman to Lieutenant Gilmore. In his testimony, Mayo described the man as over six feet tall, very heavy, and wearing a heavy shirt and no tie. *(12H 294)* The incident was not included in Mayo's report, because of an oversight on the part of Lieutenant Revill. *(12H 76)* There is no indication that the man actually got to see Ruby. It is not even known whether he got to see Lieutenant Gilmore, for Gilmore was not questioned.

About 45 minutes later, a second "great big fellow" arrived at the police building attempting to see Ruby. He was received by Officer Vaughn, the same man who was on guard at the top of the Main Street ramp. Vaughn testified that this "great big fellow" asked for a particular lieutenant, perhaps Lieutenant Cunningham, Vaughn was not sure. He took the man to the basement, where he was searched for concealed weapons by Officers Boyd and Vaughn, after which Vaughn left the man with Boyd and went back to his post. Here all information ends, for neither Boyd nor Cunningham was interrogated about this unidentified visitor.

Vaughn described the man as six feet three or four inches tall, about 250 pounds, in his middle or late twenties, without a limp. The man identified himself as an employee of Ruby's *(12H 366)*, but Ruby had no employee who corresponds with the description.

But Ruby was alleged to be a friend of one Kenneth Spivey, described as six feet three inches tall, weighing 220, age twenty-four. *(CE 1458)* Spivey denied any acquaintance with Ruby in an FBI interview on December 18, 1963, but no attempt was made to determine whether he was the man reported by Vaughn or by Mayo.

A fourth large man was reported on the afternoon of the assassination. Philip Hathaway said in an affidavit of that day that he had seen a man walking on the street and carrying a rifle; the man was about six feet six inches tall, over 250 pounds, with dirty blond hair, crewcut, about thirty years old. *(CE 2003, p. 211)*

By way of contrast to the unidentified large men, there is an unknown and mysterious thin man who comes to light in the testimony of Jimmy Turner, the television director.

> *Hubert:* Now, during our interview immediately preceding the commencement of this deposition you mentioned another person that you had seen around the court building on several occasions. . . . Tell what you know about this person when you first saw him, now, at the numerous occasions on which you saw him until the last time that you saw him?

Turner: All right. We arrived from Fort Bliss at approximately 1 a.m. Saturday, the twenty-third of November, from Fort Worth, to set up our mobile unit inside the jail. . . . When we arrived there we—there was this man that resembled John Carradine of the movies quite a lot. He was very thin faced, around forty to fifty, carrying a portfolio, and another little bag with him. Looked like a shaving kit bag, or something of that effect.

He—as soon as we got there, it was chilly and we went inside the open doors on the Commerce Street side, and he was standing inside, and he immediately started talking to us about various things which we passed off as just an average person talking to you, finding out what you were doing and everything, and he talked to us about 15 or 20 minutes. He did mention in his conversation that he had been a school teacher prior to that, about 16 months before.

Hubert: Now, did he have a press badge on?

Turner: No, he had no badge on. He was wearing a light trenchcoat or top-coat. . . . He was approximately five feet eight inches . . . only around 130 to 140 pounds. Very light in weight; very skinny. . . . I never saw him without the trenchcoat on, the whole time. . . .

We went to the cafe down the block to grab a bite to eat at this time . . . and when we got back he was still standing there talking. . . .

Hubert: Did he ever mention his name?

Turner: He never mentioned his name. . . . After they got set up, he kept coming up in the hallway. . . . On the third floor, sir. This is while we were still up on the third floor, and waiting to get shots of Oswald being transferred from the elevator door to the questioning room, and he would continually come up and give—say, "They are going to bring him down in about five minutes." And he usually was right, on each one of the tips he gave us. He mingled around in the press room up on the third floor a lot. He—I told Tom Pettit, which was the announcer up on the floor, that Oswald was coming down, and he said, "Where are you learning the information?"

Hubert: You asked this of the man?

Turner: Well, no; I didn't ever ask him where he was learning his information, but I told—Tom Pettit asked me where I was getting this information, and I said, "Well, that man back over there," and I pointed him out and he said, "Who is he?" And I said, "I don't know who he is but he is giving us some pretty good tips." And he said, "Okay, keep using him, then." From that time on, we saw him various times the whole, completely on the third.

Hubert: How many times do you think you saw him?

Turner: Oh, any number of times, 15 or 20. Just pass him in the hall. . . . He had free movement on that floor. He had free movement in the basement . . . and then Sunday morning we came over. I ran into him in the rest-room, and he seemed to just live there in the jail.

Hubert: Still had that trenchcoat?

Turner: And still carrying the little bag, same little bag. . . . And we came again Sunday morning, and then we went through the shooting of Oswald, he wasn't in the basement, to my knowledge at this point.

Hubert: When did you see him next?

Turner: The next time I saw him was approximately 15 minutes after the shooting when I started to our remote truck to pick up a mike line and a camera cable. The doors were being guarded by policemen, who stopped me, and I told them my business; why I wanted to leave the jail, and give them my name and he let me leave.

Hubert: That was at the Commerce Street entrance?

Turner: Commerce Street entrance. All right, and when I came back in, which was approximately three or four minutes after . . . well, this officer had him at the door, and he was trying to show him identification from his billfold.

Hubert: You don't know who that officer was?

Turner: No, sir; I don't. And this man turned to me and said, "That man there can identify me," and I said, "Like hell I can. I don't know who you are or what you are." . . . 15 minutes later I ran onto him in the hallway coming back out the same door, and he told me "Thanks a million," and I said, "Well, I don't know you from anyone." I said, "That's why I didn't identify you." Or something to that effect and from that point on, I have never seen the gentleman again.   *(13H 137-139)*

There is a second thin man, but his identity *is* known. The same Reserve Officer Mayo who reported the unknown fat man who claimed to be Ruby's roommate was the source of information about this new figure, which he first gave counsel off the record.

Hubert: Let the record show that Mr. Mayo wanted to acquaint me with the general nature of another matter, but that after he had spoken a few sentences, it became apparent to me that it should be a matter of record, so, I will ask you now, Mr. Mayo, just simply to repeat what you have said to me in the last few sentences off the record.

Mayo: The first individual that tried to gain entrance into the basement said that he was a minister and he had a small book in his hand and I asked him what his business was. He said he wanted to go see Lee Harvey Oswald, that he was a friend of his, a minister that was supposed to help him, and he needed him, and he needed to go down there, and I told him "No, he could not enter without"—that is when I was on the Commerce Street side, and he hung around the entrance for some 20 minutes, I think, and he kept looking in the basement and acted very peculiar, but finally he left within about 20 minutes. He was tall, skinny, looked like over six feet tall, and looked like he was a man between fifty-five and sixty. . . .

Hubert: Now, you say you reported the fact to the—

Mayo: I mentioned that to Jack Revill, and they said, well, it was probably just like lots of people trying to gain entrance. They didn't think it had much value.

Hubert: And he suggested that it be left out of your report?

Mayo: Yes.   *(12H 294)*

For once, the matter was actually followed up with Revill, when he testified a few days after Mayo.

Hubert: I understand that Sergeant Mayo, when he was interviewed by you, stated that he had been approached by some individual who was either a minister or posing to be a minister in any case, who was trying to get into the jail through the Commerce Street entrance on November 24, prior to the shooting, stating that he wanted to see Oswald, and that you had told him, well, that wasn't pertinent to your inquiry, and all I want to do is ask you what—if it is true, and just what comment do you have to make on it?

Revill: I don't recall making that, because it would have been pertinent to my inquiry. . . .

Hubert: . . . In other words, your statement is that you do not recollect that Mayo made such a statement to you?

Revill: No, sir; he might have made such a statement. . . .

Hubert: . . . regarding the minister, your thought is that he may have stated to you, but you do not remember?

Revill: I don't recall.

Hubert: Nor do you recall why he omitted it from your report?

Revill: This might have happened. It was subsequent to this I found a preacher who wanted to talk to Oswald, and he went to Chief Batchelor's office, and. . . . No, prior to the shooting . . . let's see, he arrived at City Hall at 9:30. This preacher's name is Ray Rushing. He is an evangelist, Radio Evangelist.

Hubert: And that was reported and the man was interviewed?

Revill: It was not reported because I myself found this man.

Hubert: But—

Revill: There is no report on it, because it is in—it had nothing to do with the shooting. He had gone to Sheriff Decker's office, and Decker referred him to the city . . . so, he came to the city hall and went to the third floor, and—by the way, he rode up on the elevator with Jack Ruby, now—

Hubert: This Rushing?

Revill: Yes.

Hubert: Rode to the third floor—

Revill: Now, he says this.

Hubert: Oh, he says this.

Revill: Yes, for the past seven weeks I have been assigned to the district attorney's office, the prosecution of Ruby, running down leads and interviewing witnesses and this preacher was one of the people that we located, and he related this story to me, that he rode up on the elevator with Jack Ruby on the morning of November 24. Mr. Wade did not use this man. He didn't need the testimony, because he had placed Ruby there the morning of the shooting.

Hubert: In other words, Rushing says that he rode up with Ruby on the morning of the twenty-fourth, prior to the shooting?

Revill: Yes, sir.

Hubert: What was his name? . . . You don't know how we could reach him?

Revill: . . . he lives in Richardson, Tex—correction, please,—Plano, Texas.

Hubert: . . . Did you make a report on the interview with him?

Revill: No, sir; I did not. This was an interview conducted by the—at the district attorney's office in the presence of Assistant District Attorney Alexander.

Hubert: Did Rushing say what time that was?

Revill: Nine-thirty. He was sure of the time, because he had let his wife and family out at the First Baptist Church. . . .

Hubert: How did he recognize Ruby? Did he say?

Revill: He said he recognized him from the newspaper article that appeared that day, and later days.

Hubert: Did he say whether he had any conversation with him?

Revill: He talked about the weather. I asked him. . . . What I did is, I interviewed Mr. Rushing one night and asked him if he could come to the district attorney's office and relate this to Mr. Wade. Possibility that the district attorney might use him as a witness, and Alexander was of the opinion that the man might be mistaken. That he saw this as a means of getting publicity. Of course, I disagree with that thinking. I think that the man is truthful in that he is reporting what he thinks he saw. *(12H 75-79)*

Ray Rushing told Officer Mayo that he was a "friend" of Oswald's. He told Revill that he had met and talked with Ruby on the elevator in the police building on Sunday morning at about 9:30 a.m. and that Ruby was on his way to the third floor at that time. No wonder Counsel Hubert was eager to obtain Rushing's address.

As we have come to expect, Rushing was never called before the Commission. He was not even interviewed by the FBI or the Secret Service about his important allegation that he had encountered Ruby in the police building at a time when Ruby supposedly was at home.

The failure to interrogate Rushing is not inconsequential when the Commission itself concedes that Ruby's activities and whereabouts on Sunday morning "are the subject of conflicting testimony." *(WR 352)* Three witnesses, apart from Rushing, testified that they had seen Ruby near the police building at various times between 8 and 11 a.m. And Elnora Pitts, cleaning woman, describes her telephone conversation with Ruby some time after 8 a.m. that morning in terms which raise questions about his actual whereabouts and about the supposed solitary and impulsive nature of his act of murder later in the morning.

Mrs. Pitts: ... it was after eight. I know way after eight, and when I called him he said to me, "What do you want?" And I said—

Hubert: Did you recognize his voice?

Mrs. Pitts: Well, I'll tell you how he talked to me, then I said, "What do I want?" I says, "This is Elnora." He says, "Yes, well, what—*do you need some money?*" And I says, "No; I was coming to clean today." "Coming to clean?" Like you know, like he just—

Hubert: In other words, when you told him that you were coming to clean he seemed to express some surprise, is that it?

Mrs. Pitts: Yes, sir; like he didn't know that I was going to come and clean.

Hubert: Did he recognize you?

Mrs. Pitts: I don't know if he did or not. And I says to him again, I says, "This is Elnora." And he says, "Well, what do you want?" And I said, "Well, I was coming to clean today." ... I says, "You seem funny to me." And I says, "Do you want me to come today?" And he says, "Well, yes; you can come, but you call me." And I says, "That's what I'm doing now, calling you so I won't have to call you again." ... He sounded so strange to me ... and I said, "Who am I talking to? Is this Mr. Jack Ruby?" And he said, "Yes. Why?" And I said, "Oh, nothing." But he just sounded terrible strange to me. ... *(13H 231)*

Hubert: So, there was some doubt in your mind as to whether it was Jack Ruby?

Mrs. Pitts: Yes, sir. It was a doubt in something wrong with him the way he was talking to me. ... It was him. I'm sure of that, but then he just was indifferent. He sure did talk indifferent; yes, sir. He sure did. ... *Said he was going out,* he would try to be back by two. That is what he told me. ...
[Italics added] *(13H 232)*

There are three striking aspects in Mrs. Pitts's testimony: (1) the man did not sound like Ruby and did not seem familiar with matters that Ruby knew as a matter of routine; (2) the man was expecting a request for money, more than an hour before such a request was received from another woman who telephoned; and (3) the man said that he intended to go out before receiving the phone call which caused him to go to Western Union.

It is not difficult to interpret these facts and arrive at the premise that Ruby was in collusion with persons unknown to fabricate circumstantial evidence of an unpremeditated, unaided act of murder. The Commission was duty bound to test that premise and to investigate the possibility that the man who spoke to Mrs. Pitts was impersonating Ruby, that the subsequent telephone call that sent Ruby to Western Union was rigged, and that Ruby was at the police building between the hours of 8 and 11 a.m., as several witnesses reported, for the express purpose of executing the prisoner before he left the custody of the Dallas police.

The three witnesses who reported that they saw Ruby outside the police building at various times between 8 and 11 a.m. on Sunday were WBAP (Fort Worth) television technicians Warren Richey, John Allison Smith, and Ira Walker. The Commission finds "substantial reasons to doubt the accuracy of their identifications" (WR 352), pointing out, as usual, that none of the three men had ever seen Ruby on a prior occasion. The Commission then poses a number of objections to the testimony of Richey and Smith but finds it difficult to dispose of Ira Walker's identification.

> Although Walker's identification of Ruby is the most positive, his certainty must be contrasted with the indefinite identification made by Smith, who had seen the man on one additional occasion. Both Smith and Walker saw a man resembling Ruby when the man, on two occasions, looked through the window of their mobile news unit and once asked whether Oswald had been transferred. Both saw only the man's head, and Smith was closer to the window; yet Smith would not state positively that the man was Ruby. Finally, video tapes of scenes on Sunday morning near the N.B.C. van show a man close to the Commerce Street entrance who might have been mistaken for Ruby. (WR 352-353)

The man who might have been "mistaken for Ruby" is present in a photograph taken from the video tape. (CE 3072) His resemblance to Ruby is not great. The photograph is accompanied by a memorandum by Counsel Hubert suggesting that the photograph might be shown to Richey, Smith, and Walker "to determine if they can identify this obvious newsman as the man they possibly erroneously identified as Ruby." This was never done, or if it was done, the results have been omitted. Hubert's memorandum suggested also that the newsman in the photograph should be identified, if possible—presumably to see if his account of his activities on Sunday morning corresponded with the activities of the man identified as Ruby by the television technicians. This was not done either.

An almost amusing aspect of the Commission's denial that Ruby was in the police building for some hours on Sunday morning is its reasoning that the witnesses' descriptions of the apparel and grooming of the man they identified as Ruby do not correspond with Ruby's characteristically clean and well-dressed appearance. But the Commission is undisturbed by the clean, natty, young appearance of the unidentified man in the photograph, asking us to assume that that man was mistaken for Ruby when a glance at the picture is enough to demonstrate his unlike appearance. How can the Commission suggest mistaken identity in the face of testimony like that of Ira Walker?

Hubert: When did you first see a man that you now know to be Jack Ruby, if you did see such a man?

Walker: I did see him, and I would say it was sometime after 10:30 in the morning that Oswald was shot. . . . I was sitting in the truck at the audio board. We were waiting for Oswald to be brought down. The press had been told he would not be transferred until after 10:30 in the morning . . . and Ruby came to the window of the truck and asked, "Has he been brought down yet?" He was standing on the sidewalk.

Hubert: You didn't know him to be Ruby at that time?

Walker: No; I did not.

Hubert: Can you tell us how he was dressed?

Walker: No; I can't. All I could see was his face. . . . He came to the window twice. . . . I am almost sure it was after 10:30 . . . he just said, "Has he been brought down yet?" And everybody knew who he was talking about, or I did.

Hubert: Now have you seen Ruby since?

Walker: Yes . . . I was a witness during the trial. I saw him before I was a witness, and I saw them bring him into the courtroom one morning. . . . I was asked by the district attorney's office to go look at Jack Ruby through the door of the courtroom prior to being a witness, to make sure that he was the same man that I saw come to the truck. . . .

Hubert: . . . what opinion did you reach?

Walker: I knew it was the same man. . . . I told the Dallas district attorney that the only reason I remember Jack Ruby is because within minutes after the shooting we had mug shots of Ruby on camera from the third floor of the city hall. And if it hadn't been for those mug shots being in such a close time after he came to the window, I probably would never have remembered seeing him. . . . About four of us pointed to him at the same time in the truck. I mean, we all recognized him at the same time. . . .

Hubert: . . . your opinion is that the man who did look through that window and asked you, "Have they brought him down yet?" was Jack Ruby?

Walker: Yes.

(13H 292-293)

Hubert: Has there been anything omitted here that was brought out in the trial of Ruby when you were a witness?

Walker: No; in fact, it has been covered much better. The State didn't bring out the fact that we saw mug shots, and the defense kind of tore me up on that. . . . I probably wouldn't have remembered the man coming to the window if it hadn't been for the mug shots. I told District Attorney Wade that before I went in as a witness, but he didn't follow it up.

Hubert: Well, to wrap it up, you are saying under oath now that the man at the window and the man in the mug shots and the man in the courtroom identified as Jack Ruby were one and the same person?

Walker: Yes, sir.

(13H 295)

The Commission suggests that Ira Walker's convincing identification should be rejected because of the "indefinite identification" made by John Allison Smith.

Of course, if the Commission wanted to place Ruby on the scene, Walker's testimony would be used to fortify Smith's, instead of the other way around. Obviously Ruby's presence is not desirable to the Commission.

Just how "indefinite" and "uncertain" was Smith's identification?

> *Hubert:* Have you associated the face that you have come to know as Jack Ruby from photographs and pictures and so forth, with the man that we have been talking about for the last few minutes?
>
> *Smith:* Yes. . . . The closest that I ever made the association was when we were shown a mug shot, and when I saw that mug shot, it was a straight-on photograph, and it struck me as being the same face as the one in the window.
>
> *Hubert:* Did you have any spontaneous reaction in that regard?
>
> *Smith:* Well, I was convinced to myself that that was the same man.
>
> *Hubert:* Did you make any observations to anyone to that effect?
>
> *Smith:* No, but Walker did to me . . . a couple of seconds later. . . . We were looking at the mug shot on a monitor in the truck. . . .
>
> *Hubert:* Did you at that moment associate the face that you saw on the mug shots in the monitor with the man that you had seen earlier and which you have described to us?
>
> *Smith:* I did. . . . I had noticed a distinct similarity. Now there is a difference in that, when I saw him, he had a hat on, and that was the only reason that I would not say positively that that is the same man. But that is the only reservation that I have. . . .   *(13H 282)*

Smith does not sound uncertain so much as he sounds like a good citizen who is leaning over backward to be precise and explicit about the possibility of error in identification resulting from the fact that the man who came to the window was wearing a hat, while the man in the mug shot was not.

> *Hubert:* Would you venture to say that the man on the street whose face came within three feet of yours and the man in he mug shot were, beyond any reasonable doubt, the same person?
>
> *Smith:* The only reason I would have any doubt was this thing of the hat. Now I couldn't see his hairline and I couldn't see the complete face. With that in mind, I would not say positively that is the same man; I can't say that.
>
> *Hubert:* . . . With that reservation, you would have no doubt it is the same person?
>
> *Smith:* That is true.   *(13H 283)*

It remains only to add that Ruby was wearing a hat when he shot Oswald; the unidentified newsman in the video tape photo was not.

Chapter 27
Ruby Farewell

The death of Jack Ruby, on January 3, 1967, fulfilled a common prophecy —of the man-on-the-street and the student of the Oswald case alike—that Ruby would not leave the custody of the Dallas authorities alive. The event was inexorable in its unfolding, irreversible, and in full view of the world.

Ruby died, thirty-three months after he was sentenced to death on March 14, 1964; seven months after a Texas state court on June 13, 1966 upheld his sanity; three months after the Texas Court of Criminal Appeals on October 5, 1966 upset his conviction and ordered a retrial; a month after Wichita Falls was designated on December 7, 1966 as the site of the new trial; and in a month or two he would have been likely to walk out of court a free man, credited with the time he had already served against a sentence of a few short years for murder without malice.

On December 9, 1966, Ruby was removed from the county jail and admitted to Parkland Hospital with a diagnosis of pneumonia. The next day his illness was identified as cancer. Another day or two brought the news that the malignancy was far advanced; surgery and radiation therapy were ruled out; the prognosis was that Ruby had from two weeks to five years to live. Less than four weeks after Ruby entered Parkland Hospital, he died. The rehabilitation of his image began at once: the first man to commit murder "live" on television— the ugly act of shooting a handcuffed, helpless man—was said in his funeral eulogy to be only "a misguided patriot."

"Ruby did not want to live," said Sol Dann, one of Ruby's many lawyers. "His death was a merciful release."[1]

---

1 "Ruby, Oswald Slayer, Dies of a Blood Clot in Lungs," *The New York Times,* January 4, 1967, p. 20.

A merciful release for whom? If Ruby wished to die, his accusation (when he had pneumonia) that mustard gas had been fed into his cell is strange, as is his charge (when he had cancer) that he had been injected with cancer cells.[2]

According to medical authorities cancer cannot be induced, Ruby's reported accusations notwithstanding. However, it can be neglected to the point of irreversibility, and on January 4, 1967 two Ruby lawyers charged negligence on the part of the Dallas authorities who had custody of their client.[3]

The Dallas sheriff and the doctors who had treated Ruby in jail (for a cold that turned out to be terminal cancer) scoffed at and denied suggestions of any negligence on their part. They had attributed his complaints of illness to malingering, and his vomiting to hypochondria; no prisoner in the county jail, they said, received more solicitous care than the late Jack Ruby.

Those who wonder whether Ruby took secrets to his grave may be reassured by the "secret" tape recording made at Parkland Hospital about two weeks before Ruby died and released publicly as a segment of a long-playing "documentary" record immediately after his death (though a selected number of broadcasters received it earlier).[4] On that tape recording, Ruby reiterated that he had killed Oswald by pure chance; he did not even remember the act; it was unpremeditated; and he had acted alone, not as part of any conspiracy.

That is what Ruby had declared on earlier occasions, and that is the conclusion stated in the Warren Report. *(WR 22)* But it is only one of several declarations made by Ruby. When he was examined in June of 1964 by the Chairman of the Warren Commission, Ruby made a plea to be removed from Dallas to Washington—"I want to tell the truth, and I can't tell it here" *(5H 194);* ". . . a whole new form of government is going to take over our country, and I know I won't live to see you another time" *(5H 210);* ". . . maybe certain people don't want to know the truth that may come out of me" *(5H 212).*

Almost a year later, on March 19, 1965, Ruby was seen briefly on television, en route between jail and the court where he had made a futile plea for change of counsel and removal to federal jurisdiction.[5] Notes made by this author during the telecast indicate that Ruby's remarks to reporters, as he walked purposefully down a corridor, included the words " . . . complete conspiracy . . . and the assassination too . . . if you knew the facts you would be amazed." He asserted that he was perfectly sane, in good health mentally and physically; he asked a newsman if he looked like a person who was not sane; indeed, as mentioned already, his sanity was upheld in June 1966.

In January 1966, a dealer sold by auction two letters allegedly written by Jack Ruby and smuggled out of jail. One letter said, ". . . they alone had planned the killing, by they I mean Johnson and the others . . ."[6]

The press was very restrained in reporting those Ruby statements, although when he died there was extensive coverage of his reaffirmation, on the secret

---

2   *Philadelphia Bulletin,* January 3, 1967, p. 3.
3   *New York Post,* January 4, 1967, p. 2.
4   Radio broadcast on station KLAC, Los Angeles, January 4, 1967.
5   Telecast on C.B.S.-TV, Channel 2, New York, March 19, 1965, 7-7:30 p.m.
6   Penn Jones, Jr., *Forgive My Grief,* p. 65.

tape recording, that he had acted alone and without premeditation when he murdered Oswald. Spokesmen for the legal profession reminded the public that great weight was accorded to deathbed statements like Ruby's.[7] Reminded in turn (or informed for the first time) that Oswald's last words had also been a deathbed denial, the lawyers changed the subject.

For at least a year before his death no one saw Ruby except the authorities, Warren Commission representatives, his attorneys, and members of his family. According to the *Dallas Morning News* of December 15, 1966, Dr. John Holbrook, a psychiatrist who had interviewed Ruby the day after he murdered Oswald, had "failed in an attempt to talk with Ruby at Parkland Memorial Hospital," having made the attempt apparently for "investigative and historical purposes."

---

7   The Barry Gray Program, WMCA Radio, New York, January 3, 1967, 11:05 p.m.

Epilogue
A New Investigation

No attempt has been made in this study to deal comprehensively with every aspect of the Oswald case. Such a comprehensive, all-inclusive study would involve perhaps a second set of 26 volumes, which like the Hearings and Exhibits would be read only by a minute segment of the public. The author's purpose has been to reach as many people as possible with a message that has lost none of its urgency or importance during the years which have elapsed since the publication of the Warren Report. It is hoped that message has been made apparent by means of the comparisons presented in this study between the raw evidence and the misleading and sometimes spurious presentation of that evidence by the Warren Commission.

The discrepancies, distortions, and misrepresentations of crucial points of evidence are sufficient, even on a selective rather than a comprehensive basis, to condemn the Warren Report. The Commission has issued a false indictment. It has accused Lee Harvey Oswald, after first denying posthumous defense and then systematically manipulating the evidence to build the case against him. Even so, the Warren Commission's Report leaves the case against Oswald wide open.

I have pointed to Oswald's lack of motive for the crime of assassination. Indeed, the Commission was unable to suggest a motive and resorted to insinuation and assumptions of an arbitrary nature about the emotional and ideological tendencies of the accused. Those pronouncements have no verifiable foundations, issuing as they do from a Commission committed to a specific set of conclusions. Indeed, although the evidence showed that Oswald had no motive, no means (marksmanship of the highest order), and no opportunity (his presence on the second floor of the Book Depository little more than a minute after the shooting, which to the men who encountered him at that time eliminated him from suspicion, constitutes an alibi), there is no indication in the vast collection of documentation that the Commission at any time seriously considered the possibly that Oswald was not guilty, or that he had not acted alone.

Because of the nature of the investigation, it is probable that the assassins who shot down President John F. Kennedy have gone free, undetected. The Warren Report has served merely to delay their identification and the process of justice.

No more time need be devoted to denouncing those who are responsible for this frustration of justice. They have destroyed their own case, and conceivably their reputations. What must now be done is to set about finding the assassins. Such a new investigation, if it is undertaken, must be performed by a competent and impartial body, and in the light of the bitter lesson learned from the Warren Report, the new investigation must be in the framework of an adversary proceeding.

The new investigative body should first attack the evidence against Oswald presented in the Warren Report and the Hearings and Exhibits, and present an objective and scientific evaluation of that evidence so that the ambiguity about his role in the assassination will, if possible, be dispelled. The new body must also be given access to the suppressed documents of the Warren Commission. The 75-year time vault must be opened and its contents must be put before the new body—and, at the appropriate moment, before the public, *within* our lifetime. The leads and clues which were not followed up by the Warren Commission, or which were incompletely investigated, now must be pursued with vigor, by *independent investigators* and not by the governmental agencies compromised by their role in the protection of the murdered President.

A scrupulous and disinterested investigation—even now at this late stage and despite the death of several key witnesses during the past three years—must once and for all resolve the question of Oswald's guilt or innocence and establish whether or not he was even implicated in the crimes of which he stands accused and, for all purposes, convicted and punished. It must almost inevitably point also to the identity of those who are guilty of the assassination and the collateral murders.

In advocating a new investigation, I do not have in mind the inquiry in progress in New Orleans—even though it will not have escaped notice that District Attorney Jim Garrison of the Parish of Orleans, in accusing anti-Castro Cuban exiles and CIA agents of complicity in the assassination, has postulated a theory which has much in common with the hypothetical construct elaborated in Chapter 21 (pages 384-386).

Since February 1967, when it was first revealed that Mr. Garrison was conducting his own investigation of the assassination and that he considered the Warren Report to be mistaken, his activities and pronouncements have been much in the headlines. I must admit that at the beginning, Mr. Garrison's rhetoric was disarming—"Let justice be done, though the heavens fall,"[1] for

---

[1] CBS Television Network newscast, Channel 2, New York, February 18, 1967.

example, and "I have no reason to believe at this point that Lee Harvey Oswald killed anybody in Dallas that day."[2] For the first time, a public official armed with subpoena power and ready to use it had openly repudiated the conclusions of the Warren Commission and had pledged to expose the guilty parties and bring them to justice. At a preliminary court hearing in the arrest by District Attorney Garrison of an individual whom he charged with conspiring to assassinate President Kennedy, three presiding judges rejected a motion to admit the Warren Report into evidence, on the ground that it was a compound of hearsay and error.[3]

But as the Garrison investigation continued to unfold, it gave cause for increasingly serious misgivings about the validity of his evidence, the credibility of his witnesses, and the scrupulousness of his methods. The fact that many critics of the Warren Report have remained passionate advocates of the Garrison investigation, even condoning tactics which they might not condone on the part of others, is a matter for regret and disappointment. Nothing less than strict factual accuracy and absolute moral integrity must be deemed permissible, if justice is, indeed, to be served.

June 1967

---

2 "Figure in Oswald Inquiry Is Dead in New Orleans," *The New York Times*, February 23, 1967, page 22, col. 5.

3 *The New York Times*, March 16, 1967, page 39, col. 2.

Appendix
The News Media
and the Warren Report

The news media bear a large responsibility for the tranquilization of the American public and its complacent acceptance of the Warren Report. The public mistrust of the Dallas police after their performance on the fateful days of November 22-24, 1963 had compelled the establishment of a Presidential commission to investigate the assassination and the murder of the alleged assassin. Thanks to the intensive efforts of the press, the public was persuaded to accept, or at least appear to accept, findings by the Warren Commission which in essence mirrored the suspect findings of the Dallas police.

The New York Times, most venerated of American newspapers, assumed the role of co-sponsor of the Warren Report, placing on it the stamp of both its own high reputation and its unconditional endorsement. The *Times* made the Report available, in the form of a special supplement. Within three days of the distribution of the special supplement, the *Times*—in conjunction with Bantam Books—issued a one-dollar paperback edition of the Warren Report that sold millions of copies. Then in December 1964, within a month of the release of the 26 volumes of the Hearings and Exhibits, the *Times* and Bantam Books issued a companion paperback, *The Witnesses,* which also sold for a dollar. *The Witnesses* purported to consist of "the highlights of Hearings before the Warren Commission . . . selected and edited by *The New York Times";* and, indeed, the testimony was very carefully selected and edited to present only those passages which supported the Commission's assertions and conclusions while excluding all inconsistent or inimical parts of the transcripts. Thus, for example, the excerpts from Abraham Zapruder's testimony do not include his remarks that he had believed the shots to come from behind him (the grassy knoll), and the excerpts from the testimony of Commander J. J. Humes omit his admission that he burned the first draft of the autopsy report. Excerpts from the testimony of Major Eugene D. Anderson and Sergeant James A. Zahm suggest in each case that the shots were not difficult and that Oswald had the rifle capability to have fired them; however, the Nelson Delgado testimony indicating that Oswald was a poor rifleman is omitted, and only Delgado's remarks about Oswald's views on capitalism are included in the volume, despite many elements in his testimony of far greater importance.

The Witnesses, therefore, was one of the most biased offerings ever to masquerade as objective information. In publishing this paperback, The Times engaged in uncritical partisanship, the antithesis of responsible journalism. That performance was not redeemed by an editorial slapping the Commission's wrist for its deletion, without acknowledgment, of a sentence of testimony given by one witness—a deletion which became known because a reporter had been given access to the verbatim transcript of the testimony prior to its publication in expurgated form. The editorial reprimand was solely for that deletion. (Some two years were to pass before The New York Times concerned itself with the Commission's other deletions, omissions, and irregularities of various shades and degrees.) No questions were raised about the Commission's lack of control over its own documents and records, which were repeatedly leaked or pirated. There seems to have been some correlation between the beneficiaries of those leaks and the diligent attempts by certain newspapers and periodicals to put "an end to nagging rumors" whenever evidence came to light during the Commission's investigation that threatened to compromise the lone-assassin hypothesis. Thanks to those efforts, it is clear that the Commission at no time entertained any theory other than that of Oswald's sole guilt.

The New York Times maintained a loyal silence about the Warren Report even when public controversy erupted about its main findings in many other prestigious publications. From the end of May 1966 to late in the year the Times remained aloof, but in November 1966 Harrison Salisbury, the Times' assistant managing editor and chief spokesman on the Warren Report (he provided the introduction to the Bantam edition), radically revised his earlier position by sharply criticizing the Report in The Progressive, a magazine of limited circulation. At about the same time, the Times published a cautiously worded editorial acknowledging the need for answers to the serious questions that had been raised about the Warren Report. It became an open secret that the Times had initiated its own investigation of the assassination in an attempt to rescue the Warren Commission from itself and to silence the clamor of criticism of its Report: according to Newsweek of December 12, 1966, Harrison Salisbury explained, "We will go back over all the areas of doubt and hope to eliminate them." Apparently the Times, even with all its imposing resources, did not find it possible to eliminate the areas of doubt; the investigation was aborted early in January 1967.

In 1963-1964 some magazines exhibited healthy skepticism and independence of policy. *Commentary* published a stern and prescient editorial in January 1964, voicing grave misgivings about the way in which the Warren Commission was approaching its task. Two months later, *Commentary* printed a trenchant critique of the case against Oswald written by Léo Sauvage. Then came a prolonged silence, broken in October 1966, when *Commentary* featured a major article by Professor Alexander M. Bickel of Yale University. Professor Bickel expressed some serious criticisms of the Commission (Assistant Counsel Wesley J. Liebeler said publicly that Bickel's disenchantment with the Warren Report—unlike the charges from less eminent persons—deeply distressed him) but was equally scornful of those who had preceded him in challenging its product. While Professor Bickel conceded the need for a new investigation, his pro-Commission bias was evident on every page. A few months later, a second and more balanced article by Professor Bickel appeared in *The New Republic,* no doubt adding to the burden of distress to which Liebeler had earlier admitted.

In the early days *The Nation* also took a responsible position on the Dallas events. It published an article by Harold Feldman which called attention to the enigmatic relationship between Oswald and the FBI and, upon release of the Warren Report, commissioned an appraisal by Professor Herbert Packer of Stanford University School of Law. Professor Packer made some damaging criticisms of the Commission's methods and conduct but nevertheless endorsed its central findings, on the basis of supposedly "hard" evidence which in reality is flaccid. In mid-summer of 1966, *The Nation* published a two-part article by Fred Cook dissenting from the Warren Report, but the editors carefully disassociated themselves from Cook's conclusions and reaffirmed full confidence in the Commission. And, to underline the point, *The Nation* next printed an apologia for the Warren Report by Jacob Cohen purporting to show that the autopsy report may have been tampered with, as many critics were charging, but for "innocent" reasons. Cohen elaborated his defense of the Report in the November 1966 issue of *Frontier,* in an article marred by many misstatements of fact and by pseudologic.

The New Republic also had commissioned an appraisal of the Warren Report upon its release—the caustic "Case for the Prosecution" by Murray Kempton. At that time Kempton said that in the last analysis he accepted the official findings. Two years later Kempton tore into the Warren Report with scathing contempt in an introduction to the paperback *The Second Oswald,* by Richard Popkin. Other valuable articles appearing in *The New Republic* shortly after the assassination, by Richard Dudman and by Staughton Lynd and Jack Minnis, served to inform and alert the public.

The New Leader made a major contribution to historical accuracy by publishing an article written by George and Patricia Nash, "The Other Witnesses," which clarifies the Commission's negligence and failure to find witnesses who were easily located and important to the Tippit shooting. Three witnesses located by the Nashes gave descriptions of the shooting which differed radically from the official account; one of these witnesses reported attempts by the police to intimidate and silence her. Published some weeks after the Warren Report was released, this article was later followed by several excellent critiques of the Report by Léo Sauvage, in which he emphasized the Commission's failure to prove its accusations against Oswald.

Esquire published a devastating appraisal of the Warren Report by Dwight Macdonald, who nevertheless shared Professor Packer's mistaken confidence in the so-called hard evidence and accepted the findings. Macdonald's critique was somewhat prematurely titled, "The Last Word on the Warren Report," but in any case *Esquire* had not said its last word: in November 1966, the magazine published an article by Edward Jay Epstein—in which areas of doubt and contradiction in the Report were delineated—as well as an article written by this author, "Notes for a New Investigation."

Ramparts did not enter the fray until its issues of November 1966 and January 1967, each of which included major articles on the assassination and editorial support for organizing a new investigation. Although the November 1966 issue also included material of a sophomoric and irresponsible character, the January 1967 article by David Lifton and David Welsh, "The Case for Three Assassins," was a sober, scholarly analysis of the evidence relating to the source of the shots and the autopsy findings.

In terms of giving support and comfort to the Warren Report and the thesis of the lone assassin, *Life* was the magazine counterpart of *The New York Times* for the three years following the assassination. In the days when everyone was trying to figure out how the President could have been shot in the front from behind, *Life* suggested that Kennedy had turned all the way around to receive a bullet in the throat, while in the same issue it published frames from the Zapruder film showing that he was facing forward throughout the crucial time span. Not stopping at foolish self-contradiction, *Life* exerted itself to promote the sole guilt of Oswald. The February 21, 1964 cover of the magazine displayed the notorious photograph, suitably "retouched . . . in various ways . . . for clarifying purposes," as the Warren Report was later to explain: It showed Oswald holding a rifle, with a revolver on his hip and in his hand copies of *The Worker* and *The Militant*—astonishing catholicity of reading taste for any genuine leftist, one might add. After a veritable career of devotion to the Commission's cause, *Life* finally reconsidered its posture: toward the end of 1966, *Life* published an essay by Loudon Wainwright suggesting the need for re-examination of the findings in the Warren Report, followed a few weeks later by an article dealing with the timing of the shot that struck Governor Connally and the bankruptcy of the single-missile hypothesis.

Early in 1967 *The Saturday Evening Post* joined the growing list of mass-circulation magazines which had abandoned all pretense of the legitimacy of the Warren Commission's findings and now fretted about manifest error, carelessness and lacunae in the Report (while avoiding or rejecting the thought that anything beyond slovenliness was at issue). It published a hard-hitting article by Richard Whalen whch exposed the dubious nature of some of the evidence and the un-tenability of some of the conclusions in the Report.

For *The Minority of One,* no change in position was necessary: from the beginning this extraordinary one-man-magazine had maintained an outspoken and unequivocal stand against the illusory lone-assassin hypothesis, whether it stemmed from the Dallas authorities, the FBI, or the pontifical Warren Report. Always indifferent to the unpopularity of its position and unmoved by considerations of public relations strategy or loss of revenue, the magazine consistently and freely opened its pages—more so than any other single periodical of any persuasion—to articles by such critics as Harold Feldman, Mark Lane, and Vincent J. Salandria. (Excerpts from this book and other articles by this author were published in *The Minority of One* in 1966 and 1967.)

At various times *Liberation* published articles by Mr. Salandria, including a tour de force in which he synthesized in understandable language the highly technical, abstruse medical/autopsy/ballistics evidence and demonstrated on those grounds alone that the Commission's basic conclusions were untenable.

In the daily press, several reporters and columnists have dug into the case and exposed facts or raised questions which otherwise may never have surfaced. The late Robert Ruark wrote a memorable essay showing that the ballistic findings in the Warren Report were totally absurd. The late Dorothy Kilgallen turned a skeptical eye on Dallas and wrote a number of stories challenging the official case. Other newsmen (Richard Dudman, Ronnie Dugger, and Dom Bonafede, for example) have helped to widen the scope of investigation and public knowledge. One city editor of a New York daily, Sylvan Fox, wrote the paperback, *The Unanswered Questions About President Kennedy's Assassination* (Award Books, New York, 1965), which raised some serious issues and objections to the Warren Report.

Those journalists deserve gratitude for their attempt to prod the dormant public mind and to revive the spirit of skepticism and irreverence in national affairs.

On the other side, segments of the Left and Liberal establishments have abandoned all claim to courage and integrity on the issue of the assassination in their uninformed and gratuitous stampede to sanctify the Warren Report and in their readiness to vilify and intimidate its critics. I. F. Stone is a case in point. In his weekly newsletter he published a heated defense of the Report coupled with aspersions on the morals and intelligence of his political kin, not even hesitating to instruct Lord Russell. Two years later questions about the Warren Report and demands for a re-opening of the investigation issued from every quarter of the political spectrum, and such men as Max Lerner, Harrison Salisbury, and Alistair Cooke exhibited the good grace of admitting that their first enthusiasm had been ill-founded, yet Stone never revised his original strange partisanship.

What inspired the principled and courageous Stone to such a performance? The answer may lie in public statements by A. L. Wirin, the civil libertarian, who revealed with perhaps unintended candor that his own ardent defense of the Warren Report sprang from relief and gratitude: Although finding that a Marxist committed the assassination, the Commission had absolved the Left from complicity or responsibility in the crime and thus, in his view, had averted a blood-bath against leftists. Wirin should realize that while he may have the right shoe, he has the wrong foot.

In any case, even if spokesmen for the Left suspect in their secret thoughts that the domestic or foreign Left was involved in the assassination, they may not —without yielding all claim to respect—seek to sacrifice truth or justice to a mistaken concept of self-preservation. Nothing, including "reasons of State," can justify the suppression of the truth; nothing can damage the country, including the Left, so profoundly as compounding the nightmarish events of Dallas by an American Dreyfus case.

In December 1966 a former senior counsel for the Warren Commission was interviewed on Chicago television by two newsmen. The interviewers were wholly unfamiliar with the facts and evidence and thus did not challenge a single one of the numerous misrepresentations of fact by the counsel. This sad commentary on the role of the press took place not in the immediate aftermath of the Report but after vigorous national debate criticizing the Commission's findings. All the way down the line the news media have failed in their responsibilities by choosing to act as press agents for the authorities of Government and by defaulting in their fundamental duty—to dig out the truth and to bring the facts to the people.

Nevertheless, a public opinion poll in September 1966 revealed that Americans doubted or disbelieved the findings of the Warren Commission by a margin of 3 to 5—a new "credibility gap" that caused frank anxiety in the Government and among its apologists in the academic and communications worlds.

On the one hand, Congressman Theodore Kupferman (Republican, New York) presented a bill calling for a bipartisan re-evaluation of the Warren Report, and if the re-evaluation so indicated, a new investigation of the assassination. On the other hand, die-hard establishmentarians broke two years of uncritical silence to reproach the Commission for its no longer deniable failures and defects—but only as a prelude to generally preposterous efforts to salvage the "lone assassin" for the Commission, which had not trussed him up securely enough.

More radical remedies were needed if the Warren Report was to escape re-classification as a work of fiction. As a resourceful result the missing autopsy photographs and X rays (for which some of the critics had clamored too single-mindedly throughout a summer of discontent) now mysteriously emerged. The story broke on November 1, 1966.

The Department of Justice, the press told us, had requested the missing photographs and X rays from the Kennedy family; the Kennedy family, rumored but not known to be in possession of the photographs, obligingly released them to the National Archives. However, the Kennedys imposed so many restrictions and prohibitions on their accessibility to independent examination that they might just as well have continued to keep them hidden in the family vault.

The release of the long-missing photographs and X rays was announced on the front page of The New York Times[1] and other newspapers; in smaller print, it was solemnly reported that Dr. J. J. Humes and his colleague Dr. J. Thornton

---

1 "Autopsy Photos Put in Archives by the Kennedys," The New York Times, November 3, 1966, p. 1, col. 8.

Boswell had inspected the evidence. They had pronounced the photographs and X rays authentic. They had declared that they fully corroborated the official autopsy findings.

Thus, still another spectacle of self-exoneration by those under suspicion in the first place.

For the most part, the editorial columns had no comment on this new diversion, in spite of their duty to speak out. The bizarre history of the autopsy photographs called for at least questioning, if not protest.

Despite the delinquencies of the news media and their reluctance, even now, to challenge the Warren Report, the direction of public opinion has become irreversible. If they will not lead the search for the truth about Dallas, the news media will have to follow. Ironically, reporters had great affection and admiration for President Kennedy; he enjoyed a rapport with the press unmatched by any contemporary White House incumbent. Perhaps that warmth and respect will yet impel the working press to move into the vanguard of the investigation into the assassination. The vast resources and the great power of the news media can still play a decisive role in uncovering the full truth.

Index

About the Author

Sylvia Meagher lives in New York City, where she has worked in the field of international public health both as an administrator and as a writer of analytical reports since 1947. She has appeared on radio programs and panels and has lectured in various parts of this country and Canada. Her writing on the Warren Report has appeared in such publications as *Esquire, The Minority of One,* and *Studies on the Left.*